English
PROSE *and* POETRY
1660–1800

A SELECTION

English

PROSE *and* POETRY
1660———1800

A SELECTION

Edited by

FRANK BRADY

Dartmouth College

MARTIN PRICE

Yale University

HOLT, RINEHART AND WINSTON

NEW YORK

❦ Contents ❧

Bernard Mandeville

THE FABLE OF THE BEES: REMARK M. 92

Joseph Addison and Richard Steele

THE SPECTATOR

No. 2 Friday, 2 March 1711 [Steele] 102
No. 58 Monday, 7 May 1711 [Addison] 107
No. 62 Friday, 11 May 1711 [Addison] 112
No. 335 Tuesday, 25 March 1712 [Addison] 118
No. 411 Saturday, 21 June 1712 [Addison] 121
No. 412 Monday, 23 June 1712 [Addison] 124

John Gay

THE SHEPHERD'S WEEK

Monday; or, The Squabble 129

TRIVIA; OR, THE ART OF WALKING THE STREETS OF LONDON (BOOK III) 135

FABLES

I XXIV. The Butterfly and the Snail 148
I XLIX. The Man and the Flea 149

James Thomson

THE SEASONS

Winter 153

Edward Young

THE COMPLAINT; OR, NIGHT THOUGHTS

Night I 187

William Collins

ODE ON THE POETICAL CHARACTER 201

ODE TO EVENING 204

THE PASSIONS: AN ODE FOR MUSIC 206

ODE ON THE POPULAR SUPERSTITIONS OF THE HIGHLANDS OF SCOTLAND 210

Thomas Gray

David Hume

Charles Churchill

Christopher Smart

Oliver Goldsmith

Thomas Chatterton

Edward Gibbon

❧ Preface ❧

This anthology is designed to supplement the inexpensive separate editions of the major writers of this period that are now easily available. We have omitted Dryden, Pope, Swift, Johnson, Boswell, and Blake, as well as the novelists, having learned in teaching eighteenth-century courses that the usual anthology selections of these writers were inadequate for our purposes. We have also eliminated writers of the James Beattie class because we have never found time in such courses to consider them. This anthology provides, instead, sufficiently long and substantial selections from important writers—at least, this was our aim—so that they may be studied critically with profit.

Since this anthology is intended primarily for undergraduates, the annotation has been made as comprehensive as possible: it is easy for a student to disregard a footnote which tells him what he already knows, but it is impossible for a blank page to supply what he does not. The problem of choosing which works to include presents obvious difficulties, but they have seemed minor in comparison with determining which texts of these works to reproduce. *A Song to David* offers few textual difficulties, but who is to decide which version or combination of versions of *The Jolly Beggars* is the best to present? In general, we have preferred to print almost fully normalized texts (except for Chatterton and Burns) based on what seemed the best early edition of each work; occasionally we have incorporated variant readings when that procedure seemed justifiable. In the case of Gibbon, we have expanded his footnotes to meet modern standards of documentation, a perhaps supererogatory labor, but one which will aid any reader who wishes to explore Gibbon's use of his sources.

The Introduction is meant to provide a general critical guide to the period, while the introductory sketch to each author has been restricted to a skeleton of essential information. The preparation of the anthology has been a cooperative venture, but besides writing the Introduction Mr. Price is mainly responsible for the section from Butler through Young, and Mr. Brady for the section from Collins through Crabbe.

The italicized date after the title of a work is its date of composition; the unitalicized date is its date of first publication. The names of the following periodicals have been abbreviated throughout: *English Literary History* (ELH); *Huntington Library Quarterly* (HLQ); *Modern Language Quarterly* (MLQ); *Publications of the Modern Language Association of America* (PMLA); *Review of English Studies* (RES); *Studies in Philology* (SP).

We wish to thank the following for their generous and often patient assistance: W. Kenneth Cornell, William Frost, Frederick W. Hilles, Roger H. Lonsdale, Georges C. May, Elias F. Mengel, Jr., B. Davie Napier, Henry F. and Lorna H. Pope, Frederick A. Pottle, Charles Ryskamp, Edmund T. Silk, and Warren Smith. We are indebted in particular to Charles E. Beckwith on whose unpublished dissertation, "John Gay's Eclogues and Georgics" (Yale, 1956), we drew for our annotation to Gay's works; to Wilmarth S. Lewis for permission to quote from Horace Walpole's notes on Gray's *The Candidate,* which have been published in *The Yale Edition of Horace Walpole's Correspondence;* and to David M. Vieth, who prepared the text printed here of Rochester's *Satyr against Mankind.*

F.B.
M.P.

Hanover and
New Haven
December, 1960

◈ Introduction ◈

With the return of the Stuarts to the throne in 1660, English monarchy entered a new phase. For it soon became clear, once the odes of adulation had cooled, that the King would have to rule on a new basis. In place of "the right divine of Kings to govern wrong" (as Pope was to describe the doctrines of James I), the myth of the social contract had grown into a dominant assumption of political theorists. It might, as in Hobbes, be a contract which man was forced to undertake by his own insatiable and appetitive nature; better one sovereign than the chaotic insecurity of every man seeking his own unlimited ends. But it might, as in Locke, become a free gesture of a people capable of achieving a society in their natural state, anxious to preserve and protect the freedom they already enjoy. In Locke's view the social contract becomes a myth which envisages man capable of creating order for himself, a creature of independent power and will, ready to enter into an agreement based upon an idea of justice. Instead of Hobbes's man desperately seeking to check his own savagery by surrendering his power to the will of an all-powerful sovereign, we have a man of intrinsic social reasonableness confirming in government what he approves in his nature. This secular myth of the foundation of the state does not preclude a religious end to be pursued (Swift felt, for example, that the stability of the state depended upon its established church and sense of religious purpose); but it starts from man in nature and seeks a government "of laws, not men," of principle rather than authority.

There is a similar movement in the religious thought of the day. Throughout the conflicts of the seventeenth century, the two extremes are a thorough surrender to an established authority (competent to end dispute and to interpret the ambiguous teachings of the Bible) and a thorough assertion of the inward light of the private conscience, claiming divine illumination and denying all authority which might seek to control it. The destructive "wars of truth" bred a strong desire to find a middle way, a compromise between authority and often fanatical individualism (such as produced the innumerable splintering sects of the time). The search for compromise led to suspicion of excessive emotionalism and its attendant self-deception, superstition, or arrogance (beautifully rendered by Butler in *Hudibras*). It led, in turn, to an emphasis upon those simple, common, unimpeachable truths which all men of good will could find in a disinterested reading of the Bible; for these no dubiously authoritative interpreter was needed. The fascination with religious mysteries, the love of the paradoxical and unimaginable, the adoration of inscrutable power, were sacrificed to a new vision of a God who circumscribes Himself with rational goodness, who acts—like a monarch—according to laws (which He reveals to man in nature), and who may be approached with love and trust rather than prostrate fear. God's circumscription of Himself may, indeed, render Him a more remote and equable deity, less immediate than a God who enters our lives with sudden irascibility or in miraculous descents of mercy. Increasingly, the stress becomes moral: the God in man is the God we all can know, and it is in our following of His example and His commandments that we can best do Him worship. For Pope, in the *Essay on Man*, God is a living presence, immanent in all we are and see:

> To him no high, no low, no great, no small;
> He fills, he bounds, connects, and equals all.
>
> i 279-80

To imitate God is to achieve our human counterpart to His universal love. As man's love extends from self to friend, from neighbor to country, from mankind to all the creatures who compose the cosmos, he becomes like God. As he, too, "sees with equal eye" and universal benevolence:

> Earth smiles around, with boundless bounty blest,
> And Heaven beholds its image in his breast.
>
> iv 371-72

The consequence of such a view is to place high value upon the order man achieves within himself, to see a model for this order in God's constant artistry in nature and in the encompassing love with which He includes a vast and various world (vaster than earlier ages had experienced, both in the cosmic scale of Newtonian astronomy and in the geographic scale of new colonies and spreading commerce).

The growth of experimental science in England, given impetus by Charles II's chartering of the Royal Society in 1662, was itself symptomatic of a new concern with common agreements about incontrovertible facts. The scientific temper, ludicrous as its corruptions might be, provides another model of disinterested inquiry and reverent curiosity; the natural studies of countless mariners, country gentlemen, rural clergymen, and urban societies find their counterpart in the remarkable closeness of attention a poet like Thomson or Cowper can bring to the phenomena of nature. The interest in landscape which is fed by the pastoral tradition fuses Virgilian archetypes with fresh perception, an ideal landscape with a landscape of fact. If England has her own Arcadia, she has it in a peculiar and precious English form. The very frequency of travel, as young gentlemen undertook the Grand Tour and young poets or painters went along as their tutors, awakened a new sense of the variety of scenes, stimulated a desire to find Italian counterparts in the English landscape but also to find distinctive beauties which might rival those of the Continent. Still, the act of discovery and of ordering natural phenomena was itself the greatest pleasure: at every point, whether in the laboratory or the garden, nature gave back the image of man's mind.

The desire for order which marks the search for agreement and compromise, for disinterested or practical inquiry rather than acrimonious speculation, shows itself in the new literary forms of the day. There are survivals of the wit of the Metaphysicals in the new style; but, typically, it turns back to the model of Rome for a greater simplicity, urbanity, and dignity. This looking backward is another assertion of man's intrinsic powers; for it is the literary virtues which antedate Christianity that are sought, with a humanistic confidence in the greatness of classical antiquity (and a humanistic sense of it as a "living past") that rejects the local idiosyncrasies of "Gothic" national taste. (It was later in the eighteenth century that the pre-Christian literature of the north was revived, but in the interval England had experimented, in all the arts, with the exotic forms of a great range of cultures.) The turning to classical models and examples was part of a new sense, moreover, of cultural stability. The forms of English politics were now closer to those of Republican Rome; the growth of London both in size and in importance aroused a new ideal of *urbanitas;* the sense of England's comparative freedom and enterprise (encouraged by such admiring visitors as Voltaire) gave rise to a vision of England as a robust and responsible Rome inheriting the culture of now decadent tyrannies, such as the France and Spain of the Bourbons.

The literary ideas which asserted themselves most strongly were clarity and correctness, a surrender of wayward cleverness to the integrity and order of the work itself, a surrender of the desire to astonish and confound to the end of giving rational pleasure in shapely and meaningful works of art. Dr. Johnson's words on the Metaphysicals are telling: "As they were wholly employed on something unexpected and surprising, they had no regard for that uniformity of sentiment which enables us to conceive and to excite the pains and the pleasure of other minds. . . . Their courtship was void of fondness, and their lamentation of sorrow. Their wish was only to say what they hoped had been never said before" (*Life of Cowley*). It should be observed that Johnson is writing of the Metaphysicals' neglect of the "pathetic" and that the standard he invokes is one of shared feelings, of sentiments such as we might share with Horace as well as with each other. As Pope makes clear in the *Essay on Criticism,* such common sentiments have found expression in traditional forms; Homer explored the possibilities of the epic so fully that—for the succeeding writer in that form—"Nature and Homer were, he found, the same" (i 135). The new poet, fallible and inexperienced, cannot help following the models of the past; he will, inevitably, seek to achieve uniqueness of some sort, if only to do justice to his peculiar experience, but he will depart from his models only to do better what they have done or to go farther along the path that they have marked. The danger which besets the poet is a premature fondness for his idiosyncrasies or his fame; in seeking to say what has never been said before, he may (as Johnson suggests) say ineptly what he does not know has been better said before—or produce an exhibition of strained and futile ingenuity.

Part of the tradition which the poet inherited was that of genres or traditional forms, and no English writers before the Augustans (the name suggests their loyalty to the Rome of Virgil and Horace) had taken these forms so seriously. They are set forth in a Renaissance critic like Sidney, but they are not exemplified with rigor until the eighteenth century. Thomas Hobbes set up a table of these forms and tries to relate them to levels of society; the Court produces heroic poetry and tragedy; the City, satire and comedy; the Country, pastoral (*Answer to Davenant*). This is a more rigid pattern than the age was to follow, but it establishes a hierarchy of genres and a sense of the idiom as well as manners peculiar to each. It is on the discrimination of idioms, a sense of levels of style, that many of the subtlest effects of the writing of the age are based. For, given so precise a scheme, the writer could work variations upon it or make significant departures from it in a way that would be immediately sensed by his readers.

The same advantages were given him by the dominant verse-form of the age, the heroic couplet. The use of rhyme, which had no classical precedent, was justified in a way that accords with classical discipline; as Dryden says, verse is "a rule and line by which [the poet] keeps his building compact and even, which otherwise lawless imagination would raise either irregularly or loosely. At least, if the poet commits errors with this help, he would make greater and more without it: 'tis, in short, a slow and painful, but the surest kind of working. . . . Thus then the second thoughts being usually the best, as receiving the maturest digestion from judgment, and the last and most mature product of those thoughts being artful and labored verse, it may well be inferred, that verse is a great help to a luxuriant fancy . . ." (*Essay of Dramatic Poesy*). In fact, the closed heroic couplet, with its pointed rhyme, achieves a very complex internal economy: the couplet splits into lines, the lines often break with caesuras or internal rests. The possibility of balance and opposition of phrases is enormous, especially as the opposition of phrases may be underlined by resemblances of sound:

> Beauty that shocks you, parts that none will trust;
> Wit that can creep, and pride that licks the dust.
> > Pope, *Epistle to Dr. Arbuthnot,* ll. 332-33

> Hence all thy natural worship takes the source:
> 'Tis revelation what thou thinkst discourse.
> > Dryden, *Religio Laici,* ll. 70-71

So artful and measured is the pattern of the couplet that it builds up a strong tissue of expectations, and these expectations may be rewarded or disappointed with telling effect:

> Bounded by Nature, narrowed still by Art,
> A trifling head, and a contracted heart.

> *Dunciad,* iv 503-4

The difference between *bounded,* with its suggestion of natural limits, and *narrowed,* with its suggestion of artificial reduction, is matched and yet surprisingly intensified in the second line, where the triviality is associated with intelligence and the tight, grasping closeness with the feelings. *Contracted heart* is a phrase that is earned by the ratio set up in the couplet; but it more than fulfills that function and suggests new dimensions.

The couplet, then, achieves the intensity of poetic statement less through the pursuit of extravagant metaphor than through the shrewd dislocation of familiar words. It awakens words into new life:

> Heaven visits with a Taste the wealthy fool,
> And needs no Rod but Ripley with a Rule.

> *Moral Essay* iv,17-18

Here Pope handles the word *Taste* as if it were the name of a plague (while preserving the fashionable term with which the fool contents himself); and he develops the theme of God's scourge with the well-known name of Ripley (in his eyes a mere carpenter elevated by the false taste of fashion into a prominent architect). Ripley as carpenter carries his *rule,* the physical counterpart of God's *rod;* Ripley as a man "without any genius in the art" punishes his patron's folly by his own unthinking adherence to pedantic rules. The puns make all these meanings "belong" together and give seeming logical tightness to a complicated statement, just as the alliteration makes Ripley "belong" to this role as if he were named for the sake of it. A few lines later in the same poem Pope addresses Lord Burlington:

> You show us, Rome was glorious, not profuse,
> And pompous buildings once were things of use.

> 23-24

The polysyllabics and plosive sounds of *pompous buildings* are mocked and overthrown by the simplicity of *things of use.* But in the first line, the articulated syllables of *glorious* seem to "belong" to Rome much more than the slurred first syllable and long, open second syllable of *profuse* (which is linked by sound to *pompous*). The chiastic structure and the fixing of opposites (*profuse . . . use*) in the rhyming words intensify the incongruities all the more; all the sound patterns contribute to the incongruities of sense, which converge on the paradox that what was natural or functional design for the severe Romans has become (in the hands of Ripleys) shallow decorative art created to overwhelm us with borrowed grandeur.

ii

What has been said so far is only part of the truth, and the more familiar part at that. For the Augustan compromise is earned only through a skeptical reconsideration of most of the inherited values and traditions. In Rochester's *Satyr against Mankind,* for example, we find the stunning incongruity between the noble vision of rational man and the hateful spectacle of his actual behavior. The traditionally honored godlike faculty has been corrupted into the instrument of low appetites; the franker appetites of beasts are cleaner and less contemptible. The acts and institutions in which man takes pride serve only to convict him the more readily of hypocrisy and the lust for power. One can see a similar bill of accusation drawn later in Swift's *Gulliver's Travels.* And yet the censure of man's errors may itself breed a new pride, as we see in the final misanthropic arrogance of Gulliver or, more slightly, in the proud last word of the Flea in Gay's fable of *The Man and the Flea.* The task of the critic is at once to remove himself from participation in a common moral insensibility or complacency and still to accept his own inevitable immersion in the human condition. He is "stung" into contempt, and he must relinquish the charity which would only condone and perpetuate error; his role as moral censor is a difficult and lonely one, and he may picture it as quizzical detachment, as half-mad rage, or as the terrible elevation of the Biblical prophet. But he is aware, at best, of the iridescence of his role: it shimmers between arrogance, malice, and insanity on one side; moral dignity, demanding love, and humility before a true good on the other.

The peculiar status of the critic-satirist is but one dimension of the larger issue of man's status. We can see in Halifax's detached view of Charles II the simultaneous presence of compulsion and choice, of the king who cannot help be what his somewhat trivial nature makes him and the king who rises to his station and acquits himself with charm and decency. There is little reverence in Halifax's portrait and much irony; Halifax, who accepted the title of Trimmer with pride, can hold to a mixed and middle view, one of critical acceptance. The extremes that Halifax holds together tend to split apart in the works of Shaftesbury and Mandeville. So intense is Shaftesbury's devotion to liberty and to man's self-determination that he argues constantly for man's intrinsic capacities, his moral health, his readiness to accept trust and to honor it. Man must free himself of self-imposed limitations, rather than an intrinsic evil, and train himself up to a full sense of what in his deepest nature he reverences, the best in himself. With such discipline, like that of a man trained to see a work of art with full aesthetic perception, man will immediately see what is right ("As those move easiest who have learned to dance"), and see the beauty of the good act as readily as the work of art. The enemy, for Shaftesbury, is a system that depresses man's capacities, assumes that he must be bribed into goodness or threatened away from evil, and produces a vicious world of slaves who wish to become tyrants because they worship only power. Such a view of man exalts him beyond the trust of most critics, and Mandeville opposes to it a cynical exploration of the element of self-love which is present in all man's behavior. Only such self-love or pride makes man tamable; for it makes him capable of being shamed into decency and makes most men prouder of their self-denials than they might be of open gratification. Man is controlled by "artful managers" who use their understanding to make society possible; and, in fact, man's universal self-seeking makes for the growing prosperity of a complex society. Mandeville sees man as anything but self-determined; his happiness is the result of either natural evolution or political "management," and his social order is born accidentally (a clergyman might say providentially) of man's blind appetites.

This opposition of man as a creature of choice and man as a creature of chance perpetuates the old opposition of Stoic and Epicurean systems, and the very clarity of the opposition produces innumerable possibilities for satire. In the greatest satires of the age, in Swift's *Tale of a Tub* or Pope's *Dunciad,* one can see the fullest exploration of the guise of choice concealing the rule of chance. The three brothers of Swift's allegory (who represent the church in its worldly career) have clear and sound injunctions in their father's testament; but they twist his word (or His Word) until it serves their appetites, and their appetites are controlled in turn by mercurial shifts of fashion. In *The Dunciad,* the world worships the "uncreating Word," the very negation of Being, with all the panoply and dedication of pious champions; for the mother-goddess is nothing more than their own appetites and compulsions enshrined in a mindless, indulgent version of pseudo-diety. Such a view of man's readiness for self-deception, the power he derives from foisting his will upon an image of God and worshiping as Other what is unexamined Self, informs Gibbon's study of the rise of Christianity. Needless to say, the flat hypocrisy of such a buffoon as Butler's Hudibras has little of the power which comes of sincere and thorough self-deception, and a writer like Gibbon refuses to assign motives but suggests the complexity of motives which govern any situation. Like many of the skeptical men of the period, he can see the cruelty and opportunism which are inextricably mixed with the highest intentions and are the more dangerous for the disarming mixture.

This distrust of motives expresses itself in the unsettling of genres and the emergence of what is perhaps the highest Augustan achievement, the mixed or mock form. The age was obsessed with the image of the hero, and the great translations of Dryden and Pope were attempts to give contemporary meaningfulness to the heroes of Virgil and Homer. But the distended image of heroism that we see in the heroic plays of the Restoration sets the note of quizzical skepticism for the age which follows: the heroes of Dryden's plays present the problem of heroism with something of the levity which we feel in the extreme instance and in brilliant dialectical overstatement. In the finest comedies of the age, the daring of the detached hero, often a rake, has something of the naked honesty that Rochester sees in the beast, something of the anguish one sees in the moral critic, something of the freedom from cant and self-deception that one sees in the destroyers of codes (whether courtly, religious, or moral). The problem of the hero returns us to the problematic view of man. He is held to the demands made upon him in the heroic vision and yet exposed for his inevitable failure to meet them. The heroic style is elevated and remote: the actual present stands against it, unable to realize the pattern, constantly affronting the high generality with its clumsy and petty particularities—as Gay's bumpkins in *The Shep-*

herd's Week affront the Virgilian forms they seek to fill. Yet the double mock-heroic vision is not a simple condemnation of man; often it suggests that the heroic image has a vacuous elevation, as remote from realization as the rhetorical gestures of the actor or the noble postures of antique plaster casts. Achilles is a myth and we are men. Sir Joshua Reynolds makes a related point in arguing for Shakespeare's mixed forms against the purer tragedy of the unities: "I suspect that the rigid forms to be observed in tragedy, of admitting nothing that shall divert and recreate, is formed upon what we ought to like if we were endued with perfect wisdom and taste. But that is not the case. We are governed by our passions as well as our reason. Man is both a consistent and an inconsistent being, a lover of art when it imitates nature and of nature when it imitates art, of uniformity and of variety, a creature of habit that loves novelty. The principles of art must conform to this capricious being" (*Portraits by Sir Joshua Reynolds,* ed. F. W. Hilles [1952], App. I).

The strain of the unrelieved heroic induces a sense of its unreality, and yet its myths embody aspirations we cannot abandon; they rebuke as well as inspire us. Insofar as the poet somewhat mocks their unreality he may move toward the realism of genre painting, the celebration of rustic simplicity or of urban robustness that we see in Gay (or in Swift earlier and Fielding later); in these pictures, there is sacrifice of man's dignity to a sense of his animal vigor and charm (as in Chaucer's description of the wife in *The Miller's Tale* or of the barnyard in *The Nun's Priest's Tale*). Insofar as the poet insists upon man's accountability, he may dramatize the heroic image in its perversion, as in *Hudibras* or *The Dunciad,* or in its difficult assumption by a man of conscience ("Yes, I am proud; I must be proud to see, Men not afraid of God, afraid of me"). But whatever the shading in mock-heroic or mock-pastoral works, the poet has held together disparate images of man that suggest the whole range of human dignity and squalor, boldness and low cunning, self-knowledge and blindness. Man's failure is a corruption of his moral will, but it is also presented as a failure of mind. For the failure to see himself as he is, makes man, even at the moment of highest pride, subhuman, mechanical, a lump of matter eluding form. And the clearest symptom of this failure of mind is the corruption of words. They sacrifice meaning to sound, distinctions to deceptions; they become slogans or empty cant, as does the Word in the mouths of fools and knaves.

The holding together of disparate views is characteristic not only of the view of man but of the view of art itself. It is a literature of high artifice claiming to follow nature. It is a poetry that values the "grandeur of generality"; but no poetry has been so completely enmeshed in the life of its time as Augustan satire. The age distrusts the ingenious sophistries of Metaphysical wit; yet it constantly plays logical tricks of its own. "A play . . . to be like Nature, is to be set above it . . ." (*Essay of Dramatic Poesy*). "Some, to whom Heaven in wit has been profuse, Want as much more, to turn it to its use" (*Essay on Criticism,* i 80-1). So Dryden and Pope, calling attention to paradoxes almost as flatly as Edward Young's "Teach my best reason, reason" (*Night Thoughts,* i). It is clear that the Augustans valued the ambiguity of these key terms and kept playing off their implicit, opposed meanings. Nature was both a principle of order in creation and the whole body of created things. In the first sense, Nature, it is a principle constantly seeking realization in a resistant medium (like the Aristotelian form operating in matter); at any particular moment or place man may carry its work to local perfection in a work of art (as the gardener realizes the "possibilities" of the landscape or the sculptor "frees" the form from the stone). In the second sense, nature, it is the outward mixture of ordering principle and recalcitrant matter. Dryden sees the playwright's need to carry to realization the ordering principle in his action as Nature, in its vast scale of operation, cannot and need not. (Yet the more intense and artful the artist's ordering, the greater the danger of his losing all relationship with nature.) So, "true wit" is fertility and facility in discovering relationships that have basis in reality; "false wit" is the power to discover likenesses divorced from the critical judgment which discerns simultaneous differences, or the fertility of invention divorced from the disposing judgment which rejects the irrelevant and disorderly. Pope stresses the inadequacy of false wit taken alone; in fact, it becomes false only through neglecting the judgment and claiming to be self-sufficient. Addison in *Spectator* #58 gives us a collection of pieces of rampant false wit before he goes on in succeeding papers to define "mixed wit," where the surprise of verbal devices is tamed and strengthened by the soundness of meaningful relationships. Again, "right reason" is the recognition of true relationships, perhaps intuitively and immediately perceived, but confirmed by all previous experience (tradition) and all subsequent (posterity). "Erring reason," as Pope calls it, is logically persuasive, systematic deduction from dubious principles; and their dubiousness is ignored because of the reasoner's pride or partiality. Young is asking that his seemingly rational mind be freed of the all-but-inevitable deceptions of self-interest.

One of the central metaphors of the period, and one which catches all these ambiguities, is that of dress. The "naked Nature" is beyond man's perception (like the Platonic idea) and would need, in any case, like Milton's divine truths, to be accommodated to human understanding. But to overdress Nature (as to overregularize a garden) is to obscure her utterly, to take pleasure in the art of dressing for its own sake or for its demonstration of the artist's ingenuity. At one extreme is nakedness; at the other is foppery—so frequently presented in Restoration comedy; in the allegory of Swift's *Tale of a Tub* or the formalities of the courts in the first and third voyages of *Gulliver's Travels;* in Pope's "glaring chaos and wild heap of wit" in the *Essay on Criticism* or its embodiment in Timon's Villa (*Moral Essay* iv); in the insectile glitter of Sporus (*Epistle to Dr. Arbuthnot*) or the vile splendors of Dulness' court in *The Dunciad.* (There are constant echoes of the "insectile race" in Thomson, Young, and Cowper.) True dress, like true wit, is a matter of "decency" in its Latin sense of the fitting; true dress reveals Nature rather than obscures it, reveals it through dressing it "to advantage," at once making it more accessible and familiar, and (by accommodating it to our time-bound taste) more beautiful. The metaphor keeps alive the tension between the timeless and general ("one clear, unchanged and universal light") and the local and particular ("And part admit, and part exclude the day"), between the imitation of the order of Nature and the artifices by which that imitation is most plausibly or effectively achieved, between the elusive "living grace" and the endeavors of methodical art. Like Milton in his account of Paradise, the Augustan is often (to repeat Reynolds' words) "a lover of art when it imitates nature and of nature when it imitates art." We can see this in the pastoral (where the two are fused) and in the moral and picturesque landscapes (where nature discloses the design of the painter) of Pope's *Windsor Forest,* Thomson's *Seasons,* Gray's *The Bard,* or Goldsmith's *Deserted Village.* But, if these ideal relation-

ships are admired, their incongruous upsetting is the keynote of
much satire:

> On the stage he was natural, simple, affecting;
> 'Twas only that when he was off he was acting.

Goldsmith's lines on Garrick present a gentle incongruity, as do
Gay's urban georgics and rustic mock-pastorals; in Gray's lines on
Lord Holland's Seat, there is more of the characteristic point and
shock of high Augustan satire.

iii

Throughout the period which begins with the Restoration there
are instances of a kind of poetry which reaches its ascendancy only
at the middle of the eighteenth century. Boileau had edited and
translated Longinus' treatise on the Sublime in 1674, and its emphasis upon elevation of spirit in the poet, upon the imagery which
transcends imaginable limits, upon a quality of imagination which
cuts across all genres and forms, all contribute increasingly to English literary taste in the eighteenth century. Cowley's free imitations
and translations of Pindar, as well as his linking of Pindar's sublimity
with that of the Hebrew prophets, set the tone for the "great ode."
The ode, in its irregular line and stanza lengths, and in its cul-
tivation of sudden or abrupt transitions, became the high form of
enthusiastic utterance, a "heroic" poetry whose very rule was to disdain formal bounds. Although Dryden wrote close to his best work
in the form and Swift used it for his earliest poems, the ode in the
early eighteenth century serves largely the purposes of choral music,
public celebrations, and what Johnson called the "meanness and
servility of hyperbolical adulation." Its revival in the 1740's marks
its emergence as a major rather than an incidental form: much of
Gray's and Collins' most ambitious work (as of the Romantic poets
later) is in the Pindaric ode (which Gay restores to Pindaric
regularity in *The Bard*). The emergence of the ode is not a major
event in itself but a symptomatic one; it accommodates new effects
of sound, incantatory and hypnotic rather than bound closely to
meaning; it allows the rapid apostrophe, the vivid address to a
visionary presence; it permits a "musicalization" of structure, a
greater freedom from even the surface logic of the couplet and the
discursive sequence of the verse essay. Johnson's strictures on Gray's

odes catch their effect, however unsympathetically: they are, he says, "marked by glittering accumulations of ungraceful ornaments; they strike rather than please; the images are magnified by affectation; the language is labored into harshness. The mind of the writer seems to work with unnatural violence. *Double, double, toil and trouble.* He has a kind of strutting dignity, and is tall by walking on tiptoe. His art and his struggle are too visible, and there is too little appearance of ease and nature" (*Life of Gray*).

Johnson's terms serve admirably, if one shears away their judgment of value, to define the typical poetry of an "age of sensibility." Northrop Frye has described [1] the emergence of a new age as the movement from a "literature of product" (finished, achieved, bounded, and formal) to a "literature of process," where the writer calls attention to himself as writer and to his poem as "work in progress." Characteristically for Collins and frequently for Gray, the subject matter is poetry itself or at least the poet— seen as prophet, as bard, as the power of imagination itself, calling its own visionary world into being and breaking through the shell of mundane actuality. One can see this movement foreshadowed in such enthusiastic works as Dryden's odes, obliquely through its debasement in *The Dunciad,* more explicitly in Thomson and Young; it reaches its culmination in Smart's celebration of David and in Blake's prophetic books. In its effort to break free of Augustan conventions and to assert the freedom and creative power of imagination, this poetry often becomes highly artificial and extravagantly "literary." Gray wrote to his friend Richard West, "The language of the age is never the language of poetry." Gray sees poetic diction as something heightened above a common idiom, steeped in literary usage, enriched by "foreign idioms and derivatives," by archaisms, or by new words of the poet's own invention. It is a hieratic language, peculiar to poetry, "sounding" and musical, less concerned with reference to an actual world than with a coherence of its own.

For this reason, the "struggle" may be indeed "too visible" in Gray. A poet like Young, with his imagery of thrust and drive— of bursting, soaring, plunging—also dramatizes struggle, the struggle of awakening religious consciousness. And what Young presents as

[1] In "Towards Defining an Age of Sensibility," in *Eighteenth-Century English Literature,* ed. James L. Clifford (1959).

a moral struggle, Gray and Collins often represent in the process of their poems as the struggle of the artist to rise to his prophetic status. It is the special genius of Blake to see the full power and difficulty of this struggle and to give symbolic form to the internal conflicts between the desire for order and the need for energy, between distrust of self which breeds repressive tyranny and the acceptance of self which make possible forgiveness and generous self-surrender. In the earlier poetry, the assertion of imagination (and the adherence to Young's maxim, "reverence thyself") is more sanguine and more histrionic. If it cultivates literary artifice in order to surmount the commonplace, it turns for the same reason to the primitive and attempts to re-create the spirit and idiom of the great untutored bard (as Homer and Ossian were conceived to be) or of the inspired poetry of Old Testament psalmist and prophet. These two departures from the commonplace meet again in their common exoticism (Persian eclogues and Hebrew prophecy are, first of all, Oriental poetry), in their passionate tone (the language of Milton, of Pindar, or of Old Norse sagas sounds the accent of Whiggish liberty), and in their rejection of the manners of a polite, sane, and worldly society. These works aspire to become what Joseph Warton called "pure poetry," free of the discursive speech of reasonable persuasion, committed instead to that act of vision induced by high emotion. Such effects may have, as Johnson remarked, an element of strain and self-consciousness, a "strutting dignity." There is an element of pose; the poet seems to strike an attitude in order to summon up a feeling. The poet may, in fact, strike new and outlandish attitudes in order to discover what feelings they will summon up. This introduces a note of playful detachment into the very gestures of deep feeling; we are aware of the art which is needed to reach the natural. Our interest lies in the very process of evocation or summoning-up; and the poetic process becomes more fascinating than its product. The poet tends to displace the poem (or, as in *Tristram Shandy*, the novelist the novel), and the imagination interests us more for what it is than for what it yields.

The most important critical term for such a period is the *sublime* (which Addison introduces as the "great"), for the sublime is achieved by the very act of transcending the mind's familiar categories (the corresponding term for the poet who achieves it is *genius*). The sublime seeks those forms which might cause the reason to surrender before them: suggestions of infinity in time and space, an obscurity which obliterates meaningful distinctions, a show of power which staggers the mind's security—all that over-whelms, discomforts, and thwarts the mind's preconceptions; and all that summons up new energies of resistance and self-assertion in the mind. The imagery of the sublime can take the forms of mountain, sheer cliff, ocean, mysterious night, vast ruins, sinister aliens or ancients, savage battle, and violent crime. These define the internal dimensions of the sublime (as Addison says, "a spacious prospect is an image of liberty"): the mind has its own mountains and crevasses, its own volcanic eruptions and glimmering marshes. The outward images, all too easily made mechanical and ludicrously over-insistent, are often the means for discovering inward depths. The literature of process is also a literature of self-discovery. One conse-quence is that the pictorial image is threatened, just as it is in Milton's descriptions of Hell or Heaven; the landscape is at once external and internal, a landscape of the mind at its extremes of splendor or terror. Burke insists that the sublime must transcend the image itself and pass beyond the visual as it approaches infinity: "A clear idea is therefore another name for a little idea." Conse-quently the images of nature, in the great odes particularly, tend to become magnified in scale or in "sounding" and suggestive language (like the allusive and sonorous names that ring through *Paradise Lost*); muted by mist, by twilight, or by distance, to the dimness of surmise; or, finally, invested with more than human presences. Between the external scene and the internal energies stand those tutelary deities of the age, the personified forces which the poet invokes, perceives, and locates in his landscape. They are virtually emblems of the imaginative power itself, the "shadowy tribes of mind" called forth by the poet as mythmaker.

These qualities of the literature of the period find their support in other circumstances as well: it is an age of psychology. What might have seemed objective laws of the universe are translated into the involuntary bent of man's mind. The causal necessity which seemed part of the rational structure of nature Hume sees instead as a habit of our thought. More and more the formation of ideas and beliefs is explained by the accidental association of unrelated ideas (perhaps, beyond man's knowing, providential). Some studied this association of ideas as scientists, hopeful of achieving a Newtonian system of the mind. Others were more impressed by the mysterious complexity of the mind's processes, aware of the transforming power of feeling upon our perceptions, and quick to emphasize the unpredictable felicity of association which a genius like Shakespeare might achieve. More important, the wayward and idiosyncratic patterns of the mind gained increasing respect. Burke could oppose to the inhuman rationality of the French Revolution the slow organic growth, as if by the accidents of nature, of the English constitution. And, having accepted religion as "the basis of civil society," he could defiantly accept its most questionable expressions: "there is no rust of superstition, with which the accumulated absurdity of the human mind might have crusted it over in the course of ages, that ninety-nine in a hundred of the people of England would not prefer to impiety" (*Reflections on the French Revolution*).

It is not unusual—we see it again today—for the poet who seeks new intensity of awareness and new modes of giving coherence to his awareness to turn with renewed sympathy to the "accumulated absurdity of the human mind"—to the superstitions of the Highlands; to the magical terrors of old ballads; to irrational ties of blood, locality, and shared experience; to the improbable wisdom of the child, the fool, or the dispossessed. In a poet as dry and sane as Crabbe can be, there is a fascination with the corrosive force of guilt in Peter Grimes and a minute tracing of the terrible power that the natural processes of mind can attain—the natural equivalent of the fantasies of Gothic terror and supernatural presences. Crabbe's very submission of the histrionic and "literary" inventions of earlier poets to the devices of a dry realism is in itself symptomatic of that "natural piety" which disdains the effort to exhibit the extraordinary emotion and the extreme situation. It carries over something of the Augustan emphasis upon the hard everyday reality, the limited station of man and the difficult heroism of unostentatious wisdom. Goldsmith surrounds the pretensions of the Auburn schoolmaster with irony, but the irony is suffused also with the pity that the poem's occasion casts upon the whole of the departed village life. The pity shows itself in a respect, if not a reverence, for a living community bound together by feeling and custom; and it tends to make of the absurd or ludicrous something picturesque—part of the dense and irregular harmony of genre painting. In fact, the picturesque accommodates especially the pleasure in abundant vitality—the shagginess of the worn and familiar; the accidental clutter of market or barnyard; the indistinguishable mixture of cottage, wood, and rutted paths; the scene with varied emotions caught in one composite dramatic event; the familiar occasion (the courtship, the deathbed) where simple people untidily achieve the deep and resonant feeling of traditionally high and ceremonious events. To claim for the undistinguished man the dignities or at least the attention due the traditional hero, to insist upon the preciousness of the commonplace (and to look at it with a new closeness and affection) is to rob the mock-heroic of its humor and to push it toward sentimentality. Once the edge of asserting new values is lost, the clichés of humble heroism may become a new convention and demand more and more stimulation of pathos to keep them alive.

The finest poets of the age escape sentimentality through humor or astringent indignation, through a sharpness rather than a softness of focus, through a clear view of the mysterious and often frightening processes of the heart rather than a trivial, cozy celebration of them. Perhaps most fundamental in these poets is a sense of the power of feeling; and power always tends both to exalt and appall. We can see its open terror in Cowper's lines written during madness or in the close of *The Castaway,* in Burns's studies of savage self-righteousness; but we can see something of this power, too, in the bemused picture Cowper provides of the yearning for nature producing pathetic window boxes in town, in the amusing idiosyncrasies of Goldsmith's friends, in the pressure of unrealized life that is now contained in Gray's country churchyard or of suffering yet to be endured that is evoked by the prospect of Eton. At its highest reaches this sense of the power of feeling emerges as a new conception of the mind and the imagination. The very intensity of feeling becomes a shaping and constructive power.

Significantly, the shaping power informs both the poet's vision of his characters and the characters' vision of their plight. Poet and character become more closely identified than ever before; they participate in a common imaginative life. If the poet is set off from his character by his power to find words for this experience, he often conceals this distinction in his deliberate assumption of naïve or primitive forms. He reduces the distance between himself and his material, cultivates sympathy with it, and "enacts" its attitudes. This may result in a variety of effects, from somewhat patronizing affection through whimsical contemplation to a total self-effacement in an act of identification. Whatever the effect, there is a new emphasis on the artistry of emotions and a loss of the earlier stress upon judgment as the controlling power of composition. (It was this loss which Coleridge was to protest in such an assertion as "Shakespeare's Judgment Equal to His Genius.") But this tendency need not produce sentimentalism. If tender feelings are presented, so are the terrible. Above all, their presentation exhibits curiosity and exploration as often as it does complacent indulgence.

iv

The prose of the later eighteenth century moves, in one direction, toward a much more thoroughgoing artifice than the conversational style of the Augustans (itself an artfully created version of negligent spontaneity or candid simplicity). In Gibbon, Johnson, and Burke one finds a prose that is conspicuously rhetorical, as shaped and pointed in its way as the heroic couplet of Pope, drawn toward abstractness by its use of balance and antithesis, Latinate in its generalized diction. It is a style which imposes a strong ordering by the mind upon the stuff of experience, and the order has at times a splendid irrelevance to the stubborn particularity of experience. Its spacious terms include the specific objects they name, but they include much more as well. They have the scale of those great palace doors which are opened for ceremonial occasions and into which are cut wickets to admit the daily traffic. This generality is the cost that is paid for logical precision; for the more precise the distinctions become, the more abstract the terms must be. Yet the degree of precision often seems disproportionate to the occasion, as if the mind were reluctant to stint its analytic powers to meet the limited demands of the immediate task.

Such a style moves easily toward irony. In Johnson, the complexity of a situation is often reduced to lucid patterns, but the very proliferation of distinctions, in elaborated balances, points to the number of factors which inhere in a fact. The very poise of an antithetic style insists upon the irreducible contradictions of man's plight: "Marriage has many pains, but celibacy has no pleasures." In Gibbon's prose, as in Henry Fielding's, ironic politeness and mock gravity echo and intensify the rationalizations by which men

live. Fielding writes of Dr. Blifil's pursuit of Bridget Allworthy's
fortune:

> . . . as to criminal indulgences, he certainly never thought of
> them. This was owing either to his religion, as is most prob-
> able, or to the purity of his passion, which was fixed on those
> things which matrimony only, and not criminal correspondence,
> would put him in possession of, or could give him any title to.
>
> *Tom Jones,* I x

So, too, Gibbon accounts for the way in which the image of the
New Jerusalem undergoes alteration from pastoral simplicity to
urban splendor:

> A garden of Eden, with the amusements of the pastoral life, was
> no longer suited to the advanced state of society which pre-
> vailed under the Roman Empire. A city was therefore erected
> of gold and precious stones, and a supernatural plenty of corn
> and wine was bestowed on the adjacent territory, in the free
> enjoyment of whose spontaneous productions the happy and
> benevolent people was never to be restrained by any jealous
> laws of exclusive property.
>
> Chap. xv

In both passages the note of acquisitiveness is masked in the formality
of rational and generalized argument. The words insist upon what
they do not admit; the style does not choose (or, of course, need)
to specify the unspeakable or contemptible, the particular vice
or absurdity.

In another direction, the prose of the period moves toward the
nervous accuracy with which Boswell or Sterne can catch the very
unpredictability of experience in process. In Boswell's self-scrutiny
or in Sterne's exquisite tracing of gesture and sentiment, prose
becomes a kind of precision instrument for recording fugitive states,
emerging attitudes, nuances of feeling that resist abstraction. As
Boswell says, at the opening of his London journal, "A man cannot
know himself better than by attending to the feelings of his heart
and to his external actions. . . . I shall here put down my thoughts
on different subjects at different times, the whims that may seize
me and the sallies of my luxuriant imagination." Sterne, in *Tristram
Shandy,* gives the formality of a highly logical and generalized style

to Walter Shandy, but he surrounds it with the accidents of physical existence, with the exasperated sensibility of Walter himself and the mild incomprehension of Toby, most of all with details of gesture which often communicate where words cannot.

Perhaps one can see the tendencies of the prose of the age in these two journal entries:

> I then called for Lady Mirabel. She seemed to like me a good deal. I was lively, and I looked like the game. As it was my first visit, I was very quiet. However, it was agreed that I should visit her often. This elated me, as it afforded a fine, snug, and agreeable prospect of gallantry. Yet I could not think of being unfaithful to Louisa. But, then, I thought Louisa was only in the mean time, till I got into genteel life, and that a woman of fashion was the only proper object for such a man as me. At last delicate honor prevailed, and I was resolved for some time at least to keep alive my affection for Louisa.
>
> *Boswell's London Journal, 1762-1763,*
> ed. Frederick A. Pottle (1950),
> 18 January 1763

This girl grows upon me. Though she has said nothing extraordinary, I am convinced she is sensible; perhaps it's an illusion of passion, perhaps an effect of that sympathy by which people of understanding discover one another from the merest trifles.

> *Gibbon's Journal to January 28th, 1763,*
> ed. D. M. Low (1929), 7 September 1761

Neither passage is the purest instance of its kind. Yet, in Gibbon's balance of alternatives, in his concern with the nature of Miss Chetwynd rather than his own future experiences with her, we can see a marked difference from Boswell's alternation of feelings, his concentration upon his own image, his sense of the ephemeral ("for some time at least").

In Burke, finally, we can see a sublime prose style, taking up the grandeur of generality, informing it with the passion that disdains reasonable qualifications and measured argument. Burke uses the very idiom that can, in its ironic or deliberative aloofness, express coolness and detachment. But it becomes, in the *Letter to a Noble*

Lord, a vehicle for noble resentment, and the balances give way to the headlong rush of terms: "the grave, demure, insidious, spring-nailed, velvet-pawed, green-eyed philosophers, whether going upon two legs or upon four." Again, in a passage like the following, Burke seems to be exhausting the possibilities of words; in his string of adjectives, the invective force of alliteration tends to displace the meaning:

> Nothing can be conceived more hard than the heart of a thoroughbred metaphysician. It comes nearer to the cold malignity of a wicked spirit than to the frailty and passion of a man. It is like that of the Principle of Evil himself, incorporeal, pure, unmixed, dephlegmated, defecated evil. It is no easy operation to eradicate humanity from the human breast.

Such a passage recalls that restatement of Burke's own theory of the sublime by Coleridge (in his remarks on Milton's figure of Death): "The grandest efforts of poetry are where the imagination is called forth, not to produce a distinct form, but a strong working of the mind . . . ; the result being what the poet wished to impress, namely, the substitution of a sublime feeling of the unimaginable for a mere image." For it is precisely this dramatization of the mind's movement—whether in deliberation or feeling—that marks the literature of the age. In Blake the emphasis is upon the concreteness and precision of the visionary image; he opposes Burke and all others who are primarily concerned with the natural history of the imagination. For Blake its authority and its absolute creativity are at stake. For others, like Sterne, the problematic nature of its relation to reality, its curious intermixture of the fortuitous and the formative, of the conditioned and the creative, is itself the central drama.

English
PROSE *and* POETRY
1660–1800

A SELECTION

❧ Samuel Butler ☙

Samuel Butler (1612-80) was born at Strensham, Worcestershire, of a well-to-do yeoman, and educated at King's School, Worcester. He later became familiar with the law, possibly as a student at Gray's Inn or as clerk to a justice. After the Restoration he held several appointments, notably as secretary to George Villiers, the second Duke of Buckingham. *Hudibras* had an enormous success upon its publication and in 1678 Butler was given a royal pension. Most of his minor works, including his interesting prose *Characters,* were not published until 1759, some not until this century.

The originality of *Hudibras* comes of a new combination of traditional elements. From Scarron Butler could draw the method of travesty, a reduction of high epic matter to low, familiar language. From Cervantes he has obviously drawn many mock-heroic techniques and examples of romance-parody. Also he had closer literary occasions for parody: Davenant's rational epic, *Gondibert;* the strained wit of such late metaphysical poets as Benlowes; and the canting style of many dissenting preachers. Butler's own skeptical mind comes through in his ridicule of men intoxicated with metaphysical speculation; but, even more, he forges one of the great satiric images of the cruel folly and hypocrisy (as he saw it) of the Puritan Commonwealth. His hero is named for the rash, hardy, "melancholy" knight in Spenser's *Faerie Queene* (II, ii), who woos the sour, pleasure-hating Elissa.

Editions: Collected Works, ed. A. R. Waller and René Lamar (1905-28); *Hudibras,* ed. Zachary Grey (1744), ed. Treadway Nash (1793) [both these editions since reprinted in various forms].

Biographies: René Lamar, "Du nouveau sur l'auteur d'*Hudibras,*" *Revue Anglo-Américaine* 1 (1924); E. S. de Beer, "The Later Life of Samuel Butler," *RES* 4 (1928); Jan Veldkamp, *Samuel Butler* (1924).

Critical Studies: Richmond P. Bond, *English Burlesque Poetry 1700-1750* (1932); E. A. Richards, *Hudibras in the Burlesque Tradition* (1937); Ricardo Quintana, "Samuel Butler: A Restoration Figure in a Modern Light," *ELH* 18 (1951); Ian Jack, *Augustan Satire* (1952), ch. ii.

Hudibras
Part I. Canto I.
[1663]

THE ARGUMENT

Sir Hudibras his passing worth,
The manner how he sallied forth,
His arms and equipage, are shown;
His horse's virtues and his own.
Th' adventure of the bear and fiddle
Is sung, but breaks off in the middle.

When civil dudgeon first grew high,
And men fell out, they knew not why;
When hard words,[1] jealousies, and fears
Set folks together by the ears,
And made them fight, like mad or drunk,   5
For Dame Religion as for punk;[2]
Whose honesty they all durst swear for,
Though not a man of them knew wherefore;
When gospel-trumpeter, surrounded
With long-eared rout,[3] to battle sounded;   10
And pulpit, drum ecclesiastic,
Was beat with fist instead of a stick;

[1] (1) quarrelsome words, (2) technical jargon (cf. ll. 85, 111), in this case, the cant in which sectarian groups referred to themselves or to opponents.

[2] strumpet.

[3] conventional epic term for asses; applicable to Roundheads because of their short hair and to those enthusiastic Puritans who were often pictured as cupping their ears with their hands to catch each word of a sermon.

Then did Sir Knight abandon dwelling,
And out he rode a-colonelling.
   A wight[4] he was, whose very sight would   15
Entitle him Mirror of Knighthood,[5]
That never bowed his stubborn knee
To anything but chivalry,[6]
Nor put up blow but that which laid
Right Worshipful on shoulder-blade;   20
Chief of domestic knights and errant,
Either for chartel[7] or for warrant;
Great on the bench, great in the saddle,
That could as well bind o'er as swaddle;[8]
Mighty he was at both of these,   25
And styled of war as well as peace.
(So some rats, of amphibious nature,
Are either for the land or water.)
But here our authors make a doubt
Whether he were more wise or stout.[9]   30
Some hold the one, and some the other;
But howsoe'er they make a pother,
The difference was so small, his brain
Outweighed his rage but half a grain;
Which made some take him for a tool   35
That knaves do work with, called a fool.
For 't has been held by many, that,
As Montaigne, playing with his cat,
Complains she thought him but an ass,
Much more she would Sir Hudibras;   40
(For that's the name our valiant knight
To all his challenges did write).
But they're mistaken very much;
'Tis plain enough he was no such.
We grant, although he had much wit,   45
H' was very shy of using it,

---

[4] deliberate reminiscence of romance idiom, as in Spenser.
[5] the title of a Spanish work admired by Don Quixote.
[6] (1) to be knighted, as in ll. 19-20, (2) to the vision of himself as chivalric knight.
[7] challenge.   [8] beat, cudgel.   [9] brave.

As being loath to wear it out,
And therefore bore it not about,
Unless on holidays or so,
As men their best apparel do.   50
Beside, 'tis known he could speak Greek
As naturally as pigs squeak;
That Latin was no more difficile,
Than to a blackbird 'tis to whistle.
Being rich in both, he never scanted   55
His bounty unto such as wanted;
But much of either would afford
To many that had not one word.
For Hebrew roots, although they're found
To flourish most in barren ground,[10]   60
He had such plenty as sufficed
To make some think him circumcised.
And truly so he was perhaps,
Not as a proselyte, but for claps.
    He was in logic a great critic,   65
Profoundly skilled in analytic;
He could distinguish and divide
A hair 'twixt south and southwest side;
On either which he would dispute,
Confute, change hands, and still confute.   70
He'd undertake to prove by force
Of argument, a man's no horse;
He'd prove a buzzard is no fowl,[11]
And that a lord may be an owl;[12]
A calf [13] an alderman, a goose a justice,   75
And rooks[14] committee-men[15] and trustees.

---

[10] (1) the deserts of the Holy Land, (2) the dry pedantry of some scholars, (3) the solemn addiction to Old Testament phrases and names of many simple-minded Puritans.

[11] domestic or barnyard bird.

[12] a bird variously taken as a symbol of gravity and wisdom or of pretentious dullness.

[13] with traditional overtones of harmless stupidity.

[14] (1) crowlike birds, (2) swindlers.

[15] committees established by Parliament during the Commonwealth with authority to fine and imprison whom they pleased.

He'd run in debt by disputation,
And pay with ratiocination.
All this by syllogism, true
In mood and figure,[16] he would do.   80
   For rhetoric, he could not ope
His mouth but out there flew a trope;[17]
And when he happened to break off
I' th' middle of his speech, or cough,[18]
H' had hard words ready to show why,   85
And tell what rules he did it by.
Else, when with greatest art he spoke,
You'd think he talked like other folk;
For all a rhetorician's rules
Teach nothing but to name his tools.   90
But when he pleased to show 't, his speech
In loftiness of sound was rich,
A Babylonish dialect[19]
Which learnèd pedants much affect.
It was a parti-colored dress   95
Of patched and piebald languages;
'Twas English cut on Greek and Latin,
Like fustian[20] heretofore on satin.
It had an odd promiscuous tone,
As if h' had talked three parts[21] in one;   100
Which made some think, when he did gabble,
Th' had heard three laborers of Babel,
Or Cerberus himself pronounce
A leash[22] of languages at once.
This he as volubly would vent,   105
As if his stock would ne'er be spent;
And truly, to support that charge,
He had supplies as vast and large;

---

[16] logical classifications of syllogisms.

[17] figure of speech.

[18] See note to l. 498.

[19] with reference to the division of languages at the Tower of Babel.

[20] (1) coarse material cut with holes to reveal satin through it, (2) bombast or gibberish.

[21] as in old rounds, with overtones of religious mystery.

[22] that is, one for each of Cerberus' three heads.

For he could coin or counterfeit
New words with little or no wit,   110
Words so debased and hard, no stone[23]
Was hard enough to touch them on;
And when with hasty noise he spoke 'em,
The ignorant for current[24] took 'em—
That, had the orator[25] who once   115
Did fill his mouth with pebble stones
When he harangued, but known his phrase,
He would have used no other ways.
   In mathematics he was greater
Than Tycho Brahe[26] or Erra Pater;[27]   120
For he by geometric scale
Could take the size of pots of ale;
Resolve by sines and tangents straight
If bread or butter wanted weight;
And wisely tell what hour o' th' day   125
The clock does strike, by algebra.
   Besides, he was a shrewd philosopher,
And had read every text and gloss over;
Whate'er the crabbedest author hath,
He understood b' implicit faith;[28]   130
Whatever skeptic could inquire for,
For every why he had a wherefore;
Knew more than forty of them do,
As far as words and terms could go.
All which he understood by rote,   135
And, as occasion served, would quote;
No matter whether right or wrong,
They might be either said or sung.
His notions fitted things so well,
That which was which he could not tell,   140
But oftentimes mistook the one

[23] touchstone traditionally used to test purity of gold or silver, as in coins.
[24] term used for acceptable coins.
[25] Demosthenes.
[26] eminent Danish astronomer.
[27] the English astrologer William Lilly.
[28] unquestioning trust in authority.

For th' other, as great clerks[29] have done.
He could reduce all things to acts,
And knew their natures by abstracts;
Where entity and quiddity,[30]   145
The ghosts of defunct bodies, fly;
Where Truth in person does appear,
Like words congealed in northern air.
He knew what's what, and that's as high
As metaphysic wit can fly.   150
    In school-divinity as able
As he that hight[31] Irrefragable;[32]
A second Thomas,[33] or, at once
To name them all, another Duns;[34]
Profound in all the nominal   155
And real [35] ways beyond them all;
For he a rope of sand [36] could twist
As tough as learned Sorbonist;[37]
And weave fine cobwebs, fit for skull
That's empty when the moon is full: 160
Such as take lodgings in a head
That's to be let unfurnishèd.
He could raise scruples[38] dark and nice,[39]
And after solve 'em in a trice;
As if divinity had catched   165
The itch of purpose to be scratched;

[29] scholars, men of learning.
[30] scholastic terms for being and essence. Here, as in the following lines, mental abstractions are given physical substance.
[31] romance diction for "called."
[32] irrefutable, a term applied to the English scholastic, Alexander Hales.
[33] Aquinas.
[34] John Duns Scotus, the scholastic "Doctor Subtilis," whose name was the source of the word "dunce."
[35] The nominalists held that universals or general ideas were mere names and that only particulars were real. The realists held that universals had a real, objective existence.
[36] traditional instance of futile ingenuity.
[37] The Sorbonne was the faculty of theology of the University of Paris and a center of scholastic activity.
[38] intellectual doubts or objections.
[39] subtle, foolish.

Or, like a mountebank,[40] did wound
And stab herself with doubts profound,
Only to show with how small pain
The sores of faith are cured again;   170
Although by woeful proof we find
They always leave a scar behind.
He knew the seat of Paradise,[41]
Could tell in what degree it lies,
And, as he was disposed, could prove it   175
Below the moon, or else above it;
What Adam dreamt of when his bride
Came from her closet in his side;
Whether the devil tempted her
By a High Dutch interpreter;[42]   180
If either of them had a navel;[43]
Who first made music malleable;[44]
Whether the serpent at the Fall
Had cloven feet,[45]or none at all.
All this, without a gloss or comment,   185
He could unriddle in a moment,
In proper terms, such as men smatter
When they throw out and miss the matter.
    For his religion, it was fit
To match his learning and his wit;   190
'Twas Presbyterian true blue,[46]
For he was of that stubborn crew

[40] such as performed feats of skill and illusion at fairs.

[41] a subject of much learned and fantastic speculation throughout the Middle Ages and the Renaissance.

[42] a reference to the claim by Johannes Goropius Becanus that the Teutonic was the most ancient language in the world.

[43] a matter discussed by John Evelyn and Sir Thomas Browne in Butler's own lifetime.

[44] Pythagoras was traditionally supposed to have invented music upon hearing a blacksmith strike his anvil with hammers of different weights. A similar legend grew up about the figure of Jubal, who supposedly performed the feat at the forge of his brother Tubal-cain (Genesis 4:20-22).

[45] There have been various conjectures about the serpent's form before he was made to crawl on his belly as a result of God's curse.

[46] The proverb "True blue will never stain" can suggest (1) loyalty, (2) obstinacy.

Of errant[47] saints[48] whom all men grant
To be the true church militant;[49]
Such as do build their faith upon   195
The holy text of pike and gun;
Decide all controversies by
Infallible artillery;
And prove their doctrine orthodox,
By apostolic blows[50] and knocks;   200
Call fire and sword and desolation
A godly, thorough reformation,
Which always must be carried on,
And still be doing, never done;
As if religion were intended   205
For nothing else but to be mended—
A sect whose chief devotion lies
In odd perverse antipathies,[51]
In falling out with that or this,
And finding somewhat still amiss;   210
More peevish, cross, and splenetic,
Than dog distract or monkey sick;
That with more care keep holy-day
The wrong,[52] than others the right way;
Compound for sins they are inclined to,   215
By damning those they have no mind to;
Still so perverse and opposite,
As if they worshipped God for spite.
The self-same thing they will abhor
One way, and long another for.   220
Free will [53] they one way disavow,

[47] (1) seeking a righteous cause, like the wandering chivalric knight (cf. l. 21), (2) turning away from the truth, (3) "arrant" or notorious.

[48] a term often applied by the Puritans to themselves as the "elect."

[49] (1) the church in the world fighting both temptation and persecution, (2) the rebellious and quarrelsome Puritan sects.

[50] (1) laying on of hands in ordination, (2) self-righteous use of force.

[51] ritualistic objections to innocent customs; see ll. 227-30.

[52] For example, Christmas was turned from a feast into a fast in the 1640's.

[53] denied by the Calvinistic doctrine of predestination but exercised in the radical claims of inspiration and the rejection of tradition.

Another, nothing else allow.
All piety consists therein
In them, in other men all sin.
Rather than fail, they will defy   225
That which they love most tenderly:
Quarrel with minced-pies, and disparage
Their best and dearest friend, plum-porridge;
Fat pig and goose itself oppose,
And blaspheme custard through the nose.[54]   230
Th' apostles of this fierce religion,
Like Mahomet's, were ass and widgeon,[55]
To whom our knight, by fast instinct
Of wit and temper, was so linked,
As if hypocrisy and nonsense   235
Had got th' advowson[56] of his conscience.
   Thus was he gifted and accoutered,
We mean on th' inside, not the outward:
That next of all we shall discuss;
Then listen, sirs, it followeth thus: 240
   His tawny beard was th' equal grace
Both of his wisdom and his face,
In cut and die so like a tile,
A sudden view it would beguile;
The upper part thereof was whey,   245
The nether orange mixed with gray.
This hairy meteor[57] did denounce
The fall of scepters and of crowns,
With grizzly type[58] did represent
Declining age of government,   250
And tell, with hieroglyphic spade,[59]

[54] a reference to the droning, nasal delivery of some Puritan preachers.

[55] Mahomet was given a milk-white beast, like an ass, upon which to ride to heaven. He kept a pigeon which ate out of his ear and brought him divine messages. "Pigeon" is here altered to widgeon, a species of wild duck whose stupidity was proverbial; thus a term for a fool or dolt.

[56] the right to appoint the clergyman to a specific church office.

[57] conventional term for "comet," usually taken as a portent of disaster.

[58] emblem, symbol. Butler is parodying the tortured allegory (cf. *hieroglyphic spade,* l. 251) of much theological controversy of his age.

[59] a beard trimmed in the shape of a spade.

Its own grave and the state's were made.
Like Samson's heart-breakers,[60] it grew
In time to make a nation rue;
Though it contributed its own fall,   255
To wait upon the public downfall.
It was monastic, and did grow
In holy orders by strict vow;
Of rule as sullen and severe
As that of rigid Cordelier.[61]   260
'Twas bound to suffer persecution
And martyrdom with resolution;
T' oppose itself against the hate
And vengeance of th' incensèd state,
In whose defiance it was worn,   265
Still ready to be pulled and torn,
With red-hot irons to be tortured,
Reviled, and spit upon, and martyred;
Maugre[62] all which 'twas to stand fast
As long as monarchy should last;   270
But when the state should hap to reel,
'Twas to submit to fatal steel,[63]
And fall, as it was consecrate,
A sacrifice to fall of state;
Whose thread of life the Fatal Sisters[64]   275
Did twist together with its whiskers,
And twine so close that Time should never
In life or death their fortunes sever,
But with his rusty sickle mow
Both down together at a blow.   280
   So learnèd Taliacotius,[65] from
The brawny part of porter's bum,
Cut supplemental noses, which
Would last as long as parent breech;

[60] curls, lovelocks, usually feminine.
[61] member of a strict French order of Franciscans.
[62] in spite of.
[63] (1) epic diction for "sword," (2) shears.
[64] the Three Fates, who spun and cut the thread of man's life.
[65] (1553-99); an Italian surgeon, author of a treatise on grafting and plastic surgery.

But when the date of Nock[66] was out,   285
Off dropped the sympathetic snout.
   His back, or rather burthen, showed
As if it stooped with its own load;
For as Aeneas bore his sire[67]
Upon his shoulders through the fire,   290
Our knight did bear no less a pack
Of his own buttocks on his back;
Which now had almost got the upper
Hand of his head, for want of crupper.[68]
To poise this equally, he bore   295
A paunch of the same bulk before,
Which still he had a special care
To keep well crammed with thrifty[69] fare,
As white-pot,[70] buttermilk, and curds,
Such as a country-house affords;   300
With other victual which anon
We further shall dilate upon,
When of his hose we come to treat,
The cupboard where he kept his meat.
   His doublet was of sturdy buff,[71]   305
And though not sword, yet cudgel-proof,
Whereby 'twas fitter for his use
Who feared no blows but such as bruise.
   His breeches were of rugged woollen,
And had been at the siege of Bullen;[72]   310
To old King Harry so well known,
Some writers held they were his own.
Through they were lined with many a piece
Of ammunition-bread[73] and cheese
And fat black-puddings,[74] proper food   315

---

[66] rump.

[67] Aeneas bore his father, Anchises, out of burning Troy (*Aeneid,* II).

[68] a strap used to keep the saddle from sliding forward.

[69] (1) flourishing, (2) economical (Puritan thrift was notorious).

[70] a dish of cream, flour, eggs, and spices.

[71] stout leather.

[72] Boulogne, captured by Henry VIII in 1544.

[73] supplied as rations.

[74] sausages made of blood and suet.

For warriors that delight in blood.
For, as we said, he always chose
To carry victual in his hose.[75]
That often tempted rats and mice
The ammunition to surprise;   320
And when he put a hand but in
The one or th' other magazine,[76]
They stoutly in defense on 't stood,
And from the wounded foe drew blood;
And till th' were stormed and beaten out,   325
Ne'er left the fortified redoubt.
And though knights-errant, as some think,[77]
Of old did neither eat nor drink,
Because, when thorough deserts vast
And regions desolate they passed,   330
Where belly-timber above ground
Or under was not to be found,
Unless they grazed, there's not one word
Of their provision on record;
Which made some confidently write,   335
They had no stomachs but to fight,
'Tis false; for Arthur wore in hall
Round table like a farthingal,[78]
On which, with shirt pulled out behind
And eke before, his good knights dined.   340
Though 'twas no table, some suppose,
But a huge pair of round trunk-hose,[79]
In which he carried as much meat
As he and all his knights could eat,
When, laying by their swords and truncheons,[80]   345
They took their breakfasts or their nuncheons.
But let that pass at present, lest
We should forget where we digressed,
As learnèd authors use, to whom

[75] breeches.   [76] storehouse.   [77] notably Don Quixote, I ii.
[78] a hooped petticoat. Arthur is pictured seated in a hole at the center of his round table.
[79] full, baglike breeches, sometimes stuffed with wool.
[80] cudgels.

We leave it, and to th' purpose come.   350
  His puissant sword unto his side,
Near his undaunted heart, was tied,
With basket-hilt that would hold broth,
And serve for fight and dinner both;
In it he melted lead for bullets,   355
To shoot at foes, and sometimes pullets,
To whom he bore so fell a grutch,
He ne'er gave quarter t' any such.
The trenchant blade, Toledo[81] trusty,
For want of fighting was grown rusty,   360
And ate into itself for lack
Of somebody to hew and hack.
The peaceful scabbard where it dwelt
The rancor of its edge had felt;
For of the lower end two handful   365
It had devoured, 'twas so manful,
And so much scorned to lurk in case,
As if it durst not show its face.
In many desperate attempts
Of warrants, exigents,[82] contempts,   370
It had appeared with courage bolder,
Than Sergeant Bum[83] invading shoulder;
Oft had it ta'en possession,
And prisoners too, or made them run.
  This sword a dagger had, his page,   375
That was but little for his age,
And therefore waited on him so,
As dwarfs upon knights-errant do.
It was a serviceable dudgeon,[84]
Either for fighting or for drudging;   380
When it had stabbed, or broke a head,
It would scrape trenchers[85] or chip bread,
Toast cheese or bacon; though it were

[81] city in Spain famous for swords and other armor.
[82] writs which threatened outlawry if the defendant did not appear.
[83] bumbailiffs made arrests or served warrants.
[84] dagger or short sword.
[85] serving dishes.

To bait a mouse-trap, 'twould not care;
'Twould make clean shoes, and in the earth   385
Set leeks and onions, and so forth.
It had been prentice to a brewer,
Where this and more it did endure,
But left the trade,[86] as many more
Have lately done on the same score.   390
   In th' holsters at his saddle-bow
Two agèd pistols he did stow,
Among the surplus of such meat
As in his hose he could not get.
These would inveigle rats with th' scent,   395
To forage when the cocks were bent;
And sometimes catch 'em with a snap
As cleverly as th' ablest trap.
They were upon hard duty still,
And every night stood sentinel,   400
To guard the magazine i' th' hose
From twolegg'd and from four-legg'd foes.
   Thus clad and fortified, Sir Knight
From peaceful home set forth to fight.
But first with nimble active force   405
He got on th' outside of his horse.
For having but one stirrup tied
T' his saddle on the further side,
It was so short h' had much ado
To reach it with his desperate toe;   410
But after many strains and heaves,
He got up to the saddle eaves,
From whence he vaulted into th' seat
With so much vigor, strength, and heat,
That he had almost tumbled over   415
With his own weight, but did recover
By laying hold on tail and mane,
Which oft he used instead of rein.
   But now we talk of mounting steed,
Before we further do proceed,   420

[86] like Oliver Cromwell or Colonel Pride, who reputedly had been brewers.

It doth behoove us to say something
Of that which bore our valiant bumkin.
The beast was sturdy, large, and tall,
With mouth of meal and eyes of wall—
I would say eye, for h' had but one,   425
As most agree, though some say none.
He was well stayed, and in his gait
Preserved a grave, majestic state;
At spur or switch no more he skipped
Or mended pace, than Spaniard whipped,[87]   430
And yet so fiery, he would bound,
As if he grieved to touch the ground;
That Caesar's horse, who as fame goes,
Had corns upon his feet and toes,[88]
Was not by half so tender-hoofed,   435
Nor trod upon the ground so soft;
And as that beast would kneel and stoop
(Some write) to take his rider up,
So Hudibras his ('tis well known)
Would often do to set him down.   440
We shall not need to say what lack
Of leather was upon his back,
For that was hidden under pad,
And breech of knight galled full as bad.
His strutting ribs on both sides showed   445
Like furrows he himself had plowed;
For underneath the skirt of pannel,[89]
'Twixt every two there was a channel.
His draggling tail hung in the dirt,
Which on his rider he would flirt   450
Still as his tender side he pricked
With armed heel, or with unarmed, kicked:
For Hudibras wore but one spur,

[87] a reference to a Spaniard who, in running the gantlet, refused to change his pace in order to avoid pain.
[88] The hoofs of Caesar's horse were supposed to be divided into toes like those of a human foot.
[89] cloth placed under the saddle.

As wisely knowing could he stir
To active trot one side of's horse,   455
The other would not hang an arse.
    A squire he had whose name was Ralph,[90]
That in th' adventure went his half,
Though writers, for more stately tone,
Do call him Ralpho, 'tis all one;   460
And when we can, with meter safe,
We'll call him so; if not, plain Raph;
(For rhyme the rudder is of verses,
With which like ships they steer their courses).
An equal stock of wit and valor   465
He had laid in, by birth a tailor.[91]
The mighty Tyrian queen, that gained
With subtle shreds a tract of land,[92]
Did leave it with a castle fair
To his great ancestor, her heir;   470
From him descended cross-legg'd knights,[93]
Famed for their faith[94] and warlike fights
Against the bloody cannibal,[95]
Whom they destroyed both great and small.
This sturdy Squire had, as well   475
As the bold Trojan knight,[96] seen hell;[97]
Not with a counterfeited pass
Of golden bough, but true gold-lace.
His knowledge was not far behind

[90] possibly named after the grocer's apprentice who fancies chivalric action in Beaumont and Fletcher's *Knight of the Burning Pestle*. Just as Hudibras represents the Presbyterians, so his squire does the Independents or Anabaptists.

[91] so were a number of religious enthusiasts of the age, such as John of Leyden or Lodowick Muggleton in England.

[92] Dido purchased as much land as she could surround with an ox's hide. She then cut the hide into slender strips and acquired a large territory.

[93] typical posture of tailors at work. Knights Templars were represented this way in sepulchral monuments.

[94] tailors gave much credit.

[95] (1) Saracens, (2) lice.

[96] Aeneas, who bore the *golden bough* (l. 478) to Proserpina in Hell.

[97] the tailor's receptacle for scraps of cloth.

The Knight's, but of another kind,   480
And he another way came by't.
Some call it gifts, and some new-light;[98]
A liberal art that costs no pains
Of study, industry, or brains.
His wits were sent him for a token,   485
But in the carriage cracked and broken;
Like commendation nine-pence[99] crook'd
With "To and from my love" it looked.
He ne'er considered it, as loath
To look a gift horse in the mouth,   490
And very wisely would lay forth
No more upon it than 'twas worth;
But as he got it freely, so
He spent it frank and freely too:
For saints themselves will sometimes be,   495
Of gifts that cost them nothing, free.[100]
By means of this, with hem and cough,
Prolongers to enlightened snuff,[101]
He could deep mysteries unriddle
As easily as thread a needle;   500
For as of vagabonds we say
That they are ne'er beside their way,
Whate'er men speak by this new-light,
Still they are sure to be i' th' right.
'Tis a dark lanthorn of the Spirit,[102]   505
Which none see by but those that bear it;

[98] Puritans often professed divine inspiration, and illiterate preachers were called Gifted Brethren. Butler is referring to doctrines, like that of the "inner light," which exalted the individual conscience at the expense of institutional religion.

[99] coins bent to serve as love tokens.

[100] a reference to notorious Puritan thrift.

[101] The burned wick emits flashes of light just before it goes out for want of oil. "Thus it is frequent for a single *vowel* to draw sighs from a multitude; and for a whole assembly of saints to sob to the music of one solitary liquid. . . . Hawking, spitting, and belching, the defects of other men's rhetoric, are the flowers, and figures, and ornaments" of the enthusiastic preacher's (Jonathan Swift, *Mechanical Operation of the Spirit* [1704]).

[102] Compare the Cambridge Platonists' favorite saying that "reason is the candle of the Lord."

A light that falls down from on high,[103]
For spiritual trades to cozen[104] by;
An *ignis fatuus*[105] that bewitches,
And leads men into pools and ditches,   510
To make them dip themselves[106] and sound
For Christendom in dirty pond;
To dive like wild fowl for salvation,
And fish to catch regeneration.
This light inspires and plays upon   515
The nose of saint, like bagpipe drone,[107]
And speaks through hollow empty soul,
As through a trunk or whispering hole,[108]
Such language as no mortal ear
But spiritual eavesdropper's can hear: 520
So Phoebus or some friendly Muse
Into small poets song infuse,
Which they at second hand rehearse,
Through reed or bagpipe, verse for verse.
    Thus Ralph became infallible   525
As three or four-legg'd oracle,[109]
The ancient cup, or modern chair,
Spoke truth point-blank, though unaware.
    For mystic learning, wondrous able
In magic talisman and cabal,[110]   530
Whose primitive tradition reaches
As far as Adam's first green breeches;[111]
Deep-sighted in intelligences,

---

[103] (1) from heaven, (2) through the skylight of a shop.

[104] cheat.

[105] will-of-the-wisp, also known as jack-o'-lanthorn.

[106] The Anabaptists were also called Dippers.

[107] See l. 230; also reference to Scotland, where Presbyterianism was strong.

[108] as supposedly in the oracles at Delphi, with further reference (ll. 519-20) to the Gift of Tongues.

[109] references, among others, to the three-legged stool at Delphi, to Joseph's divining cup (Genesis 44:5), and to the papal throne.

[110] magical emblem and doctrine.

[111] the apron of fig leaves (translated as "breeches" in so-called Breeches Bible of 1557). Satire on Roman Catholic reliance upon oral tradition as well as pretentious claims of occultists, alchemists, and astrologers.

Ideas, atoms, influences;[112]
And much of *Terra Incognita,*   535
Th' intelligible world, could say;
A deep occult philosopher,
As learn'd as the wild Irish[113] are,
Or Sir Agrippa,[114] for profound
And solid lying much renowned: 540
He Anthroposophus[115] and Fludd [115a]
And Jacob Behmen[116] understood;
Knew many an amulet and charm,
That would do neither good nor harm;
In Rosicrucian[117] lore as learn'd   545
As he that *Vere adeptus*[118] earned.
He understood the speech of birds
As well as they themselves do words;
Could tell what subtlest parrots mean,
That speak and think contrary clean;   550
What member 'tis of whom they talk
When they cry "Rope," and "Walk, knave, walk." [119]
He'd extract numbers[120] out of matter,[121]
And keep them in a glass, like water,
Of sovereign power to make men wise;   555
For, dropped in blear thick-sighted eyes,
They'd make them see in darkest night,

[112] technical terms for objects that are too subtle or exalted to be perceived by the senses. *Terra Incognita* (l. 535) was a regular designation on maps for unexplored land.

[113] notorious for addiction to occult practices.

[114] Cornelius Agrippa (1486-1535), scholar and writer on occult sciences.

[115] Thomas Vaughan (1626-66), alchemical writer.

[115a] physician and Rosicrucian (1574-1637).

[116] Böhme (1575-1624), the German mystic extremely influential in England.

[117] reference to the society whose members claimed magical powers.

[118] "truly a master," a title given to alchemists who had discovered the philosopher's stone.

[119] presumably, insulting phrases taught a parrot to speak to members of Parliament.

[120] The Pythagoreans and Platonists stressed the numerical structure of the world and gave magical efficacy to some numbers.

[121] for the Aristotelian, matter is always wedded to form: "pure matter" is a creation of the mind, conceivable but certainly not perceptible.

Like owls, though purblind in the light.
By help of these (as he professed)
He had First Matter seen undressed: 560
He took her naked, all alone,
Before one rag of form was on.
The Chaos,[122] too, he had descried,
And seen quite through, or else he lied:
Not that of pasteboard, which men show   565
For groats at fair of Barthol'mew;[123]
But its great grandsire, first o' th' name,
Whence that and Reformation came,
Both cousin-germans, and right able
T' inveigle and draw in the rabble.   570
But Reformation was, some say,
O' th' younger house[124] to Puppet-play.
He could foretell whats'ever was
By consequence to come to pass;
As death of great men, alterations,   575
Diseases, battles, inundations:
All this without th' eclipse of sun,
Or dreadful comet, he hath done
By inward light, a way as good,
And easy to be understood;   580
But with more lucky hit than those
That use to make the stars depose,[125]
Like Knights o' th' Post,[126] and falsely charge
Upon themselves what others forge;[127]
As if they were consenting to   585
All mischief in the world men do,
Or, like the devil, did tempt and sway 'em

[122] the materials out of which God created the cosmos, as in Milton's *Paradise Lost*, where chaos is seen only by the angels. Ralph claims more than human powers.

[123] Bartholomew Fair, where puppet shows of the Creation might be seen.

[124] of later date; perhaps imitative, as dissenters in throes of inspiration or avowing predestination might suggest puppets.

[125] testify, reveal: a reference to astrological doctrines of the stars' control of human action.

[126] hired false informers.

[127] perform.

To rogueries, and then betray 'em
They'll search a planet's house[128] to know
Who broke and robbed a house below;   590
Examine Venus and the Moon,
Who stole a thimble or a spoon;
And though they nothing will confess,
Yet by their very looks can guess,
And tell what guilty aspect[129] bodes,   595
Who stole, and who received the goods.
They'll question Mars, and by his look
Detect who 'twas that nimmed [130] a cloak;
Make Mercury confess, and peach[131]
Those thieves which he himself did teach.[132]   600
They'll find i' th' physiognomies
O' th' planets, all men's destinies,
Like him that took the doctor's bill,[133]
And swallowed it instead o' th' pill;
Cast the nativity o' th' question,   605
And from positions to be guessed on,
As sure as if they knew the moment
Of native's birth, tell what will come on't.
They'll feel the pulses of the stars,
To find out agues, cough, catarrhs,   610
And tell what crisis[134] does divine
The rot in sheep, or mange in swine;
In men, what gives or cures the itch,
What makes them cuckolds, poor or rich;
What gains or loses, hangs or saves;   615
What makes men great, what fools or knaves;
But not what wise, for only of those
The stars (they say) cannot dispose,[135]

[128] that sign of the zodiac where, in astrology, a planet has greatest influence.
[129] (1) relative position of planet (astrology), (2) countenance.
[130] stole.
[131] accuse.
[132] Mercury was god of thieves.
[133] prescription.
[134] conjunction of planets.
[135] (1) cast influence upon, (2) deceive (in next line).

No more than can the astrologians;
There they say right, and like true Trojans: 620
This Ralpho knew, and therefore took
The other course,[136] of which we spoke.
    Thus was th' accomplished Squire endued
With gifts and knowledge perilous shrewd.
Never did trusty squire with knight, 625
Or knight with squire, jump[137] more right.
Their arms and equipage did fit,
As well as virtues, parts,[138] and wit:
Their valors too were of a rate,[139]
And out they sallied at the gate. 630
    Few miles on horseback had they jogged
But Fortune unto them turned dogged;
For they a sad adventure met,
Of which anon we mean to treat.
But ere we venture to unfold 635
Achievements so resolved and bold,
We should, as learnèd poets use,
Invoke th' assistance of some Muse;
However critics count it sillier
Than jugglers[140] talking t' a familiar.[141] 640
We think 'tis no great matter which,
They're all alike, yet we shall pitch
On one that fits our purpose most,
Whom therefore thus do we accost:
    Thou that with ale or viler liquors, 645
Didst inspire Withers, Prynne, and Vicars,[142]
And force them, though it were in spite
Of nature and their stars, to write;
Who (as we find in sullen writs,[143]
And cross-grained works of modern wits) 650

[136] religious imposture rather than astrology.
[137] accord.
[138] native abilities or capacities.
[139] well matched.
[140] sorcerers.
[141] familiar spirit who comes at call.
[142] Puritan poets and pamphleteers of little skill.
[143] ill-humored satires.

With vanity, opinion, want,
The wonder of the ignorant,
The praises of the author penned
By himself or wit-ensuring friend,
The itch of picture in the front,[144]   655
With bays and wicked rhyme upon't
(All that is left o' th' forkèd hill [145]
To make men scribble without skill),
Canst make a poet, spite of Fate,
And teach all people to translate,   660
Though out of languages in which
They understand no part of speech;
Assist me but this once I 'mplore,
And I shall trouble thee no more.

    In western clime there is a town,   665
To those that dwell therein well known;
Therefore there needs no more be said here;
We unto them refer our reader;
For brevity is very good,
When w'are, or are not understood.   670
To this town people did repair
On days of market or of fair,
And to cracked fiddle and hoarse tabor,[146]
In merriment did drudge and labor.
But now a sport more formidable   675
Had raked together village rabble;
'Twas an old way of recreating,
Which learnèd butchers call bear-baiting;
A bold adventurous exercise,
With ancient heroes in high prize;   680
For authors do affirm it came
From Isthmian or Nemean game;[147]
Other derive it from the Bear
That's fixed in northern hemisphere,
And round about the pole does make   685

---

[144] frontispiece portrait of the author crowned with bays.
[145] Parnassus.
[146] drum.
[147] famous games celebrated in classical Greece.

A circle, like a bear at stake,
That at the chain's end wheels about
And overturns the rabble-rout.
For after solemn proclamation
In the bear's name (as is the fashion   690
According to the law of arms,
To keep men from inglorious harms)
That none presume to come so near
As forty foot of stake of bear,
If any yet be so foolhardy,   695
T' expose themselves to vain jeopardy,
If they come wounded off and lame,
No honor's got by such a maim;
Although the bear gain much, being bound
In honor to make good his ground   700
When he's engaged, and take no notice,
If any press upon him, who 'tis,
But lets them know, at their own cost,
That he intends to keep his post.
This to prevent and other harms   705
Which always wait on feats of arms,
(For in a hurry of a fray
'Tis hard to keep out of harm's way)
Thither the Knight his course did steer
To keep the peace 'twixt dog and bear,   710
As he believed he was bound to do
In conscience and commission too;
And therefore thus bespoke the Squire:
    "We that are wisely mounted higher[148]
Than constables in curule[149] wit,   715
When on tribunal bench[150] we sit,
Like speculators[151] should foresee,
From Pharos[152] of authority,

[148] The argument that follows is modeled on those of Don Quixote and Sancho Panza.
[149] appropriate to a Roman consul or high magistrate.
[150] as justice of the peace, the *commission* of 712.
[151] (1) watchmen, (2) students of the occult.
[152] the great lighthouse at Alexandria.

Portended mischiefs further than
Low proletarian tithing-men;[153]   720
And therefore being informed by bruit[154]
That dog and bear are to dispute,
For so of late men fighting name,
Because they often prove the same
(For where the first does hap to be,   725
The last does *coincidere*);
Quantum in nobis,[155] have thought good
To save th' expense of Christian blood,
And try if we by mediation
Of treaty and accommodation   730
Can end the quarrel, and compose
The bloody duel without blows.
Are not our liberties, our lives,
The laws, religion, and our wives
Enough at once to lie at stake   735
For Covenant[156] and the Cause's[157] sake,
But in that quarrel dogs and bears,
As well as we, must venture theirs?
This feud, by Jesuits invented,
By evil counsel is fomented;   740
There is a Machiavellian plot
(Though every *nare olfact* it[158] not)
A deep design in't to divide
The well-affected that confide,[159]
By setting brother against brother,   745
To claw and curry[160] one another.
Have we not enemies *plus satis,*[161]

---

[153] deputy constables drawn from the lowest classes.

[154] noise.

[155] "to the best of our ability."

[156] drawn up by the Scottish parliament, approved by the English, in order to unite the two nations in religion.

[157] typical Puritan cant.

[158] "nostril smell it out."

[159] have faith.

[160] thrash.

[161] "more than enough."

That *cane et angue pejus*[162] hate us?
And shall we turn our fangs and claws
Upon ourselves, without a cause?   750
That some occult design doth lie
In bloody cynarctomachy[163]
Is plain enough to him that knows
How saints lead brothers by the nose.
I wish myself a pseudo-prophet,   755
But sure some mischief will come of it,
Unless by providential wit,
Or force, we averruncate it.[164]
For what design, what interest,
Can beast have to encounter beast?   760
They fight for no espousèd Cause,[165]
Frail[166] privilege, fundamental laws,
Nor for a thorough reformation,
Nor Covenant nor Protestation,[167]
Nor liberty of consciences,   765
Nor Lords' and Commons' ordinances;[168]
Nor for the church, nor for church lands,
To get them in their own no hands;[169]
Nor evil counsellors to bring
To justice, that seduce the King;   770
Nor for the worship of us men,
Though we have done as much for them.
Th' Egyptians worshipped dogs, and for
Their faith made fierce and zealous war;
Others adored a rat, and some   775
For that church suffered martyrdom;
The Indians fought for the truth

---

[162] "worse than dog and snake."
[163] fight between dog and bear.
[164] weed-it-out.
[165] These are allusions to the claims of Parliament against King Charles I.
[166] readily violated.
[167] vow subscribed by the Long Parliament.
[168] so called because the king was driven out and could not approve them as laws.
[169] i.e., paws (?).

Of th' elephant and monkey's tooth,
And many, to defend that faith,
Fought it out *mordicus*[170] to death;   780
But no beast ever was so slight,[171]
For man, as for his god, to fight:
They have more wit, alas, and know
Themselves and us better than so.
But we, we only do infuse   785
The rage in them like *boutefeus*;[172]
'Tis our example that instils
In them th' infection of our ills.
For, as some late philosophers
Have well observed, beasts that converse   790
With man take after him, as hogs
Get pigs all th' year, and bitches dogs;
Just so, by our example, cattle
Learn to give one another battle.
We read in Nero's time, the heathen,   795
When they destroyed the Christian brethren,
They sewed them in the skins of bears,
And then set dogs about their ears;
From whence, no doubt, th' invention came
Of this lewd antichristian game."   800
   To this quoth Ralpho, "Verily
The point seems very plain to be;
It is an antichristian game,
Unlawful both in thing and name.
First, for the name; the word bear-baiting   805
Is carnal, and of man's creating,
For certainly there's no such word
In all the Scripture on record;
Therefore unlawful, and a sin:
And so is (secondly) the thing;   810
A vile assembly 'tis, that can
No more be proved by Scripture than
Provincial, classic, national,[173]

---

[170] "tooth and nail."   [171] foolish.
[172] firebrands used to ignite cannons.
[173] Ralph cites various kinds of Presbyterian assemblies of clergy.

Mere human creature-cobwebs all.
Thirdly, it is idolatrous;   815
For when men run a-whoring thus
With their inventions,[174] whatsoe'er
The thing be, whether dog or bear,
It is idolatrous and pagan,
No less than worshipping of Dagon." [175]   820
    Quoth Hudibras, "I smell a rat;
Ralpho, thou dost prevaricate:
For though the thesis which thou lay'st
Be true *ad amussim*[176] as thou say'st;
(For that bear-baiting should appear   825
Jure divino[177] lawfuller
Than synods[178] are, thou dost deny
Totidem verbis,[179] so do I)
Yet there's a fallacy in this:
For if by sly *homoeosis*,[180]   830
(*Tussis pro crepitu*, an art
Under a cough to slur a fart)
Thou wouldst sophistically imply
Both are unlawful, —I deny."
    "And I" quoth Ralpho, "do not doubt   835
But bear-baiting may be made out,
In gospel times, as lawful as is
Provincial or parochial classis;[181]
And that both are so near of kin,
And like in all, as well as sin,   840
That put 'em in a bag and shake 'em,
Yourself o' th' sudden would mistake 'em,
And not know which is which, unless
You measure by their wickedness;

[174] Ralph cites Psalm 106:39.
[175] fish-god of ancient Philistines.
[176] "exactly."
[177] "by divine law."
[178] church assemblies, but particularly the ecclesiastical courts of the Presbyterians (of whom Hudibras is an adherent).
[179] "in so many words."
[180] the explanation of a thing by something similar to it.
[181] Presbyterian assembly.

For 'tis not hard t' imagine whether   845
O' th' two is worst, though I name neither."
   Quoth Hudibras, "Thou offer'st much,
But art not able to keep touch;
Mira de lente,[182] as 'tis i' th' adage,
Id est, to make a leek a cabbage: 850
Thou canst at best but overstrain
A paradox and thy own hot brain;
For what can synods have at all
With bears that's analogical?
Or what relation has debating   855
Of church affairs with bear-baiting?
A just comparison still is
Of things *ejusdem generis;*[183]
And then what genus rightly doth
Include and comprehend them both?   860
If animal, both of us may
As justly pass for bears as they,
For we are animals no less,
Although of different specieses.
But, Ralpho, this in no fit place,   865
Nor time, to argue out the case;
For now the field is not far off
Where we must give the world a proof
Of deeds, not words, and such as suit
Another manner of dispute: 870
A controversy that affords
Actions for arguments, not words;
Which we must manage at a rate
Of prowess and conduct adequate
To what our place and fame doth promise,   875
And all the godly[184] expect from us.
Nor shall they be deceived, unless
We're slurred[185] and outed by success;
Success, the mark no mortal wit

---

[182] "a great stir about nothing"; literally, a wonder about a lentil.
[183] "of the same genus or kind."
[184] another Puritan cant term of self-approval.
[185] slighted.

Or surest hand can always hit: 880
For whatsoe'er we perpetrate,
We do but row, we're steered by Fate;[186]
Which in success oft disinherits,
For spurious causes, noblest merits.
Great actions are not always true sons   885
Of great and mighty resolutions;
Nor do the bold'st attempts bring forth
Events still equal to their worth;
But sometimes fail, and in their stead
Fortune and cowardice succeed.   890
Yet we have no great cause to doubt,
Our actions still have borne us out;
Which though they're known to be so ample,
We need no copy from example;
We're not the only person durst   895
Attempt this province, nor the first.
In northern clime a valorous knight
Did whilom kill his bear in fight,
And wound a fiddler: we have both
Of these the objects of our wroth,   900
And equal fame and glory from
Th' attempt or victory to come.
'Tis sung there is a valiant Mamaluke,[187]
In foreign land ycleped—
To whom we have been oft compared   905
For person, parts, address, and beard;
Both equally reputed stout,
And in the same cause both have fought:
He oft in such attempts as these
Came off with glory and success;   910
Nor will we fail in th' execution,
For want of equal resolution.
Honor is like a widow, won
With brisk attempt and putting on;

[186] a reference to Presbyterian doctrines of predestination.
[187] captives often raised to dignity among the Turks. The presumable rhyme is Sir Samuel Luke, a colonel in Cromwell's army and rigid Presbyterian, whom Butler served and lived with for a time.

With entering manfully, and urging,   915
Not slow approaches, like a virgin."
    This said, as once the Phrygian knight,[188]
So ours with rusty steel did smite
His Trojan horse, and just as much
He mended pace upon the touch;   920
But from his empty stomach groaned
Just as that hollow beast did sound,
And angry, answered from behind,
With brandished tail and blast of wind.
So I have seen, with armèd heel,   925
A wight bestride a Commonweal,[189]
While still the more he kicked and spurred,
The less the sullen jade has stirred.

[188] Laocoön, suspecting treachery, struck the wooden horse with his spear.
[189] probably a reference to Richard Cromwell's weakness as successor to his father.

John Wilmot
Earl of Rochester

John Wilmot, Earl of Rochester (1647-80), was born at Ditchley Manor House in Oxfordshire. His father was a landowner and Royalist general, his mother a member of a famous Puritan family. Wilmot inherited the earldom at the age of eleven; he entered Oxford two years later, and completed his education with a tour of France and Italy. He became a principal member of the group of wits at the court of Charles II; married the young heiress, Elizabeth Malet; and served with distinction in naval warfare. When Rochester became notorious as one of the most debauched of the court wits, a number of legends gathered about his name. Etherege's Dorimant in *The Man of Mode* was generally taken as a portrait of Rochester. After a period of considerable doubt and debate, Rochester renounced his libertine views and experienced a religious conversion shortly before his death. During his lifetime Rochester's poetry appeared in broadsides or was circulated in manuscript; only after his death was it collected, and both the authenticity and accuracy of many texts are still being established.

The text (as well as the material in the notes) has been supplied by Professor David M. Vieth. The following comments are his: "Rochester evidently composed this satire, his best-known poem, about 1675; it is mentioned in a letter dated 23 March 1675/6, and a single manuscript text assigns it to 1674. It is based to some extent on Boileau's eighth satire but is also indebted to Hobbes, Montaigne, and the 'libertine' tradition generally. The basic text is that of the Huntington Library copy of Rochester's *Poems on Several Occasions*, 1680. Emendations . . . are based on the readings of seventeen early manuscripts, the broadside of 1679 (main part of the poem

only), and the *Miscellaneous Works of Rochester and Roscommon,*
1707 (epilogue only)."

   The spelling *Satyr* is preserved in the title to remind the reader of
the typical Renaissance view of satire, originally based upon false
etymology, as the kind of work that might be spoken by a rough and
savage creature, harsh and direct in his manner, often brutal and
cruel.

Editions: Poems, ed. Vivian de Sola Pinto (1953); *Poems on
Several Occasions* (facsimile of 1680 text), ed. James Thorpe
(1950).

Biographies: V. de Sola Pinto, *Rochester, Portrait of a Restoration
Poet* (1935); Charles Williams, *Rochester* (1935); J. H. Wilson,
The Court Wits of the Restoration (1948).

Critical Study: Kenneth B. Murdock, *The Sun at Noon* (1939).

A Satyr against Mankind
[?1675, 1680]

   Were I (who to my cost already am
One of those strange, prodigious creatures, man)
A spirit free to choose, for my own share,
What case of flesh and blood I pleased to wear,
I'd be a dog, a monkey, or a bear,   5
Or anything but that vain animal
Who is so proud of being rational.
   The senses are too gross, and he'll contrive
A sixth, to contradict the other five,
And before certain instinct, will prefer   10
Reason, which fifty times for one does err;
Reason, an *ignis fatuus* in the mind,
Which, leaving light of nature, sense, behind,
Pathless and dangerous wandering ways it takes
Through error's fenny bogs and thorny brakes;   15
Whilst the misguided follower climbs with pain
Mountains of whimseys, heaped in his own brain;
Stumbling from thought to thought, falls headlong down

Into doubt's boundless sea, where, like to drown,
Books bear him up a while, and make him try   20
To swim with bladders of philosophy;
In hopes still to o'ertake th' escaping light,—
The vapor dances in his dazzling[1] sight
Till, spent, it leaves him to eternal night.
Then old age and experience, hand in hand,   25
Lead him to death, and make him understand,
After a search so painful and so long,
That all his life he has been in the wrong.
Huddled in dirt the reasoning engine lies,
Who was so proud, so witty, and so wise.   30
    Pride drew him in, as cheats their bubbles[1a] catch,
And made him venture to be made a wretch.
His wisdom did his happiness destroy,
Aiming to know that world he should enjoy.
And wit was his vain, frivolous pretense   35
Of pleasing others at his own expense,
For wits are treated just like common whores:
First they're enjoyed, and then kicked out of doors.
The pleasure past, a threatening doubt remains
That frights th' enjoyer with succeeding pains.   40
Women and men of wit are dangerous tools,
And ever fatal to admiring fools:
Pleasure allures, and when the fops escape,
'Tis not that they're belov'd, but fortunate,
And therefore what they fear at heart, they hate.   45
    But now, methinks, some formal band and beard [2]
Takes me to task. Come on, sir; I'm prepared.
    "Then, by your favor, anything that's writ
Against this gibing, jingling knack called wit
Likes me abundantly; but you take care   50
Upon this point, not to be too severe.
Perhaps my muse were fitter for this part,
For I profess I can be very smart

[1] an obsolete meaning of "to dazzle" is "to lose the faculty of distinct
and steady vision, especially from gazing at too bright light" (*OED*).
[1a] dupes.
[2] Many Restoration clergymen wore Geneva bands.

On wit, which I abhor with all my heart.
I long to lash it in some sharp essay,   55
But your grand indiscretion bids me stay
And turns my tide of ink another way.
   "What rage ferments in your degenerate mind
To make you rail at reason and mankind?
Blest, glorious man! to whom alone kind heaven   60
An everlasting soul has freely given,
Whom his great Maker took such care to make
That from himself he did the image take
And this fair frame in shining reason dressed
To dignify his nature above beast;   65
Reason, by whose aspiring influence
We take a flight beyond material sense,
Dive into mysteries, then soaring pierce
The flaming limits of the universe,
Search heaven and hell, find out what's acted there,   70
And give the world true grounds of hope and fear."
   Hold, mighty man, I cry, all this we know
From the pathetic pen of Ingelo,[3]
From Patrick's *Pilgrim*,[4] Sibbes's soliloquies,[5]
And 'tis this very reason I despise: 75
This supernatural gift, that makes a mite
Think he's the image of the infinite,
Comparing his short life, void of all rest,
To the eternal and the ever blest;
This busy, puzzling stirrer-up of doubt   80
That frames deep mysteries, then finds them out,
Filling with frantic crowds of thinking fools
Those reverend bedlams, colleges and schools;
Borne on whose wings, each heavy sot can pierce
The limits of the boundless universe;   85

   [3] The Reverend Nathaniel Ingelo (?1621-83) wrote a long religious-allegorical romance entitled *Bentivolio and Urania* (1660), reprinted several times during the Restoration period.
   [4] Simon Patrick (1626-1707), Bishop of Ely, wrote *The Parable of the Pilgrim* (1664), a work which resembles Bunyan's *Pilgrim's Progress*.
   [5] Richard Sibbes (1577-1635), a Puritan divine, wrote numerous religious works of an inspirational nature.

So charming ointments[6] make an old witch fly
And bear a crippled carcass through the sky.
'Tis this exalted power, whose business lies
In nonsense and impossibilities,
This made a whimsical philosopher[7]   90
Before the spacious world, his tub prefer,
And we have modern cloistered coxcombs who
Retire to think, 'cause they have nought to do.
   But thoughts are given for action's government;
Where action ceases, thought's impertinent.   95
Our sphere of action is life's happiness,
And he who thinks beyond, thinks like an ass.
Thus, whilst against false reasoning I inveigh,
I own right reason, which I would obey:
That reason which distinguishes by sense   100
And gives us rules of good and ill from thence,
That bounds desires with a reforming will
To keep them more in vigor, not to kill.
Your reason hinders, mine helps to enjoy,
Renewing appetites yours would destroy.   105
My reason is my friend, yours is a cheat;
Hunger calls out, my reason bids me eat;
Perversely, yours your appetite does mock:
This asks for food, that answers, "What's o'clock?"
This plain distinction, sir, your doubt secures: 110
'Tis not true reason I despise, but yours.
   Thus I think reason righted, but for man,
I'll ne'er recant; defend him if you can.
For all his pride and his philosophy,
'Tis evident beasts are, in their degree,   115
As wise at least, and better far than he.
Those creatures are the wisest who attain,
By surest means, the ends at which they aim.
If therefore Jowler finds and kills his hares

[6] It was popularly believed that witches anointed themselves in order to be able to fly through the air.

[7] Diogenes the Cynic, well known for dwelling in a tub, taught that virtue consists in the avoidance of all physical pleasure and that pain and hunger are positively helpful in the pursuit of goodness.

Better than Meres[8] supplies committee chairs,[9]   120
Though one's a statesman, th' other but a hound,
Jowler, in justice, would be wiser found.
   You see how far man's wisdom here extends;
Look next if human nature makes amends:
Whose principles most generous are, and just,   125
And to whose morals you would sooner trust.
Be judge yourself, I'll bring it to the test:
Which is the basest creature, man or beast?
Birds feed on birds, beasts on each other prey,
But savage man alone does man betray.   130
Pressed by necessity, they kill for food;
Man undoes man to do himself no good.
With teeth and claws by nature armed, they hunt
Nature's allowance, to supply their want.
But man, with smiles, embraces, friendship, praise,   135
Inhumanly his fellow's life betrays;
With voluntary pains works his distress,
Not through necessity, but wantonness.
   For hunger or for love they fight and tear,
Whilst wretched man is still in arms for fear.   140
For fear he arms, and is of arms afraid,
By fear to fear successively betrayed;
Base fear, the source whence his best passions came:
His boasted honor, and his dear-bought fame;
That lust of power, to which he's such a slave,   145
And for the which alone he dares be brave;
To which his various projects are designed;
Which makes him generous, affable, and kind;
For which he takes such pains to be thought wise,
And screws his actions in a forced disguise,   150
Leading a tedious life in misery
Under laborious, mean hypocrisy.
Look to the bottom of his vast design,

   [8] Sir Thomas Meres (1635-1715), a prominent member of the Country
or Whig party, M.P. for Lincoln, and a Commissioner of the Admiralty from
1679 to 1684.
   [9] The House of Commons sometimes resolved into a committee of the
whole house to allow more freedom of debate. Meres occupied the chair on
several such occasions.

Wherein man's wisdom, power, and glory join:
The good he acts, the ill he does endure,   155
'Tis all from fear, to make himself secure.
Merely for safety, after fame we thirst,
For all men would be cowards if they durst.
    And honesty's against all common sense:
Men must be knaves, 'tis in their own defense.   160
Mankind's dishonest; if you think it fair
Amongst known cheats to play upon the square,
You'll be undone.
Nor can weak truth your reputation save:
The knaves will all agree to call you knave.   165
Wronged shall he live, insulted o'er, oppressed,
Who dares be less a villain than the rest.
    Thus, sir, you see what human nature craves:
Most men are cowards, all men should be knaves.
The difference lies, as far as I can see,   170
Not in the thing itself, but the degree,
And all the subject matter of debate
Is only: Who's a knave of the first rate?

    All this with indignation have I hurled
At the pretending part of the proud world,   175
Who, swollen with selfish vanity, devise
False freedoms, holy cheats, and formal lies
Over their fellow slaves to tyrannize.
    But if in Court so just a man there be
(In Court a just man, yet unknown to me)   180
Who does his needful flattery direct,
Not to oppress and ruin, but protect
(Since flattery, which way soever laid,
Is still a tax on that unhappy trade);
If so upright a statesman you can find,   185
Whose passions bend to his unbiased mind,
Who does his arts and policies apply
To raise his country, not his family,
Nor, while his pride owned avarice withstands,
Receives close bribes through friends' corrupted hands— 190
    Is there a churchman who on God relies;
Whose life, his faith and doctrine justifies?

Not one blown up with vain prelatic pride,
Who, for reproof of sins, does man deride;
Whose envious heart makes preaching a pretense,   195
With his obstreperous, saucy eloquence,
To chide at kings, and rail at men of sense;
None of that sensual tribe whose talents lie
In avarice, pride, sloth, and gluttony;
Who hunt good livings, but abhor good lives;   200
Whose lust exalted to that height arrives
They act adultery with their own wives,
And ere a score of years completed be,
Can from the lofty pulpit proudly see
Half a large parish their own progeny;   205
Nor doting bishop who would be adored
For domineering at the council board,
A greater fop in business at fourscore,
Fonder of serious toys, affected more,
Than the gay, glittering fool at twenty proves   210
With all his noise, his tawdry clothes, and loves;
    But a meek, humble man of honest sense,
Who, preaching peace, does practice continence;
Whose pious life's a proof he does believe
Mysterious truths, which no man can conceive.   215
If upon earth there dwell such God-like men,
I'll here recant my paradox to them,
Adore those shrines of virtue, homage pay,
And, with the rabble world, their laws obey.
    If such there are, yet grant me this at least: 220
Man differs more from man, than man from beast.

George Savile
Marquess of Halifax

George Savile, Marquess of Halifax (1633-95), was the son of Sir William Savile, who fought in the Royalist cause and died in 1644. Born into a family of wealth and strong political connections, he became a Member of the Convention Parliament of 1660, was raised to the peerage in 1668. In 1679 he entered the privy council, became a favorite of Charles II, and rose to great power in public affairs. He played a large part in bringing William and Mary to the throne in 1689. His detachment from party interests won him the name of "trimmer," which he accepted with pride in his *Character of a Trimmer*. His wit was famous and, because of its unguarded play, gave rise to distrust of his principles; but these are eloquently set forth in his surviving works. In addition to his political pamphlets, he wrote *A Lady's Gift, or Advice to a Daughter* (1688), the daughter who was to become the mother of the famous Lord Chesterfield. His *Political, Moral, and Miscellaneous Reflexions* (first published with the *Character of King Charles II* in 1750) is a brilliant statement through aphorisms of his skeptical doctrine of a middle way. The prose of Halifax looks back to the "baroque" freedom of earlier style, in its Senecan point and loose sentence structure; but it catches as well that discrimination of meanings which was to shape Augustan wit and to stiffen its conversational grace with a firm sense of balance and antithesis.

Edition: Complete Works, ed. Walter Raleigh (1912).

Biographies: H. C. Foxcroft, *Life and Letters* (1898), which is also an edition; H. C. Foxcroft, *A Character of the Trimmer* (1946).

A Character of King Charles II
[?*1686*, 1750]

A character differeth from a picture only in this; every part of it must be like, but it is not necessary that every feature should be comprehended in it as in a picture, only some of the most remarkable.

This Prince at his first entrance into the world had adversity for his introducer, which is generally thought to be no ill one, but in his case it proved so, and laid the foundation of most of those misfortunes or errors that were the causes of the great objections made to him.

The first effect it had was in relation to his religion.

The ill-bred familiarity of the Scotch divines[1] had given him a distaste of that part of the Protestant religion. He was left then to the little remnant of the Church of England in the Faubourg St. Germain,[2] which made such a kind of figure as might easily be turned in such a manner as to make him lose his veneration for it. In a refined country, where religion appeared in pomp and splendor, the outward appearance of such unfashionable men was made an argument against their religion, and a young Prince not averse to raillery was the more susceptible of a contempt for it.

The company he kept, the men in his pleasures, and the arguments of state that he should not appear too much a Protestant whilst he expected assistance from a popish prince;[3] all these, together with a habit encouraged by an application to his pleasures,

---

[1] During his stay in Scotland, 1650-51; of the Scottish Presbyterians, Charles wrote (3 September 1650): "Nothing could have confirmed me more to the Church of England than being here seeing their hypocrisy" (*Letters of King Charles II*, ed. Arthur Bryant [1935], p. 16).

[2] the quarter of Paris where Charles's mother, Henrietta Maria, held her court in exile.

[3] Louis XIV (1638-1715), then largely under the influence of the queen-mother, Anne, and Cardinal Mazarin.

did so loosen and untie him from his first impressions, that I take it for granted after the first year or two he was no more a Protestant. If you ask me what he was, my answer must be that he was of the religion of a young prince in his warm blood, whose enquiries were more applied to find arguments against believing than to lay any settled foundations for acknowledging Providence, mysteries, &c. A general creed, and no very long one, may be presumed to be the utmost religion of one whose age and inclination could not well spare any thoughts that did not tend to his pleasures.

In this kind of indifference or unthinkingness, which is too natural in the beginnings of life to be heavily censured, I will suppose he might pass some considerable part of his youth. I must presume, too, that no occasions were lost during that time to insinuate everything to bend him towards Popery. Great art without intermission against youth and easiness, which are seldom upon their guard, must have its effect. A man is to be admired if he resisteth, and therefore cannot reasonably be blamed if he yieldeth to them. When the critical minute was I'll not undertake to determine, but certainly the inward conviction doth generally precede the outward declarations, at what distances dependeth upon men's several complexions and circumstances; no stated period can be fixed.

It will be said that he had not religion enough to have conviction; that is a vulgar error. Conviction, indeed, is not a proper word but where a man is convinced by reason; but in the common acceptation it is applied to those who cannot tell why they are so. If men can be at least as positive in a mistake as when they are in the right, they may be as clearly convinced when they do not know why, as when they do.

I must presume that no man of the King's age and his methods of life could possibly give a good reason for changing the religion in which he was born, let it be what it will. But our passions are much oftener convinced than our reason. He had but little reading, and that tending to his pleasures more than to his instruction. In the library of a young prince the solemn folios are not much rumpled; books of a lighter digestion have the dog's ears.

Some pretend to be very precise in the time of his reconciling—

the Cardinal de Retz,[4] &c. I will not enter into it minutely, but whenever it was, it is observable that the Government of France did not think it advisable to discover it openly; upon which such obvious reflections may be made that I will not mention them.

Such a secret can never be put into a place which is so closely stopped that there shall be no chinks. Whispers went about; particular men had intimations; Cromwell had his advertisements[5] in other things, and this was as well worth his paying for. There was enough said of it to startle a great many, though not universally diffused; so much, that if the Government here[6] had not crumbled of itself, his right alone, with that and other clogs upon it, would hardly have thrown it down. I conclude that when he came into England he was as certainly a Roman Catholic as that he was a man of pleasure, both very consistent by visible experience.

It is impertinent to give reasons for men's changing their religion. None can give them but themselves, as every man has quite a different way of arguing—a thing which may very well be accounted for. They are differing kinds of wit, to be quick to find a fault and to be capable to find out a truth. There must be industry in the last; the first requires only a lively heat that catcheth hold of the weak side of anything, but to choose the strong one is another talent. The reason why men of wit are often the laziest in their enquiries, is that their heat carrieth their thoughts so fast that they are apt to be tired, and they faint in the drudgery of a continued application. Have not men of great wit in all times permitted their understandings to give way to their first impressions? It taketh off from the diminution when a man doth not mind a thing, and the King had then other business. The inferior part of the man was then in possession, and the faculties of the brain, as to serious and painful enquiries, were laid asleep at least, though not extinguished. Careless men are most subject to superstition. Those who do not study reason enough to make it their guide have more unevenness; as they have neglects, so they have starts and frights; dreams will serve the turn; omens and sicknesses have violent and sudden effects upon them. Nor is the strength of an argument so effectual from its

[4] (1614-79); who gave aid to Charles's mother and visited Charles in London twice in 1660.

[5] reports.

[6] the Commonwealth under Richard Cromwell.

intrinsic force as by its being well suited to the temper of the party.

The genteel part of the Catholic religion might tempt a Prince that had more of the fine gentleman than his governing capacity required, and the exercise of indulgence to sinners being more frequent in it than of inflicting penance might be some recommendation. Mistresses of that faith are stronger specifics in this case than any that are in physic.

The Roman Catholics complained of his breach of promise[7] to them very early. There were broad peepings out, glimpses so often repeated, that to discerning eyes it was flaring; in the very first year there were such suspicions as produced melancholy shakings of the head, which were very significant. His unwillingness to marry a Protestant was remarkable, though both the Catholic and the Christian crown[8] would have adopted her. Very early in his youth, when any German princess was proposed, he put off the discourse with raillery. A thousand little circumstances were a kind of accumulative evidence, which in these cases may be admitted.

Men that were earnest Protestants were under the sharpness of his displeasure, expressed by raillery as well as by other ways. Men near him have made discoveries from sudden breakings out in discourse, &c., which showed there was a root. It was not the least skilful part of his concealing himself to make the world think he leaned towards an indifference in religion.

He had sicknesses before his death, in which he did not trouble any Protestant divines; those who saw him upon his deathbed saw a great deal.[9]

As to his writing those papers,[10] he might do it. Though neither his temper nor education made him very fit to be an author, yet in

---

[7] In the Declaration of Breda (1660) Charles announced his intention of granting toleration of religious opinion; when Parliament prevented this, he sought again in 1662 to use his prerogative to grant indulgence, but the seeming favor to Catholics was not permitted by the Commons.

[8] Spain and France.

[9] Charles on his deathbed refused the Anglican communion urged upon him by a group of bishops and took the last rites from a Roman Catholic priest.

[10] two papers in defense of the Roman Catholic religion, supposedly written in Charles II's hand and found in his strongbox, later published by James II; their authenticity was doubted by many.

this case (a known topic, so very often repeated) he might write it all himself and yet not one word of it his own. That Church's argument doth so agree with men unwilling to take pains, the temptation of putting an end to all the trouble of enquiring is so great that it must be very strong reason that can resist. The King had only his mere natural faculties, without any acquisitions to improve them, so that it is no wonder if an argument which gave such ease and relief to his mind made such an impression, that with thinking often of it (as men are apt to do of everything they like) he might, by the effect chiefly of his memory, put together a few lines with his own hand without any help at the time; in which there was nothing extraordinary, but that one so little inclined to write at all should prevail with himself to do it with the solemnity of a casuist.

II.—HIS DISSIMULATION

One great objection made to him was the concealing himself and disguising his thoughts. In this there ought a latitude to be given; it is a defect not to have it at all, and a fault to have it too much. Human nature will not allow the mean: like all other things, as soon as ever men get to do them well, they cannot easily hold from doing them too much. 'Tis the case even in the least things, as singing, &c.

In France he was to dissemble injuries and neglects from one reason; in England he was to dissemble, too, though for other causes. A king upon the throne hath as great temptations (though of another kind) to dissemble, as a king in exile. The King of France might have his times of dissembling as much with him as he could have to do it with the King of France; so he was in a school.

No king can be so little inclined to dissemble but he must needs learn it from his subjects, who every day give him such lessons of it. Dissimulation is like most other qualities, it hath two sides; it is necessary, and yet it is dangerous too. To have none at all layeth a man open to contempt, to have too much exposeth him to suspicion, which is only the less dishonorable inconvenience. If a man doth not take very great precautions he is never so much showed as when he endeavoreth to hide himself. One man cannot take more pains to hide himself than another will do to see into him, especially in the case of kings.

It is none of the exalted faculties of the mind, since there are chambermaids will do it better than any prince in Christendom. Men given to dissembling are like rooks[11] at play—they will cheat for shillings, they are so used to it. The vulgar definition of dissembling is downright lying; that kind of it which is less ill-bred cometh pretty near it. Only princes and persons of honor must have gentler words given to their faults than the nature of them may in themselves deserve.

Princes dissemble with too many not to have it discovered; no wonder then that he carried it so far that it was discovered. Men compared notes and got evidence, so that those whose morality would give them leave took it for an excuse for serving him ill. Those who knew his face fixed their eyes there, and thought it of more importance to see than to hear what he said. His face was as little a blab as most men's, yet though it could not be called a prattling face, it would sometimes tell tales to a good observer. When he thought fit to be angry he had a very peevish memory; there was hardly a blot that escaped him. At the same time that this showed the strength of his dissimulation, it gave warning too; it fitted his present purpose, but it made a discovery that put men more upon their guard against him. Only self-flattery furnisheth perpetual arguments to trust again; the comfortable opinion men have of themselves keepeth up human society, which would be more than half destroyed without it.

III.—HIS AMOURS, MISTRESSES, &C.

It may be said that his inclinations to love were the effects of health and a good constitution, with as little mixture of the seraphic[12] part as ever man had; and though from that foundation men often raise their passions, I am apt to think his stayed as much as any man's ever did in the lower region. This made him like easy mistresses—they were generally resigned to him while he was abroad, with an implied bargain. Heroic, refined lovers place a

[11] swindlers.

[12] a term drawn from the tradition of courtly love, as are several in the following paragraphs (*heroic, refined lovers; knight-errant*).

good deal of their pleasure in the difficulty, both for the vanity of conquest and as a better earnest of their kindness.

After he was restored, mistresses were recommended to him; which is no small matter in a court, and not unworthy the thought even of a party. A mistress either dexterous in herself, or well in-structed by those that are so, may be very useful to her friends, not only in the immediate hours of her ministry, but by her influ-ences and insinuations at other times. It was resolved generally by others whom he should have in his arms, as well as whom he should have in his councils. Of a man who was so capable of choosing, he chose as seldom as any man that ever lived.

He had more properly, at least in the beginning of his time, a good stomach to his mistresses, than any great passion for them. His taking them from others was never learnt in a romance; and indeed fitter for a philosopher than a knight-errant. His patience for their frailties showed him no exact[13] lover. It is a heresy, accord-ing to a true lover's creed, ever to forgive an infidelity, or the appearance of it. Love of ease will not do it where the heart is much engaged; but where mere nature is the motive, it is possible for a man to think righter than the common opinion, and to argue that a rival taketh away nothing but the heart and leaveth all the rest.

In his latter times he had no love, but insensible engagements that made it harder than most might apprehend to untie them. The politics might have their part; a secret, a commission, a confidence in critical things, though it doth not give a lease for a precise term of years, yet there may be difficulties in dismissing them; there may be no love all the while, perhaps the contrary.

He was said to be as little constant as they were thought to be. Though he had no love, he must have some appetite or else he could not keep them for mere ease, or for the love of sauntering. Mistresses are frequently apt to be uneasy; they are in all respects craving creatures; so that though the taste of those joys might be flattened, yet a man who loved pleasure so as to be very unwilling to part with it, might (with the assistance of his fancy, which doth not grow old so fast) reserve some supplemental entertainments that might make their personal service be still of use to him. The definition of pleasure is *what pleaseth,* and if that which grave men

[13] fastidious, precise.

may call a corrupted fancy shall administer any remedies for putting off mourning for the loss of youth, who shall blame it?

The young men seldom apply their censure to these matters; and the elder have an interest to be gentle towards a mistake that seemeth to make some kind of amends for their decays.

He had wit enough to suspect, and he had wit enough too not to care: the ladies got a great deal more than would have been allowed to be an equal bargain in Chancery[14] for what they did for it; but neither the manner, nor the measure of pleasure, is to be judged by others.

Little inducements at first grew into strong reasons by degrees. Men who do not consider circumstances but judge at a distance, by a general way of arguing, conclude if a mistress in some cases is not immediately turned off, it must needs be that the gallant is incurably subjected. This will by no means hold in private men, much less in princes, who are under more entanglements, from which they cannot so easily loosen themselves.

His mistresses were as different in their humors as they were in their looks. They gave matter of very different reflections. The last[15] especially was quite out of the definition of an ordinary mistress; the causes and the manner of her being first introduced were very different. A very peculiar distinction was spoken of, some extraordinary solemnities that might dignify, though not sanctify, her function. Her chamber was the true Cabinet Council. The King did always by his councils as he did sometimes by his meals; he sat down out of form with the Queen, but he supped below stairs. To have the secrets of a king, who happens to have too many, is to have a king in chains: he must not only not part with her, but he must in his own defense dissemble his dislike: the less kindness he hath, the more he must show. There is great difference between being muffled and being tied: he was the first, not the last. If he had quarrelled at some times, besides other advantages this mistress had a powerful second[16] (one may suppose a kind of a guarantee); this to a man that loved his ease, though his age had not helped, was sufficient.

The thing called sauntering is a stronger temptation to princes

---

[14] court of equity.

[15] the Duchess of Portsmouth, Louise de Kéroualle (1649-1734).

[16] probably the French court.

than it is to others. The being galled with importunities, pursued
from one room to another with asking faces; the dismal sound of
unreasonable complaints and ill-grounded pretenses; the deformity
of fraud ill-disguised—all these would make any man run away
from them; and I used to think it was the motive for making him
walk so fast. So it was more properly taking sanctuary. To get into
a room where all business was to stay at the door, excepting such
as he was disposed to admit, might be very acceptable to a younger
man than he was and less given to his ease. He slumbered after
dinner, had the noise of the company to divert him without their
solicitations to importune him. In these hours where he was more
unguarded, no doubt the cunning men of the court took their
times to make their observations, and there is as little doubt but
he made his upon them too: where men had chinks he would see
through them as soon as any man about him. There was much more
real business done there in his politic than there was in his personal
capacity, *stans pede in uno;*[17] and there was the French part of the
Government, which was not the least.

In short, without endeavoring to find more arguments, he
was used to it. Men do not care to put off a habit, nor do often
succeed when they go about it. His was not an unthinkingness;
he did not perhaps think so much of his subjects as they might
wish; but he was far from being wanting to think of himself.

IV.—HIS CONDUCT TO HIS MINISTERS

He lived with his ministers as he did with his mistresses; he
used them, but he was not in love with them. He showed his
judgment in this, that he cannot properly be said ever to have had
a favorite, though some might look so at a distance. The present use
he might have of them made him throw favors upon them which
might lead the lookers-on into that mistake; but he tied himself
no more to them than they did to him, which implied a sufficient
liberty on either side.

Perhaps he made dear purchases: if he seldom gave profusely
but where he expected some unreasonable thing, great rewards were
material evidences against those who received them.

He was free of access to them, which was a very gaining

---

[17] "standing in the same position" (Horace, *Satires,* I iv 10).

quality. He had at least as good a memory for the faults of his ministers as for their services; and whenever they fell, the whole inventory came out; there was not a slip omitted.

That some of his ministers seemed to have a superiority did not spring from his resignation to them, but to his ease. He chose rather to be eclipsed than to be troubled.

His brother[18] was a minister, and he had his jealousies of him. At the same time that he raised him, he was not displeased to have him lessened. The cunning observers found this out, and at the same time that he reigned in the Cabinet he was very familiarly used at the private supper.

A minister turned off is like a lady's waiting-woman, that knoweth all her washes[18a] and hath a shrewd guess at her strayings: so there is danger in turning them off as well as in keeping them.

He had back stairs to convey informations to him, as well as for other uses; and though such informations are sometimes dangerous (especially to a Prince that will not take the pains necessary to digest them), yet in the main, that humor of hearing everybody against anybody kept those about him in more awe than they would have been without it. I do not believe that ever he trusted any man, or any set of men, so entirely as not to have some secrets in which they had no share: as this might make him less well served, so in some degree it might make him the less imposed upon.

You may reckon under this article his female ministry; for though he had ministers of the council, ministers of the cabinet, and ministers of the ruelle,[19] the ruelle was often the last appeal. Those who were not well there were used because they were necessary at the time, not because they were liked; so that their tenure was a little uncertain. His ministers were to administer business to him as doctors do physic—wrap it up in something to make it less unpleasant; some skilful digressions were so far from being impertinent, that they could not many times fix him to a fair audience without them. His aversion to formality made him dislike a serious discourse, if very long, except it was mixed with something to entertain him. Some even of the graver sort, too, used to carry this very far, and, rather than fail, use the coarsest kind of youthful talk.

[18] James II, then Duke of York.
[18a] cosmetics.
[19] a lady's bedroom used as a salon for morning receptions.

In general, he was upon pretty even terms with his ministers, and could as easily bear their being hanged as some of them could his being abused.

V.—OF HIS WIT AND CONVERSATION

His wit consisted chiefly in the quickness of his apprehension. His apprehension made him find faults, and that led him to short sayings upon them, not always equal, but often very good.

By his being abroad, he contracted a habit of conversing familiarly, which, added to his natural genius, made him very apt to talk; perhaps more than a very nice judgment would approve.

He was apter to make broad allusions upon anything that gave the least occasion than was altogether suitable with the very good breeding he showed in most other things. The company he kept whilst abroad had so used him to that sort of dialect that he was so far from thinking it a fault or an indecency that he made it a matter of raillery upon those who could not prevail upon themselves to join in it. As a man who hath a good stomach loveth generally to talk of meat, so in the vigor of his age he began that style which by degrees grew so natural to him, that after he ceased to do it out of pleasure, he continued to do it out of custom. The hypocrisy of the former times inclined men to think they could not show too great an aversion to it, and that helped to encourage this unbounded liberty of talking, without the restraints of decency which were before observed. In his more familiar conversations with the ladies, even they must be passive if they would not enter into it. How far sounds as well as objects may have their effects to raise inclination might be an argument to him to use that style; or whether using liberty at its full stretch was not the general inducement without any particular motives to it.

The manner of that time of telling stories had drawn him into it; being commended at first for the faculty of telling a tale well, he might insensibly be betrayed to exercise it too often. Stories are dangerous in this, that the best expose a man most by being oftenest repeated. It might pass for an evidence for the moderns against the ancients that it is now wholly left off by all that have any pretense to be distinguished by their good sense.

He had the improvements of wine, &c., which made him pleasant and easy in company; where he bore his part and was

acceptable even to those who had no other design than to be merry
with him.

The thing called wit, a prince may taste, but it is dangerous
for him to take too much of it; it hath allurements which by
refining his thoughts take off from their dignity in applying them
less to the governing part. There is a charm in wit which a prince
must resist, and that to him was no easy matter; it was contesting
with nature upon terms of disadvantage.

His wit was not so ill-natured as to put men out of countenance.
In the case of a king especially, it is more allowable to speak sharply
of them, than to them.

His wit was not acquired by reading; that which he had above
his original stock by nature was from company, in which he was
very capable to observe. He could not so properly be said to have a
wit very much raised as a plain, gaining, well-bred, recommending
kind of wit.

But of all men that ever liked those who had wit, he could
the best endure those who had none. This leaneth more towards
a satire than a compliment, in this respect, that he could not only
suffer impertinence, but at some times seemed to be pleased with it.

He encouraged some to talk a good deal more with him than
one would have expected from a man of so good a taste. He should
rather have ordered his Attorney-General to prosecute them for a
misdemeanor in using common sense so scurvily in his presence.
However, if this was a fault, it is arrogant for any of his subjects
to object to it, since it would look like defying such a piece of
indulgence. He must, in some degree, loosen the strength of his wit
by his condescension to talk with men so very unequal to him. Wit
must be used to some equality, which may give it exercise, or else
it is apt either to languish or to grow a little vulgar, by reigning
amongst men of a lower size where there is no awe to keep a man
upon his guard.

It fell out rather by accident than choice that his mistresses
were such as did not care that wit of the best kind should have the
precedence in their apartments. Sharp and strong wit will not always
be so held in by good manners, as not to be a little troublesome in
a ruelle. But wherever impertinence[20] hath wit enough left to be
thankful for being well used, it will not only be admitted but

[20] folly, impudence.

kindly received; such charms everything hath that setteth us off by comparison.

His affability was a part, and perhaps not the least, of his wit.

It is a quality that must not always spring from the heart; men's pride as well as their weakness maketh them ready to be deceived by it. They are more ready to believe it a homage paid to their merit than a bait thrown out to deceive them. Princes have a particular advantage.

There was at first as much of art as nature in his affability, but by habit it became natural. It is an error of the better hand, but the universality taketh away a good deal of the force of it. A man that hath had a kind look seconded with engaging words, whilst he is chewing the pleasure, if another in his sight should be received just[21] as kindly, that equality would presently alter the relish. The pride of mankind will have distinction; till at last it cometh to smile for smile, meaning nothing of either side, without any kind of effect, mere drawing-room compliments; the bow alone would be better without them. He was under some disadvantages of this kind, that grew still in proportion as it came by time to be more known that there was less signification in those things than at first was thought.

The familiarity of his wit must needs have the effect of lessening the distance fit to be kept to him. The freedom used to him whilst abroad was retained by those who used it longer than either they ought to have kept it or he have suffered it, and others by their example learned to use the same. A King of Spain that will say nothing but *Tiendro cuydado*[22] will, to the generality, preserve more respect; an engine[23] that will speak but sometimes, at the same time that it will draw the raillery of the few who judge well, it will create respect in the ill-judging generality. Formality is sufficiently revenged upon the world for being so unreasonably laughed at; it is destroyed, it is true, but it hath the spiteful satisfaction of seeing everything destroyed with it.

His fine gentlemanship did him no good, encouraged in it by being too much applauded.

[21] The text reads "just received."
[22] "I will take care."
[23] contrivance, manner.

His wit was better suited to his condition before he was restored than afterwards. The wit of a gentleman and that of a crowned head ought to be different things. As there is a crown law, there is a crown wit too. To use it with reserve is very good and very rare. There is a dignity in doing things seldom, even without any other circumstance. Where wit will run continually, the spring is apt to fail; so that it groweth vulgar, and the more it is practised, the more it is debased.

He was so good at finding out other men's weak sides that it made him less intent to cure his own: that generally happeneth. It may be called a treacherous talent, for it betrayeth a man to forget to judge himself by being so eager to censure others. This doth so misguide men the first part of their lives that the habit of it is not easily recovered when the greater ripeness of their judgment inclineth them to look more into themselves than into other men.

Men love to see themselves in the false looking-glass of other men's failings. It maketh a man think well of himself at the time, and by sending his thoughts abroad to get food for laughing, they are less at leisure to see faults at home. Men choose rather to make the war in another country than to keep all well at home.

VI.—HIS TALENTS, TEMPER, HABITS, &C.

He had a mechanical head, which appeared in his inclination to shipping and fortification, &c. This would make one conclude that his thoughts would naturally have been more fixed to business if his pleasures had not drawn them away from it.

He had a very good memory, though he would not always make equal good use of it. So that if he had accustomed himself to direct his faculties to his business, I see no reason why he might not have been a good deal master of it. His chain of memory was longer than his chain of thought; the first could bear any burden, the other was tired by being carried on too long; it was fit to ride a heat, but it had not wind enough for a long course.

A very great memory often forgetteth how much time is lost by repeating things of no use. It was one reason of his talking so much; since a great memory will always have something to say and will be discharging itself, whether in or out of season, if a good judgment doth not go along with it to make it stop and turn.

One might say of his memory that it was a *beauté journalière*.[24] Sometimes he would make shrewd applications, &c., at others he would bring things out of it that never deserved to be laid in it.

He grew by age into a pretty exact distribution of his hours, both for business, pleasures, and the exercise for his health, of which he took as much care as could possibly consist with some liberties he was resolved to indulge in himself. He walked by his watch, and, when he pulled it out to look upon it, skilful men would make haste with what they had to say to him.

He was often retained in his personal against his politic capacity. He would speak upon those occasions most dexterously against himself. Charles Stuart would be bribed against the King, and in the distinction he leaned more to his natural self than his character[25] would allow. He would not suffer himself to be so much fettered by his character as was convenient; he was still starting out of it. The power of nature was too strong for the dignity of his calling, which generally yielded as often as there was a contest.

It was not the best use he made of his back stairs to admit men to bribe him against himself, to procure a defalcation, help a lame accountant to get off, or side with the farmers[25a] against the improvement of the revenue. The King was made the instrument to defraud the Crown, which is somewhat extraordinary.

That which might tempt him to it probably was his finding that those about him so often took money upon those occasions; so that he thought he might do well at least to be a partner. He did not take the money to hoard it; there were those at Court who watched those times, as the Spaniards do for the coming in of the Plate Fleet.[26] The beggars of both sexes helped to empty his cabinet, and to leave room in them for a new lading upon the next occasion. These negotiators played double with him, too, when it was for their purpose so to do. He knew it, and went on still; so he gained his present end at the time, he was less solicitous to enquire into the consequences.

He could not properly be said to be either covetous or liberal; his desire to get was not with an intention to be rich; and his spending was rather an easiness in letting money go than any

[24] "variable beauty."

[25] public role. [25a] i.e., tax-farmers, who paid a fixed sum for the right to collect taxes or revenues.

[26] the bullion fleet returning from the River Plata in Argentina.

premeditated thought for the distribution of it. He would do as much to throw off the burden of a present importunity as he would to relieve a want.

When once the aversion to bear uneasiness taketh place in a man's mind, it doth so check all the passions that they are damped into a kind of indifference; they grow faint and languishing and come to be subordinate to that fundamental maxim of not purchasing anything at the price of a difficulty. This made that he had as little eagerness to oblige as he had to hurt men; the motive of his giving bounties was rather to make men less uneasy to him than more easy to themselves; and yet no ill-nature all this while. He would slide from an asking face, and could guess very well. It was throwing a man off from his shoulders that leaned upon them with his whole weight; so that the party was not gladder to receive than he was to give. It was a kind of implied bargain; though men seldom kept it, being so apt to forget the advantage they had received that they would presume the King would as little remember the good he had done them, so as to make it an argument against their next request.

This principle of making the love of ease exercise an entire sovereignty in his thoughts would have been less censured in a private man than might be in a prince. The consequence of it to the public changeth the nature of that quality, or else a philosopher in his private capacity might say a great deal to justify it. The truth is, a king is to be such a distinct creature from a man that their thoughts are to be put in quite a differing shape, and it is such a disquieting task to reconcile them that princes might rather expect to be lamented than to be envied, for being in a station that exposeth them if they do not do more to answer men's expectations than human nature will allow.

That men have the less ease for their loving it so much is so far from a wonder that it is a natural consequence, especially in the case of a prince. Ease is seldom got without some pains, but it is yet seldomer kept without them. He thought giving would make men more easy to him, whereas he might have known it would certainly make them more troublesome.

When men receive benefits from princes, they attribute less to his generosity than to their own deserts; so that in their own opinion their merit cannot be bounded; by that mistaken rule, it can as little be satisfied. They would take it for a diminution to have it circumscribed. Merit hath a thirst upon it that can never be quenched by golden showers. It is not only still ready, but greedy to receive more. This King Charles found in as many instances as any prince that ever reigned, because the easiness of access introducing the good success of their first request, they were the more encouraged to repeat those importunities, which had been more effectually stopped in the beginning by a short and resolute denial. But his nature did not dispose him to that method; it directed him rather to put off the troublesome minute for the time, and that being his inclination, he did not care to struggle with it.

I am of an opinion, in which I am every day more confirmed by observation, that gratitude is one of those things that cannot be bought. It must be born with men, or else all the obligations in the world will not create it. An outward show may be made to satisfy decency and to prevent reproach; but a real sense of a kind thing is a gift of nature and never was, nor can be, acquired.

The love of ease is an opiate; it is pleasing for the time, quieteth the spirits; but it hath its effects that seldom fail to be most fatal. The immoderate love of ease maketh a man's mind pay a passive obedience to anything that happeneth: it reduceth the thoughts from having desire to be content.

It must be allowed he had a little over-balance on the well-natured side, not vigor enough to be earnest to do a kind thing, much less to do a harsh one; but if a hard thing was done to another man, he did not eat his supper the worse for it. It was rather a deadness than severity of nature, whether it proceeded from a dissipation of spirits, or by the habit of living in which he was engaged.

If a king should be born with more tenderness than might suit with his office, he would in time be hardened. The faults of his subjects make severity so necessary that, by the frequent occasions given to use it, it comes to be habitual, and by degrees the resistance that nature made at first groweth fainter till at last it is in a manner quite extinguished.

In short, this Prince might more properly be said to have gifts than virtues, as affability, easiness of living, inclinations to give and to forgive: qualities that flowed from his nature rather than from his virtue.

He had not more application to anything than the preservation of his health; it had an entire preference to anything else in his thoughts, and he might be said without aggravation[27] to study that with as little intermission as any man in the world. He understood it very well; only in this he failed, that he thought it was more reconcilable with his pleasures than it really was. It is natural to have such a mind to reconcile these, that 'tis the easier for any man that goeth about it to be guilty of that mistake.

This made him overdo in point of nourishment, the better to furnish to those entertainments; and then he thought by great exercise to make amends, and to prevent the ill effects of his blood being too much raised. The success he had in this method whilst he had youth and vigor to support him in it encouraged him to continue it longer than nature allowed. Age stealeth so insensibly upon us, that we do not think of suiting our way of reasoning to the several stages of life; so insensibly that, not being able to pitch upon any precise time when we cease to be young, we either flatter ourselves that we always continue to be so, or at least forget how much we are mistaken in it.

VII.—CONCLUSION

After all this, when some rough strokes of the pencil[28] have made several parts of the picture look a little hard, it is a justice that would be due to every man, much more to a prince, to make some amends and to reconcile men as much as may be to it by the last finishing.

He had as good a claim to a kind interpretation as most men. First as a prince: living and dead, generous and well-bred men will be gentle to them; next as an unfortunate prince in the beginning of his time, and a gentle one in the rest.

A prince neither sharpened by his misfortunes whilst abroad, nor by his power when restored, is such a shining character that it is a reproach not to be so dazzled with it as not to be able to see a fault in its full light. It would be a scandal in this case to have an exact memory. And if all who are akin to his vices should mourn for him, never prince would be better attended to his grave. He is under the protection of common frailty, that must engage men

[27] exaggeration.   [28] painter's brush.

for their own sakes not to be too severe where they themselves have so much to answer.

What therefore an angry philosopher would call lewdness, let frailer men call a warmth and sweetness of the blood that would not be confined in the communicating itself; an overflowing of good nature, of which he had such a stream that it would not be restrained within the banks of a crabbed and unsociable virtue.

If he had sometimes less firmness than might have been wished, let the kindest reason be given, and if that should be wanting, the best excuse. I would assign the cause of it to be his loving, at any rate, to be easy, and his deserving the more to be indulged in it by his desiring that everybody else should be so.

If he sometimes let a servant fall, let it be examined whether he did not weigh so much upon his master as to give him a fair excuse. That yieldingness, whatever foundations it might lay to the disadvantage of posterity, was a specific to preserve us in peace for his own time. If he loved too much to lie upon his own down bed of ease, his subjects had the pleasure during his reign of lolling and stretching upon theirs. As a sword is sooner broken upon a feather bed than upon a table, so his pliantness broke the blow of a present mischief much better than a more immediate resistance would perhaps have done.

Ruin saw this, and therefore removed him first to make way for further overturnings.

If he dissembled, let us remember, first, that he was a king, and that dissimulation is a jewel of the crown; next, that it is very hard for a man not to do sometimes too much of that which he concludeth necessary for him to practice. Men should consider that, as there would be no false dice if there were no true ones, so if dissembling is grown universal, it ceaseth to be foul play, having an implied allowance by the general practice. He that was so often forced to dissemble in his own defense might the better have the privilege sometimes to be the aggressor and to deal with men at their own weapon.

Subjects are apt to be as arbitrary in their censure as the most assuming kings can be in their power. If there might be matter for objections, there is not less reason for excuses; the defects laid to his charge are such as may claim indulgence from mankind.

Should nobody throw a stone at his faults but those who are free from them, there would be but a slender shower.

What private man will throw stones at him because he loved? Or what prince because he dissembled?

If he either trusted, or forgave his enemies, or in some cases neglected his friends, more than could in strictness be allowed, let not those errors be so arraigned as take away the privilege that seemeth to be due to princely frailties. If princes are under the misfortune of being accused to govern ill, their subjects have the less right to fall hard upon them, since they generally so little deserve to be governed well.

The truth is, the calling of a king, with all its glittering, hath such an unreasonable weight upon it that they may rather expect to be lamented than to be envied for being set upon a pinnacle, where they are exposed to censure if they do not do more to answer men's expectations than corrupted nature will allow.

It is but justice therefore to this Prince to give all due softenings to the less shining parts of his life; to offer flowers and leaves to hide, instead of using aggravations to expose, them.

Let his royal ashes then lie soft upon him, and cover him from harsh and unkind censures; which though they should not be unjust, can never clear themselves from being indecent.[29]

[29] unbecoming, unfitting.

❧ Matthew Prior ❧

Matthew Prior (1664-1721) was born in Wimborne Minster, East Dorset; through the patronage of the Earl of Dorset, he was educated at Westminster School and Cambridge. His distinguished career as a diplomat, under William III and Anne, made him, in his own words, "only a poet by accident." But his work was admired and supported by Pope and Swift (who sought permission to print "Jinny the Just" in their 1727 *Miscellanies*). Prior's poetry was largely occasional or casual, but the urbanity and grace of his lyrics have a basis in that skeptical, pessimistic cast of thought which is made more explicit in his philosophical poems and prose dialogues. *Alma* (1718) is a brilliant verse dialogue on the relation of mind and body, written in Prior's own modification of Butler's Hudibrastic verse. *Solomon* (1718), whose reception disappointed Prior, is his most ambitious and somber work, in a vein which anticipates Johnson's *Vanity of Human Wishes*. Prior carries into the eighteenth century the best of the Restoration lyric tradition: the detached and quizzical use of the forms of love lyrics, the frank exploitation of conventional artifice to frame a conversational tone and a modest, humorous realism. In his more ambitious works, this playfulness becomes baroque extravagance; in a poem like "To a Child of Quality," an unsentimental sense of the charm of the child in an adult posture (such as Reynolds was later to catch in many fine paintings) as well as ironic play with the conventions of courtly love.

Editions: The Literary Works, ed. H. Bunker Wright and Monroe K. Spears (1959); *Writings,* ed. A. R. Waller (1905, 1907).

Biography: C. K. Eves, *Matthew Prior; Poet and Diplomatist* (1939).

Critical Studies: Monroe K. Spears, "Some Ethical Aspects of Matthew Prior's Poetry," SP 45 (1948), and "Matthew Prior's Religion," PQ 27 (1948).

To the Honorable Charles Montague, Esq.
[1692]

Howe'er, 'tis well, that while mankind
  Through Fate's perverse meander errs,
He can imagined pleasures find,
  To combat against real cares.

Fancies and notions he pursues,   5
  Which ne'er had being but in thought:
Each, like the Grecian artist,[1] woos
  The image he himself has wrought.

Against experience he believes;
  He argues against demonstration;   10
Pleased, when his reason he deceives;
  And sets his judgment by his passion.

The hoary fool, who many days
  Has struggled with continued sorrow,
Renews his hope, and blindly lays   15
  The desperate bet upon tomorrow.

Tomorrow comes: 'tis noon, 'tis night;
  This day like all the former flies:
Yet on he runs, to seek delight
  Tomorrow, till tonight he dies.   20

Our hopes, like towering falcons, aim
  At objects in an airy height:
The little pleasure of the game
  Is from afar to view the flight.

Our anxious pains we, all the day,   25
  In search of what we like, employ:
Scorning at night the worthless prey,
  We find the labor gave the joy.

[1] Pygmalion.

At distance through an artful glass
    To the mind's eye things well appear: 30
They lose their forms, and make a mass
    Confused and black, if brought too near.

If we see right, we see our woes:
    Then what avails it to have eyes?
From ignorance our comfort flows.   35
    The only wretched are the wise.

We wearied should lie down in death:
    This cheat of life would take[2] no more;
If you thought fame but empty breath;
    I, Phillis but a perjured whore.   40

To a Child of Quality Five Years Old
[?*1700*, 1704]

Lords, knights, and squires, the numerous band
    That wear the fair Miss Mary's[1] fetters,
Were summoned by her high command,
    To show their passions by their letters.

My pen amongst the rest I took,   5
    Lest those bright eyes that cannot read
Should dart their kindling fires, and look
    The power they have to be obeyed.

Nor quality nor reputation
    Forbid me yet my flame to tell;   10
Dear Five-years-old befriends my passion,
    And I may write till she can spell.

For while she makes her silkworms beds
    With all the tender things I swear,
Whilst all the house my passion reads,   15
    In papers round her baby's[2] hair,

---

[2] deceive.

[1] Lady Mary Villiers (?1690-1735), daughter of the first Earl of Jersey, with whom Prior became familiar in 1695. By 1700 Prior was praising Mary's ability to write.   [2] doll's.

She may receive and own my flame,
   For though the strictest prudes should know it,
She'll pass for a most virtuous dame,
   And I for an unhappy poet.   20

Then too, alas! when she shall tear
   The lines some younger rival sends,
She'll give me leave to write, I fear,
   And we shall still continue friends;

For, as our different ages move,   25
   'Tis so ordained, would fate but mend it,
That I shall be past making love
   When she begins to comprehend it.

To a Lady: She Refusing to Continue a Dispute with Me, and Leaving Me in the Argument
[?1703, 1709]

Spare, generous victor, spare the slave
   Who did unequal war pursue;
That more than triumph he might have
   In being overcome by you.

In the dispute whate'er I said,   5
   My heart was by my tongue belied;
And in my looks you might have read
   How much I argued on your side.

You, far from danger as from fear,
   Might have sustained an open fight,   10
For seldom your opinions err;
   Your eyes are always in the right.

Why, fair one, would you not rely
   On Reason's force with Beauty's joined?
Could I their prevalence deny,   15
   I must at once be deaf and blind.

Alas! not hoping to subdue,
   I only to the fight aspired;
To keep the beauteous foe in view
   Was all the glory I desired.   20

But she, howe'er of victory sure,
   Contemns the wreath too long delayed,
And, armed with more immediate power,
   Calls cruel silence to her aid.

Deeper to wound, she shuns the fight;   25
   She drops her arms, to gain the field;
Secures her conquest by her flight,
   And triumphs, when she seems to yield.

So when the Parthian[1] turned his steed,
   And from the hostile camp withdrew,   30
With cruel skill the backward reed[2]
   He sent; and as he fled, he slew.

Jinny the Just
[?1704, 1907]

Released from the noise of the butcher and baker,
Who (my old friends be thanked) did seldom forsake her,
And from the soft duns of my landlord, the Quaker;

From chiding the footmen and watching the lasses,
From Nell that burned milk, and Tom that brake glasses   5
(Sad mischiefs through which a good housekeeper[1] passes!);

[1] The Parthians were famous warriors whose empire extended at one time through much of southern and middle Asia. Their tactics were proverbial: a shower of darts, then rapid flight, during which they shot arrows back at the enemy.
[2] arrow, dart.

[1] Jinny was actually Prior's housekeeper and mistress while he was at The Hague (1696-97) and at Paris (1698-99). The canceled opening stanzas indicate that Jinny was not dead at the time the poem was written, and (if the identification with Jane Ansley is correct) she may have outlived Prior.

From some real care, but more fancied vexation,
From a life parti-colored, half reason, half passion,
Here lies after all the best wench in the nation.

From the Rhine to the Po, from the Thames to the Rhône,   10
Joanna or Janneton, Jinny or Joan,
'Twas all one to her by what name she was known,

For the idiom of words very little she heeded;
Provided the matter she drove at succeeded,
She took and gave languages just as she needed.   15

So for kitchen and market, for bargain and sale,
She paid English or Dutch or French down on the nail;
But in telling a story she sometimes did fail,

Then, begging excuse as she happened to stammer,
With respect to her betters but none to her grammar,   20
Her blush helped her out and her jargon became her.

Her habit and mien she endeavored to frame
To the different *goût*² of the place where she came,
Her outside still changed, but her inside the same.

At The Hague in her slippers and hair as the mode is,   25
At Paris all falbalowed ³ fine as a goddess,
And at censuring London in smock⁴ sleeves and bodice,

She ordered affairs that few people could tell
In what part about her that mixture did dwell
Of Vrouw or Mistress or Mademoiselle.   30

For her surname and race let the heralds e'en answer,
Her own proper worth was enough to advance her,
And he who liked her, little valued her grandsire;

But from what house soever her lineage may come,
I wish my own Jinny but out of her tomb,   35
Though all her relations were there in her room.

² taste.
³ furbelowed.
⁴ smocked, gathered in a honeycomb pattern (?).

Of such terrible beauty she never could boast
As with absolute sway o'er all hearts rules the roost,
When Jacob[5] bawls out to the Chair for a toast;

But of good household features her person was made,   40
Nor by faction cried up, nor of censure afraid,
And her beauty was rather for use than parade,

Her blood so well mixed and her flesh so well pasted
That, though her youth faded, her comeliness lasted.
The blue was worn off, but the plum was well tasted.   45

Less smooth than her skin and less white than her breast
Was this polished stone beneath which she lies pressed.
Stop, reader, and sigh while thou thinkst on the rest!

With a just trim of virtue her soul was endued;
Not affectedly pious, nor secretly lewd,   50
She cut even between the coquette and the prude.

And her will with her duty so equally stood
That, seldom opposed, she was commonly good,
And did pretty well, doing just what she would.

Declining all power, she found means to persuade,   55
Was then most regarded when most she obeyed,
The mistress in truth when she seemed but the maid.

Such care of her own proper actions she took
That on other folks' lives she had no time to look;
So censure and praise were struck out of her book.   60

Her thought still confined to its own little sphere,
She minded not who did excel or did err,
But just as the matter related to her;

Then too when her private tribunal was reared,
Her mercy so mixed with her judgment appeared   65
That her foes were condemned and her friends always cleared.

Her religion so well with her learning did suit
That, in practice severe, and in controverse mute,
She showed she knew better to live than dispute.

[5] probably Jacob Tonson, the publisher, a founder of the Kit-Cat Club,
where prominent beauties were toasted.

Some parts of the Bible by heart she recited,　　　　70
And much in historical chapters delighted,
But in points about faith she was something short-sighted.

So notions and modes[6] she referred to the Schools,
And in matters of conscience adhered to two rules,
To advise with no bigots and jest with no fools;　　　　75

And, scrupling[7] but little, enough she believed.
By charity ample small sins she retrieved,
And when she had new clothes she always received.

Thus still whilst her morning unseen fled away
In ordering the linen and making the tea,　　　　80
That she scarce could have time for the Psalms of the day,

And while after dinner the night came so soon
That half she proposed very seldom was done
(With twenty God-bless-me's, how this day is gone),

While she read and accounted and paid and abated,[8]　　　　85
Ate and drank, played and worked, laughed and cried, loved and
　　　hated,
As answered the end of her being created,

In the midst of her age came a cruel disease
Which neither her broths nor receipts could appease;
So down dropped her clay, may her soul be at peace.　　　　90

Retire from this sepulchre, all the profane,
Ye that love for debauch or that marry for gain,
Retire lest ye trouble the *manes*[9] of Jane.

But thou that knowst love above interest or lust,
Strew the myrtle and rose on this once belov'd dust,　　　　95
And shed one pious tear upon Jinny the Just.

Tread soft on her grave, and do right to her honor,
Let neither rude hand nor ill tongue light upon her,
Do all the small favors that now can be done her.

[6] philosophic terms employed by theologians (Schools).
[7] objecting to doctrines on grounds of conscience.
[8] reduced in price or value.
[9] shade, spirit.

And when what thou liked shall return to her clay   100
(For so I'm persuaded she must do one day,
Whatever fantastic John Asgill [10] may say),

When, as I have done now, thou shalt set up a stone
For something however distinguished or known,
May some pious friend the misfortune bemoan,   105
And make thy concern by reflection his own.

An Ode
[1709]

The merchant, to secure his treasure,
   Conveys it in a borrowed name.
Euphelia serves to grace my measure,
   But Cloe is my real flame.

My softest verse, my darling lyre,   5
   Upon Euphelia's toilet lay;
When Cloe noted her desire
   That I should sing, that I should play.

My lyre I tune, my voice I raise,
   But with my numbers[1] mix my sighs;   10
And whilst I sing Euphelia's praise,
   I fix my soul on Cloe's eyes.

Fair Cloe blushed; Euphelia frowned;
   I sung and gazed; I played and trembled;
And Venus to the Loves around   15
   Remarked how ill we all dissembled.

[10] He published a heretical book in 1700 asserting that man might be translated to eternal life without undergoing death.

---

[1] verses.

A Better Answer (To Cloe Jealous)
[1718]

Dear Cloe, how blubbered is that pretty face!
    Thy cheek all on fire, and thy hair all uncurled!
Prithee quit this caprice; and (as old Falstaff says)[1]
    Let us e'en talk a little like folks of this world.

How canst thou presume, thou hast leave to destroy   5
    The beauties, which Venus but lent to thy keeping?
Those looks were designed to inspire love and joy;
    More ordinary eyes may serve people for weeping.

To be vexed at a trifle or two that I writ,
    Your judgment at once and my passion you wrong: 10
You take that for fact which will scarce be found wit:
    Od's life! must one swear to the truth of a song?

What I speak, my fair Cloe, and what I write shows
    The difference there is betwixt nature and art;
I court others in verse, but I love thee in prose;   15
    And they have my whimseys, but thou hast my heart.

The god of us verse-men (you know, child) the sun,
    How after his journeys he sets up his rest;
If at morning o'er earth 'tis his fancy to run,
    At night he reclines on his Thetis's[2] breast.   20

So when I am wearied with wandering all day,
    To thee my delight in the evening I come;
No matter what beauties I saw in my way—
    There were but my visits, but thou art my home.

[1] "I prithee now, deliver them like a man of this world," (2 *Henry IV*, V iii 101).

[2] a nymph who dwelt in the depths of the sea.

Then finish, dear Cloe, this pastoral war;   25
   And let us like Horace and Lydia[3] agree:
For thou art a girl as much brighter than her,
   As he was a poet sublimer than me.

An Epitaph
[1718]

Stet quicunque volet potens
Aulae culmine lubrico, &c.
SENECA[1]

Interred beneath this marble stone,
Lie sauntering Jack and idle Joan.
While rolling threescore years and one
Did round this globe their courses run,
If human things went ill or well,   5
If changing empires rose or fell,
The morning passed, the evening came,
And found this couple still the same.
They walked and eat, good folks—what then?
Why then they walked and eat again.   10
They soundly slept the night away;
They did just nothing all the day;
And having buried children four,
Would not take pains to try for more.
Nor sister either had, nor brother;   15
They seemed just tallied for each other.
   Their moral and economy

---

[3] In a dialogue (Horace, *Odes*, III ix) they boast to each other of new loves (Horace's is Chloe) but are ready nonetheless to resume their own.

---

[1] "Let him stand who will, in pride of power, on empire's slippery height; let me be filled with sweet repose; in humble station fixed, let me enjoy untroubled ease, and, to my fellow-citizens unknown, let my life's stream flow in silence. So when my days have passed noiselessly away, lowly may I die and full of years. On him does death lie heavily, who, but too well known to all, dies to himself unknown." (*Thyestes*, ll. 391-403).

Most perfectly they made agree;
Each virtue kept its proper bound,
Nor trespassed on the other's ground.   20
Nor fame nor censure they regarded;
They neither punished nor rewarded.
He cared not what the footmen did;
Her maids she neither praised nor chid;
So every servant took his course,   25
And bad at first, they all grew worse.
Slothful disorder filled his stable,
And sluttish plenty decked her table.
Their beer was strong; their wine was port;
Their meal was large; their grace was short.   30
They gave the poor the remnant-meat,
Just when it grew not fit to eat.
    They paid the church and parish rate,[2]
And took, but read not, the receipt;
For which they claimed their Sunday's due,   35
Of slumbering in an upper pew.
    No man's defects sought they to know;
So never made themselves a foe.
No man's good deeds did they commend;
So never raised themselves a friend.   40
Nor cherished they relations poor,
That might decrease their present store;
Nor barn nor house did they repair,
That might oblige their future heir.
    They neither added nor confounded;[3]   45
They neither wanted nor abounded.
Each Christmas they accompts did clear,
And wound their bottom[4] round the year.
Nor tear nor smile did they employ
At news of public grief or joy.   50
When bells were rung, and bonfires made,
If asked they ne'er denied their aid:
Their jug was to the ringers carried,

[2] tax.
[3] wasted.
[4] a skein or ball of thread.

Whoever either died or married.
Their billet⁵ at the fire was found,   55
Whoever was deposed, or crowned.
   Nor good, nor bad, nor fools, nor wise;
They would not learn, nor could advise:
Without love, hatred, joy, or fear,
They led—a kind of—as it were: 60
Nor wished, nor cared, nor laughed, nor cried;
And so they lived; and so they died.

⁵ firewood.

Anthony Ashley Cooper
Third Earl of Shaftesbury

Anthony Ashley Cooper (1671-1713) was born in London, the grandson of the famous first Earl of Shaftesbury, the original of Dryden's Achitophel. It was in his grandfather's household that the third Earl of Shaftesbury spent much of his childhood, and his education was supervised there by John Locke. Shaftesbury served in Parliament from 1695 to 1698, when his poor health required him to resign. He went to Holland, where he became familiar with the literary circle Locke had known there a decade earlier. Although he continued at times to take an active political role in England on the Whig side, he devoted himself increasingly to study and writing. The *Characteristics of Men, Manners, Opinions, Times* appeared in 1711; its three volumes included five short treatises (of which *Sensus Communis* is the second) and *Miscellaneous Reflections* on the treatises. In 1711 he settled at Naples, where he began a second large work on the arts; fragments of this have been published under the title, *Second Characters*.

Shaftesbury's work was extremely influential both in England and on the Continent throughout the eighteenth century. Drawing upon Renaissance Platonism and upon Roman Stoicism, he created a view of the universe which stressed its order and harmony (in contrast with the view that saw nature as fallen with man). Man recognized order within himself as well; he was a benevolent and sociable creature, whose natural inclination was to love and approve the beautiful and harmonious. Man's approval of a beautiful action was as ready, as spontaneous, and as just as his approval of a work of art; but in both cases this approval was the spontaneity of a trained or disciplined taste. In the *Sensus Communis* (whose title stresses man's sociability), Shaftesbury moves from the value of free, unfettered consideration of all truths to the basis of judgment in man: his aesthetic-moral sense of the harmony or form which is to be found alike in the beautiful and the just.

Editions: The Characteristics, ed. J. M. Robertson (1900); *Life, Unpublished Letters, and Philosophical Regimen*, ed. Benjamin Rand (1900); *Second Characters*, ed. Benjamin Rand (1914).

Critical Studies: R. L. Brett, *The Third Earl of Shaftesbury* (1951); Alfred Owen Aldridge, *Shaftesbury and the Deist Manifesto* (1951).

Sensus Communis; An Essay on the Freedom of Wit and Humor, in a Letter to a Friend
[1709]

> *hac urget lupus, hac canis. . . .*
> HORACE, *Satires*, II ii [64] [1]

III, 3

You have heard it, my friend, as a common saying, that interest governs the world. But, I believe, whoever looks narrowly into the affairs of it will find that passion, humor, caprice, zeal, faction, and a thousand other springs, which are counter to self-interest, have as considerable a part in the movements of this machine. There are more wheels and counterpoises in this engine than are easily imagined. 'Tis of too complex a kind to fall under one simple view or be explained thus briefly in a word or two. The studiers of this mechanism must have a very partial eye to overlook all other motions besides those of the lowest and narrowest compass. 'Tis hard that in the plan or description of this clock-work no wheel or balance should be allowed on the side of the better and more enlarged affections; that nothing should be understood to be done in kindness or generosity, nothing in pure good-nature or friendship, or through any social or natural affection of any kind; when, perhaps, the mainspring of this machine will be found to be either these very

---

[1] "on the one side a wolf attacks, on the other a dog."

natural affections themselves, or a compound kind derived from them, and retaining more than one half of their nature.

But here, my friend, you must not expect that I should draw you up a formal scheme of the passions, or pretend to show you their genealogy and relation: how they are interwoven with one another, or interfere with our happiness and interest. 'Twould be out of the genius and compass of such a letter as this to frame a just plan or model by which you might, with an accurate view, observe what proportion the friendly and natural affections seem to bear in this order of architecture.

Modern projectors, I know, would willingly rid their hands of these natural materials, and would fain build after a more uniform way. They would new-frame the human heart, and have a mighty fancy to reduce all its motions, balances, and weights, to that one principle and foundation of a cool and deliberate selfishness. Men, it seems, are unwilling to think they can be so outwitted and imposed on by Nature as to be made to serve her purposes rather than their own. They are ashamed to be drawn thus out of themselves, and forced from what they esteem their true interest.

There has been in all times a sort of narrow-minded philosophers, who have thought to set this difference to rights by conquering Nature in themselves. A primitive father and founder among these[2] saw well this power of Nature, and understood it so far, that he earnestly exhorted his followers neither to beget children nor serve their country. There was no dealing with Nature, it seems, while these alluring objects stood in the way. Relations, friends, countrymen, laws, politic constitutions, the beauty of order and government, and the interest of society and mankind, were objects which, he well saw, would naturally raise a stronger affection than any which was grounded upon the narrow bottom of mere self. His advice, therefore, not to marry, nor engage at all in the public, was wise, and suitable to his design. There was no way to be truly a disciple of this philosophy but to leave family, friends, country, and society, to cleave to it.—And, in good earnest, who would not, if it were happiness to so do? The philosopher, however, was kind in telling us his thought. 'Twas a token of his fatherly love of mankind:

[2] Epicurus.

Tu pater es rerum inventor! Tu patria nobis
Suppeditas praecepta! [3]

But the revivers of this philosophy in latter days[4] appear to be
of a lower genius. They seem to have understood less of this force
of Nature, and thought to alter the thing by shifting a name. They
would so explain all the social passions and natural affections as to
denominate them of the selfish kind. Thus civility, hospitality, humanity toward strangers or people in distress, is only a more deliberate selfishness. An honest heart is only a more cunning one; and
honesty and good-nature, a more deliberate or better-regulated self-
love. The love of kindred, children and posterity, is purely love of
self and of one's own immediate blood; as if by this reckoning all
mankind were not included: all being of one blood, and joined
by intermarriages and alliances, as they have been transplanted
in colonies and mixed one with another. And thus love of one's
country and love of mankind must also be self-love. Magnanimity
and courage, no doubt, are modifications of this universal self-love!
For courage, says our modern philosopher,[5] is constant anger; and
all men, says a witty poet,[6] would be cowards if they durst.

That the poet and the philosopher both were cowards[7] may be
yielded perhaps without dispute. They may have spoken the best of
their knowledge. But for true courage, it has so little to do with
anger, that there lies always the strongest suspicion against it where
this passion is highest. The true courage is the cool and calm. The
bravest of men have the least of a brutal bullying insolence; and
in the very time of danger are found the most serene, pleasant, and
free. Rage, we know, can make a coward forget himself and fight.
But what is done in fury or anger can never be placed to the
account of courage. Were it otherwise, womankind might claim to
be the stoutest sex; for their hatred and anger have ever been allowed
the strongest and most lasting.

[3] "Thou, Father, art the discoverer of things! Thou givest us fatherly precepts!" (Lucretius, *Of the Nature of Things,* III 9-10.) Shaftesbury's Latin
text is corrected.

[4] such materialistic philosophers as Thomas Hobbes.

[5] Hobbes, *Leviathan,* I vi.

[6] Rochester, *Satyr against Mankind,* l. 158.

[7] Hobbes openly acknowledged the large part that fear played in his life
and thought.

Other authors[8] there have been of a yet inferior kind: a sort of distributors and petty retailers of this wit, who have run changes and divisions without end, upon this article of self-love. You have the very same thought spun out a hundred ways, and drawn into mottoes and devices to set forth this riddle, that "act as disinterestedly or generously as you please, self still is at the bottom, and nothing else." Now if these gentlemen who delight so much in the play of words, but are cautious how they grapple closely with definitions, would tell us only what self-interest was, and determine happiness and good, there would be an end of this enigmatical wit. For in this we should all agree, that happiness was to be pursued, and in fact was always sought after; but whether found in following Nature, and giving way to common affection, or in suppressing it, and turning every passion towards private advantage, a narrow self-end, or the preservation of mere life, this would be the matter in debate between us. The question would not be, "who loved himself, or who not," but "who loved and served himself the rightest, and after the truest manner."

'Tis the height of wisdom, no doubt, to be rightly selfish. And to value life, as far as life is good, belongs as much to courage as to discretion. But a wretched life is no wise man's wish. To be without honesty is, in effect, to be without natural affection or sociableness of any kind. And a life without natural affection, friendship, or sociableness would be found a wretched one were it to be tried. 'Tis as these feelings and affections are intrinsically valuable and worthy that self-interest is to be rated and esteemed. A man is by nothing so much himself as by his temper and the character of his passions and affections. If he loses what is manly and worthy in these, he is as much lost to himself as when he loses his memory and understanding. The least step into villainy or baseness changes the character and value of a life. He who would preserve life at any rate must abuse himself more than anyone can abuse him. And if life be not a dear thing indeed, he who has refused to live a villain and has preferred death to a base action has been a gainer by the bargain.

[8] Shaftesbury may have in mind the *Maxims* (1665) of the Duc de La Rochefoucauld.

IV, I

By this time, my friend, you may possibly, I hope, be satisfied
that as I am in earnest in defending raillery,[9] so I can be sober too
in the use of it. 'Tis in reality a serious study to learn to temper and
regulate that humor which nature has given us as a more lenitive[10]
remedy against vice, and a kind of specific[11] against superstition and
melancholy delusion. There is a great difference between seeking
how to raise a laugh from everything, and seeking in everything
what justly may be laughed at. For nothing is ridiculous except
what is deformed; nor is anything proof against raillery except what
is handsome and just. And therefore 'tis the hardest thing in the
world to deny fair honesty the use of this weapon, which can never
bear an edge against herself, and bears against everything contrary.

If the very Italian buffoons[12] were to give us the rule in these
cases, we should learn by them that in their lowest and most scur-
rilous way of wit there was nothing so successfully to be played upon
as the passions of cowardice and avarice. One may defy the world to
turn real bravery or generosity into ridicule. A glutton or mere
sensualist is as ridiculous as the other two characters. Nor can an
unaffected temperance be made the subject of contempt to any besides the grossest and most contemptible of mankind. Now these
three ingredients make up a virtuous character, as the contrary
three a vicious one. How therefore can we possibly make a jest of
honesty? To laugh both ways is nonsensical. And if the ridicule
lie against sottishness, avarice, and cowardice, you see the consequence. A man must be soundly ridiculous who, with all the wit
imaginable, would go about to ridicule wisdom, or laugh at honesty
or good manners.

A man of thorough good breeding, whatever else he be, is
incapable of doing a rude or brutal action. He never deliberates
in this case, or considers of the matter by prudential rules of self-
interest and advantage. He acts from his nature, in a manner
necessarily, and without reflection; and if he did not, it were impossible for him to answer his character, or be found that truly
well-bred man on every occasion. 'Tis the same with the honest

---

[9] good-humored ridicule, banter.
[10] soothing.   [11] remedy.
[12] the players of farce in the *commedia dell' arte.*

man. He cannot deliberate in the case of a plain villainy. A "plum" [13] is no temptation to him. He likes and loves himself too well to change hearts with one of those corrupt miscreants, who amongst them gave that name to a round sum of money gained by rapine and plunder of the commonwealth. He who would enjoy a freedom of mind, and be truly possessor of himself, must be above the thought of stooping to what is villainous or base. He, on the other side, who has a heart to stoop, must necessarily quit the thought of manliness, resolution, friendship, merit, and a character with himself and others. But to affect these enjoyments and advantages, together with the privileges of a licentious principle; to pretend to enjoy society and a free mind in company with a knavish heart is as ridiculous as the way of children, who eat their cake and afterwards cry for it. When men begin to deliberate about dishonesty, and finding it go less against their stomach, ask slily, "Why they should stick at a good piece of knavery for a good sum?" they should be told, as children, that they can't eat their cake and have it.

When men indeed are become accomplished knaves they are past crying for their cake. They know themselves, and are known by mankind. 'Tis not these who are so much envied or admired. The moderate kind are the more taking with us. Yet had we sense we should consider 'tis in reality the thorough profligate knave, the very complete unnatural villain alone, who can any way bid for happiness with the honest man. True interest is wholly on one side or the other. All between is inconsistency, irresolution, remorse, vexation, and an ague fit: [14] from hot to cold; from one passion to another quite contrary; a perpetual discord of life; and an alternate disquiet and self-dislike. The only rest or repose must be through one determined, considerate resolution, which when once taken must be courageously kept; and the passions and affections brought under obedience to it; the temper steeled and hardened to the mind; the disposition to the judgment. Both must agree, else all must be disturbance and confusion. So that to think with one's self in good earnest, "why may not one do this little villainy, or commit this one treachery, and but for once," is the most ridiculous imagination in the world, and contrary to common sense. For a common honest

---

[13] the sum of £100,000.
[14] fever that alternates with chill.

man, whilst left to himself, and undisturbed by philosophy and subtle reasonings about his interest, gives no other answer to the thought of villainy than that he cannot possibly find in his heart to set about it or conquer the natural aversion he has to it. And this is natural and just.

The truth is, as notions stand now in the world with respect to morals, honesty is like to gain little by philosophy or deep specula-tions of any kind. In the main, 'tis best to stick to common sense and go no farther. Men's first thoughts in this matter are generally better than their second: their natural notions better than those refined by study or consultation with casuists. According to common speech, as well as common sense, honesty is the best policy: but according to refined sense, the only well-advised persons, as to this world, are errant[15] knaves; and they alone are thought to serve them-selves who serve their passions, and indulge their loosest appetites and desires. Such, it seems, are the wise, and such the wisdom of this world!

An ordinary man talking of a vile action, in a way of common sense, says naturally and heartily, "he would not be guilty of such a thing for the whole world." But speculative men find great mod-ifications in the case; many ways of evasion; many remedies; many alleviations. A good gift rightly applied; a right method of suing out a pardon; good alms-houses, and charitable foundations erected for right worshippers; and a good zeal shown for the right belief, may sufficiently atone for one wrong practice, especially when it is such as raises a man to a considerable power (as they say) of doing good, and serving the true cause.

Many a good estate, many a high station has been gained upon such a bottom as this. Some crowns too may have been purchased on these terms; and some great emperors (if I mistake not) there have been of old, who were much assisted by these or the like principles; and in return were not ingrateful to the cause and party which had assisted 'em. The forgers of such morals have been amply endowed, and the world has paid roundly for its philosophy, since the original plain principles of humanity, and the simple honest precepts of peace and mutual love, have, by a sort of spiritual chemists, been so sublimated as to become the highest corrosives, and passing

[15] arrant.

through their limbecks,[16] have yielded the strongest spirit of mutual hatred and malignant persecution.

IV, 2

But our humors, my friend, incline us not to melancholy reflections. Let the solemn reprovers of vice proceed in the manner most suitable to their genius and character. I am ready to congratulate with 'em on the success of their labors in that authoritative way which is allowed 'em. I know not, in the meanwhile, why others may not be allowed to ridicule folly, and recommend wisdom and virtue (if possibly they can) in a way of pleasantry and mirth. I know not why poets, or such as write chiefly for the entertainment of themselves and others, may not be allowed this privilege. And if it be the complaint of our standing reformers that they are not heard so well by the gentlemen of fashion; if they exclaim against those airy wits who fly to ridicule as a protection, and make successful sallies from that quarter; why should it be denied one, who is only a volunteer in this cause, to engage the adversary on his own terms, and expose himself willingly to such attacks, on the single condition of being allowed fair play in the same kind?

By gentlemen of fashion, I understand those to whom a natural good genius, or the force of good education, has given a sense of what is naturally graceful and becoming. Some by mere nature, others by art and practice, are masters of an ear in music, an eye in painting, a fancy in the ordinary things of ornament and grace, a judgment in proportions of all kinds, and a general good taste in most of those subjects which make the amusement and delight of the ingenious people of the world. Let such gentlemen as these be as extravagant as they please, or as irregular in their morals, they must at the same time discover their inconsistency, live at variance with themselves, and in contradiction to that principle on which they ground their highest pleasure and entertainment.

Of all other beauties which virtuosos[17] pursue, poets celebrate, musicians sing, and architects or artists, of whatever kind, describe or form, the most delightful, the most engaging and pathetic, is that which is drawn from real life and from the passions. Nothing

---

[16] alembics, apparatus used in distilling.
[17] learned amateurs in science or the arts; collectors or connoisseurs.

affects the heart like that which is purely from itself and of its own nature: such as the beauty of sentiments, the grace of actions, the turn of characters, and the proportions and features of a human mind. This lesson of philosophy, even a romance, a poem, or a play may teach us; whilst the fabulous author leads us with such pleasure through the labyrinth of the affections, and interests us, whether we will or no, in the passions of his heroes and heroines:

> Angit,
> Irritat, mulcet, falsis terroribus implet,
> Ut magus.[18]

Let poets or the men of harmony deny, if they can, this force of Nature or withstand this moral magic. They, for their parts, carry a double portion of this charm about them. For in the first place, the very passion which inspires them is itself the love of numbers,[19] decency[20] and proportion; and this too, not in a narrow sense, or after a selfish way (for who of them composes for himself?), but in a friendly social view, for the pleasure of others, even down to posterity and future ages. And in the next place, 'tis evident in these performers that their chief theme and subject, that which raises their genius the most, and by which they so effectually move others, is purely manners and the moral part. For this is the effect, and this the beauty of their art: "in vocal measures of syllables and sounds to express the harmony and numbers of an inward kind, and represent the beauties of a human soul by proper foils and contrarieties, which serve as graces in this limning, and render this music of the passions more powerful and enchanting."

The admirers of beauty in the fair sex would laugh, perhaps, to hear of a moral part in their amours. Yet what a stir is made about a heart! What curious search of sentiments and tender thoughts! What praises of a humor, a sense, a *je ne sais quoi*[21] of wit, and all those graces of a mind which these virtuoso-lovers delight to celebrate! Let them settle this matter among themselves, and regulate, as they think fit, the proportions which these different

---

[18] "He tortures, inflames, soothes, fills [the heart] with false terrors, like a magician" (Horace, *Epistles*, II i 211-13).

[19] verses, measures.   [20] harmony, propriety.

[21] literally, "I know not what"; an indefinable quality. This was a popular term in seventeenth-century criticism.

beauties hold one to another. They must allow still, there is a beauty of the mind, and such as is essential in the case. Why else is the very air of foolishness enough to cloy a lover at first sight? Why does an idiot look and manner destroy the effect of all those outward charms, and rob the fair one of her power, though regularly armed in all the exactness of features and complexion? We may imagine what we please of a substantial solid part of beauty; but were the subject to be well criticized we should find perhaps that what we most admired, even in the turn of outward features, was only a mysterious expression and a kind of shadow of something inward in the temper; and that when we were struck with a majestic air, a sprightly look, an Amazon bold grace, or a contrary soft and gentle one, 'twas chiefly the fancy of these characters or qualities which wrought on us: our imagination being busied in forming beauteous shapes and images of this rational kind, which entertained the mind and held it in admiration, whilst other passions of a lower species were employed another way. The preliminary addresses, the declarations, the explanations, confidences, clearings, the dependence on something mutual, something felt by way of return, the *spes animi credula mutui*[22]—all these become necessary ingredients in the affair of love, and are authentically established by the men of elegance and art in this way of passion.

Nor can the men of cooler passions and more deliberate pursuits withstand the force of beauty in other subjects. Everyone is a virtuoso of a higher or lower degree. Every one pursues a Grace and courts a Venus of one kind or another. The *venustum*,[23] the *honestum*,[24] the *decorum*[25] of things will force its way. They who refuse to give it scope in the nobler subjects of a rational and moral kind will find its prevalency elsewhere in an inferior order of things. They who overlook the main springs of action, and despise the thought of numbers and proportion in a life at large, will, in the mean particulars of it, be no less taken up and engaged, as either in the study of common arts, or in the care and culture of mere mechanic beauties. The models of houses, buildings, and their accompanying ornaments; the plans of gardens, and their compartments; the ordering of walks, plantations,[26] avenues; and a thousand

---

[22] "trustful hope of love returned" (Horace, *Odes*, iv:30).
[23] fair.   [24] noble.   [25] handsome, becoming.
[26] plantings of trees, as in avenues.

other symmetries, will succeed in the room of that happier and higher symmetry and order of a mind. The species of fair, noble, handsome, will discover itself on a thousand occasions and in a thousand subjects. The specter still will haunt us in some shape or other; and when driven from our cool thoughts, and frighted from the closet, will meet us even at court, and fill our heads with dreams of grandeur, titles, honors, and a false magnificence and beauty, to which we are ready to sacrifice our highest pleasure and ease, and for the sake of which we become the merest drudges and most abject slaves.

The men of pleasure, who seem the greatest contemners of this philosophical beauty, are forced often to confess her charms. They can as heartily as others commend honesty; and are as much struck with the beauty of a generous part. They admire the thing itself, though not the means. And, if possible, they would so order it, as to make probity and luxury agree. But the rules of harmony will not permit it. The dissonancies are too strong. However, the attempts of this kind are not unpleasant to observe. For though some of the voluptuous are found sordid pleaders for baseness and corruption of every sort, yet others, more generous, endeavor to keep measures with honesty; and understanding pleasure better, are for bringing it under some rule. They condemn *this* manner; they praise *the other.* "So far was right; but further, wrong. Such a case was allowable; but such a one not to be admitted." They introduce a justice and an order in their pleasures. They would bring reason to be of their party, account in some manner for their lives, and form themselves to some kind of consonancy and agreement. Or should they find this impracticable on certain terms, they would choose to sacrifice their other pleasures to those which arise from a generous behavior, a regularity of conduct, and a consistency of life and manners:

Et verae numerosque modosque ediscere vitae.[27]

Other occasions will put us upon this thought; but chiefly a strong view of merit, in a generous character, opposed to some detestably vile one. Hence it is that among poets, the satirists seldom fail in doing justice to virtue. Nor are any of the nobler

[27] "To master the rhythms [i.e., numbers] and measures of a genuine life" (Horace, *Epistles,* II ii 144).

poets false to this cause. Even modern wits, whose turn is all towards gallantry and pleasure, when bare-faced villainy stands in their way, and brings the contrary species in view, can sing in passionate strains the praises of plain honesty.

When we are highly friends with the world, successful with the fair, and prosperous in the possession of other beauties, we may perchance, as is usual, despise this sober mistress. But when we see, in the issue, what riot and excess naturally produce in the world; when we find that by luxury's means, and for the service of vile interests, knaves are advanced above us, and the vilest of men preferred before the honestest; we then behold virtue in a new light, and by the assistance of such a foil, can discern the beauty of honesty, and the reality of those charms which before we understood not to be either natural or powerful.

IV, 3

And thus, after all, the most natural beauty in the world is honesty and moral truth. For all beauty is truth. True features make the beauty of a face; and true proportions the beauty of architecture; as true measures that of harmony and music. In poetry, which is all fable, truth still is the perfection. And whoever is scholar enough to read the ancient philosopher,[28] or his modern copyists, upon the nature of a dramatic and epic poem, will easily understand this account of truth.

A painter, if he has any genius, understands the truth and unity of design, and knows he is even then unnatural when he follows nature too close, and strictly copies life. For his art allows him not to bring all nature into his piece, but a part only. However, his piece, if it be beautiful, and carries truth, must be a whole by itself, complete, independent, and withal as great and comprehensive as he can make it. So that particulars, on this occasion, must yield to the general design, and all things be subservient to that which is principal; in order to form a certain easiness of sight, a simple, clear, and united view, which would be broken and disturbed by the expression of any thing peculiar or distinct.

Now the variety of Nature is such, as to distinguish everything she forms, by a peculiar original character, which, if strictly ob-

---

[28] Aristotle, in the *Poetics,* esp. chs. vii and xxiii, where the problem of unity and proportion is discussed.

served, will make the subject unlike to anything extant in the world besides. But this effect the good poet and painter seek industriously to prevent. They hate minuteness, and are afraid of singularity; which would make their images, or characters, appear capricious and fantastical. The mere face-painter,[29] indeed, has little in common with the poet; but, like the mere historian, copies what he sees, and minutely traces every feature and odd mark. 'Tis otherwise with the men of invention and design. 'Tis from the many objects of nature, and not from a particular one, that those geniuses form the idea of their work. Thus the best artists are said to have been indefatigable in studying the best statues: as esteeming them a better rule than the perfectest human bodies could afford. And thus some considerable wits have recommended the best poems as preferable to the best of histories; and better teaching the truth of characters and nature of mankind.

Nor can this criticism be thought high-strained. Though few confine themselves to these rules, few are insensible of 'em. Whatever quarter we may give to our vicious poets, or other composers of irregular and short-lived works, we know very well that the standing pieces of good artists must be formed after a more uniform way. Every just work of theirs comes under those natural rules of proportion and truth. The creature of their brain must be like one of Nature's formation. It must have a body and parts proportionable; or the very vulgar will not fail to criticize the work when it has neither head nor tail. For so common sense (according to just philosophy) judges of those works which want the justness of a whole, and show their author, however curious and exact in particulars, to be in the main a very bungler:

> Infelix operis summa, quia ponere totum
> Nesciet.[30]

Such is poetical and such (if I may so call it) graphical or plastic[31] truth. Narrative or historical truth must needs be highly estimable; especially when we consider how mankind, who are be-

---

[29] portrait painter.

[30] "[There is a craftsman who will shape in bronze nails and waving locks, but] is unfortunate in the total result, because he does not know how to represent the whole figure" (Horace, *Ars Poetica*, ll. 34-35).

[31] that is, of drawing and painting or sculpture.

come so deeply interested in the subject, have suffered by the want of clearness in it. 'Tis itself a part of moral truth. To be a judge in one requires a judgment in the other. The morals, the character, and genius of an author must be thoroughly considered; and the historian or relator of things important to mankind must, whoever he be, approve himself many ways to us, both in respect of his judgment, candor, and disinterestedness, ere we are bound to take anything on his authority. And as for critical truth, or the judgment and determination of what commentators, translators, paraphrasts, grammarians and others have, on this occasion, delivered to us; in the midst of such variety of style, such different reading, such interpolations and corruptions in the originals; such mistakes of copyists, transcribers, editors, and a hundred such accidents to which ancient books[32] are subject; it becomes, upon the whole, a matter of nice speculation, considering withal that the reader, though an able linguist, must be supported by so many other helps from chronology, natural philosophy, geography, and other sciences.

And thus many previous truths are to be examined and understood in order to judge rightly of historical truth, and of the past actions and circumstances of mankind, as delivered to us by ancient authors of different nations, ages, times, and different in their characters and interests. Some moral and philosophical truths there are withal so evident in themselves, that 'twould be easier to imagine half mankind to have run mad, and joined precisely in one and the same species of folly, than to admit anything as truth which should be advanced against such natural knowledge, fundamental reason, and common sense.

This I have mentioned, the rather because some modern zealots appear to have no better knowledge of truth, nor better manner of judging it, than by counting noses. By this rule, if they can poll an indifferent number out of a mob; if they can produce a set of Lancashire noddles, remote provincial headpieces, or visionary assemblers, to attest a story of a witch upon a broomstick and a flight in the air, they triumph in the solid proof of their new prodigy, and cry, *magna est veritas et praevalebit!*[33]

---

[32] Shaftesbury is obviously alluding to such critical views of the status of the Biblical text as are expressed in Father Richard Simon's *Critical History of the Old and New Testaments.* See Dryden's *Religio Laici* (1682).

[33] "Great is truth and mighty above all things" (1 Esdras 4.41; in the Vulgate, 3 Esdras 4.41, where the reading is *praevalet*).

Religion, no doubt, is much indebted to these men of prodigy,[34] who, in such a discerning age, would set her on the foot of popular tradition and venture her on the same bottom with parish tales and gossiping stories of imps, goblins, and demoniacal pranks, invented to fright children or make practice for common exorcists and "cunning men"! For by that name, you know, country people are used to call those dealers in mystery who are thought to conjure in an honest way and foil the devil at his own weapon.

And now, my friend, I can perceive 'tis time to put an end to these reflections, lest by endeavoring to expound things any further, I should be drawn from my way of humor to harangue profoundly on these subjects. But should you find I had moralized in any tolerable manner, according to common sense and without canting, I could be satisfied with my performance, such as it is, without fearing what disturbance I might possibly give to some formal censors of the age, whose discourses and writings are of another strain. I have taken the liberty, you see, to laugh upon some occasions; and if I have either laughed wrong, or been impertinently serious, I can be content to be laughed at in my turn. If contrariwise I am railed at, I can laugh still, as before, and with fresh advantage to my cause. For though, in reality, there could be nothing less a laughing matter than the provoked rage, ill will, and fury of certain zealous gentlemen, were they armed as lately they have been known; yet as the magistrate has since taken care to pare their talons, there is nothing very terrible in their encounter. On the contrary, there is something comical in the case. It brings to one's mind the fancy of those grotesque figures and dragon faces, which are seen often in the frontispiece[35] and on the cornerstones of old buildings. They seem placed there as the defenders and supporters of the edifice; but with all their grimace are as harmless to people without as they are useless to the building within. Great efforts of anger to little purpose serve for pleasantry and farce. Exceeding fierceness, with perfect inability and impotence, make the highest ridicule.—I am, dear friend, affectionately yours, etc.

[34] Shaftesbury is attacking naive superstition first of all, but he is also looking beyond it to those who make religious truth depend upon miracles.

[35] decorated entrance, pediment over the door.

✎ Bernard Mandeville ✎

Bernard Mandeville (1670-1733) was born in Holland (probably at Rotterdam). He studied medicine and philosophy at the University of Leyden. After beginning the practice of medicine as a specialist in nerve and stomach disorders, he visited London and decided to settle there. He was married to an Englishwoman in 1699 and began to publish in English by 1703. Among his early literary works are verse fables and a burlesque poem, *Typhon*. *The Grumbling Hive* (1705) is an extended verse fable, for which Mandeville wrote a series of prose "remarks" (one of which is printed here). This volume of commentary grew, over many years, into the final two-volume work, *The Fable of the Bees* (1733). The final version consists not only of the poem and the ample remarks but several related essays and (in the second volume) six dialogues. From the early 1720's, Mandeville's work was under wide attack: the Grand Jury of Middlesex declared it a public nuisance, but the book ran through many editions and was translated into both French and German within the eighteenth century.

Mandeville's paradoxes have always been a source of confusion and excitement. By equating virtue with rigorous and ascetic self-denial Mandeville could show that it was opposed to all worldly achievements, and notably to economic expansion and prosperity. On the other hand, he equated every element of self-interest, however slight or mixed with other concerns, with vice. Thus he could prove triumphantly that private vices were public benefits, that virtue (in his sense) was what all professed but few really dared or wished to pursue. More than this, Mandeville stressed the irrational element of human nature, and man's proneness to elaborate self-deception; all human behavior was egoistic, but it could be trained to seek (for selfish reasons) patterns of socially workable behavior. Thus, society was created by artful politicians out of the selfishness of man, or (alternatively) it evolved naturally from the interaction of self-seeking individuals. (The latter view approaches the laisser-faire economic doctrine of Adam Smith.) Mandeville deliberately attacked Shaftesbury's optimism and his exalted view of human nature; in many ways he resembles Hobbes and transmits the latter's views to the eighteenth century.

Editions: The Fable of the Bees, ed. F. B. Kaye (1924); *A Letter to Dion,* ed. Bonamy Dobrée (1954).

Critical Study: J. C. Maxwell, "Ethics and Politics in Mandeville," *Philosophy* 26 (1951).

The Fable of the Bees: Or, Private Vices, Public Benefits

REMARK M.
[1714]

Pride is that natural faculty by which every mortal that has any understanding over-values and imagines better things of himself than any impartial judge, thoroughly acquainted with all his qualities and circumstances, could allow him. We are possessed of no other quality so beneficial to society, and so necessary to render it wealthy and flourishing as this, yet it is that which is most generally detested. What is very peculiar to this faculty of ours is that those who are the fullest of it are the least willing to connive at[1] it in others; whereas the heinousness of other vices is the most extenuated by those who are guilty of them themselves. The chaste man hates fornication, and drunkenness is most abhorred by the temperate; but none are so much offended at their neighbor's pride as the proudest of all; and if any one can pardon it, it is the most humble: from which I think we may justly infer, that it being odious to all the world is a certain sign that all the world is troubled with it. This all men of sense are ready to confess, and nobody denies that he has pride in general. But, if you come to particulars,

[1] condone.

you'll meet with few that will own any action you can name of theirs to have proceeded from that principle. There are likewise many who will allow that among the sinful nations of the times, pride and luxury are the great promoters of trade, but they refuse to own the necessity there is, that in a more virtuous age (such a one as should be free from pride) trade would in a great measure decay.

The Almighty, they say, has endowed us with the dominion over all things which the earth and sea produce or contain; there is nothing to be found in either but what was made for the use of man; and his skill and industry above other animals were given him that he might render both them, and every thing else within the reach of his senses, more serviceable to him. Upon this consideration they think it impious to imagine that humility, temperance, and other virtues, should debar people from the enjoyment of those comforts of life which are not denied to the most wicked nations; and so conclude, that without pride or luxury, the same things might be eat,[2] wore,[3] and consumed, the same number of handicrafts and artificers employed, and a nation be every way as flourishing as where those vices are the most predominant.

As to wearing apparel in particular, they'll tell you that pride, which sticks much nearer to us than our clothes, is only lodged in the heart, and that rags often conceal a greater portion of it than the most pompous attire; and that as it cannot be denied but that there have always been virtuous princes, who with humble hearts have wore their splendid diadems and swayed their envied scepters, void of ambition, for the good of others; so it is very probable, that silver and gold brocades, and the richest embroideries may, without a thought of pride, be wore by many whose quality and fortune are suitable to them. May not (say they) a good man of extraordinary revenues make every year a greater variety of suits than it is possible he should wear out, and yet have no other ends than to set the poor at work, to encourage trade, and by employing many, to promote the welfare of his country? And considering food and raiment to be necessaries, and the two chief articles to which all our worldly cares are extended, why may not all mankind set aside a considerable part of their income for the one as well as the other, without the least tincture of pride? Nay, is not every member of

[2] eaten.   [3] worn.

the society in a manner obliged, according to his ability, to contribute toward the maintenance of that branch of trade on which the whole has so great a dependence? Besides that, to appear decently is a civility, and often a duty, which, without any regard to ourselves, we owe to those we converse with.

These are the objections generally made use of by haughty moralists, who cannot endure to hear the dignity of their species arraigned; but if we look narrowly into them they may soon be answered.

If we had no vices, I cannot see why any man should ever make more suits than he has occasion for, though he was never so desirous of promoting the good of the nation. For though in the wearing of a well-wrought silk rather than a slight stuff, and the preferring curious[4] fine cloth to coarse, he had no other view but the setting of more people to work and consequently the public welfare, yet he could consider clothes no otherwise than lovers of their country do taxes now; they may pay them with alacrity, but nobody gives more than his due; especially where all are justly rated according to their abilities, as it could no otherwise be expected in a very virtuous age. Besides that in such golden times nobody would dress above his condition, nobody pinch his family, cheat or over-reach his neighbor to purchase finery, and consequently there would not be half the consumption, nor a third part of the people employed as now there are. But to make this more plain and demonstrate that for the support of trade there can be nothing equivalent to pride, I shall examine the several views men have in outward apparel, and set forth what daily experience may teach everybody as to dress.

Clothes were originally made for two ends, to hide our nakedness, and to fence our bodies against the weather and other outward injuries. To these our boundless pride has added a third, which is ornament; for what else but an excess of stupid vanity could have prevailed upon our reason to fancy that ornamental, which must continually put us in mind of our wants and misery, beyond all other animals that are ready clothed by nature herself? It is indeed to be admired how so sensible a creature as man, that pretends to so many fine qualities of his own, should condescend to value himself upon what it robbed from so innocent and defenseless an animal as a sheep, or what he is beholden for to the most insignificant thing

[4] rare.

upon earth, a dying worm; yet while he is proud of such trifling depredations, he has the folly to laugh at the Hottentots on the furthest promontory of Africk, who adorn themselves with the guts of their dead enemies, without considering that they are the ensigns of their valor those barbarians are fine with, the true *spolia opima*,[5] and that if their pride be more savage than ours, it is certainly less ridiculous, because they wear the spoils of the more noble animal.

But whatever reflections may be made on this head, the world has long since decided the matter. Handsome apparel is a main point, fine feathers make fine birds, and people, where they are not known, are generally honored according to their clothes and other accoutrements they have about them; from the richness of them we judge of their wealth, and by their ordering of them we guess at their understanding. It is this which encourages everybody who is conscious of his little merit, if he is any ways able, to wear clothes above his rank, especially in large and populous cities, where obscure men may hourly meet with fifty strangers to one acquaintance and consequently have the pleasure of being esteemed by a vast majority, not as what they are, but what they appear to be: which is a greater temptation than most people want[6] to be vain.

Whoever takes delight in viewing the various scenes of low life may on Easter, Whitsun, and other great holidays, meet with scores of people, especially women, of almost the lowest rank, that wear good and fashionable clothes. If coming to talk with them, you treat them more courteously and with greater respect than what they are conscious they deserve, they'll commonly be ashamed of owning what they are; and often you may, if you are a little inquisitive, discover in them a most anxious care to conceal the business they follow and the places they live in. The reason is plain; while they receive those civilities that are not usually paid them and which they think only due to their betters, they have the satisfaction to imagine that they appear what they would be, which to weak minds is a pleasure almost as substantial as they could reap from the very accomplishments of their wishes. This golden dream they are unwilling to be disturbed in, and being sure that the meanness of their condition, if it is known, must sink them very low in your opinion, they hug themselves in their disguise and take all imagin-

[5] arms wrested by a general from a general.
[6] need.

able precaution not to forfeit by a useless discovery the esteem which they flatter themselves that their good clothes have drawn from you.

Though everybody allows that as to apparel and manner of living, we ought to behave ourselves suitable to our conditions, and follow the examples of the most sensible and prudent among our equals in rank and fortune: yet how few that are not either miserably covetous, or else proud of singularity, have this discretion to boast of? We all look above ourselves, and, as fast as we can, strive to imitate those that some way or other are superior to us.

The poorest laborer's wife in the parish, who scorns to wear a strong wholesome frieze,[7] as she might, will half starve her self and her husband to purchase a second-hand gown and petticoat that cannot do her half the service; because, forsooth, it is more genteel. The weaver, the shoemaker, the tailor, the barber, and every mean working fellow that can set up with little has the impudence with the first money he gets, to dress himself like a tradesman of substance. The ordinary retailer, in the clothing of his wife, takes pattern from his neighbor that deals in the same commodity by wholesale, and the reason he gives for it is that twelve years ago the other had not a bigger shop than himself. The druggist, mercer, draper, and other creditable shopkeepers can find no difference between themselves and merchants and therefore dress and live like them. The merchant's lady, who cannot bear the assurance of those mechanics,[8] flies for refuge to the other end of the town, and scorns to follow any fashion but what she takes from thence. This haughtiness alarms the court; the women of quality are frightened to see merchants' wives and daughters dressed like themselves. This impudence of the City,[9] they cry, is intolerable; mantua-makers[10] are sent for, and the contrivance of fashions become all their study, that they may have always new modes ready to take up as soon as those saucy Cits shall begin to imitate those in being. The same emulation is continued through the several degrees of quality to an incredible expense, till at last the prince's great favorites and those of the first rank of all, having nothing else left to outstrip

---

[7] coarse woolen cloth.   [8] workmen.

[9] the commercial section of London; east of Westminster, which was the seat of the Court. Its inhabitants are scornfully called *Cits*.

[10] dress- or cloak-makers.

some of their inferiors, are forced to lay out vast estates in pompous equipages, magnificent furniture, sumptuous gardens, and princely palaces.

To this emulation and continual striving to outdo one another it is owing that after so many various shiftings and changings of modes, in trumping up new ones and renewing of old ones, there is still a *plus ultra*[11] left for the ingenious; it is this, or at least the consequence of it, that sets the poor to work, adds spurs to industry, and encourages the skillful artificer to search after further improvements.

It may be objected, that many people of good fashion, who have been used to be well dressed, out of custom wear rich clothes with all the indifferency imaginable, and that the benefit to trade accruing from them cannot be ascribed to emulation or pride. To this I answer, that it is impossible, that those who trouble their heads so little with their dress, could ever have worn those rich clothes, if both the stuffs and fashions had not been first invented to gratify the vanity of others, who took greater delight in fine apparel than they. Besides that everybody is not without pride that appears to be so; all the symptoms of that vice are not easily discovered; they are manifold, and vary according to the age, humor, circumstances, and often constitution, of the people.

The choleric City Captain seems impatient to come to action, and expressing his warlike genius by the firmness of his steps, makes his pike, for want of enemies, tremble at the valor of his arm. His martial finery, as he marches along, inspires him with an unusual elevation of mind, by which endeavoring to forget his shop as well as himself, he looks up at the balconies with the fierceness of a Saracen conqueror: while the phlegmatic Alderman, now become venerable both for his age and his authority, contents himself with being thought a considerable man; and knowing no easier way to express his vanity, looks big in his coach, where being known by his paltry livery,[12] he receives in sullen state the homage that is paid him by the meaner sort of people.

The beardless Ensign counterfeits a gravity above his years, and with ridiculous assurance strives to imitate the stern counte-

---

[11] "further step."

[12] the distinctive badge bestowed by a person on his servants or inscribed on his coach.

nance of his Colonel, flattering himself all the while that by his daring mien you'll judge of his prowess. The youthful fair, in a vast concern of being overlooked, by the continual changing of her posture betrays a violent desire of being observed, and catching, as it were, at everybody's eyes courts with obliging looks the admiration of her beholders. The conceited coxcomb, on the contrary, displaying an air of sufficiency, is wholly taken up with the contemplation of his own perfections and in public places discovers such a disregard to others that the ignorant must imagine he thinks himself to be alone.

These and such like are all manifest though different tokens of pride that are obvious to all the world; but man's vanity is not always so soon found out. When we perceive an air of humanity, and men seem not to be employed in admiring themselves nor altogether unmindful of others, we are apt to pronounce them void of pride, when perhaps they are only fatigued with gratifying their vanity and become languid from a satiety of enjoyments. That outward show of peace within and drowsy composure of careless negligence, with which a great man is often seen in his plain chariot to loll at ease, are not always so free from art as they may seem to be. *Nothing is more ravishing to the proud than to be thought happy.*

The well-bred gentleman places his greatest pride in the skill he has of covering it with dexterity, and some are so expert in concealing this frailty that when they are the most guilty of it, the vulgar think them the most exempt from it. Thus the dissembling Courtier, when he appears in state, assumes an air of modesty and good humor; and while he is ready to burst with vanity, seems to be wholly ignorant of his greatness; well knowing that those lovely qualities must heighten him in the esteem of others and be an addition to that grandeur which the coronets about his coach and harnesses, with the rest of his equipage, cannot fail to proclaim without his assistance.

And as in these pride is overlooked because industriously concealed, so in others again it is denied that they have any, when they show (or at least seem to show) it in the most public manner. The wealthy Parson being, as well as the rest of his profession, debarred from the gaiety of laymen, makes it his business to look out for an admirable black and the finest cloth that money can purchase, and distinguishes himself by the fullness of his noble and spotless garment. His wigs are as fashionable as that form he is forced to comply with will admit of, but as he is only stinted in their shape, so he takes care that for goodness of hair, and color, few noblemen shall be able to match them. His body is ever clean, as well as his clothes, his sleek face is kept constantly shaved, and his handsome nails are diligently pared; his smooth white hand and a brilliant[13] of the first water, mutually becoming, honor each other with double graces; what linen he discovers is transparently curious,[14] and he scorns ever to be seen abroad with a worse beaver than what a rich banker would be proud of on his wedding-day. To all these niceties in dress he adds a majestic gait and expresses a commanding loftiness in his carriage; yet common civility, notwithstanding the evidence of so many concurring symptoms, won't allow us to suspect any of his actions to be the result of pride. Considering the dignity of his office, it is only decency[15] in him what would be vanity in others; and in good manners to his calling we ought to believe that the worthy gentleman, without any regard to his reverend person, puts himself to all this trouble and expense merely out of a respect which is due to the divine order he belongs to and a religious zeal to preserve his holy function from the contempt of scoffers. With all my heart, nothing of all this shall be called pride; let me only be allowed to say that to our human capacities it looks very like it.

But if at last I should grant, that there are men who enjoy all the fineries of equipage and furniture as well as clothes and yet have no pride in them, it is certain that if all should be such, that emulation I spoke of before must cease, and consequently trade, which has so great a dependence upon it, suffer in every branch. For to say that if all men were truly virtuous, they might, without any regard to themselves, consume as much out of zeal to serve their neighbors and promote the public good, as they do now out of self-love and emulation, is a miserable shift and an unreasonable supposition. As there have been good people in all ages, so without doubt we are not destitute of them in this; but let us enquire of the periwig-makers and tailors in what gentlemen, even of the greatest wealth and highest quality, they ever could discover such public-spirited views. Ask the lacemen, the mercers, and the linen-drapers whether the richest, and if you will, the most virtuous

---

[13] diamond.　　[14] fine, costly.　　[15] a sense of the fitting.

ladies, if they buy with ready money, or intend to pay in any reasonable time, will not drive from shop to shop, to try the market, make as many words, and stand as hard with them to save a groat or sixpence in a yard, as the most necessitous jilts[16] in town. If it be urged that if there are not, it is possible there might be, such people; I answer that it is as possible that cats, instead of killing rats and mice, should feed them and go about the house to suckle and nurse their young ones; or that a kite[17] should call the hens to their meat, as the cock does, and sit brooding over their chickens instead of devouring them. But if they should all do so, they would cease to be cats and kites; it is inconsistent with their natures, and the species of creatures which now we mean when we name cats and kites would be extinct as soon as that could come to pass.

[16] harlots, strumpets.
[17] a bird of prey, a kind of hawk.

Joseph Addison
and Richard Steele

The son of a clergyman, Joseph Addison (1672-1719) was born at Milston, Wiltshire; he attended Oxford, where he took a master's degree in 1693. He traveled widely and studied on the Continent (1699-1703); among the works produced there were his rhymed *Letter from Italy,* his prose *Remarks on Several Parts of Italy,* and his *Dialogues on Medals.* His first great success was with *The Campaign* (1705), a celebration of Marlborough's victories. He held numerous public offices and served in Parliament steadily from 1708. In 1709 he began to aid Steele in the writing of the *Tatler* and two years later undertook the *Spectator* in full collaboration with Steele. His tragedy, *Cato* (1713), had tremendous success.

Richard Steele (1672-1729) was born in Dublin, the son of an attorney. He first met Addison at Charterhouse School and was his contemporary at Oxford. Steele left without a degree to enter the army. His early literary works include *The Christian Hero* (1701), a tract designed to correct manners with religious principles, and several sentimental comedies; his best play, *The Conscious Lovers,* came later (1722). In 1709 he began the *Tatler* and set the pattern of good-humored satire, moral reformation, popularized learning, and close attention to a new female reading-public that was to carry through the *Spectator.* Steele later edited *The Guardian* (1713) but turned increasingly to political writing for the Whigs. With the coming of George I, he was given public office and knighted.

ADDISON: *Editions: Works,* ed. H. G. Bohn (1882-83); *Miscellaneous Works,* ed. A. C. Guthkelch (1914); *Letters,* ed. Walter Graham (1941); *Spectator,* ed. G. Gregory Smith (1897-98); ed. George A. Aitken (1898).

Biography: Peter Smithers, *Addison* (1954).

Critical Studies: C. S. Lewis, "Addison," in J. L. Clifford, ed., *Eighteenth Century Literature: Modern Critical Essays* (1959); Clarence D. Thorpe, "Addison's Contribution to Criticism," in R. F. Jones, *et al., The Seventeenth Century* (1951).

STEELE: *Editions: Tracts and Pamphlets,* ed. Rae Blanchard (1944); *The Christian Hero,* ed. Rae Blanchard (1932); *Dramatic Works,* ed. George A. Aitken (1903); *Correspondence,* ed. Rae Blanchard (1941).

Biographies: George A. Aitken, *The Life of Richard Steele* (1889); Willard Connely, *Sir Richard Steele* (1934).

Critical Study: Walter Graham, *English Literary Periodicals* (1930).

The Spectator
No. 2   Friday, 2 March 1711
[Steele]

> *Haec alii sex*
> *Vel plures uno conclamant ore.*
> JUVENAL[1]

The first of our society is a gentleman of Worcestershire, of ancient descent, a baronet, his name Sir Roger de Coverley. His great-grandfather was inventor of that famous country-dance which is called after him.[2] All who know that shire are very well acquainted with the parts and merits of Sir Roger. He is a gentleman that is very singular in his behavior, but his singularities proceed from his good sense, and are contradictions to the manners of the world only as he thinks the world is in the wrong. However, this humor creates him no enemies, for he does nothing with sourness or obstinacy; and his being unconfined to modes and forms makes him but the readier and more capable to please and oblige all who know him.

---

[1] "Six others and more cry out with one voice."—*Satires,* VII 167 f.
[2] that is, after a popular dancing air with his name.

When he is in town, he lives in Soho Square. It is said he keeps himself a bachelor by reason he was crossed in love by a perverse, beautiful widow of the next county to him. Before this disappointment, Sir Roger was what you call a fine gentleman, had often supped with my Lord Rochester[3] and Sir George Etherege,[4] fought a duel upon his first coming to town, and kicked Bully Dawson in a public coffee-house for calling him "youngster." But being ill-used by the above-mentioned widow, he was very serious for a year and a half; and though, his temper being naturally jovial, he at last got over it, he grew careless of himself, and never dressed afterward. He continues to wear a coat and doublet of the same cut that were in fashion at the time of his repulse, which, in his merry humors, he tells us, has been in and out twelve times since he first wore it. 'Tis said Sir Roger grew humble in his desires after he had forgot this cruel beauty; insomuch that it is reported he has frequently offended in point of chastity with beggars and gypsies: but this is looked upon by his friends rather as matter of raillery than truth. He is now in his fifty-sixth year, cheerful, gay, and hearty; keeps a good house both in town and country; a great lover of mankind; but there is such a mirthful cast in his behavior that he is rather beloved than esteemed. His tenants grow rich, his servants look satisfied, all the young women profess love to him, and the young men are glad of his company; when he comes into a house he calls the servants by their names, and talks all the way upstairs to a visit. I must not omit that Sir Roger is a justice of the quorum;[5] that he fills the chair at a quarter-session[6] with great abilities; and, three months ago, gained universal applause by explaining a passage in the Game Act.

The gentleman next in esteem and authority among us is another bachelor, who is a member of the Inner Temple;[7] a man of great probity, wit, and understanding; but he has chosen his place of residence rather to obey the direction of an old humorsome father, than in pursuit of his own inclinations. He was placed there to

[3] See headnote to his *Satyr against Mankind.*

[4] (c. 1635-91); writer of brilliant comedies.

[5] justice of the peace who sits as part of a bench.

[6] a quarterly court of limited jurisdiction, made up of justices of the peace.

[7] one of the Inns of Court, where students of law reside.

study the laws of the land, and is the most learned of any of the house in those of the stage. Aristotle and Longinus[8] are much better understood by him than Littleton or Coke.[9] The father sends up, every post, questions relating to marriage-articles, leases, and tenures, in the neighborhood; all which questions he agrees with an attorney to answer and take care of in the lump. He is studying the passions themselves, when he should be inquiring into the debates among men which arise from them. He knows the argument of each of the orations of Demosthenes and Tully,[10] but not one case in the reports of our own courts. No one ever took him for a fool, but none, except his intimate friends, know he has a great deal of wit. This turn makes him at once both disinterested and agreeable; as few of his thoughts are drawn from business, they are most of them fit for conversation. His taste of books is a little too just for the age he lives in; he has read all, but approves of very few. His familiarity with the customs, manners, actions, and writings of the ancients makes him a very delicate[11] observer of what occurs to him in the present world. He is an excellent critic, and the time of the play is his hour of business; exactly at five he passes through New Inn, crosses through Russell Court, and takes a turn at Will's[12] till the play begins; he has his shoes rubbed and his periwig powdered at the barber's as you go into the Rose.[13] It is for the good of the audience when he is at a play, for the actors have an ambition to please him.

The person of next consideration is Sir Andrew Freeport, a merchant of great eminence in the City[14] of London, a person of indefatigable industry, strong reason, and great experience. His notions of trade are noble and generous, and (as every rich man has usually some sly way of jesting which would make no great figure were he not a rich man) he calls the sea the British Common. He is acquainted with commerce in all its parts, and will tell you that it is a stupid and barbarous way to extend dominion by arms; for

[8] as literary critics.

[9] Sir Thomas Littleton (?1407-81) and Sir Edward Coke (1552-1634), major English jurists.

[10] Cicero.

[11] fastidious.

[12] the coffeehouse near Drury Lane.

[13] the Rose Tavern, an actors' resort near Drury Lane.

[14] the financial center.

true power is to be got by arts and industry. He will often argue that if this part of our trade were well cultivated, we should gain from one nation; and if another, from another. I have heard him prove that diligence makes more lasting acquisitions than valor, and that sloth has ruined more nations than the sword. He abounds in several frugal maxims, among which the greatest favorite is, "A penny saved is a penny got." A general trader of good sense is pleasanter company than a general scholar; and Sir Andrew having a natural unaffected eloquence, the perspicuity of his discourse gives the same pleasure that wit would in another man. He has made his fortunes himself, and says that England may be richer than other kingdoms by as plain methods as he himself is richer than other men; though at the same time I can say this of him, that there is not a point in the compass but blows home a ship in which he is an owner.

Next to Sir Andrew in the clubroom sits Captain Sentry, a gentleman of great courage, good understanding, but invincible modesty. He is one of those that deserve very well, but are very awkward at putting their talents within the observation of such as should take notice of them. He was some years a captain, and behaved himself with great gallantry in several engagements and at several sieges; but having a small estate of his own, and being next heir to Sir Roger, he has quitted a way of life in which no man can rise suitably to his merit who is not something of a courtier as well as a soldier. I have heard him often lament that in a profession where merit is placed in so conspicuous a view, impudence should get the better of modesty. When he has talked to this purpose I never heard him make a sour expression, but frankly confess that he left the world because he was not fit for it. A strict honesty and an even, regular behavior are in themselves obstacles to him that must press through crowds who endeavor at the same end with himself,—the favor of a commander. He will, however, in his way of talk, excuse generals for not disposing according to men's desert, or inquiring into it: "For," says he, "that great man who has a mind to help me has as many to break through to come at me as I have to come at him." Therefore he will conclude that the man who would make a figure, especially in a military way, must get over all false modesty, and assist his patron against the importunity of other pretenders by a proper assurance in his own vindication. He says it is a civil cowardice to be backward in asserting what you ought to expect, as it is a military fear to be slow in attacking when it is your duty. With this candor does the gentleman speak of himself and others. The same frankness runs through all his conversation. The military part of his life has furnished him with many adventures, in the relation of which he is very agreeable to the company; for he is never overbearing, though accustomed to command men in the utmost degree below him; nor ever too obsequious from an habit of obeying men highly above him.

But that our society may not appear a set of humorists[15] unacquainted with the gallantries and pleasures of the age, we have among us the gallant Will Honeycomb, a gentleman who, according to his years, should be in the decline of his life, but having ever been very careful of his person, and always had a very easy fortune, time has made but very little impression either by wrinkles on his forehead or traces in his brain. His person is well turned, of a good height. He is very ready at that sort of discourse with which men usually entertain women. He has all his life dressed very well, and remembers habits as others do men. He can smile when one speaks to him, and laughs easily. He knows the history of every mode, and can inform you from which of the French king's wenches our wives and daughters had this manner of curling their hair, that way of placing their hoods; whose frailty was covered by such a sort of petticoat, and whose vanity to show her foot made that part of the dress so short in such a year. In a word, all his conversation and knowledge has been in the female world: as other men of his age will take notice to you what such a minister said upon such and such an occasion, he will tell you when the Duke of Monmouth[16] danced at court such a woman was then smitten, another was taken with him at the head of his troop in the park. In all these important relations he has ever about the same time received a kind glance or a blow of a fan from some celebrated beauty, mother of the present Lord Such-a-one. If you speak of a young Commoner that said a lively thing in the House, he starts up: "He has good blood in his veins; Tom Mirabell begot him; the rogue cheated me in that affair; that young fellow's mother used me more like a dog than any woman

---

[15] quaint or eccentric men.

[16] (1649-85); illegitimate son of Charles II, who led a rebellion against James II and died on the scaffold.

I ever made advances to." This way of talking of his very much enlivens the conversation among us of a more sedate turn; and I find there is not one of the company but myself, who rarely speak at all, but speaks of him as of that sort of man who is usually called a well-bred, fine gentleman. To conclude his character, where women are not concerned, he is an honest, worthy man.

I cannot tell whether I am to account him whom I am next to speak of as one of our company, for he visits us but seldom; but when he does, it adds to every man else a new enjoyment of himself. He is a clergyman, a very philosophic man, of general learning, great sanctity of life, and the most exact good breeding. He has the misfortune to be of a very weak constitution, and consequently cannot accept of such cares and business as preferments in his function would oblige him to; he is therefore among divines what a chamber-counselor[17] is among lawyers. The probity of his mind and the integrity of his life create him followers, as being eloquent or loud advances others. He seldom introduces the subject he speaks upon; but we are so far gone in years that he observes, when he is among us, an earnestness to have him fall on some divine topic, which he always treats with much authority, as one who has no interests in this world, as one who is hastening to the object of all his wishes, and conceives hope from his decays and infirmities. These are my ordinary companions.

No. 58   Monday, 7 May 1711
[Addison]

Ut pictura poesis erit.
HORACE [1]

Nothing is so much admired, and so little understood, as wit. No author that I know of has written professedly upon it; and as for those who make any mention of it, they only treat on the subject

---

[17] a lawyer who gives opinions in private consultation.

---

[1] "As with painting, so [it will be] with poetry" (Addison misplaces the verb, which goes with the following clause).—*Ars Poetica,* l. 361. (This was a traditional misreading.)

as it has accidentally fallen in their way, and that too in little short reflections or in general declamatory flourishes, without entering into the bottom of the matter. I hope, therefore, I shall perform an acceptable work to my countrymen, if I treat at large upon this subject; which I shall endeavor to do in a manner suitable to it, that I may not incur the censure which a famous critic[2] bestows upon one who had written a treatise upon the sublime in a low groveling style. I intend to lay aside a whole week for this undertaking, that the scheme of my thoughts may not be broken and interrupted: and I dare promise myself, if my readers will give me a week's attention, that this great city will be very much changed for the better by next Saturday night. I shall endeavor to make what I say intelligible to ordinary capacities; but if my readers meet with any paper that in some parts of it may be a little out of their reach, I would not have them discouraged, for they may assure themselves the next shall be much clearer.

As the great and only end of these my speculations is to banish vice and ignorance out of the territories of Great Britain, I shall endeavor as much as possible to establish among us a taste of polite writing. It is with this view that I have endeavored to set my readers right in several points relating to operas and tragedies; and shall from time to time impart my notions of comedy, as I think they may tend to its refinement and perfection. I find by my bookseller that these papers of criticism, with that upon humor, have met with a more kind reception than indeed I could have hoped for from such subjects; for which reason I shall enter upon my present undertaking with greater cheerfulness.

In this, and one or two following papers, I shall trace out the history of false wit, and distinguish the several kinds of it as they have prevailed in different ages of the world. This I think the more necessary at present, because I observed there were attempts on foot last winter to revive some of those antiquated modes of wit that have been long exploded out of the commonwealth of letters. There were several satires and panegyrics handed about in acrostic, by which means some of the most arrant undisputed blockheads about the town began to entertain ambitious thoughts, and to set up for

[2] Longinus at the opening of his treatise *On the Sublime* censures Caecilius.

polite authors. I shall therefore describe at length those many arts
of false wit, in which a writer does not show himself a man of a
beautiful genius, but of great industry.

The first species of false wit which I have met with is very
venerable for its antiquity, and has produced several pieces which
have lived very near as long as the *Iliad* itself: I mean those short
poems printed among the minor Greek poets, which resemble the
figure of an egg, a pair of wings, an axe, a shepherd's pipe, and an
altar.

As for the first, it is a little oval poem, and may not improperly
be called a scholar's egg. I would endeavor to hatch it, or, in more
intelligible language, to translate it into English, did not I find the
interpretation of it very difficult; for the author seems to have been
more intent upon the figure of his poem than upon the sense of it.

The pair of wings consist of twelve verses, or rather feathers,
every verse decreasing gradually in its measure according to its
situation in the wing. The subject of it (as in the rest of the poems
which follow) bears some remote affinity with the figure, for it
describes a god of love, who is always painted with wings.

The axe methinks would have been a good figure for a lampoon,
had the edge of it consisted of the most satirical parts of the work;
but, as it is in the original, I take it to have been nothing else but
the posy[3] of an axe which was consecrated to Minerva, and was
thought to have been the same that Epeus made use of in the
building of the Trojan horse; which is a hint I shall leave to the
consideration of the critics. I am apt to think that the posy was
written originally upon the axe, like those which our modern cutlers
inscribe upon their knives; and that therefore the posy still remains
in its ancient shape, though the axe itself is lost.

The shepherd's pipe may be said to be full of music, for it is
composed of nine different kinds of verses, which by their several
lengths resemble the nine stops of the old musical instrument, that
is likewise the subject of the poem.

The altar is inscribed with the Epitaph of Troilus, the son of
Hecuba; which, by the way, makes me believe that these false
pieces of wit are much more ancient than the authors to whom they
are generally ascribed; at least I will never be persuaded that so

[3] a motto inscribed on a handle.

fine a writer as Theocritus[4] could have been the author of any such simple works.

It was impossible for a man to succeed in these performances who was not a kind of painter, or at least a designer:[5] he was first of all to draw the outline of the subject which he intended to write upon, and afterwards conform the description to the figure of his subject. The poetry was to contract or dilate itself according to the mold in which it was cast. In a word, the verses were to be cramped or extended to the dimensions of the frame that was prepared for them; and to undergo the fate of those persons whom the tyrant Procrustes used to lodge in his iron bed; if they were too short he stretched them on a rack, and if they were too long chopped off a part of their legs, till they fitted the couch which he had prepared for them.

Mr. Dryden hints at this obsolete kind of wit in one of the following verses in his *MacFlecknoe* which an English reader cannot understand, who does not know that there are those little poems abovementioned in the shape of wings and altars.

> ——*choose for thy command*
> *Some peaceful province in acrostic land;*
> *There may'st thou wings display, and altars raise,*
> *And torture one poor word a thousand ways.*
>
> [ll. 205-08]

This fashion of false wit was revived by several poets of the last age, and in particular may be met with among Mr. Herbert's poems;[6] and, if I am not mistaken, in the translation of Du Bartas.[7] I do not remember any other kind of work among the moderns which more resembles the performances I have mentioned, than that famous picture of King Charles I which has the whole book of Psalms written in the lines of the face and the hair of the head. When I was last at Oxford I perused one of the whiskers; and was reading

[4] the Greek pastoral poet of the third century B.C.

[5] man skilled in drawing.

[6] *The Temple* by George Herbert (1593-1633); the relevant poems are "The Altar" and "Easter Wings."

[7] The epic by Guillaume du Bartas (1544-90) was translated from the French by Joshua Sylvester as *The Divine Weeks and Works* (1605); see the Dedication in particular.

the other, but could not go so far in it as I would have done, by reason of the impatience of my friends and fellow-travellers, who all of them pressed to see such a piece of curiosity. I have since heard, that there is now an eminent writing-master in town, who has transcribed all the Old Testament in a full-bottomed periwig; and if the fashion should introduce the thick kind of wigs which were in vogue some few years ago, he promises to add two or three supernumerary locks that shall contain all the Apocrypha. He designed this wig originally for King William, having disposed of the two books of Kings in the two forks of the foretop; but that glorious monarch dying before the wig was finished, there is a space left in it for the face of any one that has a mind to purchase it.

But to return to our ancient poems in picture, I would humbly propose, for the benefit of our modern smatterers in poetry, that they would imitate their brethren among the ancients in those ingenious devices. I have communicated this thought to a young poetical lover of my acquaintance, who intends to present his mistress with a copy of verses made in the shape of her fan; and, if he tells me true, has already finished the three first sticks of it. He has likewise promised me to get the measure of his mistress's marriage-finger, with a design to make a posy in the fashion of a ring which shall exactly fit it. It is so very easy to enlarge upon a good hint, that I do not question but my ingenious readers will apply what I have said to many other particulars; and that we shall see the town filled in a very little time with poetical tippets,[8] handkerchiefs, snuffboxes, and the like female ornaments. I shall therefore conclude with a word of advice to those admirable English authors who call themselves Pindaric writers,[9] that they would apply themselves to this kind of wit without loss of time, as being provided better than any other poets with verses of all sizes and dimensions.

[8] scarves or short cloaks.
[9] The irregular *Pindarique Odes* of Abraham Cowley (1618-67) set a fashion that was widely copied; they used lines of varied length, without regular stanzaic pattern, and thus could lend themselves to the shaping that Addison is mocking.

No. 62   Friday, 11 May 1711
[Addison]

Scribendi recte sapere est et principium et fons.
HORACE [1]

Mr. Locke has an admirable reflection upon the difference of wit and judgment, whereby he endeavors to show the reason why they are not always the talents of the same person. His words[2] are as follow: "And hence, perhaps, may be given some reason of that common observation, that men who have a great deal of wit, and prompt memories, have not always the clearest judgment, or deepest reason. For wit lying most in the assemblage of ideas, and putting those together with quickness and variety, wherein can be found any resemblance or congruity, thereby to make up pleasant pictures and agreeable visions in the fancy; judgment, on the contrary, lies quite on the other side, in separating carefully one from another, ideas wherein can be found the least difference, thereby to avoid being misled by similitude, and by affinity to take one thing for another. This is a way of proceeding quite contrary to metaphor and allusion; wherein, for the most part, lies that entertainment and pleasantry of wit which strikes so lively on the fancy, and is therefore so acceptable to all people."

This is, I think, the best and most philosophical account that I have ever met with of wit, which generally, though not always, consists in such a resemblance and congruity of ideas as this author mentions. I shall only add to it, by way of explanation, that every resemblance of ideas is not that which we call wit, unless it be such an one that gives delight and surprise to the reader: these two properties seem essential to wit, more particularly the last of them. In order, therefore, that the resemblance in the ideas be wit, it is necessary that the ideas should not lie too near one another in the nature of things; for where the likeness is obvious, it gives no surprise. To compare one man's singing to that of another, or to repre-

---

[1] "Wisdom is the first principle and source of good writing."—*Ars Poetica,* l. 309.

[2] *Essay concerning Human Understanding* (1690), II xi 2.

sent the whiteness of any object by that of milk and snow, or the variety of its colors by those of the rainbow, cannot be called wit, unless besides this obvious resemblance, there be some further congruity discovered in the two ideas that is capable of giving the reader some surprise. Thus when a poet tells us the bosom of his mistress is as white as snow, there is no wit in the comparison; but when he adds, with a sigh, that it is as cold too, it then grows into wit. Every reader's memory may supply him with innumerable instances of the same nature. For this reason the similitudes in heroic poets, who endeavor rather to fill the mind with great conceptions than to divert it with such as are new and surprising, have seldom anything in them that can be called wit. Mr. Locke's account of wit, with this short explanation, comprehends most of the species of wit, as metaphors, similitudes, allegories, enigmas, mottos, parables, fables, dreams, visions, dramatic writings, burlesque, and all the methods of allusion: as there are many other pieces of wit (how remote soever they may appear at first sight from the foregoing description) which upon examination will be found to agree with it.

As true wit generally consists in this resemblance and congruity of ideas, false wit chiefly consists in the resemblance and congruity sometimes of single letters, as in anagrams, chronograms,[3] lipograms,[4] and acrostics: sometimes of syllables, as in echoes and doggerel rimes; sometimes of words, as in puns and quibbles; and sometimes of whole sentences or poems cast into the figures of eggs, axes, or altars: nay, some carry the notion of wit so far as to ascribe it even to external mimicry, and to look upon a man as an ingenious person that can resemble the tone, posture, or face of another.

As true wit consists in the resemblance of ideas, and false wit in the resemblance of words, according to the foregoing instances, there is another kind of wit which consists partly in the resemblance of ideas, and partly in the resemblance of words, which for distinction sake I shall call mixed wit. This kind of wit is that which abounds in Cowley more than in any author that ever wrote. Mr. Waller has likewise a great deal of it. Mr. Dryden is very sparing in it. Milton had a genius much above it. Spenser is in the same class with Milton. The Italians, even in their epic poetry, are full of it.

[3] inscriptions in which certain letters are read as Roman numerals and thus as dates.

[4] poems in which a letter of the alphabet is entirely omitted.

Monsieur Boileau,[5] who formed himself upon the ancient poets, has everywhere rejected it with scorn. If we look after mixed wit among the Greek writers, we shall find it nowhere but in the epigrammatists. There are indeed some strokes of it in the little poem ascribed to Musaeus, which by that, as well as many other marks, betrays itself to be a modern composition. If we look into the Latin writers, we find none of this mixed wit in Virgil, Lucretius, or Catullus; very little in Horace, but a great deal of it in Ovid, and scarce anything else in Martial.

Out of the innumerable branches of mixed wit I shall choose one instance which may be met with in all the writers of this class. The passion of love in its nature has been thought to resemble fire; for which reason the words fire and flame are made use of to signify love. The witty poets, therefore, have taken an advantage from the double meaning of the word fire, to make an infinite number of witticisms. Cowley observing the cold regard of his mistress's eyes, and at the same time their power of producing love in him, considers them as burning-glasses made of ice; and finding himself able to live in the greatest extremities of love, concludes the torrid zone to be habitable. When his mistress has read his letter written in juice of lemon, by holding it to the fire, he desires her to read it over a second time by love's flames. When she weeps, he wishes it were inward heat that distilled those drops from the limbeck.[6] When she is absent, he is beyond eighty, that is, thirty degrees nearer the pole than when she is with him. His ambitious love is a fire that naturally mounts upwards; his happy love is the beams of heaven, and his unhappy love flames of hell. When it does not let him sleep, it is a flame that sends up no smoke; when it is opposed by counsel and advice, it is a fire that rages the more by the winds blowing upon it. Upon the dying of a tree in which he had cut his loves, he observes that his written flames had burnt up and withered the tree. When he resolves to give over his passion, he tells us that one burnt like him forever dreads the fire. His heart is an Aetna, that instead of Vulcan's shop, encloses Cupid's forge in it. His endeavoring to drown his love in wine, is throwing oil upon the fire. He would insinuate to his mistress that the fire of love,

---

[5] Nicolas Boileau-Despréaux (1636-1711); his *Art of Poetry* (1674) was translated by Dryden and Sir William Soame in 1683.

[6] alembic, distilling apparatus.

like that of the sun (which produces so many living creatures), should not only warm but beget. Love in another place cooks Pleasure at his fire. Sometimes the poet's heart is frozen in every breast and sometimes scorched in every eye. Sometimes he is drowned in tears, and burnt in love, like a ship set on fire in the middle of the sea.

The reader may observe in every one of these instances that the poet mixes the qualities of fire with those of love, and in the same sentence speaking of it both as a passion and as real fire surprises the reader with those seeming resemblances or contradictions that make up all the wit in this kind of writing. Mixed wit, therefore, is a composition of pun and true wit, and is more or less perfect as the resemblance lies in the ideas or in the words: its foundations are laid partly in falsehood and partly in truth; reason puts in her claim for one part of it, and extravagance for the other. The only province, therefore, for this kind of wit is epigram, or those little occasional poems that in their own nature are nothing else but a tissue of epigrams. I cannot conclude this head of mixed wit without owning that the admirable poet out of whom I have taken the examples of it had as much true wit as any author that ever writ, and indeed all other talents of an extraordinary genius.

It may be expected, since I am upon this subject, that I should take notice of Mr. Dryden's definition of wit;[7] which, with all the deference that is due to the judgment of so great a man, is not so properly a definition of wit as of good writing in general. Wit, as he defines it, is "a propriety of words and thoughts adapted to the subject." If this be a true definition of wit, I am apt to think that Euclid was the greatest wit that ever set pen to paper: it is certain that never was a greater propriety of words and thoughts adapted to the subject, than what that author has made use of in his *Elements*. I shall only appeal to my reader, if this definition agrees with any notion he has of wit. If it be a true one, I am sure Mr. Dryden was not only a better poet, but a greater wit, than Mr. Cowley; and Virgil a much more facetious[8] man than either Ovid or Martial.

[7] at the close of "The Author's Apology for Heroic Poetry and Poetic Licence" (1677); see *Essays*, ed. W. P. Ker (1900), I 178. Dryden wrote "elegantly adapted."

[8] witty or gay, rather than waggish.

Bouhours,[9] whom I look upon to be the most penetrating of all the French critics, has taken pains to show, that it is impossible for any thought to be beautiful which is not just, and has not its foundation in the nature of things; that the basis of all wit is truth; and that no thought can be valuable, of which good sense is not the groundwork. Boileau has endeavored to inculcate the same notion in several parts of his writings, both in prose and verse. This is that natural way of writing, that beautiful simplicity, which we so much admire in the compositions of the ancients; and which nobody deviates from, but those who want strength of genius to make a thought shine in its own natural beauties. Poets who want this strength of genius to give that majestic simplicity to nature, which we so much admire in the works of the ancients, are forced to hunt after foreign ornaments and not to let any piece of wit, of what kind soever, escape them. I look upon these writers as Goths in poetry, who, like those in architecture, not being able to come up to the beautiful simplicity of the old Greeks and Romans, have endeavored to supply its place with all the extravagancies of an irregular fancy. Mr. Dryden makes a very handsome observation[10] on Ovid's writing a letter from Dido to Aeneas, in the following words: "Ovid (says he, speaking of Virgil's fiction of Dido and Aeneas) takes it up after him, even in the same age, and makes an ancient heroine of Virgil's new-created Dido; dictates a letter for her, just before her death, to the ungrateful fugitive; and, very unluckily for himself, is for measuring a sword with a man so much superior in force to him on the same subject. I think I may be judge of this, because I have translated both. The famous author of the *Art of Love* has nothing of his own; he borrows all from a greater master in his own profession, and, which is worse, improves nothing which he finds: nature fails him, and being forced to his old shift, he has recourse to witticism. This passes, indeed, with his soft admirers, and gives him the preference to Virgil in their esteem."

Were not I supported by so great an authority as that of Mr. Dryden, I should not venture to observe, that the taste of most of our English poets, as well as readers, is extremely Gothic. He

[9] Father Dominique Bouhours, the French Jesuit critic (1628-1702), author of *The Art of Criticism; or, The Method of Making a Right Judgment upon Subjects of Wit and Learning* (1687), translated into English in 1705.
[10] "Dedication of the Aeneis" (1697), *Essays,* ed. Ker, II 193-94.

quotes[11] Monsieur Segrais for a threefold distinction of the readers of poetry: in the first of which he comprehends the rabble of readers, whom he does not treat as such with regard to their quality, but to their numbers, and the coarseness of their taste. His words are as follow: "Segrais has distinguished the readers of poetry, according to their capacity of judging, into three classes. (He might have said the same of writers too, if he had pleased.) In the lowest form he places those whom he calls *les petits esprits;* such things as are our upper-gallery audience in a playhouse; who like nothing but the husk and rind of wit; prefer a quibble, a conceit, an epigram, before solid sense and elegant expression: these are mob readers. If Virgil and Martial stood for Parliament men, we know already who would carry it. But though they make the greatest appearance in the field and cry the loudest, the best on't is they are but a sort of French Huguenots, or Dutch boors, brought over in herds but not naturalized; who have not lands of two pounds per annum in Parnassus, and therefore are not privileged to poll. Their authors are of the same level, fit to represent them on a mountebank's stage, or to be masters of the ceremonies in a bear garden: yet these are they who have the most admirers. But it often happens, to their mortification, that as their readers improve their stock of sense (as they may by reading better books and by conversation with men of judgment) they soon forsake them."

I must not dismiss this subject without observing that as Mr. Locke in the passage above mentioned has discovered the most fruitful source of wit, so there is another of quite contrary nature to it, which does likewise branch itself out into several kinds. For not only the *resemblance,* but the *opposition* of ideas, does very often produce wit; as I could show in several little points, turns, and antitheses, that I may possibly enlarge upon in some future speculation.

[11] in the same essay; II 223-24.

No. 335   Tuesday, 25 March 1712
[Addison]

Respicere exemplar vitae morumque jubebo
Doctim imitatorem, et vivas hinc ducere voces.
HORACE [1]

My friend, Sir Roger de Coverley, when we last met together
at the club, told me that he had a great mind to see the new tragedy[2]
with me, assuring me at the same time that he had not been at a
play these twenty years. "The last I saw," says Sir Roger, "was *The
Committee*,[3] which I should not have gone to neither, had not I
been told beforehand that it was a good Church of England comedy." He then proceeded to enquire of me who this distressed
mother was, and upon hearing that she was Hector's widow, he
told me that her husband was a brave man, and that when he was
a schoolboy, he had read his life at the end of the dictionary. My
friend asked me, in the next place, if there would not be some
danger in coming home late, in case the Mohocks[4] should be abroad.
"I assure you," says he, "I thought I had fallen into their hands
last night, for I observed two or three lusty black[5] men that followed
me half way up Fleet Street, and mended their pace behind me in
proportion as I put on to get away from them. You must know,"
continued the knight with a smile, "I fancied they had a mind to
hunt me; for I remember an honest gentleman in my neighborhood,
who was served such a trick in King Charles the Second's time;
for which reason he has not ventured himself in town ever since.

---

[1] "I shall urge the artist trained in representation to look at the pattern
of life and manners and to draw thence the living voices."—*Ars Poetica*,
ll. 317-18.

[2] Ambrose Philips' *The Distressed Mother,* based on Racine's *Andro-
maque,* first produced on 17 March 1712. Steele wrote the prologue and
Addison contributed to the epilogue.

[3] a comedy by Sir Robert Howard (1662).

[4] a gang of ruffian-pranksters who played savage jokes on passers-by (cf.
John Gay, *Trivia*, III 323-26 and note).

[5] masked, or with blackened faces.

I might have shown them very good sport, had this been their design, for as I am an old fox hunter, I should have turned and dodged, and have played them a thousand tricks they had never seen in their lives before." Sir Roger added that if these gentlemen had any such intention they did not succeed very well in it, "For I threw them out," says he, "at the end of Norfolk Street, where I doubled the corner and got shelter in my lodgings before they could imagine what was become of me. However," says the knight, "if Captain Sentry will make one with us tomorrow night, and if you will both of you call upon me about four o'clock that we may be at the house before it is full, I will have my own coach in readiness to attend you, for John tells me he has got the fore-wheels mended."

The captain, who did not fail to meet me there at the appointed hour, bid Sir Roger fear nothing, for that he had put on the same sword which he made use of at the Battle of Steenkirk.[6] Sir Roger's servants, and, among the rest, my old friend the butler, had, I found, provided themselves with good oaken plants,[7] to attend their master upon this occasion. When we had placed him in his coach, with myself at his left hand, the captain before him, and his butler at the head of his footmen in the rear, we convoyed him in safety to the playhouse; where, after having marched up the entry in good order, the captain and I went in with him, and seated him betwixt us in the pit. As soon as the house was full, and the candles lighted, my old friend stood up and looked about him with that pleasure which a mind seasoned with humanity naturally feels in itself at the sight of a multitude of people who seem pleased with one another, and partake of the same common entertainment. I could not but fancy to myself, as the old man stood up in the middle of the pit, that he made a very proper center to a tragic audience. Upon the entering of Pyrrhus, the knight told me that he did not believe the King of France himself had a better strut. I was indeed very attentive to my old friend's remarks, because I looked upon them as a piece of natural criticism, and was well pleased to hear him at the conclusion of almost every scene telling me that he could not imagine how the play would end. One while he appeared much concerned for Andromache, and a little while after as much for Hermione, and was extremely puzzled to think what would become of Pyrrhus.

[6] where William III defeated the French in 1692.
[7] cudgels.

When Sir Roger saw Andromache's obstinate refusal to her lover's importunities, he whispered me in the ear that he was sure she would never have him; to which he added, with a more than ordinary vehemence, "You can't imagine, sir, what 'tis to have to do with a widow." Upon Pyrrhus his threatening afterwards to leave her, the knight shook his head and muttered to himself, "Ay, do if you can." This part dwelt so much upon my friend's imagination that at the close of the third act, as I was thinking of something else, he whispered in my ear, "These widows, sir, are the most perverse creatures in the world. But pray," says he, "you that are a critic, is the play according to your dramatic rules, as you call them? Should your people in tragedy always talk to be understood? Why, there is not a single sentence in this play that I do not know the meaning of."

The fourth act very luckily begun before I had time to give the old gentleman an answer. "Well," says the knight, sitting down with great satisfaction, "I suppose we are now to see Hector's ghost." He then renewed his attention, and, from time to time, fell a-praising the widow. He made, indeed, a little mistake as to one of her pages, whom, at his first entering he took for Astyanax, but he quickly set himself right in that particular, though, at the same time, he owned he should have been very glad to have seen the little boy, who, says he, must needs be a very fine child by the account that is given of him. Upon Hermione's going off with a menace to Pyrrhus, the audience gave a loud clap, to which Sir Roger added, "On my word, a notable young baggage."

As there was a very remarkable silence and stillness in the audience during the whole action, it was natural for them to take the opportunity of the intervals between the acts to express their opinion of the players and of their respective parts. Sir Roger hearing a cluster of them praise Orestes, struck in with them and told them that he thought his friend Pylades was a very sensible man; as they were afterwards applauding Pyrrhus, Sir Roger put in a second time, "And let me tell you," says he, "though he speaks but little, I like the old fellow in whiskers as well as any of them." Captain Sentry, seeing two or three wags who sat near us lean with an attentive ear towards Sir Roger, and fearing lest they should smoke[8] the knight, plucked him by the elbow, and whispered something

[8] quiz, make fun of.

in his ear that lasted till the opening of the fifth act. The knight was wonderfully attentive to the account which Orestes gives of Pyrrhus his death, and at the conclusion of it, told me it was such a bloody piece of work that he was glad it was not done upon the stage. Seeing afterwards Orestes in his raving fit, he grew more than ordinary serious, and took occasion to moralize (in his way) upon an evil conscience, adding that Orestes in his madness looked as if he saw something.

As we were the first that came into the house, so we were the last that went out of it, being resolved to have a clear passage for our old friend, whom we did not care to venture among the justling of the crowd. Sir Roger went out fully satisfied with his entertainment, and we guarded him to his lodgings in the same manner that we brought him to the playhouse; being highly pleased, for my own part, not only with the performance of the excellent piece which had been presented, but with the satisfaction which it had given to the good old man.

No. 411   Saturday, 21 June 1712
[Addison]

Avia Pieridum peragro loca, nullius ante
Trita solo; juvat integros accedere fonteis,
Atque haurire.

LUCRETIUS[1]

Our sight is the most perfect and most delightful of all our senses. It fills the mind with the largest variety of ideas, converses with its objects at the greatest distance, and continues the longest in action without being tired or satiated with its proper enjoyments. The sense of feeling can indeed give us a notion of extension, shape, and all other ideas that enter at the eye, except colors; but at the same time it is very much straitened and confined in its operations to the number, bulk, and distance of its particular ob-

---

[1] "I traverse the pathless haunts of the Muses, never yet trodden by sole of man. I love to approach the untasted springs and to drink."—*On the Nature of the Gods,* I 725-27.

jects. Our sight seems designed to supply all these defects, and may be considered as a more delicate and diffusive kind of touch, that spreads itself over an infinite multitude of bodies, comprehends the largest figures, and brings into our reach some of the most remote parts of the universe.

It is this sense which furnishes the imagination with its ideas; so that by the pleasures of the imagination or fancy (which I shall use promiscuously) I here mean such as arise from visible objects, either when we have them actually in our view, or when we call up their ideas into our minds by paintings, statues, descriptions, or any the like occasion. We cannot indeed have a single image in the fancy that did not make its first entrance through the sight; but we have the power of retaining, altering, and compounding those images which we have once received into all the varieties of picture and vision that are most agreeable to the imagination. For by this faculty a man in a dungeon is capable of entertaining himself with scenes and landscapes more beautiful than any that can be found in the whole compass of nature.

There are few words in the English language which are employed in a more loose and uncircumscribed sense than those of the fancy and the imagination. I therefore thought it necessary to fix and determine the notion of these two words, as I intend to make use of them in the thread of my following speculations, that the reader may conceive rightly what is the subject which I proceed upon. I must therefore desire him to remember, that by the pleasures of the imagination, I mean only such pleasures as arise originally from sight, and that I divide these pleasures into two kinds: my design being first of all to discourse of those primary pleasures of the imagination, which entirely proceed from such objects as are before our eyes; and in the next place to speak of those secondary pleasures of the imagination which flow from the ideas of visible objects, when the objects are not actually before the eye, but are called up into our memories or formed into agreeable visions of things that are either absent or fictitious.

The pleasures of the imagination, taken in their full extent, are not so gross as those of sense, nor so refined as those of the understanding. The last are, indeed, more preferable because they are founded on some new knowledge or improvement in the mind of man; yet it must be confessed that those of the imagination are as great and as transporting as the other. A beautiful prospect delights the soul as much as a demonstration; and a description in Homer has charmed more readers than a chapter in Aristotle. Besides, the pleasures of the imagination have this advantage above those of the understanding, that they are more obvious and more easy to be acquired. It is but opening the eye, and the scene enters. The colors paint themselves on the fancy, with very little attention of thought or application of mind in the beholder. We are struck, we know not how, with the symmetry of anything we see, and immediately assent to the beauty of an object, without inquiring into the particular causes and occasions of it.

A man of polite imagination is let into a great many pleasures that the vulgar are not capable of receiving. He can converse with a picture and find an agreeable companion in a statue. He meets with a secret refreshment in a description, and often feels a greater satisfaction in the prospect of fields and meadows than another does in the possession. It gives him, indeed, a kind of property in everything he sees, and makes the most rude, uncultivated parts of nature administer to his pleasures: so that he looks upon the world as it were in another light, and discovers in it a multitude of charms that conceal themselves from the generality of mankind.

There are, indeed, but very few who know how to be idle and innocent, or have a relish of any pleasures that are not criminal; every diversion they take is at the expense of some one virtue or another, and their very first step out of business is into vice or folly. A man should endeavor, therefore, to make the sphere of his innocent pleasures as wide as possible that he may retire into them with safety, and find in them such a satisfaction as a wise man would not blush to take. Of this nature are those of the imagination, which do not require such a bent of thought as is necessary to our more serious employments, nor, at the same time, suffer the mind to sink into that negligence and remissness which are apt to accompany our more sensual delights, but, like a gentle exercise to the faculties, awaken them from sloth and idleness, without putting them upon any labor or difficulty.

We might here add that the pleasures of the fancy are more conducive to health than those of the understanding, which are worked out by dint of thinking, and attended with too violent a labor of the brain. Delightful scenes, whether in nature, painting, or poetry, have a kindly influence on the body as well as the mind, and not only serve to clear and brighten the imagination, but are able to disperse grief and melancholy, and to set the animal spirits in pleasing and agreeable motions. For this reason Sir Francis Bacon,[2] in his essay upon health, has not thought it improper to prescribe to his reader a poem or a prospect where he particularly dissuades him from knotty and subtile disquisitions, and advises him to pursue studies that fill the mind with splendid and illustrious objects, as histories, fables, and contemplations of nature.

I have in this paper, by way of introduction, settled the notion of those pleasures of the imagination which are the subject of my present undertaking, and endeavored, by several considerations, to recommend to my reader the pursuit of those pleasures. I shall, in my next paper, examine the several sources from whence these pleasures are derived.

No. 412   Monday, 23 June 1712
[Addison]

Divisum sic breve fiet opus.
MARTIAL[1]

I shall first consider those pleasures of the imagination which arise from the actual view and survey of outward objects. And these, I think, all proceed from the sight of what is great, uncommon, or beautiful. There may, indeed, be something so terrible or offensive, that the horror or loathsomeness of an object may overbear the pleasure which results from its greatness, novelty, or beauty; but still there will be such a mixture of delight in the very disgust it gives us, as any of these three qualifications are most conspicuous and prevailing.

By greatness, I do not only mean the bulk of any single object, but the largeness of a whole view considered as one entire

---

[2] "Of the Regiment of Health," *Essayes or Counsels Civill and Moral* (1597).

[1] "Divided, the work will be brief."—*Epigrams*, IV lxxxii 8.

piece. Such are the prospects of an open champaign country, a vast uncultivated desert, of huge heaps of mountains, high rocks and precipices, or a wide expanse of waters, where we are not struck with the novelty or beauty of the sight, but with that rude kind of magnificence which appears in many of these stupendous works of nature. Our imagination loves to be filled with an object, or to grasp at anything that is too big for its capacity. We are flung into a pleasing astonishment at such unbounded views, and feel a delightful stillness and amazement in the soul at the apprehension of them. The mind of man naturally hates everything that looks like a restraint upon it, and is apt to fancy itself under a sort of confinement, when the sight is pent up in a narrow compass, and shortened on every side by the neighborhood of walls or mountains. On the contrary, a spacious horizon is an image of liberty, where the eye has room to range abroad, to expatiate at large on the immensity of its views, and to lose itself amidst the variety of objects that offer themselves to its observation. Such wide and undetermined prospects are as pleasing to the fancy as the speculations of eternity or infinitude are to the understanding. But if there be a beauty or uncommonness joined with this grandeur, as in a troubled ocean, a heaven adorned with stars and meteors, or a spacious landskip cut out into rivers, woods, rocks, and meadows, the pleasure still grows upon us, as it arises from more than a single principle.

Everything that is new or uncommon raises a pleasure in the imagination, because it fills the soul with an agreeable surprise, gratifies its curiosity, and gives it an idea of which it was not before possessed. We are indeed so often conversant with one set of objects and tired out with so many repeated shows of the same things, that whatever is new or uncommon contributes a little to vary human life and to divert our minds, for a while, with the strangeness of its appearance: it serves us for a kind of refreshment, and takes off from that satiety we are apt to complain of in our usual and ordinary entertainments. It is this that bestows charms on a monster, and makes even the imperfections of nature please us. It is this that recommends variety, where the mind is every instant called off to something new, and the attention not suffered to dwell too long, and waste itself on any particular object. It is this, likewise, that improves what is great or beautiful, and makes it afford the mind a double entertainment. Groves, fields, and mead-ows are at any season of the year pleasant to look upon, but never so much as in the opening of the spring, when they are all new and fresh, with their first gloss upon them, and not yet too much accustomed and familiar to the eye. For this reason there is nothing that more enlivens a prospect than rivers, jetteaus,[2] or falls of water, where the scene is perpetually shifting and entertaining the sight every moment with something that is new. We are quickly tired with looking upon hills and valleys, where everything continues fixed and settled in the same place and posture, but find our thoughts a little agitated and relieved at the sight of such objects as are ever in motion and sliding away from beneath the eye of the beholder.

But there is nothing that makes its way more directly to the soul than beauty, which immediately diffuses a secret satisfaction and complacency through the imagination, and gives a finish to anything that is great or uncommon. The very first discovery of it strikes the mind with an inward joy, and spreads a cheerfulness and delight through all its faculties. There is not perhaps any real beauty or deformity more in one piece of matter than another, because we might have been so made that whatsoever now appears loathsome to us might have shown itself agreeable; but we find by experience that there are several modifications of matter which the mind, with-out any previous consideration, pronounces at first sight beautiful or deformed. Thus we see, that every different species of sensible creatures has its different notions of beauty, and that each of them is most affected with the beauties of its own kind. This is nowhere more remarkable than in birds of the same shape and proportion, where we often see the male determined in his courtship by the single grain or tincture of a feather, and never discovering any charms but in the color of its species. . . .

[Here an illustrative passage of Latin verse is omitted.]

There is a second kind of beauty that we find in the several products of art and nature, which does not work in the imagination with that warmth and violence as the beauty that appears in our proper species, but is apt however to raise in us a secret delight and a kind of fondness for the places or objects in which we discover it. This consists either in the gaiety or variety of colors, in the symmetry

[2] *jets d'eau,* ornamental sprays of water from fountains or pipes.

and proportion of parts, in the arrangement and disposition of bodies, or in a just mixture and concurrence of all together. Among these several kinds of beauty the eye takes most delight in colors. We nowhere meet with a more glorious or pleasing show in nature than what appears in the heavens at the rising and setting of the sun, which is wholly made up of those different stains of light that show themselves in clouds of a different situation. For this reason we find the poets, who are always addressing themselves to the imagination, borrowing more of their epithets from colors than from any other topic.

As the fancy delights in every thing that is great, strange, or beautiful, and is still more pleased the more it finds of these perfections in the same object, so is it capable of receiving new satisfaction by the assistance of another sense. Thus any continued sound, as the music of birds, or a fall of water, awakens every moment the mind of the beholder, and makes him more attentive to the several beauties of the place that lie before him. Thus if there arises a fragrancy of smells or perfumes, they heighten the pleasures of the imagination, and make even the colors and verdure of the landskip appear more agreeable; for the ideas of both senses recommend each other, and are pleasanter together than when they enter the mind separately: as the different colors of a picture, when they are well disposed, set off one another, and receive an additional beauty from the advantage of their situation.

๑ John Gay ๑

John Gay (1685-1732) was born and educated at Barnstaple, Devon-shire. He was apprenticed first to a London silk mercer but early turned to writing and won the friendship of Pope and Swift. He held several public appointments and places in aristocratic house-holds, meanwhile publishing many poems, translations, and plays. His greatest work was the "Newgate pastoral," *The Beggar's Opera* (1728), which had a great success and called forth a sequel, *Polly* (1729). When he lost favor at court because of political satire in his works, he retired with his patrons and friends, the Queensberrys. The *Fables* (1727) went through more than sixty editions during the century.

The first two selections from Gay show him at work in mock forms. *The Shepherd's Week* is the culmination of a literary contro-versy which opened when the *Guardian* called for a native English pastoral and praised Ambrose Philips' pastorals highly but ignored Pope's. Pope had published four pastorals representing "the golden age" when "the best of men" were shepherds, and thus sustaining the Virgilian tradition of pastoral as an ideal landscape in which nature and art are one. Pope replied to this implied criticism of his own work in his ironic *Guardian* #40, praising Philips' inept use of literal realism and of rustic manners and speech, and pushing it to absurdity. Gay, presumably with Pope's advice if not prompting, undertook his mock pastorals as a parody of Philips' unconcious incongruities; in the course of his work he shows a fine sense of country charm, but he never allows it to escape confrontation with the high style it reduces. In *Trivia*, Gay adapted the Virgilian georgic, in which the life of rural labor is presented in both contrast and likeness to a life of heroic exploit; but (as he and others, notably Swift, turned the pastoral into the town-eclogue) he presents a town-georgic. This undernote of incongruity between a life in nature and a life in the traffic of the great city is essential to the effect of the poem; and the mock-heroic allusions (such as Virgil had used, notably in the Fourth Georgic) give an edge to the elaborate realistic detail.

Editions: Poetical Works, ed. G. C. Faber (1926); also *Trivia,* ed. W. H. Williams (1922); *The Shepherd's Week,* ed. H. F. B. Brett-Smith (1924).

Biography: W. H. Irving, *John Gay: Favorite of the Wits* (1940).

Critical Studies: W. H. Irving, *John Gay's London* (1928); Sven Armens, *John Gay: Social Critic* (1954); James Sutherland, "John Gay," in J. L. Clifford, ed., *Eighteenth Century Literature: Modern Essays in Criticism* (1959); Hoyt Trowbridge, "Pope, Gay, and The Shepherd's Week," *MLQ* 5 (1944).

The Shepherd's Week[1]
[1714]

MONDAY; OR, THE SQUABBLE

LOBBIN CLOUT

Thy younglings, Cuddy, are but just awake;
No throstles shrill [2] the bramble-bush forsake,
No chirping lark the welkin[3] sheen[4] invokes,

[1] The six days of the week (Sunday is omitted) replace the twelve months of Spenser's *Shepherd's Calendar* or the four seasons of Pope's *Pastorals. Squabble* is Gay's "low" term for the traditional pastoral song-contest, used by Theocritus and Virgil, Spenser, Pope, and Philips. The wager is also reduced in scale, from a heifer or carved bowl. Finally, the names are "low" counterparts of Spenser's: Lobbin seems to fuse lobber (oaf) and Robin; Cuddy is a dialect word for ass or donkey; Cloddipole suggests blockhead; and Blouzelinda fuses Rosalind with blowze (a ruddy, fat-faced wench).

[2] Here as in *chirping,* in the next line, Gay deliberately uses inappropriate terms for these birds' songs.

[3] the same as *welken,* an old Saxon word signifying a *cloud;* by poetical license it is frequently taken for the *element* or *sky,* as may appear by this verse in the Dream of Chaucer: "Ne in all the Welkin was no Cloud" [*Book of the Duchess,* l. 343] (Gay). A parody of Philips' (and Spenser's) revival of archaisms and use of dialect.

[4] or *shine,* an old word for *shining* or *bright* (Gay).

No damsel yet the swelling udder[5] strokes;
O'er yonder hill does scant[6] the dawn appear,   5
Then why does Cuddy leave his cot[7] so rear?[8]

CUDDY

Ah Lobbin Clout, I ween[9] my plight is guessed,
For he that loves, a stranger is to rest;
If swains belie not, thou hast proved the smart,
And Blouzelinda's mistress of thy heart.   10
This rising rear betokeneth well thy mind,
Those arms are folded for thy Blouzelind.
And well, I trow, our piteous plights agree,
Thee Blouzelinda smites, Buxoma me.

LOBBIN CLOUT

Ah Blouzelind! I love thee more by half   15
Than does their fawns or cows the new-fallen calf:
Woe worth the tongue! May blisters sore it gall,
That names Buxoma, Blouzelind withal.

CUDDY

Hold, witless Lobbin Clout, I thee advise,
Lest blisters sore on thy own tongue arise.   20
Lo yonder Cloddipole, the blithesome swain,
The wisest lout of all the neighboring plain!
From Cloddipole we learnt to read the skies,
To know when hail will fall, or winds arise.
He taught us erst[10] the heifer's tail to view,   25
When stuck aloft, that showers would straight ensue;
He first that useful secret did explain,
That pricking corns foretold the gathering rain.

[5] a reference to Philips' "realistic" details, such as "spongy teat."
[6] used by ancient British authors for *scarce* (Gay).
[7] cottage.
[8] an expression in several countries of England for *early in the morning* (Gay).
[9] revived from the Saxon, *to think* or *conceive* (Gay).
[10] a contraction of *ere this*, it signifies *sometime ago* or *formerly* (Gay).

When swallows fleet soar high and sport in air,
He told us that the welkin would be clear.   30
Let Cloddipole then hear us twain rehearse
And praise his sweetheart in alternate verse.
I'll wager this same oaken staff with thee
That Cloddipole shall give the prize to me.

LOBBIN CLOUT

See this tobacco-pouch that's lined with hair,   35
Made of the skin of sleekest fallow[11] deer.
This pouch, that's tied with tape of reddest hue,
I'll wager, that the prize shall be my due.

CUDDY

Begin thy carols, then, thou vaunting[12] slouch,[13]
Be thine the oaken staff or mine the pouch.   40

LOBBIN CLOUT

My Blouzelinda is the blithest lass,
Than primrose sweeter or the clover grass.
Fair is the king-cup that in meadow blows,[14]
Fair is the daisy that beside her grows,
Fair is the gillyflower, of gardens sweet,   45
Fair is the marigold, for pottage meet.
But Blouzelind's than gillyflower more fair,
Than daisy, marigold, or king-cup rare.

CUDDY

My brown Buxoma is the featest[15] maid
That e'er at wake delightsome gambol played.   50
Clean as young lambkins or the goose's down,
And like the goldfinch in her Sunday gown.
The witless lamb may sport upon the plain,
The frisking kid delight the gaping swain,
The wanton calf may skip with many a bound,   55

---

[11] light brown.   [12] boastful.   [13] lout.   [14] blossoms.
[15] most adroit or elegant.

And my cur Tray play deftest[16] feats around;
But neither lamb nor kid, nor calf nor Tray,
Dance like Buxoma on the first of May.

LOBBIN CLOUT

Sweet is my toil when Blouzelind is near;
Of her bereft, 'tis winter all the year.   60
With her no sultry summer's heat I know;
In winter, when she's nigh, with love I glow.
Come, Blouzelinda, ease thy swain's desire,
My summer's shadow and my winter's fire!

CUDDY

As with Buxoma once I worked at hay,   65
Even noontide labor seemed an holiday;
And holidays, if haply she were gone,
Like worky-days I wished would soon be done.
Eftsoons,[17] O sweetheart kind, my love repay,
And all the year shall then be holiday.   70

LOBBIN CLOUT

As Blouzelinda in a gamesome mood
Behind a haycock loudly laughing stood,
I slyly ran and snatched a hasty kiss;
She wiped her lips, nor took it much amiss.
Believe me, Cuddy, while I'm bold to say,   75
Her breath was sweeter than the ripened hay.

CUDDY

As my Buxoma in a morning fair,
With gentle finger stroked her milky care,
I queintly[18] stole a kiss; at first, 'tis true,

[16] an old word [*deft*] signifying *brisk* or *nimble* (Gay).

[17] from *eft*, an ancient British word signifying *soon*. So that *eftsoons* is a doubling of the word *soon*, which is, as it were, to say *twice soon* or *very soon* (Gay).

[18] [queint] has various significations in the ancient English authors. I have used it in this place in the same sense as Chaucer has done in his *Miller's Tale:* "As Clerkes been ful subtil and queint" [89] (by which he means *arch* or *waggish*) and not in that obscene sense wherein he useth it in the line immediately following (Gay).

She frowned, yet after granted one or two.   80
Lobbin, I swear, believe who will my vows,
Her breath by far excelled the breathing cows.

LOBBIN CLOUT

Leek to the Welsh, to Dutchmen butter's dear,[19]
Of Irish swains potato is the cheer,
Oats for their feasts the Scottish shepherds grind,   85
Sweet turnips are the food of Blouzelind.
While she loves turnips, butter I'll despise,
Nor leeks nor oatmeal nor potato prize.

CUDDY

In good roast beef my landlord sticks his knife,
The capon fat delights his dainty wife,   90
Pudding our Parson eats, the Squire loves hare,
But white-pot[20] thick is my Buxoma's fare.
While she loves white-pot, capon ne'er shall be,
Nor hare nor beef nor pudding, food for me.

LOBBIN CLOUT

As once I played at blindman's-buff, it happed   95
About my eyes the towel thick was wrapped.
I missed the swains and seized on Blouzelind.
True speaks that ancient proverb, Love is blind.

CUDDY

As at hot-cockles[21] once I laid me down
And felt the weighty hand of many a clown,   100

[19] Gay cites Virgil, *Eclogues,* VII 61 ff.:
    The poplar is by great Alcides worn;
    The brows of Phoebus his own bays adorn;
    The branching vine the jolly Bacchus loves;
    The Cyprian queen delights in myrtle groves;
    With hazel Phyllis crowns her flowing hair;
    And while she loves that common wreath to wear,
    Nor bays, nor myrtle boughs, with hazel shall compare.
                                        Dryden, ll. 84-90
[20] a pudding made of milk, eggs, raisins, and bread.
[21] The player kneels and hides his eyes in another's lap, trying to guess
which of the others has struck him.

Buxoma gave a gentle tap, and I
Quick rose, and read soft mischief in her eye.

LOBBIN CLOUT

On two near elms the slackened cord I hung,
Now high, now low, my Blouzelinda swung.
With the rude wind her rumpled garment rose,   105
And showed her taper[22] leg and scarlet hose.

CUDDY

Across the fallen oak the plank I laid,
And myself poised against the tottering maid;
High leaped the plank, adown Buxoma fell;
I spied—but faithful sweethearts never tell.   110

LOBBIN CLOUT

This riddle, Cuddy, if thou canst, explain;
This wily riddle puzzles every swain:
What flower is that which bears the Virgin's name,
The richest metal joinèd with the same?

CUDDY

Answer, thou carle,[23] and judge this riddle right,   115
I'll frankly own thee for a cunning wight.
What flower is that which royal honor craves,[24]
Adjoin[25] the Virgin, and 'tis strown on graves.

CLODDIPOLE

Forbear, contending louts, give o'er your strains,
An oaken staff each merits for his pains.[26]   120

[22] tapering, shapely.
[23] churl.
[24] Gay cites Virgil, *Eclogues,* III 106-7:
    Nay, tell me first, in what new region springs
    A flower that bears inscribed the names of Kings . . . .
                      Dryden, ll. 163-64
[25] join to it.
[26] Gay cites Virgil, *Eclogues,* III 109:
    That both have won, or both deserved the prize . . . .
                      Dryden, l. 168

But see the sunbeams bright to labor warn,
And gild the thatch of goodman Hodges' barn.
Your herds for want of water stand adry,
They're weary of your songs—and so am I.

Trivia; Or, The Art of Walking
the Streets of London
[1716]

BOOK III. OF WALKING THE STREETS BY NIGHT

O Trivia,[1] Goddess, leave these low abodes,
And traverse o'er the wide ethereal roads,
Celestial Queen, put on thy robes of light,
Now Cynthia[2] named, fair regent of the night.
At sight of thee the villain sheathes his sword,   5
Nor scales the wall, to steal the wealthy hoard.
O may thy silver lamp from heaven's high bower
Direct my footsteps in the midnight hour!
　　When night first bids the twinkling stars appear,
Or with her cloudy vest[3] inwraps the air,   10
Then swarms the busy street; with caution tread,
Where the shop windows[4] falling threat thy head;
Now laborers home return, and join their strength
To bear the tottering plank, or ladder's length;
Still fix thy eyes intent upon the throng,   15
And as the passes open, wind along.
　　Where the fair columns of St. Clement[5] stand,
Whose straitened bounds encroach upon the Strand;
Where the low penthouse[6] bows the walker's head,

[1] Diana as goddess of the crossroads (literally, where three roads meet).
[2] Diana as goddess of the moon and the night.
[3] garment.
[4] shutters propped up during the day and let down at night.
[5] the church of St. Clement Danes, at the meeting of Fleet Street and the Strand.
[6] arcade, covered walk.

And the rough pavement wounds the yielding tread;   20
Where not a post protects the narrow space,
And strung in twines,[7] combs dangle in thy face;
Summon at once thy courage, rouse thy care,
Stand firm, look back, be resolute, beware.
Forth issuing from steep lanes, the collier's[8] steeds   25
Drag the black load; another cart succeeds,
Team follows team, crowds heaped on crowds appear,[9]
And wait impatient, till the road grow clear.
Now all the pavement sounds with trampling feet,
And the mixed hurry barricades the street.   30
Entangled here, the wagon's lengthened team[10]
Cracks the tough harness; here a ponderous beam
Lies overturned athwart; for slaughter fed
Here lowing bullocks raise their hornèd head.
Now oaths grow loud, with coaches coaches jar,   35
And the smart blow provokes the sturdy war;
From the high box[11] they whirl the thong around,
And with the twining lash their shins resound:
Their rage ferments, more dangerous wounds they try,
And the blood gushes down their painful eye.   40
And now on foot the frowning warriors light,
And with their ponderous fists renew the fight;
Blow answers blow, their cheeks are smeared with blood,
Till down they fall, and grappling roll in mud.
So when two boars, in wild Ytene[12] bred,   45
Or on Westphalia's[13] fattening chestnuts fed,
Gnash their sharp tusks, and roused with equal fire,
Dispute the reign of some luxurious mire;
In the black flood they wallow o'er and o'er,
Till their armed jaws distill with foam and gore.   50
    Where the mob gathers, swiftly shoot along,

[7] as a means of display.

[8] coal merchant's.

[9] typical epic pattern; cf. Pope, *Iliad,* XI 193-94; see l. 35, below.

[10] a long team of several horses.

[11] driver's seat.

[12] New Forest in Hampshire, anciently so called (Gay).

[13] German province renowned for its hogs.

Nor idly mingle in the noisy throng.
Lured by the silver hilt,[14] amid the swarm,
The subtle artist will thy side disarm.
Nor is thy flaxen wig with safety worn;   55
High on the shoulder, in a basket borne,
Lurks the sly boy, whose hand to rapine bred,
Plucks off the curling honors of thy head.
Here dives the skulking thief with practised slight,
And unfelt fingers make thy pocket light.   60
Where's now thy watch, with all its trinkets, flown?
And thy late snuff box is no more thy own.
But lo! his bolder theft some tradesman spies,
Swift from his prey the scudding lurcher[15] flies;
Dextrous he 'scapes the coach with nimble bounds,   65
Whilst every honest tongue "Stop thief" resounds.
So speeds the wily fox, alarmed by fear,
Who lately filched the turkey's callow care;[16]
Hounds following hounds grow louder as he flies,
And injured tenants join the hunter's cries.   70
Breathless he stumbling falls: ill-fated boy!
Why did not honest work thy youth employ?
Seized by rough hands, he's dragged amid the rout,
And stretched beneath the pump's incessant spout;[17]
Or plunged in miry ponds, he gasping lies,   75
Mud chokes his mouth, and plasters o'er his eyes.
    Let not the ballad singer's shrilling strain
Amid the swarm thy listening ear detain:
Guard well thy pocket, for these Sirens stand
To aid the labors of the diving hand;   80
Confederate in the cheat, they draw the throng
And cambric handkerchiefs reward the song.
But soon as coach or cart drives rattling on,
The rabble part, in shoals they backward run.
So Jove's loud bolts the mingled war divide,   85

[14] of a dress sword.
[15] thief.
[16] young.
[17] a frequent punishment for petty thieves.

And Greece and Troy retreat on either side.
     If the rude throng pour on with furious pace,
And hap to break thee from a friend's embrace,
Stop short; nor struggle through the crowd in vain,
But watch with careful eye the passing train.   90
Yet I (perhaps too fond) if chance the tide
Tumultuous bear my partner from my side,
Impatient venture back; despising harm,
I force my passage where the thickest swarm.
Thus his lost bride the Trojan[18] sought in vain   95
Through night, and arms, and flames, and hills of slain.
Thus Nisus[19] wandered o'er the pathless grove,
To find the brave companion of his love,
The pathless grove in vain he wanders o'er:
Euryalus, alas! is now no more.   100
     That walker who, regardless of his pace,
Turns oft to pore upon the damsel's face,
From side to side by thrusting elbows tossed,
Shall strike his aching breast against the post;
Or water, dashed from fishy stalls, shall stain   105
His hapless coat with spurts of scaly rain.
But if unwarily he chance to stray
Where twirling turnstiles[20] intercept the way,
The thwarting passenger shall force them round,
And beat the wretch half breathless to the ground.   110
     Let constant vigilance thy footsteps guide,
And wary circumspection guard thy side;
Then shalt thou walk unharmed the dangerous night,
Nor need th' officious[21] linkboy's[22] smoky light.
Thou never wilt attempt to cross the road,   115
Where alehouse benches rest the porter's load,

[18] Aeneas, who returned to burning Troy in search of his wife Creüsa (*Aeneid*, II).

[19] After his escape from Turnus' forces, he returned in search of Euryalus, only to see him die and be killed himself (*Aeneid*, IX).

[20] built to admit only pedestrians.

[21] diligent.

[22] carrier of a torch to light the way.

Grievous to heedless shins; no barrow's[23] wheel,
That bruises oft the truant schoolboy's heel,
Behind thee rolling, with insidious pace,
Shall mark thy stocking with a miry trace.   120
Let not thy venturous steps approach too nigh,
Where gaping wide, low steepy cellars lie;
Should thy shoe wrench aside, down, down you fall,
And overturn the scolding huckster's stall;
The scolding huckster shall not o'er thee moan,   125
But pence exact for nuts and pears o'erthrown.
  Though you through cleanlier alleys wind by day,
To shun the hurries of the public way,
Yet ne'er to those dark paths by night retire;
Mind only safety, and contemn the mire.   130
Then no impervious courts[24] thy haste detain,
Nor sneering alewives bid thee turn again.
  Where Lincoln's Inn,[25] wide space, is railed around,
Cross not with venturous step; there oft is found
The lurking thief, who while the daylight shone   135
Made the walls echo with his begging tone:
That crutch which late compassion moved shall wound
Thy bleeding head, and fell thee to the ground.
Though thou art tempted by the linkman's[26] call,
Yet trust him not along the lonely wall;   140
In the midway he'll quench the flaming brand,
And share the booty with the pilfering band.
Still keep the public streets, where oily rays
Shot from the crystal lamp, o'erspread the ways.
  Happy Augusta![27] law-defended town!   145
Here no dark lanthorns shade the villain's frown;
No Spanish jealousies thy lanes infest,
Nor Roman vengeance stabs th' unwary breast;
Here tyranny ne'er lifts her purple hand,
But liberty and justice guard the land;   150

[23] handcart's. [24] blind alleys.
[25] Lincoln's Inn Fields, a square then much frequented by beggars and thieves.
[26] See note to l. 114. [27] London.

No bravos[28] here profess the bloody trade,
Nor is the church the murderer's refuge made.[29]
    Let not the chairman,[30] with assuming stride,
Press near the wall, and rudely thrust thy side:
The laws have set him bounds; his servile feet   155
Should ne'er encroach where posts[31] defend the street.
Yet who the footman's arrogance can quell
Whose flambeau gilds the sashes of Pall Mall,
When in long rank a train of torches flame
To light the midnight visits of the dame?   160
Others, perhaps, by happier guidance led,
May where the chairman rests, with safety tread;
Whene'er I pass, their poles unseen below,
Make my knee tremble with the jarring blow.
    If wheels bar up the road where streets are crossed,   165
With gentle words the coachman's ear accost:
He ne'er the threat or harsh command obeys,
But with contempt the spattered shoe surveys.
Now man with utmost fortitude thy soul,
To cross the way where carts and coaches roll;   170
Yet do not in thy hardy skill confide,
Nor rashly risk the kennel's[32] spacious stride;
Stay till afar the distant wheel you hear,
Like dying thunder in the breaking air;
Thy foot will slide upon the miry stone,   175
And passing coaches crush thy tortured bone,
Or wheels enclose the road; on either hand
Pent round with perils, in the midst you stand,
And call for aid in vain; the coachman swears,
And carmen drive, unmindful of thy prayers.   180
Where wilt thou turn? ah! whither wilt thou fly?
On every side the pressing spokes are nigh.
So sailors, while Charybdis' gulf they shun,

---

[28] hired assassins.
[29] Sanctuary in English churches ended with the Reformation.
[30] bearer of a sedan chair.
[31] i.e., set between the walks and the street (cf. l. 210).
[32] gutter along the edge of the street.

Amazed, on Scylla's craggy dangers run.
   Be sure observe where brown Ostrea[33] stands,   185
Who boasts her shelly ware from Wallfleet[34] sands;
There mayst thou pass, with safe unmiry feet,
Where the raised pavement leads athwart the street.
If where Fleet Ditch[35] with muddy current flows
You chance to roam, where oyster tubs in rows   190
Are ranged beside the posts; there stay thy haste,
And with the savory fish indulge thy taste:
The damsel's knife the gaping shell commands,
While the salt liquor streams between her hands.
   The man had sure a palate covered o'er[36]   195
With brass or steel, that on the rocky shore
First broke the oozy oyster's pearly coat,
And risked the living morsel down his throat.
What will not luxury taste? Earth, sea, and air
Are daily ransacked for the bill of fare.   200
Blood stuffed in skins[37] is British Christians' food,
And France robs marshes of the croaking brood;
Spongy morels[38] in strong ragouts[39] are found,
And in the soup the slimy snail is drowned.
   When from high spouts the dashing torrents fall,   205
Ever be watchful to maintain the wall;
For shouldst thou quit thy ground, the rushing throng
Will with impetuous fury drive along;
All press to gain those honors thou hast lost,
And rudely shove thee far without the post.   210
Then to retrieve the shed you strive in vain,
Draggled [40] all o'er, and soaked in floods of rain.
Yet rather bear the shower, and toils of mud,

[33] oyster wench.
[34] town in Essex famous for oysters.
[35] an open sewer that ran into the Thames.
[36] parody of Horace, *Odes,* I iii 9 ff.
[37] blood pudding or sausage.
[38] mushroom-like fungi.
[39] French beef stews.
[40] stained with mud.

Than in the doubtful quarrel risk thy blood.
O think on Oedipus' detested state,   215
And by his woes be warned to shun thy fate.
    Where three roads joined, he met his sire unknown;
(Unhappy sire, but more unhappy son!)
Each claimed the way, their swords the strife decide,
The hoary monarch fell, he groaned and died!   220
Hence sprung the fatal plague that thinned thy reign,
Thy cursed incest! and thy children slain!
Hence wert thou doomed in endless night to stray
Through Theban streets, and cheerless grope thy way.
    Contemplate, mortal, on thy fleeting years;   225
See, with black train the funeral pomp appears!
Whether some heir attends in sable state,
And mourns with outward grief a parent's fate;
Or the fair virgin, nipped in beauty's bloom,
A crowd of lovers follow to her tomb.   230
Why is the hearse with scutcheons[41] blazoned round,
And with the nodding plume of ostrich crowned?
No: the dead know it not, nor profit gain;
It only serves to prove the living vain.
How short is life! how frail is human trust!   235
Is all this pomp for laying dust to dust?
    Where the nailed hoop[42] defends the painted stall,
Brush not thy sweeping skirt too near the wall;
Thy heedless sleeve will drink the colored oil,
And spot indelible thy pocket soil.   240
Has not wise nature strung the legs and feet
With firmest nerves,[43] designed to walk the street?
Has she not given us hands, to grope aright
Amidst the frequent dangers of the night?
And think'st thou not the double nostril meant   245
To warn from oily woes by previous scent?
    Who can the various city frauds recite
With all the petty rapines of the night?
Who now the guinea dropper's[44] bait regards,

---

[41] coats of arms.   [42] used as warning (?).   [43] sinews.
[44] confidence man who pretends to find a coin and offers to share it
with his victim, in order to set him up for cheating, as in l. 250.

Tricked by the sharper's dice, or juggler's cards? 250
Why should I warn thee ne'er to join the fray,
Where the sham quarrel interrupts the way?
Lives there in these our days so soft a clown,
Braved[45] by the bully's oaths, or threatening frown?
I need not strict enjoin the pocket's care 255
When from the crowded play thou lead'st the fair;
Who has not here, or watch, or snuff box lost,
Or handkerchiefs that India's shuttle boast?
 O! may thy virtue guard thee through the roads
Of Drury's mazy courts, and dark abodes, 260
The harlots' guileful paths, who nightly stand
Where Catherine Street[46] descends into the Strand.
Say, vagrant Muse, their wiles and subtle arts,
To lure the strangers' unsuspecting hearts;
So shall our youth on healthful sinews tread, 265
And city cheeks grow warm with rural red.
 'Tis she who nightly strolls with sauntering pace,
No stubborn stays her yielding shape embrace;
Beneath the lamp her tawdry ribbons glare,
The new-scoured manteau, and the slattern air; 270
High draggled petticoats her travels show,
And hollow cheeks with artful blushes glow;
With flattering sounds she soothes the credulous ear,
My noble captain! charmer! love! my dear!
In riding-hood near tavern doors she plies, 275
Or muffled pinners[47] hide her livid eyes.
With empty bandbox she delights to range,
And feigns a distant errand from the 'Change;[48]
Nay, she will oft the Quaker's hood profane,
And trudge demure the rounds of Drury Lane. 280
She darts from sarcenet[49] ambush wily leers,
Twitches thy sleeve, or with familiar airs
Her fan will pat thy cheek; these snares disdain,

[45] cowed.
[46] like Drury Lane nearby, a resort for prostitutes.
[47] a headdress with long flaps on either side of the face.
[48] the shopping center in the Strand.
[49] fine, soft silk.

Nor gaze behind thee, when she turns again.
    I knew a yeoman who, for thirst of gain,   285
To the great city drove from Devon's plain
His numerous lowing herd; his herds he sold,
And his deep leathern pocket bagged with gold;
Drawn by a fraudful nymph, he gazed, he sighed,
Unmindful of his home, and distant bride;   290
She leads the willing victim to his doom,
Through winding alleys to her cobweb room.
Thence through the street he reels from post to post,
Valiant with wine, nor knows his treasure lost.
The vagrant wretch th' assembled watchmen spies,   295
He waves his hanger,[50] and their poles defies;
Deep in the roundhouse[51] pent, all night he snores,
And the next morn in vain his fate deplores.
    Ah hapless swain, unused to pains and ills!
Canst thou forego roast beef for nauseous pills? [52]   300
How wilt thou lift to heaven thy eyes and hands,
When the long scroll the surgeon's fees demands!
Or else (ye gods avert that worst disgrace)
Thy ruined nose falls level with thy face;
Then shall thy wife thy loathsome kiss disdain,   305
And wholesome neighbors from thy mug refrain.
    Yet there are watchmen, who with friendly light
Will teach thy reeling steps to tread aright;
For sixpence will support thy helpless arm,
And home conduct thee, safe from nightly harm;   310
But if they shake their lanthorns, from afar
To call their brethren to confederate war
When rakes resist their power; if hapless you
Should chance to wander with the scouring crew;[53]
Though fortune yield thee captive, ne'er despair,   315

[50] sword.
[51] place of detention.
[52] prescribed for syphilis, whose later stages appear in l. 304.
[53] After drinking hard, a group of rakes often drew their swords and "scoured" the tavern of all but their company; they then went on to "scour" the streets.

But seek the constable's considerate ear;
He will reverse the watchman's harsh decree,
Moved by the rhetoric of a silver fee.
Thus would you gain some favorite courtier's word;
Fee not the petty clerks, but bribe my Lord.   320
     Now is the time that rakes their revels keep;
Kindlers of riot, enemies of sleep.
His scattered pence the flying Nicker[54] flings,
And with the copper shower the casement rings.
Who has not heard the Scourer's midnight fame?   325
Who has not trembled at the Mohock's name?
Was there a watchman took his hourly rounds,
Safe from their blows, or new-invented wounds?
I pass their desperate deeds, and mischiefs done
Where from Snow Hill[55] black steepy torrents run;   330
How matrons, hooped within the hoghead's womb,
Were tumbled furious thence, the rolling tomb
O'er the stones thunders, bounds from side to side.
So Regulus[56] to save his country died.
     Where a dim gleam the paly lanthorn throws   335
O'er the mid pavement, heapy rubbish grows;
Or archèd vaults their gaping jaws extend,
Or the dark caves to common shores[57] descend.
Oft by the winds extinct the signal lies,
Or smothered in the glimmering socket dies,   340
E'er night has half rolled round her ebon throne;
In the wide gulf the shattered coach o'erthrown
Sinks with the snorting steeds; the reins are broke,

[54] member of a gang which broke windows by throwing copper halfpence. The *Scourers* (see note to l. 314) (l. 325) and their successors, the *Mohocks* (named for the American tribe, four of whose chiefs visited London in 1709) (l. 326), were notorious wandering gangs of pranksters, given to extremely cruel jokes. While earlier groups had included aristocratic rakes, the Mohocks turned out to be common thieves.

[55] steep road from Newgate to Holborn Bridge.

[56] the Roman hero who advised his country against making peace, then returned to Carthage as a prisoner. He was put to death in a nail-studded chest.

[57] sewers.

And from the crackling axle flies the spoke.
So when famed Eddystone's far shooting ray,[58]   345
That led the sailor through the stormy way,
Was from its rocky roots by billows torn,
And the high turret in the whirlwind borne,
Fleets bulged their sides against the craggy land,
And pitchy ruins blackened all the strand.   350
        Who then through night would hire the harnessed steed,
And who would choose the rattling wheel for speed?
        But hark! distress with screaming voice draws nigher,
And wakes the slumbering street with cries of fire.
At first a glowing red enwraps the skies,   355
And borne by winds the scattering sparks arise;
From beam to beam the fierce contagion spreads;
The spiry flames now lift aloft their heads,
Through the burst sash a blazing deluge pours,
And splitting tiles descend in rattling showers.   360
Now with thick crowds th' enlightened pavement swarms,
The fireman sweats beneath his crooked arms,
A leathern casque his venturous head defends,
Boldly he climbs where thickest smoke ascends;
Moved by the mother's streaming eyes and prayers,   365
The helpless infant through the flame he bears,
With no less virtue, than through hostile fire
The Dardan hero[59] bore his aged sire.
See forceful engines spout their leveled streams,
To quench the blaze that runs along the beams;   370
The grappling hook plucks rafters from the walls,
And heaps on heaps the smoky ruin falls.
Blown by strong winds the fiery tempest roars,
Bears down new walls and pours along the floors;
The heavens are all ablaze, the face of night   375
Is covered with a sanguine[60] dreadful light:
'Twas such a light involved thy towers, O Rome,

[58] The lighthouse in Plymouth Sound was washed away in 1703.
[59] Aeneas, who bore his father from burning Troy (*Aeneid,* II).
[60] the color of blood.

The dire presage of mighty Caesar's doom,[61]
When the sun veiled in rust his mourning head,
And frightful prodigies the skies o'erspread.   380
Hark! the drum thunders! far, ye crowds, retire:
Behold! the ready match[62] is tipped with fire,
The nitrous store is laid, the smutty train
With running blaze awakes the barreled grain;[63]
Flames sudden wrap the walls; with sullen sound   385
The shattered pile[64] sinks on the smoky ground.
So when the years shall have revolved the date,
Th' inevitable hour of Naples' fate,[65]
Her sapped foundations shall with thunders shake,
And heave and toss upon the sulfurous lake;   390
Earth's womb at once the fiery flood shall rend,
And in th' abyss her plunging towers descend.
    Consider, reader, what fatigues I've known,
The toils, the perils of the wintry town;
What riots seen, what bustling crowds I bored,[66]   395
How oft I crossed where carts and coaches roared;
Yet shall I bless my labors, if mankind
Their future safety from my dangers find.
Thus the bold traveler (inured to toil,
Whose steps have printed Asia's desert soil,   400
The barbarous Arabs' haunt; or shivering crossed
Dark Greenland's mountains of eternal frost;
Whom providence in length of years restores
To the wished harbor of his native shores)
Sets forth his journals to the public view,   405
To caution, by his woes, the wandering crew.
    And now complete my generous labors lie,

[61] Caesar's fall was supposedly preceded by strange, unnatural events; see Virgil, *Georgics,* I 461 ff. and cf. *Hamlet,* I i 113-20.
[62] Houses were blown up in the path of a fire to prevent its spreading. The following lines describe this process.
[63] gunpowder.
[64] building.
[65] foreseen because of the threat of Vesuvius' eruptions, especially frequent in the early eighteenth century.
[66] penetrated.

Finished, and ripe for immortality.
Death shall entomb in dust this moldering frame,
But never reach th' eternal part, my fame.   410
When Ward and Gildon,[67] mighty names, are dead,
Or but at Chelsea[68] under custards read;
When critics crazy bandboxes repair,
And tragedies, turned rockets,[69] bounce in air;
High raised on Fleet Street posts,[70] consigned to fame,   415
This work shall shine, and walkers bless my name.

Fables
[1727]

FABLE XXIV. THE BUTTERFLY AND THE SNAIL

All upstarts, insolent in place,
Remind us of their vulgar race.

   As in the sunshine of the morn,
A Butterfly (but newly born)
Sate proudly perking on a rose,   5
With pert conceit his bosom glows.
His wings (all glorious to behold),
Bedropt with azure, jet, and gold,
Wide he displays; the spangled dew
Reflects his eyes and various hue.   10
   His now-forgotten friend, a Snail,
Beneath his house, with slimy trail
Crawls o'er the grass; whom when he spies,
In wrath he to the gardener cries:
   "What means yon peasant's daily toil   15
From choking weeds to rid the soil?

[67] Ned Ward and Charles Gildon, popular hack writers of the day.
[68] Chelsea was known for pastries. Books were often sold off to pastry-cooks for paper to line their pans.
[69] used in firecrackers.
[70] signposts or displays of booksellers.

Why wake you to the morning's care,
Why with new arts correct the year?
Why glows the peach with crimson hue,
And why the plum's inviting blue?   20
Were they to feast his taste designed,
That vermin of voracious kind?
Crush then the slow, the pilfering race;
So purge thy garden from disgrace."
   "What arrogance!" the Snail replied,   25
"How insolent is upstart pride!
Hadst thou not thus with insult vain
Provoked my patience to complain,
I had concealed thy meaner birth,
Nor traced thee to the scum of earth.   30
For scarce nine suns have waked the hours
To swell the fruit and paint the flowers,
Since I thy humbler life surveyed
In base, in sordid guise arrayed:
A hideous insect, vile, unclean,   35
You dragged a slow and noisome train,
And from your spider bowels drew
Foul film, and spun the dirty clue.[1]
I own my humbler life, good friend;
Snail was I born, and snail shall end.   40
And what's a butterfly? At best,
He's but a caterpillar dressed;
And all thy race (a numerous seed)
Shall prove of caterpillar breed."

FABLE XLIX. THE MAN AND THE FLEA

Whether on earth, in air or main,
Sure everything alive is vain!
   Does not the hawk all fowls survey
As destined only for his prey?
And do not tyrants, prouder things,   5

_____
[1] thread.

Think men were born for slaves to kings?
  When the crab views the pearly strands,[1]
Or Tagus[2] bright with golden sands,
Or crawls beside the coral grove
And hears the ocean roll above,   10
"Nature is too profuse," says he,
"Who gave all these to pleasure me!"
  When bordering pinks and roses bloom
And every garden breathes perfume,
When peaches glow with sunny dyes,   15
Like Laura's cheek when blushes rise,
When with huge figs the branches bend,
When clusters from the vine depend,
The snail looks round on flower and tree
And cries, "All these were made for me!"   20

  "What dignity's in human nature,"
Says Man, the most conceited creature,
As from a cliff he cast his eye
And viewed the sea and archèd sky.
The sun was sunk beneath the main,   25
The moon and all the starry train
Hung the vast vault of heaven. The Man
His contemplation thus began:
  "When I behold this glorious show,
And the wide wat'ry world below,   30
The scaly people of the main,
The beasts that range the wood or plain,
The winged inhabitants of air,
The day, the night, the various year,
And know all these by heaven designed   35
As gifts to pleasure humankind,
I cannot raise my worth too high:
Of what vast consequence am I!"
  "Not of th' importance you suppose,"
Replies a Flea upon his nose: 40
"Be humble, learn thyself to scan;

[1] oyster beds.
[2] river in Spain and Portugal, renowned for gold dust in its waters.

Know pride was never made for man.
'Tis vanity that swells thy mind.
What, heaven and earth for thee designed!
For thee! made only for our need,   45
That more important Fleas might feed."

❧ James Thomson ☙

James Thomson (1700-48) was born and brought up in Roxburgh-
shire, Scotland. The son of a minister, he began at Edinburgh University to prepare for the church but failed to complete a degree.
In 1725 he left for London, where he published the first version
of *Winter* in 1726 and the full *Seasons* in 1730. He wrote several
plays as well and, after travels as a tutor on the Continent, the
long poem, *Liberty*. He settled in Richmond, near London, among
many literary friends. Thomson was granted a pension by the Prince
of Wales and a government sinecure through aristocratic patronage.
He published *The Castle of Indolence,* a Spenserian poem written
earlier, in the year of his death.

    The Seasons was a work of great popularity and influence (one
can find echoes in Young, Gray, Goldsmith, Cowper, and Blake).
Its use of a Miltonic blank verse; its concern with the sublime,
particularly in closely observed natural landscape; its stress upon
the wildness and unimaginable variety that is included within the
order of God in Nature (as in Shaftesbury's *The Moralists*); and
its celebration of heroic fortitude and simplicity set it off from the
typical work of the major Augustans. There are links with other
poets of Biblical sublimity, such as Blackmore (whose hyperboles
Pope ridiculed in *The Art of Sinking in Poetry*); and Pope's own
plan for an epic about Brutus involved such scenes of northern
splendor and terror as we see in *Winter*. But Thomson's often
associative alternation of natural description and moral example or
meditation tends to produce a more purely descriptive poetry than
was common before; interest in human society and culture is present,
but more of it is displaced into a landscape which can suggest
obliquely a great range of emotion and new images of energy.

Editions: Poetical Works, ed. J. Logie Robertson (1908); *The Seasons,* a critical edition showing Thomson's revisions, ed. Otto Zippel (1908).

Biographies; Douglas Grant, *James Thomson: Poet of the Seasons* (1951); *James Thomson (1700-1748): Letters and Documents,* ed. A. D. McKillop (1958).

Critical Studies: A. D. McKillop, *The Background of Thomson's Seasons* (1942); Marjorie H. Nicolson, *Newton Demands the Muse* (1946), esp. ch. v; Patricia Ann Spacks, *The Varied God* (1959).

The Seasons

WINTER
[1726, 1746]

See, Winter comes to rule the varied year
Sullen and sad,[1] with all his rising train—
Vapors, and clouds, and storms. Be these my theme,
These that exalt the soul to solemn thought
And heavenly musing. Welcome, kindred Glooms!   5
Cogenial Horrors, hail! With frequent foot,
Pleased have I, in my cheerful morn of life,
When nursed by careless Solitude I lived
And sung of Nature with unceasing joy,
Pleased have I wandered through your rough domain;   10
Trod the pure virgin-snows, myself as pure;
Heard the winds roar, and the big torrent burst;
Or seen the deep-fermenting tempest brewed
In the grim evening sky. Thus passed the time,
Till through the lucid chambers of the south   15
Looked out the joyous Spring, looked out and smiled.
    To thee, the patron of this first essay,

[1] somber.

The Muse, O Wilmington! [2] renews her song.
Since has she rounded the revolving year: [3]
Skimmed the gay Spring; on eagle-pinions borne,   20
Attempted through the Summer-blaze to rise;
Then swept o'er Autumn with the shadowy gale;
And now among the wintry clouds again,
Rolled in the doubling storm, she tries to soar,
To swell her note with all the rushing winds,   25
To suit her sounding cadence to the floods;
As is her theme, her numbers [4] wildly great.
Thrice happy, could she fill thy judging ear
With bold description and with manly thought!
Nor art thou skilled in awful [5] schemes alone,   30
And how to make a mighty people thrive;
But equal goodness, sound integrity,
A firm, unshaken, uncorrupted soul
Amid a sliding age, and burning strong,
Not vainly blazing, for thy country's weal,   35
A steady spirit, regularly free—
These, each exalting each, the statesman light
Into the patriot; these, the public hope
And eye to thee converting, bid the Muse
Record what envy dares not flattery call.   40

Now when the cheerless empire of the sky
To Capricorn [6] the Centaur-Archer yields,
And fierce Aquarius stains th' inverted year— [7]
Hung o'er the farthest verge of heaven, the sun
Scarce spreads o'er ether the dejected day.   45
Faint are his gleams, and ineffectual shoot
His struggling rays in horizontal lines

[2] Sir Spencer Compton (1673-1743), Speaker of the Commons 1715-27; made Lord Wilmington in 1730.

[3] *Winter,* the first of *The Seasons* to be composed, was printed last in the collected edition.

[4] verses.

[5] awe-inspiring.

[6] the sun passes on 21 December from Sagittarius (the *Centaur-Archer*) to *Capricorn*; on 21 January, to *Aquarius* (l. 43).

[7] Cf. "Soon as Aquarius saddens the inverted year," Horace, *Satires,* I i 36.

Through the thick air; as clothed in cloudy storm,
Weak, wan, and broad, he skirts the southern sky;
And, soon descending, to the long dark night,   50
Wide-shading all, the prostrate world resigns.
Nor is the night unwished, while vital heat,
Light, life, and joy the dubious day forsake.
Meantime in sable cincture shadows vast,
Deep-tinged and damp, and congregated clouds,   55
And all the vapory turbulence of heaven
Involve the face of things. Thus Winter falls,
A heavy gloom oppressive o'er the world,
Through Nature shedding influence malign,
And rouses up the seeds of dark disease.   60
The soul of man dies in him, loathing life,
And black with more than melancholy views.
The cattle droop, and o'er the furrowed land,
Fresh from the plough, the dun discolored flocks,
Untended spreading, crop the wholesome root.[8]   65
Along the woods, along the moorish fens,
Sighs the sad Genius of the coming storm;
And up among the loose disjointed cliffs
And fractured mountains wild, the brawling brook
And cave, presageful, send a hollow moan,   70
Resounding long in listening Fancy's ear.
   Then comes the father of the tempest forth,
Wrapped in black glooms. First, joyless rains obscure
Drive through the mingling skies with vapor foul,
Dash on the mountain's brow, and shake the woods   75
That grumbling wave below. Th' unsightly plain
Lies a brown deluge; as the low-bent clouds
Pour flood on flood, yet unexhausted still
Combine and, deepening into night, shut up
The day's fair face. The wanderers of heaven,   80
Each to his home, retire, save those that love
To take their pastime in the troubled air,
Or skimming flutter round the dimply pool.
The cattle from th' untasted fields return

[8] turnips.

And ask, with meaning[9] low, their wonted stalls,   85
Or ruminate in the contiguous shade.
Thither the household feathery people crowd,
The crested cock with all his female train,
Pensive and dripping; while the cottage-hind [10]
Hangs o'er th' enlivening blaze and taleful there   90
Recounts his simple frolic; much he talks
And much he laughs, nor recks[11] the storm that blows
Without and rattles on his humble roof.
    Wide o'er the brim, with many a torrent swelled,
And the mixed ruin of its banks o'erspread,   95
At last the roused-up river pours along:
Resistless, roaring, dreadful, down it comes,
From the rude[12] mountain and the mossy wild,
Tumbling through rocks abrupt, and sounding far;
Then o'er the sanded valley floating spreads,   100
Calm, sluggish, silent; till again constrained
Between two meeting hills it bursts a way
Where rocks and woods o'erhang the turbid stream;
There, gathering triple force, rapid and deep,
It boils and wheels and foams and thunders through.   105
    Nature! great parent! whose unceasing hand
Rolls round the seasons of the changeful year,
How mighty, how majestic are thy works!
With what a pleasing dread they swell the soul,
That sees astonished, and astonished sings!   110
Ye too, ye winds! that now begin to blow
With boisterous sweep, I raise my voice to you.
Where are your stores, ye powerful beings! say,
Where your aërial magazines[13] reserved
To swell the brooding terrors of the storm?   115
In what far-distant region of the sky,
Hushed in deep silence, sleep you when 'tis calm?

    When from the pallid sky the sun descends,[14]
With many a spot, that o'er his glaring orb

---

[9] meaningful.   [10] rustic laborer.   [11] pays heed to.   [12] rough.
[13] armories.
[14] The account of the coming of the storm borrows from Virgil, *Georgics,*
I 351-92.

Uncertain wanders, stained; red fiery streaks   120
Begin to flush around. The reeling clouds
Stagger with dizzy poise, as doubting yet
Which master to obey; while, rising slow,
Blank in the leaden-colored east, the moon
Wears a wan circle round her blunted horns.   125
Seen through the turbid fluctuating air,
The stars obtuse[15] emit a shivering ray,
Or frequent seem to shoot athwart the gloom,
And long behind them trail the whitening blaze.
Snatched in short eddies, plays the withered leaf,   130
And on the flood the dancing feather floats.
With broadened nostrils to the sky upturned,
The conscious[16] heifer snuffs the stormy gale.
Even as the matron at her nightly task
With pensive labor draws the flaxen thread,   135
The wasted taper[17] and the crackling flame
Foretell the blast. But chief the plumy race,
The tenants of the sky, its changes speak.
Retiring from the downs, where all day long
They picked their scanty fare, a blackening train   140
Of clamorous rooks thick-urge their weary flight,
And seek the closing shelter of the grove.
Assiduous in his bower the wailing owl
Plies his sad song. The cormorant on high
Wheels from the deep and screams along the land.   145
Loud shrieks the soaring hern,[18] and with wild wing
The circling sea-fowl cleave the flaky clouds.
Ocean, unequal pressed, with broken tide
And blind commotion heaves; while from the shore,
Eat[19] into caverns by the restless wave,   150
And forest-rustling mountain, comes a voice
That solemn-sounding bids the world prepare.
Then issues forth the storm with sudden burst,

[15] dulled.
[16] alert.
[17] guttering and running candle.
[18] heron.
[19] eaten, eroded.

And hurls the whole precipitated air
Down in a torrent. On the passive main   155
Descends th' ethereal force, and with strong gust
Turns from its bottom the discolored deep.
Through the black night that sits immense around,
Lashed into foam the fierce-conflicting brine
Seems o'er a thousand raging waves to burn.   160
Meantime the mountain-billows, to the clouds
In dreadful tumult swelled, surge above surge,
Burst into chaos with tremendous roar,
And anchored navies from their stations drive,
Wild as the winds across the howling waste   165
Of mighty waters; now th' inflated wave
Straining they scale, and now impetuous shoot
Into the secret chambers of the deep,
The wintry Baltic thundering o'er their heads.
Emerging thence again, before the breath   170
Of full-exerted heaven they wing their course[20]
And dart on distant coasts—if some sharp rock
Or shoal insidious break not their career,
And in loose fragments fling them floating round.
   Nor less at land the loosened tempest reigns.   175
The mountain thunders, and its sturdy sons[21]
Stoop to the bottom of the rocks they shade.
Lone on the midnight steep and all aghast,
The dark wayfaring stranger breathless toils,
And, often falling, climbs against the blast.   180
Low waves the rooted forest, vexed, and sheds
What of its tarnished honors[22] yet remain—
Dashed down and scattered by the tearing wind's
Assiduous fury, its gigantic limbs.
Thus struggling through the dissipated[23] grove,   185
The whirling tempest raves along the plain;
And, on the cottage thatched or lordly roof
Keen-fastening, shakes them to the solid base.

[20] The sailing vessels are likened to birds.
[21] great trees.
[22] faded foliage.
[23] scattered, lain waste.

Sleep frighted flies; and round the rocking dome,[24]
For entrance eager, howls the savage blast.   190
Then too, they say, through all the burdened air
Long groans are heard, shrill sounds, and distant sighs,
That, uttered by the demon of the night,
Warn the devoted [25] wretch of woe and death.
    Huge uproar lords it wide. The clouds, commixed   195
With stars swift-gliding, sweep along the sky.
All Nature reels. Till Nature's King, who oft
Amid tempestuous darkness dwells alone,
And on the wings of the careering[26] wind
Walks dreadfully serene, commands a calm;[27]   200
Then straight air, sea, and earth are hushed at once.
    As yet 'tis midnight deep. The weary clouds,
Slow-meeting, mingle into solid gloom.
Now, while the drowsy world lies lost in sleep,
Let me associate with the serious Night,   205
And Contemplation, her sedate compeer;
Let me shake off th' intrusive cares of day,
And lay the meddling[28] senses all aside.
    Where now, ye lying vanities of life!
Ye ever-tempting, ever-cheating train!   210
Where are you now? and what is your amount?
Vexation, disappointment, and remorse.
Sad, sickening thought! and yet deluded man,
A scene of crude disjointed visions past,
And broken slumbers, rises still resolved,   215
With new-flushed hopes, to run the giddy round.
    Father of light and life! thou Good Supreme!
O teach me what is good; teach me Thyself!
Save me from folly, vanity, and vice,
From every low pursuit; and feed my soul   220

[24] building.
[25] doomed.
[26] rushing wildly. Cf. Psalm 104:3: "who walketh upon the wings of the wind."
[27] Cf. Matthew 8:26: "Then he arose, and rebuked the winds and the sea; and there was a great calm."
[28] distracting.

With knowledge, conscious peace, and virtue pure—
Sacred, substantial, never-fading bliss!

    The keener tempests come, and, fuming dun
From all the livid east or piercing north,
Thick clouds ascend, in whose capacious womb   225
A vapory deluge lies, to snow congealed.
Heavy they roll their fleecy world along,
And the sky saddens with the gathered storm.
Through the hushed air the whitening shower descends,
At first thin-wavering, till at last the flakes   230
Fall broad and wide and fast, dimming the day
With a continual flow. The cherished fields
Put on their winter robe of purest white.
'Tis brightness all, save where the new snow melts
Along the mazy current. Low the woods   235
Bow their hoar head; and, ere the languid sun
Faint from the west emits his evening ray,
Earth's universal face, deep-hid and chill,
Is one wild dazzling waste, that buries wide
The works of man. Drooping, the laborer-ox   240
Stands covered o'er with snow, and then demands
The fruit of all his toil. The fowls of heaven,
Tamed by the cruel season, crowd around
The winnowing store,[29] and claim the little boon
Which Providence assigns them. One alone,   245
The redbreast, sacred to the household gods,
Wisely regardful of the embroiling sky,
In joyless fields and thorny thickets leaves
His shivering mates, and pays to trusted man
His annual visit. Half afraid, he first   250
Against the window beats; then brisk alights
On the warm hearth; then, hopping o'er the floor,
Eyes all the smiling family askance,
And pecks, and starts, and wonders where he is—
Till, more familiar grown, the table-crumbs   255
Attract his slender feet. The foodless wilds
Pour forth their brown inhabitants. The hare,

---

[29] grain freed from chaff during winter in the barn.

Though timorous of heart, and hard beset
By death in various forms, dark snares and dogs
And more unpitying men, the garden seeks,   260
Urged on by fearless want. The bleating kind
Eye the bleak heaven, and next the glistening earth,
With looks of dumb despair; then, sad-dispersed,
Dig for the withered herb through heaps of snow.
   Now, shepherds, to your helpless charge be kind;   265
Baffle the raging year, and fill their pens
With food at will; lodge them below the storm,
And watch them strict, for from the bellowing east
In this dire season, oft the whirlwind's wing
Sweeps up the burden of whole wintry plains   270
In one wide waft, and o'er the hapless flocks,
Hid in the hollow of two neighboring hills,
The billowy tempest whelms, till, upward urged,
The valley to a shining mountain swells,
Tipped with a wreath high-curling in the sky.   275
   As thus the snows arise, and, foul and fierce,
All Winter drives along the darkened air,
In his own loose-revolving[30] fields the swain
Disastered stands; see other hills ascend
Of unknown joyless brow, and other scenes   280
Of horrid prospect shag the trackless plain;
Nor finds the river nor the forest, hid
Beneath the formless wild, but wanders on
From hill to dale, still more and more astray,
Impatient flouncing through the drifted heaps,   285
Stung with the thoughts of home—the thoughts of home
Rush on his nerves and call their vigor forth
In many a vain attempt. How sinks his soul!
What black despair, what horror fills his heart,
When, for the dusky spot which fancy feigned   290
His tufted cottage rising through the snow,
He meets the roughness of the middle waste,
Far from the track and blessed abode of man;
While round him night resistless closes fast,
And every tempest, howling o'er his head,   295

[30] seeming to move with the drifting snow.

Renders the savage wilderness more wild.
Then throng the busy shapes into his mind
Of covered pits, unfathomably deep,
A dire descent, beyond the power of frost;
Of faithless bogs; of precipices huge,   300
Smoothed up with snow; and—what is land unknown,
What water—of the still unfrozen spring
In the loose marsh or solitary lake,
Where the fresh fountain from the bottom boils.
These check his fearful steps; and down he sinks   305
Beneath the shelter of the shapeless drift,
Thinking o'er all the bitterness of death,
Mixed with the tender anguish nature shoots
Through the wrung bosom of the dying man—
His wife, his children, and his friends unseen.   310
In vain for him th' officious[31] wife prepares
The fire fair-blazing and the vestment warm;
In vain his little children, peeping out
Into the mingling storm, demand their sire
With tears of artless innocence. Alas!   315
Nor wife nor children more shall he behold,
Nor friends, nor sacred home. On every nerve
The deadly winter seizes, shuts up sense,
And, o'er his inmost vitals creeping cold,
Lays him along the snows a stiffened corse,[32]   320
Stretched out and bleaching in the northern blast.
    Ah! little think the gay licentious proud,
Whom pleasure, power, and affluence surround—
They who their thoughtless hours in giddy mirth,
And wanton, often cruel, riot waste—   325
Ah! little think they, while they dance along,
How many feel this very moment death
And all the sad variety of pain;
How many sink in the devouring flood,
Or more devouring flame; how many bleed,   330
By shameful variance betwixt man and man;
How many pine in want, and dungeon glooms,
Shut from the common air and common use

[31] dutiful.   [32] corpse.

Of their own limbs; how many drink the cup
Of baleful grief, or eat the bitter bread   335
Of misery; sore pierced by wintry winds,
How many shrink into the sordid hut
Of cheerless poverty; how many shake
With all the fiercer tortures of the mind,
Unbounded passion, madness, guilt, remorse—   340
Whence, tumbled headlong from the height of life,
They furnish matter for the Tragic Muse;
Even in the vale, where wisdom loves to dwell
With friendship, peace, and contemplation joined,
How many, racked with honest passions, droop   345
In deep retired distress; how many stand
Around the deathbed of their dearest friends,
And point[33] the parting anguish! Thought fond[34] man
Of these, and all the thousand nameless ills
That one incessant struggle render life,   350
One scene of toil, of suffering, and of fate,
Vice in his high career would stand appalled,
And heedless rambling Impulse learn to think;
The conscious[35] heart of Charity would warm,
And her wide wish Benevolence dilate;[36]   355
The social tear would rise, the social sigh;
And into clear perfection, gradual bliss
Refining still, the social passions work.
    And here can I forget the generous band [37]
Who, touched with human woe, redressive[38] searched   360
Into the horrors of the gloomy jail?
Unpitied and unheard where misery moans,
Where sickness pines, where thirst and hunger burn,
And poor misfortune feels the lash of vice;
While in the land of liberty, the land   365
Whose every street and public meeting glow
With open freedom, little tyrants[39] raged:

[33] sharpen.   [34] foolish.   [35] sensitive.   [36] spread.
[37] The Jail Committee of 1729, appointed by Parliament and led by James Oglethorpe, exposed shameful prison conditions.
[38] seeking to correct wrongs.
[39] prison keepers.

Snatched the lean morsel from the starving mouth,
Tore from cold wintry limbs the tattered weed,
Even robbed them of the last of comforts, sleep;   370
The freeborn Briton to the dungeon chained,
Or, as the lust of cruelty prevailed,
At pleasure marked him with inglorious stripes,
And crushed out lives, by secret barbarous ways,
That for their country would have toiled or bled.   375
O great design! if executed well,
With patient care and wisdom-tempered zeal.
Ye sons of Mercy! yet resume the search;
Drag forth the legal monsters into light,
Wrench from their hands Oppression's iron rod,   380
And bid the cruel feel the pains they give.
Much still untouched remains; in this rank age,
Much is the patriot's weeding hand required.
The toils[40] of law (what dark insidious men
Have cumbrous added to perplex the truth   385
And lengthen[41] simple justice into trade)
How glorious were the day that saw these broke
And every man within the reach of right!

By wintry famine roused, from all the tract
Of horrid mountains which the shining Alps   390
And wavy Apennines and Pyrenees
Branch out stupendous into distant lands,
Cruel as death, and hungry as the grave!
Burning for blood, bony and gaunt and grim,
Assembling wolves in raging troops descend;   395
And, pouring o'er the country, bear along,
Keen as the north wind sweeps the glossy snow.
All is their prize. They fasten on the steed,
Press him to earth, and pierce his mighty heart.
Nor can the bull his awful front defend,   400
Or shake the murdering savages away.
Rapacious, at the mother's throat they fly,
And tear the screaming infant from her breast.

[40] snares.
[41] a reference to the long duration of lawsuits.

The godlike face of man avails him naught.
Even Beauty, force divine, at whose bright glance[42]   405
The generous lion stands in softened gaze,
Here bleeds, a hapless undistinguished prey.
But if, apprised of the severe attack,
The country be shut up, lured by the scent,
On churchyards drear (inhuman to relate!)   410
The disappointed prowlers fall, and dig
The shrouded body from the grave, o'er which,
Mixed with foul shades and frighted ghosts, they howl.
   Among those hilly regions where, embraced
In peaceful vales, the happy Grisons[43] dwell,   415
Oft, rushing sudden from the loaded cliffs,
Mountains of snow their gathering terrors roll.
From steep to steep loud thundering down they come,
A wintry waste in dire commotion all;
And herds and flocks and travellers and swains,   420
And sometimes whole brigades of marching troops,
Or hamlets sleeping in the dead of night,
Are deep beneath the smothering ruin whelmed.
   Now, all amid the rigors of the year,
In the wild depth of winter, while without   425
The ceaseless winds blow ice, be my retreat,
Between the groaning forest and the shore
Beat by the boundless multitude of waves,
A rural, sheltered, solitary scene,
Where ruddy fire and beaming tapers join   430
To cheer the gloom. There studious let me sit,
And hold high converse with the mighty dead—
Sages of ancient time, as gods revered,
As gods beneficent, who blessed mankind
With arts and arms, and humanized a world.   435
Roused at th' inspiring thought, I throw aside
The long-lived volume, and deep-musing hail
The sacred shades that slowly-rising pass
Before my wondering eyes. First Socrates,

[42] a reference to the traditional legend that the lion respects beauty, as in the case of Una: Spenser, *Faerie Queene,* I ii.
[43] inhabitants of eastern canton of Switzerland.

Who firmly good in a corrupted state   440
Against the rage of tyrants single stood
Invincible! calm Reason's holy law,
That voice of God within th' attentive mind,
Obeying, fearless or in life or death—
Great moral teacher! wisest of mankind!   445
Solon[44] the next, who built his commonweal
On equity's wide base; by tender laws
A lively people curbing, yet undamped
Preserving still that quick peculiar fire,
Whence in the laurelled field of finer arts,   450
And of bold freedom, they unequalled shone,
The pride of smiling Greece and humankind.
Lycurgus[45] then, who bowed beneath the force
Of strictest discipline, severely wise,
All human passions. Following him I see,   455
As at Thermopylae he glorious fell,
The firm devoted chief[46] who proved by deeds
The hardest lesson which the other taught.
Then Aristides[47] lifts his honest front;
Spotless of heart, to whom th' unflattering voice   460
Of freedom gave the noblest name of Just;
In pure majestic poverty revered;
Who, even his glory to his country's weal
Submitting, swelled a haughty rival's fame.
Reared by his care, of softer ray appears   465
Cimon[48] sweet-souled, whose genius, rising strong,
Shook off the load of young debauch; abroad
The scourge of Persian pride, at home the friend
Of every worth and every splendid art;
Modest and simple in the pomp of wealth.   470
Then the last worthies of declining Greece,

[44] the lawgiver of Athens in 6th century B.C.

[45] the lawgiver of Sparta in 9/8th century B.C.

[46] Leonidas, the Spartan.

[47] Ostracized in 482 B.C., he returned to aid his "haughty rival" (l. 464),
Themistocles, in winning the battle of Salamis.

[48] hero of Marathon, follower of Aristides, both a great general and a
generous host.

Late-called to glory, in unequal times,
Pensive appear. The fair Corinthian boast,
Timoleon,[49] tempered happy, mild, and firm,
Who wept the brother while the tyrant bled.   475
And, equal to the best, the Theban pair,[50]
Whose virtues, in heroic concord joined,
Their country raised to freedom, empire, fame.
He too, with whom Athenian honor sunk,
And left a mass of sordid lees behind,—   480
Phocion[51] the Good; in public life severe,
To virtue still inexorably firm;
But when beneath his low illustrious roof
Sweet peace and happy wisdom smoothed his brow,
Not friendship softer was, nor love more kind.   485
And he, the last of old Lycurgus' sons,
The generous victim to that vain attempt
To save a rotten state—Agis,[52] who saw
Even Sparta's self to servile avarice sunk.
The two Achaian heroes close the train—   490
Aratus,[53] who a while relumed the soul
Of fondly-lingering liberty in Greece;
And he her darling as her latest hope,
The gallant Philopoemen,[54] who to arms
Turned the luxurious pomp he could not cure,   495
Or toiling in his farm a simple swain,
Or bold and skillful thundering in the field.
　　Of rougher front, a mighty people come,

　　[49] When his brother Timophanes sought to be tyrant of Corinth, Timoleon assassinated him.
　　[50] Epaminondas and Pelopidas, friends who led Thebes against Sparta in several campaigns.
　　[51] a man of public virtue; when he argued for peace with Philip of Macedon, he was condemned by the war party to die by drinking hemlock (317 B.C.).
　　[52] He tried to re-establish Lycurgus' laws in the Sparta of the third century B.C. and was finally put to death.
　　[53] chief of the Achaian League, formed to unite Greece against Macedonia; killed by poison in 213 B.C.
　　[54] successor to Aratus, regarded as "the last of the Greeks," killed in 183 B.C.

A race of heroes! in those virtuous times
Which knew no stain, save that with partial flame   500
Their dearest country they too fondly loved.
Her better founder first, the light of Rome,
Numa,[55] who softened her rapacious sons;
Servius,[56] the king who laid the solid base
On which o'er earth the vast republic spread.   505
Then the great consuls venerable rise:
The public father[57] who the private quelled,
As on the dread tribunal sternly sad;
He whom his thankless country could not lose,
Camillus,[58] only vengeful to her foes;   510
Fabricius,[59] scorner of all-conquering gold,
And Cincinnatus,[60] awful from the plough;
Thy willing victim,[61] Carthage! bursting loose
From all that pleading Nature could oppose,
From a whole city's tears, by rigid faith   515
Imperious called, and honor's dire command;
Scipio,[62] the gentle chief, humanely brave,
Who soon the race of spotless glory ran,
And, warm in youth, to the poetic shade
With friendship and philosophy retired;   520

[55] a "better founder" in that he gave laws and religion to the state founded by Romulus.

[56] the sixth King of Rome, who established new civil rights and institutions.

[57] Lucius Junius Brutus drove the Tarquins out of Rome; when his sons joined the cause of the Tarquins, he ordered them put to death.

[58] Banished unfairly, he agreed to return to Rome as dictator and defeated the Gauls; known as the "second Romulus."

[59] He refused the bribes of the invader, Pyrrhus, and after long service to Rome died in poverty.

[60] When called to assume the dictatorship, he was found at his farm, plowing his fields.

[61] Regulus; captured by Carthage, he was sent to Rome to secure peace; instead, he urged the Romans to continue the war and returned, according to his promise, to Carthage, where he was cruelly killed (cf. Gay, *Trivia* III 334).

[62] Scipio Africanus Minor, after his total defeat of Carthage in the third Punic War (146 B.C.), devoted his life to literary study as a friend of Polybius, Terence, and other writers.

Tully,[63] whose powerful eloquence a while
Restrained the rapid fate of rushing Rome;
Unconquered Cato,[64] virtuous in extreme;
And thou, unhappy Brutus,[65] kind of heart,
Whose steady arm, by awful virtue urged,   525
Lifted the Roman steel against thy friend.
Thousands besides the tribute of a verse
Demand, but who can count the stars of heaven?
Who sing their influence on this lower world?
   Behold, who yonder comes! in sober state,   530
Fair, mild, and strong as is a vernal sun:
'Tis Phoebus' [66] self, or else the Mantuan swain! [67]
Great Homer too appears, of daring wing,
Parent of song! and equal by his side,
The British Muse;[68] joined hand in hand they walk,   535
Darkling, full up the middle steep to fame.
Nor absent are those shades,[69] whose skillful touch
Pathetic drew th' impassioned heart, and charmed
Transported Athens with the moral scene;
Nor those who tuneful waked [70] th' enchanting lyre.   540
   First of your kind! society divine!
Still visit thus my nights, for you reserved,
And mount my soaring soul to thoughts like yours.
Silence, thou lonely power, the door be thine;
See on the hallowed hour that none intrude,   545
Save a few chosen friends who sometimes deign
To bless my humble roof with sense refined,
Learning digested well, exalted faith,

[63] Cicero, who exposed the conspiracy of Catiline, and was later killed by the soldiers of Antony (43 B.C.).

[64] Cato the Younger, the Stoic hero who committed suicide rather than submit to Caesar.

[65] Marcus Junius Brutus, who joined in the assassination of Caesar, and later died by his own hand (42 B.C.).

[66] Apollo as god of poetry.

[67] Virgil, *swain* as author of the *Eclogues* and the *Georgics*.

[68] Milton.

[69] the Greek tragic writers.

[70] the lyric poets.

Unstudied wit, and humor ever gay.
Or from the Muses' hill will Pope[71] descend,   550
To raise the sacred hour, to bid it smile,
And with the social spirit warm the heart;
For, though not sweeter his own Homer sings,
Yet is his life the more endearing song.
   Where art thou, Hammond?[72] thou the darling pride,   555
The friend and lover of the tuneful throng!
Ah! why, dear youth, in all the blooming prime
Of vernal genius, where disclosing[73] fast
Each active worth, each manly virtue lay,
Why wert thou ravished from our hope so soon?   560
What now avails that noble thirst of fame
Which stung thy fervent breast? that treasured store
Of knowledge early gained? that eager zeal
To serve thy country, glowing in the band
Of youthful patriots who sustain her name?   565
What now, alas! that life-diffusing charm
Of sprightly wit? that rapture for the Muse,
That heart of friendship and that soul of joy,
Which bade with softest light thy virtues smile?
Ah! only showed to check our fond pursuits   570
And teach our humbled hopes that life is vain!
   Thus in some deep retirement would I pass
The winter-glooms with friends of pliant[74] soul,
Or blithe or solemn, as the theme inspired:
With them would search[75] if nature's boundless frame   575
Was called late-rising from the void of night,
Or sprung eternal from th' eternal Mind;
Its life, its laws, its progress, and its end.
Hence larger prospects of the beauteous whole

[71] Pope, to whose translations of Homer Thomson refers (l. 553), lived very near Thomson's home at Richmond.
[72] James Hammond (1710-42), a friend of Thomson, a minor poet, and a member of the opposition (the Patriots) to Walpole; he was elected to Parliament a year before his death.
[73] revealing itself.
[74] easily varying.
[75] inquire, speculate.

Would gradual open on our opening minds, 580
And each diffusive[76] harmony unite
In full perfection to th' astonished eye.
Then would we try to scan the moral world,
Which, though to us it seems embroiled,[77] moves on
In higher order, fitted and impelled 585
By Wisdom's finest hand, and issuing all
In general good. The sage historic Muse
Should next conduct us through the deeps of time,
Show us how empire grew, declined, and fell
In scattered states; what makes the nations smile, 590
Improves their soil, and gives them double suns;[78]
And why they pine beneath the brightest skies,
In Nature's richest lap. As thus we talked,
Our hearts would burn within us, would inhale
That portion of divinity, that ray 595
Of purest Heaven which lights the public soul
Of patriots and of heroes. But, if doomed
In powerless humble fortune to repress
These ardent risings of the kindling soul,
Then, even superior to ambition, we 600
Would learn the private virtues—how to glide
Through shades and plains along the smoothest stream
Of rural life; or, snatched away by hope
Through the dim spaces of futurity,
With earnest eye anticipate those scenes 605
Of happiness and wonder, where the mind,
In endless growth and infinite ascent,
Rises from state to state, and world to world.
But, when with these the serious thought is foiled,
We, shifting for relief, would play[79] the shapes 610
Of frolic Fancy; and incessant form
Those rapid pictures, that assembled train
Of fleet ideas, never joined before,
Whence lively Wit excites to gay surprise,
Or folly-painting Humor,[80] grave himself, 615

[76] vast in scale. [77] confused. [78] doubled fertility. [79] give play to.
[80] still carries the older sense of creating extreme or eccentric characters possessed by one kind of passion or temperament.

Calls laughter forth, deep-shaking every nerve.

Meantime the village rouses up the fire;
While, well attested and as well believed,
Heard solemn, goes the goblin-story round,
Till superstitious horror creeps o'er all.   620
Or frequent in the sounding[81] hall they wake
The rural gambol. Rustic mirth goes round:
The simple joke that takes the shepherd's heart,
Easily pleased; the long loud laugh sincere;
The kiss snatched hasty from the sidelong maid   625
On purpose guardless, or pretending sleep;
The leap, the slap, the haul; and, shook to notes
Of native music, the respondent dance.
Thus jocund fleets with them the winter night.
    The city swarms intense. The public haunt,   630
Full of each theme and warm with mixed discourse,
Hums indistinct. The sons of riot flow
Down the loose stream of false enchanted joy
To swift destruction. On the rankled soul
The gaming[82] fury falls; and in one gulf   635
Of total ruin, honor, virtue, peace,
Friends, families, and fortune headlong sink.
Upsprings the dance along the lighted dome,[83]
Mixed and evolved [84] a thousand sprightly ways.
The glittering court effuses[85] every pomp;   640
The circle deepens; beamed from gaudy robes,
Tapers, and sparkling gems, and radiant eyes,
A soft effulgence o'er the palace waves—
While, a gay insect in his summer shine,
The fop, light-fluttering, spreads his mealy[86] wings.   645
    Dread o'er the scene the ghost of Hamlet stalks;
Othello rages; poor Monimia[87] mourns;

[81] resounding.
[82] gambling.
[83] hall.
[84] circled.
[85] pours forth, displays.
[86] powdery, spotted.
[87] the heroine of Thomas Otway's tragedy, *The Orphan* (1680).

And Belvidera[88] pours her soul in love.
Terror alarms the breast; the comely tear
Steals o'er the cheek; or else the Comic Muse   650
Holds to the world a picture of itself,
And raises sly the fair impartial laugh.
Sometimes she lifts her strain, and paints the scenes
Of beauteous life—whate'er can deck mankind
Or charm the heart, in generous Bevil [89] showed.   655
  O thou whose wisdom, solid yet refined,
Whose patriot virtues and consummate skill
To touch the finer springs that move the world,
Joined to whate'er the Graces can bestow,
And all Apollo's animating fire,   660
Give thee with pleasing dignity to shine
At once the guardian, ornament, and joy
Of polished life—permit the rural Muse,
O Chesterfield,[90] to grace with thee her song!
Ere to the shades again she humbly flies,   665
Indulge her fond ambition, in thy train
(For every Muse has in thy train a place)
To mark thy various full-accomplished mind—
To mark that spirit which with British scorn
Rejects the allurements of corrupted power;   670
That elegant politeness which excels,
Even in the judgment of presumptuous France,
The boasted manners of her shining court;
That wit, the vivid energy of sense,
The truth of nature, which with Attic point,[91]   675
And kind well-tempered satire, smoothly keen,
Steals through the soul and without pain corrects.
Or, rising thence with yet a brighter flame,
Oh, let me hail thee on some glorious day,
When to the listening senate ardent crowd   680
Britannia's sons to hear her pleaded cause!

[88] the heroine of Otway's tragedy, *Venice Preserved* (1682).
[89] the hero of Steele's sentimental comedy, *The Conscious Lovers* (1722).
[90] Philip Dormer Stanhope, Lord Chesterfield (1694-1773), statesman and wit, author of the famous *Letters to His Son* (1774).
[91] sharpness.

Then, dressed by thee, more amiably fair,
Truth the soft robe of mild persuasion wears;
Thou to assenting reason giv'st again
Her own enlightened thoughts: called from the heart   685
Th' obedient passions on thy voice attend;
And even reluctant Party feels a while
Thy gracious power, as through the varied maze
Of eloquence, now smooth, now quick, now strong,
Profound and clear, you roll the copious flood.   690

To thy loved haunt return, my happy Muse:
For now, behold, the joyous winter days,
Frosty, succeed; and through the blue serene,
For sight too fine, th' ethereal niter[92] flies,
Killing infectious damps, and the spent air   695
Storing afresh with elemental life.
Close crowds the shining atmosphere, and binds
Our strengthened bodies in its cold embrace,
Constringent; feeds and animates our blood;
Refines our spirits,[93] through the new-strung nerves   700
In swifter sallies darting to the brain—
Where sits the soul, intense, collected, cool,
Bright as the skies, and as the season keen.
All nature feels the renovating force
Of Winter—only to the thoughtless eye   705
In ruin seen. The frost-concocted glebe[94]
Draws in abundant vegetable soul,[95]
And gathers vigor for the coming year;
A stronger glow sits on the lively cheek
Of ruddy fire;[96] and luculent[97] along   710

[92] It was believed in Thomson's time that cold or freezing arose from the presence of salts in the air; these nitrous salts were believed to freshen the air, fertilize the soil, and dispel infections with their coming. See also l. 714 ff. below.

[93] the "animal spirits," subtle fluids believed to be carried through the nerves.

[94] soil combined with frost.

[95] fertility, power to produce vegetation.

[96] the sides of the fire burn brighter because of the salts in the air.

[97] bright and clear.

The purer rivers flow; their sullen deeps,
Transparent, open to the shepherd's gaze,
And murmur hoarser at the fixing frost.
    What art thou, Frost? and whence are thy keen stores
Derived, thou secret all-invading power,   715
Whom even th' illusive fluid [98] cannot fly?
Is not thy potent energy unseen
Myriads of little salts, or hooked or shaped
Like double wedges, and diffused immense
Through water, earth, and ether? Hence at eve,   720
Steamed eager[99] from the red horizon round,
With the fierce rage of Winter deep suffused,
An icy gale, oft shifting, o'er the pool
Breathes a blue film, and in its mid-career
Arrests the bickering stream. The loosened ice,   725
Let down the flood and half dissolved by day,
Rustles no more; but to the sedgy bank
Fast grows, or gathers round the pointed stone,
A crystal pavement, by the breath of heaven
Cemented firm; till, seized from shore to shore,   730
The whole imprisoned river growls below.
Loud rings the frozen earth and hard reflects
A double noise; while at his evening watch
The village dog deters the nightly thief;
The heifer lows; the distant waterfall   735
Swells in the breeze; and with the hasty tread
Of traveller the hollow-sounding plain
Shakes from afar. The full ethereal round,
Infinite worlds disclosing to the view,
Shines out intensely keen, and, all one cope   740
Of starry glitter, glows from pole to pole.
From pole to pole the rigid influence falls
Through the still night, incessant, heavy, strong,
And seizes nature fast. It freezes on,
Till morn, late-rising o'er the drooping world,   745
Lifts her pale eye unjoyous. Then appears
The various labor of the silent night:

[98] mercury, which freezes at 38.9° C. below zero.
[99] rising as a vapor of sharp, cold air.

Prone from the dripping eave and dumb cascade,
Whose idle torrents only seem to roar,
The pendent icicle; the frost-work fair,   750
Where transient hues and fancied figures rise;
Wide-spouted o'er the hill the frozen brook,
A livid tract, cold-gleaming on the morn;
The forest bent beneath the plumy wave;
And by the frost refined the whiter snow   755
Incrusted hard and sounding to the tread
Of early shepherd, as he pensive seeks
His pining flock or from the mountain top,
Pleased with the slippery surface, swift descends.
   On blithesome frolics bent, the youthful swains,   760
While every work of man is laid at rest,
Fond o'er the river crowd, in various sport
And revelry dissolved; where, mixing glad,
Happiest of all the train! the raptured boy
Lashes the whirling top. Or, where the Rhine   765
Branched out in many a long canal extends,
From every province swarming, void of care,
Batavia[100] rushes forth; and, as they sweep
On sounding skates a thousand different ways
In circling poise swift as the winds along,   770
The then gay land is maddened all to joy.
Nor less the northern courts wide o'er the snow
Pour a new pomp. Eager on rapid sleds
Their vigorous youth in bold contention wheel
The long-resounding course. Meantime, to raise   775
The manly strife, with highly blooming charms
Flushed by the season, Scandinavia's dames
Or Russia's buxom daughters glow around.
   Pure, quick, and sportful is the wholesome day,
But soon elapsed. The horizontal sun   780
Broad o'er the south hangs at his utmost noon,
And ineffectual strikes the gelid cliff.
His azure gloss the mountain still maintains,
Nor feels the feeble touch. Perhaps the vale

[100] Holland.

Relents awhile to the reflected ray;   785
Or from the forest falls the clustered snow,
Myriads of gems, that in the waving gleam
Gay-twinkle as they scatter. Thick around
Thunders the sport of those who with the gun,
And dog impatient bounding at the shot,   790
Worse than the season desolate the fields,
And, adding to the ruins of the year,
Distress the footed or the feathered game.
    But what is this? Our infant Winter sinks
Divested of his grandeur should our eye   795
Astonished shoot into the frigid zone,
Where for relentless months continual Night
Holds o'er the glittering waste her starry reign.
There,[101] through the prison of unbounded wilds,
Barred by the hand of Nature from escape,   800
Wide-roams the Russian exile. Naught around
Strikes his sad eye but deserts lost in snow,
And heavy-loaded groves, and solid floods
That stretch athwart the solitary vast
Their icy horrors to the frozen main,   805
And cheerless towns far distant—never blessed,
Save when its annual course the caravan
Bends to the golden coast of rich Cathay,
With news of humankind. Yet there life glows;
Yet, cherished there, beneath the shining waste   810
The furry nations harbor—tipped with jet,
Fair ermines spotless as the snows they press;
Sables of glossy black; and, dark-embrowned,
Or beauteous freaked with many a mingled hue,
Thousands besides, the costly pride of courts.   815
There, warm together pressed, the trooping deer
Sleep on the new-fallen snows; and, scarce his head
Raised o'er the heapy wreath, the branching[102] elk
Lies slumbering sullen in the white abyss.
The ruthless hunter wants nor dogs nor toils,[103]   820

---

[101] Siberia.   [102] antlered.
[103] The hunting of the deer is taken from Virgil, *Georgics,* III 371-75.

Nor with the dread of sounding bows he drives
The fearful flying race; with ponderous clubs,
As weak against the mountain-heaps they push
Their beating breast in vain and piteous bray,
He lays them quivering on th' ensanguined snows,   825
And with loud shouts rejoicing bears them home.
There, through the piny forest half-absorpt,
Rough tenant of these shades, the shapeless bear,
With dangling ice all horrid stalks forlorn;
Slow-paced, and sourer as the storms increase,   830
He makes his bed beneath th' inclement drift,
And with stern patience, scorning weak complaint,
Hardens his heart against assailing want.
    Wide o'er the spacious regions of the north
That see Boötes[104] urge his tardy wain,   835
A boisterous race, by frosty Caurus[105] pierced,
Who little pleasure know and fear no pain,
Prolific swarm. They once[106] relumed the flame
Of lost mankind in polished slavery sunk;
Drove martial horde on horde, with dreadful sweep   840
Resistless rushing o'er the enfeebled south,
And gave the vanquished world another form.
Not such the sons of Lapland: wisely they
Despise th' insensate barbarous trade of war;
They ask no more than simple Nature gives;   845
They love their mountains and enjoy their storms.
No false desires, no pride-created wants,
Disturb the peaceful current of their time,
And through the restless ever-tortured maze
Of pleasure or ambition bid it rage.   850
Their reindeer form their riches. These their tents,
Their robes, their beds, and all their homely wealth

[104] the constellation named the "ox driver" because of its closeness to the Wagon (or Big Dipper), here called the *tardy wain* because of its slow movement around the North Star.

[105] the northwest wind, associated with storm.

[106] The Gothic invaders of the Roman Empire were believed to be the founders of modern institutions of political freedom and the source of reborn heroic virtues.

Supply, their wholesome fare, and cheerful cups.
Obsequious at their call, the docile tribe
Yield to the sled their necks, and whirl them swift   855
O'er hill and dale, heaped into one expanse
Of marbled snow or, far as eye can sweep,
With a blue crust of ice unbounded glazed.
By dancing meteors then, that ceaseless shake
A waving blaze refracted o'er the heavens,   860
And vivid moons, and stars that keener play
With doubled lustre from the radiant waste,
Even in the depth of polar night they find
A wondrous day—enough to light the chase
Or guide their daring steps to Finland fairs.   865
Wished Spring returns; and from the hazy south,
While dim Aurora[107] slowly moves before,
The welcome sun, just verging up at first,
By small degrees extends the swelling curve;
Till, seen at last for gay rejoicing months,   870
Still round and round his spiral course he winds,
And, as he nearly dips his flaming orb,
Wheels up again and reascends the sky.
In that glad season from the lakes and floods,
Where pure Niëmi's fairy mountains rise,[108]   875
And fringed with roses Tenglio rolls his stream,
They draw the copious fry. With these at eve
They cheerful-loaded to their tents repair,
Where, all day long in useful cares employed,
Their kind unblemished wives the fire prepare.   880
Thrice happy race! by poverty secured
From legal plunder and rapacious power,
In whom fell interest never yet has sown
The seeds of vice, whose spotless swains ne'er knew
Injurious deed nor, blasted by the breath   885
Of faithless love, their blooming daughters woe.

[107] the goddess of the dawn seen as leading the sun's chariot.
[108] Thomson draws from Maupertuis, *La Figure de la Terre* (1738), an
account of a geodesic survey conducted in part in Lapland.

Still pressing on, beyond Tornea's lake,[109]
And Hecla[110] flaming through a waste of snow,
And farthest Greenland, to the pole itself,
Where, failing gradual, life at length goes out,   890
The Muse expands her solitary flight;
And, hovering o'er the wild stupendous scene,
Beholds new seas beneath another sky.
Throned in his palace of cerulean ice,
Here Winter holds his unrejoicing court,   895
And through his airy hall the loud misrule
Of driving tempest is forever heard;
Here the grim tyrant meditates his wrath;
Here arms his winds with all-subduing frost;
Molds his fierce hail and treasures up his snows,   900
With which he now oppresses half the globe.
    Thence winding eastward to the Tartar's coast,[111]
She sweeps the howling margin of the main,
Where, undissolving from the first of time,
Snows swell on snows amazing to the sky;   905
And icy mountains high on mountains piled
Seem to the shivering sailor from afar
Shapeless and white, an atmosphere of clouds.
Projected huge and horrid o'er the surge,
Alps frown on Alps; or, rushing hideous down,   910
As if old Chaos was again returned,
Wide-rend the deep and shake the solid pole.
Ocean itself no longer can resist
The binding fury; but, in all its rage
Of tempest taken by the boundless frost,   915
Is many a fathom to the bottom chained,
And bid to roar no more—a bleak expanse
Shagged o'er with wavy rocks, cheerless, and void
Of every life, that from the dreary months
Flies conscious southward. Miserable they!   920
Who, here entangled in the gathering ice,

[109] in Lapland, and within the Arctic circle.
[110] volcano in Iceland.
[111] Siberia.

Take their last look of the descending sun;
While, full of death and fierce with tenfold frost,
The long long night, incumbent o'er their heads,
Falls horrible. Such was the Briton's fate,[112]   925
As with first prow (what have not Britons dared?)
He for the passage sought, attempted since
So much in vain, and seeming to be shut
By jealous Nature with eternal bars.
In these fell regions, in Arzina caught,   930
And to the stony deep his idle ship
Immediate sealed, he with his hapless crew,
Each full exerted at his several task,
Froze into statues—to the cordage glued
The sailor, and the pilot to the helm.   935
   Hard by these shores, where scarce his freezing stream
Rolls the wild Oby,[113] live the last of men;
And, half enlivened by the distant sun,
That rears and ripens man as well as plants,
Here human nature wears its rudest form.   940
Deep from the piercing season sunk in caves,
Here by dull fires and with unjoyous cheer
They waste the tedious gloom. Immersed in furs
Doze the gross race, nor sprightly jest nor song
Nor tenderness they know, nor aught of life   945
Beyond the kindred bears that stalk without;
Till Morn at length, her roses drooping all,
Sheds a long twilight brightening o'er their fields,
And calls the quivered savage to the chase.
   What cannot active government perform,   950
New-molding man? Wide-stretching from these shores,
A people savage from remotest time,
A huge neglected empire, one vast mind
By Heaven inspired from Gothic darkness called.

---

[112] Sir Hugh Willoughby in 1553 sought a northern trade route to India; one vessel reached Archangel; the other two were driven back from Nova Zembla to the mouth of the *Arzina* (l. 930) in Lapland, where the frozen bodies of the crews were later found.
[113] the great Ob River in Siberia.

Immortal Peter! [114] first of monarchs! He   955
His stubborn country tamed, her rocks, her fens,
Her floods, her seas, her ill-submitting sons;
And, while the fierce barbarian he subdued,
To more exalted soul he raised the man.
Ye shades of ancient heroes, ye who toiled   960
Through long successive ages to build up
A laboring plan of state, behold at once
The wonder done! behold the matchless prince!
Who left his native throne, where reigned till then
A mighty shadow of unreal power;   965
Who greatly spurned the slothful pomp of courts;
And, roaming every land, in every port
His scepter laid aside, with glorious hand
Unwearied plying the mechanic tool,
Gathered the seeds of trade, of useful arts,   970
Of civil wisdom, and of martial skill.
Charged with the stores of Europe home he goes!
Then cities rise amid th' illumined waste;
O'er joyless deserts smiles the rural reign;
Far-distant flood to flood is social joined;[115]   975
Th' astonished Euxine hears the Baltic roar;
Proud navies ride on seas that never foamed
With daring keel before; and armies stretch
Each way their dazzling files, repressing here
The frantic Alexander of the north,[116]   980
And awing there stern Othman's shrinking sons.[117]
Sloth flies the land, and ignorance and vice
Of old dishonor proud; it glows around,
Taught by the royal hand that roused the whole,
One scene of arts, of arms, of rising trade: 985

[114] Peter the Great of Russia (1672-1725), who traveled and studied in western Europe in order to bring new technology as well as arts to Russia. His travels in 1697-98 included Germany, Holland, England, and Austria (cf. l. 967), and he worked at shipbuilding in both England and Holland (l. 969).

[115] Probably a reference to Peter's plans for connecting the Euxine (or Black) Sea with the Baltic by a series of canals.

[116] Charles XII of Sweden, defeated at Poltava in 1709.

[117] the Turks.

For, what his wisdom planned and power enforced,
More potent still his great example showed.

Muttering, the winds at eve with blunted point
Blow hollow-blustering from the south. Subdued,
The frost resolves into a trickling thaw.   990
Spotted the mountains shine; loose sleet descends
And floods the country round. The rivers swell,
Of bonds impatient. Sudden from the hills,
O'er rocks and woods, in broad brown cataracts,
A thousand snow-fed torrents shoot at once;   995
And, where they rush, the wide-resounding plain
Is left one slimy waste. Those sullen seas,
That wash th' ungenial pole, will rest no more
Beneath the shackles of the mighty north,
But, rousing all their waves, resistless heave.   1000
And hark! the lengthening roar continuous runs
Athwart the rifted deep; at once it bursts,
And piles a thousand mountains to the clouds.
Ill fares the bark, with trembling wretches charged,
That, tossed amid the floating fragments, moors   1005
Beneath the shelter of an icy isle,
While night o'erwhelms the sea, and horror looks
More horrible. Can human force endure
Th' assembled mischiefs that besiege them round—
Heart-gnawing hunger, fainting weariness,   1010
The roar of winds and waves, the crush of ice,
Now ceasing, now renewed with louder rage,
And in dire echoes bellowing round the main.
More to embroil the deep, Leviathan[118]
And his unwieldy train in dreadful sport   1015
Tempest the loosened brine; while through the gloom
Far from the bleak inhospitable shore,
Loading the winds, is heard the hungry howl
Of famished monsters, there awaiting wrecks.
Yet Providence, that ever-waking Eye,   1020
Looks down with pity on the feeble toil
Of mortals lost to hope, and lights them safe

---

[118] the whale (cf. *Paradise Lost,* VII 410-14).

Through all this dreary labyrinth of fate.
　'Tis done! Dread Winter spreads his latest glooms
And reigns tremendous o'er the conquered year.　　　　1025
How dead the vegetable kingdom lies!
How dumb the tuneful! Horror wide extends
His desolate domain. Behold, fond man!
See here thy pictured life; pass some few years,
Thy flowering Spring, thy Summer's ardent strength,　　1030
Thy sober Autumn fading into age,
And pale concluding Winter comes at last
And shuts the scene. Ah! whither now are fled
Those dreams of greatness? those unsolid hopes
Of happiness? those longings after fame?　　　　　　1035
Those restless cares? those busy bustling days?
Those gay-spent festive nights? those veering thoughts,
Lost between good and ill, that shared thy life?
All now are vanished! Virtue sole survives,
Immortal, never-failing friend of man,　　　　　　　1040
His guide to happiness on high. And see!
'Tis come, the glorious morn! the second birth
Of heaven and earth! awakening Nature hears
The new-creating Word, and starts to life
In every heightened form, from pain and death　　　1045
Forever free. The great eternal scheme,
Involving all and in a perfect whole
Uniting, as the prospect wider spreads,
To reason's eye refined clears up apace.
Ye vainly wise! ye blind presumptuous! now,　　　1050
Confounded in the dust, adore that Power
And Wisdom oft arraigned: see now the cause
Why unassuming worth in secret lived
And died neglected; why the good man's share
In life was gall and bitterness of soul;　　　　　1055
Why the lone widow and her orphans pined
In starving solitude, while Luxury
In palaces lay straining her low thought
To form unreal wants; why heaven-born Truth
And Moderation fair wore the red marks　　　　　　1060

Of Superstition's scourge; why licensed [119] Pain,
That cruel spoiler, that embosomed foe,
Embittered all our bliss. Ye good distressed!
Ye noble few! who here unbending stand
Beneath life's pressure, yet bear up a while,   1065
And what your bounded view, which only saw
A little part, deemed evil is no more.
The storms of wintry time will quickly pass,
And one unbounded Spring encircle all.

[119] permitted by Providence.

❧ *Edward Young* ☙

Edward Young (1683-1765) was born at Upham, educated at Winchester and Oxford. He sought a career in law or politics and wrote fashionable religious poetry, tragedies, and satires, notably *The Universal Passion* (1725-28) on the "Love of Fame." (These last may have influenced Pope.) He took holy orders in 1724 and, with literary success, was made one of the chaplains of the King; in 1730 he became rector of Welwyn, where he remained for the rest of his life. He married Lady Elizabeth Lee in 1731; her death ten years later may have precipitated the melancholy which Young dramatizes in *Night Thoughts*. This cycle of nine nights of meditation and argument, with its fusion of Miltonic forms and Augustan (at times Metaphysical) wit, became enormously influential, especially in Germany and France. Young's last work was his *Conjectures on Original Composition* (1759), a critical essay addressed to the novelist Richardson in which Young sets forth the doctrines of genius ("Reverence thyself") and sublimity with great eloquence. Young's use of night (as the setting of meditation on things beyond the daylight world of human involvement), of graveyard imagery (to dramatize the emptiness of this world taken as an end in itself), and of dazzling apostrophes and paradoxes (to shock conventional attitudes and to dramatize the energy of flight above them) tie him to many of the deliberately "enthusiastic" writers of his time.

Editions: Complete Works, ed. J. Nichols (1854); *Poetical Works,* ed. J. Mitford (1830-36).

Biography: H. C. Beeching, *Life and Letters of Edward Young* (1914).

Critical Studies: George Eliot, "Worldliness and Other-Worldliness: The Poet Young" (1857; see collections of her works); W. Thomas, *Le poète Edward Young* (1901); Isabel St. John Bliss, "Young's

Night Thoughts in Relation to Contemporary Christian Apologetics," *PMLA* 49 (1934).

The Complaint; Or, Night Thoughts on Life, Death, and Immortality

NIGHT I
[1742]

Tired Nature's sweet restorer, balmy Sleep!
He, like the world, his ready visit pays
Where Fortune smiles; the wretched he forsakes;
Swift on his downy pinion flies from woe,
And lights on lids unsullied with a tear.   5
   From short (as usual) and disturbed repose,
I wake: how happy they who wake no more!
Yet that were vain, if dreams infest the grave.
I wake, emerging from a sea of dreams
Tumultuous; where my wrecked desponding thought   10
From wave to wave of fancied misery
At random drove, her helm of reason lost.
Though now restored, 'tis only change of pain,
(A bitter change) severer for severe.
The day too short for my distress; and Night,   15
Even in the zenith of her dark domain,
Is sunshine to the color of my fate.
   Night, sable goddess, from her ebon throne,
In rayless majesty now stretches forth
Her leaden scepter o'er a slumbering world.   20
Silence, how dead! and darkness, how profound!
Nor eye nor listening ear an object finds;
Creation sleeps. 'Tis as the general pulse
Of life stood still, and Nature made a pause;
An awful pause, prophetic of her end.   25
And let her prophecy be soon fulfilled;
Fate, drop the curtain; I can lose no more.

Silence and Darkness, solemn sisters, twins
From ancient Night, who nurse the tender thought
To reason, and on reason build resolve   30
(That column of true majesty in man),
Assist me: I will thank you in the grave;
The grave, your kingdom: there this frame shall fall
A victim sacred to your dreary shrine.
But what are ye?—Thou who didst put to flight   35
Primeval silence, when the morning stars,
Exalted, shouted o'er the rising ball;[1]
O Thou, whose word from solid darkness struck
That spark, the sun; strike wisdom from my soul;
My soul, which flies to Thee, her trust, her treasure,   40
As misers to their gold, while others rest.
    Through this opaque of nature and of soul,
This double night, transmit one pitying ray
To lighten and to cheer. Oh, lead my mind
(A mind that fain would wander from its woe),   45
Lead it through various scenes of life and death;
And from each scene the noblest truths inspire.
Nor less inspire my conduct than my song;
Teach my best reason, reason; my best will
Teach rectitude; and fix my firm resolve   50
Wisdom to wed, and pay her long arrear:
Nor let the phial of thy vengeance, poured
On this devoted [1a] head, be poured in vain.
    The bell strikes one. We take no note of time
But from its loss. To give it then a tongue   55
Is wise in man. As if an angel spoke,
I feel the solemn sound. If heard aright,
It is the knell of my departed hours:
Where are they? With the years beyond the flood.
It is the signal that demands dispatch: 60
How much is to be done? My hopes and fears
Start up alarmed, and o'er life's narrow verge
Look down—on what? a fathomless abyss,
A dread eternity, how surely mine!

[1] Cf. Job 38:7: "When the morning stars sang together, and all the
sons of God shouted for joy."
[1a] doomed.

And can eternity belong to me,   65
Poor pensioner on the bounties of an hour?
   How poor, how rich, how abject, how august,
How complicate, how wonderful is man!
How passing wonder He who made him such!
Who centered in our make such strange extremes;   70
From different natures marvellously mixed,
Connection exquisite of distant worlds!
Distinguished link in being's endless chain,[2]
Midway from nothing to the Deity!
A beam ethereal, sullied and absorpt,   75
Though sullied and dishonored, still divine!
Dim miniature of greatness absolute:
An heir of glory! a frail child of dust!
Helpless immortal! insect infinite!
A worm! a god!—I tremble at myself,   80
And in myself am lost! At home a stranger,
Thought wanders up and down, surprised, aghast,
And wondering at her own: how reason reels!
Oh, what a miracle to man is man,
Triumphantly distressed! what joy, what dread!   85
Alternately transported and alarmed!
What can preserve my life? or what destroy?
An angel's arm can't snatch me from the grave;
Legions of angels can't confine me there.
   'Tis past conjecture; all things rise in proof: 90
While o'er my limbs sleep's soft dominion spread,
What though my soul fantastic measures trod
O'er fairy fields; or mourned along the gloom
Of pathless woods; or down the craggy steep
Hurled headlong, swam with pain the mantled[3] pool;   95
Or scaled the cliff, or danced on hollow[4] winds?
With antic shapes, wild natives of the brain?

[2] Young refers here and in surrounding lines to the Great Chain of Being, the scale which reaches from inanimate nature through vegetative forms to rational and angelic, finally to God. These lines should be compared with the opening of the second epistle of Pope's *Essay on Man.*
[3] hooded with foliage.
[4] insubstantial.

Her ceaseless flight, though devious, speaks her nature
Of subtler essence than the trodden clod;
Active, aërial, towering, unconfined,   100
Unfettered with her gross companion's[5] fall.
Even silent night proclaims my soul immortal;
Even silent night proclaims eternal day.
For human weal, Heaven husbands all events;
Dull sleep instructs, nor sport vain dreams in vain.   105
    Why then their loss deplore, that are not lost?
Why wanders wretched thought their tombs around,
In infidel distress? Are angels there?
Slumbers, raked up in dust, ethereal fire?
    They live! they greatly live a life on earth   110
Unkindled, unconceived; and from an eye
Of tenderness let heavenly pity fall
On me, more justly numbered with the dead.
This is the desert, this the solitude:
How populous, how vital, is the grave!   115
This is creation's melancholy vault,
The vale funereal, the sad cypress gloom;
The land of apparitions, empty shades!
All, all on earth is shadow, all beyond
Is substance; the reverse is Folly's creed: 120
How solid all, where change shall be no more!
    This is the bud of being, the dim dawn,
The twilight of our day, the vestibule.
Life's theater as yet is shut, and Death,
Strong Death, alone can heave the massy bar,   125
This gross impediment of clay remove,
And makes us embryos of existence free.
From real life but little more remote
Is he, not yet a candidate for light,
The future embryo slumbering in his sire.   130
Embryos we must be till we burst the shell,
Yon ambient azure shell, and spring to life,
The life of gods, oh transport! and of man.
    Yet man, fool man! here buries all his thoughts;
Inters celestial hopes without one sigh.   135

[5] body's.

Prisoner of earth and pent beneath the moon,
Here pinions all his wishes; winged by Heaven
To fly at infinite and reach it there
Where seraphs gather immortality
On life's fair tree, fast by the throne of God.   140
What golden joys ambrosial clustering glow
In His full beam and ripen for the just,
Where momentary ages are no more!
Where time, and pain, and chance, and death expire!
And is it in the flight of threescore years   145
To push eternity from human thought
And smother souls immortal in the dust?
A soul immortal, spending all her fires,
Wasting her strength in strenuous idleness,
Thrown into tumult, raptured or alarmed   150
At aught this scene can threaten or indulge,
Resembles ocean into tempest wrought
To waft a feather or to drown a fly.
   Where falls this censure? It o'erwhelms myself;
How was my heart incrusted by the world!   155
Oh, how self-fettered was my groveling soul!
How like a worm was I wrapped round and round
In silken thought which reptile Fancy spun,
Till darkened Reason lay quite clouded o'er
With soft conceit of endless comfort here,   160
Nor yet put forth her wings to reach the skies!
   Night-visions may befriend (as sung above):
Our waking dreams are fatal. How I dreamt
Of things impossible! (could sleep do more?)
Of joys perpetual in perpetual change,   165
Of stable pleasures on the tossing wave,
Eternal sunshine in the storms of life!
How richly were my noontide trances hung
With gorgeous tapestries of pictured joys,
Joy behind joy in endless perspective!   170
Till at Death's toll, whose restless iron tongue
Calls daily for his millions at a meal,
Starting I woke, and found myself undone.
Where now my frenzy's pompous furniture?

The cobwebbed cottage, with its ragged wall   175
Of moldering mud, is royalty to me!
The spider's most attenuated thread
Is cord, is cable, to man's tender tie
On earthly bliss; it breaks at every breeze.
    Oh, ye blessed scenes of permanent delight!   180
Full above measure, lasting beyond bound!
A perpetuity of bliss is bliss.
Could you, so rich in rapture, fear an end,
That ghastly thought would drink up all your joy
And quite unparadise the realms of light.   185
Safe are you lodged above these rolling spheres,[6]
The baleful influence of whose giddy dance
Sheds sad vicissitude on all beneath.
Here teems with revolutions every hour;
And rarely for the better; or the best,   190
More mortal [7] than the common births of Fate.
Each Moment has its sickle, emulous
Of Time's enormous scythe, whose ample sweep
Strikes empires from the root; each Moment plays
His little weapon in the narrower sphere   195
Of sweet domestic comfort, and cuts down
The fairest bloom of sublunary[8] bliss.
    Bliss! sublunary bliss!—proud words, and vain;
Implicit treason to divine decree.
A bold invasion of the rights of Heaven!   200
I clasped the phantoms, and I found them air.
Oh, had I weighed it ere my fond embrace,
What darts of agony had missed my heart!
    Death, great proprietor of all, 'tis thine
To tread out empire and to quench the stars.   205
The sun himself by thy permission shines,
And one day thou shalt pluck him from his sphere.

[6] planets, whose *influence* (l. 187), determined by their position at an individual's birth or at a moment of action, was traditionally believed to affect human lives.
[7] deadly.
[8] All that existed below the circle of the moon was believed subject to change; thus, earthly and transient.

Amid such mighty plunder, why exhaust
Thy partial quiver on a mark so mean?
Why thy peculiar rancor wreaked on me?   210
Insatiate archer, could not one suffice?
Thy shaft flew thrice; and thrice my peace was slain;
And thrice,[9] ere thrice yon moon had filled her horn.
O Cynthia! [10] why so pale? dost thou lament
Thy wretched neighbor? Grieve to see thy wheel   215
Of ceaseless change outwhirled in human life?
How wanes my borrowed bliss! from Fortune's smile
Precarious courtesy; not virtue's sure,
Self-given, solar ray of sound delight.
    In every varied posture, place, and hour,   220
How widowed every thought of every joy!
Thought, busy thought, too busy for my peace!
Through the dark postern[11] of time long elapsed
Led softly, by the stillness of the night—
Led like a murderer (and such it proves!)   225
Strays (wretched rover!) o'er the pleasing past;
In quest of wretchedness perversely strays;
And finds all desert now; and meets the ghosts
Of my departed joys; a numerous train.
I rue the riches of my former fate;   230
Sweet comfort's blasted clusters I lament;
I tremble at the blessings once so dear;
And every pleasure pains me to the heart.
    Yet why complain? or why complain for one?
Hangs out the sun his lustre but for me,   235
The single man? Are angels all beside?
I mourn for millions; 'tis the common lot;
In this shape or in that has fate entailed [12]
The mother's throes on all of woman born,
Not more the children, than sure heirs, of pain.   240

[9] The poet speaks of three losses within three months. Young's own stepdaughter died in 1736 and his wife four years later; the identity of Philander (l. 344) is not certain.

[10] the moon as goddess.

[11] back gate or passage.

[12] imposed.

War, famine, pest, volcano, storm, and fire,
Intestine broils, Oppression with her heart
Wrapped up in triple brass, besiege mankind.
God's image disinherited of day,
Here, plunged in mines, forgets a sun was made.   245
There, beings deathless as their haughty lord
Are hammered to the galling oar for life;
And plough the winter's wave, and reap despair.
Some, for hard masters, broken under arms,
In battle lopped away, with half their limbs,   250
Beg bitter bread through realms their valor saved,
If so the tyrant or his minion doom.
Want and incurable disease (fell pair)
On hopeless multitudes remorseless seize
At once, and make a refuge of the grave.   255
How groaning hospitals eject their dead!
What numbers groan for sad admission there!
What numbers, once in Fortune's lap high-fed,
Solicit the cold hand of Charity—
To shock us more, solicit it in vain!   260
Ye silken sons of Pleasure! since in pains
You rue more modish visits, visit here,
And breathe from your debauch: give, and reduce
Surfeit's dominion o'er you; but, so great
Your impudence, you blush at what is right.   265
    Happy! did sorrow seize on such alone.
Not prudence can defend or virtue save;
Disease invades the chastest temperance,
And punishment the guiltless; and alarm
Through thickest shades pursues the fond of peace.   270
Man's caution often into danger turns,
And, his guard falling, crushes him to death.
Not Happiness itself makes good her name!
Our very wishes give us not our wish.
How distant oft the thing we dote on most,   275
From that for which we dote, felicity!
The smoothest course of nature has its pains;
And truest friends, through error, wound our rest.
Without misfortune, what calamities,

And what hostilities, without a foe!   280
Nor are foes wanting to the best on earth—
But endless is the list of human ills,
And sighs might sooner fail, than cause to sigh.
    A part how small of the terraqueous[13] globe
Is tenanted by man! the rest a waste,   285
Rocks, deserts, frozen seas, and burning sands:
Wild haunts of monsters, poisons, stings, and death.
Such is earth's melancholy map! But, far
More sad, this earth is a true map of man.
So bounded are its haughty lord's delights   290
To woe's wide empire; where deep troubles toss,
Loud sorrows howl, envenomed passions bite,
Ravenous calamities our vitals seize,
And threatening Fate wide opens to devour.
    What then am I, who sorrow for myself?   295
In age, in infancy, from others' aid
Is all our hope, to teach us to be kind.
That, Nature's first, last lesson to mankind;
The selfish heart deserves the pain it feels;
More generous sorrow, while it sinks, exalts;   300
And conscious virtue mitigates the pang.
Nor virtue, more than prudence, bids me give
Swoln thought a second channel; who divide,
They weaken too, the torrent of their grief.
Take then, O world! thy much-indebted tear;   305
How sad a sight is human happiness
To those whose thought can pierce beyond an hour!
O thou, whate'er thou art, whose heart exults,
Wouldst thou I should congratulate thy fate?
I know thou wouldst; thy pride demands it from me.   310
Let thy pride pardon what thy nature needs,
The salutary censure of a friend.
Thou happy wretch! by blindness art thou blessed,
By dotage dandled to perpetual smiles.
Know, smiler, at thy peril art thou pleased;   315
Thy pleasure is the promise of thy pain.
Misfortune, like a creditor severe,

[13] covered with land and water.

But rises in demand for her delay;
She makes a scourge of past prosperity,
To sting thee more and double thy distress.   320
    Lorenzo,[14] Fortune makes her court to thee;
Thy fond [15] heart dances while the siren sings.
Dear is thy welfare; think me not unkind;
I would not damp,[16] but to secure[17] thy joys.
Think not that fear is sacred to the storm;   325
Stand on thy guard against the smiles of Fate.
Is Heaven tremendous in its frowns? Most sure;
And in its favors formidable too:
Its favors here are trials, not rewards,
A call to duty, not discharge from care;   330
And should alarm us, full as much as woes,
Awake us to their cause and consequence,
And make us tremble, weighed with our desert;
Awe Nature's tumult and chastise her joys,
Lest while we clasp, we kill them; nay, invert   355
To worse than simple misery, their charms.
Revolted joys, like foes in civil war,
Like bosom friendships to resentments soured,
With rage envenomed rise against our peace.
Beware what earth calls happiness; beware   340
All joys but joys that never can expire.
Who builds on less than an immortal base,
Fond as he seems, condemns his joys to death.
    Mine died with thee, Philander! thy last sight
Dissolved the charm; the disenchanted earth   345
Lost all her lustre. Where her glittering towers?
Her golden mountains, where? all darkened down
To naked waste; a dreary vale of tears:
The great magician's dead! Thou poor, pale piece
Of outcast earth, in darkness! what a change   350
From yesterday! Thy darling hope so near
(Long-labored prize), oh, how ambition flushed

---

[14] the irreligious young libertine to whom the poem is addressed.
[15] foolish.
[16] discourage.
[17] make safe.

Thy glowing cheek, ambition truly great,
Of virtuous praise. Death's subtle seed within,
(Sly, treacherous miner) working in the dark,   355
Smiled at thy well-concerted scheme, and beckoned
The worm to riot on that rose so red,
Unfaded ere it fell—one moment's prey!
   Man's foresight is conditionally wise;
Lorenzo, wisdom into folly turns   360
Oft, the first instant its idea fair
To laboring thought is born. How dim our eye!
The present moment terminates our sight;
Clouds, thick as those on doomsday, drown the next;
We penetrate, we prophesy in vain.   365
Time is dealt out by particles; and each,
Ere mingled with the streaming sands of life,
By fate's inviolable oath is sworn
Deep silence, "where eternity begins." [18]
   By Nature's law, what may be, may be now;   370
There's no prerogative in human hours.
In human hearts what bolder thought can rise
Than man's presumption on tomorrow's dawn?
Where is tomorrow? In another world.
For numbers this is certain; the reverse   375
Is sure to none; and yet on this Perhaps,
This Peradventure, infamous for lies,
As on a rock of adamant we build
Our mountain hopes, spin out eternal schemes,
As we the Fatal Sisters could outspin,   380
And, big with life's futurities, expire.
   Not even Philander had bespoke his shroud.
Nor had he cause; a warning was denied:
How many fall as sudden, not as safe;
As sudden, though for years admonished home.   385
Of human ills the last extreme beware—
Beware, Lorenzo, a slow-sudden death.
How dreadful that deliberate surprise!
Be wise today; 'tis madness to defer;
Next day the fatal precedent will plead;   390

[18] That is, *silence* as to *where* each man's *eternity begins.*

Thus on, till wisdom is pushed out of life.
Procrastination is the thief of time;
Year after year it steals, till all are fled,
And to the mercies of a moment leaves
The vast concerns of an eternal scene.   395
If not so frequent, would not this be strange?
That 'tis so frequent, this is stranger still.
   Of man's miraculous mistakes, this bears
The palm, "That all men are about to live,"
Forever on the brink of being born.   400
All pay themselves the compliment to think
They one day shall not drivel: and their pride
On this reversion[19] takes up ready praise;
At least, their own; their future selves applauds;
How excellent that life they ne'er will lead!   405
Time lodged in their own hands is Folly's vails;[20]
That lodged in Fate's, to Wisdom they consign;
The thing they can't but purpose, they postpone;
'Tis not in Folly not to scorn a fool;
And scarce in human Wisdom to do more.   410
All promise is poor dilatory man,
And that through every stage: when young, indeed,
In full content we sometimes nobly rest,
Unanxious for ourselves, and only wish,
As duteous sons, our fathers were more wise.   415
At thirty man suspects himself a fool;
Knows it at forty, and reforms his plan;
At fifty chides his infamous delay,
Pushes his prudent purpose to resolve;
In all the magnanimity[21] of thought   420
Resolves; and re-resolves; then dies the same.
   And why? Because he thinks himself immortal.
All men think all men mortal but themselves;
Themselves, when some alarming shock of Fate
Strikes through their wounded hearts the sudden dread; 425
But their hearts wounded, like the wounded air,

[19] expectation of future possession.
[20] tips, gifts (to Folly).
[21] boldness, loftiness.

Soon close; where passed the shaft no trace is found.
As from the wing no scar the sky retains,
The parted wave no furrow from the keel,
So dies in human hearts the thought of death.   430
Even with the tender tear which Nature sheds
O'er those we love, we drop it in their grave.
Can I forget Philander? That were strange!
Oh, my full heart—But should I give it vent,
The longest night, though longer far, would fail,   435
And the lark[22] listen to my midnight song.
    The sprightly lark's shrill matin wakes the morn;
Grief's sharpest thorn hard-pressing on my breast,
I strive, with wakeful melody, to cheer
The sullen gloom, sweet Philomel,[23] like thee,   440
And call the stars to listen: every star
Is deaf to mine, enamored of thy lay.
Yet be not vain; there are who thine excel
And charm through distant ages: wrapped in shade,
Prisoner of darkness, to the silent hours,   445
How often I repeat their rage divine,
To lull my griefs, and steal my heart from woe!
I roll their raptures, but not catch their fire.
Dark, though not blind like thee, Maeonides,[24]
Or, Milton, thee; ah, could I reach your strain!   450
Or his,[25] who made Maeonides our own,
Man too he sung:[26] immortal man I sing;
Oft bursts my song beyond the bounds of life;
What now but immortality can please?
Oh, had he pressed his theme, pursued the track,   455
Which opens out of darkness into day!
Oh, had he, mounted on his wing of fire,
Soared where I sink, and sung immortal man,
How had it blessed mankind, and rescued me!

[22] as bird of dawn.
[23] the nightingale.
[24] Homer.
[25] Pope's, as translator of Homer.
[26] Pope's *Essay on Man* (1733-34) to which Young both likens and contrasts his poem. See note to l. 73, above.

❧ William Collins ❧

The facts of the life of William Collins (1721-59) are few and pathetic. Born in Chichester, Sussex, he was educated at Winchester and Oxford. His *Persian Eclogues* (1742) were published while he was still at Oxford, which he left for a precarious literary existence in London. A few years after the publication of his *Odes on Several Descriptive and Allegoric Subjects* (1746), he went mad, and remained so with rational intervals until he died.

Collins used the flexible form of the ode to accommodate varied, and sometimes new, poetic subjects and attitudes. *The Passions,* a once popular declamation piece, should be compared with two of its models, Dryden's *Song for St. Cecilia's Day* and *Alexander's Feast;* the *Ode to Evening* achieves greater freshness, in spite of what it owes to Milton. The concept of Fancy in the *Ode on the Poetical Character* foreshadows Coleridge's definition of the Imagination. In this poem, Collins emphasizes rapture and sublimity as the poet's proper aims, while in the *Ode on the Popular Superstitions of the Highlands* he finds new poetic subjects in the marvelous and supernatural. At its best, Collins' poetry contains passages of descriptive vividness and rhetorical power.

Editions: Poems, ed. Christopher Stone, rev. F. Page (1937); *Drafts and Fragments of Verse,* ed. J. S. Cunningham (1956).

Biography: E. G. Ainsworth, *Poor Collins,* 1937.

Critical Studies: H. W. Garrod, *Collins* (1928); A. S. P. Woodhouse, "Collins and the Creative Imagination," *Studies in English by Members of University College, Toronto* (1931); Norman Maclean, "From Action to Image, Theories of the Lyric in the Eighteenth Century," *Critics and Criticism,* ed. R. S. Crane (1952).

Ode on the Poetical Character
[1746]

1

As once—if not with light regard
I read aright that gifted bard
(Him whose school above the rest
His loveliest Elfin queen has blessed)—
One, only one, unrivalled fair,   5
Might hope the magic girdle wear,
At solemn tourney hung on high,
The wish of each love-darting eye;

Lo! to each other nymph in turn applied,
    As if, in air unseen, some hovering hand,   10
Some chaste and angel friend to virgin fame,
    With whispered spell had burst the starting band,
It left unblessed her loathed dishonored side;
    Happier, hopeless fair, if never
Her baffled hand with vain endeavor   15
Had touched that fatal zone to her denied![1]
Young Fancy thus, to me divinest name,
    To whom, prepared and bathed in Heaven,
    The cest[2] of amplest power is given:
    To few the godlike gift assigns,   20
    To gird their blessed prophetic loins,
And gaze[3] her visions wild, and feel unmixed her flame!

[1] In Spenser's *Faerie Queene* (IV v 1-20), Florimel's girdle (zone, band)
could be worn only by a virtuous woman. Collins did not quite read Spenser
"aright."

[2] Florimel's girdle was named Cestus (Greek, *kestos,* girdle).

[3] gaze on, be struck by.

2

The band, as fairy legends say,
Was wove on that creating day,
When He who called with thought to birth   25
Yon tented sky, this laughing earth,
And dressed with springs, and forests tall,
And poured the main engirting all,
Long by the loved enthusiast[4] wooed,
Himself in some diviner mood,   30
Retiring, sate with her alone,
And placed her on his sapphire throne,
The whiles, the vaulted shrine around,
Seraphic wires[5] were heard to sound,
Now sublimest triumph swelling,   35
Now on love and mercy dwelling;
And she, from out the veiling cloud,
Breathed her magic notes aloud:
And thou, thou rich-haired Youth of Morn,[6]
And all thy subject life was born!   40
The dangerous Passions kept aloof,
Far from the sainted growing woof,[7]
But near it sate ecstatic Wonder,
Listening the deep applauding thunder,
And Truth, in sunny vest arrayed,   45
By whose the tarsel's[8] eyes were made;
All the shadowy tribes of Mind
In braided dance their murmurs joined,
And all the bright uncounted Powers
Who feed on Heaven's ambrosial flowers.   50
Where is the bard whose soul can now

[4] Fancy. "Enthusiast" implies one divinely inspired or possessed.
[5] metallic strings of a musical instrument.
[6] Apollo literally; the sun, and perhaps the poet, metaphorically.
[7] threads, cloth (of the cestus).
[8] tercel, male hawk.

Its high presuming hopes avow?
Where he who thinks, with rapture blind,
This hallowed work[9] for him designed?

3

High on some cliff, to Heaven up-piled,[10]   55
Of rude access, of prospect wild,
Where, tangled round the jealous steep,
Strange shades o'erbrow the valleys deep,
And holy genii guard the rock,
Its glooms embrown, its springs unlock,   60
While on its rich ambitious head
An Eden, like his own, lies spread,
I view that oak,[11] the fancied glades among,
By which as Milton lay, his evening ear,
From many a cloud that dropped ethereal dew,   65
Nigh sphered in Heaven, its native strains could hear;
On which that ancient trump he reached was hung.
    Thither oft, his glory greeting,
    From Waller's[12] myrtle shades retreating,
With many a vow from Hope's aspiring tongue,   70
My trembling feet his guiding steps pursue;
    In vain—such bliss to one alone,
    Of all the sons of soul was known,
    And Heaven and Fancy, kindred powers,
    Have now o'erturned th' inspiring bowers,   75
Or curtained close such scene from every future view.

[9] cestus.

[10] Collins envisages the mount of poetry (cf. Mt. Parnassus) as resembling Milton's Eden, whose "champaign head" crowns a "steep wilderness" etc. (*Paradise Lost*, iv 131-43).

[11] Milton refers to listening to the nightingale near "th' accustomed oak" in *Il Penseroso* (ll. 55-64).

[12] Edmund Waller (1606-87) was remembered for the sweetness of his lyrics (myrtle being associated with love). Apparently Collins is indicating his own shift in poetic interest from his early eclogues to his later odes.

Ode to Evening
[1746]

If aught of oaten stop[1] or pastoral song
May hope, chaste Eve, to soothe thy modest ear,[2]
   Like thy own solemn[3] springs,
   Thy springs and dying gales,

O nymph reserved, while now the bright-haired sun   5
Sits in yon western tent, whose cloudy skirts,[4]
   With brede[5] ethereal wove,
   O'erhang his wavy bed—

Now air is hushed, save where the weak-eyed bat,
With short shrill shriek, flits by on leathern wing;   10
   Or where the beetle winds
   His small but sullen horn,

As oft he rises 'midst the twilight path,
Against the pilgrim borne in heedless hum—
   Now teach me, maid composed,   15
   To breathe some softened strain,

Whose numbers,[6] stealing through thy darkening vale,
May not unseemly with its stillness suit,
   As musing slow, I hail
   Thy genial loved return!   20

For when thy folding-star[7] arising shows
His paly circlet, at his warning lamp

---

[1] shepherd's reed pipe. Here and often in this poem, Collins echoes Milton, especially *Lycidas* ("th' oaten flute") and *L'Allegro*.

[2] The text given here is that of Dodsley's *Collection* (1748). The original text reads: "May hope, O pensive Eve, to soothe thine ear."

[3] Original text reads "brawling."

[4] canopy and curtains of a tent-bed (?).

[5] braid, embroidery.

[6] verses.

[7] a star arising at the time for folding or penning sheep; evening star.

The fragrant Hours, and elves
Who slept in flowers[8] the day,

And many a nymph who wreathes her brows with sedge,   25
And sheds the freshening dew, and, lovelier still,
    The pensive Pleasures sweet
    Prepare thy shadowy car.

Then lead, calm vot'ress, where some sheety lake[9]
Cheers the lone heath, or some time-hallowed pile   30
    Or upland fallows gray
    Reflect its last cool gleam.

But when chill blustering winds or driving rain
Forbid [9a] my willing feet, be mine the hut
    That from the mountain's side   35
    Views wilds, and swelling floods,

And hamlets brown, and dim-discovered spires,
And hears their simple bell, and marks o'er all
    Thy dewy fingers draw
    The gradual dusky veil.   40

While Spring shall pour his showers, as oft he wont,
And bathe thy breathing[10] tresses, meekest Eve;
    While Summer loves to sport
    Beneath thy lingering light;

While sallow Autumn fills thy lap with leaves;   45
Or Winter, yelling through the troublous air,
    Affrights thy shrinking train,
    And rudely rends thy robes;

[8] Original text reads "buds."
[9] Original text reads:

      Then let me rove some wild and heathy scene,
      Or find some ruin midst its dreary dells,
        Whose walls more awful nod
        By thy religious gleams.

[9a] Original text reads "prevent," and in the previous line, "Or if" for
"But when."
[10] emitting fragrance.

So long, sure-found beneath the sylvan shed,[11]
Shall Fancy, Friendship, Science, rose-lipped Health,[12]   50
    Thy gentlest influence own,
    And hymn[13] thy favorite name!

The Passions: An Ode for Music
[1746]

When Music, heavenly maid, was young,
While yet in early Greece she sung,
The Passions oft, to hear her shell,[1]
Thronged around her magic cell,
Exulting, trembling, raging, fainting,   5
Possessed beyond the Muse's painting;
By turns they felt the glowing mind
Disturbed, delighted, raised, refined;
Till once, 'tis said, when all were fired,
Filled with fury, rapt, inspired,   10
From the supporting myrtles round
They snatched her instruments of sound,
And as they oft had heard apart
Sweet lessons of her forceful art,
Each, for madness ruled the hour,   15
Would prove his own expressive power.

First Fear his hand, its skill to try,
    Amid the chords bewildered laid,
And back recoiled, he knew not why,
    Even at the sound himself had made.   20

Next Anger rushed: his eyes, on fire,
    In lightnings owned his secret stings;
In one rude clash he struck the lyre,
    And swept with hurried hand the strings.

[11] Original text reads: "So long, regardful of thy quiet rule."
[12] Original text reads: "smiling Peace."
[13] Original text reads: "love."

---

[1] lyre (made of stringed tortoise shell).

With woeful measures wan Despair— 25
    Low sullen sounds—his grief beguiled,
A solemn, strange, and mingled air;
    'Twas sad by fits, by starts 'twas wild.

But thou, O Hope, with eyes so fair,
    What was thy delightful measure? 30
Still it whispered promised pleasure,
    And bade the lovely scenes at distance hail!
Still would her touch the strain prolong,
    And from the rocks, the woods, the vale,
She called on Echo still through all the song; 35
    And, where her sweetest theme[2] she chose,
    A soft responsive voice was heard at every close,
And Hope enchanted smiled, and waved her golden hair.

And longer had she sung—but with a frown
    Revenge impatient rose; 40
He threw his blood-stained sword in thunder down,
    And with a withering look
    The war-denouncing[3] trumpet took,
And blew a blast so loud and dread,
Were ne'er prophetic sounds so full of woe. 45
    And ever and anon[4] he beat
    The doubling drum with furious heat;
And though sometimes each dreary pause between,
    Dejected Pity at his side
    Her soul-subduing voice applied, 50
    Yet still he kept his wild unaltered mien,
While each strained ball of sight seemed bursting from his head.

Thy numbers, Jealousy, to naught were fixed,
    Sad proof of thy distressful state;
Of differing themes the veering song was mixed, 55
    And now it courted Love, now raving called on Hate.

With eyes upraised, as one inspired,
Pale Melancholy sate retired,
And from her wild sequestered seat,

[2] presumably love. [3] war-announcing. [4] again.

In notes by distance made more sweet,   60
Poured through the mellow horn her pensive soul;
   And dashing soft from rocks around,
   Bubbling runnels joined the sound;
Through glades and glooms the mingled measure stole,
Or o'er some haunted stream, with fond delay,   65
   Round an holy calm diffusing,
   Love of peace and lonely musing,
In hollow murmurs died away.

But O how altered was its sprightlier tone,
When Cheerfulness, a nymph of healthiest hue,   70
   Her bow across her shoulder flung,
   Her buskins gemmed with morning dew,
Blew an inspiring air, that dale and thicket rung,
   The hunter's call to faun and dryad known!
   The oak-crowned Sisters, and their chaste-eyed Queen,[5] 75
   Satyrs and sylvan boys were seen,
   Peeping from forth their alleys green;
Brown Exercise rejoiced to hear,
   And Sport leaped up, and seized his beechen spear.

Last came Joy's ecstatic trial,   80
He, with viny crown advancing,
   First to the lively pipe his hand addressed,
But soon he saw the brisk awakening viol,
   Whose sweet entrancing voice he loved the best.
   They would have thought who heard the strain,   85
   They saw in Tempe's vale[6] her native maids,
   Amidst the festal sounding shades,
To some unwearied minstrel dancing,
   While, as his flying fingers kissed the strings,
   Love framed with Mirth a gay fantastic round,   90
   Loose were her tresses seen, her zone unbound,
   And he amidst his frolic play,
As if he[7] would the charming air repay,
Shook thousand odors from his dewy wings.

[5] Artemis and her attendant wood nymphs, the dryads.
[6] a beautiful Greek valley, symbolic of the pastoral life.
[7] Love.

O Music, sphere-descended [8] maid,   95
Friend of Pleasure, Wisdom's aid,
Why, goddess, why, to us denied,
Lay'st thou thy ancient lyre aside?
As in that loved Athenian bower
You learned an all-commanding power,   100
Thy mimic soul, O nymph endeared,
Can well recall what then it heard.
Where is thy native simple heart,
Devote to Virtue, Fancy, Art?
Arise as in that elder time,   105
Warm, energic, chaste, sublime!
Thy wonders, in that godlike age,
Fill thy recording Sister's page—[9]
'Tis said, and I believe the tale,
Thy humblest reed could more prevail,   110
Had more of strength, diviner rage,
Than all which charms this laggard age,
Even all at once together found,
Cecilia's[10] mingled world of sound—
O bid our vain endeavors[11] cease;   115
Revive the just designs of Greece;
Return in all thy simple state;
Confirm the tales her sons relate!

[8] because the harmonious sound supposedly produced by the motion of the spheres is the prototype of earthly music.

[9] a reference either to Clio, the Muse of history, or to one of the Muses of poetry or drama.

[10] St. Cecilia, traditional inventor of the organ, and patron saint of music.

[11] probably a reference to the fashionable Italian opera.

Ode on the Popular Superstitions
of the Highlands of Scotland

CONSIDERED AS THE SUBJECT OF POETRY[1]
[?1749, 1788]

I

H[ome],[2] thou return'st from Thames, whose naiads long
  Have seen thee lingering with a fond delay,
  Mid those soft friends, whose hearts, some future day,
Shall melt, perhaps, to hear thy tragic song.
Go, not unmindful of that cordial youth[3]   5
  Whom, long endeared, thou leav'st by Lavant's side;[4]
Together let us wish him lasting truth,
  And joy untainted with his destined bride.
Go! nor regardless, while these numbers boast
  My short-lived bliss, forget my social name;   10
But think, far off, how, on the southern coast,
  I met thy friendship with an equal flame!
Fresh to that soil thou turn'st,[5] whose every vale
  Shall prompt the poet, and his song demand;
To thee thy copious subjects ne'er shall fail;   15
  Thou need'st but take the pencil to thy hand,
And paint what all believe who own[6] thy genial land.

II

There must thou wake perforce thy Doric[7] quill;
  'Tis Fancy's land to which thou sett'st thy feet;

[1] printed posthumously from a defective manuscript.

[2] the Reverend John Home, an aspiring Scottish dramatist, later known for his neoclassical tragedy, *Douglas*.

[3] Thomas Barrow, who had introduced Home to Collins.

[4] The Lavant runs through Chichester, Collins' home.

[5] Add "toward."

[6] acknowledge as their own.

[7] simple, rustic.

Where still, 'tis said, the fairy people meet,   20
Beneath each birken shade, on mead or hill.
There each trim lass that skims the milky store
    To the swart tribes their creamy bowls allots;[8]
By night they sip it round the cottage door,
    While airy minstrels warble jocund notes.   25
There every herd [9] by sad experience knows
    How, winged with fate, their elf-shot arrows fly,
When the sick ewe her summer food foregoes,
    Or, stretched on earth, the heart-smit heifers lie.
Such airy beings awe th' untutored swain,   30
    Nor thou, though learn'd, his homelier thoughts neglect;
Let thy sweet Muse the rural faith sustain;
    These are the themes of simple, sure effect,
That add new conquests to her boundless reign,
    And fill, with double force, her heart-commanding strain.   35

III

E'en yet preserved, how often mayst thou hear,
    Where to the pole the boreal mountains run,
    Taught by the father to his listening son,
Strange lays, whose power had [10] charmed a Spenser's ear.
At every pause, before thy mind possessed,[11]   40
    Old Runic[12] bards shall seem to rise around,
With uncouth lyres, in many-colored vest,[13]
    Their matted hair with boughs fantastic crowned:
Whether thou bidd'st the well-taught hind [14] repeat
    The choral dirge that mourns some chieftain brave,   45
When every shrieking maid her bosom beat,
    And strewed with choicest herbs his scented grave;
Or whether, sitting in the shepherd's shiel,[15]
    Thou hear'st some sounding tale of war's alarms;
When at the bugle's call, with fire and steel,   50

[8] The "swart tribes" are Brownies, who, according to folklore, helped with the farmwork. If neglected, they revenged themselves by making the animals sick.
    [9] herdsman.   [10] would have.   [11] spellbound.   [12] ancient Scottish.
    [13] vesture, apparel.   [14] peasant.   [15] summer hut.

The sturdy clans poured forth their bony[16] swarms,
And hostile brothers met, to prove each other's arms.

IV

'Tis thine to sing how, framing hideous spells,[17]
   In Skye's lone isle, the gifted wizard seer,
   Lodged in the wintry cave with [   ]   55
Or in the depth of Uist's dark forests dwells:
   How they whose sight such dreary dreams engross
With their own visions oft astonished droop,
   When o'er the watery strath or quaggy moss
They see the gliding ghosts unbodied troop;   60
   Or, if in sports, or on the festive green,
Their [   ] glance some fated youth descry,
   Who now perhaps in lusty vigor seen,
And rosy health, shall soon lamented die.
   For them the viewless forms of air obey,   65
Their bidding heed, and at their beck repair;
   They know what spirit brews the stormful day,
And, heartless,[18] oft like moody madness stare
To see the phantom train their secret work prepare.

V [19]

    .   .   .   .   .

VI

What though far off, from some dark dell espied,   95
   His glimmering mazes cheer th' excursive[20] sight,

[16] perhaps "big-boned"; more likely a form of "bonny," fine-looking or considerable in number.

[17] an account of second sight, probably based on Martin Martin's *Description of the Western Islands of Scotland* (1703). According to Martin, "the vision makes such a lively impression upon the seer[s] that they neither see nor think of anything else except the vision as long as it continues" (p. 300). Skye and the islands of North and South Uist are in the Hebrides.

[18] dismayed, dejected.

[19] A leaf, containing about twenty-five lines, was missing in the manuscript.

[20] ranging.

Yet turn, ye wanderers, turn your steps aside,
    Nor trust the guidance of that faithless light;
For, watchful, lurking mid th' unrustling reed,
    At those mirk[21] hours the wily monster[22] lies,   100
And listens oft to hear the passing steed,
    And frequent round him rolls his sullen eyes,
If chance his savage wrath may some weak wretch surprise.

VII

Ah, luckless swain, o'er all unblessed indeed!
    Whom late bewildered in the dank, dark fen,   105
    Far from his flocks and smoking hamlet then,
To that sad spot [   ]
    On him, enraged, the fiend, in angry mood,
Shall never look with pity's kind concern,
    But instant, furious, raise the whelming flood   110
O'er its drowned bank, forbidding all return.
    Or, if he meditate his wished escape
To some dim hill, that seems uprising near,
    To his faint eye the grim and grisly shape,
In all its terrors clad, shall wild appear.   115
    Meantime the watery surge shall round him rise,
Poured sudden forth from every swelling source.
    What now remains but tears and hopeless sighs?
His fear-shook limbs have lost their youthly force,
And down the waves he floats, a pale and breathless corse!   120

VIII

For him in vain his anxious wife shall wait,
    Or wander forth to meet him on his way;
For him in vain at to-fall [23] of the day,
    His babes shall linger at th' unclosing gate!
Ah, ne'er shall he return! Alone,[24] if night   125
    Her travelled [25] limbs in broken slumbers steep,

[21] murky, dark.
[22] the kelpie, a water spirit (see l. 137).
[23] close.
[24] only.
[25] travailed, wearied.

With drooping willows dressed his mournful sprite
    Shall visit sad, perchance, her silent sleep;
Then he, perhaps, with moist and watery hand,
    Shall fondly seem to press her shuddering cheek,   130
And with his blue-swoln face before her stand,
    And, shivering cold, these piteous accents speak:
"Pursue, dear wife, thy daily toils pursue,
    At dawn or dusk, industrious as before;
Nor e'er of me one hapless thought renew,   135
While I lie weltering on the osiered shore,
Drowned by the kelpie's wrath, nor e'er shall aid thee more!"

IX

Unbounded is thy range: with varied style
    Thy Muse may, like those feathery tribes which spring
    From their rude rocks, extend her skirting wing   140
Round the moist marge of each cold Hebrid isle,
    To that hoar pile which still its ruins shows;
In whose small vaults a pigmy-folk is found,[26]
    Whose bones the delver with his spade upthrows,
And culls them, wondering, from the hallowed ground!   145
Or thither where, beneath the showery West,
    The mighty kings of three fair realms are laid;[27]
Once foes, perhaps, together now they rest;
    No slaves revere them, and no wars invade:
Yet frequent now, at midnight's solemn hour,   150
    The rifted mounds their yawning cells unfold,
And forth the monarchs stalk with sovereign power,
    In pageant robes, and wreathed with sheeny gold,
And on their twilight tombs aërial council hold.

X

But O! o'er all, forget not Kilda's race,[28]   155

[26] According to Martin, certain small bones thought to be those of pigmies or birds were discovered in a stone vault on the island of Benbecula.
[27] Kings of Scotland, Ireland, and Norway were supposed to lie buried together on the island of Iona.
[28] Martin had described St. Kilda, the outermost of the Hebrides, as a place of virtuous simplicity. Collins drew on him for a number of the details in this stanza.

On whose bleak rocks, which brave the wasting tides,
  Fair Nature's daughter, Virtue, yet abides.
Go, just, as they, their blameless manners trace!
  Then to my ear transmit some gentle song
Of those whose lives are yet sincere and plain,   160
  Their bounded walks the rugged cliffs along,
And all their prospect but the wintry main.
  With sparing temperance, at the needful time,
They drain the sainted spring; or, hunger-pressed,
  Along th' Atlantic rock undreading climb,   165
And of its eggs despoil the solan's[29] nest.
  Thus blessed in primal innocence they live,
Sufficed and happy with that frugal fare
  Which tasteful toil and hourly danger give.
Hard is their shallow soil, and bleak and bare;   170
  Nor ever vernal bee was heard to murmur there!

XI

Nor need'st thou blush that such false themes engage
  Thy gentle[30] mind, of fairer stores possessed;
  For not alone they touch the village breast,
But filled in elder time, th' historic page.   175
  There Shakespeare's self, with every garland crowned,
  In musing hour his wayward Sisters found,[31]
And with their terrors dressed the magic scene.
  From them he sung, when, mid his bold design,
Before the Scot, afflicted and aghast,   180
  The shadowy kings of Banquo's fated line
Through the dark cave in gleamy pageant passed.
  Proceed, nor quit the tales which, simply told,
Could once so well my answering bosom pierce;
  Proceed—in forceful sounds and colors bold   185
The native legends of thy land rehearse;
To such adapt thy lyre, and suit thy powerful verse.

[29] solan goose, gannet.
[30] cultivated. "False" (l. 172) means wildly imaginative.
[31] The preceding line may have been lost. A line may also have been lost following l. 200.

XII

In scenes like these, which, daring to depart
  From sober truth, are still to nature true,
And call forth fresh delight to Fancy's view,   190
Th' heroic muse employed her Tasso's art! [32]
  How have I trembled, when, at Tancred's stroke,
Its gushing blood the gaping cypress poured;
  When each live plant with mortal accents spoke,
And the wild blast upheaved the vanished sword!   195
  How have I sat, when piped the pensive wind,
To hear his harp by British Fairfax strung;
  Prevailing poet! whose undoubting mind
Believed the magic wonders which he sung!
  Hence, at each sound, imagination glows;   200
  Hence his warm lay with softest sweetness flows;
Melting it flows, pure, numerous, [33] strong, and clear,
And fills th' impassioned heart, and wins th' harmonious ear.

XIII

All hail, ye scenes that o'er my soul prevail,
Ye [   ] friths and lakes, which, far away,   205
  Are by smooth Annan filled or pastoral Tay,
Or Don's romantic springs; at distance, hail!
The time shall come, when I, perhaps, may tread
  Your lowly glens, o'erhung with spreading broom;
Or, o'er your stretching heaths, by Fancy led;   210
  [   ]
Then will I dress once more the faded bower,
  Where Jonson [34] sat in Drummond's [   ] shade;
Or crop, from Tiviot's dale, each [   ]

---

[32] Edward Fairfax's translation (1600) of Tasso's *Jerusalem Delivered* was reprinted in 1749. The incident of Tancred and the bloody cypress occurs in book 13, stanzas 44 ff.

[33] musical, harmonious.

[34] Ben Jonson visited the Scottish poet, William Drummond of Hawthornden, near Edinburgh, in 1618-19. Drummond published an account of their conversation. Collins is suggesting, of course, a parallel between himself and Home and the two earlier poets.

And mourn, on Yarrow's[35] banks, [   ]   215
Meantime, ye Powers, that on the plains which bore
    The cordial youth, on Lothian's plains,[36] attend,
Where'er he dwell, on hill or lowly muir,
    To him I lose, your kind protection lend,
And, touched with love like mine, preserve my absent friend.   220

[35] The Teviot and Yarrow are Scottish rivers famous in Border ballads
and romances.
[36] Athelstaneford, Home's parish, is in the county of East Lothian.

☙ Thomas Gray ❧

Born in London, Thomas Gray (1716-71) was educated at Eton and Cambridge, and after making the Grand Tour returned to Cambridge to live. Here he spent most of his melancholy and uneventful life in private study of the classics, literature, history, and botany, though he accepted the sinecure of Professor of Modern History in 1768. Gray was a learned man with a special interest in Welsh and Norse literature, but he was temperamentally incapable of completing any of his projected critical or historical studies. He wrote a small number of highly finished poems, among which the *Elegy* was an immediate and immense success, and *The Bard,* one of his own favorites, was popularly condemned as obscure and rhapsodical. Apart from his poetry, Gray is chiefly remembered for his vivid and charming letters.

Though Gray is sometimes considered a transitional or pre-Romantic poet, he has little in common with Wordsworth, who attacked his *Sonnet on West* for its supposed artificiality. (Coleridge neatly managed to attack both the *Sonnet* and Wordsworth's comment on it in the *Biographia Literaria.*) The "romantic" elements in Gray's poetry consist rather in its restrained but intense sense of melancholy, as in the *Eton Ode* and *Elegy,* and in its attempts to reproduce the enthusiastic sublimity of Pindar, as in *The Bard.* Strength of emotion is combined with a "classical" and un-Wordsworthian detachment: the narrator in the *Eton Ode* and the *Elegy* is an onlooker, separated in time or space from the scene he describes. The prospect of Eton is "distant"; in the churchyard, the village forefathers are commented upon by a narrator, who then imagines how he himself will look from the perspective of the future. This treatment of the subject or scene described as an "other" (unlike Wordsworth's tendency to merge subject and object) appears also in the more traditional satiric mode of the two brilliant and neglected poems, *The Candidate* and *On Lord Holland's Seat.*

Editions: Works, ed. Edmund Gosse (1902-06); *Poems,* ed. A. L. Poole, rev. Leonard Whibley (1937); *Correspondence,* ed. Paget Toynbee and Leonard Whibley (1935).

Biography: R. W. Ketton-Cremer, *Thomas Gray* (1955).

Critical Studies: Cleanth Brooks, *The Well Wrought Urn* (1947); F. W. Bateson, *English Poetry* (1950); F. H. Ellis, "Gray's *Elegy,*" *PMLA* 66 (1951); Graham Hough, *The Romantic Poets* (1953); Leon Edel, *Literary Biography* (1957).

Sonnet on the Death of Richard West
[*1742, 1775*]

In vain to me the smiling mornings shine,
   And reddening Phoebus lifts his golden fire;
The birds in vain their amorous descant join,
   Or cheerful fields resume their green attire;
These ears, alas! for other notes repine,   5
   A different object do these eyes require;
My lonely anguish melts no heart but mine,
   And in my breast th' imperfect joys expire.
Yet morning smiles the busy race to cheer,
   And new-born pleasure brings to happier men;   10
The fields to all their wonted tribute bear;
   To warm their little loves the birds complain:
I fruitless mourn to him that cannot hear,
   And weep the more because I weep in vain.

Ode on a Distant Prospect of Eton College[1]
[*1742, 1747*]

"Ανθρωπος · ἱκανὴ πρόφασις εἰς τὸ δυστυχεῖν.
MENANDER[2]

Ye distant spires, ye antique towers,
That crown the wat'ry glade,
Where grateful Science[3] still adores
Her Henry's holy Shade;
And ye, that from the stately brow   5
Of Windsor's heights th' expanse below
Of grove, of lawn, of mead survey,
Whose turf, whose shade, whose flowers among
Wanders the hoary Thames along
His silver-winding way: 10

Ah happy hills, ah pleasing shade,
Ah fields beloved in vain,
Where once my careless childhood strayed,
A stranger yet to pain!
I feel the gales that from ye blow   15
A momentary bliss bestow,
As, waving fresh their gladsome wing,
My weary soul they seem to soothe,
And, redolent of joy and youth,
To breathe a second spring.   20

Say, Father Thames, for thou hast seen
Full many a sprightly race
Disporting on thy margent green
The paths of pleasure trace,

[1] Eton College (i.e., School) was founded in the fifteenth century by the pious Henry VI, whose statue stands in the outer quadrangle. The school lies opposite Windsor Castle on the Thames.

[2] I am a man, a sufficient excuse for misery [Kock, frag. 811].

[3] learning.

Who foremost now delight to cleave   25
With pliant arm thy glassy wave?
The captive linnet which enthrall?
What idle progeny succeed
To chase the rolling circle's speed,
Or urge the flying ball?   30

   While some on earnest business bent
Their murmuring labors ply
'Gainst graver hours, that bring constraint
To sweeten liberty;
Some bold adventurers disdain   35
The limits of their little reign,
And unknown regions dare descry;
Still as they run they look behind,
They hear a voice in every wind,
And snatch a fearful joy.   40

   Gay hope is theirs by fancy fed,
Less pleasing when possessed;
The tear forgot as soon as shed,
The sunshine of the breast;
Theirs buxom health of rosy hue,   45
Wild wit, invention ever new,
And lively cheer of vigor born;
The thoughtless day, the easy night,
The spirits pure, the slumbers light,
That fly th' approach of morn.   50

   Alas, regardless of their doom,
The little victims play!
No sense have they of ills to come,
Nor care beyond today:
Yet see how all around 'em wait   55
The Ministers of human fate,
And black Misfortune's baleful train!
Ah, show them where in ambush stand
To seize their prey the murtherous band!
Ah, tell them, they are men!   60

These shall the fury Passions tear,
The vultures of the mind;
Disdainful Anger, pallid Fear,
And Shame that skulks behind;
Or pining Love shall waste their youth,   65
Or Jealousy with rankling tooth,
That inly gnaws the secret heart,
And Envy wan, and faded Care,
Grim-visaged comfortless Despair,
And Sorrow's piercing dart.   70

Ambition this shall tempt to rise,
Then whirl the wretch from high,
To bitter Scorn a sacrifice,
And grinning Infamy.
The stings of Falsehood those shall try,   75
And hard Unkindness' altered eye,
That mocks the tear it forced to flow;
And keen Remorse with blood defiled,
And moody Madness laughing wild
Amid severest woe.   80

Lo, in the vale of years beneath
A grisly troop are seen,
The painful family[4] of Death,
More hideous than their queen:
This racks the joints, this fires the veins.   85
That every laboring sinew strains,
Those in the deeper vitals rage;
Lo, Poverty, to fill the band,
That numbs the soul with icy hand,
And slow-consuming Age.   90

To each his sufferings; all are men,
Condemned alike to groan:
The tender for another's pain,
Th' unfeeling for his own.
Yet, ah! why should they know their fate?   95
Since sorrow never comes too late,

[4] household companions or servants (Latin, *familia*).

And happiness too swiftly flies.
Thought would destroy their paradise.
No more: where ignorance is bliss,
'Tis folly to be wise.   100

Elegy Written in a Country Churchyard
[?1742-50, 1751]

The curfew tolls the knell of parting day,
  The lowing herd wind slowly o'er the lea,
The ploughman homeward plods his weary way,
  And leaves the world to darkness and to me.

Now fades the glimmering landscape on the sight,   5
  And all the air a solemn stillness holds,
Save where the beetle wheels his droning flight,
  And drowsy tinklings lull the distant folds;

Save that from yonder ivy-mantled tower
  The moping owl does to the moon complain   10
Of such, as wandering near her secret bower,
  Molest her ancient solitary reign.

Beneath those rugged elms, that yew-tree's shade,
  Where heaves the turf in many a moldering heap,
Each in his narrow cell forever laid,   15
  The rude forefathers of the hamlet sleep.

The breezy call of incense-breathing morn,
  The swallow twittering from the straw-built shed,
The cock's shrill clarion, or the echoing horn,
  No more shall rouse them from their lowly bed.   20

For them no more the blazing hearth shall burn,
  Or busy housewife[1] ply her evening care;
No children run to lisp their sire's return,
  Or climb his knees the envied kiss to share.

[1] pronounced *hussif.*

Oft did the harvest to their sickle yield;   25
    Their furrow oft the stubborn glebe has broke;
How jocund did they drive their team afield!
    How bowed the woods beneath their sturdy stroke!

Let not Ambition mock their useful toil,
    Their homely joys, and destiny obscure;   30
Nor Grandeur hear with a disdainful smile
    The short and simple annals of the poor.

The boast of heraldry, the pomp of power,
    And all that beauty, all that wealth e'er gave,
Awaits alike th' inevitable hour:
    The paths of glory lead but to the grave.   35

Nor you, ye proud, impute to these the fault,
    If Memory o'er their tomb no trophies raise,
Where through the long-drawn aisle and fretted vault
    The pealing anthem swells the note of praise.   40

Can storied urn or animated bust
    Back to its mansion call the fleeting breath?
Can Honor's voice provoke[2] the silent dust,
    Or Flattery soothe the dull cold ear of Death?

Perhaps in this neglected spot is laid   45
    Some heart once pregnant with celestial fire;
Hands that the rod of empire might have swayed,
    Or waked to ecstasy the living lyre.

But Knowledge to their eyes her ample page,
    Rich with the spoils of time, did ne'er unroll;   50
Chill Penury repressed their noble rage,
    And froze the genial current[3] of the soul.

Full many a gem of purest ray serene,
    The dark unfathomed caves of ocean bear;
Full many a flower is born to blush unseen,   55
    And waste its sweetness on the desert air.

[2] rouse up.
[3] natural potentialities.

Some village Hampden,[4] that with dauntless breast
    The little tyrant of his fields withstood;
Some mute inglorious Milton here may rest,
    Some Cromwell, guiltless of his country's blood.   60

Th' applause of listening senates to command,
    The threats of pain and ruin to despise,
To scatter plenty o'er a smiling land,
    And read their history in a nation's eyes,

Their lot forbade; nor circumscribed alone   65
    Their growing virtues, but their crimes confined.
Forbade to wade through slaughter to a throne,
    And shut the gates of mercy on mankind;

The struggling pangs of conscious truth to hide,
    To quench the blushes of ingenuous shame,   70
Or heap the shrine of Luxury and Pride
    With incense kindled at the Muse's flame.

Far from the madding crowd's ignoble strife,
    Their sober wishes never learned to stray;
Along the cool sequestered vale of life   75
    They kept the noiseless tenor of their way.

Yet ev'n these bones from insult to protect,
    Some frail memorial still erected nigh,
With uncouth rhymes and shapeless sculpture decked,
    Implores the passing tribute of a sigh   80

Their name, their years, spelt by th' unlettered Muse,
    The place of fame and elegy supply;
And many a holy text around she strews,
    That teach the rustic moralist to die.

For who, to dumb forgetfulness a prey,   85
    This pleasing anxious being e'er resigned,
Left the warm precincts of the cheerful day,
    Nor cast one longing lingering look behind?

[4] John Hampden, who refused to pay a special ship tax levied by
Charles I in 1636.

On some fond breast the parting soul relies,
  Some pious drops the closing eye requires;   90
Ev'n from the tomb the voice of Nature cries,
  Ev'n in our ashes live their wonted fires.

For thee, who mindful of th' unhonored dead
  Dost in these lines their artless tale relate;
If chance, by lonely contemplation led,   95
  Some kindred spirit shall inquire thy fate,

Haply some hoary-headed swain may say,
  "Oft have we seen him at the peep of dawn
Brushing with hasty steps the dews away
  To meet the sun upon the upland lawn.⁵   100

"There at the foot of yonder nodding beech
  That wreathes its old fantastic roots so high,
His listless length at noontide would he stretch,
  And pore upon the brook that babbles by.

"Hard by yon wood, now smiling as in scorn,   105
  Muttering his wayward fancies he would rove;
Now drooping, woeful-wan, like one forlorn,
  Or crazed with care, or crossed in hopeless love.

"One morn I missed him on the customed hill,
  Along the heath, and near his favorite tree;   110
Another came; nor yet beside the rill,
  Nor up the lawn, nor at the wood was he;

"The next, with dirges due, in sad array,
  Slow through the church-way path we saw him borne.
Approach and read (for thou canst read) the lay,   115
  Graved on the stone beneath yon agèd thorn." ⁶

---

⁵ glade.
⁶ In some early editions, the following stanza appeared at this point:
> There scattered oft, the earliest of the year,
>   By hands unseen, are showers of violets found;
> The redbreast loves to build and warble there,
>   And little footsteps lightly print the ground.

THE EPITAPH

Here rests his head upon the lap of earth,
  A youth to Fortune and to Fame unknown;
Fair Science⁷ frowned not on his humble birth,
  And Melancholy marked him for her own.   120

Large was his bounty, and his soul sincere;
  Heaven did a recompense as largely send:
He gave to Misery all he had, a tear;
  He gained from Heaven ('twas all he wished) a friend.

No farther seek his merits to disclose,   125
  Or draw his frailties from their dread abode,
(There they alike in trembling hope repose)
  The bosom of his Father and his God.

Ode on the Death of a Favorite Cat, Drowned in a Tub of Gold Fishes
[1747, 1748]

'Twas on a lofty vase's side,
Where China's gayest art had dyed
  The azure flowers that blow;¹
Demurest of the tabby kind,
The pensive Selima reclined,   5
  Gazed on the lake below.

Her conscious tail her joy declared;
The fair round face, the snowy beard,
  The velvet of her paws,
Her coat, that with the tortoise vies,   10
Her ears of jet, and emerald eyes,
  She saw; and purred applause.

---
⁷ knowledge.

---
¹ bloom.

Still had she gazed; but 'midst the tide
Two angel forms were seen to glide,
 The Genii of the stream: 15
Their scaly armor's Tyrian hue
Through richest purple to the view
 Betrayed a golden gleam.

The hapless nymph with wonder saw:
A whisker first and then a claw,   20
 With many an ardent wish,
She stretched in vain to reach the prize.
What female heart can gold despise?
 What cat's averse to fish?

Presumptuous maid! with looks intent   25
Again she stretched, again she bent,
 Nor knew the gulf between.
(Malignant Fate sat by, and smiled)
The slippery verge her feet beguiled,
 She tumbled headlong in.   30

Eight times emerging from the flood
She mewed to every wat'ry god,
 Some speedy aid to send.
No dolphin came, no nereid [2] stirred;
Nor cruel Tom nor Susan[3] heard.   35
  A favorite has no friend!

From hence, ye beauties, undeceived,
Know, one false step is ne'er retrieved,
  And be with caution bold.
Not all that tempts your wandering eyes 40
And heedless hearts is lawful prize.
 Nor all that glisters, gold.

[2] sea nymph.
[3] servants.

Stanzas to Mr. Bentley[1]
[*1752*, 1775]

In silent gaze the tuneful choir among,
   Half pleased, half blushing, let the Muse admire,
While Bentley leads her sister art along,
     And bids the pencil answer to the lyre.

See, in their course, each transitory thought   5
   Fixed by his touch a lasting essence take;
Each dream, in Fancy's airy coloring wrought
     To local [2] symmetry and life awake!

The tardy rhymes that used to linger on,
   To censure cold, and negligent of fame,   10
In swifter measures animated run,
     And catch a luster from his genuine flame.

Ah! could they catch his strength, his easy grace,
   His quick creation, his unerring line;
The energy of Pope they might efface,   15
     And Dryden's harmony submit to mine.

But not to one in this benighted age
   Is that diviner inspiration given,
That burns in Shakespeare's or in Milton's page,
     The pomp and prodigality of Heaven.   20

As, when conspiring[3] in the diamond's blaze,
   The meaner gems, that singly charm the sight,
Together dart their intermingled rays,
     And dazzle with a luxury of light.

[1] Richard Bentley designed the elaborate illustrations for the 1753 edition of Gray's poems.
[2] proper and concrete.
[3] harmonizing.

Enough for me, if to some feeling breast   25
  My lines a secret sympathy . . .[4]
And as their pleasing influence . . .
  A sigh of soft reflection . . .

The Bard: A Pindaric Ode[1]
[1754-57, 1757]

I.I

"Ruin seize thee, ruthless King!
Confusion on thy banners wait,[2]
Though fanned by conquest's crimson wing
They mock the air with idle state.
Helm, nor hauberk's twisted mail,   5
Nor even thy virtues, tyrant, shall avail
To save thy secret soul from nightly fears,
From Cambria's[3] curse, from Cambria's tears!"
Such were the sounds that o'er the crested pride
Of the first Edward scattered wild dismay,   10
As down the steep of Snowdon's shaggy side
He wound with toilsome march his long array.

---

[4] William Mason, who first printed this poem, explained that the corner of the manuscript had been torn off.

---

[1] In the advertisement prefixed to the poem, Gray writes: "the following ode is founded on a tradition current in Wales that Edward the First, when he completed the conquest of that country [1282-84], ordered all the bards that fell into his hands to be put to death." According to his Commonplace Book, Gray imagined the Bard, "a venerable figure seated on the summit of an inaccessible rock," reproaching Edward as he marches by with his army. A chorus of past bards, compared to the Fates, joins him in prophesying the miseries of Edward's Norman descendants. Then, after foreseeing the accession of Henry VII, who was of Welsh descent, the Bard describes the glorious reign of Elizabeth I and the subsequent revival of poetry. "His song ended, he precipitates himself from the mountain, and is swallowed up by the river that rolls at its foot."

[2] destruction seize your banners.

[3] Wales'.

Stout Gloucester[4] stood aghast in speechless trance;
"To arms!" cried Mortimer,[4] and couched his quivering lance.

I.2

On a rock whose haughty brow 15
Frowns o'er old Conway's foaming flood,
Robed in the sable garb of woe,
With haggard [5] eyes the poet stood
(Loose his beard and hoary hair
Streamed, like a meteor, to the troubled air),[6] 20
And with a master's hand and prophet's fire
Struck the deep sorrows of his lyre:
"Hark, how each giant oak and desert cave
Sighs to the torrent's awful voice beneath!
O'er thee, O King! their hundred arms they wave, 25
Revenge on thee in hoarser murmurs breathe;
Vocal no more, since Cambria's fatal day,
To high-born Hoel's[7] harp, or soft Llewellyn's[7] lay.

I.3

"Cold is Cadwallo's[7] tongue,
That hushed the stormy main; 30
Brave Urien[7] sleeps upon his craggy bed;
Mountains, ye mourn in vain
Modred,[7] whose magic song
Made huge Plinlimmon bow his cloud-topped head.
On dreary Arvon's[8] shore they lie, 35
Smeared with gore, and ghastly pale;
Far, far aloof th' affrighted ravens sail;
The famished eagle screams, and passes by.
Dear lost companions of my tuneful art,

[4] Border lords in Edward's army.
[5] Gray explains that he is using "haggard" in its metaphorical sense of wild and defiant.
[6] The image was taken from a well-known picture of Raphael, representing the Supreme Being in the vision of Ezekiel (Gray). Gray mentions elsewhere that Parmigianino's *Moses* was also a model for this description.
[7] various historical or imaginary bards.
[8] Caernarvon, a county in North Wales.

Dear as the light that visits these sad eyes,   40
Dear as the ruddy drops that warm my heart,
Ye died amidst your dying country's cries—
No more I weep. They do not sleep.
   On yonder cliffs, a grisly band,
I see them sit; they linger yet,   45
Avengers of their native land;
With me in dreadful harmony they join,
And weave with bloody hands the tissue of thy line.

II.1

" 'Weave the warp, and weave the woof,
The winding-sheet of Edward's race.   50
Give ample room, and verge enough
The characters of hell to trace.
Mark the year, and mark the night,
When Severn shall re-echo with affright
The shrieks of death through Berkeley's roofs that ring,   55
Shrieks of an agonizing king!
She-wolf of France, with unrelenting fangs,
That tear'st the bowels of thy mangled mate,
From thee be born, who o'er thy country hangs,
The scourge of Heaven. What Terrors round him wait!   60
Amazement[9] in his van, with Flight combined,
And Sorrow's faded form, and Solitude behind.[10]

II.2

" 'Mighty victor, mighty lord,
Low on his funeral couch he lies!
No pitying heart, no eye, afford   65
A tear to grace his obsequies.[11]
Is the Sable Warrior[12] fled?

[9] confusion.

[10] Edward II, son of Edward I, was murdered in Berkeley Castle near the river Severn at the instigation or with the connivance of his wife, Isabella of France. The method used to kill him was supposed to have been peculiarly painful. Their son, Edward III, conquered a good part of France.

[11] Death of that king [Edward III], abandoned by his children, and even robbed in his last moments by his courtiers and his mistress (Gray).

[12] Edward, the Black Prince, died before his father, Edward III.

Thy son is gone. He rests among the dead.
The swarm that in thy noontide beam were born?
Gone to salute the rising morn.   70
Fair laughs the morn, and soft the zephyr blows,
While proudly riding o'er the azure realm
In gallant trim the gilded vessel goes;
Youth on the prow, and Pleasure at the helm;
Regardless of the sweeping whirlwind's sway,   75
That, hushed in grim repose, expects his evening prey.

II.3

" 'Fill high the sparkling bowl,
The rich repast prepare;
Reft of a crown, he yet may share the feast;
Close by the regal chair   80
Fell Thirst and Famine scowl
A baleful smile upon their baffled guest.[13]
Heard ye the din of battle bray,[14]
Lance to lance, and horse to horse?
Long years of havoc urge their destined course,   85
And through the kindred squadrons mow their way.
Ye towers of Julius, London's lasting shame,[15]
With many a foul and midnight murther fed,
Revere his consort's faith, his father's fame,
And spare the meek usurper's holy head.[16]   90
Above, below, the rose of snow,
Twined with her blushing foe, we spread;[17]

[13] Richard II's reign was noted for its magnificence. According to one account, Richard was starved to death by his enemies.

[14] the Wars of the Roses.

[15] Henry VI, Edward V, and other members of the royal family were believed to have been murdered secretly in the Tower of London. According to tradition, the oldest part of the Tower was built by Julius Caesar.

[16] murder of Henry VI, whose father was Henry V, victor at Agincourt. Henry VI's wife, Margaret of Anjou, was "a woman of heroic spirit, who struggled hard to save her husband and her crown" (Gray). Gray also notes that Henry VI was "very near being canonized. The line of Lancaster had no right of inheritance to the Crown."

[17] The white and red roses, devices of York and Lancaster (Gray). The roses are intertwined "above, below" in a bower to represent the marriage of Henry VII, of the Lancastrian line, to Elizabeth of York.

The bristled boar in infant gore
Wallows beneath the thorny shade.[18]
Now, brothers, bending o'er th' accursèd loom,   95
Stamp we our vengeance deep, and ratify his doom.

III.1

" 'Edward, lo! to sudden fate
(Weave we the woof: the thread is spun)
Half of thy heart we consecrate.[19]
(The web is wove. The work is done.)'   100
Stay, oh stay! nor thus forlorn
Leave me unblessed, unpitied, here to mourn:
In yon bright track that fires the western skies,
They melt, they vanish from my eyes.
But oh! what solemn scenes on Snowdon's height,   105
Descending slow, their glittering skirts[20] unroll?
Visions of glory, spare my aching sight;
Ye unborn ages, crowd not on my soul!
No more our long-lost Arthur we bewail.
All hail, ye genuine kings, Britannia's issue, hail! [21]   110

III.2

"Girt with many a baron bold
Sublime their starry fronts[22] they rear;
And gorgeous dames, and statesmen old
In bearded majesty, appear.
In the midst a form divine! [23]   115
Her eye proclaims her of the Briton line;

[18] The silver boar was the badge of Richard III (Gray). Richard is represented as wallowing in the blood of the infant princes, his nephews, under "the thorny shade" of the intertwined roses. He was defeated at Bosworth Field in 1485 by his successor, Henry VII.

[19] sanctify, with the implication here of devoting to doom. Gray refers to Eleanor of Castile, Edward I's wife, who died in 1290.

[20] outlines.

[21] Gray notes that the Welsh commonly believed in the return of King Arthur. Instead, the prophecy that the Welsh would regain sovereignty over the land was fulfilled in Henry VII and his descendants.

[22] foreheads, brows.

[23] Elizabeth I. Gray quotes an account, in his note, of her "lionlike" bearing.

Her lion-port, her awe-commanding face,
Attempered sweet to virgin-grace.
What strings symphonious tremble in the air,
What strains of vocal transport round her play!   120
Hear from the grave, great Taliessin,[24] hear;
They breathe a soul to animate thy clay.
Bright Rapture calls, and soaring, as she sings,
Waves in the eye of Heaven her many-colored wings.

III.3

"The verse adorn again   125
Fierce War, and faithful Love,[25]
And Truth severe, by fairy Fiction dressed.
In buskined [26] measures move
Pale Grief, and pleasing Pain,
With Horror, tyrant of the throbbing breast.   130
A voice, as of the cherub-choir,
Gales from blooming Eden bear;[27]
And distant warblings lessen on my ear,
That lost in long futurity expire.[28]
Fond [29] impious man, think'st thou yon sanguine cloud, 135
Raised by thy breath, has quenched the orb of day?
Tomorrow he repairs the golden flood,
And warms the nations with redoubled ray.
Enough for me: with joy I see
The different doom[30] our Fates assign.   140
Be thine Despair, and sceptered Care;
To triumph, and to die, are mine."
He spoke, and headlong from the mountain's height
Deep in the roaring tide he plunged to endless night.

[24] chief of the bards (Gray). The return of a British (Welsh) monarch revives poetry.
[25] "fierce wars and faithful loves shall moralize my song" (Spenser, *Faerie Queene*, first stanza). *The Faerie Queene* is dedicated to Elizabeth I.
[26] tragic. Gray is referring to Shakespeare's plays.
[27] Milton's *Paradise Lost*.
[28] the succession of poets after Milton's time (Gray).
[29] foolish.
[30] The Bard will triumph through his poetic successors.

The Candidate[1]
[?*1764*, ?1777]

When sly Jemmy Twitcher[2] had smugged up[3] his face
With a lick of Court whitewash, and pious grimace,
A-wooing he went, where three sisters[4] of old
In harmless society guttle[5] and scold.

Lord! sister, says Physic to Law, I declare   5
Such a sheep-biting look, such a pickpocket air!
Not I, for the Indies! you know I'm no prude;
But his nose is a shame, and his eyes are so lewd!
Then he shambles and straddles[6] so oddly, I fear—
No; at our time of life, 'twould be silly, my dear,   10

I don't know, says Law, now methinks, for his look,
'Tis just like the picture in Rochester's book.[7]
But his character, Phyzzy, his morals, his life!
When she died, I can't tell, but he once had a wife.[8]
They say he's no Christian, loves drinking and whoring,   15
And all the town rings of his swearing and roaring,[9]

---

[1] This poem deals with the unsuccessful effort of John Montagu, fourth Earl of Sandwich, to be elected High Steward of Cambridge University in 1764. He was backed by the "Court party."

[2] the informer in Gay's *Beggar's Opera*. Sandwich acquired the nickname when, shortly before, he had attacked John Wilkes for obscene and blasphemous activities in which he had himself participated.

[3] smartened up.

[4] the Faculties of Medicine, Jurisprudence, and Divinity.

[5] eat greedily.

[6] swaggers, or walks with legs wide apart. Sandwich was ugly and ungainly.

[7] presumably the portrait reproduced in several early editions of Rochester's poems. In a manuscript copy of the poem, Horace Walpole noted that Sandwich was descended from Rochester, and resembled his portraits.

[8] "Lady Sandwich was confined for lunacy, but Lord S.'s enemies said she was still shut up after she recovered her senses—at least she never appeared again in the world" (Walpole).

[9] riotous behavior.

His lying, and filching, and Newgate-bird [10] tricks:—
Not I, for a coronet, chariot and six!
    Divinity heard, between waking and dozing,
Her sisters denying, and Jemmy proposing;   20
From dinner she rose with her bumper in hand,
She stroked up her belly, and stroked down her band.[11]
    What a pother is here about wenching and roaring!
Why David loved catches,[12] and Solomon whoring.
Did not Israel filch from th' Egyptians of old   25
Their jewels of silver, and jewels of gold? [13]
The prophet of Bethel,[14] we read, told a lie;
He drinks; so did Noah:[15] he swears; so do I.
To refuse him for such peccadillos were odd;
Besides, he repents, and he talks about God.   30
    Never hang down your head, you poor penitent elf;
Come buss me, I'll be Mrs. Twitcher myself.
Damn you both for a couple of Puritan bitches!
He's Christian enough, that repents, and that stitches.[16]

On Lord Holland's Seat Near Margate, Kent[1]
[*1768, 1769*]

Old, and abandoned by each venal friend,
    Here Holland took the pious resolution
To smuggle some few years, and strive to mend
    A broken character and constitution.

[10] jailbird (from Newgate prison).
[11] bands are a part of clerical dress.
[12] rounds, with an allusion to the Psalms of David. "Lord S. instituted the Catch Club" (Walpole).
[13] Exodus 12:35-36.
[14] I Kings 13.
[15] Genesis 9:20-21.
[16] has sexual intercourse.

[1] On his retirement from politics, Henry Fox, first Lord Holland, had built himself a classical mansion surrounded by artificial ruins and assorted "follies."

On this congenial spot he fixed his choice,   5
    Earl Goodwin trembled for his neighboring sand;[1a]
Here seagulls scream and cormorants rejoice,
    And mariners, though shipwrecked, dread to land.

Here reign the blustering North and blighting East,
    No tree is heard to whisper, bird to sing,   10
Yet Nature cannot furnish out the feast,
    Art he invokes new horrors still to bring.

Now moldering fanes and battlements arise,
    Arches and turrets nodding to their fall,
Unpeopled palaces delude his eyes,   15
    And mimic desolation covers all.

"Ah!" said the sighing peer, "had Bute[2] been true,
    Nor Shelburne's,[2] Rigby's,[2] Calcraft's[2] friendship vain,
Far other scenes than these had blessed our view,
    And realized the ruins that we feign.   20

"Purged by the sword and beautified by fire,
    Then had we seen proud London's hated walls;
Owls might have hooted in St. Peter's choir,
    And foxes[3] stunk and littered in St. Paul's."

[1a] The Goodwin Sands are a dangerous sandbank, named after the Saxon Earl Godwin.

[2] contemporary politicians with whom Fox had been associated in engineering the unpopular Treaty of Paris (1763). Fox received the peerage he had been promised for his services, but quarreled with his associates over the division of the political spoils, and attacked the last three mentioned here in some verses privately printed about this time.

[3] Fox was notorious for the huge fortune he had accumulated in public office, for his political jobbery, and for his disloyalty to his associates. He was universally attacked as a "traitor" to his country, and was especially detested by the City of London for his opposition to their hero, the elder Pitt.

❧ David Hume ☙

Among the remarkable group of Scottish intellectuals who radiated from Edinburgh in the later eighteenth century, David Hume (1711-76) was the most brilliant. Born in Edinburgh and educated at Edinburgh University, he was urbane in temper and cosmopolitan in outlook, characteristics accentuated by two stays of several years each in France. He supported himself by his writing and by various part-time or temporary positions, such as librarian of the Advocates' Library in Edinburgh and private secretary to the British Ambassador in Paris. Perhaps the greatest of English philosophers, Hume carried the implications of empiricism to their logical extreme in his *Treatise of Human Nature, An Enquiry concerning Human Understanding,* and *Dialogues concerning Natural Religion.* He is also notable for his essays on politics and economics, and for his *History of England,* which presented a "Tory" version of English history from the time of Julius Caesar to the Revolution of 1688. His examination of problems in aesthetics exemplifies his skeptical and psychological outlook.

Editions: Philosophical Works, ed. T. H. Green and T. H. Grose (1874-75); *Dialogues concerning Natural Religion,* ed. Norman Kemp Smith (1947); *Letters,* ed. J. Y. T. Greig (1932); *New Letters,* ed. Raymond Klibansky and E. C. Mossner (1954).

Biography: E. C. Mossner, *Life of David Hume* (1954).

Critical Studies: Norman Kemp Smith, *The Philosophy of Hume* (1941); Teddy Brunius, *Hume on Criticism* (1952); Ralph Cohen, "David Hume's Experimental Method and the Theory of Taste," *ELH* 25 (1958).

Of Tragedy
[*1749-51, 1757*]

It seems an unaccountable pleasure which the spectators of a well-written tragedy receive from sorrow, terror, anxiety, and other passions, that are in themselves disagreeable and uneasy. The more they are touched and affected, the more are they delighted with the spectacle; and as soon as the uneasy passions cease to operate, the piece is at an end. One scene of full joy and contentment and security is the utmost that any composition of this kind can bear; and it is sure always to be the concluding one. If, in the texture of the piece, there be interwoven any scenes of satisfaction, they afford only faint gleams of pleasure, which are thrown in by way of variety, and in order to plunge the actors into deeper distress by means of that contrast and disappointment. The whole art of the poet is employed in rousing and supporting the compassion and indignation, the anxiety and resentment of his audience. They are pleased in proportion as they are afflicted, and never are so happy as when they employ tears, sobs, and cries to give vent to their sorrow, and relieve their heart, swollen with the tenderest sympathy and compassion.

The few critics who have had some tincture of philosophy have remarked this singular phenomenon, and have endeavored to account for it.

L'Abbé Dubos, in his reflections on poetry and painting, asserts that nothing is in general so disagreeable to the mind as the languid, listless state of indolence into which it falls upon the removal of all passion and occupation. To get rid of this painful situation, it seeks every amusement and pursuit: business, gaming, shows, executions; whatever will rouse the passions and take its attention from itself. No matter what the passion is: let it be disagreeable, afflicting, melancholy, disordered; it is still better than that insipid languor which arises from perfect tranquility and repose.[1]

It is impossible not to admit this account as being, at least in

---

[1] from Jean Baptiste Dubos' *Critical Reflections on Poetry and Painting*, pt. I, secs. 1-2.

part, satisfactory. You may observe, when there are several tables of gaming, that all the company run to those where the deepest play is, even though they find not there the best players. The view or, at least, imagination of high passions, arising from great loss or gain, affects the spectator by sympathy, gives him more touches of the same passions, and serves him for a momentary entertainment. It makes the time pass the easier with him, and is some relief to that oppression under which men commonly labor when left entirely to their own thoughts and meditations.

We find that common liars always magnify, in their narrations, all kinds of danger, pain, distress, sickness, deaths, murders, and cruelties; as well as joy, beauty, mirth and magnificence. It is an absurd secret which they have for pleasing their company, fixing their attention, and attaching them to such marvellous relations by the passions and emotions which they excite.

There is, however, a difficulty in applying to the present subject, in its full extent, this solution, however ingenious and satisfactory it may appear. It is certain that the same object of distress which pleases in a tragedy, were it really set before us, would give the most unfeigned uneasiness, though it be then the most effectual cure to languor and indolence. Monsieur Fontenelle seeems to have been sensible of this difficulty, and accordingly attempts another solution of the phenomenon; at least makes some addition to the theory above mentioned.[2]

"Pleasure and pain," says he, "which are two sentiments so different in themselves, differ not so much in their cause. From the instance of tickling, it appears, that the movement of pleasure, pushed a little too far, becomes pain; and that the movement of pain, a little moderated, becomes pleasure. Hence it proceeds that there is such a thing as a sorrow soft and agreeable: it is a pain weakened and diminished. The heart likes naturally to be moved and affected. Melancholy objects suit it, and even disastrous and sorrowful, provided they are softened by some circumstance. It is certain that, on the theater, the representation has almost the effect of reality; yet it has not altogether that effect. However we may be hurried away by the spectacle; whatever dominion the senses and imagination may usurp over the reason, there still lurks at the bottom a certain idea of falsehood in the whole of what we see. This idea,

[2] Bernard Le Bovier de Fontenelle, *Reflections on Poetry*, sec. 36.

though weak and disguised, suffices to diminish the pain which we suffer from the misfortunes of those whom we love, and to reduce that affliction to such a pitch as converts it into a pleasure. We weep for the misfortune of a hero to whom we are attached. In the same instant we comfort ourselves by reflecting that it is nothing but a fiction; and it is precisely that mixture of sentiments which composes an agreeable sorrow, and tears that delight us. But as that affliction which is caused by exterior and sensible objects is stronger than the consolation which arises from an internal reflection, they are the effects and symptoms of sorrow that ought to predominate in the composition."

This solution seems just and convincing, but perhaps it wants still some new addition in order to make it answer fully the phenomenon which we here examine. All the passions, excited by eloquence, are agreeable in the highest degree, as well as those which are moved by painting and the theater. The epilogues[3] of Cicero are, on this account chiefly, the delight of every reader of taste; and it is difficult to read some of them without the deepest sympathy and sorrow. His merit as an orator, no doubt, depends much on his success in this particular. When he had raised tears in his judges and all his audience, they were then the most highly delighted, and expressed the greatest satisfaction with the pleader. The pathetic description of the butchery made by Verres of the Sicilian captains is a masterpiece of this kind;[4] but I believe none will affirm that the being present at a melancholy scene of that nature would afford any entertainment. Neither is the sorrow here softened by fiction, for the audience were convinced of the reality of every circumstance. What is it then which in this case raises a pleasure from the bosom of uneasiness, so to speak; and a pleasure which still retains all the features and outward symptoms of distress and sorrow?

I answer: this extraordinary effect proceeds from that very eloquence with which the melancholy scene is represented. The genius required to paint objects in a lively manner, the art employed in collecting all the pathetic circumstances, the judgment displayed in disposing them: the exercise, I say, of these noble talents, to-

---

[3] perorations or summaries.
[4] Cicero, *Verrine Orations*, II v 39-46.

gether with the force of expression and beauty of oratorial numbers,[5] diffuse the highest satisfaction on the audience, and excite the most delightful movements. By this means, the uneasiness of the melancholy passions is not only overpowered and effaced by something stronger of an opposite kind, but the whole impulse of those passions is converted into pleasure, and swells the delight which the eloquence raises in us. The same force of oratory, employed on an uninteresting subject, would not please half so much, or rather would appear altogether ridiculous; and the mind, being left in absolute calmness and indifference, would relish none of those beauties of imagination or expression which, if joined to passion, give it such exquisite entertainment. The impulse or vehemence arising from sorrow, compassion, indignation, receives a new direction from the sentiments of beauty. The latter, being the predominant emotion, seizes the whole mind, and convert the former into themselves, at least tincture them so strongly as totally to alter their nature. And the soul being, at the same time, roused by passion and charmed by eloquence, feels on the whole a strong movement which is altogether delightful.

The same principle takes place in tragedy, with this addition, that tragedy is an imitation; and imitation is always of itself agreeable. This circumstance serves still farther to smooth the motions of passion, and convert the whole feeling into one uniform and strong enjoyment. Objects of the greatest terror and distress please in painting, and please more than the most beautiful objects that appear calm and indifferent.[6] The affection, rousing the mind, excites a large stock of spirit and vehemence, which is all transformed into pleasure by the force of the prevailing movement. It is thus the fiction of tragedy softens the passion by an infusion of a new feeling,

[5] rhythms.

[6] Painters make no scruple of representing distress and sorrow as well as any other passion; but they seem not to dwell so much on these melancholy affections as the poets, who, though they copy every motion of the human breast, yet pass quickly over the agreeable sentiments. A painter represents only one instant, and if that be passionate enough, it is sure to affect and delight the spectator; but nothing can furnish to the poet a variety of scenes and incidents and sentiments except distress, terror, or anxiety. Complete joy and satisfaction is attended with security, and leaves no farther room for action (Hume).

not merely by weakening or diminishing the sorrow. You may by degrees weaken a real sorrow till it totally disappears; yet in none of its gradations will it ever give pleasure, except perhaps, by accident, to a man sunk under lethargic indolence, whom it rouses from that languid state.

To confirm this theory it will be sufficient to produce other instances where the subordinate movement is converted into the predominant, and gives force to it, though of a different, and even sometimes though of a contrary nature.

Novelty naturally rouses the mind and attracts our attention, and the movements which it causes are always converted into any passion belonging to the object, and join their force to it. Whether an event excite joy or sorrow, pride or shame, anger or good will, it is sure to produce a stronger affection when new or unusual. And though novelty of itself be agreeable, it fortifies the painful, as well as agreeable passions.

Had you any intention to move a person extremely by the narration of any event, the best method of increasing its effect would be artfully to delay informing him of it, and first to excite his curiosity and impatience before you let him into the secret. This is the artifice practiced by Iago in the famous scene[7] of Shakespeare; and every spectator is sensible that Othello's jealousy acquires additional force from his preceding impatience, and that the subordinate passion is here readily transformed into the predominant one.

Difficulties increase passions of every kind; and by rousing our attention, and exciting our active powers, they produce an emotion which nourishes the prevailing affection.

Parents commonly love that child most whose sickly infirm frame of body has occasioned them the greatest pains, trouble, and anxiety in rearing him. The agreeable sentiment of affection here acquires force from sentiments of uneasiness.

Nothing endears so much a friend as sorrow for his death. The pleasure of his company has not so powerful an influence.

Jealousy is a painful passion; yet without some share of it, the agreeable affection of love has difficulty to subsist in its full force and violence. Absence is also a great source of complaint among lovers, and gives them the greatest uneasiness; yet nothing is more favorable to their mutual passion than short intervals of that kind.

[7] *Othello,* III iii.

And if long intervals often prove fatal, it is only because, through time, men are accustomed to them, and they cease to give uneasiness. Jealousy and absence in love compose the *dolce peccante*[8] of the Italians, which they suppose so essential to all pleasure.

There is a fine observation of the elder Pliny which illustrates the principle here insisted on. "It is very remarkable," says he, "that the last works of celebrated artists, which they left imperfect, are always the most prized, such as the Iris of Aristides, the Tyndarides of Nichomachus, the Medea of Timomachus, and the Venus of Apelles. These are valued even above their finished productions: the broken lineaments of the piece, and the half-formed idea of the painter are carefully studied; and our very grief for that curious[9] hand, which had been stopped by death, is an additional increase to our pleasure." [10]

These instances (and many more might be collected) are sufficient to afford us some insight into the analogy of nature, and to show us that the pleasure which poets, orators, and musicians give us by exciting grief, sorrow, indignation, compassion, is not so extraordinary or paradoxical as it may at first sight appear. The force of imagination, the energy of expression, the power of numbers,[11] the charms of imitation: all these are naturally of themselves delightful to the mind; and when the object presented lays also hold of some affection, the pleasure still rises upon us by the conversion of this subordinate movement into that which is predominant. The passion though perhaps naturally, and when excited by the simple appearance of a real object, it may be painful; yet is so smoothed, and softened, and mollified, when raised by the finer arts, that it affords the highest entertainment.

To confirm this reasoning, we may observe that if the movements of the imagination be not predominant above those of the passion, a contrary effect follows; and the former, being now subordinate, is converted into the latter, and still farther increases the pain and affliction of the sufferer.

Who could ever think of it as a good expedient for comforting an afflicted parent to exaggerate, with all the force of elocution,

[8] correctly, *dolce peccato* ("sweet sin").
[9] skillful.
[10] Pliny, *Natural History*, XXXV xl 145.
[11] verses.

the irreparable loss which he has met with by the death of a favorite child? The more power of imagination and expression you here employ, the more you increase his despair and affliction.

The shame, confusion, and terror of Verres, no doubt, rose in proportion to the noble eloquence and vehemence of Cicero; so also did his pain and uneasiness. These former passions were too strong for the pleasure arising from the beauties of elocution; and operated, though from the same principle, yet in a contrary manner, to the sympathy, compassion, and indignation of the audience.

Lord Clarendon, when he approaches towards the catastrophe of the royal party, supposes that his narration must then become infinitely disagreeable, and he hurries over the King's death without giving us one circumstance of it. He considers it as too horrid a scene to be contemplated with any satisfaction, or even without the utmost pain and aversion. He himself, as well as the reader of that age, were too deeply concerned in the events, and felt a pain from subjects which an historian and a reader of another age would regard as the most pathetic and interesting, and, by consequence, the most agreeable.[12]

An action represented in tragedy may be too bloody and atrocious. It may excite such movements of horror as will not soften into pleasure; and the greatest energy of expression, bestowed on descriptions of that nature, serves only to augment our uneasiness. Such is that action represented in *The Ambitious Stepmother,*[13] where a venerable old man, raised to the height of fury and despair, rushes against a pillar, and striking his head upon it besmears it all over with mingled brains and gore. The English theater abounds too much with such shocking images.

Even the common sentiments of compassion require to be softened by some agreeable affection, in order to give a thorough satisfaction to the audience. The mere suffering of plaintive virtue, under the triumphant tyranny and oppression of vice, forms a disagreeable spectacle, and is carefully avoided by all masters of the drama. In order to dismiss the audience with entire satisfaction

[12] In his voluminous *History of the Rebellion* (1702-4), Edward Hyde, first Earl of Clarendon, summarizes the trial and execution of Charles I in one paragraph. He explains his brevity by the reasons Hume gives, but also refers to an extended account of these events available elsewhere.

[13] a play (1700) by Nicholas Rowe.

and contentment, the virtue must either convert itself into a noble courageous despair, or the vice receive its proper punishment.

Most painters appear in this light to have been very unhappy in their subjects. As they wrought much for churches and convents, they have chiefly represented such horrible subjects as crucifixions and martyrdoms, where nothing appears but tortures, wounds, executions, and passive suffering, without any action or affection. When they turned their pencil [14] from this ghastly mythology, they had commonly recourse to Ovid,[15] whose fictions, though passionate and agreeable, are scarcely natural or probable enough for painting.

The same inversion of that principle which is here insisted on displays itself in common life, as in the effects of oratory and poetry. Raise so the subordinate passion that it becomes the predominant, it swallows up that affection which it before nourished and increased. Too much jealousy extinguishes love; too much difficulty renders us indifferent; too much sickness and infirmity disgusts a selfish and unkind parent.

What so disagreeable as the dismal, gloomy, disastrous stories with which melancholy people entertain their companions? The uneasy passion being there raised alone, unaccompanied with any spirit, genius, or eloquence, conveys a pure uneasiness, and is attended with nothing that can soften it into pleasure or satisfaction.

Of the Standard of Taste
[1756, 1757]

The great variety of taste, as well as of opinion, which prevails in the world is too obvious not to have fallen under everyone's observation. Men of the most confined knowledge are able to remark a difference of taste in the narrow circle of their acquaintance, even where the persons have been educated under the same government, and have early imbibed the same prejudices. But those who can enlarge their view to contemplate distant nations and remote ages are still more surprised at the great inconsistence and contrariety. We are apt to call *barbarous* whatever departs widely from our own

---

[14] brush.
[15] Hume presumably refers to the tales in Ovid's *Metamorphoses*.

taste and apprehension, but soon find the epithet of reproach retorted on us. And the highest arrogance and self-conceit is at last startled on observing an equal assurance on all sides, and scruples, amidst such a contest of sentiment, to pronounce positively in its own favor.

As this variety of taste is obvious to the most careless enquirer, so will it be found, on examination, to be still greater in reality than in appearance. The sentiments of men often differ with regard to beauty and deformity of all kinds, even while their general discourse is the same. There are certain terms in every language which import blame, and others praise; and all men who use the same tongue must agree in their application of them. Every voice is united in applauding elegance, propriety, simplicity, spirit in writing; and in blaming fustian, affectation, coldness, and a false brilliancy. But when critics come to particulars, this seeming unanimity vanishes; and it is found that they had affixed a very different meaning to their expressions. In all matters of opinion and science, the case is opposite: the difference among men is there oftener found to lie in generals than in particulars, and to be less in reality than in appearance. An explanation of the terms commonly ends the controversy, and the disputants are surprised to find that they had been quarreling, while at bottom they agreed in their judgment.

Those who found morality on sentiment more than on reason are inclined to comprehend ethics under the former observation, and to maintain that in all questions which regard conduct and manners, the difference among men is really greater than at first sight it appears. It is indeed obvious that writers of all nations and all ages concur in applauding justice, humanity, magnanimity, prudence, veracity; and in blaming the opposite qualities. Even poets and other authors whose compositions are chiefly calculated to please the imagination are yet found, from Homer down to Fénelon,[1] to inculcate the same moral precepts, and to bestow their applause and blame on the same virtues and vices. This great unanimity is usually ascribed to the influence of plain reason, which, in all these cases, maintains similar sentiments in all men, and prevents those controversies to which the abstract sciences are so much exposed. So far as the unanimity is real, this account may be admitted as

[1] François de Salignac de La Mothe-Fénelon, French bishop and author of a prose epic, *Telemachus* (1699).

satisfactory. But we must also allow that some part of the seeming harmony in morals may be accounted for from the very nature of language. The word *virtue,* with its equivalent in every tongue, implies praise, as that of *vice* does blame; and no one, without the most obvious and grossest impropriety, could affix reproach to a term which in general acceptation is understood in a good sense, or bestow applause where the idiom requires disapprobation. Homer's general precepts, where he delivers any such, will never be controverted; but it is obvious that when he draws particular pictures of manners, and represents heroism in Achilles and prudence in Ulysses, he intermixes a much greater degree of ferocity in the former, and of cunning and fraud in the latter, than Fénelon would admit of. The sage Ulysses, in the Greek poet, seems to delight in lies and fictions, and often employs them without any necessity or even advantage. But his more scrupulous son, in the French epic writer, exposes himself to the most imminent perils rather than depart from the most exact line of truth and veracity.

The admirers and followers of the Alcoran[2] insist on the excellent moral precepts interspersed throughout that wild and absurd performance. But it is to be supposed that the Arabic words which correspond to the English equity, justice, temperance, meekness, charity, were such as, from the constant use of that tongue, must always be taken in a good sense, and it would have argued the greatest ignorance, not of morals but of language, to have mentioned them with any epithets besides those of applause and approbation. But would we know whether the pretended prophet had really attained a just sentiment of morals? Let us attend to his narration, and we shall soon find that he bestows praise on such instances of treachery, inhumanity, cruelty, revenge, bigotry, as are utterly incompatible with civilized society. No steady rule of right seems there to be attended to; and every action is blamed or praised so far only as it is beneficial or hurtful to the true believers.

The merit of delivering true general precepts in ethics is indeed very small. Whoever recommends any moral virtues really does no more than is implied in the terms themselves. That people who invented the word *charity,* and used it in a good sense, inculcated more clearly, and much more efficaciously, the precept, *be charitable,* than any pretended legislator or prophet who should insert such a

[2] the Koran.

maxim in his writings. Of all expressions, those which, together with their other meaning, imply a degree either of blame or approbation, are the least liable to be perverted or mistaken.

It is natural for us to seek a *Standard of Taste:* a rule by which the various sentiments of men may be reconciled; at least a decision afforded confirming one sentiment, and condemning another.

There is a species of philosophy which cuts off all hopes of success in such an attempt, and represents the impossibility of ever attaining any standard of taste. The difference, it is said, is very wide between judgment and sentiment. All sentiment is right, because sentiment has a reference to nothing beyond itself, and is always real, wherever a man is conscious of it. But all determinations of the understanding are not right, because they have a reference to something beyond themselves, to wit, real matter of fact, and are not always conformable to that standard. Among a thousand different opinions which different men may entertain of the same subject, there is one, and but one, that is just and true, and the only difficulty is to fix and ascertain it. On the contrary, a thousand different sentiments, excited by the same object, are all right, because no sentiment represents what is really in the object. It only marks a certain conformity or relation between the object and the organs or faculties of the mind; and if that conformity did not really exist, the sentiment could never possibly have being. Beauty is no quality in things themselves: it exists merely in the mind which contemplates them, and each mind perceives a different beauty. One person may even perceive deformity where another is sensible of beauty, and every individual ought to acquiesce in his own sentiment without pretending to regulate those of others. To seek the real beauty, or real deformity, is as fruitless an enquiry as to pretend to ascertain the real sweet or real bitter. According to the disposition of the organs, the same object may be both sweet and bitter; and the proverb has justly determined it to be fruitless to dispute concerning tastes. It is very natural, and even quite necessary, to extend this axiom to mental as well as bodily taste; and thus common sense, which is so often at variance with philosophy, especially with the skeptical kind, is found, in one instance at least, to agree in pronouncing the same decision.

But though this axiom by passing into a proverb seems to have attained the sanction of common sense, there is certainly a species of common sense which opposes it, at least serves to modify and restrain it. Whoever would assert an equality of genius and elegance between Ogilby[3] and Milton, or Bunyan[4] and Addison, would be thought to defend no less an extravagance than if he had maintained a molehill to be as high as Tenerife,[5] or a pond as extensive as the ocean. Though there may be found persons who give the preference to the former authors, no one pays attention to such a taste; and we pronounce without scruple the sentiment of these pretended critics to be absurd and ridiculous. The principle of the natural equality of tastes is then totally forgot, and while we admit it on some occasions where the objects seem near an equality, it appears an extravagant paradox, or rather a palpable absurdity, where objects so disproportioned are compared together.

It is evident that none of the rules of composition are fixed by reasonings *a priori,* or can be esteemed abstract conclusions of the understanding, from comparing[6] those habitudes and relations of ideas which are eternal and immutable. Their foundation is the same with that of all the practical sciences, experience; nor are they anything but general observations concerning what has been universally found to please in all countries and in all ages. Many of the beauties of poetry and even of eloquence are founded on falsehood and fiction, on hyperboles, metaphors, and an abuse or perversion of terms from their natural meaning. To check the sallies of the imagination and to reduce every expression to geometrical truth and exactness would be the most contrary to the laws of criticism because it would produce a work which, by universal experience, has been found the most insipid and disagreeable. But though poetry can never submit to exact truth, it must be confined by rules of art, discovered to the author either by genius or observation. If some negligent or irregular writers have pleased, they have not pleased by their transgressions of rule or order, but in spite of these transgressions: they have possessed other beauties which were conformable to just criticism, and the force of these beauties has been

[3] John Ogilby (1600-76), whose translations of Homer and Virgil were ridiculed by Dryden and Pope.

[4] In the eighteenth century, Bunyan was considered merely a popular religious writer for the lower classes.

[5] the great peak of the Canary Islands, proverbial for its size.

[6] arrived at by comparing.

able to overpower censure, and give the mind a satisfaction superior to the disgust arising from the blemishes. Ariosto[7] pleases, but not by his monstrous and improbable fictions, by his bizarre mixture of the serious and comic styles, by the want of coherence in his stories, or by the continual interruptions of his narration. He charms by the force and clearness of his expression, by the readiness and variety of his inventions, and by his natural pictures of the passions, especially those of the gay and amorous kind; and however his faults may diminish our satisfaction, they are not able entirely to destroy it. Did our pleasure really arise from those parts of his poem which we denominate faults, this would be no objection to criticism in general; it would only be an objection to those particular rules of criticism which would establish such circumstances to be faults, and would represent them as universally blamable. If they are found to please, they cannot be faults, let the pleasure which they produce be ever so unexpected and unaccountable.

But though all the general rules of art are founded only on experience and on the observation of the common sentiments of human nature, we must not imagine that on every occasion the feelings of men will be conformable to these rules. Those finer emotions of the mind are of a very tender and delicate nature, and require the concurrence of many favorable circumstances to make them play with facility and exactness, according to their general and established principles. The least exterior hindrance to such small springs, or the least internal disorder, disturbs their motion and confounds the operation of the whole machine. When we would make an experiment of this nature and would try the force of any beauty or deformity, we must choose with care a proper time and place, and bring the fancy to a suitable situation and disposition. A perfect serenity of mind, a recollection of thought, a due attention to the object: if any of these circumstances be wanting, our experiment will be fallacious, and we shall be unable to judge of the catholic and universal beauty. The relation which nature has placed between the form and the sentiment will at least be more obscure, and it will require greater accuracy to trace and discern it. We shall be able to ascertain its influence, not so much from the operation of each particular beauty, as from the durable admiration

[7] Lodovico Ariosto (1474-1533), author of the chivalric romance, *Orlando Furioso.*

which attends those works that have survived all the caprices of mode and fashion, all the mistakes of ignorance and envy.

The same Homer who pleased at Athens and Rome two thousand years ago is still admired at Paris and at London. All the changes of climate, government, religion, and language have not been able to obscure his glory. Authority or prejudice may give a temporary vogue to a bad poet or orator, but his reputation will never be durable or general. When his compositions are examined by posterity or by foreigners, the enchantment is dissipated and his faults appear in their true colors. On the contrary, a real genius, the longer his works endure and the more wide they are spread, the more sincere is the admiration which he meets with. Envy and jealousy have too much place in a narrow circle, and even familiar acquaintance with his person may diminish the applause due to his performances; but when these obstructions are removed, the beauties which are naturally fitted to excite agreeable sentiments immediately display their energy; and while the world endures, they maintain their authority over the minds of men.

It appears, then, that amidst all the variety and caprice of taste, there are certain general principles of approbation or blame whose influence a careful eye may trace in all operations of the mind. Some particular forms or qualities, from the original structure of the internal fabric, are calculated to please, and others to displease; and if they fail of their effect in any particular instance, it is from some apparent defect or imperfection in the organ. A man in a fever would not insist on his palate as able to decide concerning flavors; nor would one affected with the jaundice pretend to give a verdict with regard to colors. In each creature there is a sound and a defective state, and the former alone can be supposed to afford us a true standard of taste and sentiment. If in the sound state of the organ there be an entire or a considerable uniformity of sentiment among men, we may thence derive an idea of the perfect beauty; in like manner as the appearance of objects in daylight to the eye of a man in health is denominated their true and real color, even while color is allowed to be merely a phantasm of the senses.

Many and frequent are the defects in the internal organs which prevent or weaken the influence of those general principles on which depends our sentiment of beauty or deformity. Though some objects, by the structure of the mind, be naturally calculated to give pleasure, it is not to be expected that in every individual the pleasure will be equally felt. Particular incidents and situations occur which either throw a false light on the objects, or hinder the true from conveying to the imagination the proper sentiment and perception.

One obvious cause why many feel not the proper sentiment of beauty is the want of that *delicacy* of imagination which is requisite to convey a sensibility of those finer emotions. This delicacy everyone pretends to; everyone talks of it, and would reduce every kind of taste or sentiment to its standard. But as our intention in this essay is to mingle some light of the understanding with the feelings of sentiment, it will be proper to give a more accurate definition of delicacy than has hitherto been attempted. And not to draw our philosophy from too profound a source, we shall have recourse to a noted story in *Don Quixote*.[8]

It is with good reason, says Sancho to the squire with the great nose, that I pretend to have a judgment in wine: this is a quality hereditary in our family. Two of my kinsmen were once called to give their opinion of a hogshead which was supposed to be excellent, being old and of a good vintage. One of them tastes it, considers it; and, after mature reflection, pronounces the wine to be good, were it not for a small taste of leather which he perceived in it. The other, after using the same precautions, gives also his verdict in favor of the wine, but with the reserve of a taste of iron, which he could easily distinguish. You cannot imagine how much they were both ridiculed for their judgment. But who laughed in the end? On emptying the hogshead, there was found at the bottom an old key with a leathern thong tied to it.

The great resemblance between mental and bodily taste will easily teach us to apply this story. Though it be certain that beauty and deformity, no more than sweet and bitter, are not qualities in objects but belong entirely to the sentiment, internal or external, it must be allowed that there are certain qualities in objects which are fitted by nature to produce those particular feelings. Now, as these qualities may be found in a small degree or may be mixed and confounded with each other, it often happens that the taste is not affected with such minute qualities, or is not able to distinguish all the particular flavors amidst the disorder in which they are presented. Where the organs are so fine as to allow nothing

---

[8] *Don Quixote,* pt. 2, ch. 13.

to escape them, and at the same time so exact as to perceive every ingredient in the composition, this we call delicacy of taste, whether we employ these terms in the literal or metaphorical sense. Here then the general rules of beauty are of use, being drawn from established models, and from the observation of what pleases or displeases, when presented singly and in a high degree; and if the same qualities, in a continued composition and in a smaller degree, affect not the organs with a sensible delight or uneasiness, we exclude the person from all pretensions to this delicacy. To produce these general rules or avowed patterns of composition is like finding the key with the leathern thong, which justified the verdict of Sancho's kinsmen, and confounded those pretended judges who had condemned them. Though the hogshead had never been emptied, the taste of the one was still equally delicate, and that of the other equally dull and languid; but it would have been more difficult to have proved the superiority of the former, to the conviction of every bystander. In like manner, though the beauties of writing had never been methodized, or reduced to general principles; though no excellent models had ever been acknowledged, the different degrees of taste would still have subsisted, and the judgment of one man been preferable to that of another; but it would not have been so easy to silence the bad critic, who might always insist upon his particular sentiment, and refuse to submit to his antagonist. But when we show him an avowed principle of art; when we illustrate this principle by examples, whose operation, from his own particular taste, he acknowledges to be conformable to the principle; when we prove that the same principle may be applied to the present case, where he did not perceive or feel its influence: he must conclude, upon the whole, that the fault lies in himself, and that he wants the delicacy which is requisite to make him sensible of every beauty and every blemish in any composition or discourse.

It is acknowledged to be the perfection of every sense or faculty to perceive with exactness its most minute objects, and allow nothing to escape its notice and observation. The smaller the objects are which become sensible to the eye, the finer is that organ, and the more elaborate its make and composition. A good palate is not tried by strong flavors, but by a mixture of small ingredients, where we are still sensible of each part, notwithstanding its minuteness and its confusion with the rest. In like manner, a quick and acute perception of beauty and deformity must be the perfection of our mental taste; nor can a man be satisfied with himself while he suspects that any excellence or blemish in a discourse has passed him unobserved. In this case, the perfection of the man and the perfection of the sense or feeling are found to be united. A very delicate palate, on many occasions, may be a great inconvenience both to a man himself and to his friends; but a delicate taste of wit or beauty must always be a desirable quality, because it is the source of all the finest and most innocent enjoyments of which human nature is susceptible. In this decision the sentiments of all mankind are agreed. Wherever you can ascertain a delicacy of taste, it is sure to meet with approbation; and the best way of ascertaining it is to appeal to those models and principles which have been established by the uniform consent and experience of nations and ages.

But though there be naturally a wide difference in point of delicacy between one person and another, nothing tends further to increase and improve this talent than *practice* in a particular art, and the frequent survey or contemplation of a particular species of beauty. When objects of any kind are first presented to the eye or imagination, the sentiment which attends them is obscure and confused; and the mind is, in a great measure, incapable of pronouncing concerning their merits or defects. The taste cannot perceive the several excellencies of the performance, much less distinguish the particular character of each excellency, and ascertain its quality and degree. If it pronounce the whole in general to be beautiful or deformed, it is the utmost that can be expected; and even this judgment, a person so unpracticed will be apt to deliver with great hesitation and reserve. But allow him to acquire experience in those objects, his feeling becomes more exact and nice: he not only perceives the beauties and defects of each part, but marks the distinguishing species of each quality, and assigns it suitable praise or blame. A clear and distinct sentiment attends him through the whole survey of the objects; and he discerns that very degree and kind of approbation or displeasure which each part is naturally fitted to produce. The mist dissipates which seemed formerly to hang over the object; the organ acquires greater perfection in its operations, and can pronounce, without danger of mistake, concerning the merits of every performance. In a word, the same address and dexterity which practice gives to the execution of any work is also acquired by the same means in the judging of it.

So advantageous is practice to the discernment of beauty that, before we can give judgment on any work of importance, it will even be requisite that that very individual performance be more than once perused by us, and be surveyed in different lights with attention and deliberation. There is a flutter or hurry of thought which attends the first perusal of any piece, and which confounds the genuine sentiment of beauty. The relation of the parts is not discerned; the true characters of style are little distinguished; the several perfections and defects seem wrapped up in a species of confusion, and present themselves indistinctly to the imagination. Not to mention that there is a species of beauty which, as it is florid and superficial, pleases at first; but being found incompatible with a just expression either of reason or passion soon palls upon the taste, and is then rejected with disdain, at least rated at a much lower value.

It is impossible to continue in the practice of contemplating any order of beauty without being frequently obliged to form *comparisons* between the several species and degrees of excellence, and estimating their proportion to each other. A man who has had no opportunity of comparing the different kinds of beauty is indeed totally unqualified to pronounce an opinion with regard to any object presented to him. By comparison alone we fix the epithets of praise or blame, and learn how to assign the due degree of each. The coarsest daubing contains a certain luster of colors and exactness of imitation, which are so far beauties, and would affect the mind of a peasant or Indian with the highest admiration. The most vulgar ballads are not entirely destitute of harmony or nature; and none but a person familiarized to superior beauties would pronounce their numbers[9] harsh, or narration uninteresting. A great inferiority of beauty gives pain to a person conversant in the highest excellence of the kind, and is for that reason pronounced a deformity; as the most finished object with which we are acquainted is naturally supposed to have reached the pinnacle of perfection, and to be entitled to the highest applause. One accustomed to see, and examine, and weigh the several performances admired in different ages and nations can alone rate the merits of a work exhibited to

[9] verses.

his view, and assign its proper rank among the productions of genius.

But to enable a critic the more fully to execute this undertaking, he must preserve his mind free from all *prejudice,* and allow nothing to enter into his consideration but the very object which is submitted to his examination. We may observe that every work of art, in order to produce its due effect on the mind, must be surveyed in a certain point of view, and cannot be fully relished by persons whose situation, real or imaginary, is not conformable to that which is required by the performance. An orator addresses himself to a particular audience, and must have a regard to their particular genius, interests, opinions, passions, and prejudices; otherwise he hopes in vain to govern their resolutions, and inflame their affections. Should they even have entertained some prepossessions against him, however unreasonable, he must not overlook this disadvantage; but, before he enters upon the subject, must endeavor to conciliate their affection and acquire their good graces. A critic of a different age or nation, who should peruse this discourse, must have all these circumstances in his eye, and must place himself in the same situation as the audience in order to form a true judgment of the oration. In like manner, when any work is addressed to the public, though I should have a friendship or enmity with the author, I must depart from this situation, and considering myself as a man in general forget, if possible, my individual being and my peculiar circumstances. A person influenced by prejudice complies not with this condition, but obstinately maintains his natural position, without placing himself in that point of view which the performance supposes. If the work be addressed to persons of a different age or nation, he makes no allowance for their peculiar views and prejudices; but full of the manners of his own age and country rashly condemns what seemed admirable in the eyes of those for whom alone the discourse was calculated. If the work be executed for the public, he never sufficiently enlarges his comprehension, or forgets his interest as a friend or enemy, as a rival or commentator. By this means his sentiments are perverted; nor have the same beauties and blemishes the same influence upon him as if he had imposed a proper violence on his imagination, and had forgotten himself for a moment. So far his taste evidently departs from the true standard, and of consequence loses all credit and authority.

It is well known that in all questions submitted to the understanding prejudice is destructive of sound judgment, and perverts all operations of the intellectual faculties: it is no less contrary to good taste; nor has it less influence to corrupt our sentiment of beauty. It belongs to *good sense* to check its influence in both cases; and in this respect, as well as in many others, reason, if not an essential part of taste, is at least requisite to the operations of this latter faculty. In all the nobler productions of genius, there is a mutual relation and correspondence of parts; nor can either the beauties or blemishes be perceived by him whose thought is not capacious enough to comprehend all those parts and compare them with each other, in order to perceive the consistence and uniformity of the whole. Every work of art has also a certain end or purpose for which it is calculated; and is to be deemed more or less perfect, as it is more or less fitted to attain this end. The object of eloquence is to persuade, of history to instruct, of poetry to please, by means of the passions and the imagination. These ends we must carry constantly in our view when we peruse any performance; and we must be able to judge how far the means employed are adapted to their respective purposes. Besides, every kind of composition, even the most poetical, is nothing but a chain of propositions and reasonings; not always, indeed, the justest and most exact, but still plausible and specious,[10] however disguised by the coloring of the imagination. The persons introduced in tragedy and epic poetry must be represented as reasoning, and thinking, and concluding, and acting suitably to their characters and circumstances; and without judgment, as well as taste and invention, a poet can never hope to succeed in so delicate an undertaking. Not to mention that the same excellence of faculties which contributes to the improvement of reason, the same clearness of conception, the same exactness of distinction, the same vivacity of apprehension, are essential to the operations of true taste, and are its infallible concomitants. It seldom or never happens that a man of sense, who has experience in any art, cannot judge of its beauty; and it is no less rare to meet with a man who has a just taste without a sound understanding.

Thus, though the principles of taste be universal, and nearly, if not entirely, the same in all men, yet few are qualified to give judgment on any work of art, or establish their own sentiment as

[10] attractive at first glance. "Specious" does not necessarily carry its modern meaning of "deceptive."

the standard of beauty. The organs of internal sensation are seldom so perfect as to allow the general principles their full play, and produce a feeling correspondent to those principles. They either labor under some defect, or are vitiated by some disorder; and by that means excite a sentiment which may be pronounced erroneous. When the critic has no delicacy, he judges without any distinction, and is only affected by the grosser and more palpable qualities of the object; the finer touches pass unnoticed and disregarded. Where he is not aided by practice, his verdict is attended with confusion and hesitation. Where no comparison has been employed, the most frivolous beauties, such as rather merit the name of defects, are the object of his admiration. Where he lies under the influence of prejudice, all his natural sentiments are perverted. Where good sense is wanting, he is not qualified to discern the beauties of design and reasoning, which are the highest and most excellent. Under some or other of these imperfections, the generality of men labor; and hence a true judge in the finer arts is observed, even during the most polished ages, to be so rare a character: strong sense, united to delicate sentiment, improved by practice, perfected by comparison, and cleared of all prejudice, can alone entitle critics to this valuable character; and the joint verdict of such, wherever they are to be found, is the true standard of taste and beauty.

But where are such critics to be found? By what marks are they to be known? How distinguish them from pretenders? These questions are embarrassing; and seem to throw us back into the same uncertainty from which during the course of this essay we have endeavored to extricate ourselves.

But if we consider the matter aright, these are questions of fact, not of sentiment. Whether any particular person be endowed with good sense and a delicate imagination, free from prejudice, may often be the subject of dispute, and be liable to great discussion and inquiry: but that such a character is valuable and estimable will be agreed in by all mankind. Where these doubts occur, men can do no more than in other disputable questions which are submitted to the understanding: they must produce the best arguments that their invention suggests to them; they must acknowledge a true and decisive standard to exist somewhere, to wit, real existence and matter of fact; and they must have indulgence to such as differ from them in their appeals to this standard. It is sufficient for our present purpose if we have proved that the taste of all individuals is not upon an equal footing, and that some men in general, however difficult to be particularly pitched upon, will be acknowledged by universal sentiment to have a preference above others.

But in reality the difficulty of finding, even in particulars, the standard of taste, is not so great as it is represented. Though in speculation we may readily avow a certain criterion in science,[11] and deny it in sentiment, the matter is found in practice to be much more hard to ascertain in the former case than in the latter. Theories of abstract philosophy, systems of profound theology, have prevailed during one age; in a successive period these have been universally exploded, their absurdity has been detected; other theories and systems have supplied their place, which again gave place to their successors, and nothing has been experienced more liable to the revolutions of chance and fashion than these pretended decisions of science. The case is not the same with the beauties of eloquence and poetry. Just expressions of passion and nature are sure, after a little time, to gain public applause, which they maintain forever. Aristotle and Plato and Epicurus and Descartes may successively yield to each other; but Terence and Virgil maintain an universal, undisputed empire over the minds of men. The abstract philosophy of Cicero has lost its credit; the vehemence of his oratory is still the object of our admiration.

Though men of delicate taste be rare, they are easily to be distinguished in society by the soundness of their understanding, and the superiority of their faculties above the rest of mankind. The ascendant which they acquire gives a prevalence to that lively approbation with which they receive any productions of genius, and renders it generally predominant. Many men, when left to themselves, have but a faint and dubious perception of beauty, who yet are capable of relishing any fine stroke which is pointed out to them. Every convert to the admiration of the real poet or orator is the cause of some new conversion. And though prejudices may prevail for a time, they never unite in celebrating any rival to the true genius, but yield at last to the force of nature and just sentiment. Thus, though a civilized nation may easily be mistaken in the choice of their admired philosopher, they never have been

[11] branches of knowledge.

found long to err in their affection for a favorite epic or tragic author.

But notwithstanding all our endeavors to fix a standard of taste, and reconcile the discordant apprehensions of men, there still remain two sources of variation, which are not sufficient indeed to confound all the boundaries of beauty and deformity, but will often serve to produce a difference in the degrees of our approbation or blame. The one is the different humors of particular men; the other, the particular manners and opinions of our age and country. The general principles of taste are uniform in human nature; where men vary in their judgments, some defect or perversion in the faculties may commonly be remarked, proceeding either from prejudice, from want of practice, or want of delicacy; and there is just reason for approving one taste and condemning another. But where there is such a diversity in the internal frame or external situation as is entirely blameless on both sides, and leaves no room to give one the preference above the other, in that case a certain degree of diversity in judgment is unavoidable, and we seek in vain for a standard by which we can reconcile the contrary sentiments.

A young man, whose passions are warm, will be more sensibly touched with amorous and tender images than a man more advanced in years, who takes pleasure in wise, philosophical reflections concerning the conduct of life and moderation of the passions. At twenty, Ovid may be the favorite author, Horace at forty, and perhaps Tacitus at fifty. Vainly would we, in such cases, endeavor to enter into the sentiments of others and divest ourselves of those propensities which are natural to us. We choose our favorite author as we do our friend, from a conformity of humor and disposition. Mirth or passion, sentiment or reflection: whichever of these most predominates in our temper, it gives us a peculiar sympathy with the writer who resembles us.

One person is more pleased with the sublime, another with the tender, a third with raillery. One has a strong sensibility to blemishes, and is extremely studious of correctness; another has a more lively feeling of beauties, and pardons twenty absurdities and defects for one elevated or pathetic stroke. The ear of this man is entirely turned towards conciseness and energy; that man is delighted with a copious, rich, and harmonious expression. Simplicity is affected by one; ornament by another. Comedy, tragedy, satire, odes have each its partisans who prefer that particular species of writing to all others. It is plainly an error in a critic to confine his approbation to one species or style of writing, and condemn all the rest. But it is almost impossible not to feel a predilection for that which suits our particular turn and disposition. Such preferences are innocent and unavoidable, and can never reasonably be the object of dispute because there is no standard by which they can be decided.

For a like reason, we are more pleased in the course of our reading with pictures and characters that resemble objects which are found in our own age or country than with those which describe a different set of customs. It is not without some effort that we reconcile ourselves to the simplicity of ancient manners, and behold princesses carrying water from the spring, and kings and heroes dressing[12] their own victuals. We may allow in general that the representation of such manners is no fault in the author, nor deformity in the piece; but we are not so sensibly touched with them. For this reason, comedy is not easily transferred from one age or nation to another. A Frenchman or Englishman is not pleased with the *Andria* of Terence, or *Clitia* of Machiavel: where the fine lady, upon whom all the play turns, never once appears to the spectators, but is always kept behind the scenes, suitably to the reserved humor of the ancient Greeks and modern Italians. A man of learning and reflection can make allowance for these peculiarities of manners; but a common audience can never divest themselves so far of their usual ideas and sentiments as to relish pictures which nowise resemble them.

But here there occurs a reflection which may, perhaps, be useful in examining the celebrated controversy concerning ancient and modern learning;[13] where we often find the one side excusing any seeming absurdity in the ancients from the manners of the age, and the other refusing to admit this excuse, or at least admitting it only as an apology for the author, not for the performance. In my opinion, the proper boundaries in this subject have seldom been

---

[12] preparing.

[13] This controversy, which erupted at the end of the seventeenth century over whether modern writers were superior to those of Greece and Rome, is best remembered for Swift's burlesque of it in *The Battle of the Books*.

fixed between the contending parties. Where any innocent peculiarities of manners are represented, such as those above mentioned, they ought certainly to be admitted; and a man who is shocked with them gives an evident proof of false delicacy and refinement. The poet's *monument more durable than brass*[14] must fall to the ground like common brick or clay, were men to make no allowance for the continual revolutions of manners and customs, and would admit of nothing but what was suitable to the prevailing fashion. Must we throw aside the pictures of our ancestors because of their ruffs and farthingales? But where the ideas of morality and decency alter from one age to another, and where vicious manners[15] are described, without being marked with the proper characters of blame and disapprobation, this must be allowed to disfigure the poem, and to be a real deformity. I cannot, nor is it proper I should, enter into such sentiments; and however I may excuse the poet, on account of the manners of his age, I never can relish the composition. The want of humanity and of decency so conspicuous in the characters drawn by several of the ancient poets, even sometimes by Homer and the Greek tragedians, diminishes considerably the merit of their noble performances, and gives modern authors an advantage over them. We are not interested in the fortunes and sentiments of such rough heroes; we are displeased to find the limits of vice and virtue so much confounded; and whatever indulgence we may give to the writer on account of his prejudices, we cannot prevail on ourselves to enter into his sentiments, or bear an affection to characters which we plainly discover to be blamable.

The case is not the same with moral principles as with speculative[16] opinions of any kind. These are in continual flux and revolution. The son embraces a different system from the father. Nay, there scarcely is any man who can boast of great constancy and uniformity in this particular. Whatever speculative errors may be found in the polite[17] writings of any age or country, they detract but little from the value of those compositions. There needs but a certain turn of thought or imagination to make us enter into all the opinions which then prevailed, and relish the sentiments or con-

---

[14] Horace, *Odes*, III xxx 1.

[15] ways of life, customs; also, characters.

[16] theoretical.

[17] polished, civilized.

clusions derived from them. But a very violent effort is requisite to change our judgment of manners, and excite sentiments of approbation or blame, love or hatred, different from those to which the mind, from long custom, has been familiarized. And where a man is confident of the rectitude of that moral standard by which he judges, he is justly jealous of it, and will not pervert the sentiments of his heart for a moment, in complaisance to any writer whatsoever.

Of all speculative errors, those which regard religion are the most excusable in compositions of genius; nor is it ever permitted to judge of the civility[18] or wisdom of any people, or even of single persons, by the grossness or refinement of their theological principles. The same good sense that directs men in the ordinary occurrences of life is not hearkened to in religious matters, which are supposed to be placed altogether above the cognizance of human reason. On this account, all the absurdities of the pagan system of theology must be overlooked by every critic who would pretend to form a just notion of ancient poetry; and our posterity, in their turn, must have the same indulgence to their forefathers. No religious principles can ever be imputed as a fault to any poet, while they remain merely principles, and take not such strong possession of his heart as to lay him under the imputation of *bigotry* or *superstition*. Where that happens, they confound[19] the sentiments of morality, and alter the natural boundaries of vice and virtue. They are therefore eternal blemishes, according to the principle above mentioned; nor are the prejudices and false opinions of the age sufficient to justify them.

It is essential to the Roman Catholic religion to inspire a violent hatred of every other worship, and to represent all pagans, Mahometans, and heretics, as the objects of divine wrath and vengeance. Such sentiments, though they are in reality very blamable, are considered as virtues by the zealots of that communion, and are represented in their tragedies and epic poems as a kind of divine heroism. This bigotry has disfigured two very fine tragedies of the French theater, *Polyeucte*[20] and *Athalia*, where an

---

[18] culture.   [19] confuse, upset.

[20] Corneille's *Polyeucte* (?1642) tells the story of a Christian executed by the Romans for refusing to renounce his beliefs. Racine's *Athalia* (1691) tells how Joad, the Jewish high priest, overthrows the idolatrous queen Athalia, and places the rightful ruler, the child Joas, on the throne of Judah.

intemperate zeal for particular modes of worship is set off with all the pomp imaginable, and forms the predominant character of the heroes. "What is this," says the sublime Joad to Josabet, finding her in discourse with Mathan, the priest of Baal, "Does the daughter of David speak to this traitor? Are you not afraid lest the earth should open, and pour forth flames to devour you both? Or lest these holy walls should fall and crush you together? What is his purpose? Why comes that enemy of God hither to poison the air which we breathe, with his horrid presence?" Such sentiments are received with great applause on the theater of Paris; but at London the spectators would be full as much pleased to hear Achilles tell Agamemnon that he was a dog in his forehead and a deer in his heart; or Jupiter threaten Juno with a sound drubbing, if she will not be quiet.[21]

Religious principles are also a blemish in any polite composition, when they rise up to superstition, and intrude themselves into every sentiment, however remote from any connection with religion. It is no excuse for the poet that the customs of his country had burthened life with so many religious ceremonies and observances that no part of it was exempt from that yoke. It must for ever be ridiculous in Petrarch to compare his mistress, Laura, to Jesus Christ. Nor is it less ridiculous in that agreeable libertine, Boccace,[22] very seriously to give thanks to God Almighty and the ladies, for their assistance in defending him against his enemies.

[21] two incidents from the *Iliad*, i 225, 560-67.
[22] Giovanni Boccaccio (1313-75), author of *The Decameron*.

❧ Charles Churchill ❧

Charles Churchill (1732-64), a remarkable scholar at Westminster School, made an early and quick marriage which probably prevented him from attending Cambridge; like his father, he became a minister. Debts and dissatisfaction with the ministry led him to write, and publish at his own expense, *The Rosciad* (1761), a very successful satire on contemporary actors. Soon afterward he met John Wilkes, the extraordinary politician, man of the world, and rabble rouser, and joined with him in producing a periodical, *The North Briton* (1762-63). Their main object of attack was the Ministry of the Scottish Earl of Bute, the favorite of the young George III, and the Scots who descended like locusts, according to the dissatisfied, upon London after Bute's appointment. The rest of Churchill's brief life was mainly taken up with writing personal and political satires at high speed, including *The Author, Gotham, The Times, The Candidate* (like Gray's *Candidate*, an attack on Lord Sandwich), and the fragmentary *Dedication to the Sermons* (an attack on Bishop Warburton).

Edition: Poetical Works, ed. Douglas Grant (1956).

Biography: Wallace C. Brown, *Charles Churchill* (1953).

Critical Studies: J. M. Beatty, "The Political Satires of Charles Churchill," SP 16 (1919); Wallace C. Brown, *The Triumph of Form* (1948).

The Prophecy of Famine

A SCOTS PASTORAL
[*1762, 1763*]

Carmina tum melius, cum venerit ipse, canemus—
DR. KING, OXON.[1]

When Cupid first instructs his darts to fly
From the sly corner of some cook-maid's eye,
The stripling raw, just entered in his teens,
Receives the wound, and wonders what it means;
His heart like dripping melts, and new desire   5
Within him stirs, each time she stirs the fire;
Trembling and blushing, he the fair one views,
And fain would speak, but can't—without a Muse.
   So, to the sacred mount he takes his way,
Prunes his young wings, and tunes his infant lay;   10
His oaten reed to rural ditties frames,
To flocks and rocks, to hills and rills, proclaims,
In simplest notes, and all unpolished strains,
The loves of nymphs, and eke the loves of swains.
   Clad, as your nymphs were always clad of yore,   15
In rustic weeds—a cook-maid now no more—
Beneath an agèd oak Lardella lies,
Green moss her couch; her canopy the skies.
From aromatic shrubs the roguish gale
Steals young perfumes, and wafts them through the vale. 20
The youth, turned swain, and skilled in rustic lays,
Fast by her side his amorous descant plays.
Herds low, flocks bleat, pies[2] chatter, ravens scream,

---

[1] "We shall sing better songs when he himself [the Pretender] arrives." William King was an Oxford don, and head of the Jacobite party at Oxford until his recantation at the accession of George III. In *North Briton*, no. 32, he is described as a "factious, pestilent, vain old man."

[2] magpies.

And the full chorus dies a-down the stream.
The streams, with music freighted, as they pass   25
Present the fair Lardella with a glass,
And Zephyr, to complete the lovesick plan,
Waves his light wings and serves her for a fan.
  But when maturer Judgment takes the lead,
These childish toys on Reason's altar bleed;   30
Formed after some great man,[3] whose name breeds awe,
Whose every sentence Fashion makes a law,
Who on mere credit his vain trophies rears,
And founds his merit on our servile fears;
Then we discard the workings of the heart,   35
And nature's banished by mechanic art;
Then, deeply read, our reading must be shown;
Vain is that knowledge which remains unknown.
Then Ostentation marches to our aid,
And lettered Pride stalks forth in full parade;   40
Beneath their care behold the work refine,
Pointed each sentence,[4] polished every line.
Trifles are dignified, and taught to wear
The robes of ancients with a modern air;
Nonsense with classic ornaments is graced,   45
And passes current with the stamp of Taste.
  Then the rude Theocrite[5] is ransacked o'er,
And courtly Maro[6] called from Mincio's shore;
Sicilian Muses on our mountains roam,
Easy and free as if they were at home;   50
Nymphs, Naiads, Nereids, Dryads, Satyrs, Fauns,
Sport in our floods and trip it o'er our lawns;
Flowers which once flourished fair in Greece and Rome,
More fair revive in England's meads to bloom;
Skies without cloud exotic suns adorn,   55
And roses blush, but blush without a thorn;
Landscapes unknown to dowdy Nature rise,

[3] Bute.
[4] thought or maxim, as well as grammatical unit.
[5] the rustic Theocritus, Greek writer of Sicilian pastorals.
[6] Virgil (Publius Virgilius Maro) was born near Mantua on the Mincio River.

And new creations strike our wondering eyes.
For bards like these, who neither sing nor say,
Grave without thought, and without feeling gay,   60
Whose numbers[7] in one even tenor flow,
Attuned to pleasure, and attuned to woe;
Who, if plain Common-sense her visit pays,
And mars one couplet in their happy lays,
As at some ghost affrighted, start and stare,   65
And ask the meaning of her coming there;
For bards like these a wreath shall Mason[8] bring,
Lined with the softest down of Folly's wing;
In Love's Pagoda[9] shall they ever doze,
And Gisbal[10] kindly rock them to repose;   70
My Lord[11]—to letters as to faith most true—
At once their patron and example too—
Shall quaintly fashion his love-labored dreams,
Sigh with sad winds, and weep with weeping streams,
Curious[11a] in grief (for real grief, we know,   75
Is curious to dress up the tale of woe)
From the green umbrage of some Druid's seat
Shall his own works in his own way repeat.
Me, whom no Muse of heavenly birth inspires,
No judgment tempers when rash genius fires;   80
Who boast no merit but mere knack of rhyme,
Short gleams of sense, and satire out of time;
Who cannot follow where trim fancy leads
By prattling streams, o'er flower-empurpled meads;
Who often, but without success, have prayed   85
For apt Alliteration's artful aid;

---

[7] verses.

[8] William Mason wove "an ivy chaplet" for the "blessed Shade" of Pope in his pastoral monody, *Musaeus* (1747).

[9] the Great Pagoda erected at Kew, the seat of the Dowager Princess of Wales, George III's mother. She and Bute were lovers, according to contemporary slander.

[10] a pretended Ossianic fragment, actually a satire on Bute (Gisbal) and his public and private life.

[11] George Lyttelton, first Baron Lyttelton, author of some feeble pastorals, and a long monody on the death of his first wife. For his "faith," see note on l. 232. [11a] skillful, careful.

Who would, but cannot, with a master's skill,
Coin fine new epithets, which mean no ill;
Me, thus uncouth, thus every way unfit
For pacing poesy, and ambling wit,   90
Taste with contempt beholds, nor deigns to place
Amongst the lowest of her favored race.
     Thou, Nature, art my goddess—to thy law
Myself I dedicate—hence, slavish awe,
Which bends to fashion, and obeys the rules   95
Imposed at first, and since observed by fools.[12]
Hence those vile tricks which mar fair Nature's hue,
And bring the sober matron forth to view
With all that artificial, tawdry glare
Which virtue scorns, and none but strumpets wear.   100
Sick of those pomps, those vanities, that waste
Of toil, which critics now mistake for Taste,
Of false refinements sick, and labored ease,
Which Art, too thinly veiled, forbids to please,
By Nature's charms (inglorious truth!) subdued,   105
However plain her dress, and 'havior rude,
To northern climes my happier course I steer,
Climes where the goddess reigns throughout the year;
Where, undisturbed by Art's rebellious plan,
She rules the loyal laird and faithful clan.[13]   110
     To that rare soil, where virtues clustering grow,
What mighty blessings doth not England owe,
What wagon-loads of courage, wealth, and sense,
Doth each revolving day import from thence?
To us she gives, disinterested friend,   115
Faith without fraud, and Stuarts without end.[14]
When we prosperity's rich trappings wear,

[12] So Edmund rejects the accepted moral and social order in *King Lear* (I ii 1-6).

[13] an ironic allusion to the Scottish support of Prince Charles Edward in the '45.

[14] "It was noticed by the Opposition papers of the day that out of sixteen names in one list of gazette [that is, official] promotions there were eleven Stuarts and four M'Kenzies" (Tooke). James Stuart-Mackenzie was the political manager of Scotland for his brother, John Stuart, third Earl of Bute.

Come not her generous sons and take a share?
And if, by some disastrous turn of fate,
Change should ensue, and ruin seize our state,   120
Shall we not find, safe in that hallowed ground,
Such refuge as the holy martyr[15] found?
   Nor less our debt in science,[16] though denied
By the weak slaves of prejudice and pride.
Thence came the Ramsays,[17] names of worthy note,   125
Of whom one paints as well as t'other wrote;
Thence, Home,[18] disbanded from the sons of prayer
For loving plays, though no dull dean[19] was there;
Thence issued forth, at great Macpherson's call,
That old, new, epic pastoral, *Fingal;*[20]   130
Thence Malloch,[21] friend alike of church and state,
Of Christ and Liberty, by grateful Fate
Raised to rewards, which, in a pious reign,[22]
All daring infidels should seek in vain;
Thence simple bards, by simple prudence taught,   135
To this wise town by simple patrons brought,
In simple manner utter simple lays,

[15] Charles I, whom the Scots handed over to the English Parliamentary forces for part of a sum of money due them.

[16] arts.

[17] Allan Ramsay, author of a pastoral drama, *The Gentle Shepherd* (which Churchill parodies in ll. 343-402), and his son, Allan Ramsay, later Painter in Ordinary to George III, to whom he had been introduced by Bute. The elder Ramsay had been a Jacobite, and the younger Ramsay was falsely suspected of being one.

[18] The Rev. John Home (see Collins' *Ode on the Popular Superstitions of the Highlands*, note on l. 1) was forced to resign from the ministry for allowing his neoclassical tragedy, *Douglas*, to be staged in 1756. Bute procured a sinecure office and government pension for him.

[19] apparently Zachary Pearce, Dean of Westminster, who had reprimanded Churchill for his unclerical dress and conduct.

[20] For Macpherson, see Goldsmith's *Retaliation*, note on l. 87. *Fingal* was one of his Ossianic productions. The advertisement prefixed to it contains a eulogy of Bute.

[21] David Mallet (originally, Malloch) was a Scottish skeptic, who published an edition of the deistic works of Bolingbroke. Mallet's tragedy, *Elvira* (1763), was dedicated to Bute "as a friend to all the liberal arts." Bute gave him a sinecure.

[22] Churchill thought George III's piety was hypocritical.

And take, with simple pensions, simple praise.
   Waft me, some Muse, to Tweed's inspiring stream,
Where all the little loves and graces dream;   140
Where, slowly winding, the dull waters creep,
And seem themselves to own the power of sleep;[23]
Where on the surface lead, like feathers, swims;
There let me bathe my yet unhallowed limbs,
As once a Syrian bathed in Jordan's flood,[24]   145
Wash off my native stains, correct that blood
Which mutinies at call of English pride,
And, deaf to prudence, rolls a patriot[25] tide.
   From solemn thought which overhangs the brow
Of patriot care, when things are—God knows how;   150
From nice trim points, where Honor, slave to rule,
In compliment to folly plays the fool;
From those gay scenes, where mirth exalts his power,
And easy humor wings the laughing hour;
From those soft better moments, when desire   155
Beats high, and all the world of man's on fire;
When mutual ardors of the melting fair
More than repay us for whole years of care,
At friendship's summons will my Wilkes retreat,[26]
And see, once seen before, that ancient seat,   160
That ancient seat, where majesty displayed
Her ensigns, long before the world was made?
   Mean narrow maxims which enslave mankind
Ne'er from its bias warp thy settled mind.
Not duped by party nor opinion's slave,   165
Those faculties which bounteous nature gave

[23] As often elsewhere in the poem, Churchill alludes to Pope, here to his attack on dull poetry (*Essay on Criticism*, ll. 352-53):

> If crystal streams "with pleasing murmurs creep,"
> The reader's threatened (not in vain) with "sleep."

[24] Naaman was cured of leprosy by bathing in the Jordan (II Kings 5).

[25] here used both in its modern sense, and for one in Opposition to the Ministry.

[26] For Wilkes, see introductory sketch. He had toured Scotland in 1758, but the rest of the allusion has not been satisfactorily explained. *The Prophecy of Famine* is inscribed to Wilkes.

Thy honest spirit into practice brings,
Nor courts the smile, nor dreads the frown of kings.
Let rude, licentious Englishmen comply
With tumult's voice, and curse they know not why;   170
Unwilling to condemn, thy soul disdains
To wear vile faction's arbitrary chains,
And strictly weighs, in apprehension clear,
Things as they are, and not as they appear.
With thee Good Humor tempers lively Wit;   175
Enthroned with Judgment, Candor loves to sit,
And nature gave thee, open to distress,
A heart to pity and a hand to bless.
    Oft have I heard thee mourn the wretched lot
Of the poor, mean, despised, insulted Scot,   180
Who, might calm reason credit idle tales,
By rancor forged where prejudice prevails,
Or starves at home, or practices, through fear
Of starving, arts which damn all conscience here.
When scribblers, to the charge by interest led,   185
The fierce *North Briton* foaming at their head,
Pour forth invectives, deaf to candor's call,
And, injured by one alien, rail at all;
On northern Pisgah[27] when they take their stand,
To mark the weakness of that Holy Land,   190
With needless truths their libels to adorn,
And hang a nation up to public scorn,
Thy generous soul condemns the frantic rage,
And hates the faithful but ill-natured page.
    The Scots are poor, cries surly English pride;   195
True is the charge, nor by themselves denied.
Are they not then in strictest reason clear,
Who wisely come to mend their fortunes here?
If, by low supple arts successful grown,
They sapped our vigor to increase their own,   200
If, mean in want, and insolent in power,
They only fawned more surely to devour,
Roused by such wrongs should Reason take alarm,

[27] the mountain from which Moses viewed the Promised Land he was
not allowed to enter (Deuteronomy 3:23-29; 34:1-4).

And e'en the Muse for public safety arm;
But if they own ingenuous virtue's sway,   205
And follow where true honor points the way,
If they revere the hand by which they're fed,
And bless the donors for their daily bread,
Or by vast debts of higher import bound,
Are always humble, always grateful found;   210
If they, directed by Paul's holy pen,
Become discreetly all things to all men,[28]
That all men may become all things to them,
Envy may hate, but justice can't condemn.
"Into our places, states, and beds they creep":   215
They've sense to get what we want sense to keep.
   Once, be the hour accursed, accursed the place,
I ventured to blaspheme the chosen race.
Into those traps, which men, called patriots, laid,
By specious arts unwarily betrayed,   220
Madly I leagued against that sacred earth,
Vile parricide! which gave a parent birth.[29]
But shall I meanly error's path pursue,
When heavenly Truth presents her friendly clue?
Once plunged in ill, shall I go farther in?   225
To make the oath, was rash; to keep it, sin.
Backward I tread the paths I trod before,
And calm reflection hates what passion swore.
Converted (blessèd are the souls which know
Those pleasures which from true conversion flow,   230
Whether to reason, who now rules my breast,
Or to pure faith, like Lyttelton and West),[30]
Past crimes to expiate, be my present aim
To raise new trophies to the Scottish name;
To make (what can the proudest Muse do more?)   235
E'en faction's sons her brighter worth adore;

[28] "I am made all things to all men, that I might by all means save some" (I Corinthians 9:22).

[29] Apparently Churchill's mother was Scottish.

[30] Lyttelton, a skeptic, was brought to accept Christianity by Gilbert West, to whom he addressed his *Observations on the Conversion of St. Paul* (1747). It was commonly printed together with West's own *Observations on the Resurrection* (1747).

To make her glories, stamped with honest rhymes,
In fullest tide roll down to latest times.
   "Presumptuous wretch! and shall a Muse like thine,
An English Muse, the meanest of the nine,   240
Attempt a theme like this? Can her weak strain
Expect indulgence from the mighty Thane?[31]
Should he from toils of government retire,
And for a moment fan the poet's fire;
Should he, of sciences the moral friend,   245
Each curious, each important search suspend,
Leave unassisted Hill [32] of herbs to tell,
And all the wonders of a cockleshell,
Having the Lord's good grace[33] before his eyes,
Would not the Home[34] step forth and gain the prize?   250
Or if this wreath of honor might adorn
The humble brows of one in England born,
Presumptuous still thy daring must appear;
Vain all thy towering hopes whilst I am here."
   Thus spake a form, by silken smile, and tone   255
Dull and unvaried, for the Laureate[35] known,
Folly's chief friend, Decorum's eldest son,
In every party found, and yet of none.
This airy substance, this substantial shade,
Abashed I heard, and with respect obeyed.   260
   From themes too lofty for a bard so mean,
Discretion beckons to an humbler scene;
The restless fever of ambition laid,
Calm I retire, and seek the sylvan shade.
Now be the Muse disrobed of all her pride,   265

---

[31] Bute.

[32] John Hill, apothecary, actor, botanist, and hack writer. He wrote *The British Herbal* (1756), *A General Natural History* (1748-52), etc. Bute, his patron, was himself a botanist.

[33] favor (a parody of various Biblical passages, e.g., Genesis 6:8; 47:25; II Samuel 16:4).

[34] John Home (see note on l. 127). Churchill mocks the Scottish custom of calling a clan chieftain "the ——" (e.g., the MacNeil).

[35] William Whitehead, who had attacked Churchill in his *Charge to the Poets* (1762). Churchill here imitates Pope's treatment of Cibber in *The Dunciad.*

Be all the glare of verse by truth supplied,
And if plain nature pours a simple strain,
Which Bute may praise, and Ossian not disdain,
Ossian, sublimest, simplest bard of all,
Whom English infidels, Macpherson call,   270
Then round my head shall Honor's ensigns wave,
And pensions mark me for a willing slave.
    Two boys, whose birth, beyond all question, springs
From great and glorious, though forgotten, kings,
Shepherds of Scottish lineage, born and bred   275
On the same bleak and barren mountain's head,
By niggard nature doomed on the same rocks
To spin out life, and starve themselves and flocks,
Fresh as the morning, which, enrobed in mist,
The mountain top with usual dullness kissed,   280
Jockey and Sawney to their labors rose;
Soon clad I ween, where nature needs no clothes;
Where, from their youth enured to winter skies,
Dress and her vain refinements they despise.
    Jockey, whose manly high-boned cheeks to crown   285
With freckles spotted, flamed the golden down,
With mickle art could on the bagpipes play,
E'en from the rising to the setting day;
Sawney as long without remorse could bawl
Home's madrigals, and ditties from *Fingal*.   290
Oft at his strains, all natural though rude,
The Highland lass forgot her want of food,
And, whilst she scratched her lover into rest,
Sunk pleased, though hungry, on her Sawney's breast.
    Far as the eye could reach, no tree was seen;[36]   295
Earth, clad in russet, scorned the lively green.
The plague of locusts they secure defy,
For in three hours a grasshopper must die.
No living thing, whate'er its food, feasts there,
But the chameleon, who can feast on air.   300
No birds, except as birds of passage, flew;
No bee was known to hum, no dove to coo.
No streams, as amber smooth, as amber clear,

[36] The treelessness of Scotland was a standard English joke.

Were seen to glide, or heard to warble here.
Rebellion's spring, which through the country ran,   305
Furnished, with bitter draughts, the steady clan.
No flowers embalmed the air, but one white rose,[37]
Which, on the tenth of June, by instinct blows,
By instinct blows at morn, and when the shades
Of drizzly eve prevail, by instinct fades.   310
  One, and but one poor solitary cave,
Too sparing of her favors, nature gave;
That one alone (hard tax on Scottish pride!)
Shelter at once for man and beast supplied.
Their snares without[38] entangling briars spread,   315
And thistles, armed against th' invader's head,
Stood in close ranks, all entrance to oppose,
Thistles now held more precious than the rose.[39]
All creatures which, on nature's earliest plan,
Were formed to loathe, and to be loathed by man,   320
Which owed their birth to nastiness and spite,
Deadly to touch, and hateful to the sight,
Creatures, which when admitted in the ark
Their savior shunned, and rankled in the dark,
Found place within; marking her noisome road   325
With poison's trail, here crawled the bloated toad;
There webs were spread of more than common size,
And half-starved spiders preyed on half-starved flies;
In quest of food, efts[40] strove in vain to crawl;
Slugs, pinched with hunger, smeared the slimy wall;   330
The cave around with hissing serpents rung;
On the damp roof unhealthy vapor hung;
And Famine, by her children always known,
As proud as poor, here fixed her native throne.
  Here, for the sullen sky was overcast,   335
And summer shrunk beneath a wintry blast—
A native blast, which, armed with hail and rain,

[37] the Jacobite emblem, worn on Charles Edward's birthday.
[38] outside.
[39] The thistle and the rose are the Scottish and English national emblems respectively.
[40] newts.

Beat unrelenting on the naked swain—
The boys for shelter made; behind, the sheep,
Of which those shepherds every day take keep,   340
Sickly crept on, and with complainings rude,
On nature seemed to call, and bleat for food.

JOCKEY

Sith to this cave, by tempest, we're confined,
And within ken our flocks, under the wind,
Safe from the pelting of this perilous storm,   345
Are laid emong yon thistles, dry and warm,
What, Sawney, if by shepherds' art we try
To mock the rigor of this cruel sky?
What if we tune some merry roundelay?
Well dost thou sing, nor ill doth Jockey play.   350

SAWNEY

Ah! Jockey, ill advisest thou, I wis,[41]
To think of songs at such a time as this.
Sooner shall herbage crown these barren rocks,
Sooner shall fleeces clothe these ragged flocks,
Sooner shall want seize shepherds of the south,   355
And we forget to live from hand to mouth,
Than Sawney, out of season, shall impart
The songs of gladness with an aching heart.

JOCKEY

Still have I known thee for a silly swain;
Of things past help what boots it to complain?   360
Nothing but mirth can conquer fortune's spite;
No sky is heavy if the heart be light:
Patience is sorrow's salve; what can't be cured,
So Donald right areeds,[42] must be endured.

SAWNEY

Full silly swain, I wot,[43] is Jockey now.   365
How didst thou bear thy Maggy's falsehood? how,

---

[41] I know (pseudoarchaic form).
[42] counsels.   [43] I know.

When with a foreign loon[44] she stole away,
Didst thou forswear thy pipe and shepherd's lay?
Where was thy boasted wisdom then, when I
Applied those proverbs, which you now apply?   370

JOCKEY

O she was bonny! all the Highlands round
Was there a rival to my Maggy found?
More precious (though that precious is to all)
Than the rare medicine which we brimstone call,
Or that choice plant, so grateful to the nose,[45]   375
Which, in I know not what far country, grows,
Was Maggy unto me; dear do I rue
A lass so fair should ever prove untrue.

SAWNEY

Whether with pipe or song to charm the ear,
Through all the land did Jamie find a peer?   380
Cursed be that year by every honest Scot,
And in the shepherd's calendar forgot,
That fatal year,[46] when Jamie, hapless swain,
In evil hour forsook the peaceful plain.
Jamie, when our young laird discreetly fled,   385
Was seized, and hanged till he was dead, dead, dead.

JOCKEY

Full sorely may we all lament that day:
For all were losers in the deadly fray.
Five brothers had I on the Scottish plains,
Well dost thou know were none more hopeful swains;   390
Five brothers there I lost, in manhood's pride;
Two in the field, and three on gibbets died;
Ah! silly swains, to follow war's alarms;
Ah! what hath shepherd's life to do with arms?

[44] lout, rascal.
[45] tobacco (brimstone) and snuff.
[46] 1745.

SAWNEY

Mention it not—there saw I strangers clad   395
In all the honors of our ravished plaid;[47]
Saw the Ferrara,[48] too, our nation's pride,
Unwilling grace the awkward victor's side.
There fell our choicest youth, and from that day
Mote[49] never Sawney tune the merry lay;   400
Blessed those which fell! cursed those which still survive,
To mourn fifteen[50] renewed in forty-five.

Thus plained the boys, when from her throne of turf,
With boils embossed, and overgrown with scurf,
Vile humors, which, in life's corrupted well,   405
Mixed at the birth, not abstinence could quell,
Pale Famine reared the head; her eager eyes,
Where hunger e'en to madness seemed to rise,
Speaking aloud her throes and pangs of heart,
Strained to get loose, and from their orbs to start;   410
Her hollow cheeks were each a deep-sunk cell,
Where wretchedness and horror loved to dwell;
With double rows of useless teeth supplied,
Her mouth from ear to ear extended wide,
Which, when for want of food her entrails pined,   415
She oped, and cursing, swallowed naught but wind;
All shrivelled was her skin; and here and there,
Making their way by force, her bones lay bare;
Such filthy sight to hide from human view,
O'er her foul limbs a tattered plaid she threw.   420
  "Cease," cried the goddess, "cease, despairing swains,
And from a parent hear what Jove ordains!
  "Pent in this barren corner of the isle,
Where partial fortune never deigned to smile;
Like nature's bastards, reaping for our share   425

---

[47] After the '45, the clans were forbidden to wear the tartan or to carry arms.
[48] a city famous for its swords. The Highlanders' claymore is meant.
[49] might.
[50] 1715, when the Scots had risen in favor of the Old Pretender.

What was rejected by the lawful heir;
Unknown amongst the nations of the earth,
Or only known to raise contempt and mirth;
Long free, because the race of Roman braves
Thought it not worth their while to make us slaves;   430
Then into bondage by that nation brought,
Whose ruin we for ages vainly sought,
Whom still with unslacked hate we view, and still,
The power of mischief lost, retain the will;
Considered as the refuse of mankind,   435
A mass till the last moment left behind,
Which frugal nature doubted, as it lay,
Whether to stamp with life or throw away;
Which, formed in haste, was planted in this nook,
But never entered in creation's book;   440
Branded as traitors who for love of gold
Would sell their God, as once their king they sold;
Long have we borne this mighty weight of ill,
These vile injurious taunts, and bear them still;
But times of happier note are now at hand,   445
And the full promise of a better land:
There, like the sons of Israel, having trod,
For the fixed term of years ordained by God,
A barren desert, we shall seize rich plains,
Where milk with honey flows, and plenty reigns.   450
With some few natives joined, some pliant few,
Who worship interest and our track pursue,
There shall we, though the wretched people grieve,
Ravage at large, nor ask the owner's leave.

"For us, the earth shall bring forth her increase;   455
For us, the flocks shall wear a golden fleece;
Fat beeves shall yield us dainties not our own,
And the grape bleed a nectar yet unknown;
For our advantage shall their harvests grow,
And Scotsmen reap what they disdained to sow;   460
For us, the sun shall climb the eastern hill;
For us, the rain shall fall, the dew distill;
When to our wishes Nature cannot rise,
Art shall be tasked to grant us fresh supplies.

His brawny arm shall drudging Labor strain,   465
And for our pleasure suffer daily pain;
Trade shall for us exert her utmost powers,
Hers all the toil, and all the profit ours;
For us, the oak shall from his native steep
Descend, and fearless travel through the deep;   470
The sail of Commerce, for our use unfurled,
Shall waft the treasures of each distant world;
For us, sublimer heights shall science reach;
For us, their statesmen plot, their churchmen preach;
Their noblest limbs of council we'll disjoint,   475
And, mocking, new ones of our own appoint;
Devouring War, imprisoned in the north,
Shall, at our call, in horrid pomp break forth,
And when, his chariot-wheels with thunder hung,
Fell Discord braying with her brazen tongue,   480
Death in the van, with Anger, Hate, and Fear,
And Desolation stalking in the rear,
Revenge, by Justice guided, in his train,
He drives impetuous o'er the trembling plain,
Shall, at our bidding, quit his lawful prey,   485
And to meek, gentle, generous Peace give way.
    "Think not, my sons, that this so blessed estate
Stands at a distance on the roll of fate;
Already big with hopes of future sway,
E'en from this cave I scent my destined prey.   490
Think not that this dominion o'er a race
Whose former deeds shall time's last annals grace,
In the rough face of peril must be sought,
And with the lives of thousands dearly bought;
No—fooled by cunning, by that happy art   495
Which laughs to scorn the blundering hero's heart,
Into the snare shall our kind neighbors fall
With open eyes, and fondly give us all.
    "When Rome, to prop her sinking empire, bore
Their choicest levies to a foreign shore,   500
What if we seized, like a destroying flood,
Their widowed plains, and filled the realm with blood,
Gave an unbounded loose to manly rage,

And, scorning mercy, spared nor sex nor age?
When, for our interest too mighty grown,   505
Monarchs of warlike bent possessed the throne,
What if we strove divisions to foment,
And spread the flames of civil discontent,
Assisted those who 'gainst their king made head,
And gave the traitors refuge when they fled?   510
When restless Glory bade her sons advance,
And pitched her standard in the fields of France,
What if, disdaining oaths, an empty sound,
By which our nation never shall be bound,
Bravely we taught unmuzzled war to roam   515
Through the weak land, and brought cheap laurels home.
When the bold traitors leagued for the defense
Of law, religion, liberty, and sense,
When they against their lawful monarch rose,
And dared the Lord's anointed to oppose,[51]   520
What if we still revered the banished race,
And strove the royal vagrants to replace,[52]
With fierce rebellions shook th' unsettled state,
And greatly dared, though crossed by partial fate?
These facts, which might, where wisdom held the sway,   525
Awake the very stones to bar our way,
There shall be nothing, nor one trace remain
In the dull region of an English brain.
Blessed with that faith which mountains can remove,
First they shall dupes, next saints, last martyrs, prove. 530
    "Already is this game of fate begun
Under the sanction of my darling son;[53]
That son, whose nature, royal as his name,
Is destined to redeem our race from shame;
His boundless power, beyond example great,   535
Shall make the rough way smooth, the crooked straight,
Shall for our ease the raging floods restrain,
And sink the mountain level to the plain.

[51] the deposition of James II in favor of William III of Orange in
1688.
[52] reseat on the throne.
[53] Bute.

Discord, whom in a cavern under ground
With massy fetters their late patriot[54] bound,   540
Where her own flesh the furious hag might tear,
And vent her curses to the vacant air,
Where, that she never may be heard of more,
He planted Loyalty to guard the door,
For better purpose shall our chief release,   545
Disguise her for a time, and call her peace.
    "Lured by that name, fine engine of deceit,
Shall the weak English help themselves to cheat;
To gain our love, with honors shall they grace
The old adherents of the Stuart race,   550
Who, pointed out, no matter by what name,
Tories or Jacobites, are still the same;
To soothe our rage, the temporizing brood
Shall break the ties of truth and gratitude,
Against their savior venomed falsehoods frame,   555
And brand with calumny their William's[55] name;
To win our grace (rare argument of wit),
To our untainted faith shall they commit
(Our faith which, in extremest perils tried,
Disdained, and still disdains to change her side)   560
That sacred Majesty they all approve,
Who most enjoys, and best deserves their love."

[54] William Pitt, whose place as Prime Minister Bute had taken. Bute had concluded the preliminaries of the unpopular Treaty of Paris (1763) ending the Seven Years' War, as this poem was being written.
[55] William Augustus, Duke of Cumberland, victor at Culloden in 1745 over the Jacobite forces, and much hated in Scotland for his severe treatment of the rebels. In a notorious Jacobite oration delivered at Oxford in 1749, King implied that Cumberland feared everything but God.

❧ Christopher Smart ❧

Christopher Smart (1722-71) was born in Shipbourne, Kent, and educated at Cambridge, where he became a Fellow of Pembroke College. In 1749, tired of a restrictive academic life and burdened with debts, he left Cambridge and found work in London as a hack writer for John Newbery, a bookseller and publisher, whose daughter Smart married. Smart developed religious mania and had to be confined for seven years (1756-63). He spent the rest of his life in a losing struggle against poverty, and died in debtors' prison.

Though Smart's writings range from comic prose pieces in *The Midwife*, one of Newbery's magazines, to both prose and verse translations of Horace, he is remembered almost entirely for his religious poetry: *A Song to David*, a translation of the Psalms, and the strange, highly imaginative *Jubilate Agno* (*Rejoice in the Lamb*). *Jubilate Agno* shows the influence of Old Testament prophetic verse in its repetitive and rhapsodic formulations, in contrast to *A Song to David*, which is distinguished by its elaborately patterned structure.

Editions: Collected Poems, ed. N. C. Callan (1949); *Poems*, ed. Robert Brittain (1950); *Rejoice in the Lamb*, ed. William F. Stead (1939); *Jubilate Agno*, ed. W. H. Bond (1954).

Biography: E. G. Ainsworth and C. E. Noyes, *Christopher Smart: A Biographical and Critical Study* (1943).

Critical Studies: R. D. Havens, "The Structure of Smart's *Song to David*," *RES* 14 (1938); Brittain (listed above).

A Song to David
[1763]

David the son of Jesse said, and the man who was raised up on high, the anointed of the God of Jacob, and the sweet psalmist of Israel, said, "The Spirit of the Lord spake by me, and His word was in my tongue."   II SAMUEL 23:1-2.

O thou, that sit'st upon a throne,
With harp of high majestic tone,
   To praise the King of kings;
And voice of heaven-ascending swell,
Which, while its deeper notes excel,   5
   Clear as a clarion rings:

To bless each valley, grove, and coast,
And charm the cherubs to the post
   Of gratitude in throngs;
To keep the days on Zion's mount,   10
And send the year to his account,
   With dances and with songs;

O Servant of God's holiest charge,
The minister of praise at large,
   Which thou mayst now receive;   15
From thy blessed mansion hail and hear,
From topmost eminence appear
   To this the wreath I weave.

Great, valiant, pious, good, and clean,
Sublime, contemplative, serene,   20
   Strong, constant, pleasant, wise!
Bright effluence of exceeding grace;
Best man!—the swiftness and the race,
   The peril and the prize!

Great—from the luster of his crown,   25
From Samuel's horn[1] and God's renown,[2]

[1] the horn of oil with which Samuel anointed David (I Samuel 16:13).
[2] commendation.

Which is the people's voice;
For all the host, from rear to van,
Applauded and embraced the man—
    The man of God's own choice.   30

Valiant—the word and up he rose—
The fight—he triumphed o'er the foes
    Whom God's just laws abhor;
And armed in gallant faith he took
Against the boaster, from the brook,   35
    The weapons of the war.[3]

Pious—magnificent and grand;
'Twas he the famous temple planned:[4]
    (The seraph in his soul)
Foremost to give his Lord his dues,   40
Foremost to bless the welcome news,
    And foremost to condole.[5]

Good—from Jehudah's[6] genuine vein,
From God's best nature good in grain,[7]
    His aspect and his heart;   45
To pity, to forgive, to save:
Witness En-gedi's conscious cave,[8]
    And Shimei's blunted dart.[9]

Clean—if perpetual prayer be pure,
And love, which could itself inure   50
    To fasting and to fear—
Clean in his gestures, hands, and feet,

[3] David took pebbles from the brook for his sling to kill the "boaster," Goliath (I Samuel 17:40).

[4] God reserved the building of the temple of Jerusalem, which David had planned, for Solomon (I Chronicles 28).

[5] probably, grieve or lament (see David's lamentation over Saul and Jonathan—II Samuel 1:17-27).

[6] Judah, the tribe to which David belonged.

[7] indelibly good.

[8] the cave where David deliberately refrained from killing Saul (I Samuel 24).

[9] David forgave Shimei for cursing and throwing stones at him (II Samuel 16:5-14; 19:16-23).

To smite the lyre, the dance complete,
　　To play the sword and spear.

Sublime—invention ever young,　　　　　　　55
Of vast conception, towering tongue,
　　To God th' eternal theme;
Notes from yon exaltations caught,
Unrivaled royalty of thought,
　　O'er meaner strains supreme.　　　　　　60

Contemplative—on God to fix
His musings, and above the six
　　The sabbath-day he blessed;
'Twas then his thoughts self-conquest pruned,
And heavenly melancholy tuned,　　　　　　65
　　To bless and bear the rest.

Serene—to sow the seeds of peace,
Remembering, when he watched the fleece,
　　How sweetly Kidron[10] purled—
To further knowledge, silence vice,　　　　70
And plant perpetual paradise
　　When God had calmed the world.

Strong—in the Lord, who could defy
Satan, and all his powers that lie
　　In sempiternal night;　　　　　　　　　75
And hell and horror and despair
Were as the lion and the bear[11]
　　To his undaunted might.

Constant—in love to God the Truth,
Age, manhood, infancy, and youth—　　　　80
　　To Jonathan his friend
Constant, beyond the verge of death;
And Ziba and Mephibosheth
　　His endless fame attend.[12]

[10] a brook east of Jerusalem.
[11] See I Samuel 17:32-37.
[12] David restored the land of Saul to Mephibosheth, the son of his beloved friend Jonathan. Ziba, Saul's former servant, was placed in Mephibosheth's service.

Pleasant—and various as the year;   85
Man, soul, and angel, without peer,
    Priest, champion, sage, and boy;
In armour, or in ephod [13] clad,
His pomp, his piety was glad;
    Majestic was his joy.   90

Wise—in recovery from his fall,
Whence rose his eminence o'er all,
    Of all the most reviled;
The light of Israel in his ways,
Wise are his precepts, prayer, and praise,   95
    And counsel to his child.[14]

His Muse, bright angel of his verse,
Gives balm for all the thorns that pierce,
    For all the pangs that rage;
Blessed light, still gaining on the gloom,   100
The more than Michal [15] of his bloom,
    Th' Abishag[16] of his age.

He sung of God—the mighty source
Of all things—the stupendous force
    On which all strength depends;   105
From whose right arm, beneath whose eyes,
All period, power, and enterprise
    Commences, reigns, and ends.

Angels—their ministry and meed,
Which to and fro with blessings speed,   110
    Or with their citterns[17] wait;

[13] Jewish ceremonial vestment. David wore a linen ephod when he "danced before the Lord" (II Samuel 6:14).

[14] David's "fall" refers to his treatment of Uriah and Bathsheba (II Samuel 11-12). Patrick Delany, whose *Historical Account of David* (1740-42) Smart drew upon, considered part of the Book of Proverbs as David's instructions to Solomon.

[15] David's first wife.

[16] The young Abishag was used in an attempt to revive David in his old age (I Kings 1).

[17] The cittern is the ancestor of the zither.

Where Michael with his millions bows,
Where dwells the seraph and his spouse,
    The cherub and her mate.

Of man—the semblance and effect   115
Of God and love, the saint elect
    For infinite applause—
To rule the land, and briny broad,
To be laborious in his laud,
    And heroes in his cause.   120

The world—the clustering spheres he made,
The glorious light, the soothing shade,
    Dale, champaign, grove, and hill;
The multitudinous abyss,
Where secrecy remains in bliss,   125
    And wisdom hides her skill.

Trees, plants, and flowers—of virtuous[18] root;
Gem[19] yielding blossom, yielding fruit,
    Choice gums and precious balm;
Bless ye the nosegay in the vale,   130
And with the sweeteners of the gale
    Enrich the thankful psalm.

Of fowl—e'en every beak and wing
Which cheer the winter, hail the spring,
    That live in peace or prey;   135
They that make music, or that mock,
The quail, the brave domestic cock,
    The raven, swan, and jay.

Of fishes—every size and shape,
Which nature frames of light escape,   140
    Devouring man to shun;
The shells are in the wealthy deep,
The shoals[20] upon the surface leap,
    And love the glancing sun.

[18] potent, medicinal, beneficial.
[19] bud.   [20] schools of fish.

Of beasts—the beaver plods his task;   145
While the sleek tigers roll and bask,
    Nor yet the shades arouse;
Her cave the mining coney scoops;
Where o'er the mead the mountain stoops
    The kids exult and browse.   150

Of gems—their virtue and their price,
Which hid in earth from man's device,[21]
    Their darts of luster sheathe:
The jasper of the master's stamp,
The topaz blazing like a lamp   155
    Among the mines beneath.

Blessed was the tenderness he felt
When to his graceful harp he knelt,
    And did for audience call;
When Satan with his hand he quelled,   160
And in serene suspense he held
    The frantic throes of Saul.[22]

His furious foes no more maligned
As he such melody divined,
    And sense and soul detained;   165
Now striking strong, now soothing soft,
He sent the godly sounds aloft,
    Or in delight refrained.

When up to heaven his thoughts he piled,
From fervent lips fair Michal smiled,   170
    As blush to blush she stood,
And chose herself the queen, and gave
Her utmost from her heart, "so brave,
    And plays his hymns so good." [23]

[21] contrivance.

[22] David drove away the "evil spirit" (Satan) from Saul by playing on
his harp (I Samuel 16:23).

[23] Michal "loved David" (I Samuel 18:18-20), but Smart invents her
remark.

The pillars of the Lord are seven,[24]   175
Which stand from earth to topmost heaven;
   His wisdom drew the plan;
His Word accomplished the design,
From brightest gem to deepest mine,
   From Christ enthroned to man.   180

Alpha, the cause of causes, first
In station, fountain, whence the burst
   Of light, and blaze of day;
Whence bold attempt and brave advance
Have motion, life, and ordinance,   185
   And heaven itself its stay.

Gamma supports the glorious arch
On which angelic legions march,
   And is with sapphires paved;
Thence the fleet clouds are sent adrift,   190
And thence the painted folds, that lift
   The crimson veil, are waved.[25]

Eta with living sculpture breathes,
With verdant carvings, flowery wreathes
   Of never-wasting bloom;   195
In strong relief his goodly base
All instruments of labor grace,
   The trowel, spade, and loom.

Next Theta stands to the Supreme—
Who formed, in number, sign,[26] and scheme,   200
   Th' illustrious lights that are;
And one[27] addressed [28] his saffron robe,

[24] Smart correlates the seven pillars of the house of Wisdom (Proverbs 9:1) with the days of the week of creation. The significance of the Greek letters has not been satisfactorily explained, although the passage apparently has Masonic overtones.

[25] Not satisfactorily explained. Perhaps Smart refers to the furnishings of the temple in Jerusalem.

[26] division of the Zodiac.

[27] sun.

[28] put on, donned.

And one,[29] clad in a silver globe,
    Held rule with every star.

Iota's tuned to choral hymns   205
Of those that fly, while he that swims
    In thankful safety lurks;
And foot, and chapiter,[30] and niche,
The various histories enrich
    Of God's recorded works.   210

Sigma presents the social droves,
With him that solitary roves,
    And man of all the chief;
Fair on whose face, and stately frame,
Did God impress his hallowed name,   215
    For ocular belief.

Omega! Greatest and the Best,
Stands sacred to the day of rest,
    For gratitude and thought;
Which blessed the world upon his pole,   220
And gave the universe his goal,
    And closed th' infernal draught.[31]

O David, scholar of the Lord!
Such is thy science, whence reward
    And infinite degree;[32]   225
O strength, O sweetness, lasting ripe!
God's harp thy symbol, and thy type[33]
    The lion and the bee! [34]

There is but One who ne'er rebelled,
But One by passion unimpelled,   230
    By pleasures unenticed;

[29] moon.

[30] the head of a pillar.

[31] Perhaps (1) separated the created cosmos from chaos; (2) closed off hell ("draught" can mean "privy" or "cesspool").

[32] ascent in divine favor; possibly "degree" has Masonic overtones.

[33] model, emblem.

[34] Samson, finding honey in the carcass of a lion he had killed, said, "Out of the strong came forth sweetness" (Judges 14:14).

He from himself his semblance sent,
Grand object of his own content,
   And saw the God in Christ.

"Tell them I am," Jehovah said[35]   235
To Moses; while earth heard in dread,[36]
   And smitten to the heart,
At once above, beneath, around,
All nature, without voice or sound,
   Replied, "O Lord, Thou art."   240

Thou art—to give and to confirm
For each his talent and his term;
   All flesh thy bounties share.
Thou shalt not call thy brother fool;[37]
The porches[38] of the Christian school   245
   Are meekness, peace, and prayer.

Open, and naked of offence,
Man's made of mercy, soul, and sense;
   God armed the snail and wilk;[39]
Be good to him that pulls thy plough;   250
Due food and care, due rest, allow
   For her that yields thee milk.

Rise up before the hoary head,
And God's benign commandment dread,
   Which says thou shalt not die: 255
"Not as I will, but as thou wilt," [40]
Prayed He whose conscience knew no guilt;
   With whose blessed pattern vie.

Use all thy passions!—love is thine,
And joy, and jealousy[41] divine,   260

[35] In these nine stanzas Smart presents most of the Commandments in various forms.

[36] Exodus 3:14.

[37] Matthew 5:22.

[38] entrances or approaches, with an allusion to the Porch, a public walk in Athens associated with the Stoic philosophers.

[39] whelk, a marine snail.

[40] Matthew 26:39.

[41] zeal.

Thine hope's eternal fort;
And care thy leisure to disturb,
With fear concupiscence to curb,
    And rapture to transport.

Act simply, as occasion asks;[42]   265
Put mellow wine in seasoned casks,
    Till not with ass and bull.
Remember thy baptismal bond;
Keep from commixtures foul and fond,
    Nor work thy flax with wool.   270

Distribute: pay the Lord his tithe,
And make the widow's heartstrings blithe;
    Resort[43] with those that weep;
As you from all and each expect,
For all and each thy love direct,   ·   275
    And render as you reap.

The slander and its bearer spurn,
And propagating praise sojourn
    To make thy welcome last;
Turn from old Adam to the New;[44]   280
By hope futurity pursue;
    Look upwards to the past.

Control thine eye, salute success,
Honor the wiser, happier bless,
    And for thy neighbor feel;   285
Grutch[45] not of Mammon and his leaven,
Work emulation up to heaven
    By knowledge and by zeal.

O David, highest in the list
Of worthies, on God's ways insist,   290
    The genuine word repeat:[46]

[42] Smart paraphrases various Biblical injunctions in these three stanzas.
[43] consort.
[44] The New Adam is Christ (see I Corinthians 15:22, 45).
[45] complain.
[46] Psalm 119 (Smart).

Vain are the documents of men,
And vain the flourish of the pen
  That keeps the fool's conceit.

Praise above all—for praise prevails;   295
Heap up the measure, load the scales,
  And good to goodness add.
The generous soul her Savior aids,
But peevish obloquy degrades;
  The Lord is great and glad.   300

For Adoration all the ranks
Of angels yield eternal thanks,
  And David in the midst;
With God's good poor, which, last and least
In man's esteem, thou to thy feast,   305
  O blessed bridegroom, bidst.[47]

For Adoration seasons change,
And order, truth, and beauty range,
  Adjust, attract, and fill:
The grass the polyanthus checks;[48]   310
And polished porphyry reflects,
  By the descending rill.

Rich almonds color to the prime
For Adoration; tendrils climb,
  And fruit trees pledge their gems,   315
And Ivis[48a] with her gorgeous vest
Builds for her eggs her cunning nest,
  And bellflowers bow their stems.

With vinous syrup[49] cedars spout;
From rocks pure honey gushing out,[50]   320
  For Adoration springs.
All scenes of painting crowd the map

[47] See Revelation 22:16-17.
[48] perhaps meaning both "restrains" and "variegates."
[48a] hummingbird (Smart).
[49] sap (Psalm 104:16).
[50] Psalm 81:16.

Of nature; to the mermaid's pap
    The scalèd infant clings.

The spotted ounce and playsome cubs   325
Run rustling 'mongst the flowering shrubs,
    And lizards feed [51] the moss;
For Adoration beasts embark,[52]
While waves upholding halcyon's ark
    No longer roar and toss.   330

While Israel sits beneath his fig,[53]
With coral root and amber sprig
    The weaned adventurer sports;
Where to the palm the jasmine cleaves,
For Adoration 'mongst the leaves   335
    The gale his peace reports.

Increasing days their reign exalt,
Nor in the pink and mottled vault
    Th' opposing spirits[54] tilt;
And, by the coasting reader spied,   340
The silverlings[55] and crusions[56] glide
    For Adoration gilt.

For Adoration ripening canes
And cocoa's purest milk detains
    The western pilgrim's staff;   345
Where rain in clasping boughs inclosed,
And vines with oranges disposed,
    Embower the social laugh.

[51] feed upon.

[52] To explain "beasts embark," Smart added a footnote in the 1765 edition describing "a large quadruped" (the beaver?) that paddles around on "a piece of timber." But some reference to Noah's ark seems likely, as well as to the legend that the sea becomes calm when the kingfisher (halcyon) builds its nest on it.

[53] The image of Israel sitting beneath the fig tree suggests peace and security (see I Kings 4:25).

[54] winds.

[55] tarpons.

[56] crucians, carplike fish.

Now labor his reward receives,
For Adoration counts his sheaves   350
  To peace, her bounteous prince;
The nect'rine his strong tint imbibes,
And apples of ten thousand tribes,
  And quick peculiar quince.

The wealthy crops of whitening rice,   355
'Mongst thyine[57] woods and groves of spice,
  For Adoration grow;
And, marshalled in the fencèd land,
The peaches and pomegranates stand,
  Where wild carnations blow.   360

The laurels with the winter strive;
The crocus burnishes alive
  Upon the snow-clad earth;
For Adoration myrtles stay
To keep the garden from dismay,   365
  And bless the sight from dearth.

The pheasant shows his pompous neck;
And ermine, jealous of a speck,
  With fear eludes offence;
The sable, with his glossy pride,   370
For Adoration is descried,
  Where frosts the wave condense.

The cheerful holly, pensive yew,
And holy thorn, their trim renew;
  The squirrel hoards his nuts;   375
All creatures batten o'er their stores,
And careful nature all her doors
  For Adoration shuts.

For Adoration, David's psalms
Lift up the heart to deeds of alms;   380
  And he who kneels and chants
Prevails his passions to control,

[57] a precious wood mentioned in Revelation 18:12.

Finds meat and medicine to the soul,
    Which for translation[58] pants.

For Adoration, beyond match,   385
The scholar bullfinch[58a] aims to catch
    The soft flute's ivory touch;
And, careless on the hazel spray,
The daring redbreast keeps at bay
    The damsel's greedy clutch.   390

For Adoration, in the skies,
The Lord's philosopher espies
    The Dog, the Ram, and Rose;
The planet's ring, Orion's sword;
Nor is his greatness less adored   395
    In the vile worm that glows.

For Adoration on the strings[59]
The western breezes work their wings,
    The captive ear to soothe.
Hark! 'tis a voice[60]—how still and small—   400
That makes the cataracts to fall,
    Or bids the sea be smooth.

For Adoration, incense comes
From bezoar,[61] and Arabian gums,
    And on the civet's fur.   405
But as for prayer, or ere it faints,[62]
Far better is the breath of saints
    Than galbanum[63] and myrrh.

For Adoration, from the down
Of damsons to th' anana's[64] crown,   410

---

[58] removal to heaven.

[58a] a bird taught to imitate sounds, like the parrot.

[59] Aeolian harp (Smart).

[60] of God (I Kings 19:11-12).

[61] a concretion found in the stomach or intestines of some animals; it is used as an antidote to poison, not for incense.

[62] before it dies away.

[63] an aromatic gum.

[64] properly ananas', the pineapple's.

God sends to tempt the taste;
And while the luscious zest invites
The sense, that in the scene delights,
   Commands desire be chaste.

For Adoration, all the paths   415
Of grace are open, all the baths
   Of purity refresh;
And all the rays of glory beam
To deck the man of God's esteem,
   Who triumphs o'er the flesh.   420

For Adoration, in the dome
Of Christ the sparrows find an home,
   And on his olives perch;
The swallow also dwells with thee,
O man of God's humility,   425
   Within his savior Church.[65]

Sweet is the dew that falls betimes,
And drops upon the leafy limes;
   Sweet Hermon's[66] fragrant air;
Sweet is the lily's silver bell,   430
And sweet the wakeful tapers smell
   That watch for early prayer.

Sweet the young nurse with love intense,
Which smiles o'er sleeping innocence;
   Sweet when the lost arrive;   435
Sweet the musician's ardor beats,
While his vague mind's in quest of sweets,
   The choicest flowers to hive.

Sweeter in all the strains of love,
The language of thy turtle dove,   440
   Paired to thy swelling chord;
Sweeter with every grace endued,
The glory of thy gratitude,
   Respired unto the Lord.

[65] Psalm 84:3.
[66] The dew of Mt. Hermon is mentioned in Psalm 133.

Strong is the horse upon his speed; 445
Strong in pursuit the rapid glede,[67]
   Which makes at once his game;
Strong the tall ostrich on the ground;
Strong through the turbulent profound
   Shoots xiphias[68] to his aim. 450

Strong is the lion—like a coal
His eyeball—like a bastion's mole
   His chest against the foes;
Strong, the gier-eagle[69] on his sail,
Strong against tide, th' enormous whale 455
   Emerges as he goes.

But stronger still, in earth and air,
And in the sea, the man of prayer;
   And far beneath the tide;
And in the seat to faith assigned, 460
Where ask is have, where seek is find,
   Where knock is open wide.[70]

Beauteous the fleet before the gale;
Beauteous the multitudes in mail,
   Ranked arms and crested heads; 465
Beauteous the garden's umbrage mild,
Walk, water, meditated [71] wild,
   And all the bloomy beds.

Beauteous the moon full on the lawn;
And beauteous, when the veil's withdrawn, 470
   The virgin to her spouse;
Beauteous the temple decked and filled,
When to the heaven of heavens they build
   Their heart-directed vows.

Beauteous, yea beauteous more than these, 475
The shepherd king upon his knees,

[67] kite (bird).
[68] the swordfish (Smart).
[69] a Biblical bird, probably the vulture.
[70] Matthew 7:7.
[71] planned, artificial.

For his momentous trust;
With wish of infinite conceit,[72]
For man, beast, mute, the small and great,
   And prostrate dust to dust.   480

Precious the bounteous widow's mite;[73]
And precious, for extreme delight,
   The largess from the churl;[74]
Precious the ruby's blushing blaze,
And alba's blessed imperial rays,[75]   485
   And pure cerulean pearl.

Precious the penitential tear;
And precious is the sigh sincere,
   Acceptable to God;
And precious are the winning flowers,   490
In gladsome Israel's feast of bowers,
   Bound on the hallowed sod.[76]

More precious that diviner part
Of David, even the Lord's own heart,[77]
   Great, beautiful, and new;   495
In all things where it was intent,
In all extremes, in each event,
   Proof—answering true to true.

Glorious the sun in mid-career;
Glorious th' assembled fires appear;   500
   Glorious the comet's train;
Glorious the trumpet and alarm;
Glorious th' almighty stretched-out arm;
   Glorious th' enraptured main;

Glorious the northern lights astream;   505
Glorious the song, when God's the theme;
   Glorious the thunder's roar;

[72] conception, imagination.
[73] Mark 12:42-44.
[74] A reference to the story of Nabal and Abigail (I Samuel 25).
[75] "the white stone" of Revelation 2:17.
[76] the Feast of Tabernacles (see Leviticus 23:34-44).
[77] David is called the man after God's own heart (Acts 13:22).

Glorious hosanna from the den;[78]
Glorious the catholic amen;
   Glorious the martyr's gore;   510

Glorious—more glorious is the crown
Of Him that brought salvation down
   By meekness, called thy Son;
Thou at stupendous truth believed,
And now the matchless deed's achieved,   515
   Determined, Dared, and Done.

[78] the lion's den in which Daniel was preserved (Daniel 6:22-23).

❧ *Oliver Goldsmith* ❧

Oliver Goldsmith (?1730-74) was born in Ireland, educated at Trinity College, Dublin, and studied medicine at Edinburgh and Leyden. After making a vagabond version of the Grand Tour later recalled in his poem, *The Traveller,* he settled in London in 1757 as a hack writer. His career was increasingly successful, but his generosity, expensive tastes, and financial ineptitude kept him drudging at compilations and other ephemeral work for most of his remaining life. A clumsy and ugly man whose desire to shine made him the amusement of his friends, he was nevertheless a highly regarded and much-liked member of the Johnson circle.

Goldsmith was the most versatile of all major eighteenth-century writers. As essayist (*The Bee,* 1759; *The Citizen of the World,* 1762), novelist (*The Vicar of Wakefield,* 1766), dramatist (*She Stoops to Conquer,* 1773), and poet, the easiness and elegance of his style, his mild but shrewd comic view of life, and his command of combined pathos and irony make him still worth reading. His once highly popular histories of Greece, Rome, England, and even of "Earth and Animated Nature" hardly pretended to be more than readable surveys.

Editions: Works, ed. J. W. M. Gibbs (1884-86); *Poetical Works,* ed. Austin Dobson (1906); *Plays, together with The Vicar of Wakefield,* ed. C. E. Doble and G. Ostler (1909); *New Essays,* ed. R. S. Crane (1927); *Letters,* ed. K. C. Balderston (1928); *The Vicar of Wakefield and Other Writings,* ed. F. W. Hilles (1955).

Biography: R. M. Wardle, *Oliver Goldsmith* (1957).

Critical Studies: T. S. Eliot, Introduction to Johnson's *London* (1930); Donald Davie, *"The Deserted Village," Twentieth Century* 156 (1954); Earl Miner, "The Making of *The Deserted Village,"* *HLQ* 22 (1959).

The Deserted Village[1]
[1770]

Sweet Auburn, loveliest village of the plain,
Where health and plenty cheered the laboring swain,
Where smiling spring its earliest visit paid,
And parting summer's lingering blooms delayed;
Dear lovely bowers of innocence and ease,   5
Seats of my youth, when every sport could please,
How often have I loitered o'er thy green,
Where humble happiness endeared each scene;
How often have I paused on every charm,
The sheltered cot,[2] the cultivated farm,   10
The never failing brook, the busy mill,
The decent[3] church that topped the neighboring hill,
The hawthorn bush, with seats beneath the shade,
For talking age and whispering lovers made;
How often have I blessed the coming day,   15
When toil remitting lent its turn to play,
And all the village train, from labor free,
Led up their sports beneath the spreading tree;
While many a pastime circled in the shade,
The young contending as the old surveyed;   20
And many a gambol frolicked o'er the ground,
And sleights of art and feats of strength went round;
And still, as each repeated pleasure tired,
Succeeding sports the mirthful band inspired;
The dancing pair that simply[4] sought renown,   25
By holding out to tire each other down;
The swain mistrustless of his smutted face,
While secret laughter tittered round the place;

[1] Goldsmith's dedicatory note to Sir Joshua Reynolds, in which he
deplores the depopulation of the countryside and the increase of luxury, is
omitted.
 [2] cottage.
 [3] seemly.
 [4] artlessly.

The bashful virgin's sidelong looks of love,
The matron's glance that would those looks reprove: 30
These were thy charms, sweet village; sports like these,
With sweet succession, taught even toil to please;
These round thy bowers their cheerful influence shed;
These were thy charms—but all these charms are fled.
　　Sweet smiling village, loveliest of the lawn,[5]   35
Thy sports are fled and all thy charms withdrawn;
Amidst thy bowers the tyrant's hand is seen,
And desolation saddens all thy green;
One only master grasps the whole domain,[6]
And half a tillage stints[7] thy smiling plain;   40
No more thy glassy brook reflects the day,
But choked with sedges works its weedy way;
Along thy glades, a solitary guest,
The hollow-sounding bittern guards its nest;
Amidst thy desert walks the lapwing flies,   45
And tires their echoes with unvaried cries.
Sunk are thy bowers in shapeless ruin all,
And the long grass o'ertops the moldering wall;
And, trembling, shrinking from the spoiler's hand,
Far, far away thy children leave the land.   50
　　Ill fares the land, to hastening ills a prey,
Where wealth accumulates and men decay;
Princes and lords may flourish or may fade;
A breath can make them as a breath has made;
But a bold peasantry, their country's pride,   55
When once destroyed, can never be supplied.
　　A time there was, ere England's griefs began,
When every rood of ground maintained its man;
For him light labor spread her wholesome store,
Just gave what life required, but gave no more: 60
His best companions, innocence and health;
And his best riches, ignorance of wealth.

[5] stretch of untilled ground, plain.
[6] Enclosure bills passed in the eighteenth century enabled a lord of the manor to enclose the "common" land, forcing many small farmers to emigrate to the cities or the colonies.
[7] limits unduly by only half cultivating.

But times are altered; trade's unfeeling train
Usurp the land, and dispossess the swain;
Along the lawn, where scattered hamlets rose,   65
Unwieldy wealth and cumbrous pomp repose;
And every want to luxury allied,
And every pang that folly pays to pride.
Those gentle hours that plenty bade to bloom,
Those calm desires that asked but little room,   70
Those healthful sports that graced the peaceful scene,
Lived in each look, and brightened all the green;
These, far departing, seek a kinder shore,
And rural mirth and manners are no more.

   Sweet Auburn! parent of the blissful hour,   75
Thy glades forlorn confess the tyrant's power.
Here, as I take my solitary rounds
Amidst thy tangling walks and ruined grounds,
And, many a year elapsed, return to view
Where once the cottage stood, the hawthorn grew,   80
Here, as with doubtful, pensive steps I range,
Trace every scene, and wonder at the change,
Remembrance wakes with all her busy train,
Swells at my breast, and turns the past to pain.

   In all my wanderings round this world of care,   85
In all my griefs—and God has given my share—
I still had hopes, my latest hours to crown,
Amidst these humble bowers to lay me down;
My anxious day to husband near the close,
And keep life's flame from wasting by repose.   90
I still had hopes, for pride attends us still,
Amidst the swains to show my book-learned skill,
Around my fire an evening group to draw,
And tell of all I felt, and all I saw;
And, as an hare whom hounds and horns pursue,   95
Pants to the place from whence at first she flew,
I still had hopes, my long vexations past,
Here to return—and die at home at last.

   O blessed retirement, friend to life's decline,
Retreats from care that never must be mine,   100

How blessed is he who crowns in shades like these
A youth of labor with an age of ease;
Who quits a world where strong temptations try,
And, since 'tis hard to combat, learns to fly.
For him no wretches, born to work and weep,   105
Explore the mine, or tempt[8] the dangerous deep;
No surly porter stands in guilty state
To spurn imploring famine from his gate;
But on he moves to meet his latter end,
Angels around befriending virtue's friend;   110
Sinks to the grave with unperceived decay,
While resignation gently slopes the way;
And all his prospects brightening to the last,
His heaven commences ere the world be past!
    Sweet was the sound, when oft at evening's close 115
Up yonder hill the village murmur rose;
There, as I passed with careless steps and slow,
The mingling notes came softened from below;
The swain responsive as the milkmaid sung,
The sober herd that lowed to meet their young,   120
The noisy geese that gabbled o'er the pool,
The playful children just let loose from school,
The watchdog's voice that bayed the whispering wind,
And the loud laugh that spoke the vacant[9] mind;
These all in soft confusion sought the shade,   125
And filled each pause the nightingale had made.
But now the sounds of population fail,
No cheerful murmurs fluctuate in the gale,
No busy steps the grass-grown footway tread,
For all the bloomy flush of life is fled;   130
All but yon widowed, solitary thing
That feebly bends beside the plashy spring;
She, wretched matron, forced in age, for bread,
To strip the brook with mantling[10] cresses spread,
To pick her wintry faggot from the thorn,   135
To seek her nightly shed,[11] and weep till morn;
She only left of all the harmless train,

[8] attempt.   [9] carefree.   [10] covering.   [11] cottage.

The sad historian of the pensive[12] plain.
   Near yonder copse, where once the garden smiled,
And still where many a garden flower grows wild,   140
There, where a few torn shrubs the place disclose,
The village preacher's modest mansion rose.
A man he was, to all the country dear,
And passing rich with forty pounds a year;
Remote from towns he ran his godly race,   145
Nor e'er had changed, nor wished to change his place;
Unskillful he to fawn, or seek for power,
By doctrines fashioned to the varying hour;
Far other aims his heart had learned to prize,
More bent to raise the wretched than to rise.   150
His house was known to all the vagrant train;
He chid their wanderings, but relieved their pain;
The long remembered beggar was his guest,
Whose beard descending swept his agèd breast;
The ruined spendthrift, now no longer proud,   155
Claimed kindred there, and had his claims allowed;
The broken soldier, kindly bade to stay,
Sate by his fire and talked the night away;
Wept o'er his wounds, or, tales of sorrow done,
Shouldered his crutch and showed how fields were won.   160
Pleased with his guests, the good man learned to glow,
And quite forgot their vices in their woe;
Careless their merits or their faults to scan,
His pity gave ere charity began.
   Thus to relieve the wretched was his pride,   165
And even his failings leaned to Virtue's side;
But in his duty prompt at every call,
He watched and wept, he prayed and felt for all.
And, as a bird each fond endearment tries
To tempt its new-fledged offspring to the skies,   170
He tried each art, reproved each dull delay,
Allured to brighter worlds, and led the way.
   Beside the bed where parting life was laid,
And sorrow, guilt, and pain by turns dismayed,

[12] melancholy.

The reverend champion stood. At his control   175
Despair and anguish fled the struggling soul;
Comfort came down the trembling wretch to raise,
And his last faltering accents whispered praise.
    At church, with meek and unaffected grace,
His looks adorned the venerable place;   180
Truth from his lips prevailed with double sway,
And fools, who came to scoff, remained to pray.
The service past, around the pious man,
With ready zeal, each honest rustic ran;
Even children followed with endearing wile,   185
And plucked his gown, to share the good man's smile.
His ready smile a parent's warmth expressed,
Their welfare pleased him and their cares distressed;
To them his heart, his love, his griefs were given,
But all his serious thoughts had rest in Heaven.   190
As some tall cliff, that lifts its awful form,
Swells from the vale, and midway leaves the storm,
Though round its breast the rolling clouds are spread,
Eternal sunshine settles on its head.
    Beside yon straggling fence that skirts the way,   195
With blossomed furze unprofitably gay,
There, in his noisy mansion, skilled to rule,
The village master taught his little school.
A man severe he was, and stern to view;
I knew him well, and every truant knew;   200
Well had the boding tremblers learned to trace
The day's disasters in his morning face;
Full well they laughed with counterfeited glee
At all his jokes, for many a joke had he;
Full well the busy whisper, circling round,   205
Conveyed the dismal tidings when he frowned;
Yet he was kind, or, if severe in aught,
The love he bore to learning was in fault;
The village all declared how much he knew;
'Twas certain he could write, and cipher too;   210
Lands he could measure, terms and tides presage,[13]

[13] calculate court terms and ecclesiastical seasons or tides (like Whitsun-tide).

And even the story ran that he could gauge;[14]
In arguing too, the parson owned his skill,
For e'en though vanquished, he could argue still;
While words of learnèd length and thundering sound   215
Amazed the gazing rustics ranged around;
And still they gazed, and still the wonder grew
That one small head could carry all he knew.
    But past is all his fame. The very spot
Where many a time he triumphed is forgot.   220
Near yonder thorn that lifts its head on high,
Where once the signpost caught the passing eye,
Low lies that house where nut-brown draughts inspired,
Where graybeard mirth and smiling toil retired,
Where village statesmen talked with looks profound,   225
And news much older than their ale went round.
Imagination fondly stoops to trace
The parlor splendors of that festive place;
The whitewashed wall, the nicely sanded floor,
The varnished clock that clicked behind the door;   230
The chest contrived a double debt to pay,
A bed by night, a chest of drawers by day;
The pictures placed for ornament and use,
The twelve good rules,[15] the royal game of goose;[16]
The hearth, except when winter chilled the day,   235
With aspen boughs and flowers and fennel gay;
While broken teacups, wisely kept for show,
Ranged o'er the chimney, glistened in a row.
    Vain transitory splendors! Could not all
Reprieve the tottering mansion from its fall?   240
Obscure it sinks, nor shall it more impart
An hour's importance to the poor man's heart;
Thither no more the peasant shall repair
To sweet oblivion of his daily care;
No more the farmer's news, the barber's tale,   245
No more the woodman's ballad shall prevail;

[14] measure the contents of casks.

[15] King Charles I's "twelve good rules" hung in broadside form in many houses. Typical rules were "reveal no secrets" and "lay no wagers."

[16] a dice game somewhat like parcheesi.

No more the smith his dusky brow shall clear,
Relax his ponderous strength, and lean to hear;
The host himself no longer shall be found
Careful to see the mantling[16a] bliss go round;   250
Nor the coy maid, half willing to be pressed,
Shall kiss the cup[17] to pass it to the rest.
   Yes! let the rich deride, the proud disdain,
These simple blessings of the lowly train;
To me more dear, congenial to my heart,   255
One native charm, than all the gloss of art;
Spontaneous joys, where Nature has its play,
The soul adopts, and owns their first-born sway;
Lightly they frolic o'er the vacant mind,
Unenvied, unmolested, unconfined.   260
But the long pomp, the midnight masquerade,
With all the freaks of wanton wealth arrayed,
In these, ere triflers half their wish obtain,
The toiling pleasure sickens into pain;
And ev'n while fashion's brightest arts decoy,   265
The heart distrusting asks if this be joy.
   Ye friends to truth, ye statesmen, who survey
The rich man's joys increase, the poor's decay,
'Tis yours to judge how wide the limits stand
Between a splendid and an happy land.   270
Proud swells the tide with loads of freighted ore,
And shouting Folly hails them from her shore;
Hoards even beyond the miser's wish abound,
And rich men flock from all the world around.
Yet count our gains. This wealth is but a name   275
That leaves our useful products still the same.
Not so the loss. The man of wealth and pride
Takes up a space that many poor supplied;
Space for his lake, his park's extended bounds,
Space for his horses, equipage, and hounds;   280
The robe that wraps his limbs in silken sloth
Has robbed the neighboring fields of half their growth;
His seat, where solitary sports are seen,

[16a] foaming, frothing.
[17] take a sip.

Indignant spurns the cottage from the green;
Around the world each needful product flies,   285
For all the luxuries the world supplies;
While thus the land adorned for pleasure all
In barren splendor feebly waits the fall.
   As some fair female, unadorned and plain,
Secure to please[18] while youth confirms her reign,   290
Slights every borrowed charm that dress supplies,
Nor shares with art the triumph of her eyes;
But when those charms are past, for charms are frail,
When time advances and when lovers fail,
She then shines forth, solicitous to bless,   295
In all the glaring impotence of dress:
Thus fares the land, by luxury betrayed,
In nature's simplest charms at first arrayed;
But verging to decline, its splendors rise,
Its vistas strike, its palaces surprise;   300
While scourged by famine from the smiling land,
The mournful peasant leads his humble band;
And while he sinks, without one arm to save,
The country blooms—a garden and a grave.
   Where then, ah where, shall poverty reside,   305
To 'scape the pressure of contiguous pride?
If to some common's fenceless limits strayed,
He drives his flock to pick the scanty blade,
Those fenceless fields the sons of wealth divide,
And even the bare-worn common is denied.   310
   If to the city sped—what waits him there?
To see profusion that he must not share;
To see ten thousand baneful arts combined
To pamper luxury, and thin mankind;
To see each joy the sons of pleasure know   315
Extorted from his fellow-creature's woe.
Here while the courtier glitters in brocade,
There the pale artist[19] plies the sickly trade;
Here while the proud their long drawn pomps display,
There the black gibbet glooms beside the way;   320

[18] certain of pleasing.
[19] artisan, workman.

The dome where Pleasure holds her midnight reign,
Here, richly decked, admits the gorgeous train;
Tumultuous grandeur crowds the blazing square,
The rattling chariots clash, the torches glare:
Sure scenes like these no trouble e'er annoy!   325
Sure these denote one universal joy!
Are these thy serious thoughts?—Ah, turn thine eyes
Where the poor houseless shivering female lies.
She once, perhaps, in village plenty blessed,
Has wept at tales of innocence distressed;   330
Her modest looks the cottage might adorn,
Sweet as the primrose peeps beneath the thorn;
Now lost to all; her friends, her virtue fled,
Near her betrayer's door she lays her head,
And pinched with cold, and shrinking from the shower,   335
With heavy heart deplores that luckless hour,
When idly first, ambitious of the town,
She left her wheel and robes of country brown.
    Do thine, sweet Auburn, thine, the loveliest train,
Do thy fair tribes participate her pain?   340
Ev'n now, perhaps, by cold and hunger led,
At proud men's doors they ask a little bread!
    Ah, no. To distant climes, a dreary scene,
Where half the convex world intrudes between,
To torrid tracts with fainting steps they go,   345
Where wild Altama[20] murmurs to their woe.
Far different there from all that charmed before,
The various terrors of that horrid shore;
Those blazing suns that dart a downward ray,
And fiercely shed intolerable day;   350
Those matted woods where birds forget to sing,
But silent bats in drowsy clusters cling;
Those poisonous fields with rank luxuriance crowned
Where the dark scorpion gathers death around;
Where at each step the stranger fears to wake   355
The rattling terrors of the vengeful snake;

[20] The Altamaha River was the boundary between General Oglethorpe's colony in Georgia and the Spaniards in Florida. Two settlements were founded near its mouth in 1735.

Where crouching tigers[21] wait their hapless prey,
And savage men more murderous still than they;
While oft in whirls the mad tornado flies,
Mingling the ravaged landscape with the skies.   360
Far different these from every former scene,
The cooling brook, the grassy-vested green,
The breezy covert of the warbling grove,
That only sheltered thefts of harmless love.

    Good Heaven! what sorrows gloomed that parting day   365
That called them from their native walks away;
When the poor exiles, every pleasure past,
Hung round their bowers, and fondly looked their last,
And took a long farewell, and wished in vain
For seats like these beyond the western main;   370
And shuddering still to face the distant deep,
Returned and wept, and still returned to weep.
The good old sire the first prepared to go
To new-found worlds, and wept for others' woe;
But for himself, in conscious virtue brave,   375
He only wished for worlds beyond the grave.
His lovely daughter, lovelier in her tears,
The fond companion of his helpless years,
Silent went next, neglectful of her charms,
And left a lover's for her father's arms.   380
With louder plaints the mother spoke her woes,
And blessed the cot where every pleasure rose,
And kissed her thoughtless babes with many a tear,
And clasped them close, in sorrow doubly dear;
Whilst her fond husband strove to lend relief   385
In all the decent manliness of grief.

    O Luxury! thou cursed by heaven's decree,
How ill exchanged are things like these for thee!
How do thy potions, with insidious joy,
Diffuse their pleasures only to destroy!   390
Kingdoms by thee, to sickly greatness grown,
Boast of a florid vigor not their own:
At every draught more large and large they grow,

<hr>
[21] In his *Animated Nature,* Goldsmith mentions the cougar or "red tiger."

A bloated mass of rank, unwieldy woe;
Till sapped their strength, and every part unsound,   395
Down, down they sink, and spread a ruin round.
    Even now the devastation is begun,
And half the business of destruction done;
Even now, methinks, as pondering here I stand,
I see the rural virtues leave the land: 400
Down where yon anchoring vessel spreads the sail,
That idly waiting flaps with every gale,
Downward they move, a melancholy band,
Pass from the shore, and darken all the strand.
Contented Toil, and hospitable Care,   405
And kind connubial Tenderness are there;
And Piety with wishes placed above,
And steady Loyalty, and faithful Love.
And thou, sweet Poetry, thou loveliest maid,
Still first to fly where sensual joys invade,   410
Unfit, in these degenerate times of shame,
To catch the heart, or strike for honest fame;
Dear charming nymph, neglected and decried,
My shame in crowds, my solitary pride;
Thou source of all my bliss and all my woe,   415
That found'st me poor at first, and keep'st me so;
Thou guide by which the nobler arts excel,
Thou nurse of every virtue, fare thee well!
Farewell, and O where'er thy voice be tried,
On Torno's cliffs, or Pambamarca's[22] side,   420
Whether where equinoctial fervors glow,
Or winter wraps the polar world in snow,
Still let thy voice, prevailing over time,
Redress the rigors of th' inclement clime;
Aid slighted truth, with thy persuasive strain   425
Teach erring man to spurn the rage of gain;
Teach him that states of native strength possessed,
Though very poor, may still be very blessed;
That trade's proud empire hastes to swift decay,

[22] Tornea is in Lapland, Pambamarca in Ecuador.

As ocean sweeps the labored mole away;   430
While self-dependent power can time defy,
As rocks resist the billows and the sky.[23]

Retaliation[1]
[1774, 1774]

Of old, when Scarron[2] his companions invited,
Each guest brought his dish, and the feast was united;
If our landlord supplies us with beef and with fish,
Let each guest bring himself, and he brings the best dish:
Our Dean[3] shall be venison, just fresh from the plains;   5
Our Burke shall be tongue, with a garnish of brains;
Our Will shall be wild fowl, of excellent flavor,
And Dick with his pepper shall heighten their savor;[4]
Our Cumberland's[5] sweetbread its place shall obtain,
And Douglas's[6] pudding, substantial and plain;   10
Our Garrick's a salad, for in him we see
Oil, vinegar, sugar, and saltness agree;
To make out the dinner full certain I am,
That Ridge is anchovy, and Reynolds is lamb;
That Hickey's[7] a capon, and by the same rule,   15
Magnanimous Goldsmith, a gooseberry fool.[8]

[23] Dr. Johnson wrote the last four lines of the poem, beginning "That trade's proud empire. . . ."

[1] Goldsmith wrote this poem, left incomplete at his death, in response to some mock epitaphs composed by certain of his friends who met regularly at the St. James's Coffeehouse. Garrick's epitaph survives:
> Here lies Nolly Goldsmith, for shortness called Noll,
> Who wrote like an angel, but talked like poor Poll.

[2] Goldsmith was translating the *Roman comique* of Paul Scarron (1610-60), French burlesque writer, at the time this poem was written.

[3] Thomas Barnard, Dean of Derry.

[4] Edmund Burke, his brother Richard, and his relative William.

[5] Richard Cumberland, who wrote sentimental plays.

[6] John Douglas, a Scot, later Bishop of Salisbury.

[7] John Ridge and Joseph Hickey, both lawyers, and Sir Joshua Reynolds.

[8] literally, a dish of stewed gooseberries and cream.

At a dinner so various, at such a repast,
Who'd not be a glutton, and stick to the last:
Here, waiter, more wine, let me sit while I'm able,
Till all my companions sink under the table;   20
Then, with chaos and blunders encircling my head,
Let me ponder, and tell what I think of the dead.
   Here lies the good Dean, reunited to earth,
Who mixed reason with pleasure, and wisdom with mirth:
If he had any faults, he has left us in doubt,   25
At least, in six weeks I could not find 'em out;
Yet some have declared, and it can't be denied 'em,
That sly-boots was cursedly cunning to hide 'em.
   Here lies our good Edmund, whose genius was such,
We scarcely can praise it, or blame it too much;   30
Who, born for the universe, narrowed his mind,
And to party gave up what was meant for mankind:
Though fraught with all learning, yet[9] straining his throat
To persuade Tommy Townshend[10] to lend him a vote;
Who, too deep for his hearers, still went on refining,   35
And thought of convincing, while they thought of dining;[11]
Though equal to all things, for all things unfit;
Too nice[12] for a statesman, too proud for a wit;
For a patriot[13] too cool; for a drudge, disobedient;
And too fond of the right to pursue the expedient.   40
In short, 'twas his fate, unemployed or in place,[14] sir,
To eat mutton cold, and cut blocks with a razor.[15]
   Here lies honest William, whose heart was a mint,
While the owner ne'er knew half the good that was in't;
The pupil of impulse, it forced him along,   45
His conduct still right, with his argument wrong;

[9] First edition reads "kept."

[10] Townshend earned his mention here by having recently attacked the granting of a pension to Goldsmith's friend, Dr. Johnson.

[11] Burke later acquired the nickname of the "Dinner Bell" from the frequent thinning of the House of Commons when he rose to speak.

[12] fastidious.

[13] unthinking member of the Opposition.

[14] office.

[15] apply his abilities incongruously or absurdly.

Still aiming at honor, yet fearing to roam,
The coachman was tipsy, the chariot drove home.
Would you ask for his merits, alas! he had none;
What was good was spontaneous, his faults were his own.   50
    Here lies honest Richard, whose fate I must sigh at;
Alas, that such frolic should now be so quiet!
What spirits were his, what wit and what whim,
Now breaking a jest, and now breaking a limb;
Now wrangling and grumbling to keep up the ball,[16]   55
Now teasing and vexing, yet laughing at all!
In short, so provoking a devil was Dick,
That we wished him full ten times a day at Old Nick;
But missing his mirth and agreeable vein,
As often we wished to have Dick back again.   60
    Here Cumberland lies, having acted his parts,
The Terence[17] of England, the mender of hearts;
A flattering painter, who made it his care
To draw men as they ought to be, not as they are.
His gallants are all faultless, his women divine,   65
And Comedy wonders at being so fine:
Like a tragedy queen he has dizened her out,
Or rather like Tragedy giving a rout.[18]
His fools have their follies so lost in a crowd
Of virtues and feelings, that folly grows proud;   70
And coxcombs alike in their failings alone,
Adopting his portraits, are pleased with their own.
Say, where has our poet this malady caught,
Or wherefore his characters thus without fault?
Say, was it that vainly directing his view   75
To find out men's virtues, and finding them few,
Quite sick of pursuing each troublesome elf,
He grew lazy at last, and drew from himself?
    Here Douglas retires from his toils to relax,
The scourge of impostors, the terror of quacks: 80
Come, all ye quack bards, and ye quacking divines,

[16] keep the ball rolling.
[17] Roman writer of comedies.
[18] ball.

Come and dance on the spot where your tyrant reclines: [19]
When satire and censure encircled his throne,
I feared for your safety, I feared for my own;
But now he is gone, and we want a detector;   85
Our Dodds shall be pious, our Kenricks[20] shall lecture;
Macpherson[21] write bombast, and call it a style;
Our Townshend [22] make speeches, and I shall compile;[23]
New Lauders and Bowers the Tweed shall cross over,
No countryman living their tricks to discover;   90
Detection her taper shall quench to a spark,
And Scotchman meet Scotchman, and cheat in the dark.
    Here lies David Garrick, describe me who can,
An abridgment of all that was pleasant in man:
As an actor, confessed without rival to shine;   95
As a wit, if not first, in the very first line;
Yet, with talents like these, and an excellent heart,
The man had his failings, a dupe to his art;
Like an ill-judging beauty, his colors he spread,
And beplastered with rouge his own natural red.   100
On the stage he was natural, simple, affecting;
'Twas only that when he was off he was acting:
With no reason on earth to go out of his way,
He turned and he varied full ten times a day;
Though secure of our hearts, yet confoundedly sick   105

[19] Douglas had exposed the two Scotsmen mentioned below, William Lauder and Archibald Bower. Lauder had tried to prove, by means of forgeries, that Milton was a plagiarist. Bower's *History of the Popes* was discredited when it was discovered that he was a secret Jesuit, and when Douglas showed that his *Motives of Conversion from Popery to Protestantism* was deceitful.

[20] The Rev. William Dodd, a sensational preacher over repentant prostitutes, was hanged for forgery in 1777. William Kenrick, a hack writer, made a career of attacking well-known men, including Goldsmith. He lectured on Shakespeare at the Devil Tavern in 1774.

[21] James Macpherson, who produced vague rhetorical pieces which he claimed were translations from the ancient Gaelic poet, Ossian. Goldsmith refers here to his badly received translation of the *Iliad* (1773).

[22] See note to l. 34.

[23] Goldsmith made a good part of his living by doing compilations for booksellers.

If they were not his own by finessing and trick:
He cast off his friends, as a huntsman his pack,
For he knew when he pleased he could whistle them back.
Of praise a mere[24] glutton, he swallowed what came,
And the puff [25] of a dunce, he mistook it for fame;   110
Till his relish grown callous, almost to disease,
Who peppered the highest was surest to please.
But let us be candid, and speak out our mind;
If dunces applauded, he paid them in kind.
Ye Kenricks, ye Kellys, and Woodfalls[26] so grave,   115
What a commerce was yours while you got and you gave!
How did Grub Street re-echo the shouts that you raised,
While he was be-Rosciused,[27] and you were be-praised!
But peace to his spirit, wherever it flies,
To act as an angel, and mix with the skies;   120
Those poets who owe their best fame to his skill
Shall still be his flatterers, go where he will;
Old Shakespeare receive him with praise and with love,
And Beaumonts and Bens[28] be his Kellys above.

Here Hickey reclines, a most blunt, pleasant creature,   125
And slander itself must allow him good nature;
He cherished his friend, and he relished a bumper;
Yet one fault he had, and that one was a thumper:
Perhaps you may ask if the man was a miser?
I answer, no, no, for he always was wiser.   130

---

[24] absolute.   [25] praise.

[26] Though Garrick, as joint-patentee and manager of the Drury Lane
Theater, had produced two of Kenrick's plays, Kenrick published a libelous
attack on him, which he was forced to retract. Hugh Kelly's sentimental
comedy, *False Delicacy* (1768), had been produced very successfully at
Drury Lane in competition with Goldsmith's *Good-Natured Man,* but a
performance of Kelly's *Word to the Wise* in 1770 ran into such trouble that
Kelly took his next play to Garrick's competitor, George Colman, at Covent
Garden. William Woodfall, a young critic, quarreled with Garrick in 1773
and wrote a letter of apology to him, which Mrs. Garrick endorsed, "Puppy
Woodfall's answer." Woodfall had defended sentimental comedy and attacked
She Stoops to Conquer in the *Monthly Review.*

[27] compared to the great Roman actor, Roscius. The reading of the first
edition, "be-Rosciad," suggests an allusion to Charles Churchill's praise of
Garrick in *The Rosciad.* Churchill later attacked Garrick in *The Apology.*

[28] Francis Beaumont and Ben Jonson.

Too courteous, perhaps, or obligingly flat? [29]
His very worst foe can't accuse him of that.
Perhaps he confided in men as they go,
And so was too foolishly honest? Ah, no.
Then what was his failing? come, tell it, and burn ye.[30]   135
He was, could he help it? a special attorney.[31]
   Here Reynolds is laid, and, to tell you my mind,
He has not left a better or wiser behind.
His pencil [32] was striking, resistless, and grand;
His manners were gentle, complying, and bland;   140
Still born to improve us in every part,
His pencil our faces, his manners our heart:
To coxcombs averse, yet most civilly steering,[33]
When they judged without skill he was still hard of hearing:
When they talked of their Raphaels, Correggios, and stuff,   145
He shifted his trumpet[34] and only took snuff.

An Essay on the Theater; or, A Comparison between Laughing and Sentimental Comedy [1773]

   The theater, like all other amusements, has its fashions and its prejudices; and when satiated with its excellence, mankind began to mistake change for improvement. For some years tragedy was the reigning entertainment; but of late it has entirely given way to comedy, and our best efforts are now exerted in these lighter kinds of composition. The pompous train,[1] the swelling phrase, and the unnatural rant are displaced for that natural portrait of human folly

[29] insipid, or perhaps slang for easily cheated.

[30] damn you. An Irish greeting, according to a contemporary footnote.

[31] an attorney who practiced in one court only. In fact, Hickey, who was an attorney of the Court of King's Bench, was also a solicitor of the Court of Chancery. The point apparently is that attorneys or solicitors, as distinct from barristers, were held in very low esteem.

[32] brush.

[33] First edition reads "staring," which quite possibly rhymed with "hearing" in Anglo-Irish.

[34] Reynolds used an ear trumpet.

---

[1] either stage procession or heroic retinue.

and frailty, of which all are judges, because all have sat for the picture.

But, as in describing nature it is presented with a double face, either of mirth or sadness, our modern writers find themselves at a loss which chiefly to copy from; and it is now debated, whether the exhibition of human distress is likely to afford the mind more entertainment than that of human absurdity?

Comedy is defined by Aristotle to be a picture of the frailties of the lower part of mankind, to distinguish it from tragedy, which is an exhibition of the misfortunes of the great.[2] When comedy therefore ascends to produce the characters of princes or generals upon the stage, it is out of its walk, since low life and middle life are entirely its object. The principal question therefore is whether, in describing low or middle life, an exhibition of its follies be not preferable to a detail of its calamities? Or, in other words, which deserves the preference? The weeping sentimental comedy, so much in fashion at present, or the laughing and even low comedy, which seems to have been last exhibited by Vanbrugh and Cibber?[3]

If we apply to authorities, all the great masters in the dramatic art have but one opinion. Their rule is, that as tragedy displays the calamities of the great, so comedy should excite our laughter, by ridiculously exhibiting the follies of the lower part of mankind. Boileau, one of the best modern critics, asserts that comedy will not admit of tragic distress:

> Le Comique, ennemi des soupirs et des pleurs,
> N'admet point dans ses vers de tragiques douleurs.[4]

Nor is this rule without the strongest foundation in nature, as the distresses of the mean by no means affect us so strongly as the calamities of the great. When tragedy exhibits to us some great

[2] Aristotle distinguishes comedy and tragedy by saying that "one would make its personages worse, and the other better, than the men of the present day"; further, that comedy imitates one particular kind of fault, the ridiculous (*Poetics,* trans. Ingram Bywater, 1448a, 1449a).

[3] Sir John Vanbrugh, author of *The Relapse* (1696) and *The Provoked Wife* (1697). His *Journey to London* was completed and somewhat moralized by Colley Cibber under the title of *The Provoked Husband* (1728). Cibber's own most important play was *The Careless Husband* (1704).

[4] "The comic, enemy of sighs and tears, never admits tragic sorrows into its verses" (*Art of Poetry,* iii 401-2).

man fallen from his height, and struggling with want and adversity, we feel his situation in the same manner as we suppose he himself must feel, and our pity is increased in proportion to the height from whence he fell. On the contrary, we do not so strongly sympathize with one born in humbler circumstances, and encountering accidental distress: so that while we melt for Belisarius,[5] we scarcely give halfpence to the beggar who accosts us in the street. The one has our pity, the other our contempt. Distress, therefore, is the proper object of tragedy, since the great excite our pity by their fall; but not equally so of comedy, since the actors employed in it are originally so mean that they sink but little by their fall.

Since the first origin of the stage, tragedy and comedy have run in distinct channels, and never till of late encroached upon the provinces of each other. Terence, who seems to have made the nearest approaches, yet always judiciously stops short before he comes to the downright pathetic; and yet he is even reproached by Caesar for wanting the *vis comica*.[6] All the other comic writers of antiquity aim only at rendering folly or vice ridiculous, but never exalt their characters into buskined [7] pomp, or make what Voltaire humorously calls a *tradesman's tragedy*.[8]

Yet notwithstanding this weight of authority, and the universal practice of former ages, a new species of dramatic composition has been introduced under the name of *sentimental* comedy,[9] in which the virtues of private life are exhibited, rather than the vices exposed; and the distresses rather than the faults of mankind make our interest in the piece. These comedies have had of late great success,[10] perhaps from their novelty, and also from their flattering

[5] sixth-century Byzantine general, who, according to one account, was reduced to live by begging in the streets.

[6] Suetonius quotes Julius Caesar as saying that Terence equaled the Greek comic writers in grace, but lacked their "comic force" (*Life of Terence*, end).

[7] tragic. The buskin was the half boot worn by the classical tragedian.

[8] Voltaire condemns the contemporary tearful comedy as a "bastard species" which aims more at "bourgeois tragedy" than at a faithful representation of ridiculous people ("The Dramatic Art," *Philosophic Dictionary*).

[9] comedy appealing to benevolent or refined emotions, based on the idea that man naturally responds to the idea of the good. Sentimental comedy reached its peak in the 1760's and 1770's.

[10] Hugh Kelly's *False Delicacy* (see *Retaliation*, note to l. 115) sold ten thousand copies in its first season.

every man in his favorite foible. In these plays almost all the characters are good, and exceedingly generous; they are lavish enough of their *tin* money on the stage, and, though they want humor, have abundance of sentiment and feeling. If they happen to have faults or foibles, the spectator is taught not only to pardon, but to applaud them, in consideration of the goodness of their hearts; so that folly, instead of being ridiculed, is commended, and the comedy aims at touching our passions without the power of being truly pathetic. In this manner we are likely to lose one great source of entertainment on the stage; for while the comic poet is invading the province of the tragic muse, he leaves her lovely sister quite neglected. Of this, however, he is no way solicitous, as he measures his fame by his profits.

But it will be said that the theater is formed to amuse mankind, and that it matters little, if this end be answered, by what means it is obtained. If mankind find delight in weeping at comedy, it would be cruel to abridge them in that or any other innocent pleasure. If those pieces are denied the name of comedies, yet call them by any other name, and if they are delightful, they are good. Their success, it will be said, is a mark of their merit, and it is only abridging our happiness to deny us an inlet to amusement.

These objections, however, are rather specious than solid. It is true that amusement is a great object of the theater; and it will be allowed that these sentimental pieces do often amuse us; but the question is, whether the true comedy would not amuse us more? The question is, whether a character supported throughout a piece with its ridicule still attending, would not give us more delight than this species of bastard tragedy, which only is applauded because it is new?

A friend of mine, who was sitting unmoved at one of these sentimental pieces, was asked how he could be so indifferent? "Why, truly," says he, "as the hero is but a tradesman, it is indifferent to me whether he be turned out of his countinghouse on Fish Street Hill, since he will still have enough left to open shop in St. Giles's."

The other objection is as ill-grounded; for though we should give these pieces another name, it will not mend their efficacy. It will continue a kind of *mulish* production, with all the defects of its opposite parents, and marked with sterility. If we are permitted to make comedy weep, we have an equal right to make tragedy laugh, and to set down in blank verse the jests and repartees of all the attendants in a funeral procession.

But there is one argument in favor of sentimental comedy which will keep it on the stage, in spite of all that can be said against it. It is of all others the most easily written. Those abilities that can hammer out a novel are fully sufficient for the production of a sentimental comedy. It is only sufficient to raise the characters a little; to deck out the hero with a riband, or give the heroine a title; then to put an insipid dialogue, without character or humor, into their mouths, give them mighty good hearts, very fine clothes, furnish a new set of scenes,[11] make a pathetic scene or two, with a sprinkling of tender melancholy conversation through the whole; and there is no doubt but all the ladies will cry and all the gentlemen applaud.

Humor at present seems to be departing from the stage, and it will soon happen that our comic players will have nothing left for it but a fine coat and a song. It depends upon the audience whether they will actually drive those poor merry creatures from the stage, or sit at a play as gloomy as at the Tabernacle.[12] It is not easy to recover an art when once lost; and it would be but a just punishment that when, by our being too fastidious, we have banished humor from the stage, we should ourselves be deprived of the art of laughing.

[11] group of stage sets.
[12] a Methodist chapel in London.

❧ Thomas Chatterton ❧

Thomas Chatterton (1752-70) was born and grew up in Bristol, where he was apprenticed at fourteen as a scrivener (copyist) in an attorney's office. He escaped this dull job by threatening to commit suicide, and went to London in April, 1770, to earn his living as a poet and hack writer. In August he killed himself by swallowing poison, perhaps by mistake, but more probably from despair at neglect and poverty.

Though Chatterton wrote a fair amount of conventional verse, he is remembered only for his Rowley Poems, which he claimed were the work of a fifteenth-century monk, Thomas Rowley. Chatterton's imitations of Middle English are childishly simple and imperfect, but the general contemporary ignorance of earlier English provided him with defenders. Actually, that these poems were forgeries is not important; they survive because they attempt to re-create the life and spirit of medieval England.

Editions: Works, ed. Robert Southey and Joseph Cottle (1803); *Poetical Works,* ed. W. W. Skeat (1871); *Poetical Works,* ed. Henry D. Roberts (1906); *Rowley Poems,* reprinted from Tyrwhitt's third edition (1778), ed. Maurice E. Hare (1911).

Biography: E. H. W. Meyerstein, *Life of Thomas Chatterton* (1930).

Critical Studies: F. S. Miller, "The Historic Sense of Thomas Chatterton," *ELH* 11 (1944); B. H. Bronson, "Thomas Chatterton," in *The Age of Johnson: Essays Presented to C. B. Tinker* (1949).

Aella: A Tragycal Enterlude

MYNSTRELLES SONGE[1]
[1777]

O! synge untoe mie roundelaie,
O! droppe the brynie teare wythe mee,
Daunce ne moe atte hallie daie,[2]
Lycke a reynynge[3] ryver bee;
        Mie love ys dedde,   5
        Gon to hys death-bedde,
        Al under the wyllowe tree.

Blacke hys cryne[4] as the wyntere nyghte,
Whyte hys rode[5] as the sommer snowe,
Rodde[6] hys face as the mornynge lyghte,   10
Cale[7] he lyes ynne the grave belowe;
        Mie love ys dedde,
        Gon to hys deathe-bedde,
        Al under the wyllowe tree.

Swote[8] hys tyngue as the throstles note,   15
Quycke ynn daunce as thoughte canne bee,
Defte hys taboure, codgelle stote,
O! hee lyes bie the wyllowe tree:
        Mie love ys dedde,
        Gonne to hys deathe-bedde,   20
        Alle underre the wyllowe tree.

---

[1] In *Aella: A Tragycal Enterlude,* the minstrels sing to comfort Birtha, the heroine, as she waits for word from the battlefield of her heroic husband, Aella.

[2] holiday.

[3] running (Chatterton). "Chatterton" following a note means that it is Chatterton's gloss.

[4] hair (Chatterton).

[5] complexion (Chatterton).

[6] red.   [7] cold.   [8] sweet.

Harke! the ravenne flappes hys wynge,
In the briered delle belowe;
Harke! the dethe-owle loude dothe synge,
To the nyghte-mares[9] as heie[10] goe;   25
  Mie love ys dedde,
  Gon to hys deathe-bedde,
  Al under the wyllowe tree.

See! the whyte moone sheenes onne hie;
Whyterre ys mie true loves shroude;   30
Whyterre yanne[11] the mornynge skie,
Whyterre yanne the evenynge cloude;
  Mie love ys dedde,
  Gon to hys deathe-bedde,
  Al under the wyllowe tree.   35

Heere, uponne mie true loves grave,
Schalle the baren fleurs be layde,
Nee one hallie Seyncte to save
Al the celness[12] of a mayde.
  Mie love ys dedde,   40
  Gonne to hys death-bedde,
  Alle under the wyllowe tree.

Wythe mie hondes I'lle dente[13] the brieres
Rounde his hallie corse to gre,[14]
Ouphante[15] fairie, lyghte youre fyres,   45
Heere mie boddie stylle[16] schalle bee.
  Mie love ys dedde,
  Gon to hys deathe-bedde,
  Al under the wyllowe tree.

Comme, wythe acorne-coppe & thorne,   50
Drayne mie hartys blodde awaie;
Lyfe & all yttes goode I scorne,
Daunce bie nete, or feaste by daie.
  Mie love ys dedde,
  Gon to hys death-bedde,   55
  Al under the wyllowe tree.

[9] incubi; female spirits supposed to settle on people in their sleep.
[10] they. [11] than. [12] coldness. [13] plant. [14] grow. [15] elfin.
[16] still, always.

Waterre wytches, crownede wythe reytes,[17]
Bere mee to yer leathalle tyde.
I die; I comme; mie true love waytes.
Thos the damselle spake, and dyed.   60

An Excelente Balade of Charitie:

AS WROTEN BIE THE GODE PRIEST THOMAS ROWLEY, 1464[1]
[1777]

In Virgyne[2] the sweltrie sun gan sheene,
And hotte upon the mees[3] did caste his raie;
The apple rodded[4] from its palie greene,
And the mole[5] peare did bende the leafy spraie;
The peede chelandri[6] sunge the livelong daie;   5
'Twas nowe the pride, the manhode of the yeare,
And eke the grounde was dighte[7] in its mose defte[8] aumere.[9]

The sun was glemeing in the midde of daie,
Deadde still the aire, and eke the welken[10] blue,
When from the sea arist[11] in drear arraie   10
A hepe of cloudes of sable sullen hue,
The which full fast unto the woodlande drewe,

---

[17] water-flags (Chatterton).

---

[1] Thomas Rowley, the author, was born at Norton Mal-reward in Somersetshire, educated at the convent of St. Kenna at Keynesham, and died at Westbury in Gloucestershire (Chatterton).
[2] The sign of Virgo, August 23—September 22.
[3] meads (Chatterton).
[4] reddened, ripened (Chatterton).
[5] soft (Chatterton).
[6] pied goldfinch (Chatterton).
[7] dressed, arrayed (Chatterton).
[8] neat, ornamental (Chatterton).
[9] a loose robe or mantle (Chatterton). An "aumere" actually is a purse.
[10] the sky, the atmosphere (Chatterton).
[11] arose (Chatterton).

Hiltring[12] attenes[13] the sunnis fetive[14] face,
And the blacke tempeste swolne and gatherd up apace.

Beneath an holme,[15] faste by a pathwaie side,   15
Which dide unto Seyncte Godwine's covent[16] lede,
A hapless pilgrim moneynge[17] did abide,
Pore in his viewe, ungentle[18] in his weede,[19]
Longe bretful[20] of the miseries of neede,
Where from the hail-stone coulde the almer[21] flie?   20
He had no housen theere, ne anie covent nie.

Look in his glommed[22] face, his sprighte there scanne;
Howe woe-be-gone, how withered, forwynd,[23] deade!
Haste to thie church-glebe-house,[24] asshrewed[25] manne!
Haste to thie kiste,[26] thie onlie dortoure[27] bedde.   25
Cale, as the claie whiche will gre on thie hedde,
Is Charitie and Love aminge highe elves;[28]
Knightis and Barons live for pleasure and themselves.

The gatherd storme is rype; the bigge drops falle;
The forswat[29] meadowes smethe,[30] and drenche[31] the raine;   30

[12] hiding, shrouding (Chatterton).
[13] at once (Chatterton).
[14] beauteous (Chatterton).
[15] oak.
[16] convent, monastery. "It would have been *charitable* if the author had not pointed at personal characters in this *Ballad of Charity*. The Abbot of St. Godwin's at the time of the writing of this was Ralph de Bellomont, a great stickler for the Lancastrian family. Rowley was a Yorkist" (Chatterton).
[17] moaning.
[18] beggarly (Chatterton).
[19] clothes.
[20] filled with (Chatterton).
[21] beggar (Chatterton).
[22] clouded, dejected (Chatterton).
[23] dry, sapless (Chatterton).
[24] the grave (Chatterton).
[25] accursed, unfortunate (Chatterton).
[26] coffin (Chatterton).
[27] a sleeping room (Chatterton).
[28] knights, lords.
[29] sunburnt (Chatterton).
[30] smoke (Chatterton).
[31] drink (Chatterton).

The comyng ghastness do the cattle pall,[32]
And the full flockes are drivynge ore the plaine;
Dashde from the cloudes the waters flott[33] againe;
The welkin opes; the yellow levynne[34] flies;
And the hot fierie smothe[35] in the wide lowings[36] dies.   35

Liste! now the thunder's rattling clymmynge[37] sound
Cheves[38] slowlie on, and then embollen[39] clangs,
Shakes the hie spyre, and losst, dispended, drown'd,
Still on the gallard [40] eare of terroure hanges;   40
The windes are up; the lofty elmen swanges;[41]
Again the levynne and the thunder poures,
And the full cloudes are braste[42] attenes in stonen showers.[43]

Spurreynge his palfrie oere the watrie plaine,
The Abbote of Scynctc Godwynes convente came;
His chapournette[44] was drented with the reine,   45
And his pencte[45] gyrdle met with mickle shame;
He aynewarde tolde his bederoll [46] at the same;
The storme encreasen, and he drew aside,
With the mist[47] almes craver neere to the holme to bide.

His cope[48] was all of Lyncolne clothe so fyne,   50
With a gold button fasten'd neere his chynne;

[32] *pall,* a contraction from *appall,* to fright (Chatterton).
[33] fly (Chatterton).
[34] lightning (Chatterton).
[35] steam, or vapors (Chatterton).
[36] flames (Chatterton).
[37] noisy (Chatterton).
[38] moves (Chatterton).
[39] swelled, strengthened (Chatterton).
[40] frighted (Chatterton).
[41] swings.
[42] burst (Chatterton).
[43] showers of (hail) stones.
[44] a small round hat (Chatterton).
[45] painted (Chatterton).
[46] he told his [rosary] beads backwards; a figurative expression to signify cursing (Chatterton).
[47] poor, needy (Chatterton).
[48] a cloak (Chatterton).

His autremete[49] was edged with golden twynne,
And his shoone pyke[50] a loverds[51] mighte have binne;
Full well it shewn he thoughten coste no sinne:
The trammels[52] of the palfrye pleasde his sighte,   55
For the horse-millanare his head with roses dighte.

An almes, sir prieste! the droppynge pilgrim saide,
O! let me waite within your covente dore,
Till the sunne sheneth hie above our heade,
And the loude tempeste of the aire is oer;   60
Helpless and ould am I alas! and poor;
No house, ne friend, ne moneie in my pouche;
All yatte I call my owne is this my silver crouche.[53]

Varlet, replyd the Abbatte, cease your dinne;
This is no season almes and prayers to give;   65
Mie porter never lets a faitour[54] in;
None touch mie rynge[55] who not in honour live.
And now the sonne with the blacke cloudes did stryve,
And shettynge[56] on the grounde his glairie raie,
The Abbatte spurrde his steede, and eftsoones[57] roadde awaie. 70

Once moe the skie was blacke, the thunder rolde;
Faste reyneynge oer the plaine a prieste was seen;
Ne dighte full proude, ne buttoned up in golde;
His cope and jape[58] were graie, and eke were clene;
A Limitoure[59] he was of order seene;   75
And from the pathwaie side then turned hee,
Where the pore almer laie binethe the holmen tree.

[49] a loose white robe, worn by priests (Chatterton).
[50] peaked or pointed shoes.
[51] a lord['s] (Chatterton).
[52] shackles used to teach a horse to amble.
[53] crucifix.
[54] a beggar or vagabond (Chatterton).
[55] door-knocker.
[56] shedding.
[57] immediately, forthwith.
[58] a short surplice, worn by friars of an inferior class and secular priests (Chatterton).
[59] a friar licensed to beg within certain limits or territories.

An almes, sir priest! the droppynge pilgrim sayde,
For sweete Seyncte Marie and your order sake.
The Limitoure then loosen'd his pouche threade,   80
And did thereoute a groate of silver take;
The mister[60] pilgrim dyd for halline[61] shake.
Here take this silver, it maie eathe[62] thie care;
We are Goddes stewards all, nete[63] of oure owne we bare.

But ah! unhailie[64] pilgrim, lerne of me,   85
Scathe anie give a rentrolle to their Lorde.
Here take my semecope,[65] thou arte bare I see;
Tis thyne; the Seynctes will give me mie rewarde.
He left the pilgrim, and his waie aborde.[66]
Virgynne and hallie Seyncte, who sitte yn gloure,[67]   90
Or give the mittee[68] will,[69] or give the gode man power.

[60] poor.
[61] joy (Chatterton).
[62] ease (Chatterton).
[63] nought (Chatterton).
[64] unhappy (Chatterton).
[65] a short undercloak (Chatterton).
[66] went on.
[67] glory (Chatterton).
[68] mighty, rich (Chatterton).
[69] will to do good.

❧ Edward Gibbon ✍

The historian of the Roman Empire, Edward Gibbon (1737-94), was under five feet in height, fat, and baby-faced. He was born in Putney, Surrey, and educated at Westminster School and Magdalen College, Oxford. At Oxford he became a Roman Catholic, which caused his father to ship him off to Lausanne in 1753 to be reconverted to Protestantism. (In the end he became a deist and skeptic.) In 1758, his engagement to Suzanne Curchod—later the wife of the French Finance Minister Jacques Necker, and the mother of Mme. de Staël—was broken off because of his father's disapproval, and he never married. Gibbon served as a captain in the Hampshire militia, and in the House of Commons (1774-83), but his life project was *The Decline and Fall of the Roman Empire*, inspired by his visit to Rome in 1764. Begun in 1768, the first volume appeared in 1776, the next two in 1781, and the last three in 1788. Gibbon retired to the congenial and inexpensive surroundings of Lausanne in 1783, and did not return permanently to England until shortly before his death.

The Decline and Fall covers an immense period of time, from the accession of Commodus in A.D. 180 to the fall of Constantinople in 1453, though about half the work deals with the period up to the fall of the Roman Empire in the West around 476. Much of Gibbon's account, especially the part dealing with the Byzantine Empire, is inadequate by modern historical standards, but his ability to balance generalization and detail satisfactorily, his command of irony, and the brilliance and clarity of his presentation make his work the greatest of histories written in English. His unfinished *Memoirs* (or *Autobiographies*) are well worth reading.

Editions: The Decline and Fall of the Roman Empire, ed. J. B. Bury (1926-29); *Miscellaneous Works*, ed. John, Lord Sheffield (1814); *Autobiographies*, ed. John Murray (1896); *Memoirs*, ed. G. B. Hill (1900); *Letters*, ed. J. E. Norton (1956); *Journal to Jan. 28, 1763*, ed. D. M. Low (1929); *Journal à Lausanne*, ed. Georges Bonnard (1945).

Biographies: G. M. Young, *Gibbon* (1932); D. M. Low, *Edward Gibbon* (1937).

Critical Studies: S. T. McCloy, *Gibbon's Antagonism to Christianity* (1933); L. P. Curtis, "Gibbon's Paradise Lost," in *The Age of Johnson: Essays Presented to C. B. Tinker* (1949); E. M. W. Tillyard, *The English Epic and Its Background* (1954); W. R. Keast, "The Element of Art in Gibbon's *History*," ELH 23 (1956); H. L. Bond, *The Literary Art of Edward Gibbon* (1960).

The History
of the
Decline and Fall of the Roman Empire
[1768-76, 1776]

CHAPTER XV

The Progress of the Christian Religion, and the Sentiments, Manners, Numbers, and Condition, of the Primitive Christians

A candid [1] but rational enquiry into the progress and establishment of Christianity may be considered as a very essential part of the

---

[1] well-intentioned. [Gibbon's notes, which form an integral part of his text, have been retained throughout, but his varying modes of citing sources have, to some extent, been changed to conform to modern practice. Additions to his citations, such as titles, page numbers, and authors' first names or initials have been made silently, when a mere listing of authorities is involved; they have been enclosed in square brackets when the rhythm of a phrase or sentence seems to be altered. Dates of modern editions, if the possibility of confusion exists, have been added in square brackets, as have corrections of Gibbon's references. His spelling of authors' names has ordinarily been preserved (e.g., Dion Cassius, Augustin, but Jerome for Hieronymus). Titles and quotations in foreign languages have been translated, and such titles silently expanded when necessary. Apparent inconsistencies sometimes result, because Gibbon sometimes supplied a title or date of an edition inconsistently and these references have almost always been retained. No attempt to correct or modify Gibbon's historical account has been made, except in cases where a clear and significant misstatement of fact is involved. We have, in general, preferred readings of the first, third (1777), and fourth (1781) editions to those of the "new edition" of 1782 followed by Bury.]

history of the Roman empire. While that great body was invaded by open violence, or undermined by slow decay, a pure and humble religion gently insinuated itself into the minds of men, grew up in silence and obscurity, derived new vigor from opposition, and finally erected the triumphant banner of the cross on the ruins of the Capitol. Nor was the influence of Christianity confined to the period or to the limits of the Roman empire. After a revolution of thirteen or fourteen centuries, that religion is still professed by the nations of Europe, the most distinguished portion of human-kind in arts and learning as well as in arms. By the industry and zeal of the Europeans it has been widely diffused to the most distant shores of Asia and Africa; and by the means of their colonies has been firmly established from Canada to Chile, in a world unknown to the ancients.

But this enquiry, however useful or entertaining, is attended with two peculiar difficulties. The scanty and suspicious materials of ecclesiastical history seldom enable us to dispel the dark cloud that hangs over the first age of the church. The great law of impartiality too often obliges us to reveal the imperfections of the uninspired teachers and believers of the gospel; and, to a careless observer, *their* faults may seem to cast a shade on the faith which they professed. But the scandal of the pious Christian, and the fallacious triumph of the infidel, should cease as soon as they recollect not only *by whom,* but likewise *to whom,* the Divine Revelation was given. The theologian may indulge the pleasing task of describing religion as she descended from heaven, arrayed in her native purity. A more melancholy duty is imposed on the historian. He must discover the inevitable mixture of error and corruption which she contracted in a long residence upon earth, among a weak and degenerate race of beings.

Our curiosity is naturally prompted to enquire by what means the Christian faith obtained so remarkable a victory over the estab-lished religions of the earth. To this enquiry, an obvious but satis-factory answer may be returned; that it was owing to the convincing evidence of the doctrine itself, and to the ruling providence of its great Author. But as truth and reason seldom find so favorable a reception in the world, and as the wisdom of Providence frequently condescends to use the passions of the human heart, and the general circumstances of mankind, as instruments to execute its purpose, we may still be permitted, though with becoming submission, to ask not indeed what were the first, but what were the secondary causes of the rapid growth of the Christian church. It will, perhaps, appear that it was most effectually favored and assisted by the five following causes: I. The inflexible and, if we may use the expression, the intolerant zeal of the Christians, derived, it is true, from the Jewish religion, but purified from the narrow and unsocial spirit which, instead of inviting, had deterred the Gentiles from embracing the law of Moses. II. The doctrine of a future life, improved by every additional circumstance which could give weight and efficacy to that important truth. III. The miraculous powers ascribed to the primitive church. IV. The pure and austere morals of the Christians. V. The union and discipline of the Christian republic, which gradually formed an independent and increasing state in the heart of the Roman empire.

I. We have already described the religious harmony of the ancient world, and the facility with which the most different and even hostile nations embraced, or at least respected, each other's superstitions. A single people refused to join in the common intercourse of mankind. The Jews, who, under the Assyrian and Persian monarchies, had languished for many ages the most despised portion of their slaves,[2] emerged from obscurity under the successors of Alexander; and as they multiplied to a surprising degree in the East, and afterwards in the West, they soon excited the curiosity and wonder of other nations.[3] The sullen obstinacy with which they maintained their peculiar rites and unsocial manners seemed to mark them out a distinct species of men, who boldly professed, or who faintly disguised, their implacable hatred to the rest of human-

[2] "When the Assyrians, Medes, and Persians ruled the East, the Jews were regarded as the lowest of their subjects" (Tacitus, *Histories*, v 8). Herodotus, who visited Asia whilst it obeyed the last of those empires, slightly mentions the Syrians of Palestine, who, according to their own confession, had received from Egypt the rite of circumcision (see *History*, ii 104).

[3] Diodorus Siculus, *Library of History*, xl; Dion Cassius, *Roman History* [1750-52], i 121 (xxxvii 17); Tacitus, *Histories*, v 1-9; Justin, *Philipian History*, xxxvi 2-3.

kind.[4] Neither the violence of Antiochus, nor the arts of Herod, nor the example of the circumjacent nations, could ever persuade the Jews to associate with the institutions of Moses the elegant mythology of the Greeks.[5] According to the maxims of universal toleration, the Romans protected a superstition which they despised.[6] The polite Augustus condescended to give orders that sacrifices should be offered for his prosperity in the temple of Jerusalem;[7] while the meanest of the posterity of Abraham, who should have paid the same homage to the Jupiter of the Capitol, would have been an object of abhorrence to himself and to his brethren. But the moderation of the conquerors was insufficient to appease the jealous prejudices of their subjects, who were alarmed and scandalized at the ensigns of paganism, which necessarily introduced themselves into a Roman province.[8] The mad attempt of Caligula to place his own statue in the temple of Jerusalem was defeated by the unanimous resolution of a people who dreaded death much

[4] ["Accustomed to disregard the laws of Rome, they learn and follow and revere Jewish law] and all that Moses put in his secret book, forbidding them to show the way to any not practising the same rites, and leading only the circumcised to the wished-for fountain" [Juvenal, *Satires*, xiv 102-4]. The letter of this law is not to be found in the present volume of Moses. But the wise, the humane Maimonides openly teaches that if an idolater fall into the water, a Jew ought not to save him from instant death. See Jacques Basnage, *History of the Jews*, vi 28 [(1706-7), v 24].

[5] A Jewish sect, which indulged themselves in a sort of occasional conformity, derived from Herod, by whose example and authority they had been seduced, the name of Herodians. But their numbers were so inconsiderable, and their duration so short, that Josephus has not thought them worthy of his notice (see Humphrey Prideaux's *Connection* [*The Old and New Testament Connected*], ii 285 [end of pt. ii, bk. 5]). ["Occasional conformity" refers to the practice of some Nonconformists of taking the Anglican communion on one occasion in order to escape certain legal disqualifications.]

[6] Cicero, *In Defense of Flaccus*, ch. 28.

[7] Philo, *On the Embassy to Gaius*. Augustus left a foundation for a perpetual sacrifice. Yet he approved of the neglect which his grandson Caius expressed towards the temple of Jerusalem (see Suetonius in "Augustus" [*Lives of the Twelve Caesars*], ch. 93, and Isaac Casaubon's notes on that passage).

[8] See, in particular, Josephus, *Jewish Antiquities*, xvii 6, xviii 3, and *The Jewish War*, i 33 and ii 9, ed. Sigebert Havercamp [1726].

less than such an idolatrous profanation.[9] Their attachment to the law of Moses was equal to their detestation of foreign religions. The current of zeal and devotion, as it was contracted into a narrow channel, ran with the strength, and sometimes with the fury, of a torrent.

This inflexible perseverance, which appeared so odious or so ridiculous to the ancient world, assumes a more awful character, since Providence has deigned to reveal to us the mysterious history of the chosen people. But the devout and even scrupulous attachment to the Mosaic religion, so conspicuous among the Jews who lived under the second temple, becomes still more surprising, if it is compared with the stubborn incredulity of their forefathers. When the law was given in thunder from Mount Sinai, when the tides of the ocean and the course of the planets were suspended for the convenience of the Israelites, and when temporal rewards and punishments were the immediate consequences of their piety or disobedience, they perpetually relapsed into rebellion against the visible majesty of their Divine King, placed the idols of the nations in the sanctuary of Jehovah, and imitated every fantastic ceremony that was practised in the tents of the Arabs or in the cities of Phoenicia.[10] As the protection of Heaven was deservedly withdrawn from the ungrateful race, their faith acquired a proportionable degree of vigor and purity. The contemporaries of Moses and Joshua had beheld with careless indifference the most amazing miracles. Under the pressure of every calamity, the belief of those miracles has preserved the Jews of a later period from the universal contagion of idolatry; and, in contradiction to every known principle of the human mind, that singular people seems to have yielded a

[9] "When Caligula commanded the Jews to erect his statue in their temple, they preferred to fight" (Tacitus, *Histories*, v 9). Philo and Josephus gave a very circumstantial, but a very rhetorical, account of this transaction, which exceedingly perplexed the governor of Syria. At the first mention of this idolatrous proposal, King Agrippa fainted away and did not recover his senses till the third day.

[10] For the enumeration of the Syrian and Arabian deities, it may be observed that Milton has comprised in one hundred and thirty very beautiful lines [*Paradise Lost*, i 381-505] the two large and learned syntagmas [*The Syrian Gods*] which [John] Selden had composed on that abstruse subject.

stronger and more ready assent to the traditions of their remote ancestors than to the evidence of their own senses.[11]

The Jewish religion was admirably fitted for defense, but it was never designed for conquest; and it seems probable that the number of proselytes was never much superior to that of apostates. The divine promises were originally made, and the distinguishing rite of circumcision was enjoined, to a single family. When the posterity of Abraham had multiplied like the sands of the sea, the Deity, from whose mouth they received a system of laws and ceremonies, declared himself the proper and, as it were, the national God of Israel; and with the most jealous care separated his favorite people from the rest of mankind. The conquest of the land of Canaan was accompanied with so many wonderful and with so many bloody circumstances that the victorious Jews were left in a state of irreconcilable hostility with all their neighbors. They had been commanded to extirpate some of the most idolatrous tribes; and the execution of the Divine will had seldom been retarded by the weakness of humanity. With the other nations they were forbidden to contract any marriages or alliances; and the prohibition of receiving them into the congregation, which in some cases was perpetual, almost always extended to the third, to the seventh, or even to the tenth generation. The obligation of preaching to the Gentiles the faith of Moses had never been inculcated as a precept of the law, nor were the Jews inclined to impose it on themselves as a voluntary duty. In the admission of new citizens, that unsocial people was actuated by the selfish vanity of the Greeks, rather than by the generous policy of Rome. The descendants of Abraham were flattered by the opinion that they alone were the heirs of the covenant; and they were apprehensive of diminishing the value of their inheritance, by sharing it too easily with the strangers of the earth. A larger acquaintance with mankind extended their knowledge without correcting their prejudices; and whenever the God of Israel acquired any new votaries, he was much more indebted to the inconstant humor of polytheism than to the active zeal of his

[11] "How long will this people provoke me? and how long will it be ere they *believe* me, for all the *signs* which I have shown among them?" (Numbers 14:11.) It would be easy, but it would be unbecoming, to justify the complaint of the Deity from the whole tenor of the Mosaic history.

own missionaries.[12] The religion of Moses seems to be instituted for a particular country, as well as for a single nation; and, if a strict obedience had been paid to the order that every male, three times in the year, should present himself before the Lord Jehovah, it would have been impossible that the Jews could ever have spread themselves beyond the narrow limits of the promised land.[13] That obstacle was indeed removed by the destruction of the temple of Jerusalem; but the most considerable part of the Jewish religion was involved in its destruction; and the pagans, who had long wondered at the strange report of an empty sanctuary,[14] were at a loss to discover what could be the object, or what could be the instruments, of a worship which was destitute of temples and of altars, of priests and of sacrifices. Yet even in their fallen state, the Jews, still asserting their lofty and exclusive privileges, shunned, instead of courting, the society of strangers. They still insisted with inflexible rigor on those parts of the law which it was in their power to practice. Their peculiar distinctions of days, of meats, and a variety of trivial though burdensome observances, were so many objects of disgust and aversion for the other nations, to whose habits and prejudices they were diametrically opposite. The painful and even dangerous rite of circumcision was alone capable of repelling a willing proselyte from the door of the synagogue.[15]

Under these circumstances, Christianity offered itself to the world, armed with the strength of the Mosaic law, and delivered from the weight of its fetters. An exclusive zeal for the truth of religion and the unity of God was as carefully inculcated in the new as in the ancient system; and whatever was now revealed to

[12] All that relates to the Jewish proselytes has been very ably treated by Basnage, *History of the Jews*, vi [v] 6-7.

[13] See Exodus 24[34]:23, Deuteronomy 16:16, the commentators, and a very sensible note in the *Universal History*, i 603, folio edition [1744].

[14] When Pompey, using or abusing the right of conquest, entered into the Holy of Holies, it was observed with amazement, "there were no representations of the gods inside; the place was empty, and the secret shrine contained nothing" (Tacitus, *Histories*, v 9). It was a popular saying with regard to the Jews, "They worship only the clouds and the Spirit of the heavens" [Juvenal, xiv 97].

[15] A second kind of circumcision was inflicted on a Samaritan or Egyptian proselyte. The sullen indifference of the Talmudists, with respect to the conversion of strangers, may be seen in Basnage, *History of the Jews*, vi [v] 6.

mankind concerning the nature and designs of the Supreme Being was fitted to increase their reverence for that mysterious doctrine. The divine authority of Moses and the prophets was admitted, and even established, as the firmest basis of Christianity. From the beginning of the world, an uninterrupted series of predictions had announced and prepared the long expected coming of the Messiah, who, in compliance with the gross apprehensions of the Jews, had been more frequently represented under the character of a king and conqueror, than under that of a prophet, a martyr, and the Son of God. By his expiatory sacrifice, the imperfect sacrifices of the temple were at once consummated and abolished. The ceremonial law, which consisted only of types and figures, was succeeded by a pure and spiritual worship, equally adapted to all climates as well as to every condition of mankind; and to the initiation of blood was substituted a more harmless initiation of water. The promise of divine favor, instead of being partially confined to the posterity of Abraham, was universally proposed to the freeman and the slave, to the Greek and to the barbarian, to the Jew and to the Gentile. Every privilege that could raise the proselyte from earth to heaven, that could exalt his devotion, secure his happiness, or even gratify that secret pride which, under the semblance of devotion, insinuates itself into the human heart, was still reserved for the members of the Christian church; but at the same time all mankind was permitted, and even solicited, to accept the glorious distinction, which was not only proffered as a favor, but imposed as an obligation. It became the most sacred duty of a new convert to diffuse among his friends and relations the inestimable blessing which he had received, and to warn them against a refusal that would be severely punished as a criminal disobedience to the will of a benevolent but all-powerful Deity.

The enfranchisement of the church from the bonds of the synagogue was a work however of some time and of some difficulty. The Jewish converts, who acknowledged Jesus in the character of the Messiah foretold by their ancient oracles, respected him as a prophetic teacher of virtue and religion; but they obstinately adhered to the ceremonies of their ancestors, and were desirous of imposing them on the Gentiles, who continually augmented the number of believers. These Judaizing Christians seem to have argued with some degree of plausibility from the divine origin of the Mosaic law, and from the immutable perfections of its great Author. They affirmed *that,* if the Being, who is the same through all eternity, had designed to abolish those sacred rites which had served to distinguish his chosen people, the repeal of them would have been no less clear and solemn than their first promulgation: *that,* instead of those frequent declarations, which either suppose or assert the perpetuity of the Mosaic religion, it would have been represented as a provisionary scheme intended to last only till the coming of the Messiah, who should instruct mankind in a more perfect mode of faith and of worship:[16] *that* the Messiah himself, and his disciples who conversed with him on earth, instead of authorizing by their example the most minute observances of the Mosaic law,[17] would have published to the world the abolition of those useless and obsolete ceremonies, without suffering Christianity to remain during so many years obscurely confounded among the sects of the Jewish church. Arguments like these appear to have been used in the defense of the expiring cause of the Mosaic law; but the industry of our learned divines has abundantly explained the ambiguous language of the Old Testament, and the ambiguous conduct of the apostolic teachers. It was proper gradually to unfold the system of the gospel, and to pronounce with the utmost caution and tenderness a sentence of condemnation so repugnant to the inclination and prejudices of the believing Jews.

The history of the church of Jerusalem affords a lively proof of the necessity of those precautions, and of the deep impression which the Jewish religion had made on the minds of its sectaries. The first fifteen bishops of Jerusalem were all circumcised Jews; and the congregation over which they presided, united the law of

[16] These arguments were urged with great ingenuity by the Jew [Isaac] Orobio [de Castro], and refuted with equal ingenuity and candor by the Christian [Philipp van] Limborch. See the *Friendly Debate [on the Truth of the Christian Religion* (1687)] (it well deserves that name) or account of the dispute between them.

[17] "Jesus . . . was circumcised; he ate the same food as the Jews; was clothed as they were; those who were cured of leprosy he sent to the priests; he religiously observed the Passover and the other feast days. If he cured some on the Sabbath, he showed not merely by the law but also by common opinion that such works were not forbidden on the Sabbath" (Grotius, *The Truth of the Christian Religion,* v 7). A little afterwards (ch. 12) he expatiates on the condescension of the apostles.

Moses with the doctrine of Christ.[18] It was natural that the primitive tradition of a church which was founded only forty days after the death of Christ, and was governed almost as many years under the immediate inspection of his apostles, should be received as the standard of orthodoxy.[19] The distant churches very frequently appealed to the authority of their venerable parent, and relieved her distresses by a liberal contribution of alms. But when numerous and opulent societies were established in the great cities of the empire, in Antioch, Alexandria, Ephesus, Corinth, and Rome, the reverence which Jerusalem had inspired to all the Christian colonies insensibly diminished. The Jewish converts, or, as they were afterwards called, the Nazarenes, who had laid the foundations of the church, soon found themselves overwhelmed by the increasing multitudes that from all the various religions of polytheism inlisted under the banner of Christ; and the Gentiles, who with the approbation of their peculiar apostle[20] had rejected the intolerable weight of Mosaic ceremonies, at length refused to their more scrupulous brethren the same toleration which at first they had humbly solicited for their own practice. The ruin of the temple, of the city, and of the public religion of the Jews, was severely felt by the Nazarenes; as in their manners, though not in their faith, they maintained so intimate a connection with their impious countrymen, whose misfortunes were attributed by the pagans to the contempt, and more justly ascribed by the Christians to the wrath, of the Supreme Deity. The Nazarenes retired from the ruins of Jerusalem to the little town of Pella beyond the Jordan, where that ancient church languished above sixty years in solitude and obscurity.[21] They still enjoyed the comfort of making frequent and devout

[18] "Almost all believed that Christ was God while continuing to observe the Mosaic laws" (Sulpicius Severus, *Sacred History*, ii 31). See Eusebius, *Ecclesiastical History*, iv 5.

[19] J. L. Mosheim, *Commentaries on the Affairs of the Christians before the Time of Constantine the Great* [1753], p. 153. In this masterly performance, which I shall often have occasion to quote, he enters much more fully into the state of the primitive church than he has an opportunity of doing in his general history [*An Ecclesiastical History from the Birth of Christ to the Beginning of the Present Century*].

[20] [St. Paul.]

[21] Eusebius, iii 5. Jean Le Clerc, *Ecclesiastical History* [1716], p. 605.

visits to the *Holy City,* and the hope of being one day restored to those seats which both nature and religion taught them to love as well as to revere. But at length, under the reign of Hadrian, the desperate fanaticism of the Jews filled up the measure of their calamities; and the Romans, exasperated by their repeated rebellions, exercised the rights of victory with unusual rigor. The emperor founded, under the name of Aelia Capitolina, a new city on Mount Sion,[22] to which he gave the privileges of a colony; and, denouncing the severest penalties against any of the Jewish people who should dare to approach its precincts, he fixed a vigilant garrison of a Roman cohort to enforce the execution of his orders. The Nazarenes had only one way left to escape the common proscription, and the force of truth was on this occasion assisted by the influence of temporal advantages. They elected Marcus for their bishop, a prelate of the race of the Gentiles, and most probably a native either of Italy or of some of the Latin provinces. At his persuasion, the most considerable part of the congregation renounced the Mosaic law, in the practice of which they had persevered above a century. By this sacrifice of their habits and prejudices they purchased a free admission into the colony of Hadrian, and more firmly cemented their union with the Catholic church.[23]

When the name and honors of the church of Jerusalem had been restored to Mount Sion, the crimes of heresy and schism were imputed to the obscure remnant of the Nazarenes which refused to accompany their Latin bishop. They still preserved their former habitation of Pella, spread themselves into the villages adjacent to Damascus, and formed an inconsiderable church in the city of

---

During this occasional absence, the bishop and church of Pella still retained the title of Jerusalem. In the same manner, the Roman pontiffs resided seventy years at Avignon, and the patriarchs of Alexandria have long since transferred their episcopal seat to Cairo. [Bury notes that the Nazarenes retired before the capture and destruction of Jerusalem in A.D. 70.]

[22] Dion Cassius, lxix 12. The exile of the Jewish nation from Jerusalem is attested by Aristo of Pella (according to Eusebius, iv 6), and is mentioned by several ecclesiastical writers, though some of them too hastily extend this interdiction to the whole country of Palestine.

[23] Eusebius, iv 6. Sulpicius Severus, ii 31. By comparing their unsatisfactory accounts, Mosheim (pp. 327 etc.) has drawn out a very distinct representation of the circumstances and motives of this revolution.

Boerea, or, as it is now called, of Aleppo, in Syria.[24] The name of Nazarenes was deemed too honorable for those Christian Jews, and they soon received from the supposed poverty of their understanding, as well as of their condition, the contemptuous epithet of Ebionites.[25] In a few years after the return of the church of Jerusalem, it became a matter of doubt and controversy whether a man who sincerely acknowledged Jesus as the Messiah, but who still continued to observe the law of Moses, could possibly hope for salvation. The humane temper of Justin Martyr inclined him to answer this question in the affirmative; and, though he expressed himself with the most guarded diffidence, he ventured to determine in favor of such an imperfect Christian, if he were content to practise the Mosaic ceremonies, without pretending to assert their general use or necessity. But, when Justin was pressed to declare the sentiment of the church, he confessed that there were very many among the orthodox Christians, who not only excluded their Judaizing brethren from the hope of salvation, but who declined any intercourse with them in the common offices of friendship, hospitality, and social life.[26] The more rigorous opinion prevailed, as it was natural to expect, over the milder; and an external bar of separation was fixed between the disciples of Moses and those of Christ. The unfortunate Ebionites, rejected from one religion as apostates, and from the other as heretics, found themselves compelled to assume a more decided character; and, although some traces of that obsolete sect

[24] Le Clerc (*Ecclesiastical History*, pp. 477, 535) seems to have collected from Eusebius, Jerome, Epiphanius, and other writers, all the principal circumstances that relate to the Nazarenes or Ebionites. The nature of their opinions soon divided them into a stricter and a milder sect; and there is some reason to conjecture that the family of Jesus Christ remained members, at least, of the latter and more moderate party.

[25] Some writers have been pleased to create an Ebion, the imaginary author of their sect and name. But we can more safely rely on the learned Eusebius than on the vehement Tertullian or the credulous Epiphanius. According to Le Clerc, the Hebrew word *Ebjonim* may be translated into Latin by that of *Pauperes* (see the *Ecclesiastical History*, p. 477).

[26] See the very curious *Dialogue* of Justin Martyr with the Jew Tryphon. The conference between them was held at Ephesus, in the reign of Antoninus Pius, and about twenty years after the return of the church of Pella to Jerusalem. For this date consult the accurate note of [Louis Sebastien Le Nain de] Tillemont, *Ecclesiastical Memoirs*, ii 511 [Gibbon owned the edition of 1706].

may be discovered as late as the fourth century, they insensibly melted away either into the church or the synagogue.[27]

While the orthodox church preserved a just medium between excessive veneration and improper contempt for the law of Moses, the various heretics deviated into equal but opposite extremes of error and extravagance. From the acknowledged truth of the Jewish religion the Ebionites had concluded that it could never be abolished. From its supposed imperfections the Gnostics as hastily inferred that it never was instituted by the wisdom of the Deity. There are some objections against the authority of Moses and the prophets, which too readily present themselves to the skeptical mind; though they can only be derived from our ignorance of remote antiquity, and from our incapacity to form an adequate judgment of the divine economy. These objections were eagerly embraced and as petulantly urged by the vain science of the Gnostics.[28] As those heretics were, for the most part, averse to the pleasures of sense, they morosely arraigned the polygamy of the patriarchs, the gallantries of David, and the seraglio of Solomon. The conquest of the land of Canaan, and the extirpation of the unsuspecting natives, they were at a loss how to reconcile with the common notions of humanity and justice. But when they recollected the sanguinary list of murders, of executions, and of massacres, which stain almost every page of the Jewish annals, they acknowledged that the barbarians of Palestine had exercised as much compassion towards

[27] Of all the systems of Christianity, that of Abyssinia is the only one which still adheres to the Mosaic rites (Michael Geddes's *Church History of Ethiopia*, and the *Dissertations* of Joachim Le Grand on the *Voyage to Abyssinia* of Father Jerome Lobo). The eunuch of the queen Candace might suggest some suspicions; but, as we are assured (Socrates, *Ecclesiastical History*, i 19; Sozomen, *Ecclesiastical History*, ii 24; Ludolphus, *History of Ethiopia* [1691], p. 281) that the Ethiopians were not converted till the fourth century, it is more reasonable to believe that they respected the Sabbath, and distinguished the forbidden meats, in imitation of the Jews, who, in a very early period, were seated on both sides of the Red Sea. Circumcision had been practised by the most ancient Ethiopians, from motives of health and cleanliness which seem to be explained in the *Philosophical Studies on the Americans* [by Cornelius de Pauw (1769)], ii 117.

[28] [Isaac de] Beausobre, *Critical History of Manichaeanism* [1734-39], i 3, has stated their objections, particularly those of Faustus, the adversary of Augustin, with the most learned impartiality.

their idolatrous enemies as they had ever shown to their friends or countrymen.[29] Passing from the sectaries of the law to the law itself, they asserted that it was impossible that a religion which consisted only of bloody sacrifices and trifling ceremonies, and whose rewards as well as punishments were all of a carnal and temporal nature, could inspire the love of virtue, or restrain the impetuosity of passion. The Mosaic account of the creation and fall of man was treated with profane derision by the Gnostics, who would not listen with patience to the repose of the Deity after six days' labor, to the rib of Adam, the garden of Eden, the trees of life and of knowledge, the speaking serpent, the forbidden fruit, and the condemnation prounounced against humankind for the venial offense of their first progenitors.[30] The God of Israel was impiously represented by the Gnostics as a being liable to passion and to error, capricious in his favor, implacable in his resentment, meanly jealous of his superstitious worship, and confining his partial providence to a single people and to this transitory life. In such a character they could discover none of the features of the wise and omnipotent father of the universe.[31] They allowed that the religion of the Jews was somewhat less criminal than the idolatry of the Gentiles; but it was their fundamental doctrine that the Christ whom they adored as the first and brightest emanation of the Deity appeared upon earth to rescue mankind from their various errors, and to reveal a *new* system of truth and perfection. The most learned of the fathers, by a very singular condescension, have imprudently admitted the sophistry of the Gnostics. Acknowledging that the literal sense is repugnant to every principle of faith as

[29] "They show great loyalty and are always ready to be compassionate to each other, but they hate and are hostile to all other peoples" (Tacitus, *Histories*, v 4). Surely Tacitus had seen the Jews with too favorable an eye. The perusal of Josephus must have destroyed the antithesis.

[30] Dr. [Thomas] Burnet (*Philosophical Archaeology*, ii 7) has discussed the first chapters of Genesis with too much wit and freedom. [Burnet included in his work a ludicrous account of the conversation between Eve and the serpent, which gave great offense.]

[31] The milder Gnostics considered Jehovah, the Creator, as a Being of a mixed nature between God and the Demon. Others confounded him with the evil principle. Consult the second century of the general history [*Ecclesiastical History*] of Mosheim, which gives a very distinct though concise account of their strange opinions on this subject.

well as reason, they deem themselves secure and invulnerable behind the ample veil of allegory, which they carefully spread over every tender part of the Mosaic dispensation.[32]

It has been remarked, with more ingenuity than truth, that the virgin purity of the church was never violated by schism or heresy before the reign of Trajan or Hadrian, about one hundred years after the death of Christ.[33] We may observe, with much more propriety, that, during that period, the disciples of the Messiah were indulged in a freer latitude both of faith and practice than has ever been allowed in succeeding ages. As the terms of communion were insensibly narrowed, and the spiritual authority of the prevailing party was exercised with increasing severity, many of its most respectable adherents, who were called upon to renounce, were provoked to assert, their private opinions, to pursue the consequences of their mistaken principles, and openly to erect the standard of rebellion against the unity of the church. The Gnostics were distinguished as the most polite, the most learned, and the most wealthy of the Christian name, and that general appellation which expressed a superiority of knowledge was either assumed by their own pride or ironically bestowed by the envy of their adversaries.[34] They were, almost without exception, of the race of the Gentiles; and their principal founders seem to have been natives of Syria or Egypt, where the warmth of the climate disposes both the mind and the body to indolent and contemplative devotion. The Gnostics blended with the faith of Christ many sublime but obscure tenets which they derived from oriental philosophy, and even from the religion of Zoroaster, concerning the eternity of matter, the existence of two principles, and the mysterious hierarchy of the invisible world.[35] As soon as they launched out into that vast abyss, they delivered themselves to the guidance of a disordered imagination; and, as the paths of error are various and infinite, the Gnostics were

[32] See Beausobre, *History of Manichaeanism*, i 4. Origen and St. Augustin were among the allegorists.

[33] Hegesippus, according to Eusebius, iii 32, iv 22; Clemens of Alexandria, *Miscellanies*, vii 17.

[34] [Gnostic is derived from Greek *gnostikos*, sagacious.]

[35] In the account of the Gnostics of the second and third centuries, Mosheim is ingenious and candid; Le Clerc, dull but exact; Beausobre, almost always an apologist; and it is much to be feared that the primitive fathers are very frequently calumniators.

imperceptibly divided into more than fifty particular sects,[36] of
whom the most celebrated appear to have been the Basilidians, the
Valentinians, the Marcionites, and, in a still later period, the
Manichaeans. Each of these sects could boast of its bishops and
congregations, of its doctors and martyrs,[37] and, instead of the four
gospels adopted by the church, the heretics produced a multitude of
histories, in which the actions and discourses of Christ and of his
apostles were adapted to their respective tenets.[38] The success of
the Gnostics was rapid and extensive.[39] They covered Asia and
Egypt, established themselves in Rome, and sometimes penetrated
into the provinces of the West. For the most part they arose in the
second century, flourished during the third, and were suppressed
in the fourth or fifth, by the prevalence of more fashionable controversies, and by the superior ascendant of the reigning power.
Though they constantly disturbed the peace, and frequently disgraced the name, of religion, they contributed to assist rather than
to retard the progress of Christianity. The Gentile converts, whose
strongest objections and prejudices were directed against the law
of Moses, could find admission into many Christian societies, which

[36] See the catalogues of Irenaeus and Epiphanius. It must indeed be
allowed that those writers were inclined to multiply the number of sects
which opposed the *unity* of the church.

[37] Eusebius, iv 15; Sozomen, ii 32. See in [Pierre] Bayle [*Historical and
Critical Dictionary*] in the article of *Marcion*, a curious detail of a dispute
on that subject. It should seem that some of the Gnostics (the Basilidians)
declined, and even refused, the honor of martyrdom. Their reasons were
singular and abstruse (see Mosheim, p. 359).

[38] See a very remarkable passage of Origen (Proem to *Homilies on Luke*,
[First Homily]). That indefatigable writer, who had consumed his life in the
study of the Scriptures, relies for their authenticity on the inspired authority
of the Church. It was impossible that the Gnostics could receive our present
Gospels, many parts of which (particularly in the resurrection of Christ) are
directly, and as it might seem designedly, pointed against their favorite tenets.
It is therefore somewhat singular that Ignatius (*Epistle to the Smyrnaeans*
[iii 2], *Apostolic Fathers* [1724], ii 34) should choose to employ a vague
and doubtful tradition, instead of quoting the certain testimony of the
Evangelists.

[39] "As wasps make combs, so the Marcionites set up churches" is the
strong expression of Tertullian, which I am obliged to quote from memory
[*Against Marcion*, iv 5]. In the time of Epiphanius (*Eighty Antidotes against
Heresies* [1622], p. 302) the Marcionites were very numerous in Italy,
Syria, Egypt, Arabia, and Persia.

required not from their untutored mind any belief of an antecedent revelation. Their faith was insensibly fortified and enlarged, and the church was ultimately benefited by the conquests of its most inveterate enemies.[40]

But whatever difference of opinion might subsist between the Orthodox, the Ebionites, and the Gnostics, concerning the divinity or the obligation of the Mosaic law, they were all equally animated by the same exclusive zeal and by the same abhorrence for idolatry which had distinguished the Jews from the other nations of the ancient world. The philosopher, who considered the system of polytheism as a composition of human fraud and error, could disguise a smile of contempt under the mask of devotion, without apprehending that either the mockery, or the compliance, would expose him to the resentment of any invisible, or, as he conceived them, imaginary powers. But the established religions of paganism were seen by the primitive Christians in a much more odious and formidable light. It was the universal sentiment both of the church and of heretics that the demons were the authors, the patrons, and the objects of idolatry.[41] Those rebellious spirits who had been degraded from the rank of angels, and cast down into the infernal pit, were still permitted to roam upon earth, to torment the bodies, and to seduce the minds, of sinful men. The demons soon discovered and abused the natural propensity of the human heart towards devotion; and, artfully withdrawing the adoration of mankind from their Creator, they usurped the place and honors of the Supreme Deity. By the success of their malicious contrivances, they at once gratified their own vanity and revenge, and obtained the only comfort of which they were yet susceptible, the hope of involving the human species in the participation of their guilt and misery. It was confessed, or at least it was imagined, that they had distributed among themselves the most important characters of polytheism, one demon assuming the name and attributes of Jupiter, another of Aesculapius, a third of Venus, and a fourth perhaps of

[40] Augustin is a memorable instance of this gradual progress from reason to faith. He was, during several years, engaged in the Manichaean sect.

[41] The unanimous sentiment of the primitive church is very clearly explained by Justin Martyr, *First Apology*, ch. 25, by Athenagoras, *Plea for the Christians*, chs. 22 etc., and by Lactantius, *The Divine Institutes*, ii 14-19.

Apollo;[42] and that, by the advantage of their long experience and
aërial nature, they were enabled to execute, with sufficient skill and
dignity, the parts which they had undertaken. They lurked in the
temples, instituted festivals and sacrifices, invented fables, pronounced oracles, and were frequently allowed to perform miracles.
The Christians, who, by the interposition of evil spirits, could so
readily explain every preternatural appearance, were disposed and
even desirous to admit the most extravagant fictions of the pagan
mythology. But the belief of the Christian was accompanied with
horror. The most trifling mark of respect to the national worship he
considered as a direct homage yielded to the demon, and as an act
of rebellion against the majesty of God.

In consequence of this opinion, it was the first but arduous
duty of a Christian to preserve himself pure and undefiled by the
practice of idolatry. The religion of the nations was not merely a
speculative doctrine professed in the schools or preached in the
temples. The innumerable deities and rites of polytheism were
closely interwoven with every circumstance of business or pleasure,
of public or of private life; and it seemed impossible to escape the
observance of them, without, at the same time, renouncing the
commerce of mankind and all the offices and amusements of society.[43] The important transactions of peace and war were prepared
or concluded by solemn sacrifices, in which the magistrate, the
senator, and the soldier were obliged to preside or to participate.[44]
The public spectacles were an essential part of the cheerful devotion
of the pagans, and the gods were supposed to accept, as the most
grateful offering, the games that the prince and people celebrated
in honor of their peculiar festivals.[45] The Christian, who with pious

[42] Tertullian (*Apology*, ch. 23) alleges the confessions of the demons
themselves as often as they were tormented by the Christian exorcists.

[43] Tertullian has written a most severe treatise against idolatry, to caution his brethren against the hourly danger of incurring that guilt. "Think
of what a forest it is, and how many thorns are concealed in it" (*The
Soldier's Chaplet*, ch. 10).

[44] The Roman senate was always held in a temple or consecrated place
(Aulus Gellius, *Attic Nights*, xiv 7). Before they entered on business, every
senator dropped some wine and frankincense on the altar (Suetonius in
"Augustus," ch. 35).

[45] See Tertullian, *On Spectacles*. This severe reformer shows no more
indulgence to a tragedy of Euripides than to a combat of gladiators. The

horror avoided the abomination of the circus or the theater, found himself encompassed with infernal snares in every convivial entertainment, as often as his friends, invoking the hospitable deities, poured out libations to each other's happiness.[46] When the bride, struggling with well-affected reluctance, was forced in hymeneal pomp over the threshold of her new habitation,[47] or when the sad procession of the dead slowly moved towards the funeral pile;[48] the Christian, on these interesting occasions, was compelled to desert the persons who were the dearest to him, rather than contract the guilt inherent to those impious ceremonies. Every art and every trade that was in the least concerned in the framing or adorning of idols was polluted by the stain of idolatry;[49] a severe sentence, since it devoted to eternal misery the far greater part of the community, which is employed in the exercise of liberal or mechanic professions. If we cast our eyes over the numerous remains of antiquity, we shall perceive that, besides the immediate representations of the gods, and the holy instruments of their worship, the elegant forms and agreeable fictions consecrated by the imagination of the Greeks were introduced as the richest ornaments of the houses, the dress, and the furniture of the pagans.[50] Even the arts of music and painting, of eloquence and poetry, flowed from the same impure origin. In the style of the fathers, Apollo and the Muses were the

dress of the actors particularly offends him. By the use of the lofty buskin, they impiously strive to add a cubit to their stature (ch. 23).

[46] The ancient practice of concluding the entertainment with libations may be found in every classic. Socrates and Seneca, in their last moments, made a noble application of this custom. "As a last resort, he [Seneca] got into a hot bath and sprinkled some of the water on the nearest slaves, remarking that he offered the liquid to Jove the Liberator" (Tacitus, *Annals*, xv 64).

[47] See the elegant but idolatrous hymn of Catullus, on the nuptials of Manlius and Julia: "O Hymen, Hymenaee hail. . . . What god would dare compare himself to this god?" (*Poems*, 61).

[48] The ancient funerals (in those of Misenus and Pallas) are no less accurately described by Virgil than they are illustrated by his commentator, Servius. The pile itself was an altar, the flames were fed with the blood of victims, and all the assistants were sprinkled with lustral water.

[49] Tertullian, *On Idolatry*, ch. 11.

[50] See every part of [Bernard de] Montfaucon's *Antiquities* [*Antiquity in Sculptures*]. Even the reverses of the Greek and Roman coins were frequently of an idolatrous nature. Here indeed the scruples of the Christian were suspended by a stronger passion.

organs of the infernal spirit, Homer and Virgil were the most eminent of his servants, and the beautiful mythology which pervades and animates the compositions of their genius is destined to celebrate the glory of the demons. Even the common language of Greece and Rome abounded with familiar but impious expressions, which the imprudent Christian might too carelessly utter, or too patiently hear.[51]

The dangerous temptations which on every side lurked in ambush to surprise the unguarded believer assailed him with redoubled violence on the days of solemn festivals. So artfully were they framed and disposed throughout the year that superstition always wore the appearance of pleasure, and often of virtue.[52] Some of the most sacred festivals in the Roman ritual were destined to salute the new calends of January with vows of public and private felicity, to indulge the pious remembrance of the dead and living, to ascertain the inviolable bounds of property, to hail, on the return of spring, the genial powers of fecundity, to perpetuate the two memorable eras of Rome, the foundation of the city and that of the republic, and to restore, during the humane license of the Saturnalia, the primitive equality of mankind. Some idea may be conceived of the abhorrence of the Christians for such impious ceremonies, by the scrupulous delicacy which they displayed on a much less alarming occasion. On days of general festivity, it was the custom of the ancients to adorn their doors with lamps and with branches of laurel, and to crown their heads with a garland of flowers. This innocent and elegant practice might, perhaps, have been tolerated as a mere civil institution. But it most unluckily happened that the doors were under the protection of the household gods, that the laurel was sacred to the lover of Daphne, and that garlands of flowers, though frequently worn as a symbol either of joy or mourning, had been dedicated in their first origin to the service of superstition. The trembling Christians, who were persuaded in this instance to comply with the fashion of their country and the commands of the magistrate, la-

[51] Tertullian, *On Idolatry*, chs. 20-22. If a pagan friend (on the occasion perhaps of sneezing) used the familiar expression of "Jupiter bless you," the Christian was obliged to protest against the divinity of Jupiter.

[52] Consult the most labored work of Ovid, his imperfect *Fasti*. He finished no more than the first six months of the year. The compilation of Macrobius is called the *Saturnalia,* but it is only a small part of the first book that bears any relation to the title.

bored under the most gloomy apprehensions, from the reproaches of their own conscience, the censures of the church, and the denunciations of divine vengeance.[53]

Such was the anxious diligence which was required to guard the chastity of the gospel from the infectious breath of idolatry. The superstitious observances of public or private rites were carelessly practiced, from education and habit, by the followers of the established religion. But as often as they occurred, they afforded the Christians an opportunity of declaring and confirming their zealous opposition. By these frequent protestations, their attachment to the faith was continually fortified, and, in proportion to the increase of zeal, they combated with the more ardor and success in the holy war which they had undertaken against the empire of the demons.

II. The writings of Cicero[54] represent, in the most lively colors, the ignorance, the errors, and the uncertainty of the ancient philosophers with regard to the immortality of the soul. When they are desirous of arming their disciples against the fear of death, they inculcate, as an obvious though melancholy position, that the fatal stroke of our dissolution releases us from the calamities of life, and that those can no longer suffer who no longer exist. Yet there were a few sages of Greece and Rome who had conceived a more exalted, and, in some respects, a juster idea of human nature; though it must be confessed that, in the sublime enquiry, their reason had been often guided by their imagination, and that their imagination had been prompted by their vanity. When they viewed with complacency the extent of their own mental powers, when they exercised the various faculties of memory, of fancy, and of judgment in the most profound speculations, or the most important labors, and when they

[53] Tertullian has composed a defense, or rather panegyric, of the rash action of a Christian soldier who, by throwing away his crown of laurel, had exposed himself and his brethren to the most imminent danger. By the mention of the *emperors* (Severus and Caracalla) it is evident, notwithstanding the wishes of M. de Tillemont, that Tertullian composed his treatise, *The Soldier's Chaplet*, long before he was engaged in the errors of the Montanists (see *Ecclesiastical Memoirs*, iii 384). [Bury says that Tertullian joined the Montanist heretics in 207, and that the date of *The Soldier's Chaplet* is 211.]

[54] In particular, the first book of the *Tusculan Questions*, and the treatise *On Old Age*, and the *Dream of Scipio* contain, in the most beautiful language, everything that Grecian philosophy, or Roman good sense, could possibly suggest on this dark but important subject.

reflected on the desire of fame, which transported them into future ages far beyond the bounds of death and of the grave, they were unwilling to confound themselves with the beasts of the field, or to suppose that a being, for whose dignity they entertained the most sincere admiration, could be limited to a spot of earth and to a few years of duration. With this favorable prepossession, they summoned to their aid the science, or rather the language, of metaphysics. They soon discovered that, as none of the properties of matter will apply to the operations of the mind, the human soul must consequently be a substance distinct from the body, pure, simple, and spiritual, incapable of dissolution, and susceptible of a much higher degree of virtue and happiness after the release from its corporeal prison. From these specious and noble principles, the philosophers who trod in the footsteps of Plato deduced a very unjustifiable conclusion, since they asserted, not only the future immortality, but the past eternity of the human soul, which they were too apt to consider as a portion of the infinite and self-existing spirit which pervades and sustains the universe.[55] A doctrine thus removed beyond the senses and the experience of mankind might serve to amuse the leisure of a philosophic mind; or, in the silence of solitude, it might sometimes impart a ray of comfort to desponding virtue; but the faint impression which had been received in the schools was soon obliterated by the commerce and business of active life. We are sufficiently acquainted with the eminent persons who flourished in the age of Cicero and of the first Caesars, with their actions, their characters, and their motives, to be assured that their conduct in this life was never regulated by any serious conviction of the rewards or punishments of a future state. At the bar and in the senate of Rome, the ablest orators were not apprehensive of giving offense to their hearers by exposing that doctrine as an idle and extravagant opinion, which was rejected with contempt by every man of a liberal education and understanding.[56]

Since, therefore, the most sublime efforts of philosophy can

[55] The pre-existence of human souls, so far at least as that doctrine is compatible with religion, was adopted by many of the Greek and Latin fathers (see Beausobre, *History of Manichaeanism*, vi 4).

[56] See Cicero, *In Defense of Cluentius*, ch. 61; Caesar, according to Sallust, *The War with Catiline*, ch. 50 [51]; Juvenal, *Satires*, ii 149, 152: "that such things exist as subterranean realms and divine ancestral spirits . . . even boys do not believe, except those who are too young to be charged for their bath."

extend no farther than feebly to point out the desire, the hope, or at most the probability, of a future state, there is nothing, except a divine revelation, that can ascertain the existence, and describe the condition, of the invisible country which is destined to receive the souls of men after their separation from the body. But we may perceive several defects inherent to the popular religions of Greece and Rome, which rendered them very unequal to so arduous a task. 1. The general system of their mythology was unsupported by any solid proofs; and the wisest among the pagans had already disclaimed its usurped authority. 2. The description of the infernal regions had been abandoned to the fancy of painters and of poets, who peopled them with so many phantoms and monsters, who dispensed their rewards and punishments with so little equity, that a solemn truth, the most congenial to the human heart, was oppressed and disgraced by the absurd mixture of the wildest fictions.[57] 3. The doctrine of a future state was scarcely considered among the devout polytheists of Greece and Rome as a fundamental article of faith. The providence of the gods, as it related to public communities rather than to private individuals, was principally displayed on the visible theater of the present world. The petitions which were offered on the altars of Jupiter or Apollo expressed the anxiety of their worshippers for temporal happiness, and their ignorance or indifference concerning a future life.[58] The important truth of the immortality of the soul was inculcated with more diligence as well as success in India, in Assyria, in Egypt, and in Gaul; and, since we cannot attribute such a difference to the superior knowledge of the barbarians, we must ascribe it to the influence of an established priesthood, which employed the motives of virtue as the instrument of ambition.[59]

[57] The eleventh book of the *Odyssey* gives a very dreary and incoherent account of the infernal shades. Pindar and Virgil have embellished the picture, but even those poets, though more correct than their great model, are guilty of very strange inconsistencies (see Pierre Bayle, *Replies to the Questions of a Provincial*, iii 22).

[58] See the sixteenth epistle of the first book of Horace, the thirteenth satire of Juvenal, and the second satire of Persius: these popular discourses express the sentiment and language of the multitude.

[59] If we confine ourselves to the Gauls, we may observe that they intrusted not only their lives, but even their money, to the security of another world. "I heard of an old Celtic custom" (says Valerius Maximus [*Memorable Deeds and Sayings*], II v 10), "which is that they often lend each other considerable sums of money to be repaid in the other world." The same

We might naturally expect that a principle so essential to religion would have been revealed in the clearest terms to the chosen people of Palestine, and that it might safely have been intrusted to the hereditary priesthood of Aaron. It is incumbent on us to adore the mysterious dispensations of Providence,[60] when we discover that the doctrine of the immortality of the soul is omitted in the law of Moses; it is darkly insinuated by the prophets, and during the long period which elapsed between the Egyptian and the Babylonian servitudes, the hopes as well as fears of the Jews appear to have been confined within the narrow compass of the present life.[61] After Cyrus had permitted the exiled nation to return into the promised land, and after Ezra had restored the ancient records of their religion, two celebrated sects, the Sadducees and the Pharisees, insensibly arose at Jerusalem.[62] The former, selected from the more opulent and distinguished ranks of society, were strictly attached to the literal sense of the Mosaic law; and they piously rejected the immortality of the soul, as an opinion that received no countenance from the divine book, which they revered as the only rule of their faith. To the authority of Scripture the Pharisees added that of tradition, and they accepted, under the name of traditions, several speculative tenets from the philosophy or religion of the eastern nations. The doctrines of fate or predestination, of angels and spirits, and of a future state of rewards and punishments were in the

---

custom is more darkly insinuated by [Pomponius] Mela [*Description of the World*], iii 2. It is almost needless to add that the profits of trade hold a just proportion to the credit of the merchant, and that the Druids derived from their holy profession a character of responsibility which could scarcely be claimed by any other order of men.

[60] The Right Reverend author of the *Divine Legation of Moses* assigns a very curious reason for the omission, and most ingeniously retorts it on the unbelievers. [William Warburton, Bishop of Gloucester, maintained that Moses deliberately refrained from introducing the doctrine of immortality to the Israelites so that they would not fancy themselves gods.]

[61] See Le Clerc (Prolegomena to *Ecclesiastical History*, i 8). His authority seems to carry the greater weight, as he has written a learned and judicious commentary on the books of the Old Testament.

[62] Josephus, *Jewish Antiquities*, xiii 10; *The Jewish War*, ii 8. According to the most natural interpretation of his words, the Sadducees admitted only the Pentateuch, but it has pleased some modern critics to add the Prophets to their creed, and to suppose that they contented themselves with rejecting the traditions of the Pharisees. Dr. [John] Jortin has argued that point in his *Remarks on Ecclesiastical History* [1767], ii 103.

number of these new articles of belief; and as the Pharisees, by the austerity of their manners, had drawn into their party the body of the Jewish people, the immortality of the soul became the prevailing sentiment of the synagogue, under the reign of the Asmonean princes and pontiffs. The temper of the Jews was incapable of contenting itself with such a cold and languid assent as might satisfy the mind of a polytheist; and as soon as they admitted the idea of a future state, they embraced it with the zeal which has always formed the characteristic of the nation. Their zeal, however, added nothing to its evidence, or even probability; and it was still necessary that the doctrine of life and immortality, which had been dictated by nature, approved by reason, and received by superstition, should obtain the sanction of divine truth from the authority and example of Christ.

When the promise of eternal happiness was proposed to mankind, on condition of adopting the faith and of observing the precepts of the gospel, it is no wonder that so advantageous an offer should have been accepted by great numbers of every religion, of every rank, and of every province in the Roman empire. The ancient Christians were animated by a contempt for their present existence, and by a just confidence of immortality, of which the doubtful and imperfect faith of modern ages cannot give us any adequate notion. In the primitive church, the influence of truth was very powerfully strengthened by an opinion which, however it may deserve respect for its usefulness and antiquity, has not been found agreeable to experience. It was universally believed that the end of the world and the kingdom of heaven were at hand. The near approach of this wonderful event had been predicted by the apostles; the tradition of it was preserved by their earliest disciples, and those who understood in their literal sense the discourses of Christ himself were obliged to expect the second and glorious coming of the Son of Man in the clouds before that generation was totally extinguished which had beheld his humble condition upon earth, and which might still be witness of the calamities of the Jews under Vespasian or Hadrian. The revolution of seventeen centuries has instructed us not to press too closely the mysterious language of prophecy and revelation; but, as long as, for wise purposes, this error was permitted to subsist in the church, it was productive of the most salutary effects on the faith and practice of Christians, who lived in the awful expectation of that moment when the globe itself, and all the various race of mankind, should tremble at the appearance of their divine judge.[63]

The ancient and popular doctrine of the millennium was intimately connected with the second coming of Christ. As the works of the creation had been finished in six days, their duration in their present state, according to a tradition which was attributed to the prophet Elijah, was fixed to six thousand years.[64] By the same analogy it was inferred that this long period of labor and contention, which was now almost elapsed,[65] would be succeeded by a joyful sabbath of a thousand years; and that Christ, with the triumphant band of the saints and the elect who had escaped death, or who had been miraculously revived, would reign upon earth till the time appointed for the last and general resurrection. So pleasing was this hope to the mind of believers that the *New Jerusalem*, the seat of this blissful kingdom, was quickly adorned with all the gayest colors of the imagination. A felicity consisting only of pure and spiritual pleasure would have appeared too refined for its inhabitants, who were still supposed to possess their human nature and senses. A garden of Eden, with the amusements of the pastoral life, was no longer suited to the advanced state of society which prevailed under the Roman empire. A city was therefore erected of gold and precious stones, and a supernatural plenty of corn and wine was bestowed on the adjacent territory, in the free enjoyment of whose spontaneous productions the happy and benevolent people was never to be re-

[63] This expectation was countenanced by the twenty-fourth chapter of St. Matthew, and by the first epistle of St. Paul to the Thessalonians. Erasmus removes the difficulty by the help of allegory and metaphor, and the learned Grotius ventures to insinuate that, for wise purposes, the pious deception was permitted to take place.

[64] See Thomas Burnet's *Sacred Theory of the Earth*, iii 5. This tradition may be traced as high as the author of the *Epistle of Barnabas*, who wrote in the first century and who seems to have been half a Jew.

[65] The primitive church of Antioch computed almost 6000 years from the creation of the world to the birth of Christ. Africanus, Lactantius, and the Greek church have reduced that number to 5500, and Eusebius has contented himself with 5200 years. These calculations were formed on the Septuagint, which was universally received during the six first [first six?] centuries. The authority of the Vulgate and of the Hebrew text has determined the moderns, Protestants as well as Catholics, to prefer a period of about 4000 years, though, in the study of profane antiquity, they often find themselves straitened by those narrow limits.

strained by any jealous laws of exclusive property.⁶⁶ The assurance of such a millennium was carefully inculcated by a succession of fathers from Justin Martyr⁶⁷ and Irenaeus, who conversed with the immediate disciples of the apostles, down to Lactantius, who was preceptor to the son of Constantine.⁶⁸ Though it might not be universally received, it appears to have been the reigning sentiment of the orthodox believers; and it seems so well adapted to the desires and apprehensions of mankind that it must have contributed in a very considerable degree to the progress of the Christian faith. But when the edifice of the church was almost completed, the temporary support was laid aside. The doctrine of Christ's reign upon earth was at first treated as a profound allegory, was considered by degrees as a doubtful and useless opinion, and was at length rejected as the absurd invention of heresy and fanaticism.⁶⁹ A mysterious prophecy, which still forms a part of the sacred canon, but which was thought to favor the exploded sentiment, has very narrowly escaped the proscription of the church.⁷⁰

⁶⁶ Most of these pictures were borrowed from a misinterpretation of Isaiah, Daniel, and the Apocalypse. One of the grossest images may be found in Irenaeus (*Against Heresies* [1702], v 455 [ch. 33]), the disciple of Papias, who had seen the apostle St. John.

⁶⁷ The testimony of Justin of his own faith and that of his orthodox brethren, in the doctrine of a millennium, is delivered in the clearest and most solemn manner (*Dialogue with Trypho the Jew*, pp. 177-78, Benedictine edition [1742]). If in the beginning of this important passage there is anything like an inconsistency, we may impute it, as we think proper, either to the author or to his transcribers.

⁶⁸ See the second dialogue of Justin with Tryphon, and the seventh book of Lactantius [*The Divine Institutes*]. It is unnecessary to allege all the intermediate fathers, as the fact is not disputed. Yet the curious reader may consult [Jean] Daillé, *Treatise on the Right Use of the Fathers*, ii 4. [This note and the preceding one were misplaced in early editions.]

⁶⁹ Louis Ellies Dupin, *New Library of Ecclesiastical Authors* [1690-1715], i 223, ii 366, and Mosheim, p. 720, though the latter of these learned divines is not altogether candid on this occasion.

⁷⁰ In the Council of Laodicea (about the year 360) the Apocalypse was tacitly excluded from the sacred canon by the same churches of Asia to which it is addressed; and we may learn from the complaint of Sulpicius Severus that their sentence had been ratified by the greater number of Christians of his time. From what causes, then, is the Apocalypse at present so generally received by the Greek, the Roman, and the Protestant churches? The following ones may be assigned: 1. The Greeks were subdued by the authority of an impostor who, in the sixth century, assumed the character

Whilst the happiness and glory of a temporal reign were promised to the disciples of Christ, the most dreadful calamities were denounced against an unbelieving world. The edification of the new Jerusalem was to advance by equal steps with the destruction of the mystic Babylon; and as long as the emperors who reigned before Constantine persisted in the profession of idolatry, the epithet of Babylon was applied to the city and to the empire of Rome. A regular series was prepared of all the moral and physical evils which can afflict a flourishing nation; intestine discord, and the invasion of the fiercest barbarians from the unknown regions of the North; pestilence and famine, comets and eclipses, earthquakes and inundations.[71] All these were only so many preparatory and alarming signs of the great catastrophe of Rome, when the country of the Scipios and Caesars should be consumed by a flame from heaven, and the city of the seven hills, with her palaces, her temples, and her triumphal arches, should be buried in a vast lake of fire and brimstone. It might, however, afford some consolation to Roman vanity, that the period of their empire would be that of the world itself; which, as it had once perished by the element of water, was destined to experience a second and a speedy destruction from the element of fire. In the opinion of a general conflagration, the faith of the Christian very happily coincided with the tradition of the East, the philosophy of the Stoics, and the analogy of Nature; and even the country, which from religious motives had been chosen for the origin and principal scene of the conflagration, was the best adapted for that purpose by natural and physical causes; by its deep caverns, beds of sulphur, and numerous volcanoes, of which

---

of Dionysius the Areopagite. 2. A just apprehension that the grammarians might become more important than the theologians engaged the Council of Trent to fix the seal of their infallibility on all the books of Scripture contained in the Latin Vulgate, in the number of which the Apocalypse was fortunately included (Father Paolo [Sarpi], *History of the Council of Trent,* bk. ii). 3. The advantage of turning those mysterious prophecies against the See of Rome inspired the Protestants with uncommon veneration for so useful an ally. See the ingenious and elegant discourses of the present Bishop of Lichfield on that unpromising subject [Richard Hurd, *An Introduction to the Study of the Prophecies concerning the Christian Church, and in particular concerning the Church of Papal Rome*].

    [71] Lactantius (*Divine Institutes,* vii 15 etc.) relates the dismal tale of futurity with great spirit and eloquence.

those of Aetna, of Vesuvius, and of Lipari, exhibit a very imperfect representation. The calmest and most intrepid skeptic could not refuse to acknowledge that the destruction of the present system of the world by fire was in itself extremely probable. The Christian, who founded his belief much less on the fallacious arguments of reason than on the authority of tradition and the interpretation of Scripture, expected it with terror and confidence, as a certain and approaching event; and, as his mind was perpetually filled with the solemn idea, he considered every disaster that happened to the empire as an infallible symptom of an expiring world.[72]

The condemnation of the wisest and most virtuous of the pagans, on account of their ignorance or disbelief of the divine truth, seems to offend the reason and the humanity of the present age.[73] But the primitive church, whose faith was of a much firmer consistence, delivered over, without hesitation, to eternal torture the far greater part of the human species. A charitable hope might perhaps be indulged in favor of Socrates, or some other sages of antiquity, who had consulted the light of reason before that of the gospel had arisen.[74] But it was unanimously affirmed that those who, since the birth or the death of Christ, had obstinately persisted in the worship of the demons, neither deserved, nor could expect, a pardon from the irritated justice of the Deity. These rigid sentiments, which had been unknown to the ancient world, appear to have infused a spirit of bitterness into a system of love and harmony.

[72] On this subject every reader of taste will be entertained with the third part of [Thomas] Burnet's *Sacred Theory*. He blends philosophy, Scripture, and tradition into one magnificent system, in the description of which he displays a strength of fancy not inferior to that of Milton himself.

[73] And yet, whatever may be the language of individuals, it is still the public doctrine of all the Christian churches; nor can even our own refuse to admit the conclusions which must be drawn from the eighth and the eighteenth of her Articles. The Jansenists, who have so diligently studied the works of the fathers, maintain this sentiment with distinguished zeal, and the learned M. de Tillemont never dismisses a virtuous emperor without pronouncing his damnation. Zuinglius [Zwingli] is perhaps the only leader of a party who has ever adopted the milder sentiment, and he gave no less offense to the Lutherans than to the Catholics (see Jacques Bossuet, *History of the Variations of the Protestant Churches*, ii 19-22).

[74] Justin and Clemens of Alexandria allow that some of the philosophers were instructed by the Logos, confounding its double signification of the human reason and of the Divine Word.

The ties of blood and friendship were frequently torn asunder by
the difference of religious faith; and the Christians, who, in this
world, found themselves oppressed by the power of the pagans,
were sometimes seduced by resentment and spiritual pride to
delight in the prospect of their future triumph. "You are fond of
spectacles," exclaims the stern Tertullian; "expect the greatest of
all spectacles, the last and eternal judgment of the universe. How
shall I admire, how laugh, how rejoice, how exult, when I behold
so many proud monarchs, and fancied gods, groaning in the lowest
abyss of darkness; so many magistrates who persecuted the name
of the Lord liquefying in fiercer fires than they ever kindled against
the Christians; so many sage philosophers blushing in red hot flames
with their deluded scholars; so many celebrated poets trembling
before the tribunal, not of Minos, but of Christ; so many tragedians,
more tuneful in the expression of their own sufferings; so many
dancers——." But the humanity of the reader will permit me to
draw a veil over the rest of this infernal description, which the
zealous African pursues in a long variety of affected and unfeeling
witticisms.[75]

Doubtless there were many among the primitive Christians
of a temper more suitable to the meekness and charity of their
profession. There were many who felt a sincere compassion for
the danger of their friends and countrymen, and who exerted the
most benevolent zeal to save them from the impending destruction.
The careless polytheist, assailed by new and unexpected terrors,
against which neither his priests nor his philosophers could afford
him any certain protection, was very frequently terrified and subdued by the menace of eternal tortures. His fears might assist the
progress of his faith and reason; and if he could once persuade
himself to suspect that the Christian religion might possibly be true,
it became an easy task to convince him that it was the safest and
most prudent party that he could possibly embrace.

III. The supernatural gifts, which even in this life were

[75] Tertullian, *On Spectacles*, ch. 30. In order to ascertain the degree of
authority which the zealous African had acquired, it may be sufficient to
allege the testimony of Cyprian, the doctor and guide of all the Western
churches (see Prudentius, *Hymns*, xiii 100). As often as he applied himself
to his daily study of the writings of Tertullian, he was accustomed to say,
"Da mihi magistrum (give me my master)" (Jerome, *Of Illustrious Men*,
i 284 [ch. 53]). [The correct reading is *da magistrum*.]

ascribed to the Christians above the rest of mankind, must have conduced to their own comfort, and very frequently to the conviction of infidels. Besides the occasional prodigies which might sometimes be effected by the immediate interposition of the Deity when he suspended the laws of nature for the service of religion, the Christian church, from the time of the apostles and their first disciples,[76] has claimed an uninterrupted succession of miraculous powers, the gift of tongues, of vision and of prophecy, the power of expelling demons, of healing the sick, and of raising the dead. The knowledge of foreign languages was frequently communicated to the contemporaries of Irenaeus, though Irenaeus himself was left to struggle with the difficulties of a barbarous dialect whilst he preached the gospel to the natives of Gaul.[77] The divine inspiration, whether it was conveyed in the form of a waking or of a sleeping vision, is described as a favor very liberally bestowed on all ranks of the faithful, on women as on elders, on boys as well as upon bishops. When their devout minds were sufficiently prepared by a course of prayer, of fasting, and of vigils, to receive the extraordinary impulse, they were transported out of their senses, and delivered in ecstasy what was inspired, being mere organs of the Holy Spirit, just as a pipe or flute is of him who blows into it.[78] We may add that the design of these visions was, for the most part, either to disclose the future history, or to guide the present administration, of the church. The expulsion of the demons from the bodies of those unhappy persons whom they had been permitted to torment was considered as a signal, though ordinary, triumph of religion, and is repeatedly alleged by the ancient apologists as the most convincing evidence of the truth of Christianity. The

[76] Notwithstanding the evasions of Dr. [Conyers] Middleton, it is impossible to overlook the clear traces of visions and inspiration which may be found in the apostolic fathers. [Conyers Middleton was a skeptical divine, who derided all miracles occurring subsequent to the first era of Christianity.]

[77] Irenaeus, *Against Heresies,* Preface, p. 3. Dr. Middleton (*Free Inquiry* [1749], pp. 96 etc.) observes that as this pretension of all others was the most difficult to support by art, it was the soonest given up. The observation suits his hypothesis.

[78] Athenagoras in *Plea for the Christians;* Justin Martyr, *Hortatory Address to the Greeks;* Tertullian, *Against Marcion,* iv. These descriptions are not very unlike the prophetic fury for which Cicero (*On Divination,* ii 54) expresses so little reverence.

awful ceremony was usually performed in a public manner, and in the presence of a great number of spectators; the patient was relieved by the power or skill of the exorcist, and the vanquished demon was heard to confess that he was one of the fabled gods of antiquity, who had impiously usurped the adoration of mankind.[79] But the miraculous cure of diseases of the most inveterate, or even preternatural, kind can no longer occasion any surprise when we recollect that in the days of Irenaeus, about the end of the second century, the resurrection of the dead was very far from being esteemed an uncommon event; that the miracle was frequently performed on necessary occasions, by great fasting and the joint supplication of the church of the place, and that the persons thus restored to their prayers had lived afterwards among them many years.[80] At such a period, when faith could boast of so many wonderful victories over death, it seems difficult to account for the skepticism of those philosophers who still rejected and derided the doctrine of the resurrection. A noble Grecian had rested on this important ground the whole controversy, and promised Theophilus, Bishop of Antioch, that if he could be gratified with the sight of a single person who had been actually raised from the dead, he would immediately embrace the Christian religion. It is somewhat remarkable that the prelate of the first eastern church, however anxious for the conversion of his friend, thought proper to decline this fair and reasonable challenge.[81]

The miracles of the primitive church, after obtaining the sanction of ages, have been lately attacked in a very free and ingenious inquiry;[82] which, though it has met with the most favorable reception from the public, appears to have excited a general scandal among the divines of our own as well as of the other Protestant

[79] Tertullian (*Apology,* ch. 23) throws out a bold defiance to the pagan magistrates. Of the primitive miracles, the power of exorcising is the only one which has been assumed by Protestants.

[80] Irenaeus, *Against Heresies,* ii 56-57, v 6. Mr. [Henry] Dodwell (*Dissertations on Irenaeus,* ii 42) concludes that the second century was still more fertile in miracles than the first.

[81] Theophilus, *To Autolycus,* i 345 (Benedictine edition, Paris, 1742).

[82] Dr. Middleton sent out his *Introduction* [*Introductory Discourse*] in the year 1747, published his *Free Inquiry* in 1749, and before his death, which happened in 1750, he had prepared a vindication [*A Vindication of the Free Inquiry* (1751)] of it against his numerous adversaries.

churches of Europe.[83] Our different sentiments on this subject will be much less influenced by any particular arguments than by our habits of study and reflection; and, above all, by the degree of the evidence which we have accustomed ourselves to require for the proof of a miraculous event. The duty of an historian does not call upon him to interpose his private judgment in this nice and important controversy; but he ought not to dissemble the difficulty of adopting such a theory as may reconcile the interest of religion with that of reason, of making a proper application of that theory, and of defining with precision the limits of that happy period, exempt from error and from deceit, to which we might be disposed to extend the gift of supernatural powers. From the first of the fathers to the last of the popes, a succession of bishops, of saints, of martyrs, and of miracles is continued without interruption, and the progress of superstition was so gradual and almost imperceptible that we know not in what particular link we should break the chain of tradition. Every age bears testimony to the wonderful events by which it was distinguished, and its testimony appears no less weighty and respectable than that of the preceding generation, till we are insensibly led on to accuse our own inconsistency, if in the eighth or in the twelfth century we deny to the venerable Bede, or to the holy Bernard, the same degree of confidence which, in the second century, we had so liberally granted to Justin or to Irenaeus.[84] If the truth of any of those miracles is appreciated [85] by their apparent use and propriety, every age had unbelievers to convince, heretics to confute, and idolatrous nations to convert; and sufficient motives might always be produced to justify the interposition of heaven. And yet, since every friend to revelation is persuaded of the reality, and every reasonable man is convinced of the cessation, of miraculous powers, it is evident that there must have been *some*

[83] The University of Oxford conferred degrees on his opponents. From the indignation of Mosheim (p. 221), we may discover the sentiments of the Lutheran divines.

[84] It may seem somewhat remarkable that Bernard of Clairvaux, who records so many miracles of his friend St. Malachi, never takes any notice of his own, which in their turn, however, are carefully related by his companions and disciples. In the long series of ecclesiastical history, does there exist a single instance of a saint asserting that he himself possessed the gift of miracles?

[85] [estimated.]

period in which they were either suddenly or gradually withdrawn from the Christian church. Whatever era is chosen for that purpose, the death of the apostles, the conversion of the Roman empire, or the extinction of the Arian heresy,[86] the insensibility of the Christians who lived at that time will equally afford a just matter of surprise. They still supported their pretensions after they had lost their power. Credulity performed the office of faith; fanaticism was permitted to assume the language of inspiration, and the effects of accident or contrivance were ascribed to supernatural causes. The recent experience of genuine miracles should have instructed the Christian world in the ways of Providence, and habituated their eye (if we may use a very inadequate expression) to the style of the Divine Artist. Should the most skillful painter of modern Italy presume to decorate his feeble imitations with the name of Raphael or of Correggio, the insolent fraud would be soon discovered and indignantly rejected.

Whatever opinion may be entertained of the miracles of the primitive church since the time of the apostles, this unresisting softness of temper, so conspicuous among the believers of the second and third centuries, proved of some accidental benefit to the cause of truth and religion. In modern times, a latent and even involuntary skepticism adheres to the most pious dispositions. Their admission of supernatural truths is much less an active consent than a cold and passive acquiescence. Accustomed long since to observe and to respect the invariable order of nature, our reason, or at least our imagination, is not sufficiently prepared to sustain the visible action of the Deity. But in the first ages of Christianity, the situation of mankind was extremely different. The most curious, or the most credulous, among the pagans were often persuaded to enter into a society which asserted an actual claim of miraculous powers. The primitive Christians perpetually trod on mystic ground, and their minds were exercised by the habits of believing the most extraordinary events. They felt, or they fancied, that on every side they were incessantly assaulted by demons, comforted by visions, instructed by prophecy, and surprisingly delivered from danger,

---

[86] The conversion of Constantine is the era which is most usually fixed by Protestants. The more rational divines are unwilling to admit the miracles of the fourth, whilst the more credulous are unwilling to reject those of the fifth century.

sickness, and from death itself, by the supplications of the church. The real or imaginary prodigies, of which they so frequently conceived themselves to be the objects, the instruments, or the spectators, very happily disposed them to adopt with the same ease, but with far greater justice, the authentic wonders of the evangelic history; and thus miracles that exceeded not the measure of their own experience inspired them with the most lively assurance of mysteries which were acknowledged to surpass the limits of their understanding. It is this deep impression of supernatural truths which has been so much celebrated under the name of faith; a state of mind described as the surest pledge of the divine favor and of future felicity, and recommended as the first or perhaps the only merit of a Christian. According to the more rigid doctors, the moral virtues, which may be equally practiced by infidels, are destitute of any value or efficacy in the work of our justification.

IV. But the primitive Christian demonstrated his faith by his virtues; and it was very justly supposed that the divine persuasion which enlightened or subdued the understanding must, at the same time, purify the heart and direct the actions of the believer. The first apologists of Christianity who justify the innocence of their brethren, and the writers of a later period who celebrate the sanctity of their ancestors, display, in the most lively colors, the reformation of manners which was introduced into the world by the preaching of the gospel. As it is my intention to remark only such human causes as were permitted to second the influence of revelation, I shall slightly mention two motives which might naturally render the lives of the primitive Christians much purer and more austere than those of their pagan contemporaries, or their degenerate successors: repentance for their past sins, and the laudable desire of supporting the reputation of the society in which they were engaged.

It is a very ancient reproach, suggested by the ignorance or the malice of infidelity, that the Christians allured into their party the most atrocious criminals, who, as soon as they were touched by a sense of remorse, were easily persuaded to wash away, in the water of baptism, the guilt of their past conduct, for which the temples of the gods refused to grant them any expiation. But this reproach, when it is cleared from misrepresentation, contributes as

much to the honor as it did to the increase of the church.[87] The
friends of Christianity may acknowledge without a blush that many
of the most eminent saints had been before their baptism the most
abandoned sinners. Those persons who in the world had followed,
though in an imperfect manner, the dictates of benevolence and
propriety, derived such a calm satisfaction from the opinion of their
own rectitude as rendered them much less susceptible of the sudden
emotions of shame, of grief, and of terror, which have given birth
to so many wonderful conversions. After the example of their Divine
Master, the missionaries of the gospel disdained not the society of
men, and especially of women, oppressed by the consciousness, and
very often by the effects, of their vices. As they emerged from sin
and superstition to the glorious hope of immortality, they resolved
to devote themselves to a life, not only of virtue, but of penitence.
The desire of perfection became the ruling passion of their soul;
and it is well known that, while reason embraces a cold mediocrity,
our passions hurry us, with rapid violence, over the space which
lies between the most opposite extremes.

When the new converts had been enrolled in the number
of the faithful and were admitted to the sacraments of the church,
they found themselves restrained from relapsing into their past
disorders by another consideration of a less spiritual, but of a very
innocent and respectable nature. Any particular society that has
departed from the great body of the nation or the religion to which
it belonged immediately becomes the object of universal as well as
invidious observation. In proportion to the smallness of its numbers,
the character of the society may be affected by the virtues and vices
of the persons who compose it; and every member is engaged to
watch with the most vigilant attention over his own behavior and
over that of his brethren, since, as he must expect to incur a part
of the common disgrace, he may hope to enjoy a share of the
common reputation. When the Christians of Bithynia were brought
before the tribunal of the younger Pliny, they assured the proconsul
that, far from being engaged in any unlawful conspiracy, they were
bound by a solemn obligation to abstain from the commission of

[87] The imputations of Celsus and Julian, with the defense of the
fathers, are very fairly stated by [Baron Ezechiel von] Spanheim, Commentary on *The Caesars* of Julian, p. 468 [(1728), Proofs, pp. 130 ff.].

those crimes which disturb the private or public peace of society, from theft, robbery, adultery, perjury, and fraud.[88] Near a century afterwards, Tertullian, with an honest pride, could boast that very few Christians had suffered by the hand of the executioner, except on account of their religion.[89] Their serious and sequestered life, averse to the gay luxury of the age, inured them to chastity, temperance, economy, and all the sober and domestic virtues. As the greater number were of some trade or profession, it was incumbent on them, by the strictest integrity and the fairest dealing, to remove the suspicions which the profane are too apt to conceive against the appearances of sanctity. The contempt of the world exercised them in the habits of humility, meekness, and patience. The more they were persecuted, the more closely they adhered to each other. Their mutual charity and unsuspecting confidence has been remarked by infidels, and was too often abused by perfidious friends.[90]

It is a very honorable circumstance for the morals of the primitive Christians, that even their faults, or rather errors, were derived from an excess of virtue. The bishops and doctors of the church, whose evidence attests, and whose authority might influence, the professions, the principles, and even the practice of their contemporaries, had studied the Scriptures with less skill than devotion, and they often received, in the most literal sense, those rigid precepts of Christ and the apostles to which the prudence of succeeding commentators has applied a looser and more figurative mode of interpretation. Ambitious to exalt the perfection of the gospel above the wisdom of philosophy, the zealous fathers have carried the duties of self-mortification, of purity, and of patience, to a height which it is scarcely possible to attain, and much less to preserve, in our present state of weakness and corruption. A doctrine so extraordinary and so sublime must inevitably command the veneration of the people; but it was ill calculated to obtain the suffrage of

[88] Pliny, *Epistles,* x 97 [96, ed. Schuster].
[89] Tertullian, *Apology,* ch. 44. He adds, however, with some degree of hesitation, "Or if he is charged with anything further, he is no Christian."
[90] The philosopher Peregrinus (of whose life and death Lucian has left us so entertaining an account) imposed, for a long time, on the credulous simplicity of the Christians of Asia.

those worldly philosophers who, in the conduct of this transitory life, consult only the feelings of nature and the interest of society.[91]

There are two very natural propensities which we may distinguish in the most virtuous and liberal dispositions, the love of pleasure and the love of action. If the former is refined by art and learning, improved by the charms of social intercourse, and corrected by a just regard to economy, to health, and to reputation, it is productive of the greatest part of the happiness of private life. The love of action is a principle of a much stronger and more doubtful nature. It often leads to anger, to ambition, and to revenge; but, when it is guided by the sense of propriety and benevolence, it becomes the parent of every virtue; and if those virtues are accompanied with equal abilities, a family, a state, or an empire may be indebted for their safety and prosperity to the undaunted courage of a single man. To the love of pleasure we may therefore ascribe most of the agreeable, to the love of action we may attribute most of the useful and respectable, qualifications. The character in which both the one and the other should be united and harmonized would seem to constitute the most perfect idea of human nature. The insensible and inactive disposition, which should be supposed alike destitute of both, would be rejected, by the common consent of mankind, as utterly incapable of procuring any happiness to the individual, or any public benefit to the world. But it was not in *this* world that the primitive Christians were desirous of making themselves either agreeable or useful.

The acquisition of knowledge, the exercise of our reason or fancy, and the cheerful flow of unguarded conversation, may employ the leisure of a liberal mind. Such amusements, however, were rejected with abhorrence, or admitted with the utmost caution, by the severity of the fathers, who despised all knowledge that was not useful to salvation, and who considered all levity of discourse as a criminal abuse of the gift of speech. In our present state of existence, the body is so inseparably connected with the soul that it seems to be our interest to taste, with innocence and moderation, the enjoyments of which that faithful companion is susceptible. Very different was the reasoning of our devout predecessors: vainly aspiring to imitate the perfection of angels, they disdained, or they

[91] See a very judicious treatise of [Jean] Barbeyrac, *On the Morality of the Church Fathers* [1728].

affected to disdain, every earthly and corporeal delight.[92] Some of our senses indeed are necessary for our preservation, others for our subsistence, and others again for our information, and thus far it was impossible to reject the use of them. The first sensation of pleasure was marked as the first moment of their abuse. The unfeeling candidate for heaven was instructed, not only to resist the grosser allurements of the taste or smell, but even to shut his ears against the profane harmony of sounds, and to view with indifference the most finished productions of human art. Gay apparel, magnificent houses, and elegant furniture were supposed to unite the double guilt of pride and of sensuality: a simple and mortified appearance was more suitable to the Christian, who was certain of his sins and doubtful of his salvation. In their censures of luxury, the fathers are extremely minute and circumstantial;[93] and among the various articles which excite their pious indignation, we may enumerate false hair, garments of any color except white, instruments of music, vases of gold or silver, downy pillows (as Jacob reposed his head on a stone), white bread, foreign wines, public salutations,[93a] the use of warm baths, and the practice of shaving the beard, which, according to the expression of Tertullian, is a lie against our own faces, and an impious attempt to improve the works of the Creator.[94] When Christianity was introduced among the rich and the polite, the observation of these singular laws was left, as it would be at present, to the few who were ambitious of superior sanctity. But it is always easy, as well as agreeable, for the inferior ranks of mankind to claim a merit from the contempt of that pomp and pleasure which fortune has placed beyond their reach. The virtue of the primitive Christians, like that of the first Romans, was very frequently guarded by poverty and ignorance.

The chaste severity of the fathers, in whatever related to the commerce of the two sexes, flowed from the same principle: their abhorrence of every enjoyment which might gratify the sensual,

[92] Lactantius, *Divine Institutes,* vi 20-22.

[93] Consult a work of Clemens of Alexandria, intitled *The Pedagogue,* which contains the rudiments of ethics as they were taught in the most celebrated of the Christian schools.

[93a] kisses.

[94] Tertullian, *On Spectacles,* ch. 23; Clemens of Alexandria, *Pedagogue,* iii 8.

and degrade the spiritual, nature of man. It was their favorite opinion that if Adam had preserved his obedience to the Creator, he would have lived for ever in a state of virgin purity, and that some harmless mode of vegetation might have peopled paradise with a race of innocent and immortal beings.[95] The use of marriage was permitted only to his fallen posterity as a necessary expedient to continue the human species, and as a restraint, however imperfect, on the natural licentiousness of desire. The hesitation of the orthodox casuists on this interesting subject betrays the perplexity of men unwilling to approve an institution which they were compelled to tolerate.[96] The enumeration of the very whimsical laws which they most circumstantially imposed on the marriage bed would force a smile from the young, and a blush from the fair. It was their unanimous sentiment that a first marriage was adequate to all the purposes of nature and of society. The sensual connection was refined into a resemblance of the mystic union of Christ with his church, and was pronounced to be indissoluble either by divorce or by death. The practice of second nuptials was branded with the name of a legal adultery; and the persons who were guilty of so scandalous an offense against Christian purity were soon excluded from the honors, and even from the alms, of the church.[97] Since desire was imputed as a crime, and marriage was tolerated as a defect, it was consistent with the same principles to consider a state of celibacy as the nearest approach to the divine perfection. It was with the utmost difficulty that ancient Rome could support the institution of six vestals;[98] but the primitive church was filled with a great number of persons of either sex who had devoted

[95] Beausobre, *History of Manichaeanism,* vii 3. Justin, Gregory of Nyssa, Augustin, etc. strongly inclined to this opinion.

[96] Some of the Gnostic heretics were more consistent; they rejected the use of marriage.

[97] See a chain of tradition, from Justin Martyr to Jerome, in the *Morality of the Church Fathers,* iv 6-26.

[98] See a very curious "Dissertation on the Vestals" [by Augustin Nadal] in the *Memoirs of the Royal Academy of Inscriptions* [1723], iv 161-227. Notwithstanding the honors and rewards which were bestowed on those virgins, it was difficult to procure a sufficient number; nor could the dread of the most horrible death always restrain their incontinence.

themselves to the profession of perpetual chastity.[99] A few of these, among whom we may reckon the learned Origen, judged it the most prudent to disarm the tempter.[100] Some were insensible and some were invincible against the assaults of the flesh. Disdaining an ignominious flight, the virgins of the warm climate of Africa encountered the enemy in the closest engagement; they permitted priests and deacons to share their bed, and gloried amidst the flames in their unsullied purity. But insulted Nature sometimes vindicated her rights, and this new species of martyrdom served only to introduce a new scandal into the church.[101] Among the Christian ascetics, however (a name which they soon acquired from their painful exercise), many, as they were less presumptuous, were probably more successful. The loss of sensual pleasure was supplied and compensated by spiritual pride. Even the multitude of pagans were inclined to estimate the merit of the sacrifice by its apparent difficulty; and it was in the praise of these chaste spouses of Christ that the fathers have poured forth the troubled stream of their eloquence.[102] Such are the early traces of monastic principles and institutions which, in a subsequent age, have counterbalanced all the temporal advantages of Christianity.[103]

The Christians were not less averse to the business than to the

---

[99] "In wishing to procreate, we have either one wife or none" (Minucius Felix, *Octavius*, xxxi 5). Justin Martyr, *First Apology*, ch. 29; Athenagoras in *Plea for the Christians*, ch. 28; Tertullian, *On the Apparel of Women*, bk. ii.

[100] Eusebius, vi 8. Before the fame of Origen had excited envy and persecution, this extraordinary action [he had himself castrated] was rather admired than censured. As it was his general practice to allegorize Scripture, it seems unfortunate that, in this instance only, he should have adopted the literal sense.

[101] Cyprian, *Epistles*, 4, and Henry Dodwell, *Dissertations on Cyprian*, bk. iii. Something like this rash attempt was long afterwards imputed to the founder of the order of Fontevrault [Robert d'Arbrissel]. Bayle has amused himself and his readers on that very delicate subject.

[102] Dupin (*New Library*, i 195) gives a particular account of the dialogue of the ten virgins, as it was composed by Methodius, Bishop of Tyre. The praises of virginity are excessive.

[103] The ascetics (as early as the second century) made a public profession of mortifying their bodies, and of abstaining from the use of flesh and wine (Mosheim, p. 310).

pleasures of this world. The defense of our persons and property they knew not how to reconcile with the patient doctrine which enjoined an unlimited forgiveness of past injuries and commanded them to invite the repetition of fresh insults. Their simplicity was offended by the use of oaths, by the pomp of magistracy, and by the active contention of public life, nor could their humane ignorance be convinced that it was lawful on any occasion to shed the blood of our fellow creatures, either by the sword of justice or by that of war; even though their criminal or hostile attempts should threaten the peace and safety of the whole community.[104] It was acknowledged that, under a less perfect law, the powers of the Jewish constitution had been exercised, with the approbation of heaven, by inspired prophets and by anointed kings. The Christians felt and confessed that such institutions might be necessary for the present system of the world, and they cheerfully submitted to the authority of their pagan governors. But while they inculcated the maxims of passive obedience, they refused to take any active part in the civil administration or the military defense of the empire. Some indulgence might perhaps be allowed to those persons who, before their conversion, were already engaged in such violent and sanguinary occupations;[105] but it was impossible that the Christians, without renouncing a more sacred duty, could assume the character of soldiers, of magistrates, or of princes.[106] This indolent or even criminal disregard to the public welfare exposed them to the contempt and reproaches of the pagans, who very frequently asked, what must be the fate of the empire, attacked on every side by the barbarians, if all mankind should adopt the pusillanimous sentiments

[104] See the *Morality of the Church Fathers.* The same patient principles have been revived since the Reformation by the Socinians, the modern Anabaptists, and the Quakers. [Robert] Barclay, the apologist of the Quakers, has protected his brethren by the authority of the primitive Christians [*An Apology for the True Christian Divinity*], pp. 542-49 [1736, pp. 542-71].

[105] Tertullian, *Apology,* ch. 21, *On Idolatry,* chs. 17-18; Origen, *Against Celsus* [1677], v 253, vii 348, viii 423-28.

[106] Tertullian (*The Soldier's Chaplet,* ch. 11) suggests to them the expedient of deserting, a counsel which, if it had been generally known, was not very proper to conciliate the favor of the emperors towards the Christian sect.

of the new sect? [107] To this insulting question the Christian apologists returned obscure and ambiguous answers, as they were unwilling to reveal the secret cause of their security: the expectation that, before the conversion of mankind was accomplished, war, government, the Roman empire, and the world itself would be no more. It may be observed that, in this instance likewise, the situation of the first Christians coincided very happily with their religious scruples, and that their aversion to an active life contributed rather to excuse them from the service, than to exclude them from the honors, of the state and army.

V. But the human character, however it may be exalted or depressed by a temporary enthusiasm, will return by degrees to its proper and natural level, and will resume those passions that seem the most adapted to its present condition. The primitive Christians were dead to the business and pleasures of the world; but their love of action, which could never be entirely extinguished, soon revived, and found a new occupation in the government of the church. A separate society, which attacked the established religion of the empire, was obliged to adopt some form of internal policy, and to appoint a sufficient number of ministers, intrusted not only with the spiritual functions, but even with the temporal direction of the Christian commonwealth. The safety of that society, its honor, its aggrandizement, were productive, even in the most pious minds, of a spirit of patriotism, such as the first of the Romans had felt for the republic, and sometimes of a similar indifference in the use of whatever means might probably conduce to so desirable an end. The ambition of raising themselves or their friends to the honors and offices of the church was disguised by the laudable intention of devoting to the public benefit the power and consideration which, for that purpose only, it became their duty to solicit. In the exercise of their functions, they were frequently called upon to detect the errors of heresy or the arts of faction, to oppose the designs of perfidious brethren, to stigmatize their characters with deserved infamy, and to expel them from the bosom of a society whose peace and happiness they had attempted to disturb. The ecclesiastical

[107] As well as we can judge from the mutilated representation of Origen (viii 423), his adversary, Celsus, had urged his objection with great force and candor.

governors of the Christians were taught to unite the wisdom of the
serpent with the innocence of the dove; but as the former was refined, so the latter was insensibly corrupted, by the habits of government. In the church, as well as in the world, the persons who
were placed in any public station rendered themselves considerable
by their eloquence and firmness, by their knowledge of mankind,
and by their dexterity in business; and while they concealed from
others, and perhaps from themselves, the secret motives of their
conduct, they too frequently relapsed into all the turbulent passions
of active life, which were tinctured with an additional degree of
bitterness and obstinacy from the infusion of spiritual zeal.

The government of the church has often been the subject, as
well as the prize, of religious contention. The hostile disputants of
Rome, of Paris, of Oxford, and of Geneva have alike struggled to
reduce the primitive and apostolic model [108] to the respective
standards of their own policy. The few who have pursued this
inquiry with more candor and impartiality are of opinion[109] that
the apostles declined the office of legislation, and rather chose to
endure some partial scandals and divisions than to exclude the
Christians of a future age from the liberty of varying their forms of
ecclesiastical government according to the changes of times and
circumstances. The scheme of policy which, under their approbation,
was adopted for the use of the first century may be discovered from
the practice of Jerusalem, of Ephesus, or of Corinth. The societies
which were instituted in the cities of the Roman empire were united
only by the ties of faith and charity. Independence and equality
formed the basis of their internal constitution. The want of discipline
and human learning was supplied by the occasional assistance of
the *prophets*,[110] who were called to that function without distinction
of age, of sex, or of natural abilities, and who, as often as they
left the divine impulse, poured forth the effusions of the Spirit in
the assembly of the faithful. But these extraordinary gifts were

[108] The aristocratical party in France, as well as in England, has
strenuously maintained the divine origin of bishops. But the Calvinistical
presbyters were impatient of a superior, and the Roman pontiff refused to
acknowledge an equal (see Father Paolo [Sarpi]).

[109] In the history of the Christian hierarchy, I have, for the most part,
followed the learned and candid Mosheim.

[110] For the prophets of the primitive church, see Mosheim, *Dissertations
Pertaining to Ecclesiastical History* [1767], ii 132-208.

frequently abused or misapplied by the prophetic teachers. They displayed them at an improper season, presumptuously disturbed the service of the assembly, and by their pride or mistaken zeal they introduced, particularly into the apostolic church of Corinth, a long and melancholy train of disorders.[111] As the institution of prophets became useless, and even pernicious, their powers were withdrawn and their office abolished. The public functions of religion were solely intrusted to the established ministers of the church, the *bishops* and the *presbyters;* two appellations which, in their first origin, appear to have distinguished the same office and the same order of persons. The name of presbyter was expressive of their age, or rather of their gravity and wisdom. The title of bishop denoted their inspection over the faith and manners of the Christians who were committed to their pastoral care. In proportion to the respective numbers of the faithful, a larger or smaller number of these *episcopal presbyters* guided each infant congregation with equal authority and with united councils.[112]

But the most perfect equality of freedom requires the directing hand of a superior magistrate; and the order of public deliberations soon introduces the office of a president, invested at least with the authority of collecting the sentiments, and of executing the resolutions, of the assembly. A regard for the public tranquillity, which would so frequently have been interrupted by annual or by occasional elections, induced the primitive Christians to constitute an honorable and perpetual magistracy, and to choose one of the wisest and most holy among their presbyters to execute, during his life, the duties of their ecclesiastical governor. It was under these circumstances that the lofty title of bishop began to raise itself above the humble appellation of presbyter; and while the latter remained the most natural distinction for the members of every Christian senate, the former was appropriated to the dignity of its new president.[113] The advantages of this episcopal form of government,

[111] See the Epistles of St. Paul, and of Clemens, to the Corinthians.

[112] Richard Hooker's *Ecclesiastical Polity,* bk. vii.

[113] See Jerome, *Commentary on Titus,* ch. 1, and *Letters,* 85 [in the edition of 1623] (in the Benedictine edition [1693-1706], 101), and the elaborate apology of [David] Blondel, *In Defense of the Opinions of Jerome on Bishops and Presbyters.* The ancient state, as it is described by Jerome, of the bishop and presbyters of Alexandria, receives a remarkable confirmation from the patriarch Eutychius (*Annals,* i 330, trans. by Edward Pocock [into

which appears to have been introduced before the end of the first
century,[114] were so obvious, and so important for the future greatness, as well as the present peace, of Christianity, that it was
adopted without delay by all the societies which were already
scattered over the empire, had acquired in a very early period the
sanction of antiquity,[115] and is still revered by the most powerful
churches, both of the East and of the West, as a primitive and
even as a divine establishment.[116] It is needless to observe that the
pious and humble presbyters who were first dignified with the
episcopal title could not possess, and would probably have rejected,
the power and pomp which now encircles the tiara of the Roman
pontiff, or the mitre of a German prelate. But we may define, in a
few words, the narrow limits of their original jurisdiction, which
was chiefly of a spiritual, though in some instances of a temporal,
nature.[117] It consisted in the administration of the sacraments and
discipline of the church, the superintendency of religious ceremonies, which imperceptibly increased in number and variety, the
consecration of ecclesiastical ministers, to whom the bishop assigned
their respective functions, the management of the public fund, and
the determination of all such differences as the .faithful were unwilling to expose before the tribunal of an idolatrous judge. These
powers, during a short period, were exercised according to the
advice of the presbyteral college, and with the consent and ap-

---

Latin, 1654-56]), whose testimony I know not how to reject, in spite of all
the objections of the learned [John] Pearson in his *Vindication of the Letters
of St. Ignatius*, i 11.

[114] See the introduction to the Apocalypse. Bishops, under the name of
angels, were already instituted in seven cities of Asia. And yet the *Epistle* of
Clemens [Romanus] (which is probably of as ancient a date) does not lead
us to discover any traces of episcopacy either at Corinth or Rome.

[115] "No church without a bishop" has been a fact as well as a maxim
since the time of Tertullian and Irenaeus.

[116] After we have passed the difficulties of the first century, we find the
episcopal government universally established, till it was interrupted by the
republican genius of the Swiss and German reformers.

[117] See Mosheim, in the first and second centuries [of his *Commentaries*].
Ignatius (*Epistle to the Smyrnaeans*, chs. 3 etc.) is fond of exalting the
episcopal dignity. Le Clerc (*Ecclesiastical History*, p. 569) very bluntly censures his conduct. Mosheim, with a more critical judgment (p. 161) suspects
the purity [that is, authenticity] even of the smaller epistles [of Ignatius].

probation of the assembly of Christians. The primitive bishops were considered only as the first of their equals, and the honorable servants of a free people. Whenever the episcopal chair became vacant by death, a new president was chosen among the presbyters by the suffrage of the whole congregation, every member of which supposed himself invested with a sacred and sacerdotal character.[118]

Such was the mild and equal constitution by which the Christians were governed more than an hundred years after the death of the apostles. Every society formed within itself a separate and independent republic; and, although the most distant of these little states maintained a mutual as well as friendly intercourse of letters and deputations, the Christian world was not yet connected by any supreme authority or legislative assembly. As the numbers of the faithful were gradually multiplied, they discovered the advantages that might result from a closer union of their interest and designs. Towards the end of the second century, the churches of Greece and Asia adopted the useful institutions of provincial synods, and they may justly be supposed to have borrowed the model of a representative council from the celebrated examples of their own country, the Amphictyons, the Achaean league, or the assemblies of the Ionian cities. It was soon established as a custom and as a law that the bishops of the independent churches should meet in the capital of the province at the stated periods of spring and autumn. Their deliberations were assisted by the advice of a few distinguished presbyters, and moderated by the presence of a listening multitude.[119] Their decrees, which were styled canons, regulated every important controversy of faith and discipline; and it was natural to believe that a liberal effusion of the Holy Spirit would be poured on the united assembly of the delegates of the Christian people. The institution of synods was so well suited to private ambition and to public interest that in the space of a few

[118] "And are we laymen not priests?" (Tertullian, *Exhortation to Chastity,* ch. 7). As the human heart is still the same, several of the observations which Mr. Hume has made on enthusiasm (["Of Superstition and Enthusiasm"], *Essays,* i 76, quarto edition [1768]) may be applied even to real inspiration.

[119] *Acts of the Council of Carthage,* according to Cyprian, *Works,* ed. John Fell [1700], p. 158. This council was composed of eighty-seven bishops from the provinces of Mauritania, Numidia, and Africa; some presbyters and deacons assisted at the assembly; "a great number of the people were present."

years it was received throughout the whole empire. A regular correspondence was established between the provincial councils, which mutually communicated and approved their respective proceedings; and the catholic church soon assumed the form, and acquired the strength, of a great federative republic.[120]

As the legislative authority of the particular churches was insensibly superseded by the use of councils, the bishops obtained by their alliance a much larger share of executive and arbitrary power; and as soon as they were connected by a sense of their common interest, they were enabled to attack, with united vigor, the original rights of their clergy and people. The prelates of the third century imperceptibly changed the language of exhortation into that of command, scattered the seeds of future usurpations, and supplied, by scripture allegories and declamatory rhetoric, their deficiency of force and of reason. They exalted the unity and power of the church, as it was represented in the *Episcopal Office,* of which every bishop enjoyed an equal and undivided portion.[121] Princes and magistrates, it was often repeated, might boast an earthly claim to a transitory dominion; it was the episcopal authority alone which was derived from the Deity, and extended itself over this and over another world. The bishops were the vice-gerents of Christ, the successors of the apostles, and the mystic substitutes of the high priest of the Mosaic law. Their exclusive privilege of conferring the sacerdotal character invaded the freedom both of clerical and of popular elections; and if, in the administration of the church, they still consulted the judgment of the presbyters or the inclination of the people, they most carefully inculcated the merit of such a voluntary condescension. The bishops acknowledged the supreme authority which resided in the assembly of their brethren; but in the government of his peculiar diocese, each of them exacted from his *flock* the same implicit obedience as if that favorite metaphor had been literally just, and as if the shepherd had

[120] "Moreover, throughout the Greek provinces, councils gathered from the universal churches are held in definite places" etc. (Tertullian, *On Fasting,* ch. 13). The African mentions it as a recent and foreign institution. The coalition of the Christian churches is very ably explained by Mosheim, pp. 164-70.

[121] Cyprian, in his admired treatise, *On the Unity of the Church,* pp. 75-86.

been of a more exalted nature than that of his sheep.[122] This obedience, however, was not imposed without some efforts on one side, and some resistance on the other. The democratical part of the constitution was, in many places, very warmly supported by the zealous or interested opposition of the inferior clergy. But their patriotism received the ignominious epithets of faction and schism; and the episcopal cause was indebted for its rapid progress to the labors of many active prelates, who, like Cyprian of Carthage, could reconcile the arts of the most ambitious statesman with the Christian virtues which seem adapted to the character of a saint and martyr.[123]

The same causes which at first had destroyed the equality of the presbyters introduced among the bishops a pre-eminence of rank, and from thence a superiority of jurisdiction. As often as in the spring and autumn they met in provincial synod, the difference of personal merit and reputation was very sensibly felt among the members of the assembly, and the multitude was governed by the wisdom and eloquence of the few. But the order of public proceedings required a more regular and less invidious distinction: the office of perpetual presidents in the councils of each province was conferred on the bishops of the principal city, and these aspiring prelates, who soon acquired the lofty titles of Metropolitans and Primates, secretly prepared themselves to usurp over their episcopal brethren the same authority which the bishops had so lately assumed above the college of presbyters.[124] Nor was it long before an emulation of pre-eminence and power prevailed among the metropolitans themselves, each of them affecting to display, in the most pompous terms, the temporal honors and advantages of the city over which he presided; the numbers and opulence of the Christians who were subject to their pastoral care; the saints and martyrs who had arisen

[122] We may appeal to the whole tenor of Cyprian's conduct, of his doctrine, and of his *Epistles*. Le Clerc, in a short life of Cyprian (*Universal Library*, xii 207-378), has laid him open with great freedom and accuracy.

[123] If Novatus, Felicissimus, etc., whom the Bishop of Carthage expelled from his church and from Africa, were not the most detestable monsters of wickedness, the zeal of Cyprian must occasionally have prevailed over his veracity. For a very just account of these obscure quarrels, see Mosheim, pp. 497-512.

[124] Mosheim, pp. 269, 574; Dupin, *Historical Dissertations on the Ancient Discipline of the Church* [1691], pp. 19-20.

among them; and the purity with which they preserved the tradition of the faith, as it had been transmitted through a series of orthodox bishops from the apostle or the apostolic disciple to whom the foundation of their church was ascribed.[125] From every cause, either of a civil or of an ecclesiastical nature, it was easy to foresee that Rome must enjoy the respect, and would soon claim the obedience, of the provinces. The society of the faithful bore a just proportion to the capital of the empire; and the Roman church was the greatest, the most numerous, and, in regard to the West, the most ancient of all the Christian establishments, many of which had received their religion from the pious labors of her missionaries. Instead of *one* apostolic founder, the utmost boast of Antioch, of Ephesus, or of Corinth, the banks of the Tiber were supposed to have been honored with the preaching and martyrdom of the *two* most eminent among the apostles;[126] and the bishops of Rome very prudently claimed the inheritance of whatsoever prerogatives were attributed either to the person or to the office of St. Peter.[127] The bishops of Italy and of the provinces were disposed to allow them a primacy of order and association (such was their very accurate expression) in the Christian aristocracy.[128] But the power of a monarch was rejected with abhorrence, and the aspiring genius of Rome experienced, from the nations of Asia and Africa, a more vigorous resistance to her spiritual, than she had formerly done to

[125] Tertullian, in a distinct treatise [*The Prescription against Heretics*], has pleaded against the heretics the right of prescription, as it was held by the apostolic churches.

[126] The journey of St. Peter to Rome is mentioned by most of the ancients (see Eusebius, ii 25), maintained by all the Catholics, allowed by some Protestants (see [John] Pearson and [Henry] Dodwell, *On the Succession of the First Bishops of Rome*), but has been vigorously attacked by [Friedrich] Spanheim (*Sacred Miscellanies,* iii 3). According to Father [Jean] Hardouin ["Pseudo-Virgil," *Posthumous Works*], the monks of the thirteenth century, who composed the *Aeneid,* represented St. Peter under the allegorical character of the Trojan hero.

[127] It is in French only that the famous allusion to St. Peter's name is exact: "Tu es *Pierre* et sur cette *pierre* . . . ." The same is imperfect in Greek, Latin, Italian, etc., and totally unintelligible in our Teutonic languages.

[128] Irenaeus, *Against Heresies,* iii 3, Tertullian, *The Prescription against Heretics,* ch. 36, and Cyprian, *Epistles,* 27, 55, 71, 75. Le Clerc (*Ecclesiastical History,* p. 764) and Mosheim (pp. 258, 578) labor in the interpretation of these passages. But the loose and rhetorical style of the fathers often appears favorable to the pretensions of Rome.

her temporal, dominion. The patriotic Cyprian, who ruled with the most absolute sway the church of Carthage and the provincial synods, opposed with resolution and success the ambition of the Roman pontiff, artfully connected his own cause with that of the eastern bishops, and, like Hannibal, sought out new allies in the heart of Asia.[129] If this Punic War was carried on without any effusion of blood, it was owing much less to the moderation than to the weakness of the contending prelates. Invectives and ex-communications were *their* only weapons; and these, during the progress of the whole controversy, they hurled against each other with equal fury and devotion. The hard necessity of censuring either a pope, or a saint and martyr, distresses the modern Catholics, whenever they are obliged to relate the particulars of a dispute in which the champions of religion indulged such passions as seem much more adapted to the senate or to the camp.[130]

The progress of the ecclesiastical authority gave birth to the memorable distinction of the laity and of the clergy, which had been unknown to the Greeks and Romans.[131] The former of these appellations comprehended the body of the Christian people; the latter, according to the signification of the word, was appropriated to the chosen portion that had been set apart for the service of religion: a celebrated order of men which has furnished the most important, though not always the most edifying, subjects for modern history. Their mutual hostilities sometimes disturbed the peace of the infant church, but their zeal and activity were united in the common cause; and the love of power, which (under the most artful disguises) could insinuate itself into the breasts of bishops and martyrs, animated them to increase the number of their sub-jects, and to enlarge the limits of the Christian empire. They were destitute of any temporal force, and they were for a long time discouraged and oppressed, rather than assisted, by the civil magis-trate; but they had acquired, and they employed within their own society, the two most efficacious instruments of government, rewards

[129] See the sharp epistle from Firmilianus, Bishop of Caesarea, to Stephen, Bishop of Rome, according to Cyprian, *Epistles,* 75.

[130] Concerning this dispute of the rebaptism of heretics, see the *Epistles* of Cyprian and the seventh book of Eusebius.

[131] For the origin of these words, see Mosheim, p. 141; Friedrich Span-heim, *Ecclesiastical History* [1701], p. 633. The distinction of *clerus* and *laicus* was established before the time of Tertullian.

and punishments: the former derived from the pious liberality, the latter from the devout apprehensions, of the faithful.

I. The community of goods, which had so agreeably amused the imagination of Plato,[132] and which subsisted in some degree among the austere sect of the Essenians,[133] was adopted for a short time in the primitive church. The fervor of the first proselytes prompted them to sell those worldly possessions which they despised, to lay the price of them at the feet of the apostles, and to content themselves with receiving an equal share out of the general distribution.[134] The progress of the Christian religion relaxed, and gradually abolished, this generous institution, which, in hands less pure than those of the apostles, would too soon have been corrupted and abused by the returning selfishness of human nature; and the converts who embraced the new religion were permitted to retain the possession of their patrimony, to receive legacies and inheritances, and to increase their separate property by all the lawful means of trade and industry. Instead of an absolute sacrifice, a moderate proportion was accepted by the ministers of the gospel; and in their weekly or monthly assemblies, every believer, according to the exigency of the occasion, and the measure of his wealth and piety, presented his voluntary offering for the use of the common fund.[135] Nothing, however inconsiderable, was refused; but it was diligently inculcated that, in the article of tithes, the Mosaic law was still of divine obligation; and that since the Jews, under a less perfect discipline, had been commanded to pay a tenth part of all that they possessed, it would become the disciples of Christ to distinguish themselves by a superior degree of liberality,[136] and

---

[132] The community instituted by Plato is more perfect than that which Sir Thomas More had imagined for his *Utopia*. The community of women, and that of temporal goods, may be considered as inseparable parts of the same system.

[133] Josephus, *Jewish Antiquities*, xviii 2; Philo, *On the Contemplative Life*.

[134] See the Acts of the Apostles 2:4-5, with Grotius's *Commentary*. Mosheim, in a particular dissertation, attacks the common opinion with very inconclusive arguments.

[135] Justin Martyr, *First Apology*, ch. 89; Tertullian, *Apology*, ch. 39.

[136] Irenaeus, *Against Heresies*, iv 27, 34; Origen in *Homilies on Numbers*, 2; Cyprian, *On the Unity of the Church*; *Apostolical Constitutions*, ii 34-35, with the notes of Cotelerius [1724]. The *Constitutions* introduce this divine precept by declaring that priests are as much above kings as the soul is above the

to acquire some merit by resigning a superfluous treasure, which must so soon be annihilated with the world itself.[137] It is almost unnecessary to observe that the revenue of each particular church, which was of so uncertain and fluctuating a nature, must have varied with the poverty or the opulence of the faithful, as they were dispersed in obscure villages, or collected in the great cities of the empire. In the time of the emperor Decius, it was the opinion of the magistrates that the Christians of Rome were possessed of very considerable wealth; that vessels of gold and silver were used in their religious worship; and that many among their proselytes had sold their lands and houses to increase the public riches of the sect, at the expense, indeed, of their unfortunate children, who found themselves beggars because their parents had been saints.[138] We should listen with distrust to the suspicions of strangers and enemies: on this occasion, however, they receive a very specious and probable color from the two following circumstances, the only ones that have reached our knowledge, which define any precise sums, or convey any distinct idea. Almost at the same period, the bishop of Carthage, from a society less opulent than that of Rome, collected an hundred thousand sesterces (above eight hundred and fifty pounds sterling), on a sudden call of charity, to redeem the

---

body. Among the tithable articles, they enumerate corn, wine, oil, and wool. On this interesting subject, consult Prideaux's *History of Tithes* [*The Original and Right of Tithes*], and Father Paolo [Sarpi], *Of Beneficiary Matters,* two writers of a very different character.

[137] The same opinion which prevailed about the year 1000 was productive of the same effects. Most of the donations express their motive, "the approaching end of the world" (see Mosheim's general history of the church [*Ecclesiastical History*], i 457 [trans. Archibald Maclaine (1767-68), ii 216-18].

[138] "Also, according to common report, it is the brotherhood's chief concern to sell their properties and hand over thousands of sesterces. The disinherited heir, impoverished by his holy parents, sighs for the estates of his ancestors which have been sold up in shameful auctions. This concealed wealth is hidden in obscure church corners, and the highest piety is believed to consist in leaving your beloved children destitute" (Prudentius, *Crowns of Martyrdom,* ii 73-84). The subsequent conduct of the deacon Laurence [in Prudentius' poem] only proves how proper a use was made of the wealth of the Roman church; it was undoubtedly very considerable, but Father Paolo (ch. 3) appears to exaggerate when he supposes that the successors of Commodus were urged to persecute the Christians by their own avarice, or that of their Praetorian prefects.

brethren of Numidia, who had been carried away captives by the barbarians of the desert.[139] About an hundred years before the reign of Decius, the Roman church had received, in a single donation, the sum of two hundred thousand sesterces from a stranger of Pontus, who proposed to fix his residence in the capital.[140] These oblations, for the most part, were made in money; nor was the society of Christians either desirous or capable of acquiring, to any considerable degree, the incumbrance of landed property. It had been provided by several laws, which were enacted with the same design as our statutes of mortmain, that no real estates should be given or bequeathed to any corporate body, without either a special privilege or a particular dispensation from the emperor or from the senate,[141] who were seldom disposed to grant them in favor of a sect, at first the object of their contempt, and at last of their fears and jealousy. A transaction, however, is related under the reign of Alexander Severus, which discovers that the restraint was sometimes eluded or suspended, and that the Christians were permitted to claim and to possess lands within the limits of Rome itself.[142] The progress of Christianity and the civil confusions of the empire contributed to relax the severity of the laws, and before the close of the third century, many considerable estates were bestowed on the opulent churches of Rome, Milan, Carthage, Antioch, Alexandria, and the other great cities of Italy and the provinces.

The bishop was the natural steward of the church; the public stock was intrusted to his care, without account or control; the presbyters were confined to their spiritual functions, and the more dependent order of deacons was solely employed in the management and distribution of the ecclesiastical revenue.[143] If we may give

[139] Cyprian, *Epistles,* 62.

[140] Tertullian, *The Prescription against Heretics,* ch. 30. [The stranger was Marcion, against whom Tertullian later wrote.]

[141] Diocletian gave a rescript, which is only a declaration of the old law: "Undoubtedly a corporate body, if not authorized by special statute, cannot receive inheritances." Father Paolo (ch. 4) thinks that these regulations had been much neglected since the reign of Valerian.

[142] *Augustan History* [1620], p. 131 ["Alexander Severus," xlix 6]. The ground had been public, and was now disputed between the society of Christians and that of butchers.

[143] *Apostolical Constitutions,* ii 35.

credit to the vehement declamations of Cyprian, there were too many among his African brethren who, in the execution of their charge, violated every precept, not only of evangelic perfection, but even of moral virtue. By some of these unfaithful stewards the riches of the church were lavished in sensual pleasures, by others they were perverted to the purposes of private gain, of fraudulent purchases, and of rapacious usury.[144] But, as long as the contributions of the Christian people were free and unconstrained, the abuse of their confidence could not be very frequent, and the general uses to which their liberality was applied reflected honor on the religious society. A decent portion was reserved for the maintenance of the bishop and his clergy; a sufficient sum was allotted for the expenses of the public worship, of which the feasts of love, the *agapoe,* as they were called, constituted a very pleasing part. The whole remainder was the sacred patrimony of the poor. According to the discretion of the bishop, it was distributed to support widows and orphans, the lame, the sick, and the aged of the community; to comfort strangers and pilgrims, and to alleviate the misfortunes of prisoners and captives, more especially when their sufferings had been occasioned by their firm attachment to the cause of religion.[145] A generous intercourse of charity united the most distant provinces, and the smaller congregations were cheerfully assisted by the alms of their more opulent brethren.[146] Such an institution, which paid less regard to the merit than to the distress of the object, very materially conduced to the progress of Christianity. The pagans who were actuated by a sense of humanity, while they derided the doctrines, acknowledged the benevolence, of the new sect.[147] The prospect of immediate relief and of future protection allured into its hospitable bosom many of those unhappy persons whom the neglect of the world would have abandoned to the miseries of want, of sickness, and of old age. There

[144] Cyprian, *On the Lapsed,* p. 89; *Epistles,* 65. The charge is confirmed by the nineteenth and twentieth canon[s] of the council of Illiberis.

[145] See the apologies of Justin, Tertullian, etc.

[146] The wealth and liberality of the Romans to their most distant brethren is gratefully celebrated by Dionysius of Corinth, according to Eusebius, iv 23.

[147] See Lucian in *The Passing of Peregrinus.* Julian (*Letters* [in *Works* (1696)], 49) [84a, ed. Bidez and Cumont] seems mortified that the Christian charity maintains not only their own, but likewise the heathen poor.

is some reason likewise to believe that great numbers of infants who, according to the inhuman practice of the times, had been exposed by their parents were frequently rescued from death, baptized, educated, and maintained by the piety of the Christians, and at the expense of the public treasure.[148]

II. It is the undoubted right of every society to exclude from its communion and benefits such among its members as reject or violate those regulations which have been established by general consent. In the exercise of this power, the censures of the Christian church were chiefly directed against scandalous sinners, and particularly those who were guilty of murder, of fraud, or of incontinence; against the authors, or the followers, of any heretical opinions which had been condemned by the judgment of the episcopal order; and against those unhappy persons who, whether from choice or from compulsion, had polluted themselves after their baptism by any act of idolatrous worship. The consequences of excommunication were of a temporal as well as a spiritual nature. The Christian against whom it was pronounced was deprived of any part in the oblations of the faithful. The ties both of religious and of private friendship were dissolved; he found himself a profane object of abhorrence to the persons whom he the most esteemed, or by whom he had been the most tenderly beloved; and as far as an expulsion from a respectable society could imprint on his character a mark of disgrace, he was shunned or suspected by the generality of mankind. The situation of these unfortunate exiles was in itself very painful and melancholy; but, as it usually happens, their apprehensions far exceeded their sufferings. The benefits of the Christian communion were those of eternal life; nor could they erase from their minds the awful opinion that to those ecclesiastical governors by whom they were condemned the Deity had committed the keys of hell and of paradise. The heretics, indeed, who might be supported by the consciousness of their intentions, and by the flattering hope that they alone had discovered the true path of salvation, endeavored to regain, in their separate

---

[148] Such, at least, has been the laudable conduct of more modern missionaries, under the same circumstances. Above three thousand new-born infants are annually exposed in the streets of Pekin (see Louis Le Comte, *New Memoirs of China,* and the *Studies on the Chinese and the Egyptians,* i 61 [by Cornelius de Pauw (1773), i 61 [57]].

assemblies, those comforts, temporal as well as spiritual, which they no longer derived from the great society of Christians. But almost all those who had reluctantly yielded to the power of vice or idolatry were sensible of their fallen condition, and anxiously desirous of being restored to the benefits of the Christian communion.

With regard to the treatment of these penitents, two opposite opinions, the one of justice, the other of mercy, divided the primitive church. The more rigid and inflexible casuists refused them for ever, and without exception, the meanest place in the holy community which they had disgraced or deserted; and, leaving them to the remorse of a guilty conscience, indulged them only with a faint ray of hope that the contrition of their life and death might possibly be accepted by the Supreme Being.[149] A milder sentiment was embraced, in practice as well as in theory, by the purest and most respectable of the Christian churches.[150] The gates of reconciliation and of heaven were seldom shut against the returning penitent; but a severe and solemn form of discipline was instituted, which, while it served to expiate his crime, might powerfully deter the spectators from the imitation of his example. Humbled by a public confession, emaciated by fasting, and clothed in sackcloth, the penitent lay prostrate at the door of the assembly, imploring with tears the pardon of his offenses, and soliciting the prayers of the faithful.[151] If the fault was of a very heinous nature, whole years of penance were esteemed an inadequate satisfaction to the divine justice; and it was always by slow and painful gradations that the sinner, the heretic, or the apostate was readmitted into the bosom of the church. A sentence of perpetual excommunication was, however, reserved for some crimes of an extraordinary magnitude, and particularly for the inexcusable relapses of those penitents who had already experienced and abused the clemency of their ecclesiastical superiors. According to the circumstances or the number of the guilty, the exercise of the

[149] The Montanists and the Novatians, who adhered to this opinion with the greatest rigor and obstinacy, found *themselves* at last in the number of excommunicated heretics (see the learned and copious Mosheim, second and third centuries).

[150] Dionysius, according to Eusebius, iv 23; Cyprian, *On the Lapsed.*

[151] William Cave's *Primitive Christianity,* iii 5. The admirers of antiquity regret the loss of this public penance.

Christian discipline was varied by the discretion of the bishops. The councils of Ancyra and Illiberis were held about the same time, the one in Galatia, the other in Spain; but their respective canons, which are still extant, seem to breathe a very different spirit. The Galatian, who after his baptism had repeatedly sacrificed to idols, might obtain his pardon by a penance of seven years, and if he had seduced others to imitate his example, only three years more were added to the term of his exile. But the unhappy Spaniard who had committed the same offense was deprived of the hope of reconciliation, even in the article of death; and his idolatry was placed at the head of a list of seventeen other crimes, against which a sentence no less terrible was pronounced. Among these we may distinguish the inexpiable guilt of calumniating a bishop, a presbyter, or even a deacon.[152]

The well-tempered mixture of liberality and rigor, the judicious dispensation of rewards and punishments, according to the maxims of policy as well as justice, constituted the *human* strength of the church. The bishops, whose paternal care extended itself to the government of both worlds, were sensible of the importance of these prerogatives, and, covering their ambition with the fair pretense of the love of order, they were jealous of any rival in the exercise of a discipline so necessary to prevent the desertion of those troops which had inlisted themselves under the banner of the cross, and whose numbers every day became more considerable. From the imperious declamations of Cyprian we should naturally conclude that the doctrines of excommunication and penance formed the most essential part of religion; and that it was much less dangerous for the disciples of Christ to neglect the observance of the moral duties than to despise the censures and authority of their bishops. Sometimes we might imagine that we were listening to the voice of Moses when he commanded the earth to open, and to swallow up, in consuming flames, the rebellious race which

---

[152] See in Dupin (*New Library of Ecclesiastical Authors,* ii 304-13) a short but rational exposition of the canons of those councils which were assembled in the first moments of tranquillity after the persecution of Diocletian. This persecution had been much less severely felt in Spain than in Galatia, a difference which may, in some measure, account for the contrast of their regulations.

refused obedience to the priesthood of Aaron; and we should sometimes suppose that we heard a Roman consul asserting the majesty of the republic, and declaring his inflexible resolution to enforce the rigor of the laws. "If such irregularities are suffered with impunity (it is thus that the bishop of Carthage chides the lenity of his colleague), if such irregularities are suffered, there is an end of *Episcopal Vigor;*[153] an end of the sublime and divine power of governing the church, an end of Christianity itself." Cyprian had renounced those temporal honors which it is probable he would never have obtained; but the acquisition of such absolute command over the consciences and understanding of a congregation, however obscure or despised by the world, is more truly grateful to the pride of the human heart than the possession of the most despotic power imposed by arms and conquest on a reluctant people.

In the course of this important, though perhaps tedious, inquiry, I have attempted to display the secondary causes which so efficaciously assisted the truth of the Christian religion. If among these causes we have discovered any artificial ornaments, any accidental circumstances, or any mixture of error and passion, it cannot appear surprising that mankind should be the most sensibly affected by such motives as were suited to their imperfect nature. It was by the aid of these causes, exclusive zeal, the immediate expectation of another world, the claim of miracles, the practice of rigid virtue, and the constitution of the primitive church, that Christianity spread itself with so much success in the Roman empire. To the first of these the Christians were indebted for their invincible valor, which disdained to capitulate with the enemy whom they were resolved to vanquish. The three succeeding causes supplied their valor with the most formidable arms. The last of these causes united their courage, directed their arms, and gave their efforts that irresistible weight which even a small band of well-trained and intrepid volunteers has so often possessed over an undisciplined multitude, ignorant of the subject, and careless of the event, of the war. In the various religions of polytheism, some wandering fanatics of Egypt and Syria, who addressed themselves to the credulous superstition of the populace, were perhaps

[153] Cyprian, *Epistles,* 59.

the only order of priests[154] that derived their whole support and credit from their sacerdotal profession, and were very deeply affected by a personal concern for the safety or prosperity of their tutelar deities. The ministers of polytheism, both in Rome and in the provinces, were, for the most part, men of a noble birth and of an affluent fortune, who received, as an honorable distinction, the care of a celebrated temple or of a public sacrifice; exhibited, very frequently at their own expense, the sacred games;[155] and with cold indifference performed the ancient rites, according to the laws and fashion of their country. As they were engaged in the ordinary occupations of life, their zeal and devotion were seldom animated by a sense of interest, or by the habits of an ecclesiastical character. Confined to their respective temples and cities, they remained without any connection of discipline or government; and whilst they acknowledged the supreme jurisdiction of the senate, of the college of pontiffs, and of the emperor, those civil magistrates contented themselves with the easy task of maintaining, in peace and dignity, the general worship of mankind. We have already seen how various, how loose, and how uncertain were the religious sentiments of polytheists. They were abandoned, almost without control, to the natural workings of a superstitious fancy. The accidental circumstances of their life and situation determined the object as well as the degree of their devotion; and as long as their adoration was successively prostituted to a thousand deities, it was scarcely possible that their hearts could be susceptible of a very sincere or lively passion for any of them.

When Christianity appeared in the world, even these faint and imperfect impressions had lost much of their original power. Human reason, which by its unassisted strength is incapable of perceiving the mysteries of faith, had already obtained an easy

[154] The arts, the manners, and the vices of the priests of the Syrian goddess are very humorously described by Apuleius, in the eighth book of his *Metamorphoses* [*The Golden Ass*].

[155] The office of Asiarch was of this nature, and it is frequently mentioned in Aristides, the inscriptions, etc. It was annual and elective. None but the vainest citizens could desire the honor; none but the most wealthy could support the expense. See in the *Apostolic Fathers,* ii 200 [*Epistle of the Smyrnaean Church on the Martyrdom of Polycarp,* ch. 12] with how much indifference Philip the Asiarch conducted himself in the martyrdom of Polycarp. There were likewise Bithyniarchs, Lyciarchs, etc.

triumph over the folly of paganism; and when Tertullian or
Lactantius employ their labors in exposing its falsehood and extravagance, they are obliged to transcribe the eloquence of Cicero
or the wit of Lucian. The contagion of these skeptical writings had
been diffused far beyond the number of their readers. The fashion
of incredulity was communicated from the philosopher to the man
of pleasure or business, from the noble to the plebeian, and from
the master to the menial slave who waited at his table, and who
eagerly listened to the freedom of his conversation. On public
occasions the philosophic part of mankind affected to treat with
respect and decency the religious institutions of their country; but
their secret contempt penetrated through the thin and awkward
disguise; and even the people, when they discovered that their
deities were rejected and derided by those whose rank or understanding they were accustomed to reverence, were filled with
doubts and apprehensions concerning the truth of those doctrines to
which they had yielded the most implicit belief. The decline of
ancient prejudice exposed a very numerous portion of humankind
to the danger of a painful and comfortless situation. A state of
skepticism and suspense may amuse a few inquisitive minds. But
the practice of superstition is so congenial to the multitude that, if
they are forcibly awakened, they still regret the loss of their
pleasing vision. Their love of the marvellous and supernatural,
their curiosity with regard to future events, and their strong
propensity to extend their hopes and fears beyond the limits of
the visible world, were the principal causes which favored the
establishment of polytheism. So urgent on the vulgar is the
necessity of believing, that the fall of any system of mythology
will most probably be succeeded by the introduction of some other
mode of superstition. Some deities of a more recent and fashionable
cast might soon have occupied the deserted temples of Jupiter
and Apollo, if, in the decisive moment, the wisdom of Providence
had not interposed a genuine revelation, fitted to inspire the most
rational esteem and conviction, whilst, at the same time, it was
adorned with all that could attract the curiosity, the wonder, and
the veneration of the people. In their actual disposition, as many
were almost disengaged from their artificial prejudices, but equally
susceptible and desirous of a devout attachment, an object much
less deserving would have been sufficient to fill the vacant place in

their hearts, and to gratify the uncertain eagerness of their passions. Those who are inclined to pursue this reflection, instead of viewing with astonishment the rapid progress of Christianity, will perhaps be surprised that its success was not still more rapid and still more universal.

It has been observed, with truth as well as propriety, that the conquests of Rome prepared and facilitated those of Christianity. In the second chapter of this work we have attempted to explain in what manner the most civilized provinces of Europe, Asia, and Africa were united under the dominion of one sovereign, and gradually connected by the most intimate ties of laws, of manners, and of language. The Jews of Palestine, who had fondly expected a temporal deliverer, gave so cold a reception to the miracles of the divine prophet that it was found unnecessary to publish, or at least to preserve, any Hebrew gospel.[156] The authentic histories of the actions of Christ were composed in the Greek language, at a considerable distance from Jerusalem, and after the Gentile converts were grown extremely numerous.[157] As soon as those histories were translated into the Latin tongue, they were perfectly intelligible to all the subjects of Rome, excepting only to the peasants of Syria and Egypt, for whose benefit particular versions were afterwards made. The public highways, which had been constructed for the use of the legions, opened an easy passage for the Christian missionaries from Damascus to Corinth, and from Italy to the extremity of Spain or Britain; nor did those spiritual conquerors encounter any of the obstacles which usually retard or prevent the introduction of a foreign religion into a distant country. There is the strongest reason to believe that before the reigns of Diocletian and Constantine the faith of Christ had been preached in every province, and in all the great cities of the empire; but the foundation of the several congregations, the numbers of the faithful who composed them, and their proportion

---

[156] The modern critics are not disposed to believe what the fathers almost unanimously assert, that St. Matthew composed a Hebrew gospel, of which only the Greek translation is extant. It seems, however, dangerous to reject their testimony.

[157] Under the reigns of Nero and Domitian, and in the cities of Alexandria, Antioch, Rome, and Ephesus (see [John] Mill, *Prolegomena to the New Testament,* and Dr. [Nathaniel] Lardner's fair and extensive collection [*The Credibility of the Gospel History,* 1755], xv).

to the unbelieving multitude, are now buried in obscurity, or disguised by fiction and declamation. Such imperfect circumstances, however, as have reached our knowledge concerning the increase of the Christian name in Asia and Greece, in Egypt, in Italy, and in the West, we shall now proceed to relate, without neglecting the real or imaginary acquisitions which lay beyond the frontiers of the Roman empire.

The rich provinces that extend from the Euphrates to the Ionian sea were the principal theater on which the apostle of the Gentiles[158] displayed his zeal and piety. The seeds of the gospel, which he had scattered in a fertile soil, were diligently cultivated by his disciples; and it should seem that, during the two first centuries, the most considerable body of Christians was contained within those limits. Among the societies which were instituted in Syria, none were more ancient or more illustrious than those of Damascus, of Beroea or Aleppo, and of Antioch. The prophetic introduction of the Apocalypse has described and immortalized the seven churches of Asia: Ephesus, Smyrna, Pergamus, Thyatira,[159] Sardes, Laodicea, and Philadelphia; and their colonies were soon diffused over that populous country. In a very early period, the islands of Cyprus and Crete, the provinces of Thrace and Macedonia, gave a favorable reception to the new religion; and Christian republics were soon founded in the cities of Corinth, of Sparta, and of Athens.[160] The antiquity of the Greek and Asiatic churches allowed a sufficient space of time for their increase and multiplication, and even the swarms of Gnostics and other heretics serve to display the flourishing condition of the orthodox church, since the appellation of heretics has always been applied to the less numerous party. To these domestic testimonies we may add the confession, the complaints, and the apprehensions of the Gentiles themselves. From the writings of Lucian, a philosopher who had

[158] [St. Paul.]
[159] The Alogians (Epiphanius, *Antidotes against Eighty Heresies*, 51 [p. 455]) disputed the genuineness of the Apocalypse, because the church of Thyatira was not yet founded. Epiphanius, who allows the fact, extricates himself from the difficulty by ingeniously supposing that St. John wrote in the spirit of prophecy (see Firmin Abauzit, *Discourse on the Apocalypse*).
[160] The epistles of Ignatius and Dionysius (according to Eusebius, iv 23) point out many churches in Asia and Greece. That of Athens seems to have been one of the least flourishing.

studied mankind, and who describes their manners in the most lively colors, we may learn that, under the reign of Commodus, his native country of Pontus was filled with Epicureans and Christians.[161] Within fourscore years after the death of Christ,[162] the humane Pliny laments the magnitude of the evil which he vainly attempted to eradicate. In his very curious epistle to the emperor Trajan, he affirms that the temples were almost deserted, that the sacred victims scarcely found any purchasers, and that the superstition had not only infected the cities, but had even spread itself into the villages and the open country of Pontus and Bithynia.[163]

Without descending into a minute scrutiny of the expressions, or of the motives, of those writers who either celebrate or lament the progress of Christianity in the East, it may in general be observed that none of them have left us any grounds from whence a just estimate might be formed of the real numbers of the faithful in those provinces. One circumstance, however, has been fortunately preserved, which seems to cast a more distinct light on this obscure but interesting subject. Under the reign of Theodosius, after Christianity had enjoyed during more than sixty years the sunshine of imperial favor, the ancient and illustrious church of Antioch consisted of one hundred thousand persons, three thousand of whom were supported out of the public oblations.[164] The splendor and dignity of the queen of the East, the acknowledged populousness of Caesarea, Seleucia, and Alexandria, and the destruction of two hundred and fifty thousand souls in the earthquake which afflicted Antioch under the elder Justin,[165] are so

[161] Lucian in *Alexander, The False Prophet*, ch. 25. Christianity, however, must have been very unequally diffused over Pontus, since in the middle of the third century there were no more than seventeen believers in the extensive diocese of Neo-Caesarea (see M. de Tillemont, *Ecclesiastical Memoirs,* iv 675, from Basil and Gregory of Nyssa, who were themselves natives of Cappadocia).

[162] According to the ancients, Jesus Christ suffered under the consulship of the two Gemini, in the year 29 of our present era. Pliny was sent into Bithynia (according to Antoine Pagi [*Historical-Chronological Critique of the Annals of Baronius*]) in the year 110. [Both dates are disputed.]

[163] Pliny, *Epistles*, x 97 [96].

[164] Chrysostom, *Works* [1734-41], vii 658, 810.

[165] John Malala, *Chronicle History* [1691], ii 144. He draws the same conclusion with regard to the populousness of Antioch.

many convincing proofs that the whole number of its inhabitants was not less than half a million, and that the Christians, however multiplied by zeal and power, did not exceed a fifth part of that great city. How different a proportion must we adopt when we compare the persecuted with the triumphant church, the West with the East, remote villages with populous towns, and countries recently converted to the faith with the place where the believers first received the appellation of Christians! It must not, however, be dissembled that, in another passage, Chrysostom, to whom we are indebted for this useful information, computes the multitude of the faithful as even superior to that of the Jews and pagans.[166] But the solution of this apparent difficulty is easy and obvious. The eloquent preacher draws a parallel between the civil and the ecclesiastical constitution of Antioch; between the list of Christians who had acquired heaven by baptism and the list of citizens who had a right to share the public liberality. Slaves, strangers, and infants were comprised in the former; they were excluded from the latter.

The extensive commerce of Alexandria, and its proximity to Palestine, gave an easy entrance to the new religion. It was at first embraced by great numbers of the Therapeutae, or Essenians of the lake Mareotis, a Jewish sect which had abated much of its reverence for the Mosaic ceremonies. The austere life of the Essenians, their fasts and excommunications, the community of goods, the love of celibacy, their zeal for martyrdom, and the warmth though not the purity of their faith, already offered a very lively image of the primitive discipline.[167] It was in the school of Alexandria that the Christian theology appears to have assumed a regular and scientifical form; and when Hadrian visited Egypt,

[166] Chrysostom, i 592. I am indebted for these passages, though not for my inference, to the learned Dr. Lardner, *Credibility of the Gospel History,* xii 370.

[167] Basnage, *History of the Jews,* ii 20-23 [ii 13], has examined with the most critical accuracy the curious treatise of Philo [*On the Contemplative Life*] which describes the Therapeutae. By proving that it was composed as early as the time of Augustus, Basnage has demonstrated, in spite of Eusebius (ii 17) and a crowd of modern Catholics, that the Therapeutae were neither Christians nor monks. It still remains probable that they changed their name, preserved their manners, adopted some new articles of faith, and gradually became the fathers of the Egyptian ascetics.

he found a church, composed of Jews and of Greeks, sufficiently important to attract the notice of that inquisitive prince.[168] But the progress of Christianity was for a long time confined within the limits of a single city, which was itself a foreign colony, and, till the close of the second century, the predecessors of Demetrius were the only prelates of the Egyptian church. Three bishops were consecrated by the hands of Demetrius, and the number was increased to twenty by his successor Heraclas.[169] The body of the natives, a people distinguished by a sullen inflexibility of temper,[170] entertained the new doctrine with coldness and reluctance; and even in the time of Origen it was rare to meet with an Egyptian who had surmounted his early prejudices in favor of the sacred animals of his country.[171] As soon, indeed, as Christianity ascended the throne, the zeal of those barbarians obeyed the prevailing impulsion; the cities of Egypt were filled with bishops, and the deserts of Thebais swarmed with hermits.

A perpetual stream of strangers and provincials flowed into the capacious bosom of Rome. Whatever was strange or odious, whoever was guilty or suspected, might hope in the obscurity of that immense capital to elude the vigilance of the law. In such a various conflux of nations, every teacher, either of truth or of falsehood, every founder, whether of a virtuous or a criminal association, might easily multiply his disciples or accomplices. The Christians of Rome, at the time of the accidental persecution of Nero, are represented by Tacitus as already amounting to a very great multitude,[172] and the language of that great historian is almost similar to the style employed by Livy when he relates the introduction and the suppression of the rites of Bacchus. After the Bacchanals had awakened the severity of the senate, it was likewise apprehended

[168] See a letter of Hadrian, in the *Augustan History,* p. 245 ["Firmus," viii. Bury notes that the letter is spurious.]

[169] For the succession of Alexandrian bishops, consult [Eusèbe] Renaudot's *History [of the Alexandrian Jacobite Patriarchs* (1713)], pp. 24 etc. This curious fact is preserved by the patriarch Eutychius (*Annals,* i 334, trans. Pocock), and its internal evidence would alone be a sufficient answer to all the objections which Bishop Pearson has urged in the *Vindication of the Letters of St. Ignatius.*

[170] Ammianus Marcellinus, *History,* xxii 16.

[171] Origen, *Against Celsus,* i 40.

[172] *Ingens multitudo* is the expression of Tacitus, xv 44.

that a very great multitude, as it were *another people,* had been initiated into those abhorred mysteries. A more careful inquiry soon demonstrated that the offenders did not exceed seven thousand: a number indeed sufficiently alarming, when considered as the object of public justice.[173] It is with the same candid allowance that we should interpret the vague expressions of Tacitus, and, in a former instance, of Pliny, when they exaggerate the crowds of deluded fanatics who had forsaken the established worship of the gods. The church of Rome was undoubtedly the first and most populous of the empire; and we are possessed of an authentic record which attests the state of religion in that city about the middle of the third century, and after a peace of thirty-eight years. The clergy, at that time, consisted of a bishop, forty-six presbyters, seven deacons, as many sub-deacons, forty-two acolythes, and fifty readers, exorcists, and porters. The number of widows, of the infirm, and of the poor, who were maintained by the oblations of the faithful, amounted to fifteen hundred.[174] From reason, as well as from the analogy of Antioch, we may venture to estimate the Christians of Rome at about fifty thousand. The populousness of that great capital cannot, perhaps, be exactly ascertained; but the most modest calculation will not surely reduce it lower than a million of inhabitants, of whom the Christians might constitute at the most a twentieth part.[175]

The western provincials appeared to have derived the knowledge of Christianity from the same source which had diffused among them the language, the sentiments, and the manners of Rome. In this more important circumstance, Africa, as well as Gaul, was gradually fashioned to the imitation of the capital. Yet, notwithstanding the many favorable occasions which might invite

[173] Titus Livius, *History of Rome,* xxxix 13-17. Nothing could exceed the horror and consternation of the senate on the discovery of the Bacchanalians, whose depravity is described, and perhaps exaggerated, by Livy.

[174] Eusebius, vi 43. The Latin translator [of Eusebius] (M. [Henri] de Valois) has thought proper to reduce the number of presbyters to forty-four.

[175] This proportion of the presbyters and of the poor to the rest of the people was originally fixed by [Gilbert] Burnet (*Travels into Italy* [1737], p. 168), and is approved by [Walter] Moyle [*Works* (1726-27)], ii 151. They were both unacquainted with the passage of Chrysostom, which converts their conjecture almost into a fact.

the Roman missionaries to visit their Latin provinces, it was late before they passed either the sea or the Alps;[176] nor can we discover in those great countries any assured traces either of faith or of persecution that ascend higher than the reign of the Antonines.[177] The slow progress of the gospel in the cold climate of Gaul was extremely different from the eagerness with which it seems to have been received on the burning sands of Africa. The African Christians soon formed one of the principal members of the primitive church. The practice introduced into that province of appointing bishops to the most inconsiderable towns, and very frequently to the most obscure villages, contributed to multiply the splendor and importance of their religious societies, which during the course of the third century were animated by the zeal of Tertullian, directed by the abilities of Cyprian, and adorned by the eloquence of Lactantius. But if, on the contrary, we turn our eyes towards Gaul, we must content ourselves with discovering, in the time of Marcus Antoninus, the feeble and united congregations of Lyons and Vienna;[178] and, even as late as the reign of Decius, we are assured that in a few cities only, Arles, Narbonne, Toulouse, Limoges, Clermont, Tours, and Paris, some scattered churches were supported by the devotion of a small number of Christians.[179]

[176] "God's religion was accepted somewhat late beyond the Alps" (Sulpicius Severus, ii 32). According to the Donatists, whose assertion is confirmed by the tacit acknowledgment of Augustin, Africa was the last of the provinces which received the gospel (Tillemont, *Ecclesiastical Memoirs,* i 754). One of the adversaries of Apuleius seems to have been a Christian (Apuleius, *Apology,* pp. 496-97, Delphin edition [1688]).

[177] "Then first did martyrdoms take place in Gaul" (Sulpicius Severus, ii 32). These were the celebrated martyrs of Lyons (see Eusebius, v 1; Tillemont, *Ecclesiastical Memoirs,* ii 316). With regard to Africa, see Tertullian, *To Scapula,* ch. 3. It is imagined that the Scillitan martyrs were the first (Thierry Ruinart, *Selected and Genuine Acts of the First Martyrs* [1713], p. 34 [84]). [Apparently this note and the preceding one were badly intermingled in the original editions; they are rearranged here.]

[178] [Vienne.]

[179] "A few churches rise in some cities through the devotion of a small number of Christians" (Ruinart, *Selected Acts of the Martyrs,* p. 130). Gregory of Tours, *Ecclesiastical History of the Franks,* i 28; Mosheim, pp. 207, 449. There is some reason to believe that, in the beginning of the fourth century, the extensive dioceses of Liège, of Treves, and of Cologne composed a single bishopric, which had been very recently founded (see *Memoirs* of Tillemont, vol. vi, pt. 1, pp. 43, 411).

Silence is indeed very consistent with devotion, but as it is seldom compatible with zeal, we may perceive and lament the languid state of Christianity in those provinces which had exchanged the Celtic for the Latin tongue; since they did not, during the three first centuries, give birth to a single ecclesiastical writer. From Gaul, which claimed a just pre-eminence of learning and authority over all the countries on this side of the Alps, the light of the gospel was more faintly reflected on the remote provinces of Spain and Britain; and, if we may credit the vehement assertions of Tertullian, they had already received the first rays of the faith when he addressed his apology to the magistrates of the emperor Severus.[180] But the obscure and imperfect origin of the western churches of Europe has been so negligently recorded that, if we would relate the time and manner of their foundation, we must supply the silence of antiquity by those legends which avarice or superstition long afterwards dictated to the monks in the lazy gloom of their convents.[181] Of these holy romances, that of the apostle St. James can alone, by its singular extravagance, deserve to be mentioned. From a peaceful fisherman of the lake of Gennesareth, he was transformed into a valorous knight, who charged at the head of the Spanish chivalry in their battles against the Moors. The gravest historians have celebrated his exploits; the miraculous shrine of Compostella displayed his power; and the sword of a military order, assisted by the terrors of the Inquisition, was sufficient to remove every objection of profane criticism.[182]

The progress of Christianity was not confined to the Roman empire; and, according to the primitive fathers, who interpret facts by prophecy, the new religion, within a century after the death of its divine Author, had already visited every part of the globe.

[180] The date of Tertullian's *Apology* is fixed, in a dissertation of Mosheim, to the year 198.

[181] In the fifteenth century, there were few who had either inclination or courage to question whether Joseph of Arimathea founded the monastery of Glastonbury, and whether Dionysius the Areopagite preferred the residence of Paris to that of Athens.

[182] The stupendous metamorphosis was performed in the ninth century. See [Jean] Mariana, *History of Spain*, vii 13 (vol. i, p. 285, The Hague edition [1733]), who, in every sense, imitates Livy, and the honest detection of the legend of St. James by Dr. [Michael] Geddes, *Miscellanies* [*Miscellaneous Tracts* (1730)], ii 221.

"There exists not," says Justin Martyr, "a people, whether Greek or barbarian, or any other race of men, by whatsoever appellation or manners they may be distinguished, however ignorant of arts or agriculture, whether they dwell under tents, or wander about in covered wagons, among whom prayers are not offered up in the name of a crucified Jesus to the Father and Creator of all things." [183] But this splendid exaggeration, which even at present it would be extremely difficult to reconcile with the real state of mankind, can be considered only as the rash sally of a devout but careless writer, the measure of whose belief was regulated by that of his wishes. But neither the belief nor the wishes of the fathers can alter the truth of history. It will still remain an undoubted fact that the barbarians of Scythia and Germany, who afterwards subverted the Roman monarchy, were involved in the darkness of paganism; and that even the conversion of Iberia, of Armenia, or of Ethiopia, was not attempted with any degree of success till the sceptre was in the hands of an orthodox emperor.[184] Before that time the various accidents of war and commerce might indeed diffuse an imperfect knowledge of the gospel among the tribes of Caledonia,[185] and among the borderers of the Rhine, the Danube, and the Euphrates.[186] Beyond the last-mentioned river, Edessa was distinguished by a firm and early adherence to the faith.[187] From

[183] Justin Martyr, *Dialogue with Trypho*, p. 341; Irenaeus, *Against Heresies*, i 10; Tertullian, *Answer to the Jews*, ch. 7. See Mosheim, p. 203.

[184] See the fourth century of Mosheim's history of the church [*Ecclesiastical History*]. Many, though very confused, circumstances that relate to the conversion of Iberia and Armenia may be found in Moses of Chorene [*History of Armenia*], ii 78-89. [Milman notes that Gibbon intended to delete "of Armenia" in later editions.]

[185] According to Tertullian, the Christian faith had penetrated into parts of Britain inaccessible to the Roman arms. About a century afterwards, Ossian, the son of Fingal, is *said* to have disputed, in his extreme old age, with one of the foreign missionaries, and the dispute is still extant, in verse and in the Erse language. See Mr. James Macpherson's Dissertation on the Antiquity of Ossian's Poems [*The Works of Ossian* (1765)], p. 10.

[186] The Goths who ravaged Asia in the reign of Gallienus carried away great numbers of captives, some of whom were Christians and became missionaries (see Tillemont, *Ecclesiastical Memoirs*, iv 44).

[187] The legend of Abgarus, fabulous as it is, affords a decisive proof that many years before Eusebius wrote his history the greatest part of the inhabitants of Edessa had embraced Christianity. Their rivals, the citizens of Carrhae, adhered, on the contrary, to the cause of paganism as late as the sixth century.

Edessa the principles of Christianity were easily introduced into the Greek and Syrian cities which obeyed the successors of Artaxerxes; but they do not appear to have made any deep impression on the minds of the Persians, whose religious system, by the labors of a well-disciplined order of priests, had been constructed with much more art and solidity than the uncertain mythology of Greece and Rome.[188]

From this impartial though imperfect survey of the progress of Christianity, it may perhaps seem probable that the number of its proselytes has been excessively magnified by fear on the one side and by devotion on the other. According to the irreproachable testimony of Origen,[189] the proportion of the faithful was very inconsiderable when compared with the multitude of an unbelieving world; but as we are left without any distinct information, it is impossible to determine, and it is difficult even to conjecture, the real numbers of the primitive Christians. The most favorable calculation, however, that can be deduced from the examples of Antioch and of Rome will not permit us to imagine that more than a twentieth part of the subjects of the empire had inlisted themselves under the banner of the cross before the important conversion of Constantine. But their habits of faith, of zeal, and of union seemed to multiply their numbers; and the same causes which contributed to their future increase served to render their actual strength more apparent and more formidable.

Such is the constitution of civil society that, whilst a few persons are distinguished by riches, by honors, and by knowledge, the body of the people is condemned to obscurity, ignorance, and poverty. The Christian religion, which addressed itself to the whole human race, must consequently collect a far greater number of proselytes from the lower than from the superior ranks of life. This innocent and natural circumstance has been improved into a very odious imputation, which seems to be less strenuously denied by the apologists than it is urged by the adversaries of the faith: that the new sect of Christians was almost entirely composed of the

[188] According to Bardesanes (according to Eusebius, *Anticipations of the Gospel*), there were some Christians in Persia before the end of the second century. In the time of Constantine (see his Epistle to Sapor [in Eusebius'] *Life of Constantine*, iv 13), they composed a flourishing church. Consult Beausobre, *Critical History of Manichaeanism*, i 180 [bk. ii, ch. 3], and the *Clement-Vatican Oriental Library* of Giuseppe Luigi Assemani.

[189] Origen, *Against Celsus*, viii 424.

dregs of the populace, of peasants and mechanics, of boys and women, of beggars and slaves; the last of whom might sometimes introduce the missionaries into the rich and noble families to which they belonged. These obscure teachers (such was the charge of malice and infidelity) are as mute in public as they are loquacious and dogmatical in private. Whilst they cautiously avoid the dangerous encounter of philosophers, they mingle with the rude and illiterate crowd, and insinuate themselves into those minds whom their age, their sex, or their education has the best disposed to receive the impression of superstitious terrors.[190]

· This unfavorable picture, though not devoid of a faint resemblance, betrays, by its dark coloring and distorted features, the pencil of an enemy. As the humble faith of Christ diffused itself through the world, it was embraced by several persons who derived some consequence from the advantages of nature or fortune. Aristides, who presented an eloquent apology to the emperor Hadrian, was an Athenian philosopher.[191] Justin Martyr had sought divine knowledge in the schools of Zeno, of Aristotle, of Pythagoras, and of Plato, before he fortunately was accosted by the old man, or rather the angel, who turned his attention to the study of the Jewish prophets.[192] Clemens of Alexandria had acquired much various reading in the Greek, and Tertullian in the Latin, language. Julius Africanus and Origen possessed a very considerable share of the learning of their times; and although the style of Cyprian is very different from that of Lactantius, we might almost discover that both those writers had been public teachers of rhetoric. Even the study of philosophy was at length introduced among the Christians, but it was not always productive of the most salutary effects: knowledge was as often the parent of heresy as of devotion, and the description which was designed for the followers of Artemon[193] may, with equal propriety, be applied to the various sects that

---

[190] Minucius Felix, ch. 8, with Wowerus's notes; Celsus, according to Origen, iii 138, 142; Julian, according to Cyril of Alexandria, *Against Julian,* vi 206, ed. Ezechiel Spanheim [1696].

[191] Eusebius, *Ecclesiastical History,* iv 3; Jerome, *Letters,* 83 [84].

[192] The story is prettily told in Justin's Dialogues [*Dialogue with Trypho,* pp. 3 ff.]. Tillemont (*Ecclesiastical Memoirs,* ii 334), who relates it after him, is sure that the old man was a disguised angel.

[193] [a third-century heretic, who held that Christ was a prophet rather than divine.]

resisted the successors of the apostles: "They presume to alter the Holy Scriptures, to abandon the ancient rule of faith, and to form their opinions according to the subtile precepts of logic. The science of the church is neglected for the study of geometry, and they lose sight of heaven while they are employed in measuring the earth. Euclid is perpetually in their hands. Aristotle and Theophrastus are the objects of their admiration; and they express an uncommon reverence for the works of Galen. Their errors are derived from the abuse of the arts and sciences of the infidels, and they corrupt the simplicity of the gospel by the refinements of human reason."[194]

Nor can it be affirmed with truth that the advantages of birth and fortune were always separated from the profession of Christianity. Several Roman citizens were brought before the tribunal of Pliny, and he soon discovered that a great number of persons of *every order* of men in Bithynia had deserted the religion of their ancestors.[195] His unsuspected testimony may, in this instance, obtain more credit than the bold challenge of Tertullian, when he addresses himself to the fears as well as to the humanity of the proconsul of Africa, by assuring him that, if he persists in his cruel intentions, he must decimate Carthage, and that he will find among the guilty many persons of his own rank, senators and matrons of noblest extraction, and the friends or relations of his most intimate friends.[196] It appears, however, that about forty years afterwards the emperor Valerian was persuaded of the truth of this assertion, since in one of his rescripts he evidently supposes that senators, Roman knights, and ladies of quality were engaged in the Christian sect.[197] The church still continued to increase its outward splendor as it lost its internal purity; and in the reign of Diocletian the palace, the courts of justice, and even the army concealed a multitude of Christians who endeavored to reconcile the interests of the present with those of a future life.

---

[194] Eusebius, v 28. It may be hoped that none, except the heretics, gave occasion to the complaint of Celsus (according to Origen, ii 77) that the Christians were perpetually correcting and altering their Gospels.

[195] Pliny, *Epistles,* x 97 [96]: "Others felt the same infatuation . . . Roman citizens. . . . Persons of every age, *of every order,* of both sexes, are, and will be, affected by the prosecution."

[196] Tertullian, *To Scapula.* Yet even his rhetoric rises no higher than to claim a tenth part of Carthage.

[197] Cyprian, *Epistles,* 80.

And yet these exceptions are either too few in number, or too recent in time, entirely to remove the imputation of ignorance and obscurity which has been so arrogantly cast on the first proselytes of Christianity. Instead of employing in our defense the fictions of later ages, it will be more prudent to convert the occasion of scandal into a subject of edification. Our serious thoughts will suggest to us that the apostles themselves were chosen by Providence among the fishermen of Galilee, and that the lower we depress the temporal condition of the first Christians, the more reason we shall find to admire their merit and success. It is incumbent on us diligently to remember that the kingdom of heaven was promised to the poor in spirit, and that minds afflicted by calamity and the contempt of mankind cheerfully listen to the divine promise of future happiness; while, on the contrary, the fortunate are satisfied with the possession of this world; and the wise abuse in doubt and dispute their vain superiority of reason and knowledge.

We stand in need of such reflections to comfort us for the loss of some illustrious characters, which in our eyes might have seemed the most worthy of the heavenly present. The names of Seneca, of the elder and the younger Pliny, of Tacitus, of Plutarch, of Galen, of the slave Epictetus, and of the emperor Marcus Antoninus, adorn the age in which they flourished, and exalt the dignity of human nature. They filled with glory their respective stations, either in active or contemplative life; their excellent understandings were improved by study; philosophy had purified their minds from the prejudices of the popular superstition; and their days were spent in the pursuit of truth and the practice of virtue. Yet all these sages (it is no less an object of surprise than of concern) overlooked or rejected the perfection of the Christian system. Their language or their silence equally discover their contempt for the growing sect, which in their time had diffused itself over the Roman empire. Those among them who condescend to mention the Christians consider them only as obstinate and perverse enthusiasts, who exacted an implicit submission to their mysterious doctrines, without being able to produce a single argument that could engage the attention of men of sense and learning.[198]

[198] Dr. Lardner, in his first and second volume[s] of Jewish and Christian testimonies [*Ancient Jewish and Heathen Testimonies*], collects and illustrates those of Pliny the younger, of Tacitus, of Galen, of Marcus Antoninus,

It is at least doubtful whether any of these philosophers perused the apologies which the primitive Christians repeatedly published in behalf of themselves and of their religion; but it is much to be lamented that such a cause was not defended by abler advocates. They expose with superfluous wit and eloquence the extravagance of polytheism. They interest our compassion by displaying the innocence and sufferings of their injured brethren. But when they would demonstrate the divine origin of Christianity, they insist much more strongly on the predictions which announced, than on the miracles which accompanied, the appearance of the Messiah. Their favorite argument might serve to edify a Christian or to convert a Jew, since both the one and the other acknowledge the authority of those prophecies, and both are obliged, with devout reverence, to search for their sense and their accomplishment. But this mode of persuasion loses much of its weight and influence when it is addressed to those who neither understand nor respect the Mosaic dispensation and the prophetic style.[199] In the unskillful hands of Justin and of the succeeding apologists, the sublime meaning of the Hebrew oracles evaporates in distant types, affected conceits, and cold allegories; and even their authenticity was rendered suspicious to an unenlightened Gentile by the mixture of pious forgeries, which, under the names of Orpheus, Hermes, and the Sibyls,[200] were obtruded on him as of equal value with the genuine inspirations of heaven. The adoption of fraud and sophistry in the defense of revelation too often reminds us of the injudicious

and perhaps of Epictetus (for it is doubtful whether that philosopher means to speak of the Christians). The new sect is totally unnoticed by Seneca, the elder Pliny, and Plutarch.

[199] If the famous prophecy of the Seventy Weeks had been alleged to a Roman philosopher, would he not have replied in the words of Cicero, "Tell me by what principle of augury does he arrive at years rather than at months or days?" (*On Divination*, ii 30). Observe with what irreverence Lucian (in *Alexander*, ch. 13) and his friend Celsus, according to Origen (vii 327), express themselves concerning the Hebrew prophets.

[200] The philosophers, who derided the more ancient predictions of the Sibyls, would easily have detected the Jewish and Christian forgeries, which have been so triumphantly quoted by the fathers, from Justin Martyr to Lactantius. When the Sibylline verses had performed their appointed task, they, like the system of the millennium, were quietly laid aside. The Christian Sibyl had unluckily fixed the ruin of Rome for the year 195, A.U.C. [*ab urbe condita*, from the founding of the City] 948.

conduct of those poets who load their *invulnerable* heroes with a useless weight of cumbersome and brittle armor.

But how shall we excuse the supine inattention of the pagan and philosophic world to those evidences which were presented by the hand of Omnipotence, not to their reason, but to their senses? During the age of Christ, of his apostles, and of their first disciples, the doctrine which they preached was confirmed by innumerable prodigies. The lame walked, the blind saw, the sick were healed, the dead were raised, demons were expelled, and the laws of nature were frequently suspended for the benefit of the church. But the sages of Greece and Rome turned aside from the awful spectacle, and, pursuing the ordinary occupations of life and study, appeared unconscious of any alterations in the moral or physical government of the world. Under the reign of Tiberius, the whole earth,[201] or at least a celebrated province of the Roman empire,[202] was involved in a preternatural darkness of three hours. Even this miraculous event, which ought to have excited the wonder, the curiosity, and the devotion of mankind, passed without notice in an age of science and history.[203] It happened during the lifetime of Seneca and the elder Pliny, who must have experienced the immediate effects, or received the earliest intelligence, of the prodigy. Each of these philosophers, in a laborious work, has recorded all the great phenomena of nature, earthquakes, meteors, comets, and eclipses, which his indefatigable curiosity could collect.[204] Both the one and the other have omitted to mention the greatest phenomenon to which the mortal eye has been witness since the creation of the

[201] The fathers, as they are drawn out in battle array by Dom [Augustin] Calmet (*Dissertations on the Bible,* iii 295-308 [1734, ii 322-27]), seem to cover the whole earth with darkness, in which they are followed by most of the moderns.

[202] Origen, *Commentary on Matthew* 27:45, and a few modern critics, [Theodore] Beza, Le Clerc, Lardner, etc., are desirous of confining it to the land of Judea.

[203] The celebrated passage of Phlegon is now wisely abandoned. When Tertullian assures the pagans that the mention of the prodigy is found in *arcanis* (not *archivis*) *vestris* (see his *Apology,* ch. 21), he probably appeals to the Sibylline verses, which relate it exactly in the words of the Gospel. [Modern editors of Tertullian agree in reading *arcanis.*]

[204] Seneca, *Nature Questions,* i 1, 15, vi 1, vii 17; Pliny, *Natural History,* ii.

globe. A distinct chapter of Pliny[205] is designed for eclipses of an extraordinary nature and unusual duration; but he contents himself with describing the singular defect of light which followed the murder of Caesar, when, during the greatest part of a year, the orb of the sun appeared pale and without splendor. This season of obscurity, which cannot surely be compared with the preternatural darkness of the Passion, had been already celebrated by most of the poets[206] and historians of that memorable age.[207]

[205] Pliny, *Natural History,* ii 30.

[206] Virgil, *Georgics,* i 466; Tibullus, *Poems,* II v 75; Ovid, *Metamorphoses,* xv 782; Lucan, *Concerning the Civil War,* i 540. The last of these poets places this prodigy before the civil war [between Caesar and Pompey].

[207] See a public epistle of M. Antony in Josephus, *Jewish Antiquities,* xiv 12. Plutarch in "Caesar" [*Works,* 1599], i 471 [741] [ch. 69]; Appian, *Civil Wars,* iv; Dion Cassius, i 431 (bk. xlv, ch. 17); Julius Obsequens [*Of Prodigies*], ch. 128. His little treatise is an abstract of Livy's prodigies.

❧ William Cowper ❧

William Cowper (1731-1800) was born in Great Berkhamsted, Hertfordshire, and educated at Westminster School. He studied law at the Middle and Inner Temples, but the prospect of making his way in public life brought on the first of a series of attacks of insanity in 1763. His conversion to Evangelicalism only relieved in part his feelings of guilt and helplessness, which were represented by his conviction that he was damned for eternity. For most of his remaining life he lived in retirement with his friend Mrs. Unwin, first in Olney, Buckinghamshire, where he benefited or suffered from the strong religious influence of the Rev. John Newton, and later in the neighboring village of Weston.

Cowper published a joint volume of hymns with Newton in 1779, and most of his poetry was written and published thereafter, when he was over fifty. His moral satires, written in heroic couplets, on such topics as hope, the progress of error, expostulation, and retirement, are largely ignored today, as are his many translations, including his version of Homer. He also wrote poems attacking "public" schools and polygamy. Cowper's reputation rests on *The Task* and on some of his shorter pieces, both serious and amusing; his letters are among the finest of the eighteenth century.

Editions: Life and Works, ed. Robert Southey (1835-37); *Poetical Works,* ed. H. S. Milford (1934); *Correspondence,* ed. Thomas Wright (1904); *Unpublished and Uncollected Letters,* ed. Thomas Wright (1925).

Biographies: M. J. Quinlan, *William Cowper* (1953); Charles Ryskamp, *William Cowper to 1768* (1959).

Critical Studies: Kenneth Maclean, "William Cowper," in *The Age of Johnson: Essays Presented to C. B. Tinker* (1949); Norman Nicholson, *William Cowper* (1951).

Lines Written During a Period of Insanity[1]
[?*1763*, 1816]

Hatred and vengeance, my eternal portion,
Scarce can endure delay of execution,
Wait with impatient readiness to seize my
        Soul in a moment.

Damned below Judas; more abhorred than he was,   5
Who for a few pence sold his holy Master.
Twice-betrayed Jesus me, the last delinquent,
        Deems the profanest.

Man disavows, and Deity disowns me;
Hell might afford my miseries a shelter;   10
Therefore Hell keeps her ever-hungry mouths all
        Bolted against me.

Hard lot! encompassed with a thousand dangers,
Weary, faint, trembling with a thousand terrors,
I'm called, if vanquished, to receive a sentence   15
        Worse than Abiram's.[2]

Him the vindictive rod of angry Justice
Sent quick and howling to the center headlong;
I, fed with judgment,[3] in a fleshly tomb, am
        Buried above ground.   20

[1] For the origin of this poem, see introductory sketch. Metrically it imitates the classical Sapphic line, especially if the Sapphic is given its Anglicized pronunciation.

[2] When Korah, Dathan, and Abiram rebelled against Moses, they and their followers were swallowed up by the earth (Numbers 16:1-35). In an account of his early life, Cowper wrote that at this period he expected "every moment that the earth would open her mouth and swallow me" (*Memoir* [1816], p. 58).

[3] The wicked leaders of the flock will be fed with God's judgment (that is, divine punishment), according to Ezekiel (34:7-16).

Olney Hymns
[1779]

XV. PRAISE FOR THE FOUNTAIN OPENED
[?1771-72]

ZECHARIAH 13:1[1]

There is a fountain filled with blood
    Drawn from Emmanuel's veins;
And sinners, plunged beneath that flood,
    Lose all their guilty stains.

The dying thief [2] rejoiced to see   5
    That fountain in his day;
And there have I, as vile as he,
    Washed all my sins away.

Dear dying Lamb, thy precious blood
    Shall never lose its power;   10
Till all the ransomed church of God
    Be saved, to sin no more.

E'er since, by faith, I saw the stream
    Thy flowing wounds supply;
Redeeming love has been my theme,   15
    And shall be till I die.

Then in a nobler sweeter song
    I'll sing thy power to save:
When this poor lisping stammering tongue
    Lies silent in the grave.   20

Lord, I believe thou hast prepared
    (Unworthy though I be)
For me a blood-bought free reward,
    A golden harp for me!

[1] "In that day [of the destruction and restoration of Jerusalem] there shall be a fountain [of purgation] opened to the house of David and to the inhabitants of Jerusalem for sin and for uncleanness."

[2] one of the two thieves hanged with Christ (Luke 23:39-43).

'Tis strung, and tuned, for endless years,　　25
　　And formed by power divine;
To sound in God the Father's ears,
　　No other name but thine.

XXXV. LIGHT SHINING OUT OF DARKNESS
[1773]

God moves in a mysterious way,
　　His wonders to perform;
He plants his footsteps in the sea,
　　And rides upon the storm.

Deep in unfathomable mines　　5
　　Of never failing skill,
He treasures up his bright designs,
　　And works his sovereign will.

Ye fearful saints[1] fresh courage take,
　　The clouds ye so much dread　　10
Are big with mercy, and shall break
　　In blessings on your head.

Judge not the Lord by feeble sense,
　　But trust him for his grace;
Behind a frowning providence,　　15
　　He hides a smiling face.

His purposes will ripen fast,
　　Unfolding every hour;
The bud may have a bitter taste,
　　But sweet will be the flower.　　20

Blind unbelief is sure to err,[2]
　　And scan[3] his work in vain;
God is his own interpreter,
　　And he will make it plain.

[1] believers.
[2] The original edition refers to John 13:7, where Jesus says, "What I do thou knowest not now; but thou shalt know hereafter."
[3] judge critically.

XXXVIII. TEMPTATION
[?1771-72]

The billows swell, the winds are high,
Clouds overcast my wintry sky;
Out of the depths to thee I call,
My fears are great, my strength is small.

O Lord, the pilot's part perform,   5
And guard and guide me through the storm;
Defend me from each threatening ill,
Control the waves, say, "Peace! be still."

Amidst the roaring of the sea,
My soul still hangs her hope on thee;   10
Thy constant love, thy faithful care,
Is all that saves me from despair.

Dangers of every shape and name
Attend the followers of the Lamb,
Who leave the world's deceitful shore,   15
And leave it to return no more.

Though tempest-tossed and half a wreck,
My Savior through the floods I seek;
Let neither winds nor stormy main
Force back my shattered bark again.   20

Verses
Supposed to Be Written by Alexander Selkirk,
During His Solitary Abode in the Island
of Juan Fernandez[1]
[1782]

I am monarch of all I survey,
    My right there is none to dispute,

---

[1] Selkirk quarreled with the captain of the ship on which he served, and disembarked or was abandoned on the island of Juan Fernandez off the coast of Chile. He was picked up by another ship in 1709, four years and four months later.

From the center all round to the sea,
    I am lord of the fowl and the brute.
Oh, solitude! where are the charms   5
    That sages have seen in thy face?
Better dwell in the midst of alarms
    Than reign in this horrible place.

I am out of humanity's reach,
    I must finish my journey alone,   10
Never hear the sweet music of speech,
    I start at the sound of my own.
The beasts that roam over the plain
    My form with indifference see;
They are so unacquainted with man,   15
    Their tameness is shocking to me.

Society, friendship, and love,
    Divinely bestowed upon man,
Oh, had I the wings of a dove,
    How soon would I taste you again!   20
My sorrows I then might assuage
    In the ways of religion and truth,
Might learn from the wisdom of age,
    And be cheered by the sallies of youth.

Religion! what treasure untold   25
    Resides in that heavenly word!
More precious than silver and gold,
    Or all that this earth can afford.
But the sound of the church-going bell
    These valleys and rocks never heard,   30
Ne'er sighed at the sound of a knell,
    Or smiled when a sabbath appeared.

Ye winds, that have made me your sport,
    Convey to this desolate shore
Some cordial endearing report   35
    Of a land I shall visit no more.
My friends, do they now and then send
    A wish or a thought after me?
O tell me I yet have a friend,
    Though a friend I am never to see.   40

How fleet is a glance of the mind!
   Compared with the speed of its flight,
The tempest itself lags behind,
   And the swift winged arrows of light.
When I think of my own native land,   45
   In a moment I seem to be there;
But alas! recollection at hand
   Soon hurries me back to despair.

But the sea-fowl is gone to her nest,
   The beast is laid down in his lair,   50
Even here is a season of rest,
   And I to my cabin repair.
There is mercy in every place,
   And mercy, encouraging thought!
Gives even affliction a grace,   55
   And reconciles man to his lot.

Epitaph on a Hare
[*1783*, 1784]

Here lies whom hound did ne'er pursue
   Nor swifter greyhound follow,
Whose foot ne'er tainted [1] morning dew,
   Nor ear heard huntsman's halloo.

Old Tiney, surliest of his kind,   5
   Who, nursed with tender care,
And to domestic bounds confined,
   Was still a wild jack hare.

Though duly from my hand he took
   His pittance every night,   10
He did it with a jealous look,
   And, when he could, would bite.

[1] imbued with his scent.

His diet was of wheaten bread,
   And milk, and oats, and straw,
Thistles, or lettuces instead,   15
   With sand to scour his maw.

On twigs of hawthorn he regaled,
   On pippins' russet peel,
And, when his juicy salads failed,
   Sliced carrot pleased him well.   20

A Turkey carpet was his lawn,
   Whereon he loved to bound,
To skip and gambol like a fawn,
   And swing his rump around.

His frisking was at evening hours,   25
   For then he lost his fear;
But most before approaching showers,
   Or when a storm drew near.

Eight years and five round-rolling moons
   He thus saw steal away,   30
Dozing out all his idle noons,
   And every night at play.

I kept him for his humor sake,
   For he would oft beguile
My heart of thoughts that made it ache,   35
   And force me to a smile.

But now beneath this walnut shade
   He finds his long, last home,
And waits, in snug concealment laid,
   Till gentler Puss[2] shall come.   40

He, still more agèd, feels the shocks
   From which no care can save,
And, partner once of Tiney's box,
   Must soon partake his grave.

[2] another of Cowper's hares. He died three years after Tiney, aged
almost twelve years.

The Task[1]

IV. THE WINTER EVENING
[*1783-84*, 1785]

Hark! 'tis the twanging horn! o'er yonder bridge
That with its wearisome but needful length
Bestrides the wintry flood, in which the moon
Sees her unwrinkled face reflected bright,
He comes, the herald of a noisy world,   5
With spattered boots, strapped waist, and frozen locks,
News from all nations lumbering at his back.
True to his charge, the close-packed load behind,
Yet careless what he brings, his one concern
Is to conduct it to the destined inn,[2]   10
And having dropped th' expected bag—pass on.
He whistles as he goes, light-hearted wretch,
Cold and yet cheerful: messenger of grief
Perhaps to thousands, and of joy to some;
To him indifferent whether grief or joy.   15
Houses in ashes, and the fall of stocks,
Births, deaths, and marriages, epistles wet
With tears that trickled down the writer's cheeks
Fast as the periods[3] from his fluent quill,
Or charged with amorous sighs of absent swains   20
Or nymphs responsive, equally affect
His horse and him, unconscious of them all.
But oh th' important budget![4] ushered in
With such heart-shaking music, who can say
What are its tidings? Have our troops awaked?   25
Or do they still, as if with opium drugged,

---

[1] When Cowper complained of being unable to find a subject for poetry, his friend Lady Austen assigned him the "task" of writing about a sofa, which led him to compose this didactic-descriptive poem in six books.

[2] which served as a post office.

[3] sentences.

[4] bag, pouch; figuratively, newspaper.

Snore to the murmurs of th' Atlantic wave?[5]
Is India free, and does she wear her plumed
And jewelled turban with a smile of peace,
Or do we grind her still?[6] The grand debate,   30
The popular harangue, the tart reply,
The logic, and the wisdom, and the wit,
And the loud laugh—I long to know them all;
I burn to set th' imprisoned wranglers free,
And give them voice and utterance once again.   35
    Now stir the fire, and close the shutters fast,
Let fall the curtains, wheel the sofa round,
And while the bubbling and loud-hissing urn
Throws up a steamy column, and the cups
That cheer but not inebriate, wait on each,[7]   40
So let us welcome peaceful evening in.
Not such his evening, who with shining face
Sweats in the crowded theater, and, squeezed
And bored with elbow-points through both his sides,
Outscolds the ranting actor on the stage;   45
Nor his, who patient stands till his feet throb,
And his head thumps, to feed upon the breath
Of patriots[8] bursting with heroic rage,
Or placemen,[9] all tranquillity and smiles.
This folio of four pages,[10] happy work!   50
Which not even critics criticize; that holds
Inquisitive attention, while I read,
Fast bound in chains of silence, which the fair,
Though eloquent themselves, yet fear to break;

[5] After the surrender of Yorktown in October, 1781, little action took place in America for the rest of the Revolutionary War.

[6] The British, under Warren Hastings, were involved in a war with Hyder 'Ali of Mysore and, after his death, with his son Tipu. Though peace negotiations had been opened, hostilities kept breaking out and were not definitely concluded until early 1784.

[7] Perhaps a reference not to tea but to Bishop Berkeley's favorite remedy, tar water, which Berkeley said was of a nature "to cheer but not inebriate" (*Siris,* sec. 217).

[8] members of the Opposition in Parliament.

[9] government officeholders and supporters (here, in Parliament).

[10] a common size for eighteenth-century newspapers.

What is it but a map of busy life,   55
Its fluctuations and its vast concerns?
Here runs the mountainous and craggy ridge
That tempts ambition. On the summit, see,
The seals of office glitter in his eyes;
He climbs, he pants, he grasps them. At his heels,   60
Close at his heels, a demagogue ascends,
And with a dexterous jerk soon twists him down,
And wins them, but to lose them in his turn.
Here rills of oily eloquence in soft
Meanders lubricate the course they take;   65
The modest speaker is ashamed and grieved
T' engross a moment's notice, and yet begs,
Begs a propitious ear for his poor thoughts,
However trivial all that he conceives.
Sweet bashfulness! it claims at least this praise: 70
The dearth of information and good sense,
That it foretells us, always comes to pass.
Cataracts of declamation thunder here;
There forests of no-meaning spread the page,
In which all comprehension wanders lost;   75
While fields of pleasantry amuse us there
With merry descants on a nation's woes.
The rest appears a wilderness of strange
But gay confusion: roses for the cheeks,
And lilies for the brows of faded age,   80
Teeth for the toothless, ringlets for the bald,
Heaven, earth, and ocean, plundered of their sweets,
Nectareous essences, Olympian dews,
Sermons, and city feasts, and favorite airs,
Ethereal journeys, submarine exploits,[11]   85
And Katterfelto,[12] with his hair on end

[11] The first balloon ascents were made in 1783. "Submarines" had been experimented with in the 1770's, but it is not known what Cowper specifically had in mind.

[12] a conjuror and quack doctor, who demonstrated such things as a "solar microscope" and who held "grand medley entertainments." His newspaper advertisements were headed, "Wonders! Wonders! Wonders! and Wonders!"

At his own wonders, wondering for his bread.
  'Tis pleasant through the loopholes of retreat
To peep at such a world. To see the stir
Of the great Babel and not feel the crowd;   90
To hear the roar she sends through all her gates,
At a safe distance, where the dying sound
Falls a soft murmur on th' uninjured ear.
Thus sitting, and surveying thus at ease
The globe and its concerns, I seem advanced   95
To some secure and more than mortal height,
That liberates and exempts me from them all.
It turns submitted to my view, turns round
With all its generations; I behold
The tumult, and am still. The sound of war   100
Has lost its terrors ere it reaches me;
Grieves but alarms me not. I mourn the pride
And avarice that make man a wolf to man;
Hear the faint echo of those brazen throats
By which he speaks the language of his heart,   105
And sigh, but never tremble at the sound.
He travels and expatiates,[13] as the bee
From flower to flower, so he from land to land;
The manners, customs, policy[14] of all
Pay contribution to the store he gleans;   110
He sucks intelligence in every clime,
And spreads the honey of his deep research
At his return, a rich repast for me.
He travels, and I too. I tread his deck,
Ascend his topmast, through his peering eyes   115
Discover countries, with a kindred heart
Suffer his woes, and share in his escapes;
While fancy, like the finger of a clock,
Runs the great circuit, and is still at home.
  O Winter! ruler of th' inverted year,   120
Thy scattered hair with sleet like ashes filled,
Thy breath congealed upon thy lips, thy cheeks
Fringed with a beard made white with other snows

[13] roams about.
[14] system of government.

Than those of age, thy forehead wrapped in clouds,
A leafless branch thy scepter, and thy throne   125
A sliding car indebted to no wheels,
But urged by storms along its slippery way,
I love thee, all unlovely as thou seem'st,
And dreaded as thou art. Thou hold'st the sun
A prisoner in the yet undawning east,   130
Shortening his journey between morn and noon,
And hurrying him, impatient of his stay,
Down to the rosy west; but kindly still
Compensating his loss with added hours
Of social converse and instructive ease,   135
And gathering at short notice in one group
The family dispersed, and fixing thought,
Not less dispersed by daylight and its cares.
I crown thee king of intimate delights,
Fireside enjoyments, home-born happiness,   140
And all the comforts that the lowly roof
Of undisturbed retirement and the hours
Of long uninterrupted evening know.
No rattling wheels stop short before these gates;
No powdered pert,[15] proficient in the art   145
Of sounding an alarm, assaults these doors
Till the street rings; no stationary steeds
Cough their own knell, while, heedless of the sound,
The silent circle fan themselves, and quake.
But here the needle plies its busy task,   150
The pattern grows, the well-depicted flower,
Wrought patiently into the snowy lawn,
Unfolds its bosom; buds and leaves and sprigs
And curling tendrils, gracefully disposed,
Follow the nimble finger of the fair;   155
A wreath that cannot fade, of flowers that blow
With most success when all besides decay.
The poet's or historian's page, by one
Made vocal for th' amusement of the rest;
The sprightly lyre, whose treasure of sweet sounds   160
The touch from many a trembling chord shakes out;

[15] impertinent person.

And the clear voice symphonious, yet distinct,
And in the charming strife triumphant still,
Beguile the night, and set a keener edge
On female industry: the threaded steel   165
Flies swiftly, and unfelt the task proceeds.
The volume closed, the customary rites
Of the last meal commence. A Roman meal,
Such as the mistress of the world once found
Delicious, when her patriots of high note,   170
Perhaps by moonlight, at their humble doors,
And under an old oak's domestic shade,
Enjoyed, spare feast! a radish and an egg.
Discourse ensues, not trivial, yet not dull,
Nor such as with a frown forbids the play   175
Of fancy, or proscribes the sound of mirth.
Nor do we madly, like an impious world,
Who deem religion frenzy, and the God
That made them an intruder on their joys,
Start at his awful name, or deem his praise   180
A jarring note. Themes of a graver tone,
Exciting oft our gratitude and love,
While we retrace with memory's pointing wand,
That calls the past to our exact review,
The dangers we have 'scaped, the broken snare,   185
The disappointed foe, deliverance found
Unlooked for, life preserved and peace restored,
Fruits of omnipotent eternal love.
"Oh evenings worthy of the gods!" exclaimed
The Sabine bard.[16] "Oh evenings," I reply,   190
"More to be prized and coveted than yours,
As more illumined, and with nobler truths,
That I, and mine, and those we love, enjoy."
    Is winter hideous in a garb like this?
Needs he the tragic fur,[17] the smoke of lamps,   195
The pent-up breath of an unsavory throng,
To thaw him into feeling; or the smart

[16] "O nights and banquets of the gods!" (Horace, *Satires*, II vi 65).
Horace here is also praising a rural evening.
[17] presumably the fur (e.g., royal ermine) worn by the tragedian.

And snappish dialogue, that flippant wits
Call comedy, to prompt him with a smile?
The self-complacent actor, when he views   200
(Stealing a sidelong glance at a full house)
The slope of faces, from the floor to th' roof,
(As if one master-spring controlled them all)
Relaxed into an universal grin,
Sees not a countenance there that speaks a joy   205
Half so refined or so sincere as ours.
Cards were superfluous here, with all the tricks
That idleness has ever yet contrived
To fill the void of an unfurnished brain,
To palliate dullness, and give time a shove.   210
Time, as he passes us, has a dove's wing,
Unsoiled and swift and of a silken sound;
But the world's Time is Time in masquerade.
Theirs, should I paint him, has his pinions fledged
With motley plumes; and, where the peacock shows   215
His azure eyes, is tinctured black and red
With spots quadrangular of diamond form,
Ensanguined hearts, clubs typical of strife,
And spades, the emblem of untimely graves.
What should be and what was an hourglass once,   220
Becomes a dice-box, and a billiard mast[18]
Well does the work of his destructive scythe.
Thus decked, he charms a world whom fashion blinds
To his true worth, most pleased when idle most,
Whose only happy are their wasted hours.   225
Even misses, at whose age their mothers wore
The back-string[19] and the bib, assume the dress
Of womanhood, sit pupils in the school
Of card-devoted time, and night by night
Placed at some vacant corner of the board,   230
Learn every trick, and soon play all the game.
But truce with censure. Roving as I rove,
Where shall I find an end, or how proceed?
As he that travels far, oft turns aside

[18] cue.
[19] leading string for children.

To view some rugged rock or moldering tower,   235
Which seen delights him not; then, coming home,
Describes and prints it, that the world may know
How far he went for what was nothing worth;
So I with brush in hand and palette spread,
With colors mixed for a far different use,   240
Paint cards and dolls and every idle thing
That fancy finds in her excursive flights.
　　Come, Evening, once again, season of peace;
Return, sweet Evening, and continue long!
Methinks I see thee in the streaky west,   245
With matron step slow-moving, while the night
Treads on thy sweeping train; one hand employed
In letting fall the curtain of repose
On bird and beast, the other charged for man
With sweet oblivion of the cares of day;   250
Not sumptuously adorned, nor needing aid,
Like homely featured night, of clustering gems;
A star or two, just twinkling on thy brow,
Suffices thee; save that the moon is thine
No less than hers, not worn indeed on high   255
With ostentatious pageantry, but set
With modest grandeur in thy purple zone,[20]
Resplendent less, but of an ampler round.
Come then, and thou shalt find thy vot'ry calm,
Or make me so. Composure is thy gift;   260
And, whether I devote thy gentle hours
To books, to music, or the poet's toil;
To weaving nets for bird-alluring fruit;
Or twining silken threads round ivory reels
When they command whom man was born to please;   265
I slight thee not, but make thee welcome still.
　　Just when our drawing rooms begin to blaze
With lights, by clear reflection multiplied
From many a mirror, in which he of Gath,
Goliah[21] might have seen his giant bulk   270
Whole without stooping, towering crest and all,

[20] encircling band, girdle.
[21] Goliath.

My pleasures too begin. But me perhaps
The glowing hearth may satisfy awhile
With faint illumination, that uplifts
The shadow to the ceiling, there by fits   275
Dancing uncouthly to the quivering flame.
Not undelightful is an hour to me
So spent in parlor twilight; such a gloom
Suits well the thoughtful or unthinking mind,
The mind contemplative, with some new theme   280
Pregnant, or indisposed alike to all.
Laugh ye, who boast your more mercurial powers,
That never feel a stupor, know no pause,
Nor need one; I am conscious, and confess,
Fearless, a soul that does not always think.   285
Me oft has fancy, ludicrous and wild,
Soothed with a waking dream of houses, towers,
Trees, churches, and strange visages, expressed
In the red cinders, while with poring eye
I gazed, myself creating what I saw.   290
Nor less amused have I quiescent watched
The sooty films that play upon the bars,
Pendulous,[21a] and foreboding in the view
Of superstition, prophesying still,
Though still deceived, some stranger's near approach.   295
'Tis thus the understanding takes repose
In indolent vacuity of thought,
And sleeps and is refreshed. Meanwhile the face
Conceals the mood lethargic with a mask
Of deep deliberation, as the man   300
Were tasked to his full strength, absorbed and lost.
Thus oft, reclined at ease, I lose an hour
At evening, till at length the freezing blast,
That sweeps the bolted shutter, summons home
The recollected powers; and, snapping short   305
The glassy threads with which the fancy weaves
Her brittle toys, restores me to myself.
How calm is my recess; and how the frost,
Raging abroad, and the rough wind, endear

[21a] the ashes hanging on the grate or fire-screen.

The silence and the warmth enjoyed within.   310
I saw the woods and fields, at close of day,
A variegated show: the meadows green,
  Though faded; and the lands, where lately waved
The golden harvest, of a mellow brown,
Upturned so lately by the forceful share.   315
I saw far off the weedy fallows smile
With verdure not unprofitable, grazed
By flocks, fast feeding, and selecting each
His favorite herb; while all the leafless groves
That skirt th' horizon wore a sable hue,   320
Scarce noticed in the kindred dusk of eve.
To-morrow brings a change, a total change!
Which even now, though silently performed,
And slowly, and by most unfelt, the face
Of universal nature undergoes.   325
Fast falls a fleecy shower. The downy flakes,
Descending, and with never-ceasing lapse,
Softly alighting upon all below,
Assimilate all objects. Earth receives
Gladly the thickening mantle, and the green   330
And tender blade, that feared the chilling blast,
Escapes unhurt beneath so warm a veil.
    In such a world, so thorny, and where none
Finds happiness unblighted, or, if found,
Without some thistly sorrow at its side,   335
It seems the part of wisdom, and no sin
Against the law of love, to measure lots
With less distinguished than ourselves, that thus
We may with patience bear our moderate ills,
And sympathize with others, suffering more.   340
Ill fares the traveller now, and he that stalks
In ponderous boots beside his reeking team.
The wain goes heavily, impeded sore
By congregated loads adhering close
To the clogged wheels; and in its sluggish pace,[22]   345
Noiseless, appears a moving hill of snow.
The toiling steeds expand the nostril wide,

[22] course, way.

While every breath, by respiration strong
Forced downward, is consolidated soon
Upon their jutting chests. He, formed to bear   350
The pelting brunt of the tempestuous night,
With half-shut eyes, and puckered cheeks, and teeth
Presented bare against the storm, plods on.
One hand secures his hat, save when with both
He brandishes his pliant length of whip,   355
Resounding oft, and never heard in vain.
Oh happy! and, in my account,[23] denied
That sensibility of pain with which
Refinement is endued, thrice happy thou!
Thy frame, robust and hardy, feels indeed   360
The piercing cold, but feels it unimpaired.
The learnèd finger never need explore
Thy vigorous pulse; and the unhealthful east,
That breathes the spleen,[24] and searches every bone
Of the infirm, is wholesome air to thee.   365
Thy days roll on, exempt from household care;
Thy wagon is thy wife; and the poor beasts
That drag the dull companion to and fro,
Thine helpless charge, dependent on thy care.
Ah, treat them kindly! rude as thou appear'st,   370
Yet show that thou hast mercy, which the great,
With needless hurry whirled from place to place,
Humane as they would seem, not always show.
    Poor, yet industrious, modest, quiet, neat;
Such claim compassion in a night like this,   375
And have a friend in every feeling heart.
Warmed, while it lasts, by labor, all day long
They brave the season, and yet find at eve,
Ill clad and fed but sparely, time to cool.
The frugal housewife trembles when she lights   380
Her scanty stock of brushwood, blazing clear
But dying soon, like all terrestrial joys.
The few small embers left she nurses well;
And, while her infant race, with outspread hands

[23] estimation.
[24] spreads melancholy.

And crowded knees, sit cowering o'er the sparks,   385
Retires, content to quake, so they be warmed.
The man feels least, as more inured than she
To winter, and the current in his veins
More briskly moved by his severer toil;
Yet he, too, finds his own distress in theirs.   390
The taper soon extinguished, which I saw
Dangled along at the cold finger's end
Just when the day declined, and the brown loaf
Lodged on the shelf, half eaten, without sauce
Of savory cheese, or butter costlier still,   395
Sleep seems their only refuge. For alas!
Where penury is felt the thought is chained,
And sweet colloquial pleasures are but few.
With all this thrift they thrive not. All the care
Ingenious parsimony takes but just   400
Saves the small inventory, bed and stool,
Skillet, and old carved chest, from public sale.
They live, and live without extorted alms
From grudging hands; but other boast have none
To soothe their honest pride that scorns to beg,   405
Nor comfort else, but in their mutual love.
I praise you much, ye meek and patient pair,
For ye are worthy; choosing rather far
A dry but independent crust, hard earned,
And eaten with a sigh, than to endure   410
The rugged frowns and insolent rebuffs
Of knaves in office, partial in the work
Of distribution: liberal of their aid
To clamorous importunity in rags,
But ofttimes deaf to suppliants who would blush   415
To wear a tattered garb however coarse,
Whom famine cannot reconcile to filth:
These ask with painful shyness, and, refused
Because deserving, silently retire.
But be ye of good courage. Time itself   420
Shall much befriend you. Time shall give increase,
And all your numerous progeny, well-trained
But helpless, in few years shall find their hands,

And labor too. Meanwhile ye shall not want
What, conscious of your virtues, we can spare,   425
Nor what a wealthier than ourselves may send.
I mean the man, who, when the distant poor
Need help, denies them nothing but his name.[25]
    But poverty, with most who whimper forth
Their long complaints, is self-inflicted woe,   430
Th' effect of laziness or sottish waste.
Now goes the nightly thief prowling abroad
For plunder; much solicitous how best
He may compensate for a day of sloth
By works of darkness and nocturnal wrong.   435
Woe to the gardener's pale, the farmer's hedge,
Plashed [26] neatly, and secured with driven stakes
Deep in the loamy bank. Uptorn by strength,
Resistless in so bad a cause, but lame
To better deeds, he bundles up the spoil,   440
As ass's burden, and, when laden most
And heaviest, light of foot steals fast away.
Nor does the boarded hovel better guard
The well-stacked pile of riven logs and roots
From his pernicious force. Nor will he leave   445
Unwrenched the door, however well secured,
Where chanticleer amidst his harem sleeps
In unsuspecting pomp. Twitched from the perch,
He gives the princely bird with all his wives
To his voracious bag, struggling in vain,   450
And loudly wondering at the sudden change.
Nor this to feed his own. 'Twere some excuse
Did pity of their sufferings warp aside
His principle, and tempt him into sin
For their support, so destitute. But they   455
Neglected pine at home; themselves, as more
Exposed than others, with less scruple made
His victims, robbed of their defenseless all.
Cruel is all he does. 'Tis quenchless thirst

---

[25] Robert Smith, later first Baron Carrington.
[26] made with interwoven branches, etc.

Of ruinous ebriety[27] that prompts   460
His every action, and imbrutes the man.
Oh for a law to noose the villain's neck
Who starves his own, who persecutes the blood
He gave them in his children's veins, and hates
And wrongs the woman he has sworn to love.   465
   Pass where we may, through city or through town,
Village or hamlet of this merry land,
Though lean and beggared, every twentieth pace
Conducts th' unguarded nose to such a whiff
Of stale debauch, forth-issuing from the sties   470
That law has licensed, as makes temperance reel.
There sit involved and lost in curling clouds
Of Indian fume, and guzzling deep, the boor,
The lackey, and the groom. The craftsman there
Takes a Lethean leave of all his toil;   475
Smith, cobbler, joiner, he that plies the shears,
And he that kneads the dough; all loud alike,
All learnèd, and all drunk. The fiddle screams
Plaintive and piteous, as it wept and wailed
Its wasted tones and harmony unheard: 480
Fierce the dispute, whate'er the theme; while she,
Fell Discord, abitress of such debate,
Perched on the signpost, holds with even hand
Her undecisive scales. In this she lays
A weight of ignorance, in that, of pride,   485
And smiles delighted with th' eternal poise.
Dire is the frequent curse and its twin sound
The cheek-distending oath, not to be praised
As ornamental, musical, polite,
Like those which modern senators employ,   490
Whose oath is rhetoric, and who swear for fame.
Behold the schools in which plebeian minds,
Once simple, are initiated in arts
Which some may practise with politer grace,
But none with readier skill! 'tis here they learn   495
The road that leads from competence[28] and peace

[27] drunkenness.
[28] financial sufficiency.

To indigence and rapine; till at last
Society, grown weary of the load,
Shakes her incumbered lap, and casts them out.
But censure profits little. Vain th' attempt   500
To advertise in verse a public pest,
That, like the filth with which the peasant feeds
His hungry acres, stinks, and is of use.
Th' excise is fattened with the rich result
Of all this riot; and ten thousand casks,   505
Forever dribbling out their base contents,
Touched by the Midas finger of the state,
Bleed gold for ministers to sport away.
Drink and be mad then. 'Tis your country bids.
Gloriously drunk, obey th' important call.   510
Her cause demands th' assistance of your throats;
Ye all can swallow, and she asks no more.
    Would I had fallen upon those happier days
That poets celebrate. Those golden times
And those Arcadian scenes that Maro[29] sings,   515
And Sidney,[30] warbler of poetic prose.
Nymphs were Dianas then, and swains had hearts
That felt their virtues. Innocence it seems,
From courts dismissed, found shelter in the groves;
The footsteps of simplicity, impressed   520
Upon the yielding herbage (so they sing)
Then were not all effaced. Then, speech profane
And manners profligate were rarely found,
Observed as prodigies, and soon reclaimed.
Vain wish! those days were never. Airy dreams   525
Sat for the picture. And the poet's hand,
Imparting substance to an empty shade,
Imposed a gay delirium for a truth.
Grant it. I still must envy them an age
That favored such a dream, in days like these   530
Impossible, when virtue is so scarce
That to suppose a scene where she presides,

[29] Virgil (Publius Virgilius Maro). His *Eclogues* are pastoral or Arcadian.
[30] Sir Philip Sidney, author of the *Arcadia* (1593), a long pastoral prose
romance.

Is tramontane,[31] and stumbles all belief.
No. We are polished now. The rural lass,
Whom once her virgin modesty and grace,   535
Her artless manners, and her neat attire,
So dignified, that she was hardly less
Than the fair shepherdess of old romance,
Is seen no more. The character is lost.
Her head, adorned with lappets[32] pinned aloft,   540
And ribands streaming gay, superbly[33] raised
And magnified beyond all human size,
Indebted to some smart wig-weaver's hand
For more than half the tresses it sustains;
Her elbows ruffled, and her tottering form   545
Ill propped upon French heels, she might be deemed
(But that the basket dangling on her arm
Interprets her more truly) of a rank
Too proud for dairy work, or sale of eggs.
Expect her soon with footboy at her heels,   550
No longer blushing for her awkward load,
Her train and her umbrella all her care.
   The town has tinged the country. And the stain
Appears a spot upon a vestal's robe,
The worse for what it soils. The fashion runs   555
Down into scenes still rural, but alas!
Scenes rarely graced with rural manners now.
Time was when in the pastoral retreat
Th' unguarded door was safe. Men did not watch
T' invade another's right, or guard their own.   560
Then sleep was undisturbed by fear, unscared
By drunken howlings; and the chilling tale
Of midnight murther was a wonder heard
With doubtful credit, told to frighten babes.
But farewell now to unsuspicious nights,   565
And slumbers unalarmed. Now, ere you sleep,
See that your polished arms be primed with care,
And drop the night-bolt. Ruffians are abroad,

[31] beyond the mountain; figuratively, strange, foreign.
[32] loose flaps or folds of headdress.
[33] magnificently; but also with the sense of its Latin root, proudly.

And the first larum of the cock's shrill throat
May prove a trumpet, summoning your ear   570
To horrid sounds of hostile feet within.
Even daylight has its dangers. And the walk
Through pathless wastes and woods, unconscious once
Of other tenants than melodious birds,
Or harmless flocks, is hazardous and bold.   575
Lamented change! to which full many a cause
Inveterate, hopeless of a cure, conspires.
The course of human things from good to ill,
From ill to worse, is fatal,[34] never fails.
Increase of power begets increase of wealth,   580
Wealth luxury, and luxury excess;
Excess, the scrofulous and itchy plague
That seizes first the opulent, descends
To the next rank contagious, and in time
Taints downward all the graduated scale   585
Of order, from the chariot to the plough.
The rich, and they that have an arm to check
The license of the lowest in degree,
Desert their office; and themselves intent
On pleasure haunt the capital, and thus   590
To all the violence of lawless hands
Resign the scenes their presence might protect.
Authority herself not seldom sleeps,
Though resident, and witness of the wrong.
The plump convivial parson often bears   595
The magisterial sword in vain, and lays
His reverence and his worship both to rest
On the same cushion of habitual sloth.[35]
Perhaps timidity restrains his arm;
When he should strike, he trembles, and sets free,   600
Himself enslaved by terror of the band,
Th' audacious convict, whom he dares not bind.
Perhaps, though by profession ghostly[36] pure,

[34] destined, fated.
[35] The parson might serve as the local J.P., thus being entitled both "His Reverence" and "His Worship."
[36] spiritually.

He too may have his vice, and sometimes prove
Less dainty than becomes his grave outside,   605
In lucrative concerns. Examine well
His milk-white hand. The palm is hardly clean—
But here and there an ugly smutch appears.
Foh! 'twas a bribe that left it. He has touched
Corruption. Whoso seeks an audit here   610
Propitious, pays his tribute, game or fish,
Wildfowl or venison, and his errand speeds.
    But faster far and more than all the rest,
A noble cause, which none who bears a spark
Of public virtue ever wished removed,   615
Works the deplored and mischievous effect.
'Tis universal soldiership has stabbed
The heart of merit in the meaner class.
Arms, through the vanity and brainless rage
Of those that bear them, in whatever cause,   620
Seem most at variance with all moral good,
And incompatible with serious thought.
The clown, the child of nature, without guile,
Blessed with an infant's ignorance of all
But his own simple pleasures, now and then   625
A wrestling match, a foot-race, or a fair,
Is balloted,[37] and trembles at the news.
Sheepish he doffs his hat, and mumbling swears
A Bible-oath to be whate'er they please,
To do he knows not what. The task performed,   630
That instant he becomes the sergeant's care,
His pupil, and his torment, and his jest.
His awkward gait, his introverted toes,
Bent knees, round shoulders, and dejected looks,
Procure him many a curse. By slow degrees,   635
Unapt to learn and formed of stubborn stuff,
He yet by slow degrees puts off himself,
Grows conscious of a change, and likes it well.
He stands erect, his slouch becomes a walk,
He steps right onward, martial in his air,   640
His form, and movement; is as smart above

[37] chosen by lot; drafted.

As meal [38] and larded locks can make him; wears
His hat, or his plumed helmet, with a grace,
And, his three years of heroship expired,
Returns indignant to the slighted plough.   645
He hates the field in which no fife or drum
Attends him, drives his cattle to a march,
And sighs for the smart comrades he has left.
'Twere well if his exterior change were all—
But with his clumsy port the wretch has lost   650
His ignorance and harmless manners too.
To swear, to game, to drink, to show at home
By lewdness, idleness, and sabbath-breach,
The great proficiency he made abroad;
T' astonish and to grieve his gazing friends,   655
To break some maiden's and his mother's heart;
To be a pest where he was useful once,
Are his sole aim, and all his glory now.
     Man in society is like a flower
Blown[39] in its native bed. 'Tis there alone   660
His faculties expanded in full bloom
Shine out, there only reach their proper use.
But man, associated and leagued with man
By regal warrant, or self-joined by bond
For interest sake, or swarming into clans   665
Beneath one head for purposes of war,
Like flowers selected from the rest, and bound
And bundled close to fill some crowded vase,
Fades rapidly, and, by compression marred,
Contracts defilement not to be endured.   670
Hence chartered boroughs[40] are such public plagues,
And burghers, men immaculate perhaps
In all their private functions, once combined
Become a loathsome body, only fit
For dissolution, hurtful to the main.   675
Hence merchants, unimpeachable of sin

---

[38] used for powdering the hair.
[39] blossomed.
[40] municipal governments established by royal charter. (Cf. the use of "chartered" in Blake's *London.*)

Against the charities of domestic life,
Incorporated, seem at once to lose
Their nature, and, disclaiming all regard
For mercy and the common rights of man,   680
Build factories[41] with blood, conducting trade
At the sword's point, and dyeing the white robe
Of innocent commercial justice red.
Hence, too, the field of glory, as the world
Misdeems it, dazzled by its bright array,   685
With all the majesty of its thundering pomp,
Enchanting music and immortal wreaths,
Is but a school where thoughtlessness is taught
On principle, where foppery atones
For folly, gallantry[42] for every vice.   690
   But slighted as it is, and by the great
Abandoned, and, which still I more regret,
Infected with the manners and the modes
It knew not once, the country wins me still.
I never framed a wish, or formed a plan   695
That flattered me with hopes of earthly bliss,
But there I laid the scene. There early strayed
My fancy, ere yet liberty of choice
Had found me, or the hope of being free.
My very dreams were rural, rural, too,   700
The first-born efforts of my youthful Muse,
Sportive, and jingling her poetic bells
Ere yet her ear was mistress of their powers.
No bard could please me but whose lyre was tuned
To Nature's praises. Heroes and their feats   705
Fatigued me, never weary of the pipe
Of Tityrus,[43] assembling, as he sang,
The rustic throng beneath his favorite beech.
Then Milton had indeed a poet's charm.
New to my taste, his Paradise surpassed   710
The struggling efforts of my boyish tongue
To speak its excellence; I danced for joy.

[41] trading stations of a merchant company, as in India.
[42] amorous intrigue.
[43] one of the shepherds in Virgil's first *Eclogue*.

I marvelled much that, at so ripe an age
As twice seven years, his beauties had then first
Engaged my wonder, and admiring still,   715
And still admiring, with regret supposed
The joy half lost because not sooner found.
Thee too enamored of the life I loved,
Pathetic in its praise, in its pursuit
Determined, and possessing it at last   720
With transports such as favored lovers feel,
I studied, prized, and wished that I had known,
Ingenious Cowley! [44] and, though now reclaimed,
By modern lights from an erroneous taste,
I cannot but lament thy splendid wit   725
Entangled in the cobwebs of the schools.[45]
I still revere thee, courtly though retired,
Though stretched at ease in Chertsey's[46] silent bowers
Not unemployed, and finding rich amends
For a lost world in solitude and verse.   730
'Tis born with all. The love of Nature's works
Is an ingredient in the compound, man,
Infused at the creation of the kind.
And, though th' Almighty Maker has throughout
Discriminated each from each, by strokes   735
And touches of his hand, with so much art
Diversified, that two were never found
Twins at all points—yet this obtains in all,
That all discern a beauty in his works,
And all can taste them: minds that have been formed   740
And tutored, with a relish more exact,
But none without some relish, none unmoved.
It is a flame that dies not even there,
Where nothing feeds it. Neither business, crowds,
Nor habits of luxurious city life,   745
Whatever else they smother of true worth
In human bosoms, quench it or abate.

[44] Abraham Cowley (1618-67), last of the Metaphysical poets.
[45] scholastic philosophy.
[46] a village in Surrey, where Cowley retired after having failed to receive
the rewards he had hoped for at the Restoration.

The villas with which London stands begirt,
Like a swarth Indian with his belt of beads,
Prove it. A breath of unadulterate air,   750
The glimpse of a green pasture, how they cheer
The citizen, and brace his languid frame!
Even in the stifling bosom of the town,
A garden, in which nothing thrives, has charms
That soothe the rich possessor; much consoled,   755
That here and there some sprigs of mournful mint,
Of nightshade, or valerian grace the well [47]
He cultivates. These serve him with a hint
That nature lives, that sight-refreshing green
Is still the livery she delights to wear,   760
Though sickly samples of th' exuberant whole.
What are the casements lined with creeping herbs,
The prouder sashes fronted with a range
Of orange, myrtle, or the fragrant weed,
The Frenchman's darling? [48] are they not all proofs   765
That man, immured in cities, still retains
His inborn inextinguishable thirst
Of rural scenes, compensating his loss
By supplemental shifts, the best he may?
The most unfurnished with the means of life,   770
And they that never pass their brick-wall bounds
To range the fields and treat their lungs with air,
Yet feel the burning instinct: overhead
Suspend their crazy [49] boxes planted thick
And watered duly. There the pitcher stands   775
A fragment, and the spoutless teapot there;
Sad witnesses how close-pent man regrets
The country, with what ardor he contrives
A peep at nature, when he can no more.
  Hail, therefore, patroness of health and ease   780
And contemplation, heart-consoling joys
And harmless pleasures, in the thronged abode
Of multitudes unknown! hail, rural life!

[47] presumably the space between buildings which lets in light and air.
[48] mignonette (Cooper).
[49] shaky, infirm.

Address himself who will to the pursuit
Of honors, or emolument, or fame,   785
I shall not add myself to such a chase,
Thwart his attempts, or envy his success.
Some must be great. Great offices will have
Great talents. And God gives to every man
The virtue, temper, understanding, taste,   790
That lifts him into life, and lets him fall
Just in the niche he was ordained to fill.
To the deliverer of an injured land
He gives a tongue t' enlarge upon, an heart
To feel, and courage to redress her wrongs;   795
To monarchs dignity, to judges sense,
To artists ingenuity and skill;
To me an unambitious mind, content
In the low vale of life, that early felt
A wish for ease and leisure, and ere long   800
Found here that leisure and that ease I wished.

On the Death of Mrs. Throckmorton's Bullfinch[1]
[1788, 1789]

Ye nymphs! if e'er your eyes were red
With tears o'er hapless favorites shed,
   O share Maria's grief!
Her favorite, even in his cage
(What will not hunger's cruel rage?)   5
   Assassined by a thief.

Where Rhenus[2] strays his vines among,
The egg was laid from which he sprung,
   And though by nature mute,
Or only with a whistle blessed,   10
Well-taught, he all the sounds expressed
   Of flageolet or flute.[3]

---

[1] Cowper and Mrs. Unwin lived in a house at Weston belonging to their friends and neighbors, John (later Sir John) and Maria Catherine Throckmorton.

[2] Rhine.   [3] See Smart, *Song to David,* ll. 386-87.

The honors[4] of his ebon poll
Were brighter than the sleekest mole;
   His bosom of the hue   15
With which Aurora decks the skies,
When piping winds shall soon arise
   To sweep up all the dew.

Above, below, in all the house,
Dire foe, alike to bird and mouse,   20
   No cat had leave to dwell;
And Bully's cage supported stood,
On props of smoothest-shaven wood,
   Large built and latticed well.

Well-latticed—but the grate, alas!   25
Not rough with wire of steel or brass,
   For Bully's plumage sake,
But smooth with wands from Ouse's[5] side,
With which, when neatly peeled and dried,
   The swains their baskets make.   30

Night veiled the pole. All seemed secure.
When led by instinct sharp and sure,
   Subsistence to provide,
A beast forth sallied on the scout,
Long backed, long tailed, with whiskered snout,   35
   And badger-colored hide.

He, entering at the study door,
Its ample area 'gan explore;
   And something in the wind
Conjectured, sniffing round and round,   40
Better than all the books he found,
   Food, chiefly, for the mind.

Just then, by adverse fate impressed,
A dream disturbed poor Bully's rest;
   In sleep he seemed to view   45
A rat, fast-clinging to the cage,
And, screaming at the sad presage,
   Awoke and found it true.

[4] ornamental hairs.   [5] the nearby river.

For, aided both by ear and scent,
Right to his mark the monster went—   50
   Ah, Muse! forbear to speak
Minute the horrors that ensued;
His teeth were strong, the cage was wood—
   He left poor Bully's beak.

He left it—but he should have ta'en   55
That beak, whence issued many a strain
   Of such mellifluous tone,
Might have repaid him well, I wote,[6]
For silencing so sweet a throat,
   Fast set within his own.   60

Maria weeps—the Muses mourn—
So, when by Bacchanalians torn,
   On Thracian Hebrus' side
The tree-enchanter Orpheus fell,
His head alone remained to tell   65
   The cruel death he died.[7]

The Castaway[1]

[*1799*, 1803]

Obscurest night involved the sky,
   Th' Atlantic billows roared,

---

[6] know.

[7] Orpheus was so great a musician that trees and rocks followed the sounds of his lyre. He was torn to pieces and his head thrown into the Hebrus by Thracian women during a Bacchanalian orgy (see Ovid, *Metamorphoses*, xi 1-60, and Milton, *Lycidas*, ll. 58-63).

[1] Taken from an incident in Richard Walter's *A Voyage Round the World by George Anson* (1748), which Cowper recollected many years after reading the book. While rounding Cape Horn in a storm, Walter says, "one of our ablest seamen was canted overboard; and notwithstanding the

When such a destined wretch as I,
    Washed headlong from on board,
Of friends, of hope, of all bereft,   5
His floating home for ever left.

No braver chief [2] could Albion boast
    Than he with whom he went,
Nor ever ship left Albion's coast,
    With warmer wishes sent.   10
He loved them both, but both in vain,
Nor him beheld, nor her again.

Not long beneath the whelming brine,
    Expert to swim, he lay;
Nor soon he felt his strength decline,   15
    Or courage die away;
But waged with death a lasting strife,
Supported by despair of life.

He shouted: nor his friends had failed
    To check the vessel's course,   20
But so the furious blast prevailed,
    That, pitiless perforce,
They left their outcast mate behind,
And scudded still before the wind.

Some succour yet they could afford;   25
    And, such as storms allow,
The cask, the coop,[3] the floated cord,
    Delayed not to bestow.
But he (they knew) nor ship, nor shore,
Whate'er they gave, should visit more.   30

---

prodigious agitation of the waves, we perceived that he swam very strong,
and it was with the utmost concern that we found ourselves incapable of
assisting him; and we were the more grieved at his unhappy fate since we
lost sight of him struggling with the waves, and conceived from the manner
in which he swam that he might continue sensible for a considerable time
longer of the horror attending his irretrievable situation" (bk. i, ch. 8).

[2] George Anson, later an admiral and first Baron Anson, led this expedi-
tion against the Spanish.

[3] wicker basket used in catching fish.

Nor, cruel as it seemed, could he
   Their haste himself condemn,
Aware that flight, in such a sea,
   Alone could rescue them;
Yet bitter felt it still to die   35
Deserted, and his friends so nigh.

He long survives, who lives an hour
   In ocean, self-upheld;
And so long he, with unspent power,
   His destiny repelled;   40
And ever, as the minutes flew,
Entreated help, or cried, "Adieu!"

At length, his transient respite past,
   His comrades, who before
Had heard his voice in every blast,   45
   Could catch the sound no more.
For then, by toil subdued, he drank
The stifling wave, and then he sank.

No poet wept him: but the page
   Of narrative sincere,   50
That tells his name, his worth, his age,
   Is wet with Anson's tear.
And tears by bards or heroes shed
Alike immortalize the dead.

I therefore purpose not, or dream,   55
   Descanting on his fate,
To give the melancholy theme
   A more enduring date:
But misery still delights to trace
Its semblance in another's case.   60

No voice divine the storm allayed,
   No light propitious shone;
When, snatched from all effectual aid,
   We perished, each alone:
But I beneath a rougher sea,   65
And whelmed in deeper gulfs than he.

❧ Robert Burns ❧

Robert Burns (1759-96), the son of a poor tenant farmer, was born in Alloway, Ayrshire. His education was largely self-acquired, and he was an unknown Ayrshire farmer himself when, in 1786, he had a book of poems printed locally at Kilmarnock. This book brought him a brief season of attention in Edinburgh, after which he leased an unproductive farm and worked as an exciseman. In 1791, he gave up the farm and moved to Dumfries to attend better to his excise duties; he spent the rest of his brief life there.

Burns's best poetry, which comes out of, and serves as climax to, the Scots vernacular tradition, consists of two main kinds: satires and lyrics. The satires, several of which remained unpublished during his lifetime, concentrate on the rigidity and hypocrisy of contemporary Presbyterianism; in their outlook they naturally complement the liberal and passionate attitude of the lyrics. Satire and lyric, with their emphasis on the natural goodness and equally natural imperfections of man, are fused in the most brilliant of Burns's poems, *The Jolly Beggars*.

Editions: Poetry, ed. William E. Henley and T. F. Henderson (1896-97); *Songs*, ed. James C. Dick (1903); *Letters*, ed. J. De Lancey Ferguson (1931).

Biographies: F. B. Snyder, *Life of Robert Burns* (1932); De Lancey Ferguson, *Pride and Passion* (1939).

Critical Studies: John Speirs, *The Scots Literary Tradition* (1940); David Daiches, *Robert Burns* (1950); Thomas Crawford, *Burns: A Study of the Poems and Songs* (1960).

The Holy Fair[1]
[?*1785*, 1786]

A robe of seeming truth and trust
Hid crafty observation;
And secret hung, with poison'd crust,
The dirk of defamation:
A mask that like the gorget show'd,
Dye-varying on the pigeon;
And for a mantle large and broad,
He wrapt him in Religion.

HYPOCRISY À LA MODE.

Upon a simmer Sunday morn,
  When Nature's face is fair,
I walkèd forth to view the corn,
  An' snuff the caller[2] air.
The rising sun, owre Galston muirs,   5
  Wi' glorious light was glintin;
The hares were hirplin[3] down the furs,[4]
  The lav'rocks[5] they were chantin
         Fu' sweet that day.

As lightsomely I glowr'd [6] abroad,   10
  To see a scene sae gay,
Three hizzies,[7] early at the road,
  Cam skelpin[8] up the way.
Twa had manteeles o' dolefu' black,
  But ane[9] wi' lyart[10] lining;   15
The third, that gaed a wee aback,[11]
  Was in the fashion shining,
         Fu' gay that day.

---

[1] "Holy Fair" is a common phrase in the West of Scotland for a sacramental occasion (Burns). The taking of Communion was generally a once-a-year affair, which was accompanied by outdoor preaching.
  [2] cool.   [3] hopping.   [4] furrows.   [5] larks.   [6] glanced.
  [7] hussies, young women.
  [8] hurrying noisily.
  [9] one.   [10] gray.
  [11] came a little behind.

The twa appear'd like sisters twin,
    In feature, form, an' claes;[12]   20
Their visage wither'd, lang an' thin,
    An' sour as ony slaes:[13]
The third cam up, hap-step-an'-lowp,[14]
    As light as ony lambie,
An' wi' a curchie[15] low did stoop,   25
    As soon as e'er she saw me,
                            Fu' kind that day.

Wi' bonnet aff, quoth I, "Sweet lass,
    I think ye seem to ken me;
I'm sure I've seen that bonie[16] face,   30
    But yet I canna name ye."
Quo' she, an' laughin as she spak,
    An' taks me by the han's,
"Ye, for my sake, hae gi'en the feck[17]
    Of a' the Ten Comman's   35
                            A screed [18] some day.

"My name is Fun—your cronie dear,
    The nearest friend ye hae;
An' this is Superstition here,
    An' that's Hypocrisy.   40
I'm gaun to Mauchline[19] Holy Fair,
    To spend an hour in daffin:[20]
Gin[21] ye'll go there, yon runkl'd [22] pair,
    We will get famous laughin[23]
                            At them this day."   45

Quoth I, "Wi' a' my heart, I'll do't;
    I'll get my Sunday's sark[24] on,
An' meet you on the holy spot;
    Faith, we'se hae fine remarkin!"
Then I gaed hame at crowdie-time[25]   50

---

[12] clothes.   [13] sloes.   [14] jump.
[15] curtsy.   [16] bonny, pretty.
[17] the greater part.   [18] rip, tear.
[19] a small Ayrshire town.
[20] having fun.   [21] if.   [22] wrinkled.
[23] a great laugh.   [24] shirt.
[25] porridge time, breakfast.

An' soon I made me ready;
For roads were clad, frae side to side,
  Wi' mony a wearie body,
        In droves that day.

Here farmers gash[26] in ridin graith[27]   55
  Gaed hoddin by their cotters;[28]
There swankies young[29] in braw[30] braid-claith
  Are springin owre the gutters.
The lasses, skelpin barefit, thrang,[31]
  In silks an' scarlets glitter;   60
Wi' sweet-milk cheese, in mony a whang,[32]
  An' farls[33] bak'd wi' butter
        Fu' crump[34] that day.

When by the plate we set our nose,
  Weel heapèd up wi' ha'pence,   65
A greedy glow'r Black Bonnet[35] throws,
  An' we maun draw[36] our tippence.
Then in we go to see the show,
  On ev'ry side they're gath'rin,
Some carryin dails,[37] some chairs an' stools,   70
  An' some are busy bleth'rin[38]
        Right loud that day.

Here stands a shed to fend the show'rs,
  An' screen our countra gentry;
There Racer Jess[39] an' twa-three whores   75
  Are blinkin at the entry.[40]

[26] well-dressed.   [27] gear.
[28] went jogging past their tenants.
[29] robust young men.
[30] "brave," fine.
[31] thronged.   [32] slice.
[33] small oatcakes.
[34] crisp.
[35] an elder of the church.
[36] must draw out.
[37] deal planks.
[38] blithering, gabbling.
[39] a half-witted woman, noted for her swiftness.
[40] leering at the door.

Here sits a raw o' tittlin jads,[41]
  Wi' heavin breasts an' bare neck,
An' there a batch o' wabster[42] lads,
    Blackguardin frae Kilmarnock   80
        For fun this day.

Here some are thinkin on their sins,
  An' some upo' their claes;
Ane curses feet that fyl'd[43] his shins,
  Anither sighs an' prays: 85
On this hand sits a chosen swatch,[44]
  Wi' screw'd up, grace-proud faces;
On that a set o' chaps, at watch,
  Thrang[45] winkin on the lasses
        To chairs[46] that day.   90

O happy is that man an' blest![47]
  Nae wonder that it pride him!
Whase ain dear lass, that he likes best,
  Comes clinkin down beside him!
Wi' arm repos'd on the chair-back   95
  He sweetly does compose him;
Which, by degrees, slips round her neck,
  An's loof[48] upon her bosom
        Unkend[49] that day.

Now a'[50] the congregation o'er   100
  Is silent expectation;
For Moodie[51] speels the holy door,[52]

[41] row of tittering wenches.
[42] webster, weaver.
[43] defiled, dirtied.
[44] sample.
[45] busy.
[46] to come take chairs (beside them).
[47] Psalm 146:5 (Scottish Metrical Version).
[48] and his palm.
[49] unperceived.
[50] all.
[51] the Rev. Alexander Moodie, known for his violent fire and brimstone preaching.
[52] climbs (enters) the pulpit.

Wi' tidings o' damnation.[53]
Should Hornie,[54] as in ancient days,
  'Mang sons o' God present him,[55]   105
The very sight o' Moodie's face
  To's ain het hame[56] had sent him
                Wi' fright that day.

Hear how he clears the points o' faith
  Wi' rattlin an' thumpin!   110
Now meekly calm, now wild in wrath,
  He's stampin an' he's jumpin!
His lengthen'd chin, his turn'd-up snout,
  His eldritch[57] squeel an' gestures,
O how they fire the heart devout—   115
  Like cantharidian[58] plaisters,
              On sic[59] a day!

But, hark! the tent has chang'd its voice;
  There's peace an' rest nae langer:
For a' the real judges rise,   120
  They canna sit for anger.
Smith[60] opens out his cauld harangues,
  On practice and on morals;
An' aff the godly[61] pour in thrangs,
  To gie the jars an' barrels[62]   125
              A lift that day.

What signifies his barren shine
  Of moral pow'rs an' reason?
His English style an' gesture fine
  Are a' clean out o' season.   130

---

[53] "salvation" in first edition.
[54] the Devil.
[55] as in Job 1:6.
[56] to his own hot home.
[57] unearthly.
[58] aphrodisiac.
[59] such.
[60] the Rev. George Smith, a moderate or "New Light."
[61] the "Old Lights" or fundamentalists.
[62] of whisky and ale.

Like Socrates or Antonine,[63]
  Or some auld pagan heathen,
The moral man he does define,
  But ne'er a word o' faith in
        That's right that day.   135

In guid time comes an antidote
  Against sic poison'd nostrum;
For Peebles,[64] frae the water-fit,[65]
  Ascends the holy rostrum:
See, up he's got the word o' God,   140
  An' meek an' mim[66] has view'd it,
While Common Sense has taen the road,
  An' aff, an' up the Cowgate,[67]
        Fast, fast, that day.

Wee Miller,[68] niest, the Guard[69] relieves,   145
  An' orthodoxy raibles,[70]
Tho' in his heart he weel believes,
  An' thinks it auld wives' fables:
But, faith! the birkie[71] wants a manse,[72]
  So, cannilie he hums[73] them;   150
Altho' his carnal wit an' sense
  Like hafflins-wise[74] o'ercomes him
        At times that day.

Now, butt an' ben, the change-house fills,
  Wi' yill caup commentators.[75]   155

[63] Marcus Aurelius Antoninus, Roman emperor and Stoic philosopher.
[64] the Rev. William Peebles of Newton-on-Ayr, one of the "Old Lights."
He condemned this poem in his anonymous *Burnomania* (1811).
[65] water's foot, river mouth.
[66] prim, affectedly meek.
[67] a street facing the preaching tent in Mauchline.
[68] the Rev. Alexander Miller, who was short and very fat.
[69] next, the Guard (of "Old Light" preachers).
[70] rattles off.
[71] fellow.
[72] clerical residence; figuratively, a living.
[73] humbugs.
[74] almost half.
[75] Now, inner and outer rooms, the tavern fills, /With ale-cup commentators (on the preachers, texts, etc.).

Here's crying out for bakes[76] an' gills,
　　An' there the pint-stowp[77] clatters;
While thick an' thrang, an' loud an' lang,
　　Wi' logic, an' wi' Scripture,
They raise a din, that, in the end,　　　　　　160
　　Is like to breed a rupture
　　　　　　　　O' wrath that day.

Leeze me[78] on drink! it gies[79] us mair
　　Than either school or college:
It kindles wit, it waukens lear,[80]　　　　　165
　　It pangs us fou[81] o' knowledge.
Be't whisky gill, or penny wheep,[82]
　　Or ony stronger potion,
It never fails, on drinkin deep,
　　To kittle up[83] our notion[84]　　　　　170
　　　　　　　　By night or day.

The lads an' lasses, blythely bent
　　To mind baith saul an' body,
Sit round the table, weel content,
　　An' steer[85] about the toddy.　　　　　175
On this ane's dress, an' that ane's leuk,
　　They're makin observations;
While some are cozie i' the neuk,[86]
　　An' formin assignations
　　　　　　　　To meet some day.　　　　　180

But now the Lord's ain trumpet touts,[87]
　　Till a' the hills are rairin,
An' echoes back return the shouts;
　　Black Russel[88] is na spairin:

---

[76] biscuits.　　　[77] pint flagon.
[78] blessings.　　　[79] gives.
[80] learning.
[81] crams us full of (or, tipsy with).
[82] small beer.　　　[83] tickle.
[84] imagination, ideas.
[85] stir.　　　[86] nook, corner.
[87] toots, blares.
[88] the Rev. John Russel, noted for his Calvinistic severity. His voice is said to have been audible a mile away.

His piercin words, like Highlan' swords,   185
    Divide the joints an' marrow;[89]
His talk o' Hell, whare devils dwell,
    Our verra "sauls does harrow" [90]
                Wi' fright that day!

A vast, unbottom'd, boundless pit,   190
    Fill'd fou o' lowin[91] brunstane,
Whase ragin flame, an' scorchin heat,
    Wad melt the hardest whun-stane!
The half-asleep start up wi' fear
    An' think they hear it roarin,   195
When presently it does appear
    'Twas but some neebor snorin
                Asleep that day.

'Twad be owre lang a tale, to tell
    How mony stories past,   200
An' how they crowded to the yill,
    When they were a' dismist;
How drink gaed round, in cogs[92] an' caups,
    Amang the furms[93] an' benches;
An' cheese an' bread, frae women's laps,   205
    Was dealt about in lunches,[94]
                An' dawds[95] that day.

In comes a gawsie, gash[96] guidwife,
    An' sits down by the fire,
Syne[97] draws her kebbuck[98] an' her knife;   210
    The lasses they are shyer.
The auld guidmen, about the grace,
    Frae side to side they bother,
Till some ane by his bonnet lays,
    An' gies them't like a tether,[99]   215
                Fu' lang that day.

[89] See Hebrews 4:12.
[90] See *Hamlet*, I v 16.   [91] blazing.
[92] small wooden dishes.
[93] forms.   [94] large portions.
[95] chunks.   [96] jolly, talkative.
[97] then.   [98] cheese.   [99] rope.

Waesucks![100] for him that gets nae lass,
   Or lasses that hae naething!
Sma' need has he to say a grace,
   Or melvie[101] his braw claithing!   220
O wives, be mindfu', ance yoursel
   How bonie lads ye wanted,
An' dinna, for a kebbuck-heel,
   Let lasses be affronted
               On sic a day!   225

Now Clinkumbell,[102] wi' rattlin tow,[103]
   Begins to jow an' croon;[104]
Some swagger hame the best they dow,[105]
   Some wait the afternoon.
At slaps the billies[106] halt a blink,   230
   Till lasses strip their shoon:
Wi' faith an' hope, an' love an' drink,
   They're a' in famous tune
               For crack[107] that day.

How mony hearts this day converts   235
   O' sinners and o' lasses!
Their hearts o' stane, gin[108] night, are gane
   As saft as ony flesh is.
There's some are fou o' love divine;
   There's some are fou o' brandy;   240
An' mony jobs that day begin,
   May end in houghmagandie[109]
               Some ither day.

[100] alas.
[101] soil with meal (crumbs).
[102] the bell ringer.
[103] rope.
[104] toll and sound.
[105] can.
[106] at fence (or hedge) gaps the fellows.
[107] talk.
[108] by.
[109] fornication.

Address to the Deil
[?*1785*, *1786*]

O Prince! O Chief of many thronèd pow'rs!
That led th' embattl'd seraphim to war.
MILTON[1]

O thou! whatever title suit thee,
Auld Hornie, Satan, Nick, or Clootie,[2]
Wha in yon cavern grim an' sootie,
   Clos'd under hatches,
Spairges about the brunstane cootie,[3]   5
   To scaud poor wretches!

Hear me, auld Hangie, for a wee,
An' let poor damnèd bodies be;
I'm sure sma' pleasure it can gie,
   Ev'n to a deil,   10
To skelp[4] an' scaud poor dogs like me,
   An' hear us squeel.

Great is thy pow'r, an' great thy fame;
Far kend an' noted is thy name;
An' tho' yon lowin heugh's[5] thy hame,   15
   Thou travels far;
An' faith! thou's neither lag[6] nor lame,
   Nor blate nor scaur.[7]

Whyles,[8] ranging like a roarin lion
For prey, a' holes an' corners tryin;   20
Whyles on the strong-wing'd tempest flyin,
   Tirlin[9] the kirks;

---

[1] *Paradise Lost,* i 128-29.
[2] Cloven-foot.
[3] scatters around from the brimstone tub.
[4] slap. [5] flaming pit's. [6] laggard.
[7] nor bashful nor fearful.
[8] sometimes.
[9] unroofing.

Whyles, in the human bosom pryin,
      Unseen thou lurks.

I've heard my reverend graunie say,   25
In lanely glens ye like to stray;
Or where auld ruin'd castles grey
      Nod to the moon,
Ye fright the nightly wand'rer's way,
      Wi' eldritch croon.[10]   30

When twilight did my graunie summon,
To say her pray'rs, douce,[11] honest woman!
Aft yont the dyke[13] she's heard you bummin,[13]
      Wi' eerie drone;
Or, rustlin, thro' the boortrees[14] comin,   35
      Wi' heavy groan.

Ae dreary, windy, winter night,
The stars shot down wi' sklentin[15] light,
Wi' you mysel I gat a fright
      Ayont the lough;[16]   40
Ye, like a rash-buss[17] stood in sight
      Wi' waving sugh.[18]

The cudgel in my nieve[19] did shake,
Each bristl'd hair stood like a stake,
When, wi' an eldritch, stoor[20] quaick, quaick,   45
      Amang the springs,
Awa ye squatter'd, like a drake,
      On whistling wings.

[10] unearthly sound.
[11] sober-minded.
[12] often beyond the fence.
[13] humming.
[14] elder bushes.
[15] slanting, deceptive.
[16] on the other side of the lake.
[17] clump of rushes.
[18] sough, moan.
[19] fist.
[20] harsh.

Let warlocks grim, an' wither'd hags,
Tell how wi' you on ragweed nags,   50
They skim the muirs, an' dizzy crags,
          Wi' wicked speed;
And in kirk-yards renew their leagues,
          Owre howkit[21] dead.

Thence countra wives, wi' toil an' pain,   55
May plunge an' plunge the kirn[22] in vain;
For, oh! the yellow treasure's taen
          By witching skill;
An' dawtit, twal-pint hawkie's gaen
          As yell's the bill.[23]   60

Thence mystic knots mak great abuse
On young guidmen,[24] fond, keen, an' crouse;[25]
When the best wark-lume[26] i' the house,
          By cantraip wit,[27]
Is instant made no worth a louse,   65
          Just at the bit.[28]

When thowes dissolve the snawy hoord,
An' float the jinglin icy boord,
Then water-kelpies[29] haunt the foord,
          By your direction,   70
An' nighted trav'llers are allur'd
          To their destruction.

An' aft your moss-traversing spunkies[30]
Decoy the wight that late an' drunk is:
The bleezin,[31] curst, mischievous monkies   75
          Delude his eyes,
Till in some miry slough he sunk is,
          Ne'er mair to rise.

---

[21] disinterred.   [22] churn.
[23] And the petted, twelve-pint cow is gone,/As dry as the bull.
[24] married men.   [25] cocksure.
[26] work loom, tool.
[27] magic art.   [28] critical moment.
[29] mischievous spirits.
[30] morass-crossing will-o'-the-wisps.
[31] blazing.

When Masons' mystic word an' grip
In storms an' tempests raise you up,   80
Some cock or cat your rage maun[32] stop,
    Or, strange to tell!
The youngest brother ye wad whip
    Aff straught to hell.

Lang syne,[33] in Eden's bonie yard,   85
When youthfu' lovers first were pair'd,
An' all the soul of love they shar'd,
    The raptur'd hour,
Sweet on the fragrant flow'ry swaird,
    In shady bow'r: 90

Then you, ye auld, snick-drawing[34] dog!
Ye cam to Paradise incog,
An' play'd on man a cursed brogue[35]
    (Black be you fa'! [36]),
An' gied the infant warld a shog,[37]   95
    'Maist ruin'd a'.

D'ye mind that day, when in a bizz,[38]
Wi' reekit duds, an' reestit gizz,[39]
Ye did present your smoutie phiz
    'Mang better folk,   100
An' sklented[40] on the man of Uzz[41]
    Your spitefu' joke?

An' how ye gat him i' your thrall,
An' brak him out o' house an' hal',
While scabs an' botches[42] did him gall   105
    Wi' bitter claw,
An' lows'd [43] his ill-tongu'd, wicked scaul,[44]
    Was warst ava?

[32] must.   [33] since, ago.
[34] latch-lifting, scheming.
[35] trick.   [36] fate.
[37] jog.   [38] hurry.
[39] with smoky clothes and singed wig.
[40] cast, played.   [41] Job.   [42] boils.
[43] loosed.
[44] scold (wife).

But a' your doings to rehearse,
Your wily snares an' fechtin[45] fierce,   110
Sin' that day Michael did you pierce,[46]
      Down to this time,
Wad ding[47] a' Lallan[48] tongue, or Erse,[49]
      In prose or rhyme.

An' now, auld Cloots,[50] I ken ye're thinkin,   115
A certain Bardie's rantin, drinkin,
Some luckless hour will send him linkin,[51]
      To your black pit;
But faith! he'll turn a corner jinkin,[52]
      An' cheat you yet.   120

But fare you weel, auld Nickie-ben! [53]
O wad ye tak a thought an' men'!
Ye aiblins[54] might—I dinna ken—
      Still hae a stake:[55]
I'm wae[56] to think upo' yon den,   125
      Ev'n for your sake!

To a Mouse

ON TURNING HER UP IN HER NEST WITH THE PLOUGH,
NOVEMBER, 1785
[*1785, 1786*]

Wee, sleekit, cowrin, tim'rous beastie,
O, what a panic's in thy breastie!
Thou need na start awa sae hasty,
      Wi' bickering brattle![1]

---

[45] fighting.
[46] See *Paradise Lost*, vi 320-34.
[47] beat.   [48] Lowland.
[49] Gaelic, which was still spoken extensively in the Highlands.
[50] Hoofs.   [51] careering.   [52] dodging.   [53] Nick boy.
[54] perhaps.   [55] gambler's wager.   [56] sad.

---

[1] with noisy scamper.

I wad be laith to rin an' chase thee,   5
   Wi' murdering pattle! [2]

I'm truly sorry man's dominion
Has broken Nature's social union,
An' justifies that ill opinion
   Which makes thee startle   10
At me, thy poor earth-born companion
   An' fellow-mortal!

I doubt na, whyles,[3] but thou may thieve;
What then? poor beastie, thou maun live!
A daimen icker in a thrave[4]   15
   'S a sma' request;
I'll get a blessin wi' the lave,[5]
   An' never miss't!

Thy wee bit housie, too, in ruin!
Its silly wa's[6] the win's are strewin!   20
An' naething, now, to big[7] a new ane,
   O' foggage[8] green!
An' bleak December's winds ensuin,
   Baith snell [9] an' keen!

Thou saw the fields laid bare an' waste,   25
An' weary winter comin fast,
An' cozie here, beneath the blast,
   Thou thought to dwell,
Till crash! the cruel coulter past
   Out thro' thy cell.   30

That wee bit heap o' leaves an' stibble[10]
Has cost thee mony a weary nibble!
Now thou's turned out, for a' thy trouble,
   But house or hald,[11]

---

[2] plowstaff. [3] sometimes.
[4] an occasional ear in twenty-four sheaves.
[5] rest. [6] feeble walls. [7] build.
[8] grass left in the fields.
[9] sharp. [10] stubble.
[11] without house or hold (home).

To thole[12] the winter's sleety dribble,   35
    An' cranreuch[13] cauld!

But, Mousie, thou art no thy lane,[14]
In proving foresight may be vain:
The best laid schemes o' mice an' men
    Gang aft agley,[15]   40
An' lea'e us nought but grief an' pain
    For promised joy!

Still thou art blest, compared wi' me!
The present only toucheth thee:
But och! I backward cast my e'e   45
    On prospects drear!
An' forward, tho' I canna see,
    I guess an' fear!

To the Rev. John M'Math

INCLOSING A COPY OF *Holy Willie's Prayer,*
WHICH HE HAD REQUESTED
[*1785,* 1808]

While at the stook[1] the shearers cow'r
To shun the bitter blaudin[2] show'r,
Or, in gulravage rinnin, scowr[3]
    To pass the time,
To you I dedicate the hour   5
    In idle rhyme.

My Musie, tir'd wi' mony a sonnet
On, gown, an' ban', an' douse black bonnet,[4]

---

[12] endure.   [13] hoarfrost.
[14] not alone.   [15] awry.

---

[1] shock.   [2] pelting.
[3] Or, running in horseplay, scamper.
[4] that is, on ministers and elders.

Is grown right eerie[5] now she's done it,
         Lest they should blame her,   10
An' rouse their holy thunder on it,
         And anathem[6] her.

I own 'twas rash, an' rather hardy,
That I, a simple countra bardie,
Should meddle wi' a pack sae sturdy,   15
         Wha, if they ken me,
Can easy wi' a single wordie
         Louse hell upon me.

But I gae mad at their grimaces,
Their sighin, cantin, grace-proud faces,   20
Their three-mile prayers, an' hauf-mile graces,
         Their raxin[7] conscience,
Whase greed, revenge, an' pride disgraces
         Waur nor[8] their nonsense.

There's Gau'n,[9] misca'd waur than a beast,   25
Wha has mair honor in his breast
Than mony scores as guid's the priest
         Wha sae abus't him:
And may a bard no crack his jest
         What way they've use't him?   30

See him, the poor man's friend in need,
The gentleman in word an' deed—
An' shall his fame an' honor bleed
         By worthless skellums,[10]
An' not a Muse erect her head   35
         To cowe the blellums?[11]

O Pope, had I thy satire's darts
To gie the rascals their deserts,

[5] fearful.
[6] anathematize.
[7] elastic.
[8] worse than.
[9] Gavin Hamilton (see *Holy Willie's Prayer*).
[10] no-goods.
[11] blusterers.

I'd rip their rotten, hollow hearts,
            An' tell aloud   40
Their jugglin hocus-pocus arts
            To cheat the crowd!

God knows, I'm no the thing I should be,
Nor am I even the thing I could be,
But, twenty times, I rather would be   45
            An atheist clean
Than under gospel colors hid be
            Just for a screen.

An honest man may like a glass,
An honest man may like a lass;   50
But mean revenge an' malice fause
            He'll still disdain,
An' then cry zeal for gospel laws,
            Like some we ken.

They take religion in their mouth,   55
They talk o' mercy, grace, an' truth:
For what? to gie their malice skouth[12]
            On some puir wight;
An' hunt him down, o'er right an' ruth,[13]
            To ruin streight.   60

All hail, Religion! Maid divine,
Pardon a Muse sae mean as mine,
Who in her rough imperfect line
            Thus daurs to name thee;
To stigmatise false friends of thine   65
            Can ne'er defame thee.

Tho' blotch't an' foul wi' mony a stain
An' far unworthy of thy train,
Wi' trembling voice I tune my strain
            To join with those   70
Who boldly dare thy cause maintain
            In spite of foes:

[12] scope.
[13] against right and compassion.

468   *English Texts: 1660-1800*

In spite o' crowds, in spite o' mobs,
In spite of undermining jobs,
In spite o' dark banditti stabs   75
   At worth an' merit,
By scoundrels, even wi' holy robes
   But hellish spirit!

O Ayr! my dear, my native ground,
Within thy presbyterial bound[14]   80
A candid lib'ral band is found
   Of public teachers,
As men, as Christians too, renown'd,
   An' manly preachers.

Sir, in that circle you are nam'd;   85
Sir, in that circle you are fam'd;
An' some, by whom your doctrine's blam'd
   (Which gies you honor),
Even, sir, by them your heart's esteem'd,
   An' winning manner.   90

Pardon this freedom I have taen,
An' if impertinent I've been,
Impute it not, good sir, in ane
   Whase heart ne'er wrang'd ye,
But to his utmost would befriend   95
   Ought that belang'd ye.[15]

[14] within the bounds of the presbytery or church district.
[15] belonged to you.

Holy Willie's Prayer[1]
[*1785, 1789*]

And send the godly in a pet to pray.
POPE[2]

O Thou, wha in the heavens dost dwell,
Wha, as it pleases best Thysel,
Sends ane to heaven an' ten to hell,
      A' for Thy glory,
And no for ony guid or ill   5
      They've done afore Thee!

I bless and praise Thy matchless might,
Whan thousands Thou hast left in night,
That I am here afore Thy sight,
      For gifts an' grace   10
A burnin an' a shinin light,
      To a' this place.

What was I, or my generation,[3]
That I should get sic[4] exaltation?

[1] Holy Willie was William Fisher, a Calvinistic elder of the Mauchline church, "justly famed," according to Burns, "for that polemical chattering which ends in tippling orthodoxy, and for that spiritualized bawdry which refines to liquorish [that is, lecherous] devotion. In a sessional process [church complaint against one of its members for irreligious speech or behavior] with a gentleman in Mauchline—a Mr. Gavin Hamilton—Holy Willie and his priest, Father Auld, after full hearing in the Presbytery of Ayr, came off but second best, owing partly to the oratorical powers of Mr. Robert Aiken, Mr. Hamilton's counsel; but chiefly to Mr. Hamilton's being one of the most irreproachable and truly respectable characters in the country. On losing his process, the Muse overheard him at his devotions, as follows. . . ." The text printed here is a composite one, based on Stewart and Meikle's (1799).
[2] *Rape of the Lock,* iv 64.
[3] begetting, ancestry.
[4] such.

I, wha deserve sic just damnation,   15
   For broken laws,
Five thousand years 'fore my creation,
   Thro' Adam's cause!

When frae my mither's womb I fell,
Thou might hae plungèd me in hell,   20
To gnash my gums, to weep and wail,
   In burnin lake,
Where damnèd devils roar and yell,
   Chain'd to a stake;

Yet I am here, a chosen sample,   25
To show Thy grace is great an' ample;
I'm here a pillar in Thy temple,
   Strong as a rock,
A guide, a buckler, and example
   To a' Thy flock.   30

O Lord, Thou kens what zeal I bear,
When drinkers drink, an' swearers swear,
And singin here and dancin there,
   Wi' great an' sma':
For I am keepit by Thy fear   35
   Free frae them a'.

But yet, O Lord! confess I must,
At times I'm fash'd [5] wi' fleshy lust;
An' sometimes too, in warldly trust,
   Vile self gets in;[6]   40
But thou remembers we are dust,
   Defil'd wi' sin.

O Lord! yestreen,[7] Thou kens, wi' Meg—
Thy pardon I sincerely beg;
O! may't ne'er be a livin plague   45
   To my dishonour,
An' I'll ne'er lift a lawless leg
   Again upon her.

---

[5] troubled.
[6] Willie was reputed to have helped himself to the church collection.
[7] last night.

Besides I farther maun[8] allow,
Wi' Leezie's lass, three times I trow—   50
But, Lord, that Friday I was fou,[9]
        When I cam near her,
Or else, Thou kens, the servant true
        Wad ne'er hae steer'd [10] her.

May be Thou lets this fleshly thorn   55
Beset Thy servant e'en and morn
Lest he owre high and proud should turn,
        Cause he's sae gifted;
If sae, Thy han' maun e'en be borne,
        Until Thou lift it.   60

Lord, bless Thy chosen in this place,
For here Thou hast a chosen race;
But God confound their stubborn face,
        And blast their name,
Wha bring Thy elders to disgrace   65
        An' public shame!

Lord, mind Gau'n Hamilton's deserts,
He drinks, an' swears, an' plays at cartes,
Yet has sae mony takin arts
        Wi' great and sma',   70
Frae God's ain priest the people's hearts
        He steals awa'.

An' when we chasten'd him therefore,
Thou kens how he bred sic a splore[11]
As set the warld in a roar   75
        O' laughin at us;
Curse thou his basket and his store,
        Kail an' potatoes.

Lord, hear my earnest cry an' pray'r,
Against that Presbyt'ry o' Ayr;   80
Thy strong right hand, Lord, mak it bare
        Upo' their heads;

[8] must.   [9] drunk.
[10] stirred, meddled with.
[11] riot.

Lord, weigh it down, and dinna spare,
      For their misdeeds!

O Lord my God, that glib-tongu'd Aiken,   85
My vera heart and saul are quakin,
To think how we stood sweatin, shakin,
      An' piss'd wi' dread,
While he, wi' hingin lips and snakin,[12]
      Held up his head.   90

Lord, in the day of vengeance try him;
Lord, visit him wha did employ him,
And pass not in Thy mercy by them,
      Nor hear their pray'r;
But, for Thy people's sake, destroy them,   95
      And dinna spare!

But, Lord, remember me and mine
Wi' mercies temp'ral and divine,
That I for grace an' gear[13] may shine
      Excell'd by nane;   100
And a' the glory shall be Thine,
      Amen, Amen!

The Jolly Beggars

A CANTATA
[?1785, 1799]

RECITATIVO

I

When lyart[1] leaves bestrow the yird,[2]
Or, wavering like the bauckie-bird,[3]
    Bedim cauld Boreas' blast;

---

[12] sneering.   [13] wealth.

[1] withered.   [2] ground.
[3] bat ("baucks" are crossbeams).

When hailstanes drive wi' bitter skyte,[4]
And infant frosts begin to bite, 5
  In hoary cranreuch[5] drest;
Ae[6] night at e'en a merry core[7]
  O' randie, gangrel[8] bodies
In Poosie Nansie's[9] held the splore,[10]
  To drink their orra duddies:[11] 10
    Wi' quaffing and laughing,
      They ranted an' they sang,
    Wi' jumping an' thumping
      The vera girdle[12] rang.

II

First, niest[13] the fire, in auld red rags 15
Ane sat, weel brac'd wi' mealy bags[14]
  And knapsack a' in order;
His doxy[15] lay within his arm;
Wi' usquebae[16] an' blankets warm,
  She blinket on[17] her sodger. 20
An' aye[18] he gies the tozie[19] drab
  The tither skelpin[20] kiss,
While she held up her greedy gab,[21]
  Just like an aumous dish:[22]
    Ilk[23] smack still did crack still 25
      Just like a cadger's[24] whip;

[4] stroke.　[5] rime.　[6] one.
[7] corps, company.
[8] disorderly, vagrant.
[9] Pussy or Pushing Nancy—"pushing school" was a slang term for a brothel—was the nickname of Agnes Gibson, who kept a tavern in the Cowgate, Mauchline.
[10] spree.
[11] spare duds or ragged clothes.
[12] griddle.　[13] next to.
[14] bags for oatmeal, standard begging equipment.
[15] whore.　[16] whisky.
[17] leered at.　[18] over and over.
[19] tipsy.　[20] smacking.
[21] mouth.　[22] alms.　[23] each.
[24] peddler's.

Then swaggering an' staggering
He roar'd this ditty up:—

AIR

Tune: *Soldier's Joy*

I

I am a son of Mars, who have been in many wars,
 And show my cuts and scars wherever I come: 30
This here was for a wench, and that other in a trench
 When welcoming the French at the sound of the drum.
    Lal de daudle, *etc.*

II

My prenticeship I pass'd, where my leader breath'd his last,
 When the bloody die was cast on the Heights of Abram;[25] 35
And I servèd out my trade when the gallant game was play'd,
 And the Moro[26] low was laid at the sound of the drum.

III

I lastly was with Curtis,[27] among the floating batt'ries,
 And there I left for witness an arm and a limb;
Yet let my country need me, with Eliott[28] to head me 40
 I'd clatter on my stumps at the sound of the drum.

IV

And now, tho' I must beg with a wooden arm and leg
 And many a tatter'd rag hanging over my bum,
I'm as happy with my wallet,[29] my bottle, and my callet[30]
 As when I us'd in scarlet to follow a drum.   45

[25] Wolfe decisively defeated Montcalm at Quebec in 1759 on the Heights of Abraham. Wolfe died there.

[26] El Moro (Morro Castle), the chief fortification of Havana, which the British captured in 1762.

[27] Admiral Sir Roger Curtis, who destroyed the French floating batteries before Gibraltar in 1782.

[28] George Augustus Eliott, later first Baron Heathfield, famous for his defense of Gibraltar in 1779-83.

[29] oatmeal bag. [30] whore.

V

What tho' with hoary locks I must stand the winter shocks,
    Beneath the woods and rocks oftentimes for a home?
When the tother bag[31] I sell, and the tother bottle tell,
    I could meet a troop of hell at the sound of a drum.
              Lal de daudle, *etc.*   50

RECITATIVO

He ended; and the kebars sheuk[32]
    Aboon[33] the chorus roar;
While frighted rattons[34] backward leuk,
    An' seek the benmost bore:[35]
A fairy[36] fiddler frae the neuk,[37]   55
    He skirl'd out *Encore!*
But up arose the martial chuck,[38]
    An' laid the loud uproar:—

AIR

Tune: *Sodger Laddie*

I

I once was a maid, tho' I cannot tell when,
And still my delight is in proper young men.   60
Some one of a troop of dragoons was my daddie:
No wonder I'm fond of a sodger laddie!
            Sing, lal de dal, *etc.*

II

The first of my loves was a swaggering blade,
To rattle the thundering drum was his trade;   65
His leg was so tight, and his cheek was so ruddy,
Transported I was with my sodger laddie.

[31] of oatmeal, which was used as a medium of exchange.
[32] rafters shook.
[33] above.   [34] rats.
[35] innermost hole.
[36] diminutive.
[37] nook, corner.
[38] sweetheart.

III

But the godly old chaplain left him in the lurch;[39]
The sword I forsook for the sake of the church;
He risk**è**d the soul, and I ventur'd the body: 70
'Twas then I prov'd false to my sodger laddie.

IV

Full soon I grew sick of my sanctified sot;
The regiment at large for a husband I got;
From the gilded spontoon[40] to the fife I was ready:
I ask**è**d no more but a sodger laddie.   75

V

But the Peace[41] it reduc'd me to beg in despair,
Till I met my old boy in a Cunningham[42] fair;
His rags regimental they flutter'd so gaudy:
My heart it rejoic'd at a sodger laddie.

VI

And now I have liv'd—I know not how long!   80
And still I can join in a cup and a song;
But whilst with both hands I can hold the glass steady,
Here's to thee, my hero, my sodger laddie!
                              Sing, lal de dal, *etc.*

RECITATIVO

Poor Merry-Andrew[43] in the neuk   85
    Sat guzzling wi' a tinkler-hizzie;[44]
They mind't na wha the chorus teuk,
    Between themselves they were sae busy.
    At length, wi' drink an' courting dizzy,
He stoiter'd [45] up an' made a face;   90
    Then turn'd an' laid a smack on Grizzie,
Syne[46] tun'd his pipes wi' grave grimace:—

---

[39] got ahead of him.
[40] short pike carried by junior officers.
[41] of 1783.
[42] the most northern Ayrshire district.
[43] clown.   [44] tinker-wench.
[45] staggered.   [46] then.

AIR

Tune: *Auld Sir Symon*

I

Sir Wisdom's a fool when he's fou;[47]
  Sir Knave is a fool in a session:[48]
He's there but a prentice I trow,   95
  But I am a fool by profession.

II

My grannie she bought me a beuk,[49]
  An' I held awa[50] to the school:
I fear I my talent misteuk,
  But what will ye hae of a fool?   100

III

For drink I wad venture my neck;
  A hizzie's the half o' my craft:
But what could ye other expect
  Of ane that's avowedly daft?

IV

I ance was tyed up like a stirk[51]   105
  For civilly swearing and quaffing;
I ance was abus'd i' the kirk
  For towsing[52] a lass i' my daffin.[53]

V

Poor Andrew that tumbles for sport
  Let naebody name wi' a jeer;
There's even, I'm tauld, i' the Court   110
  A tumbler ca'd the Premier.

[47] drunk.   [48] court.
[49] book.
[50] went off.
[51] young bullock or heifer. It was tied in an iron collar.
[52] rumpling.
[53] fun.

VI

Observ'd ye yon reverend lad
    Maks faces to tickle the mob?
He rails at our mountebank squad—   115
    It's rivalship just i' the job!

VII

And now my conclusion I'll tell,
    For faith! I'm confoundedly dry:
The chiel [54] that's a fool for himsel,
    Guid Lord! he's far dafter than I.   120

RECITATIVO

Then niest outspak a raucle carlin,[55]
Wha kent fu' weel to cleek the sterlin,[56]
For mony a pursie she had hookèd,
And had in mony a well been doukèd.
Her love had been a Highland laddie,   125
But weary fa' the waefu' woodie! [57]
Wi' sighs and sobs, she thus began
To wail her braw[58] John Highlandman:—

AIR

Tune: *O, An' Ye Were Dead, Guidman*

I

A Highland lad my love was born,
The Lalland [59] laws he held in scorn,   130
But he still was faithfu' to his clan,
My gallant, braw John Highlandman.

---

[54] fellow.
[55] rough old woman.
[56] pinch the cash.
[57] put a plague upon the woeful gallows.
[58] fine, gaily dressed.
[59] Lowland.

Chorus[60]

Sing hey, my braw John Highlandman!
Sing ho, my braw John Highlandman!
There's not a lad in a' the lan'   135
Was match for my John Highlandman!

II

With his philibeg[61] an' tartan plaid,
And guid claymore[62] down by his side,
The ladies' hearts he did trepan,
My gallant, braw John Highlandman.   140

III

We rangèd a' from Tweed to Spey,[63]
And liv'd like lords an' ladies gay,
For a Lalland face he fearèd none,
My gallant, braw John Highlandman.

IV

They banish'd him beyond the sea,   145
But ere the bud was on the tree,
Adown my cheeks the pearls ran,
Embracing my John Highlandman.

V

But, och! they catch'd him at the last,
And bound him in a dungeon fast.   150
My curse upon them every one—
They've hang'd my braw John Highlandman.

VI

And now a widow I must mourn
The pleasures that will ne'er return;
No comfort but a hearty can[64]   155
When I think on John Highlandman.

[60] The Chorus is repeated after each stanza.
[61] kilt.   [62] Highland sword.
[63] from one end of Scotland to the other.
[64] wooden drinking vessel.

RECITATIVO

I

A pigmy scraper wi' his fiddle,
Wha us'd to trystes[65] an' fairs to driddle,[66]
Her strappin limb and gawsie[67] middle
       (He reach'd nae higher)   160
Had hol'd his heartie like a riddle,[68]
       And blawn't on fire.

II

Wi' hand on hainch, and upward e'e,
He croon'd his gamut, one, two, three,
Then, in an *arioso*[69] key,   165
       The wee Apollo
Set aff, wi' *allegretto* glee,
       His *giga*[70] solo:—

AIR

Tune: *Whistle Owre the Lave*[71] *O't*

I

Let me ryke[72] up to dight[73] that tear;
And go wi' me an' be my dear,   170
And then your every care an' fear
   May whistle owre the lave o't.

Chorus[74]

I am a fiddler to my trade,
And a' the tunes that e'er I play'd,
The sweetest still to wife or maid   175
   Was *Whistle Owre the Lave O't.*

[65] markets, fairs.
[66] toddle.   [67] buxom.
[68] had riddled his heart.
[69] aria-like.   [70] lively.
[71] rest. The title means "say no more."
[72] reach.   [73] wipe.
[74] The Chorus is sung after each stanza.

II

At kirns[75] and weddings we'se be there,
And O, sae nicely's we will fare!
We'll bowse[76] about till Daddie Care
  Sings *Whistle Owre the Lave O't.*　　　　180

III

Sae merrily the banes[77] we'll pyke,[78]
And sun oursels about the dyke;[79]
And at our leisure, when ye like,
  We'll—whistle owre the lave o't!

IV

But bless me wi' your heav'n o' charms,　　　　185
And while I kittle hair on thairms,[80]
Hunger, cauld, an a' sic harms,
  May whistle owre the lave o't.

RECITATIVO

I

Her charms had struck a sturdy caird,[81]
  As weel as poor gut-scraper;　　　　190
He taks the fiddler by the beard,
  An' draws a roosty rapier;
He swoor by a' was swearing worth
  To speet him like a pliver,[82]
Unless he would from that time forth　　　　195
  Relinquish her for ever.

II

Wi' ghastly ee, poor Tweedle-Dee
  Upon his hunkers[83] bended,

[75] harvest-homes.
[76] booze, drink.
[77] bones.　　[78] pick.
[79] fence.
[80] And while I tickle the hair of the fiddlestrings.
[81] tinker.　　[82] plover.　　[83] haunches.

And pray'd for grace wi' ruefu' face,
   And sae the quarrel ended.   200
But tho' his little heart did grieve
   When round the tinkler prest her,
He feign'd to snirtle[84] in his sleeve,
   When thus the caird address'd her:—

AIR

Tune: *Clout*[85] *the Cauldron*

I

My bonie lass, I work in brass,   205
   A tinkler is my station;[86]
I've travell'd round all Christian ground
   In this my occupation;
I've taen the gold, an' been enrolled
   In many a noble squadron;   210
But vain they search'd, when off I march'd
   To go an' clout the cauldron.

II

Despise that shrimp, that wither'd imp,
   Wi' a' his noise and cap'rin,
An' tak a share wi' those that bear   215
   The budget[87] and the apron!
And by that stowp,[88] my faith and houpe!
   And by that dear Kilbaigie! [89]
If e'er ye want, or meet wi' scant,
   May I ne'er weet my craigie! [90]   220

[84] snigger.
[85] patch.
[86] calling.
[87] tinker's tool bag.
[88] flagon.
[89] a particular kind of whisky.
[90] throat.

RECITATIVO

I

The caird prevail'd: th' unblushing fair
  In his embraces sunk,
Partly wi' love o'ercome sae sair,
  An' partly she was drunk.
Sir Violino, with an air   225
  That show'd a man o' spunk,
Wish'd unison between the pair,
  And made the bottle clunk[91]
          To their health that night.

II

But hurchin[92] Cupid shot a shaft,   230
  That play'd a dame a shavie:[93]
The fiddler rak'd her fore and aft,
  Behint the chicken cavie.[94]
Her lord, a wight of Homer's[95] craft,
  Tho' limpin' wi' the spavie,[96]   235
He hirpl'd up, an' lap like daft,[97]
  And shor'd [98] them *Dainty Davie*[99]
         O' boot[100] that night.

III

He was a care-defying blade
  As ever Bacchus listed! [101]   240

[91] gurgle.
[92] urchin, rascal.
[93] trick.
[94] coop.
[95] Homer is allowed to be the oldest ballad singer on record (Burns).
[96] spavin.
[97] He hobbled up, and leapt like mad.
[98] offered.
[99] a ballad in which a man is hidden in a girl's bed by her mother.
[100] to boot.
[101] enlisted.

Tho' Fortune sair upon him laid,
　His heart, she ever miss'd it.
He had no wish—but to be glad,
　Nor want but—when he thristed;
He hated nought but—to be sad,   245
　An' thus the Muse suggested
　　His sang that night:—

AIR

Tune: *For A' That, An' A' That*

I

I am a bard of no regard
　Wi' gentle folks, an' a' that,
But Homer-like, the glowrin byke,[102]   250
　Frae town to town I draw that.

Chorus[103]

For a' that, an' a' that,
　And twice as muckle's[104] a' that;
I've lost but ane,[105] I've twa behin',
　I've wife eneugh for a' that.   255

II

I never drank the Muses' stank,[106]
　Castalia's burn[107] an' a' that;
But there it[108] streams, an' richly reams[109]—
　My Helicon[110] I ca' that.

---

[102] staring swarm.
[103] The Chorus is repeated after each stanza, except the last.
[104] much as.
[105] one (girl).
[106] pond.
[107] Castalia's stream, or fountain, on Mt. Parnassus, sacred to Apollo and the Muses.
[108] ale.
[109] foams.
[110] A mountain in Boeotia, usually snow-covered, sacred to Apollo and the Muses.

III

Great love I bear to a' the fair,   260
   Their humble slave, an' a' that;
But lordly will, I hold it still
   A mortal sin to thraw[111] that.

IV

In raptures sweet this hour we meet
   Wi' mutual love, an' a' that;   265
But for how lang the flie may stang,
   Let inclination law that.

V

Their tricks an' craft hae put me daft.
   They've taen me in, an' a' that;
But clear your decks, an' here's "the Sex!"   270
   I like the jads for a' that.

Chorus

For a' that, an' a' that,
   And twice as muckle's a' that,
My dearest bluid, to do them guid,
   They're welcome till't for a' that!   275

RECITATIVO

So sung the bard, and Nansie's wa's[112]
Shook with a thunder of applause,
   Re-echo'd from each mouth!
They toom'd their pocks,[113] they pawn'd their duds,
They scarcely left to coor their fuds,[114]   280
   To quench their lowin[115] drouth.
Then owre again the jovial thrang
   The poet did request

[111] thwart.
[112] walls.
[113] emptied their bags.
[114] cover their rears.
[115] burning.

To lowse[116] his pack, an' wale[117] a sang,
  A ballad o' the best: 285
    He rising, rejoicing,
      Between his twa Deborahs,
    Looks round him, an' found them
      Impatient for the chorus:—

AIR

Tune: Jolly Mortals, Fill Your Glasses

I

See the smoking bowl before us!   290
  Mark our jovial, ragged ring!
Round and round take up the chorus,
  And in raptures let us sing:

Chorus

A fig for those by law protected!
  Liberty's a glorious feast,   295
Courts for cowards were erected,
  Churches built to please the priest!

II

What is title? what is treasure?
  What is reputation's care?
If we lead a life of pleasure,   300
  'Tis no matter how or where!

III

With the ready trick and fable
  Round we wander all the day;
And at night, in barn or stable,
  Hug our doxies on the hay.   305

[116] loose, untie.
[117] choose.

IV

Does the train-attended carriage
  Thro' the country lighter rove?
Does the sober bed of marriage
  Witness brighter scenes of love?

V

Life is all a variorum,   310
  We regard not how it goes;
Let them prate about decorum
  Who have character to lose.

VI

Here's to budgets, bags, and wallets!
  Here's to all the wandering train!   315
Here's our ragged brats and callets!
  One and all, cry out, Amen!

Chorus

A fig for those by law protected!
  Liberty's a glorious feast,
Courts for cowards were erected,   320
  Churches built to please the priest!

Tam O' Shanter
[*1790, 1791*]

Of Brownyis and of Bogillis full is this Buke.
GAWIN DOUGLAS [1]

When chapman billies[2] leave the street,
And drouthy[3] neebors, neebors meet,
As market days are wearing late,

[1] Gavin Douglas, *Prologue to the Sixth Book of the Aeneid*, l. 18.
[2] peddlers.
[3] thirsty.

An' folk begin to tak the gate;[4]
While we sit bousing at the nappy,[5]   5
An' getting fou[6] and unco[7] happy,
We think na on the lang Scots miles,[8]
The mosses, waters, slaps, and styles,[9]
That lie between us and our hame,
Whare sits our sulky, sullen dame,   10
Gathering her brows like gathering storm,
Nursing her wrath to keep it warm.
　　This truth fand honest Tam o' Shanter,
As he frae Ayr ae[10] night did canter,
(Auld Ayr, wham ne'er a town surpasses   15
For honest men and bonie[11] lasses).
　　O Tam! hadst thou but been sae wise,
As taen thy ain wife Kate's advice!
She tauld thee weel thou was a skellum,[12]
A bletherin,[13] blusterin, drunken blellum;[14]   20
That frae November till October,
Ae market-day thou was nae sober;
That ilka melder,[15] wi' the miller
Thou sat as lang as thou had siller;[16]
That every naig was ca'd a shoe on,   25
The smith and thee gat roarin fou on;
That at the Lord's house, even on Sunday,
Thou drank wi' Kirkton Jean[17] till Monday.
She prophesied that, late or soon,
Thou would be found deep drown'd in Doon;[18]   30

[4] road.　　[5] ale.　　[6] drunk.
[7] uncommonly.
[8] A Scots mile is about 1975 yards.
[9] the bogs, pools, hedge (or fence) openings, and stiles.
[10] one.
[11] bonny, pretty.
[12] no-good.
[13] chattering.
[14] babbler.
[15] every grist-time.
[16] silver.
[17] Kirkton Jean and her sister kept a tavern sometimes called the Ladies' House.
[18] a river that runs by Alloway Kirk.

Or catch'd wi' warlocks in the mirk,[19]
By Alloway's auld, haunted kirk.
   Ah, gentle dames! it gars me greet[20]
To think how mony counsels sweet,
How mony lengthen'd sage advices,   35
The husband frae the wife despises!
   But to our tale: ae market night,
Tam had got planted unco right;
Fast by an ingle, bleezing finely,
Wi' reamin swats,[21] that drank divinely;   40
And at his elbow, Souter[22] Johnie,
His ancient, trusty, drouthy crony;
Tam lo'ed him like a vera brither;
They had been fou for weeks thegither.
The night drave on wi' sangs and clatter;   45
And ay[23] the ale was growing better:
The landlady and Tam grew gracious,
Wi' secret favours, sweet and precious:
The souter tauld his queerest stories;
The landlord's laugh was ready chorus: 50
The storm without might rair and rustle,
Tam did na mind the storm a whistle.
   Care, mad to see a man sae happy,
E'en drown'd himsel amang the nappy.
As bees flee hame wi' lades o' treasure,   55
The minutes wing'd their way wi' pleasure;
Kings may be blest, but Tam was glorious,
O'er a' the ills o' life victorious!
   But pleasures are like poppies spread,
You seize the flow'r, its bloom is shed;   60
Or like the snow falls in the river,
A moment white—then melts for ever;
Or like the borealis race,
That flit ere you can point their place;

[19] murk, dark.
[20] makes me weep.
[21] foaming new ale.
[22] Cobbler.
[23] always.

Or like the rainbow's lovely form   65
Evanishing amid the storm—
Nae man can tether time or tide;
The hour approaches Tam maun[24] ride;
That hour, o' night's black arch the key-stane,
That dreary hour, he mounts his beast in;   70
And sic[25] a night he taks the road in,
As ne'er poor sinner was abroad in.

    The wind blew as 'twad [26] blawn its last;
The rattling show'rs rose on the blast;
The speedy gleams the darkness swallow'd;   75
Loud, deep, and lang, the thunder bellow'd:
That night, a child might understand,
The Deil had business on his hand.

    Weel mounted on his grey mare, Meg,
A better never lifted leg,   80
Tam skelpit[27] on thro' dub[28] and mire,
Despising wind, and rain, and fire;
Whiles[29] holding fast his guid blue bonnet;
Whiles crooning o'er some auld Scots sonnet;[30]
Whiles glow'ring round wi' prudent cares,   85
Lest bogles[31] catch him unawares:
Kirk-Alloway was drawing nigh,
Whare ghaists and houlets[32] nightly cry.

    By this time he was cross the ford,
Where in the snaw the chapman smoor'd;[33]   90
And past the birks[34] and meikle[35] stane,
Where drunken Charlie brak's neck-bane;
And thro' the whins,[36] and by the cairn,
Where hunters fand the murder'd bairn;
And near the thorn, aboon[37] the well,   95
Where Mungo's mither hang'd hersel.

---

[24] must.   [25] such.
[26] would have.   [27] hurried.
[28] puddle.   [29] sometimes.
[30] song.   [31] bogies.
[32] owls.   [33] smothered.
[34] birches.   [35] great.
[36] furze.   [37] above.

Before him Doon pours all his floods;
The doubling storm roars thro' the woods;
The lightnings flash from pole to pole;
Near and more near the thunders roll: 100
When, glimmering thro' the groaning trees,
Kirk-Alloway seem'd in a bleeze;
Thro' ilka bore[38] the beams were glancing,
And loud resounded mirth and dancing.

    Inspiring bold John Barleycorn!   105
What dangers thou canst make us scorn!
Wi' tippenny,[39] we fear nae evil;
Wi' usquebae[40] we'll face the devil!
The swats sae ream'd in Tammie's noddle,
Fair play, he car'd na deils a boddle.[41]   110
But Maggie stood right sair astonish'd,
Till, by the heel and hand admonish'd,
She ventur'd forward on the light;
And, vow! Tam saw an unco sight!

    Warlocks and witches in a dance;   115
Nae cotillon brent[42] new frae France,
But hornpipes, jigs, strathspeys, and reels,
Put life and mettle in their heels.
A winnock-bunker[43] in the east,
There sat auld Nick, in shape o' beast;   120
A tousie tyke,[44] black, grim, and large!
To gie them music was his charge:
He screw'd the pipes and gart them skirl,[45]
Till roof and rafters a' did dirl.[46]
Coffins stood round like open presses,[47]   125
That shaw'd the dead in their last dresses;
And, by some devilish cantraip sleight,[48]
Each in its cauld hand held a light,
By which heroic Tam was able
To note upon the haly table   130

---

[38] chink.   [39] twopenny ale.   [40] whisky.
[41] Given fair play, he cared not two cents about devils.
[42] brand.   [43] window seat.   [44] shaggy hound.
[45] made them squeal.   [46] rattle.   [47] clothes cupboards.
[48] magic trick.

A murderer's banes in gibbet-airns;[49]
Twa span-lang, wee, unchristen'd bairns;
A thief new-cutted frae a rape,[50]
Wi' his last gasp his gab[51] did gape;
Five tomahawks, wi' blude red-rusted;   135
Five scymitars, wi' murder crusted;
A garter which a babe had strangled;
A knife a father's throat had mangled,
Whom his ain son o' life bereft,
The gray hairs yet stack to the heft;   140
Wi' mair of horrible and awefu',
Which even to name wad be unlawfu'.[52]
   As Tammie glowr'd, amaz'd, and curious,
The mirth and fun grew fast and furious:
The piper loud and louder blew,   145
The dancers quick and quicker flew,
They reel'd, they set, they cross'd, they cleekit,[53]
Till ilka carlin swat and reekit,
And coost her duddies to the wark,[54]
And linket[55] at it in her sark! [56]   150
   Now Tam, O Tam! had thae been queans,[57]
A' plump and strapping in their teens;
Their sarks, instead o' creeshie[58] flannen,
Been snaw-white seventeen hunder[59] linen!
Thir[60] breeks o' mine, my only pair,   155
That ance were plush, o' guid blue hair,
I wad hae gi'en them off my hurdies,[61]

[49] bones in gibbet irons.
[50] rope.   [51] mouth.
[52] At this point four lines appeared in early editions:
   Three lawyers' tongues, turn'd inside out,
   Wi' lies seam'd like a beggar's clout [patched garment];
   Three priests' hearts, rotten black as muck,
   Lay stinking, vile, in every neuk.
[53] linked themselves.
[54] Till every woman sweated and steamed,/And cast off her clothes to dance better.
[55] danced along.   [56] shift.   [57] girls.
[58] greasy.   [59] finely woven.   [60] those.
[61] buttocks.

For ae blink o' the bonie burdies! [62]
    But wither'd beldams, auld and droll,
Rigwoodie[63] hags wad spean[64] a foal,   160
Louping and flinging on a crummock,[65]
I wonder did na turn thy stomach!
    But Tam kend what was what fu' brawlie:[66]
There was ae winsome wench and wawlie[67]
That night enlisted in the core[68]   165
(Lang after kend on Carrick[69] shore;
For mony a beast to dead she shot,
And perished mony a bonie boat,
And shook[70] baith meikle corn and bear,[71]
And kept the country-side in fear),   170
Her cutty sark, o' Paisley harn,[72]
That while a lassie she had worn,
In longitude tho' sorely scanty,
It was her best, and she was vauntie.[73]
Ah! little kend thy reverend grannie   175
That sark she coft[74] for her wee Nannie
Wi' twa pund Scots[75] ('twas a' her riches)
Wad ever grac'd a dance of witches!
    But here my Muse her wing maun cour;[76]
Sic flights are far beyond her pow'r: 180
To sing how Nannie lap and flang,[77]
(A souple jad she was, and strang),
And how Tam stood, like ane bewitch'd,
And thought his very een enrich'd;

[62] pretty creatures.
[63] ropy.   [64] wean.
[65] leaping and capering with a crooked staff.
[66] full well.   [67] buxom.   [68] corps.
[69] the southernmost district of Ayrshire.
[70] scattered. Possibly, stole.
[71] barley.
[72] her short shift, of coarse Paisley cloth.
[73] proud of it.
[74] bought.
[75] The Scots pound was worth one twelfth of the English.
[76] curb.
[77] leaped and flung about.

Even Satan glowr'd, and fidg'd fu' fain,[78]   185
And hotch'd [79] and blew wi' might and main:
Till first ae caper, syne anither,
Tam tint[80] his reason a' thegither,
And roars out, "Weel done, Cutty-sark!"
And in an instant all was dark,   190
And scarcely had he Maggie rallied,
When out the hellish legion sallied.
    As bees bizz out wi' angry fyke,[81]
When plundering herds[82] assail their byke;[82a]
As open pussie's[83] mortal foes,   195
When, pop! she starts before their nose;
As eager runs the market-crowd,
When "Catch the thief!" resounds aloud;
So Maggie runs; the witches follow,
Wi' mony an eldritch skriech and hollo.   200
    Ah, Tam! ah, Tam! thou'll get thy fairin! [84]
In hell they'll roast thee like a herrin!
In vain thy Kate awaits thy comin!
Kate soon will be a woefu' woman!
Now do thy speedy utmost, Meg,   205
And win the key-stane o' the brig;[85]
There at them thou thy tail may toss,
A running stream they dare na cross.
But ere the key-stane she could make,
The fient a[86] tail she had to shake;   210
For Nannie, far before the rest,
Hard upon noble Maggie prest,
And flew at Tam wi' furious ettle;[87]
But little wist she Maggie's mettle!
Ae spring brought off her master hale,   215
But left behind her ain gray tail:

[78] fidgeted with fondness.
[79] jerked (his arm about).
[80] lost.   [81] fuss.
[82] herdsmen.   [82a] hive.
[83] hare's.   [84] reward.
[85] bridge.   [86] devil a.
[87] purpose.

The carlin claught[88] her by the rump,
And left poor Maggie scarce a stump.
   Now, wha this tale o' truth shall read,
Ilk man and mother's son, take heed: 220
Whene'er to drink you are inclined,
Or cutty-sarks run in your mind,
Think! ye may buy the joys o'er dear;
Remember Tam o' Shanter's mare.

Green Grow the Rashes[1]
[?*1784*, 1787]

Green grow the rashes, O;
   Green grow the rashes, O;
The sweetest hours that e'er I spend,
   Are spent amang the lasses, O!

There's nought but care on ev'ry han',   5
   In ev'ry hour that passes, O;
What signifies the life o' man,
   An' 'twere na for the lasses, O.

The warly[2] race may riches chase,
   An' riches still may fly them, O;   10
An' tho' at last they catch them fast,
   Their hearts can ne'er enjoy them, O.

But gie me a canny[3] hour at e'en,
   My arms about my dearie, O;
An' warly cares, an' warly men,   15
   May a' gae tapsalteerie,[4] O!

---

[88] witch seized.

---

[1] rushes. This is Burns's version of an old ballad. Stanza I (the Chorus) is repeated after every stanza.
[2] worldly.
[3] pleasant.
[4] topsy-turvy.

For you sae douce,[5] ye sneer at this,
   Ye're nought but senseless asses, O;
The wisest man[6] the warl' e'er saw,
   He dearly lov'd the lasses, O.   20

Auld Nature swears, the lovely dears
   Her noblest work she classes, O;
Her prentice han' she try'd on man,
   An' then she made the lasses, O.

Ae[1] Fond Kiss
[*1791*, 1792]

Ae fond kiss, and then we sever;
Ae fareweel and then for ever!
Deep in heart-wrung tears I'll pledge thee,
Warring sighs and groans I'll wage[2] thee.
Who shall say that fortune grieves him   5
While the star of hope she leaves him?
Me, nae cheerfu' twinkle lights me;
Dark despair around benights me.

I'll ne'er blame my partial fancy,
Naething could resist my Nancy: 10
But to see her was to love her,
Love but her, and love for ever.
Had we never lov'd sae kindly,
Had we never lov'd sae blindly,
Never met, or never parted,   15
We had ne'er been broken-hearted.

Fare thee weel, thou first and fairest!
Fare thee weel, thou best and dearest!
Thine be ilka[3] joy and treasure,
Peace, enjoyment, love, and pleasure!   20

[5] sedate.   [6] Solomon.

[1] one.   [2] pledge.
[3] every.

Ae fond kiss, and then we sever;
Ae fareweel, alas! for ever!
Deep in heart-wrung tears I'll pledge thee,
Warring sighs and groans I'll wage thee.

For A'[1] That and A' That
[*1794, 1795*]

Is there,[2] for honest poverty,
    That hings his head, and a' that;
The coward-slave, we pass him by,
    We dare be poor for a' that!
        For a' that, and a' that,   5
            Our toils obscure, and a' that,
        The rank is but the guinea's stamp,
            The man's the gowd[3] for a' that.

What though on hamely fare we dine,
    Wear hoddin grey,[4] and a' that;   10
Gie fools their silks, and knaves their wine,
    A man's a man for a' that.
        For a' that, and a' that,
            Their tinsel show, and a' that;
        The honest man, tho' e'er sae poor,   15
            Is king o' men for a' that.

Ye see yon birkie, ca'd[5] a lord,
    Wha struts, and stares, and a' that;
Tho' hundreds worship at his word,
    He's but a coof[6] for a' that.   20
        For a' that, and a' that,
            His ribband, star,[7] and a' that,

---

[1] all. This poem, inspired by the French Revolution, is based on an old song.

[2] is there one.   [3] gold.

[4] coarse gray woolen.

[5] fellow, called.   [6] fool.

[7] order, decoration.

The man of independent mind,
 He looks and laughs at a' that.

A prince can mak a belted knight,   25
 A marquis, duke, and a' that;
But an honest man's aboon[8] his might,
 Guid faith, he mauna fa'[9] that!
  For a' that, and a' that,
   Their dignities, and a' that,   30
  The pith o' sense, and pride o' worth,
   Are higher rank than a' that.

Then let us pray that come it may,
 As come it will for a' that,
That sense and worth, o'er a' the earth, 35
 Shall bear the gree,[10] and a' that.
  For a' that and a' that,
   It's coming yet, for a' that,
  That man to man, the warld o'er,
   Shall brothers be for a' that.   40

A Red, Red Rose[1]
[1794]

O my luve's like a red, red rose,
 That's newly sprung in June;
O my luve's like the melodie
 That's sweetly play'd in tune.

As fair art thou, my bonie lass,   5
 So deep in luve am I;
And I will luve thee still, my dear,
 Till a' the seas gang dry.

[8] above.
[9] must not lay claim to make.
[10] take first place.

---

[1] This is Burns's combination and alteration of several old songs.

Till a' the seas gang dry, my dear,
  And the rocks melt wi' the sun;   10
And I will luve thee still, my dear,
  While the sands o' life shall run.

And fare thee weel, my only luve!
  And fare thee weel a while!
And I will come again, my luve,   15
  Tho' it were ten thousand mile!

❧ Edmund Burke ❧

Born in Dublin, Edmund Burke (1729-97) was educated at Trinity College there, and studied law at the Middle Temple in London. He first became known for his *Philosophical Enquiry into the Origin of Our Ideas of the Sublime and Beautiful* (1757); in 1765, he became private secretary to the Prime Minister, the Marquess of Rockingham, and an M.P. The intellectual leader of the Rockingham Whigs, with whom he took office briefly in 1782 (he also served in the Fox-North Coalition Ministry of 1783), he became famous as a brilliant, intemperate, and tiresome orator in the House of Commons. There he vigorously supported conciliation with the American colonies (and not merely because he was Agent of the State of New York), economic and administrative reform, and Catholic emancipation. The last years of his life were spent on two great causes: the impeachment and trial of Warren Hastings, who was accused of oppression and the illegal acquisition of enormous wealth as Governor-General of India, and opposition to the French Revolution and the spread of its doctrines in England.

Burke is remembered today as an intellectual who distrusted reason, and as a political theorist who condemned theory. Profoundly moved by concrete injustice, he opposed any attempt to alter existing institutions on the basis of abstract principles, or to apply a "delusive geometrical accuracy in moral arguments." The best forms of government, he felt, were based on tradition: they had evolved through, and were tested by, time. This belief is the basis for his analysis of party politics, *Thoughts on the Cause of the Present Discontents* (1770), and for his best-known work, *Reflections on the Revolution in France* (1790). Burke's fundamental ideas, his learning and capacious mind, and his mastery of a balanced, incisive style are well illustrated in his *apologia pro vita sua*, the *Letter to a Noble Lord*.

Editions: Works (1854-89); *Works* (1865-67); *Select Works,* ed. E. J. Payne (1874-78); *Burke's Politics: Selected Writings and Speeches,* ed. Ross J. S. Hoffman and Paul Levack (1949); *The Sublime and Beautiful,* ed. J. T. Boulton (1958); *Correspondence,* Vols. I-II, ed. Thomas W. Copeland and L. S. Sutherland (1958-60).

Biographies: Rev. Robert H. Murray, *Edmund Burke* (1931); Sir Philip Magnus, *Edmund Burke* (1939).

Critical Studies: Thomas W. Copeland, *Our Eminent Friend, Edmund Burke* (1949); Charles Parkin, *The Moral Basis of Burke's Political Thought* (1956); Carl B. Cone, *Burke and the Nature of Politics,* Vol. I (1957).

Letter to a Noble Lord [1]
[*1795,* 1796]

My Lord,

I could hardly flatter myself with the hope that so very early in the season[2] I should have to acknowledge obligations to the Duke of Bedford, and to the Earl of Lauderdale. These noble persons have lost no time in conferring upon me that sort of honor which it is alone within their competence, and which it is certainly most congenial to their nature, and their manners, to bestow.

To be ill spoken of, in whatever language they speak, by the zealots of the new sect[3] in philosophy and politics, of which these noble persons think so charitably, and of which others think so

---

[1] On Burke's retirement from the House of Commons in 1794, he was granted a pension of £3,700 a year by the Prime Minister, the younger William Pitt. The pension was attacked in Parliament by Francis Russell, fifth Duke of Bedford, and James Maitland, eighth Earl of Lauderdale, on the grounds that it should have been submitted to Parliament for approval, and that it violated Burke's own plan for economic reform. Burke's *Letter* is addressed to William FitzWilliam, fourth Earl FitzWilliam, nephew and heir to Burke's old political chief, Charles Watson-Wentworth, second Marquess of Rockingham.

[2] Parliamentary season. Parliament had been convened on 29 October 1795; Bedford and Lauderdale's attack was made on 13 November.

[3] sympathizers with the French Revolution and its ideas.

justly, to me, is no matter of uneasiness or surprise. To have incurred the displeasure of the Duke of Orléans[4] or the Duke of Bedford, to fall under the censure of Citizen Brissot[5] or of his friend the Earl of Lauderdale, I ought to consider as proofs, not the least satisfactory, that I have produced some part of the effect I proposed by my endeavors. I have labored hard to earn what the noble Lords are generous enough to pay. Personal offense I have given them none. The part they take against me is from zeal to the cause. It is well! It is perfectly well! I have to do homage to their justice. I have to thank the Bedfords and the Lauderdales for having so faithfully and so fully acquitted towards me whatever arrear of debt was left undischarged by the Priestleys[6] and the Paines.[7]

Some, perhaps, may think them executors in their own wrong:[8] I at least have nothing to complain of. They have gone beyond the demands of justice. They have been (a little perhaps beyond their intention) favorable to me. They have been the means of bringing out, by their invectives, the handsome things which Lord Grenville[9] has had the goodness and condescension to say on my behalf. Retired as I am from the world and from all its affairs and all its pleasures, I confess it does kindle, in my nearly extinguished feelings, a very vivid satisfaction to be so attacked and so commended. It is soothing to my wounded mind to be commended by an able, vigorous, and well-informed statesman, and at the very moment when he stands forth with a manliness and resolution, worthy of himself and of his cause, for the preservation of the person and government of our sovereign, and therein for the security of the laws, the liberties, the morals, and the lives of his people. To be in any fair way connected with such things is indeed a distinction. No philosophy can make

[4] Philippe Egalité, a cousin of Louis XVI, had voted for his execution.

[5] Jacques Pierre Brissot, a moderate among the French Revolutionists. Like Philippe Egalité, he himself eventually was guillotined by the Jacobins. "Citizen" had replaced "Monsieur" as the French mode of address.

[6] Joseph Priestley, the noted chemist, wrote a reply to Burke's *Reflections on the Revolution in France.*

[7] Thomas Paine's *Rights of Man* was the most famous of the replies to Burke's *Reflections.*

[8] a legal phrase defining strangers who take it upon themselves to act as executors without any right to do so.

[9] William Wyndham Grenville, Baron Grenville, Foreign Secretary, who had replied in the House of Lords to Bedford's attack.

me above it; no melancholy can depress me so low as to make me wholly insensible to such an honor.

Why will they not let me remain in obscurity and inaction? Are they apprehensive that if an atom of me remains, the sect has something to fear? Must I be annihilated, lest, like old John Zisca's,[10] my skin might be made into a drum to animate Europe to eternal battle against a tyranny that threatens to overwhelm all Europe and all the human race?

My Lord, it is a subject of awful meditation. Before this of France, the annals of all time have not furnished an instance of a *complete* revolution. That Revolution seems to have extended even to the constitution of the mind of man. It has this of wonderful in it, that it resembles what Lord Verulam says of the operations of nature: it was perfect, not only in all its elements and principles, but in all its members and its organs from the very beginning.[11] The moral scheme of France furnishes the only pattern ever known which they who admire will *instantly* resemble. It is indeed an inexhaustible repertory of one kind of examples. In my wretched condition, though hardly to be classed with the living, I am not safe from them. They have tigers to fall upon animated strength. They have hyenas to prey upon carcasses. The national menagerie is collected by the first physiologists[12] of the time, and it is defective in no description of savage nature. They pursue even such as me into the obscurest retreats, and haul them before their revolutionary tribunals. Neither sex, nor age—not the sanctuary of the tomb is sacred to them. They have so determined a hatred to all privileged orders that they deny even to the departed the sad immunities of the grave. They are not wholly without an object. Their turpitude purveys to their malice; and they unplumb the dead[13] for bullets to assassinate the living. If all revolutionists were not proof against all caution, I should recommend it to their consideration that no persons were ever known in history, either sacred or profane, to vex

[10] a Bohemian leader of the Hussites in the early fifteenth century, of whom it was said that he wanted his skin to be made into a drumhead after his death to frighten his enemies.

[11] Francis Bacon, Lord Verulam. A passage suggesting Burke's allusion occurs in the *Novum Organum,* ii 4.

[12] naturalists.

[13] the French Revolutionists melted down the lead from coffins for bullets.

the sepulchre, and, by their sorceries, to call up the prophetic dead with any other event than the prediction of their own disastrous fate: "Leave me, oh leave me to repose!" [14]

In one thing I can excuse the Duke of Bedford for his attack upon me and my mortuary pension. He cannot readily comprehend the transaction he condemns. What I have obtained was the fruit of no bargain; the production of no intrigue; the result of no compromise; the effect of no solicitation. The first suggestion of it never came from me, mediately or immediately, to his Majesty or any of his Ministers. It was long known that the instant my engagements[15] would permit it, and before the heaviest of all calamities[16] had for ever condemned me to obscurity and sorrow, I had resolved on a total retreat. I had executed that design. I was entirely out of the way of serving or of hurting any statesman, or any party, when the Ministers so generously and so nobly carried into effect the spontaneous bounty of the Crown. Both descriptions[17] have acted as became them. When I could no longer serve them, the Ministers have considered my situation. When I could no longer hurt them, the revolutionists have trampled on my infirmity. My gratitude, I trust, is equal to the manner in which the benefit was conferred. It came to me indeed at a time of life and in a state of mind and body in which no circumstance of fortune could afford me any real pleasure. But this was no fault in the royal donor or in his Ministers, who were pleased, in acknowledging the merits of an invalid servant of the public, to assuage the sorrows of a desolate old man.

It would ill become me to boast of anything. It would as ill become me, thus called upon, to depreciate the value of a long life spent with unexampled toil in the service of my country. Since the total body of my services, on account of the industry which was shown in them, and the fairness of my intentions, have obtained the acceptance of my sovereign, it would be absurd in me to range myself on the side of the Duke of Bedford and the Corresponding Society,[18] or, as far as in me lies, to permit a dispute on the rate

[14] the Prophetess's repeated reply from the grave, slightly misquoted, to the questions of Odin in Gray's *Descent of Odin*.

[15] particularly Burke's involvement in the trial of Warren Hastings.

[16] the death of his son, Richard, in 1794.

[17] groups.

[18] a political society in sympathy with the French Revolutionists.

at which the authority appointed by *our* constitution to estimate such things has been pleased to set them.

Loose libels ought to be passed by in silence and contempt. By me they have been so always. I knew that as long as I remained in public, I should live down the calumnies of malice and the judgments of ignorance. If I happened to be now and then in the wrong (as who is not?), like all other men I must bear the consequence of my faults and my mistakes. The libels of the present day are just of the same stuff as the libels of the past. But they derive an importance from the rank of the persons they come from, and the gravity of the place where they were uttered. In some way or other I ought to take some notice of them. To assert myself thus traduced is not vanity or arrogance. It is a demand of justice; it is a demonstration of gratitude. If I am unworthy, the Ministers are worse than prodigal. On that hypothesis, I perfectly agree with the Duke of Bedford.

For whatever I have been (I am now no more) I put myself on my country. I ought to be allowed a reasonable freedom, because I stand upon my deliverance;[19] and no culprit ought to plead in irons. Even in the utmost latitude of defensive liberty, I wish to preserve all possible decorum. Whatever it may be in the eyes of these noble persons themselves, to me their situation calls for the most profound respect. If I should happen to trespass a little, which I trust I shall not, let it always be supposed that a confusion of characters may produce mistakes; that, in the masquerades of the grand carnival of our age, whimsical adventures happen; odd things are said and pass off. If I should fail a single point in the high respect I owe to those illustrious persons, I cannot be supposed to mean the Duke of Bedford and the Earl of Lauderdale of the House of Peers, but the Duke of Bedford and the Earl of Lauderdale of Palace Yard[20]—the dukes and earls of Brentford.[21] There they are on the pavement; there they seem to come nearer to my humble level; and, virtually at least, to have waived their high privilege.

---

[19] am concerned about securing my release.

[20] Old Palace Yard, in front of the House of Lords.

[21] a London suburb, whose two chief magistrates were made kings, according to tradition, by a Saxon ruler. These "kings" are introduced as ridiculous characters in Buckingham's play, *The Rehearsal* (1671), and are referred to satirically elsewhere.

Making this protestation, I refuse all revolutionary tribunals, where men have been put to death for no other reason than that they had obtained favors from the Crown. I claim, not the letter, but the spirit of the old English law, that is, to be tried by my peers. I decline his Grace's[22] jurisdiction as a judge. I challenge the Duke of Bedford as a juror to pass upon the value of my services. Whatever his natural parts[23] may be, I cannot recognize, in his few and idle years,[24] the competence to judge of my long and laborious life. If I can help it, he shall not be on the inquest of my *quantum meruit*.[25] Poor rich man! He can hardly know anything of public industry in its exertions, or can estimate its compensations when its work is done. I have no doubt of his Grace's readiness in all the calculations of vulgar arithmetic; but I shrewdly suspect that he is little studied in the theory of moral proportions; and has never learned the rule of three[26] in the arithmetic of policy and state.

His Grace thinks I have obtained too much. I answer that my exertions, whatever they have been, were such as no hopes of pecuniary reward could possibly excite; and no pecuniary compensation can possibly reward them. Between them and money there is no common measurer. Such services, if done by abler men than I am, are quantities incommensurable. Money is made for the comfort and convenience of animal life. It cannot be a reward for what mere animal life must indeed sustain, but never can inspire. With submission to his Grace, I have not had more than sufficient. As to any noble use, I trust I know how to employ, as well as he, a much greater fortune than he possesses. In a more confined application, I certainly stand in need of every kind of relief and easement much more than he does. When I say I have not received more than I deserve, is this the language I hold to Majesty? No! Far, very far, from it! Before that presence, I claim no merit at all. Every thing towards me is favor and bounty. One style to a gracious benefactor; another to a proud and insulting foe.

His Grace is pleased to aggravate my guilt, by charging my

[22] the form of address for a duke (here the Duke of Bedford).

[23] talents, capacities.

[24] Bedford was about thirty.

[25] law Latin for "how much was it worth?"

[26] the rule that the product of the means of a proportion equals the product of the extremes.

acceptance of his Majesty's grant as a departure from my ideas, and the spirit of my conduct with regard to economy. If it be, my ideas of economy were false and ill founded. But they are the Duke of Bedford's ideas of economy I have contradicted, and not my own. If he means to allude to certain bills brought in by me on a Message from the Throne in 1782, I tell him that there is nothing in my conduct that can contradict either the letter or the spirit of those acts. Does he mean the Pay Office Act?[27] I take it for granted he does not. The Act to which he alludes, is, I suppose, the Establishment Act.[28] I greatly doubt whether his Grace has ever read the one or the other. The first of these systems cost me, with every assistance which my then situation gave me, pains incredible. I found an opinion common through all the offices, and general in the public at large, that it would prove impossible to reform and methodize the office of Paymaster General. I undertook it, however; and I succeeded in my undertaking. Whether the military service, or whether the general economy of our finances have profited by that act, I leave to those who are acquainted with the army and with the treasury to judge.

An opinion full as general prevailed also at the same time that nothing could be done for the regulation of the Civil-List Establishment. The very attempt to introduce method into it, and any limitations to its services, was held absurd. I had not seen the man who so much as suggested one economical principle, or an economical expedient, upon that subject. Nothing but coarse amputation, or coarser taxation, were then talked of, both of them without design, combination, or the least shadow of principle. Blind and headlong zeal, or factious fury, were the whole contribution brought by the most noisy on that occasion towards the satisfaction of the public or the relief of the Crown.

Let me tell my youthful censor[29] that the necessities of that time required something very different from what others then sug-

---

[27] Burke, who had himself been Paymaster General at the time, had reformed the Paymaster's Office. He is said to have saved the country £47,000 a year by his reforms, which included giving up some of the Paymaster's perquisites in disbursing money to the military.

[28] the act of 1782 reforming the Establishment (composed of the royal household, great officers of state, ambassadors, etc.) supported by money voted on the Civil List.

[29] ironic, since the Roman Censor was usually an elderly man.

gested, or what his Grace now conceives. Let me inform him that it was one of the most critical periods in our annals.

Astronomers have supposed that if a certain comet[30] whose path intercepted the ecliptic had met the earth in some (I forget what) sign, it would have whirled us along with it, in its eccentric course, into God knows what regions of heat and cold. Had the portentous comet of the Rights of Man[31] (which "from its horrid hair shakes pestilence and war," and "with fear of change perplexes monarchs"[32]), had that comet crossed upon us in that internal state[33] of England, nothing human could have prevented our being irresistibly hurried out of the highway of heaven into all the vices, crimes, horrors, and miseries of the French Revolution.

Happily, France was not then Jacobinized. Her hostility was at a good distance. We had a limb cut off, but we preserved the body: we lost our colonies, but we kept our constitution. There was, indeed, much intestine heat; there was a dreadful fermentation. Wild and savage insurrection quitted the woods and prowled about our streets in the name of reform. Such was the distemper of the public mind, that there was no madman,[34] in his maddest ideas and maddest projects, that might not count upon numbers to support his principles and execute his designs.

Many of the changes, by a great misnomer called parliamentary reforms, went, not in the intention of all the professors and supporters of them, undoubtedly, but went in their certain, and, in my opinion, not very remote effect, home to the utter destruction of the constitution of this kingdom. Had they taken place, not

[30] perhaps the Great Comet of 1680, which Halley calculated might have hit the earth if its course had been slightly altered.

[31] an allusion to the statement of the natural Rights of Man which the French National Assembly adopted in 1789 as the basis of the constitution.

[32] *Paradise Lost*, ii 710-11 (its *for* his); i 589-99. In the first quotation Satan is compared to a comet, and in the second to the sun in eclipse.

[33] There was considerable pressure for both an economic and a political reform of Parliament in the early 1780's. Burke opposed such political reforms as the abolition of the rotten boroughs and universal suffrage.

[34] Burke seems to be referring particularly to Lord George Gordon, who in 1780 had led a mob of 60,000 to petition Parliament against the repeal of anti-Catholic laws. The mob got out of hand, and burned and sacked London for almost a week.

France, but England would have had the honor of leading up the death-dance[35] of democratic revolution. Other projects, exactly coincident in time with those, struck at the very existence of the kingdom under any constitution. There are who remember the blind fury of some, and the lamentable helplessness of others; here, a torpid confusion, from a panic fear of the danger; there, the same inaction from a stupid insensibility to it; here, well-wishers to the mischief; there, indifferent lookers-on. At the same time, a sort of National Convention,[36] dubious in its nature and perilous in its example, nosed Parliament in the very seat of its authority; sat with a sort of superintendence over it; and little less than dictated to it, not only laws, but the very form and essence of legislature itself. In Ireland[37] things ran in a still more eccentric course. Government was unnerved, confounded, and in a manner suspended. Its equipoise was totally gone. I do not mean to speak disrespectfully of Lord North. He was a man of admirable parts; of general knowledge; of a versatile understanding fitted for every sort of business; of infinite wit and pleasantry; of a delightful temper; and with a mind most perfectly disinterested. But it would be only to degrade myself by a weak adulation, and not to honor the memory of a great man, to deny that he wanted something of the vigilance and spirit of command that the time required. Indeed, a darkness, next to the fog of this awful day, loured over the whole region. For a little time the helm appeared abandoned—

> *Ipse diem noctemque negat discernere caelo,*
> *Nec meminisse viae media Palinurus in unda.*[38]

[35] a popular allegory of the late Middle Ages, illustrating the power of death in the midst of scenes of apparent vitality.

[36] probably a reference to the Society for Constitutional Information, to which Burke applies the name of the revolutionary French National Convention. In 1782 it had recommended that popular assemblies petition Parliament for reform, since Parliament would not reform itself of its own accord.

[37] The Irish wished the severe restrictions on their exports removed, and were opposed by the English manufacturing towns. Lord North, then Prime Minister, veered back and forth in this conflict.

[38] *Aeneid*, iii 201-2. Dryden translates:
> Even Palinurus [the pilot] no distinction found
> Betwixt the night and day; such darkness reigned around.

At that time I was connected with men of high place[39] in the community. They loved liberty as much as the Duke of Bedford can do; and they understood it at least as well. Perhaps their politics, as usual, took a tincture from their character, and they cultivated what they loved. The liberty they pursued was a liberty inseparable from order, from virtue, from morals, and from religion, and was neither hypocritically nor fanatically followed. They did not wish that liberty, in itself one of the first of blessings, should in its perversion become the greatest curse which could fall upon mankind. To preserve the constitution entire, and practically equal to all the great ends of its formation, not in one single part but in all its parts, was to them the first object. Popularity and power they regarded alike. They were with them different means of obtaining that object, and had no other preference over each other in their minds than as they furnished the surer or the less certain means of arriving at that end. It is some consolation to me in the cheerless gloom which darkens the evening of my life, that with them I commenced my political career, and never for a moment, in reality nor in appearance, for any length of time was separated from their good wishes and good opinion.

By what accident it matters not, nor upon what desert, but just then, and in the midst of that hunt of obloquy[40] which ever has pursued me with a full cry through life, I had obtained a very considerable degree of public confidence. I know well enough how equivocal a test this kind of popular opinion forms of the merit that obtained it. I am no stranger to the insecurity of its tenure. I do not boast of it. It is mentioned to show, not how highly I prize the thing, but my right to value the use I made of it. I endeavored to turn that short-lived advantage to myself into a permanent benefit to my country. Far am I from detracting from the merit of some gentlemen, out of office or in it, on that occasion. No!—It is not my way to refuse a full and heaped measure of justice to the aids that I receive. I have, through life, been willing to give everything to others; and to reserve nothing for myself but the inward con-

[39] the Rockingham Whigs.

[40] Among other accusations, Burke was charged with being a Roman Catholic (Catholics could not sit in Parliament or vote), as well as with having made a fortune by unscrupulous means.

science that I had omitted no pains to discover, to animate, to discipline, to direct the abilities of the country for its service, and to
place them in the best light to improve their age or to adorn it.
This conscience I have. I have never suppressed any man; never
checked him for a moment in his course by any jealousy or by any
policy. I was always ready to the height of my means, which were
always infinitely below my desires, to forward those abilities that
overpowered my own. He is an ill-furnished undertaker[41] who has
no machinery but his own hands to work with. Poor in my own
faculties, I thought myself rich in theirs. I then consulted and
sincerely co-operated with men of all parties who seemed disposed
to the same ends, or to any main part of them. Nothing to prevent
disorder was omitted; when it appeared, nothing to subdue it was
left uncounselled nor unexecuted, as far as I could prevail. At the
time I speak of, and having a momentary lead, so aided and so
encouraged and as a feeble instrument in a mighty hand—I do
not say I saved my country; I am sure I did my country important
service. There were few, indeed, that did not at that time acknowledge it, and that time was thirteen years ago. It was but one voice,
that no man in the kingdom better deserved an honorable provision
should be made for him.

So much for my general conduct through the whole of the
portentous crisis from 1780 to 1782, and the general sense then
entertained of that conduct by my country. But my character as
a reformer, in the particular instances which the Duke of Bedford
refers to, is so connected in principle with my opinions on the
hideous changes which have since barbarized France, and, spreading
thence, threaten the political and moral order of the whole world,
that it seems to demand something of a more detailed discussion.

My economical reforms[42] were not, as his Grace may think,
the suppression of a paltry pension or employment, more or less.
Economy in my plans was, as it ought to be, secondary, subordinate,
instrumental. I acted on state principles. I found a great distemper
in the commonwealth; and, according to the nature of the evil and

[41] one who undertakes a project.
[42] Burke stated, in 1780, that his reform plan was primarily aimed at
restoring administrative vigor to the government, and at securing Parliamentary independence of the King and Ministry.

of the object, I treated it. The malady was deep; it was complicated, in the causes and in the symptoms. Throughout it was full of contraindicants. On one hand Government, daily growing more invidious for an apparent increase of the means of strength, was every day growing more contemptible by real weakness.[43] Nor was this dissolution confined to Government commonly so called. It extended to Parliament, which was losing not a little in its dignity and estimation, by an opinion of its not acting on worthy motives.[44] On the other hand, the desires of the people[45] (partly natural and partly infused into them by art) appeared in so wild and inconsiderate a manner, with regard to the economical object (for I set aside for a moment the dreadful tampering with the body of the constitution itself), that if their petitions had literally been complied with, the state would have been convulsed; and a gate would have been opened through which all property might be sacked and ravaged. Nothing could have saved the public from the mischiefs of the false reform but its absurdity, which would soon have brought itself, and with it all real reform, into discredit. This would have left a rankling wound in the hearts of the people, who knew they had failed in the accomplishment of their wishes, but who, like the rest of mankind in all ages, would impute the blame to anything rather than to their own proceedings. But there were then persons in the world who nourished complaint, and would have been thoroughly disappointed if the people were ever satisfied. I was not of that humor. I wished that they *should* be satisfied. It was my aim to give to the people the substance of what I knew they desired, and what I thought was right whether they desired it or not, before it had been modified for them into senseless petitions. I knew that there is a manifest marked distinction, which ill [46] men, with ill designs, or weak men incapable of any design, will constantly be confounding, that is, a marked distinction between change and

[43] Burke means that the Ministerial hold on Parliament weakened the government rather than strengthened it, since the Ministers were indecisive and were quarreling among themselves.

[44] that it was controlled by Ministerial powers of patronage.

[45] the lower classes, who were in general disqualified from voting by property clauses.

[46] evil.

reformation. The former alters the substance of the objects them-selves, and gets rid of all their essential good, as well as of all the accidental evil, annexed to them. Change is novelty; and whether it is to operate any one of the effects of reformation at all, or whether it may not contradict the very principle upon which ref-ormation is desired, cannot be certainly known beforehand. Reform is not a change in the substance, or in the primary modification of the object, but a direct application of a remedy to the grievance complained of. So far as that is removed, all is sure. It stops there; and, if it fails, the substance which underwent the operation, at the very worst, is but where it was.

All this, in effect, I think but am not sure, I have said elsewhere. It cannot at this time be too often repeated, line upon line,[47] precept upon precept, until it comes into the currency of a proverb, *to inno-vate is not to reform*. The French revolutionists complained of every-thing; they refused to reform anything; and they left nothing, no, nothing at all *unchanged*. The consequences are *before* us,—not in remote history; not in future prognostication: they are about us; they are upon us. They shake the public security; they menace private enjoyment. They dwarf the growth of the young; they break the quiet of the old. If we travel, they stop our way. They infest us in town; they pursue us to the country. Our business is interrupted; our repose is troubled; our pleasures are saddened; our very studies are poisoned and perverted, and knowledge is rendered worse than ignorance by the enormous evils of this dreadful innovation. The revolution harpies of France, sprung from night and hell, or from that chaotic anarchy which generates equivocally[48] "all monstrous, all prodigious things,"[49] cuckoo-like, adulterously lay their eggs, and brood over, and hatch them in the nest of every neighboring state. These obscene harpies, who deck themselves in I know not what divine attributes, but who in reality are foul and ravenous birds of prey (both mothers and daughters), flutter over our heads, and souse[50] down upon our tables, and leave nothing unrent, un-

[47] Burke condenses Isaiah 28:10.

[48] literally, conceives by spontaneous generation; figuratively, its offspring cannot claim parents, or is ambiguous in its origins.

[49] from Milton's description of Chaos (*Paradise Lost,* ii 625).

[50] swoop.

rifled, unravaged, or unpolluted with the slime of their filthy offal.[51]

If his Grace can contemplate the result of this complete innovation, or, as some friends of his will call it, *reform,* in the whole body
of its solidity and compound mass, at which, as Hamlet says,[62] the
face of heaven glows with horror and indignation, and which, in
truth, makes every reflecting mind, and every feeling heart, perfectly
thought-sick, without a thorough abhorrence of everything they say,
and everything they do, I am amazed at the morbid strength, or the
natural infirmity of his mind.

It was then not my love, but my hatred, to innovation, that
produced my plan of reform. Without troubling myself with the
exactness of the logical diagram, I considered them as things sub-
stantially opposite. It was to prevent that evil, that I proposed the
measures which his Grace is pleased, and I am not sorry he is
pleased, to recall to my recollection. I had (what I hope that noble
duke will remember in all its operations) a state to preserve, as well
as a state to reform. I had a people to gratify, but not to inflame
or to mislead. I do not claim half the credit for what I did, as for
what I prevented from being done. In that situation of the public
mind, I did not undertake, as was then proposed, to new model [53]
the House of Commons or the House of Lords; or to change the authority under which any officer of the Crown acted, who was suffered
at all to exist. Crown, Lords, Commons, judicial system, system of

[51] Burke supplies in Latin, Virgil's description of the Harpies (*Aeneid,*
iii 214-18), given here in Dryden's translation:
> Monsters more fierce offended heaven ne'er sent
> From hell's abyss, for human punishment—
> With virgin-faces, but with wombs obscene,
> Foul paunches, and with ordure still unclean;
> With claws for hands, and looks for ever lean.

Here the poet breaks the line [the Latin ends in a broken line], because
he (and that he is Virgil) had not verse or language enough to describe
that monster even as he had conceived her. Had he lived in our time, he
would have been more overpowered with the reality than he was with the
imagination. Virgil only knew the horror of the times before him. Had he
lived to see the Revolutionists and Constitutionalists of France, he would
have had more horrid and disgusting features of his Harpies to describe, and
more frequent failures in the attempt to describe them (Burke).

[52] III iv 49-52.

[53] Cromwell organized the New Model army, on a professional basis,
with which he finally overthrew Parliament.

administration, existed as they had existed before, and in the mode and manner in which they had always existed. My measures were, what I then truly stated them to the House[54] to be, in their intent, healing and mediatorial. A complaint was made of too much influence[55] in the House of Commons; I reduced it in both Houses; and I gave my reasons article by article for every reduction, and showed why I thought it safe for the service of the state. I heaved the lead [56] every inch of way I made. A disposition to expense was complained of; to that I opposed not mere retrenchment, but a system of economy which would make a random expense without plan or foresight, in future not easily practicable. I proceeded upon principles of research to put me in possession of my matter; on principles of method to regulate it; and on principles in the human mind and in civil affairs to secure and perpetuate the operation. I conceived nothing arbitrarily; nor proposed anything to be done by the will and pleasure of others, or my own, but by reason, and by reason only. I have ever abhorred, since the first dawn of my understanding to this its obscure twilight, all the operations of opinion, fancy, inclination, and will, in the affairs of government, where only a sovereign reason, paramount to all forms of legislation and administration, should dictate. Government is made for the very purpose of opposing that reason to will and caprice, in the reformers or in the reformed, in the governors or in the governed, in kings, in senates, or in people.

On a careful review, therefore, and analysis of all the component parts of the Civil List, and on weighing them against each other, in order to make, as much as possible, all of them a subject of estimate (the foundation and cornerstone of all regular provident economy), it appeared to me evident that this was impracticable whilst that part, called the pension list, was totally discretionary in its amount. For this reason, and for this only, I proposed to reduce it, both in its gross quantity and in its larger individual proportions, to a certainty; lest if it were left without a *general* limit, it might eat up the Civil-List service; if suffered to be granted in portions too

[54] of Commons.

[55] In 1780, the House of Commons passed Dunning's resolution that "the influence of the Crown has increased, is increasing, and ought to be diminished."

[56] took soundings.

great for the fund, it might defeat its own end; and by unlimited allowances to some, it might disable the Crown in means of providing for others. The pension list was to be kept as a sacred fund, but it could not be kept as a constant, open fund, sufficient for growing demands, if some demands would wholly devour it. The tenor of the Act will show that it regarded the Civil List *only,* the reduction of which to some sort of estimate was my great object.

No other of the crown funds did I meddle with, because they had not the same relations. This of the four and a half per cents,[57] does his Grace imagine had escaped me, or had escaped all the men of business who acted with me in those regulations? I knew that such a fund existed and that pensions had been always granted on it, before his Grace was born. This fund was full in my eye. It was full in the eyes of those who worked with me. It was left on principle. On principle I did what was then done; and on principle what was left undone was omitted. I did not dare to rob the nation of all funds to reward merit. If I pressed this point too close, I acted contrary to the avowed principles on which I went. Gentlemen are very fond of quoting me; but if any one thinks it worth his while to know the rules that guided me in my plan of reform, he will read my printed speech on that subject, at least what is contained from page 230 to page 241 in the second volume of the collection which a friend has given himself the trouble to make of my publications.[58] Be this as it may, these two bills[59] (though achieved with the greatest labor and management of every sort, both within and without the House) were only a part, and but a small part, of a very large system, comprehending all the objects I stated in opening my proposition,[60] and, indeed, many more, which I just hinted at in my speech to the electors of Bristol,[61] when I was put out of that representation. All these, in some state or other of forwardness, I have long had by me.

[57] a fund derived from West Indian duties, on which Burke's pension was charged.

[58] Dr. French Laurence brought out a three-volume edition of Burke's writings in 1792.

[59] the Pay Office Act and the Establishment Act.

[60] Burke's Speech on Economical Reform, given in 1780.

[61] perhaps Burke's most famous speech, addressed to his constituents in 1780.

But do I justify his Majesty's grace on these grounds? I think them the least of my services! The time gave them an occasional [62] value: what I have done in the way of political economy[63] was far from confined to this body of measures. I did not come into Parliament to con my lesson. I had earned my pension before I set my foot in St. Stephen's Chapel.[64] I was prepared and disciplined to this political warfare. The first session I sat in Parliament, I found it necessary to analyze the whole commercial, financial, constitutional, and foreign interests of Great Britain and its empire. A great deal was then done; and more, far more, would have been done, if more had been permitted by events. Then, in the vigor of my manhood, my constitution sunk under my labor. Had I then died (and I seemed to myself very near death), I had then earned for those who belonged to me more than the Duke of Bedford's ideas of service are of power to estimate. But, in truth, these services I am called to account for are not those on which I value myself the most. If I were to call for a reward (which I have never done), it should be for those in which for fourteen years, without intermission, I showed the most industry and had the least success: I mean in the affairs of India.[65] They are those on which I value myself the most; most for the importance; most for the labor; most for the judgment; most for constancy and perseverance in the pursuit. Others may value them most for the *intention*. In that, surely, they are not mistaken.

Does his Grace think that they who advised the Crown to make my retreat easy considered me only as an economist? That, well understood, however, is a good deal. If I had not deemed it of some value, I should not have made political economy an object of my humble studies from my very early youth to near the end of my service in Parliament, even before (at least to any knowledge of mine) it had employed the thoughts of speculative men[66] in other parts of Europe. At that time it was still in its infancy in

[62] temporary.
[63] the study of national finances and resources.
[64] where the House of Commons sat.
[65] From 1780 to 1794 Burke concerned himself closely with Indian affairs, including of course the trial of Warren Hastings, who was acquitted.
[66] theorists.

England, where, in the last century, it had its origin.[67] Great and learned men thought my studies were not wholly thrown away, and deigned to communicate with me now and then on some particulars of their immortal works. Something of these studies may appear incidentally in some of the earliest things I published. The House has been witness to their effect, and has profited of them more or less, for above eight and twenty years.

To their estimate I leave the matter. I was not, like his Grace of Bedford, swaddled and rocked and dandled into a legislator; *"Nitor in adversum"*[68] is the motto for a man like me. I possessed not one of the qualities, nor cultivated one of the arts that recommend men to the favor and protection of the great. I was not made for a minion or a tool. As little did I follow the trade of winning the hearts, by imposing on the understandings, of the people. At every step of my progress in life (for in every step was I traversed [69] and opposed), and at every turnpike[70] I met, I was obliged to show my passport, and again and again to prove my sole title to the honor of being useful to my country by a proof that I was not wholly unacquainted with its laws and the whole system of its interests both abroad and at home. Otherwise no rank, no toleration even, for me. I had no arts but manly arts. On them I have stood, and, please God, in spite of the Duke of Bedford and the Earl of Lauderdale, to the last gasp will I stand.

Had his Grace condescended to enquire concerning the person whom he has not thought it below him to reproach, he might have found that in the whole course of my life I have never, on any pretense of economy or on any other pretense, so much as in a single instance, stood between any man and his reward of service, or his encouragement in useful talent and pursuit, from the highest of those services and pursuits to the lowest. On the contrary I have, on an hundred occasions, exerted myself with singular zeal to forward every man's even tolerable pretensions. I have more than once had good-natured reprehensions from my friends for carrying the matter to something bordering on abuse. This line of conduct, whatever its merits might be, was partly owing to natural disposition,

[67] Burke presumably refers to William Petty and John Locke among others.

[68] "I make my way against opposition" (Ovid, *Metamorphoses*, ii 72).

[69] crossed.

[70] barrier or tollgate.

but I think full as much to reason and principle. I looked on the consideration of public service, or public ornament, to be real and very justice: and I ever held a scanty and penurious justice to partake of the nature of a wrong. I held it to be, in its consequences, the worst economy in the world. In saving money, I soon can count up all the good I do; but when by a cold penury I blast the abilities of a nation and stunt the growth of its active energies, the ill I may do is beyond all calculation. Whether it be too much or too little, whatever I have done has been general and systematic. I have never entered into those trifling vexations and oppressive details that have been falsely, and most ridiculously, laid to my charge.

Did I blame the pensions given to Mr. Barré and Mr. Dunning[71] between the proposition and execution of my plan? No! surely no! Those pensions were within my principles. I assert it, those gentlemen deserved their pensions, their titles—all they had; and if more they had, I should have been but pleased the more. They were men of talents; they were men of service. I put the profession of the law out of the question in one of them.[72] It is a service that rewards itself. But their *public service,* though, from their abilities unquestionably of more value than mine, in its quantity and in its duration, was not to be mentioned with it. But I never could drive a hard bargain in my life concerning any matter whatever; and least of all do I know how to haggle and huckster with merit. Pension for myself I obtained none; nor did I solicit any. Yet I was loaded with hatred for everything that was withheld, and with obloquy for everything that was given. I was thus left to support the grants of a name ever dear[73] to me, and ever venerable to the world, in favor of those who were no friends of mine or of his, against the rude attacks of those who were at that time friends to the grantees and their own zealous partisans. I have never heard the Earl of Lauderdale complain of these pensions. He finds nothing wrong till he comes to me. This is impartiality, in the true modern revolutionary style.

[71] Isaac Barré and John Dunning, created Baron Ashburton, were granted enormous pensions.

[72] Burke means he disregarded Dunning's large income from his law practice.

[73] Rockingham, who had died before the granting of these pensions, as Prime Minister had approved them in writing, as his successor Shelburne demonstrated.

Whatever I did at that time, so far as it regarded order and economy, is stable and eternal as all principles must be. A particular order of things may be altered; order itself cannot lose its value. As to other particulars, they are variable by time and by circumstances. Laws of regulation are not fundamental laws. The public exigencies are the masters of all such laws. They rule the laws, and are not to be ruled by them. They who exercise the legislative power at the time must judge.

It may be new to his Grace, but I beg leave to tell him that mere parsimony is not economy. It is separable in theory from it; and in fact it may, or it may not, be a *part* of economy, according to circumstances. Expense, and great expense, may be an essential part in true economy. If parsimony were to be considered as one of the kinds of that virtue, there is however another and an higher economy. Economy is a distributive virtue, and consists not in saving but in selection. Parsimony requires no providence, no sagacity, no powers of combination, no comparison, no judgment. Mere instinct, and that not an instinct of the noblest kind, may produce this false economy in perfection. The other economy has larger views. It demands a discriminating judgment, and a firm, sagacious mind. It shuts one door to impudent importunity, only to open another, and a wider, to unpresuming merit. If none but meritorious service or real talent were to be rewarded, this nation has not wanted, and this nation will not want, the means of rewarding all the service it ever will receive, and encouraging all the merit it ever will produce. No state, since the foundation of society, has been impoverished by that species of profusion. Had the economy of selection and proportion been at all times observed, we should not now have had an overgrown Duke of Bedford [74] to oppress the industry of humble men, and to limit, by the standard of his own conceptions, the justice, the bounty, or, if he pleases, the charity of the Crown.

His Grace may think as meanly as he will of my deserts in the far greater part of my conduct in life. It is free for him to do so. There will always be some difference of opinion in the value of political services. But there is one merit of mine, which he, of all men living, ought to be the last to call in question. I have supported

[74] The immense fortune of the Russells was founded on grants given to their ancestor John Russell, first Earl of Bedford, by Henry VIII.

with very great zeal, and I am told with some degree of success, those opinions, or if his Grace likes another expression better, those old prejudices which buoy up the ponderous mass of his nobility, wealth, and titles. I have omitted no exertion to prevent him and them from sinking to that level to which the meretricious French faction his Grace at least coquets with omit no exertion to reduce both. I have done all I could to discountenance their enquiries into the fortunes of those who hold large portions of wealth without any apparent merit of their own. I have strained every nerve to keep the Duke of Bedford in that situation which alone makes him my superior. Your Lordship has been a witness of the use he makes of that pre-eminence.

But be it, that this is virtue! Be it, that there is virtue in this well-selected rigor; yet all virtues are not equally becoming to all men and at all times. There are crimes, undoubtedly there are crimes which in all seasons of our existence ought to put a generous antipathy in action: crimes that provoke an indignant justice, and call forth a warm and animated pursuit. But all things that concern what I may call the preventive police of morality, all things merely rigid, harsh, and censorial, the antiquated moralists at whose feet I was brought up would not have thought these the fittest matter to form the favorite virtues of younger men of rank. What might have been well enough, and have been received with a veneration mixed with awe and terror, from an old, severe, crabbed Cato,[75] would have wanted something of propriety in the young Scipios, the ornament of the Roman nobility, in the flower of their life. But the times, the morals, the masters, the scholars, have all undergone a thorough revolution. It is a vile illiberal school, this new French academy of the *sans-culottes*.[76] There is nothing in it that is fit for a gentleman to learn.

Whatever its vogue may be, I still flatter myself that the parents of the growing generation will be satisfied with what is to be taught to their children in Westminster, in Eton, or in Winchester: I still

[75] the famous Censor, M. Porcius Cato, who especially attacked the Scipios. But Burke may be recalling Cicero's dialogue, *Of Old Age*, in which Cato is represented as conversing with P. Cornelius Scipio Africanus Minor.

[76] literally, "without knee breeches," the contemptuous name given by the French aristocracy to the middle and lower classes, who wore trousers.

indulge the hope that no *grown* gentleman or nobleman of our time will think of finishing at Mr. Thelwall's lecture[77] whatever may have been left incomplete at the old universities of his country. I would give to Lord Grenville and Mr. Pitt for a motto, what was said of a Roman censor or praetor (or what was he?) who, in virtue of a *Senatus consultum,*[78] shut up certain academies,

> *Cludere ludum impudentiae jussit.*

Every honest father of a family in the kingdom will rejoice at the breaking up for the holidays, and will pray that there may be a very long vacation in all such schools.

The awful state of the time, and not myself or my own justification, is my true object in what I now write; or in what I shall ever write or say. It little signifies to the world what becomes of such things as me, or even as the Duke of Bedford. What I say about either of us is nothing more than a vehicle, as you, my Lord, will easily perceive, to convey my sentiments on matters far more worthy of your attention. It is when I stick to my apparent first subject that I ought to apologize, not when I depart from it. I therefore must beg your Lordship's pardon for again resuming it after this very short digression; assuring you that I shall never altogether lose sight of such matter as persons abler than I am may turn to some profit.

The Duke of Bedford conceives that he is obliged to call the attention of the House of Peers to his Majesty's grant to me, which he considers as excessive and out of all bounds.

I know not how it has happened, but it really seems that, whilst his Grace was meditating his well-considered censure upon me, he fell into a sort of sleep. Homer nods, and the Duke of Bedford may dream; and as dreams (even his golden dreams) are apt to be ill-pieced and incongruously put together, his Grace preserved his idea of reproach to *me,* but took the subject matter from the crown grants *to his own family.* This is "the stuff of which his dreams are

---

[77] John Thelwall, a popular radical, expressed his opinions on contemporary politics through a series of lectures on Roman history. He answered Burke in his *Sober Reflections on the Seditious and Inflammatory Letter . . .* , 1796.

[78] decree of the Senate. The line below, adapted from Tacitus, reads, "He ordered the school of impudence closed" (*On Orators,* sec. 35).

made." [79] In that way of putting things together his Grace is perfectly in the right. The grants to the house of Russell were so enormous as not only to outrage economy, but even to stagger credibility. The Duke of Bedford is the Leviathan among all the creatures of the Crown. He tumbles about his unwieldy bulk; he plays and frolics in the ocean of the royal bounty. Huge as he is, and whilst "he lies floating many a rood," [80] he is still a creature. His ribs, his fins, his whalebone, his blubber, the very spiracles[81] through which he spouts a torrent of brine against his origin, and covers me all over with the spray,—everything of him and about him is from the throne. Is it for *him* to question the dispensation of the royal favor?

I really am at a loss to draw any sort of parallel between the public merits of his Grace, by which he justifies the grants he holds, and these services of mine, on the favorable construction of which I have obtained what his Grace so much disapproves. In private life, I have not at all the honor of acquaintance with the noble Duke. But I ought to presume, and it costs me nothing to do so, that he abundantly deserves the esteem and love of all who live with him. But as to public service, why truly it would not be more ridiculous for me to compare myself in rank, in fortune, in splendid descent, in youth, strength, or figure, with the Duke of Bedford, than to make a parallel between his services and my attempts to be useful to my country. It would not be gross adulation, but uncivil irony, to say that he has any public merit of his own to keep alive the idea of the services by which his vast landed pensions were obtained. My merits, whatever they are, are original and personal; his are derivative. It is his ancestor, the original pensioner, that has laid up this inexhaustible fund of merit[82] which makes his Grace so very delicate and exceptious about the merit of all other grantees of the Crown. Had he permitted me to remain in quiet, I should have said, 'tis his estate; that's enough. It is his by law; what have I to do with it or its history? He would naturally have said on his

---

[79] paraphrased from *The Tempest*, IV i 156-57.

[80] altered from Milton's comparison of Satan to Leviathan and other gigantic creatures (*Paradise Lost,* i 196).

[81] blowholes.

[82] the Catholic concept that the merits of Christ, the Virgin Mary, and the saints provide an infinite "treasury" for indulgences that the Church grants to the faithful.

side, 'tis this man's fortune.—He is as good now as my ancestor was two hundred and fifty years ago. I am a young man with very old pensions; he is an old man with very young pensions—that's all.

Why will his Grace, by attacking me, force me reluctantly to compare my little merit with that which obtained from the Crown those prodigies of profuse donation by which he tramples on the mediocrity of humble and laborious individuals? I would willingly leave him to the Heralds' College,[83] which the philosophy of the *sans-culottes* (prouder by far than all the Garters, and Norroys, and Clarencieux, and Rouge Dragons, that ever pranced in a procession of what his friends call aristocrats and despots[84]) will abolish with contumely and scorn. These historians, recorders, and blazoners of virtues and arms, differ wholly from that other description of historians, who never assign any act of politicians to a good motive. These gentle historians, on the contrary, dip their pens in nothing but the milk of human kindness. They seek no further for merit than the preamble of a patent, or the inscription on a tomb. With them every man created a peer is first an hero ready made. They judge of every man's capacity for office by the offices he has filled, and the more offices the more ability. Every general officer with them is a Marlborough; every statesman a Burleigh; every judge a Murray or a Yorke. They, who alive were laughed at or pitied by all their acquaintance, make as good a figure as the best of them in the pages of Guillim, Edmondson, and Collins.[85]

To these recorders, so full of good nature to the great and prosperous, I would willingly leave the first Baron Russell and Earl of Bedford, and the merits of his grants. But the aulnager,[86] the weigher, the meter[87] of grants, will not suffer us to acquiesce in the judgment of the prince reigning at the time when they were made. They are never good to those who earn them. Well then; since the new grantees have war made on them by the old, and that the word of the sovereign is not to be taken, let us turn our eyes to

[83] the College of Arms, which registers armorial bearings, etc. The titles mentioned below are those of officers of the College.

[84] "Aristocrat" was a word formed at the time of the French Revolution; "despot" originally meant absolute ruler, and came to mean "tyrant" at this time also.

[85] authorities on heraldry and genealogy.

[86] inspector of woolen goods.

[87] official measurer.

history, in which great men have always a pleasure in contemplating the heroic origin of their house.

The first peer of the name, the first purchaser[88] of the grants, was a Mr. Russell, a person of an ancient gentleman's family, raised by being a minion of Henry the Eighth. As there generally is some resemblance of character to create these relations, the favorite was in all likelihood much such another as his master. The first of those immoderate grants was not taken from the ancient demesne of the Crown, but from the recent confiscation of the ancient nobility of the land. The lion having sucked the blood of his prey threw the offal carcass to the jackal in waiting. Having tasted once the food of confiscation, the favorites became fierce and ravenous. This worthy favorite's first grant was from the lay nobility. The second, infinitely improving on the enormity of the first, was from the plunder of the church. In truth his Grace is somewhat excusable for his dislike to a grant like mine, not only in its quantity but in its kind so different from his own.

Mine was from a mild and benevolent sovereign; his from Henry the Eighth.

Mine had not its fund in the murder of any innocent person of illustrious rank,[89] or in the pillage of any body of unoffending men.[90] His grants were from the aggregate and consolidated funds[91] of judgments iniquitously legal, and from possessions voluntarily surrendered by the lawful proprietors with the gibbet at their door.

The merit of the grantee whom he derives from was that of being a prompt and greedy instrument of a *levelling*[92] tyrant, who oppressed all descriptions of his people, but who fell with particular fury on everything that was *great and noble*. Mine has been, in endeavoring to screen every man, in every class, from oppression, and

[88] (1) one who acquires land or property other than by inheritance; (2) robber or beggar.

[89] "See the history of the melancholy catastrophe of the Duke of Buckingham" in the time of Henry VIII (Burke). Edward Strafford, Duke of Buckingham, was executed simply because Henry wished it.

[90] churchmen.

[91] Burke alludes to excise and custom revenues "consolidated" into a fund about ten years before, on which all public debts were secured.

[92] a word which alludes not only to Henry's crushing of opposition, but which associates him with the radical Levellers of Cromwell's time, and with the "levellers" of the French Revolution.

particularly in defending the high and eminent, who in the bad times of confiscating princes, confiscating chief governors, or confiscating demagogues, are the most exposed to jealousy, avarice, and envy.

The merit of the original grantee of his Grace's pensions was in giving his hand to the work, and partaking the spoil with a prince who plundered a part of the national church of his time and country. Mine was in defending the whole of the national church of my own time and my own country, and the whole of the national churches of all countries, from the principles and the examples which lead to ecclesiastical pillage, thence to a contempt of *all* prescriptive titles,[93] thence to the pillage of *all* property, and thence to universal desolation.

The merit of the origin of his Grace's fortune was in being a favorite and chief adviser to a prince who left no liberty to their native country. My endeavor was to obtain liberty for the municipal country[94] in which I was born, and for all descriptions and denominations in it. Mine was to support with unrelaxing vigilance every right, every privilege, every franchise, in this my adopted, my dearer, and more comprehensive country; and not only to preserve those rights in this chief seat of empire, but in every nation, in every land, in every climate, language and religion, in the vast domain that still is under the protection, and the larger that was once under the protection, of the British Crown.

His founder's merits were, by arts in which he served his master and made his fortune, to bring poverty, wretchedness, and depopulation on his country. Mine were under a benevolent prince, in promoting the commerce, manufactures, and agriculture of his kingdom; in which his Majesty shows an eminent example, who even in his amusements is a patriot, and in hours of leisure an improver of his native soil.

His founder's merit was the merit of a gentleman raised by the arts of a court, and the protection of a Wolsey, to the eminence of a great and potent lord. His merit in that eminence was by in-

[93] titles established by long possession or by possession during a period fixed by law.

[94] Ireland, called municipal here, because its citizens should have enjoyed the full rights of English citizenship. A *municipium* under the Roman Empire was a town whose inhabitants held the right of Roman citizenship.

stigating a tyrant to injustice to provoke a people to rebellion. My merit was to awaken the sober part of the country, that they might put themselves on their guard against any one potent lord, or any greater number of potent lords, or any combination of great leading men of any sort, if ever they should attempt to proceed in the same courses, but in the reverse order, that is, by instigating a corrupted populace to rebellion, and through that rebellion should introduce a tyranny yet worse than the tyranny which his Grace's ancestor supported, and of which he profited in the manner we behold in the despotism of Henry the Eighth.

The political merit of the first pensioner of his Grace's house was that of being concerned as a counsellor of state in advising, and in his person executing, the conditions of a dishonorable peace with France: the surrendering the fortress of Boulogne, then our out-guard on the Continent. By that surrender, Calais, the key of France, and the bridle in the mouth of that power, was not many years afterwards finally lost. My merit has been in resisting the power and pride of France under any form of its rule, but in opposing it with the greatest zeal and earnestness when that rule appeared in the worst form it could assume; the worst indeed which the prime cause and principle of all evil could possibly give it. It was my endeavor by every means to excite a spirit in the House where I had the honor of a seat for carrying on with early vigor and decision the most clearly just and necessary war that this or any nation ever carried on; in order to save my country from the iron yoke of its power, and from the more dreadful contagion of its principles; to preserve, while they can be preserved, pure and untainted, the ancient, inbred integrity, piety, good nature, and good humor of the people of England from the dreadful pestilence, which beginning in France threatens to lay waste the whole moral and in a great degree the whole physical world, having done both in the focus of [95] its most intense malignity.

The labor of his Grace's founder merited the curses, not loud but deep,[96] of the Commons of England, on whom *he* and his master had effected a *complete parliamentary reform,* by making them in their slavery and humiliation the true and adequate repre-sentatives of a debased, degraded, and undone people. My merits

[95] having concentrated.
[96] *Macbeth,* V iii 27.

were in having had an active, though not always an ostentatious share, in every one act, without exception, of undisputed constitutional utility in my time, and in having supported on all occasions the authority, the efficiency, and the privileges of the Commons of Great Britain. I ended my services by a recorded and fully reasoned assertion on their own journals of their constitutional rights, and a vindication of their constitutional conduct.[97] I labored in all things to merit their inward approbation, and (along with the assistants of the largest, the greatest, and best of my endeavors[98]) I received their free, unbiased, public, and solemn thanks.

Thus stands the account of the comparative merits of the crown grants which compose the Duke of Bedford's fortune as balanced against mine. In the name of common sense, why should the Duke of Bedford think that none but of the house of Russell are entitled to the favor of the Crown? Why should he imagine that no king of England has been capable of judging of merit but King Henry the Eighth? Indeed, he will pardon me; he is a little mistaken; all virtue did not end in the first Earl of Bedford. All discernment did not lose its vision when his creator closed his eyes. Let him remit his rigor on the disproportion between merit and reward in others, and they will make no enquiry into the origin of his fortune. They will regard with much more satisfaction, as he will contemplate with infinitely more advantage, whatever in his pedigree has been dulcified[99] by an exposure to the influence of heaven in a long flow of generations from the hard, acidulous, metallic tincture of the spring. It is little to be doubted that several of his forefathers in that long series have degenerated[100] into honor and virtue. Let the Duke of Bedford (I am sure he will) reject with scorn and horror the counsels of the lecturers, those wicked panders to avarice and ambition, who would tempt him in the troubles of his country to seek another enormous fortune from the forfeitures of another nobility and the plunder of another

[97] Burke was influential in having the trial of Warren Hastings continued in 1790 after the election of a new Parliament. Not to have continued the trial would have meant that any impeachment proceedings could be stopped by the dissolution of Parliament.

[98] the impeachment of Hastings. The House of Commons passed a vote of thanks to the managers of the impeachment in 1794.

[99] sweetened; originally, to have neutralized the acidity of.

[100] Burke's sarcasm is reinforced by the literal meaning of "degenerate," to change from the genus or kind.

church. Let him (and I trust that yet he will) employ all the energy of his youth, and all the resources of his wealth, to crush rebellious principles which have no foundation in morals, and rebellious movements that have no provocation in tyranny.

Then will be forgot the rebellions which, by a doubtful priority in crime, his ancestor had provoked and extinguished. On such a conduct in the noble Duke, many of his countrymen might, and with some excuse might, give way to the enthusiasm of their gratitude, and in the dashing style of some of the old declaimers cry out, that if the fates had found no other way in which they could give a Duke of Bedford [101] and his opulence as props to a tottering world, then the butchery of the Duke of Buckingham might be tolerated; it might be regarded even with complacency, whilst in the heir of confiscation they saw the sympathizing comforter of the martyrs who suffer under the cruel confiscation of this day; whilst they beheld with admiration his zealous protection of the virtuous and loyal nobility of France, and his manly support of his brethren, the yet standing nobility and gentry of his native land. Then his Grace's merit would be pure and new and sharp, as fresh from the mint of honor. As he pleased he might reflect honor on his predecessors, or throw it forward on those who were to succeed him. He might be the propagator of the stock of honor, or the root of it, as he thought proper.

Had it pleased God to continue to me the hopes of succession, I should have been, according to my mediocrity and the mediocrity of the age I live in, a sort of founder of a family: I should have left a son, who, in all the points in which personal merit can be viewed, in science,[102] in erudition, in genius, in taste, in honor, in generosity, in humanity, in every liberal sentiment, and every liberal accomplishment, would not have shown himself inferior to the Duke of Bedford, or to any of those whom he traces in his line.[102a] His Grace very soon would have wanted all plausibility in his attack upon that provision which belonged more to mine than to me. He[103] would soon have supplied every deficiency, and symmetrized every

[101] Burke footnotes here in Latin, "For if Fate could discover no other means for Nero to come upon the scene, etc." The passage in Lucan (*Pharsalia,* i 33 ff.) ends, "Even such crimes and such guilt are not too much to bear."

[102] knowledge.   [102a] See *Macbeth,* IV i 153.

[103] Richard Burke. Burke's eulogy, according to contemporary opinion, was more generous than accurate.

disproportion. It would not have been for that successor to resort to any stagnant wasting reservoir of merit in me, or in any ancestry. He had in himself a salient, living spring of generous and manly action. Every day he lived he would have repurchased the bounty of the Crown, and ten times more, if ten times more he had received. He was made a public creature; and had no enjoyment whatever but in the performance of some duty. At this exigent moment, the loss of a finished man is not easily supplied.

But a Disposer whose power we are little able to resist, and whose wisdom it behooves us not at all to dispute, has ordained it in another manner, and (whatever my querulous weakness might suggest) a far better. The storm has gone over me; and I lie like one of those old oaks which the late hurricane[104] has scattered about me. I am stripped of all my honors; I am torn up by the roots, and lie prostrate on the earth! There, and prostrate there, I most unfeignedly recognize the divine justice, and in some degree submit to it. But whilst I humble myself before God, I do not know that it is forbidden to repel the attacks of unjust and inconsiderate men. The patience of Job is proverbial. After some of the convulsive struggles of our irritable nature, he submitted himself, and repented in dust and ashes.[105] But even so, I do not find him blamed for reprehending, and with a considerable degree of verbal asperity, those ill-natured neighbors of his, who visited his dunghill to read moral, political, and economical lectures on his misery. I am alone. I have none to meet my enemies in the gate.[106] Indeed, my Lord, I greatly deceive myself, if in this hard season I would give a peck of refuse wheat for all that is called fame and honor in the world. This is the appetite but of a few. It is a luxury, it is a privilege, it is an indulgence for those who are at their ease. But we are all of us made to shun disgrace, as we are made to shrink from pain and poverty and disease. It is an instinct; and under the direction of reason, instinct is always in the right. I live in an inverted order. They who ought to have succeeded me are gone before me. They who should have been to me as posterity are in the place of an-

---

[104] of 6 November 1795.

[105] "Wherefore I abhor myself, and repent in dust and ashes" (Job 42:6).

[106] "Happy is the man that hath his quiver full of them [children]: they shall not be ashamed, but they shall speak [bargain] with the enemies in the gate" (Psalm 127:5).

cestors. I owe to the dearest relation (which ever must subsist in memory) that act of piety which he would have performed to me; I owe it to him to show that he was not descended, as the Duke of Bedford would have it, from an unworthy parent.

The Crown has considered me after long service; the Crown has paid the Duke of Bedford by advance. He has had a long credit for any service which he may perform hereafter. He is secure, and long may he be secure, in his advance, whether he performs any services or not. But let him take care how he endangers the safety of that constitution which secures his own utility or his own insignificance; or how he discourages those who take up even puny arms to defend an order of things which, like the sun of heaven, shines alike[107] on the useful and the worthless. His grants are engrafted on the public law of Europe, covered with the awful hoar of innumerable ages. They are guarded by the sacred rules of prescription, found in that full treasury of jurisprudence from which the jejuneness and penury of our municipal law[108] has, by degrees, been enriched and strengthened. This prescription I had my share (a very full share) in bringing to its perfection.[109] The Duke of Bedford will stand as long as prescriptive law endures: as long as the great stable laws of property, common to us with all civilized nations, are kept in their integrity, and without the smallest intermixture of laws, maxims, principles, or precedents of the grand Revolution. They are secure against all changes but one.[110] The whole revolutionary system, institutes,[111] digest, code, novels, text, gloss, comment, are not only not the same, but they are the very reverse, and the reverse fundamentally, of all the laws on which civil life has hitherto been upheld in all the governments of the world. The learned professors of the Rights of Man regard prescription not as a title to bar all claim set up against old possession—but they look

---

[107] God "maketh his sun to rise on the evil and on the good" (Matthew 5:45).

[108] local, in this case British, law, as opposed to international law, "that full treasury of jurisprudence."

[109] Sir George Savile's Act, called the *Nullum Tempus* Act (Burke). An act, passed in 1769, which limited the claims of the Crown against private property possessed for more than a certain length of time.

[110] revolution.

[111] Burke uses terms connected with Justinian's codification of Roman law. "Novels" were new laws promulgated during Justinian's reign.

on prescription as itself a bar against the possessor and proprietor. They hold an immemorial possession to be no more than a long continued, and therefore an aggravated, injustice.

Such are *their* ideas; such *their* religion, and such *their* law. But as to *our* country and *our* race, as long as the well-compacted structure of our church and state, the sanctuary, the holy of holies of that ancient law, defended by reverence, defended by power, a fortress at once and a temple,[112] shall stand inviolate on the brow of the British Sion—as long as the British monarchy, not more limited than fenced by the orders of the state, shall, like the proud Keep of Windsor,[113] rising in the majesty of proportion, and girt with the double belt of its kindred and coeval towers, as long as this awful structure shall oversee and guard the subjected land— so long the mounds and dykes of the low, fat Bedford Level [114] will have nothing to fear from all the pickaxes of all the levellers of France. As long as our Sovereign Lord the King, and his faithful subjects, the Lords and Commons of this realm—the triple cord,[115] which no man can break; the solemn, sworn, constitutional frank-pledge of this nation; the firm guarantees of each other's being and each other's rights; the joint and several securities, each in its place and order, for every kind and every quality, of property and of dignity—as long as these endure, so long the Duke of Bedford is safe: and we are all safe together—the high from the blights of envy and the spoliations of rapacity; the low from the iron hand of oppression and the insolent spurn of contempt. Amen! and so be it: and so it will be,

> *Dum domus Aeneae Capitoli immobile saxum*
> *Accolet imperiumque pater Romanus habebit.*—[116]

[112] *Templum in modum arcis* (Tacitus [*Histories,* v 12], of the temple of Jerusalem) (Burke).

[113] of Windsor Castle, symbolizing the British government. Its "coeval towers" stand for the two Houses of Parliament.

[114] a large area of flat land, named for a seventeenth-century Earl of Bedford and his son, who were leaders in draining its fens. The pickaxes of the "levellers" would destroy the dykes and flood the crops of this land.

[115] an allusion to the "threefold cord [which] is not quickly broken" of Ecclesiastes 4:12.

[116] *Aeneid,* ix 448-49. Dryden translates:

Fixed as the Capitol's foundation lies,
And spread where'er the Roman eagle flies!

But if the rude inroad of Gallic tumult, with its sophistical Rights of Man to falsify the account, and its sword as a make-weight[117] to throw into the scale, shall be introduced into our city by a misguided populace set on by proud great men, themselves blinded and intoxicated by a frantic ambition, we shall, all of us, perish and be overwhelmed in a common ruin. If a great storm blow on our coast, it will cast the whales on the strand as well as the periwinkles. His Grace will not survive the poor grantee he despises, no, not for a twelvemonth. If the great look for safety in the services they render to this Gallic cause, it is to be foolish, even above the weight of privilege allowed to wealth. If his Grace be one of these whom they endeavor to proselytize, he ought to be aware of the character of the sect whose doctrines he is invited to embrace. With them insurrection is the most sacred of revolutionary duties to the state. Ingratitude to benefactors is the first of revolutionary virtues. Ingratitude is indeed their four cardinal virtues compacted and amalgamated into one; and he will find it in everything that has happened since the commencement of the philosophic Revolution to this hour. If he pleads the merit of having performed the duty of insurrection against the order he lives in (God forbid he ever should), the merit of others will be to perform the duty of insurrection against him. If he pleads (again God forbid he should, and I do not suspect he will) his ingratitude to the Crown for its creation of his family, others will plead their right and duty to pay him in kind. They will laugh, indeed they will laugh, at his parchment and his wax. His deeds will be drawn out with the rest of the lumber[118] of his evidence room,[119] and burnt to the tune of *ça ira*[120] in the courts of Bedford (then Equality) House.

Am I to blame if I attempt to pay his Grace's hostile reproaches to me with a friendly admonition to himself? Can I be blamed to point out to him in what manner he is likely to be affected, if the sect of the cannibal philosophers of France should proselytize any considerable part of this people, and by their joint proselytizing

[117] The Celts, who had besieged Rome in the fourth century B.C., had agreed to retire for a thousand pounds of gold. As the gold was being weighed, their leader cast his sword onto the scale, crying, "Woe to the vanquished."

[118] refuse.

[119] room in which title deeds are kept.

[120] "that will go," part of the refrain of a famous French Revolutionary song. "String up the aristocrats" is its next line.

arms should conquer that government to which his Grace does not seem to me to give all the support his own security demands? Surely it is proper that he, and that others like him, should know the true genius of this sect, what their opinions are, what they have done, and to whom; and what (if a prognostic is to be formed from the dispositions and actions of men) it is certain they will do hereafter. He ought to know that they have sworn assistance, the only engagement they ever will keep, to all in this country who bear a resemblance to themselves, and who think as such, that *the whole duty of man*[121] consists in destruction. They are a misallied and disparaged [122] branch of the house of Nimrod.[123] They are the Duke of Bedford's natural hunters, and he is their natural game. Because he is not very profoundly reflecting, he sleeps in profound security; they, on the contrary, are always vigilant, active, enterprising, and, though far removed from any knowledge which makes men estimable or useful, in all the instruments and resources of evil their leaders are not meanly instructed or insufficiently furnished. In the French Revolution everything is new; and, from want of preparation to meet so unlooked-for an evil, everything is dangerous. Never before this time was a set of literary men converted into a gang of robbers and assassins. Never before did a den of bravoes and banditti assume the garb and tone of an academy of philosophers.

Let me tell his Grace that an union of such characters, monstrous as it seems, is not made for producing despicable enemies. But if they are formidable as foes, as friends they are dreadful indeed. The men of property in France, confiding in a force which seemed to be irresistible because it had never been tried, neglected to prepare for a conflict with their enemies at their own weapons. They were found in such a situation as the Mexicans were when they were attacked by the dogs, the cavalry, the iron, and the gunpowder of an handful of bearded men,[124] whom they did not know to exist in nature. This is a comparison that some, I think, have made; and it is just. In France they had their enemies within their houses. They were even in the bosoms of many of them. But they

---

[121] "Fear God, and keep his commandments: for this is the whole duty of man" (Ecclesiastes 12:13).

[122] from *mésallier* and *desparagier*, both meaning "to marry beneath one."

[123] Nimrod seen as usurping tyrant (*Paradise Lost*, xii 24 ff.).

[124] Cortez and his forces.

had not sagacity to discern their savage character. They seemed tame, and even caressing. They had nothing but *douce humanité*[125] in their mouth. They could not bear the punishment of the mildest laws on the greatest criminals. The slightest severity of justice made their flesh creep. The very idea that war existed in the world disturbed their repose. Military glory was no more than, with them, a splendid infamy. Hardly would they hear of self-defense, which they reduced within such bounds as to leave it no defense at all. All this while they meditated the confiscations and massacres we have seen. Had any one told these unfortunate noblemen and gentlemen how, and by whom, the grand fabric of the French monarchy under which they flourished would be subverted, they would not have pitied him as a visionary, but would have turned from him as what they call a *mauvais plaisant*.[126] Yet we have seen what has happened. The persons who have suffered from the cannibal philosophy of France are so like the Duke of Bedford that nothing but his Grace's probably not speaking quite so good French could enable us to find out any difference. A great many of them had as pompous titles as he, and were of full as illustrious a race; some few of them had fortunes as ample; several of them, without meaning the least disparagement to the Duke of Bedford, were as wise, and as virtuous, and as valiant, and as well-educated, and as complete in all the lineaments of men of honor, as he is: and to all this they had added the powerful outguard of a military profession, which, in its nature, renders men somewhat more cautious than those who have nothing to attend to but the lazy enjoyment of undisturbed possessions. But security was their ruin. They are dashed to pieces in the storm, and our shores are covered with the wrecks. If they had been aware that such a thing might happen, such a thing never could have happened.

I assure his Grace that if I state to him the designs of his enemies in a manner which may appear to him ludicrous and impossible, I tell him nothing that has not exactly happened, point by point, but twenty-four miles from our own shore. I assure him that the Frenchified faction, more encouraged than others are warned by what has happened in France, look at him and his landed possessions as an object at once of curiosity and rapacity. He

[125] brotherhood.
[126] one who makes ill-considered jokes.

is made for them in every part of their double character. As robbers, to them he is a noble booty; as speculatists,[127] he is a glorious subject for their experimental philosophy. He affords matter for an extensive analysis in all the branches of their science, geometrical, physical, civil, and political. These philosophers are fanatics; independent of any interest,[128] which if it operated alone would make them much more tractable, they are carried with such an headlong rage towards every desperate trial that they would sacrifice the whole human race to the slightest of their experiments. I am better able to enter into the character of this description of men than the noble Duke can be. I have lived long and variously in the world. Without any considerable pretensions to literature in myself, I have aspired to the love of letters. I have lived for a great many years in habitudes with those who professed them. I can form a tolerable estimate of what is likely to happen from a character, chiefly dependent for fame and fortune on knowledge and talent, as well in its morbid and perverted state, as in that which is sound and natural. Naturally men so formed and finished are the first gifts of Providence to the world. But when they have once thrown off the fear of God, which was in all ages too often the case, and the fear of man, which is now the case, and when in that state they come to understand one another and to act in corps, a more dreadful calamity cannot arise out of hell to scourge mankind. Nothing can be conceived more hard than the heart of a thoroughbred metaphysician. It comes nearer to the cold malignity of a wicked spirit than to the frailty and passion of a man. It is like that of the principle of evil himself, incorporeal, pure, unmixed, dephlegmated, defecated[129] evil. It is no easy operation to eradicate humanity from the human breast. What Shakespeare calls "the compunctious visitings of nature" [130] will sometimes knock at their hearts, and protest against their murderous speculations. But they have a means of compounding with their nature. Their humanity is not dissolved. They only give it a long prorogation. They are ready to declare that they do not think two thousand years too long a period for the good that they pursue. It is remarkable that they never see any way to their pro-

[127] theorists.
[128] share in something, especially legal right or title to property.
[129] purified, unmitigated.
[130] *Macbeth,* I v 46.

jected good but by the road of some evil. Their imagination is not fatigued with the contemplation of human suffering through the wild waste of centuries added to centuries of misery and desolation. Their humanity is at their horizon—and, like the horizon, it always flies before them. The geometricians and the chemists bring, the one from the dry bones of their diagrams, and the other from the soot of their furnaces, dispositions that make them worse than indifferent about those feelings and habitudes which are the supports of the moral world. Ambition is come upon them suddenly; they are intoxicated with it, and it has rendered them fearless of the danger which may from thence arise to others or to themselves. These philosophers consider men, in their experiments, no more than they do mice in an air pump, or in a recipient[131] of mephitic gas. Whatever his Grace may think of himself, they look upon him and everything that belongs to him with no more regard than they do upon the whiskers of that little long-tailed animal that has been long the game of the grave, demure, insidious, spring-nailed, velvet-pawed, green-eyed philosophers, whether going upon two legs or upon four.

His Grace's landed possessions are irresistibly inviting to an *agrarian*[132] experiment. They are a downright insult upon the Rights of Man. They are more extensive than the territory of many of the Grecian republics; and they are without comparison more fertile than most of them. There are now republics in Italy, in Germany, and in Switzerland which do not possess anything like so fair and ample a domain. There is a scope for seven philosophers to proceed in their analytical experiments, upon Harrington's[133] seven different forms of republics, in the acres of this one Duke. Hitherto they have been wholly unproductive to speculation; fitted for nothing but to fatten bullocks, and to produce grain for beer, still more to stupefy the dull English understanding. Abbé Sieyès[134] has whole nests of pigeonholes full of constitutions ready made,

[131] receptacle.

[132] An agrarian was one who favored redistribution of landed property.

[133] James Harrington, author of *The Commonwealth of Oceana* (1656), in which forms of government are defined according to the distribution of property among the various classes.

[134] As Burke indicates, Emmanuel Joseph Sieyès was one of the leading French constitutional theorists.

ticketed, sorted, and numbered; suited to every season and every fancy; some with the top of the pattern at the bottom, and some with the bottom at the top; some plain, some flowered; some distinguished for their simplicity, others for their complexity; some of blood color; some of *boue de Paris*;[135] some with directories, others without a direction; some with councils of elders, and councils of youngsters; some without any council at all. Some, where the electors choose the representatives; others, where the representatives choose the electors. Some in long coats, and some in short cloaks; some with pantaloons; some without breeches. Some with five-shilling qualifications; some totally unqualified. So that no constitution-fancier may go unsuited from his shop, provided he loves a pattern of pillage, oppression, arbitrary imprisonment, confiscation, exile, revolutionary judgment, and legalized premeditated murder, in any shapes into which they can be put. What a pity it is that the progress of experimental philosophy should be checked by his Grace's monopoly! Such are their sentiments, I assure him; such is their language when they dare to speak; and such are their proceedings when they have the means to act.

Their geographers and geometricians have been some time out of practice. It is some time since they have divided their own country into squares.[136] That figure has lost the charms of its novelty. They want new lands for new trials. It is not only the geometricians of the republic that find him a good subject, the chemists have bespoke him after the geometricians have done with him. As the first set have an eye on his Grace's lands, the chemists are not less taken with his buildings. They consider mortar as a very antirevolutionary[137] invention in its present state, but, properly employed, an admirable material for overturning all establishments. They have found that the gunpowder of *ruins* is far the fittest for making other *ruins*, and so ad infinitum. They have calculated what quantity of matter convertible into niter is to be found in Bedford House, in Woburn Abbey,[138] and in what his Grace and his trustees have still suffered

---

[135] Parisian mud, which was notable for its stench.

[136] The newly created French *départements* were roughly equal in size, though of course they were not squares.

[137] since mortar preserves rather than destroys.

[138] the Duke of Bedford's London house and country seat, respectively.

to stand of that foolish royalist Inigo Jones, in Covent Garden.[139] Churches, playhouses, coffeehouses, all alike are destined to be mingled and equalized and blended into one common rubbish; and well-sifted and lixiviated [140] to crystallize into true, democratic, explosive, insurrectionary niter. Their Academy *del Cimento* (*per antiphrasin*),[141] with Morveau and Hassenfratz[142] at its head, have computed that the brave *sans-culottes* may make war on all the aristocracy of Europe for a twelvemonth out of the rubbish of the Duke of Bedford's buildings.[143]

While these experiments are going on upon the Duke of Bedford's houses by the Morveaux and Priestleys, the Sieyès and

[139] Inigo Jones (1573-1652), King's Surveyor of Works, designed the church of St. Paul's, Covent Garden, and the piazza of Covent Garden for the fourth Earl of Bedford. Jones was fined under the Commonwealth as a "malignant." Covent Garden was famous for its theaters and coffeehouses.

[140] separated by washing with a solvent.

[141] The Italian Accademia del Cimento was founded in 1657 for experimental research. *Cimento* means "test," but its closeness in sound to *cemento* (cement) suggested *per antiphrasin* (by opposition of words) Burke's sarcastic reference.

[142] Louis Bernard Guyton de Morveau and Jean Henri Hassenfratz, two French chemists. Morveau was experimenting with explosives, and Hassenfratz had been head of the ordnance.

[143] There is nothing on which the leaders of the Republic, one and indivisible, value themselves more than on the chemical operations by which, through science, they convert the pride of aristocracy to an instrument of its own destruction—on the operations by which they reduce the magnificent, ancient country seats of the nobility, decorated with the *feudal* titles of Duke, Marquis, or Earl, into magazines of what they call *revolutionary* gunpowder. They tell us that hitherto things "had not yet been properly and in a *revolutionary* manner explored. . . . The strong *chateaus*, those *feudal* fortresses that *were ordered to be demolished*, attracted next the attention of your committee. *Nature* there had *secretly* regained her *rights*, and had produced saltpeter for the *purpose*, as it should seem, *of facilitating the execution of your decree by preparing the means of destruction*. From these *ruins*, which *still frown* on the liberties of the Republic, we have extracted the means of producing good; and those piles which have hitherto glutted the *pride of despots* and covered the plots of La Vendée will soon furnish wherewithal to tame the traitors and to overwhelm the disaffected. . . . The *rebellious cities* also have afforded a large quantity of saltpeter. *Commune Affranchie* (that is, the noble city of Lyons reduced in many parts to an heap of ruins) and Toulon will pay a *second* tribute to our artillery" (*Report*, 1st February 1794) (Burke).

the rest of the analytical [144] legislators and constitution-venders are quite as busy in their trade of decomposing organization, in forming his Grace's vassals into primary assemblies, national guards, first, second and third requisitioners, committees of research, conductors of the travelling guillotine, judges of revolutionary tribunals, legislative hangmen, supervisors of domiciliary visitation, exactors of forced loans, and assessors of the maximum.

The din of all this smithery may some time or other possibly wake this noble Duke, and push him to an endeavor to save some little matter from their experimental philosophy. If he pleads his grants from the Crown, he is ruined at the outset. If he pleads he has received them from the pillage of superstitious corporations,[145] this indeed will stagger them a little, because they are enemies to all corporations and to all religion. However, they will soon recover themselves and will tell his Grace, or his learned council,[146] that all such property belongs to the *nation,* and that it would be more wise for him, if he wishes to live the natural term of a *citizen* (that is, according to Condorcet's[147] calculation, six months on an average), not to pass for an usurper upon the national property. This is what the *serjeants-at-law*[148] of the Rights of Man will say to the puny *apprentices*[149] of the common law of England.

Is the genius[150] of philosophy not yet known? You may as well think the garden of the Tuileries was well protected with the cords of ribbon insultingly stretched by the National Assembly to keep the sovereign canaille from intruding on the retirement of the poor king of the French, as that such flimsy cobwebs will stand between the savages of the Revolution and their natural prey. Deep philosophers are no triflers; brave *sans-culottes* are no formalists. They will no more regard a Marquis of Tavistock than an Abbot

---

[144] breaking into parts.

[145] monasteries.

[146] counsel.

[147] Marie Jean Antoine Nicolas de Caritat, Marquis de Condorcet (1743-94), philosopher and mathematician, was a republican who denounced the Jacobins and died in prison. Famous for his studies on the laws of probability, he wished to apply these laws to political questions.

[148] a special class of high-ranking lawyers.

[149] "puny" means "puisne" (junior); a barrister of less than sixteen years' standing was once called an apprentice.

[150] nature.

of Tavistock; the Lord of Woburn will not be more respectable in their eyes than the Prior of Woburn; they will make no difference between the Superior of a Covent Garden of nuns and of a Covent Garden of another description.[151] They will not care a rush whether his coat is long or short; whether the color be purple or blue and buff.[152] They will not trouble *their* heads with what part of *his* head, his hair is cut from; and they will look with equal respect on a tonsure and a crop.[153] Their only question will be that of their Legendre,[154] or some other of their legislative butchers, how he cuts up?[155] how he tallows in the caul,[156] or on the kidneys?

Is it not a singular phenomenon that whilst the *sans-culotte* carcass butchers and the philosophers of the shambles are pricking their dotted lines upon his hide, and like the print of the poor ox that we see at the shop windows at Charing Cross, alive as he is and thinking no harm in the world, he is divided into rumps, and sirloins, and briskets, and into all sorts of pieces for roasting, boiling, and stewing, that all the while they are measuring *him,* his Grace is measuring *me;* is invidiously comparing the bounty of the Crown with the deserts of the defender of his order, and in the same moment fawning on those who have the knife half out of the sheath—poor innocent!

> *Pleased to the last, he crops the flowery food,*
> *And licks the hand just raised to shed his blood.*[157]

No man lives too long who lives to do with spirit, and suffer with resignation, what Providence pleases to command or inflict; but indeed they are sharp incommodities which beset old age. It was but the other day that, on putting in order some things which had

[151] Tavistock, Woburn, and Covent Garden were all confiscated religious properties given to the first Earl of Bedford. The Duke of Bedford was also Marquess of Tavistock and Lord of the Manor of Woburn. Covent (convent) Garden had become known for its whores.

[152] the royal color and the colors of the liberal Whigs, respectively.

[153] monks, of course, were tonsured; only Bedford and some of his friends had discarded the usual powdered wigs and begun to wear their hair short at this time.

[154] Louis Legendre, a butcher who became a popular Revolutionary orator.

[155] how much "meat" there is to the Bedford estate.

[156] whether there is much tallow fat in his abdominal region.

[157] Pope, *Essay on Man,* i 83-84.

been brought here[158] on my taking leave of London for ever, I looked over a number of fine portraits, most of them of persons now dead, but whose society in my better days made this a proud and happy place. Amongst these was the picture of Lord Keppel.[159] It was painted by an artist[160] worthy of the subject, the excellent friend of that excellent man from their earliest youth, and a common friend of us both, with whom we lived for many years without a moment of coldness, of peevishness, of jealousy, or of jar, to the day of our final separation.

I ever looked on Lord Keppel as one of the greatest and best men of his age; and I loved and cultivated him accordingly. He was much in my heart, and I believe I was in his to the very last beat. It was after his trial at Portsmouth that he gave me this picture. With what zeal and anxious affection I attended him through that his agony of glory, what part my son took in the early flush and enthusiasm of his virtue, and the pious passion[161] with which he attached himself to all my connections, with what prodigality we both squandered ourselves in courting almost every sort of enmity for his sake, I believe he felt, just as I should have felt such friendship on such an occasion. I partook indeed of this honor with several of the first and best and ablest in the kingdom, but I was behindhand with none of them; and I am sure that if to the eternal disgrace of this nation, and to the total annihilation of every trace of honor and virtue in it, things had taken a different turn from what they did, I should have attended him to the quarter-deck[162] with no less goodwill and more pride, though with far other feelings, than I partook of the general flow of national joy that attended the justice that was done to his virtue.

Pardon, my Lord, the feeble garrulity of age, which loves to diffuse itself in discourse of the departed great. At my years we live in retrospect alone: and wholly unfitted for the society of vigorous

---

[158] Gregories, Burke's country house at Beaconsfield near Windsor.

[159] Admiral Augustus Keppel (1725-86) was court-martialed in 1779 on charges of poor management in battle against the French fleet. He was acquitted and was made a Viscount and First Lord of the Admiralty in 1782.

[160] Sir Joshua Reynolds (1723-92).

[161] filial love.

[162] the place of naval executions.

life we enjoy the best balm to all wounds, the consolation of friendship, in those only whom we have lost for ever. Feeling the loss of Lord Keppel at all times, at no time did I feel it so much as on the first day when I was attacked in the House of Lords.

Had he lived, that reverend form would have risen in its place, and with a mild, parental reprehension to his nephew the Duke of Bedford, he would have told him that the favor of that gracious Prince, who had honored his virtues with the government of the navy of Great Britain, and with a seat in the hereditary great council [163] of his kingdom, was not undeservedly shown to the friend of the best portion of his life, and his faithful companion and counsellor under his rudest trials. He would have told him that to whomever else these reproaches might be becoming, they were not decorous in his near kindred. He would have told him that when men in that rank lose decorum,[164] they lose everything.

On that day I had a loss in Lord Keppel; but the public loss of him in this awful crisis—! I speak from much knowledge of the person; he never would have listened to any compromise with the rabble rout of this *sans-culotterie* of France. His goodness of heart, his reason, his taste, his public duty, his principles, his prejudices, would have repelled him for ever from all connection with that horrid medley of madness, vice, impiety, and crime.

Lord Keppel had two countries: one of descent,[165] and one of birth. Their interest and their glory are the same, and his mind was capacious of [166] both. His family was noble and it was Dutch: that is, he was of the oldest and purest nobility that Europe can boast, among a people renowned above all others for love of their native land. Though it was never shown in insult to any human being, Lord Keppel was something high.[167] It was a wild stock of pride, on which the tenderest of all hearts had grafted the milder virtues. He valued ancient nobility, and he was not disinclined to augment it with new honors. He valued the old nobility and the new, not

[163] the House of Lords.

[164] sense of appropriateness.

[165] Keppel's grandfather was Dutch, and came to England with William III, who made him Earl of Albemarle.

[166] able to contain.

[167] somewhat proud.

as an excuse for inglorious sloth but as an incitement to virtuous activity. He considered it as a sort of cure for selfishness and a narrow mind; conceiving that a man born in an elevated place in himself was nothing, but everything in what went before and what was to come after him. Without much speculation, but by the sure instinct of ingenuous feelings, and by the dictates of plain, unsophisticated, natural understanding, he felt that no great commonwealth could by any possibility long subsist without a body of some kind or other of nobility, decorated with honor and fortified by privilege. This nobility forms the chain that connects the ages of a nation, which otherwise (with Mr. Paine) would soon be taught that no one generation can bind another. He felt that no political fabric could be well made without some such order of things as might, through a series of time, afford a rational hope of securing unity, coherence, consistency, and stability to the state. He felt that nothing else can protect it against the levity of courts, and the greater levity of the multitude. That to talk of hereditary monarchy, without anything else of hereditary reverence in the commonwealth, was a low-minded absurdity; fit only for those detestable "fools aspiring to be knaves," [168] who began to forge in 1789 the false money of the French constitution.—That it is one fatal objection to all *new* fancied and *new fabricated* republics (among a people who, once possessing such an advantage, have wickedly and insolently rejected it), that the *prejudice*[169] of an old nobility is a thing that *cannot* be made. It may be improved, it may be corrected, it may be replenished: men may be taken from it or aggregated to it, but the *thing itself* is matter of *inveterate* opinion, and therefore *cannot* be matter of mere positive[170] institution. He felt that this nobility in fact does not exist in wrong of other orders of the state, but by them and for them.

I knew the man I speak of; and if we can divine the future out of what we collect from the past, no person living would look with more scorn and horror on the impious parricide committed on all their ancestry, and on the desperate attainder passed on all their posterity, by the Orléans, and the Rochefoucaulds, and the

---

[168] Pope, *Epilogue to the Satires,* i 164.
[169] long-standing conviction or habit of mind.
[170] formally decreed, artificial.

Fayettes, and the Vicomtes de Noailles, and the false Périgords,[171] and the long et cetera of the perfidious *sans-culottes* of the court, who like demoniacs, possessed with a spirit of fallen pride and inverted ambition, abdicated their dignities, disowned their families, betrayed the most sacred of all trusts, and by breaking to pieces a great link of society and all the cramps and holdings of the state, brought eternal confusion and desolation on their country. For the fate of the miscreant parricides themselves he would have had no pity. Compassion for the myriads of men of whom the world was not worthy,[172] who by their means have perished in prisons, or on scaffolds, or are pining in beggary and exile, would leave no room in his, or in any well-formed mind, for any such sensation. We are not made at once to pity the oppressor and the oppressed.

Looking to his Batavian[173] descent, how could he bear to behold his kindred, the descendants of the brave nobility of Holland, whose blood prodigally poured out had more than all the canals, meres, and inundations of their country protected their independence, to behold them bowed in the basest servitude to the basest and vilest of the human race; in servitude to those who in no respect were superior in dignity, or could aspire to a better place than that of hangmen to the tyrants, to whose sceptered pride they had opposed an elevation of soul that surmounted and overpowered the loftiness of Castile, the haughtiness of Austria, and the overbearing arrogance of France?

Could he with patience bear that the children of that nobility, who would have deluged their country and given it to the sea[174] rather than submit to Louis XIV, who was then in his meridian glory, when his arms were conducted by the Turennes, by the Luxembourgs, by the Boufflers; when his councils were directed by the Colberts and the Louvois; when his tribunals were filled

[171] Among these other noblemen who renounced old feudal rights, Charles Maurice de Talleyrand-Périgord, once Bishop of Autun, proposed that feudal privileges be abolished and that Church property be confiscated for the use of the nation. Talleyrand became famous for his political flexibility.

[172] Burke compares these men to the faithful described in Hebrews 11:36-38.

[173] In Roman times, the fierce Batavi inhabited what is now Holland.

[174] When William of Orange was attacked by the French under Louis XIV, he proposed that the country be submerged and that the people found a new Holland in the East Indies.

by the Lamoignons and the D'Aguesseaus—that these should be given up to the cruel sport of the Pichegrus, the Jourdans, the Santerres, under the Rolands, and Brissots, and Gorsas, and Robespierres, the Reubels, the Carnots, and Talliens, and Dantons, and the whole tribe of regicides, robbers, and revolutionary judges that from the rotten carcass of their own murdered country have poured out innumerable swarms of the lowest, and at once the most destructive of the classes of animated nature, which like columns of locusts have laid waste the fairest part of the world?

Would Keppel have borne to see the ruin of the virtuous patricians, that happy union of the noble and the burgher, who with signal prudence and integrity had long governed the cities of the confederate republic,[175] the cherishing fathers of their country who, denying commerce to themselves, made it flourish in a manner unexampled under their protection? Could Keppel have borne that a vile faction[176] should totally destroy this harmonious construction in favor of a robbing democracy founded on the spurious rights of man?

He was no great clerk,[177] but he was perfectly well versed in the interests of Europe, and he could not have heard with patience that the country of Grotius,[178] the cradle of the law of nations, and one of the richest repositories of all law, should be taught a new code by the ignorant flippancy of Thomas Paine, the presumptuous foppery of Lafayette, with his stolen[179] Rights of Man in his hand, the wild, profligate intrigue and turbulency of Marat, and the impious sophistry of Condorcet, in his insolent addresses[180] to the Batavian republic?

Could Keppel, who idolized the house of Nassau,[181] who was himself given to England, along with the blessings of the British

[175] Holland, or the United Provinces.

[176] The Dutch provinces began to go over to the French in the autumn of 1794.

[177] scholar.

[178] Dutch jurist and statesman, who wrote a standard work on international law.

[179] because modeled on the American Declaration of Independence.

[180] In 1792, Condorcet had invited the Dutch, or Batavians, as he called them, to unite with France. The Batavian Republic was formed in May, 1795, the Stadholder having fled in January before the conquering French.

[181] the Dutch ruling family.

and Dutch revolutions;[182] with revolutions of stability; with revolutions which consolidated and married the liberties and the interests of the two nations for ever, could he see the fountain of British liberty itself in servitude to France? Could he see with patience a Prince of Orange expelled as a sort of diminutive despot, with every kind of contumely, from the country which that family of deliverers had so often rescued from slavery, and obliged to live in exile in another country, which owes its liberty to his house?

Would Keppel have heard with patience that the conduct to be held on such occasions was to become short by the knees[183] to the faction of the homicides, to intreat them quietly to retire? or if the fortune of war should drive them from their first wicked and unprovoked invasion, that no security should be taken, no arrangement made, no barrier formed, no alliance entered into for the security of that, which under a foreign name is the most precious part of England? What would he have said if it was even proposed that the Austrian Netherlands[184] (which ought to be a barrier to Holland, and the tie of an alliance, to protect her against any species of rule that might be erected, or even be restored in France) should be formed into a republic under her influence, and dependent upon her power?

But above all, what would he have said if he had heard it made a matter of accusation against me, by his nephew the Duke of Bedford, that I was the author of the war? [185] Had I a mind to keep that high distinction to myself, as from pride I might but from justice I dare not, he would have snatched his share of it from my hand, and held it with the grasp of a dying convulsion to his end.

It would be a most arrogant presumption in me to assume to myself the glory of what belongs to his Majesty, and to his Ministers, and to his Parliament, and to the far greater majority of his faithful people; but had I stood alone to counsel, and that all were determined to be guided by my advice and to follow it implicitly—

---

[182] of 1688 and 1672, respectively.

[183] kneel. Burke was angry at the temporizing behavior of the British government.

[184] Belgium, which had been conquered by the French in 1794.

[185] Burke was, in fact, very influential in bringing about the war with France in 1793.

then I should have been the sole author of a war. But it should have been a war on my ideas and my principles. However, let his Grace think as he may of my demerits with regard to the war with regicide, he will find my guilt confined to that alone. He never shall, with the smallest color of reason, accuse me of being the author of a peace with regicide.[186] But that is high matter; and ought not to be mixed with anything of so little moment as what may belong to me, or even to the Duke of Bedford.

I have the honor to be, etc.

EDMUND BURKE.

[186] Pitt was considering negotiations with the French, which Burke opposed in his *Letters on a Regicide Peace*.

❧ George Crabbe ☙

George Crabbe (1754-1832) combined three careers: doctor, minister, and writer. Born in Aldeburgh, a fishing village in Suffolk, he served an apprenticeship to an apothecary, and then set up as a surgeon-apothecary in 1775. He abandoned this career four years later and went to London to earn his living as a writer. In 1782 he was ordained priest and became chaplain to the Duke of Rutland. He held several livings thereafter, and finally in 1814 became rector of Trowbridge, Wiltshire, where he spent the rest of his life.

Crabbe's long literary career divides into two parts: the poems, notably *The Village* (1783), published during or shortly after his early stay in London; and the long series of works beginning with *Poems* (1807), which includes *The Parish Register* and *Sir Eustace Grey*; *The Borough* (1810), *Tales in Verse* (1812), *Tales of the Hall* (1819), and the inferior *Posthumous Tales* (1834). This series shows Crabbe moving from static description and portrait toward narrative, until he achieves something which approaches a group of linked short stories in verse. His work, in its low-keyed, realistic, unsentimental picture of rural life, represents less the last gasp of eighteenth-century poetry than a reaction to it different in direction from Wordsworth's. It is indicative of the kind of work Crabbe produced that Thomas Hardy admired and was influenced by him.

Editions: Poetical Works, with His Letters and Journals, and His Life, by His Son (1834); *Poems*, ed. Adolphus A. Ward (1905-7).

Biography: René Huchon, *George Crabbe*, trans. Frederick Clarke (1907).

Critical Studies: E. M. Forster, *Two Cheers for Democracy* (1951); Arthur Sale, "The Development of Crabbe's Narrative Art," *Cambridge Journal* 5 (1952); Lilian Haddakin, *The Poetry of Crabbe* (1955).

The Borough[1]
[*1804-1809*, 1810]

LETTER XXII. THE POOR OF THE BOROUGH

PETER GRIMES

> ———————— *was a sordid soul,*
> *Such as does murder for a meed;*
> *Who, but for fear, knows no control,*
> *Because his conscience, seared and foul,*
> *Feels not the import of the deed;*
> *One whose brute feeling ne'er aspires*
> *Beyond his own more brute desires.*
>   SCOTT, *Marmion* [II xxii]

> *Methought the souls of all that I had murdered*
> *Came to my tent; and every one did threat . . .*
>   SHAKESPEARE, *Richard III* [V iii 204-5]

> *the time hath been,*
> *That, when the brains were out, the man would die,*
> *And there an end; but now they rise again,*
> *With twenty mortal murders on their crowns,*
> *And push us from our stools . . . .*
>   SHAKESPEARE, *Macbeth* [III iv 78-82]

Old Peter Grimes made fishing his employ,
His wife he cabined with him and his boy,

---

[1] *The Borough* is made up of twenty-four Letters which illustrate various aspects of a small fishing village. "What I thought I could best describe," Crabbe says, "that I attempted: the sea, and the country in the immediate vicinity; the dwellings and the inhabitants; some incidents and characters, with an exhibition of morals and manners, offensive perhaps to those of extremely delicate feelings, but sometimes, I hope, neither unamiable nor unaffecting."

Of Peter Grimes, Crabbe says, "The mind here exhibited is one untouched by pity, unstung by remorse, and uncorrected by shame; yet is this hardihood of temper and spirit broken by want, disease, solitude, and disappointment, and he becomes the victim of a distempered and horror-stricken fancy."

And seemed that life laborious to enjoy:
To town came quiet Peter with his fish,
And had of all a civil word and wish.   5
He left his trade upon the Sabbath day,
And took young Peter in his hand to pray;
But soon the stubborn boy from care broke loose,
At first refused, then added his abuse;
His father's love he scorned, his power defied,   10
But, being drunk, wept sorely when he died.
   Yes! then he wept, and to his mind there came
Much of his conduct, and he felt the shame:
How he had oft the good old man reviled,
And never paid the duty of a child;   15
How, when the father in his Bible read,
He in contempt and anger left the shed;[2]
"It is the word of life," the parent cried;
"This is the life itself," the boy replied;
And while old Peter in amazement stood,   20
Gave the hot spirit to his boiling blood:
How he, with oath and furious speech, began
To prove his freedom and assert the man;
And when the parent checked his impious rage,
How he had cursed the tyranny of age—   25
Nay, once had dealt the sacrilegious blow
On his bare head, and laid his parent low:
The father groaned—"If thou art old," said he,
"And hast a son—thou wilt remember me;
Thy mother left me in a happy time,   30
Thou kill'dst not her—Heaven spares the double crime."
   On an inn-settle, in his maudlin grief,
This he revolved, and drank for his relief.
   Now lived the youth in freedom, but debarred
From constant pleasure, and he thought it hard;   35
Hard that he could not every wish obey,
But must awhile relinquish ale and play;[3]
Hard! that he could not to his cards attend,
But must acquire the money he would spend.

[2] cottage.
[3] gambling.

With greedy eye he looked on all he saw,   40
He knew not justice, and he laughed at law;
On all he marked he stretched his ready hand;
He fished by water, and he filched by land.
Oft in the night has Peter dropped his oar,
Fled from his boat and sought for prey on shore;   45
Oft up the hedgerow glided, on his back
Bearing the orchard's produce in a sack,
Or farmyard load, tugged fiercely from the stack;
And as these wrongs to greater numbers rose,
The more he looked on all men as his foes.   50

He built a mud-walled hovel, where he kept
His various wealth, and there he ofttimes slept;
But no success could please his cruel soul,
He wished for one to trouble and control;
He wanted some obedient boy to stand   55
And bear the blow of his outrageous hand;
And hoped to find in some propitious hour
A feeling creature subject to his power.

Peter had heard there were in London then—
Still have they being!—workhouse-clearing men,   60
Who, undisturbed by feelings just or kind,
Would parish boys to needy tradesmen bind;
They[4] in their want a trifling sum would take,
And toiling slaves of piteous orphans make.

Such Peter sought, and when a lad was found,   65
The sum was dealt him, and the slave was bound.
Some few in town observed in Peter's trap
A boy, with jacket blue and woolen cap;
But none inquired how Peter used the rope,
Or what the bruise, that made the stripling stoop; 70
None could the ridges on his back behold,
None sought him shivering in the winter's cold;
None put the question, "Peter, dost thou give
The boy his food?—What, man! the lad must live.
Consider, Peter, let the child have bread,   75
He'll serve thee better if he's stroked and fed."

---

[4] the tradesmen. The premium paid to Grimes would have been 50
shillings for sea-clothing and bedding, according to the law of 1704.

None reasoned thus—and some, on hearing cries,
Said calmly, "Grimes is at his exercise."
    Pined,[5] beaten, cold, pinched, threatened, and abused—
His efforts punished and his food refused—   80
Awake tormented—soon aroused from sleep—
Struck if he wept, and yet compelled to weep,
The trembling boy dropped down and strove to pray,
Received a blow, and trembling turned away,
Or sobbed and hid his piteous face; while he,   85
The savage master, grinned in horrid glee.
He'd now the power he ever loved to show,
A feeling being subject to his blow.
    Thus lived the lad, in hunger, peril, pain,
His tears despised, his supplications vain;   90
Compelled by fear to lie, by need to steal,
His bed uneasy and unblessed his meal,
For three sad years the boy his tortures bore,
And then his pains and trials were no more.
    "How died he, Peter?" when the people said,   95
He growled—"I found him lifeless in his bed";
Then tried for softer tone, and sighed, "Poor Sam is dead."
Yet murmurs were there, and some questions asked—
How he was fed, how punished, and how tasked?
Much they suspected, but they little proved,   100
And Peter passed untroubled and unmoved.
    Another boy with equal ease was found,
The money granted, and the victim bound;
And what his fate? One night it chanced he fell
From the boat's mast and perished in her well,   105
Where fish were living kept, and where the boy
(So reasoned men) could not himself destroy:—
    "Yes! so it was," said Peter, "in his play
(For he was idle both by night and day),
He climbed the mainmast and then fell below";   110
Then showed his corpse and pointed to the blow.
"What said the jury?" They were long in doubt,
But sturdy Peter faced the matter out.
So they dismissed him, saying at the time,

[5] exhausted by suffering or hunger.

"Keep fast your hatchway when you've boys who climb."   115
This hit the conscience, and he colored more
Than for the closest questions put before.
　　Thus all his fears the verdict set aside,
And at the slave shop Peter still applied.
　　Then came a boy, of manners soft and mild—   120
Our seamen's wives with grief beheld the child;
All thought (the poor themselves) that he was one
Of gentle blood, some noble sinner's son,
Who had, belike, deceived some humble maid,
Whom he had first seduced and then betrayed.   125
However this, he seemed a gracious lad,
In grief submissive and with patience sad.
　　Passive he labored, till his slender frame
Bent with his loads, and he at length was lame:
Strange that a frame so weak could bear so long   130
The grossest insult and the foulest wrong;
But there were causes—in the town they gave
Fire, food, and comfort, to the gentle slave;
And though stern Peter, with a cruel hand,
And knotted rope, enforced the rude[6] command,   135
Yet he considered what he'd lately felt,
And his vile blows with selfish pity dealt.
　　One day such draughts the cruel fisher made,
He could not vend them in his borough trade,
But sailed for London mart; the boy was ill,   140
But ever humbled to his master's will;
And on the river, where they smoothly sailed,
He strove with terror and awhile prevailed;
But new to danger on the angry sea,
He clung affrighted to his master's knee: 145
The boat grew leaky and the wind was strong,
Rough was the passage and the time was long;
His liquor failed, and Peter's wrath arose—
No more is known—the rest we must suppose,
Or learn of Peter—Peter says, he "spied   150
The stripling's danger and for harbor tried;
Meantime the fish, and then th' apprentice died."

[6] harsh.

The pitying women raised a clamor round,
And weeping said, "Thou hast thy prentice drowned."
    Now the stern man was summoned to the hall,   155
To tell his tale before the burghers all:
He gave th' account; professed the lad he loved,
And kept his brazen features all unmoved.
    The mayor himself with tone severe replied,
"Henceforth with thee shall never boy abide;   160
Hire thee a freeman, whom thou durst not beat,
But who, in thy despite, will sleep and eat;
Free thou art now!—again shouldst thou appear,
Thou'lt find thy sentence, like thy soul, severe."
    Alas! for Peter not a helping hand,   165
So was he hated, could he now command;
Alone he rowed his boat, alone he cast
His nets beside, or made his anchor fast;
To hold a rope or hear a curse was none—
He toiled and railed, he groaned and swore alone.   170
    Thus by himself compelled to live each day,
To wait for certain hours the tide's delay;
At the same times the same dull views to see,
The bounding marshbank and the blighted tree;
The water only, when the tides were high,   175
When low, the mud half-covered and half-dry;
The sunburnt tar that blisters on the planks,
And bankside stakes in their uneven ranks;
Heaps of entangled weeds that slowly float,
As the tide rolls by th' impeded boat.   180
    When tides were neap, and, in the sultry day,
Through the tall bounding mudbanks made their way,
Which on each side rose swelling, and below
The dark warm flood ran silently and slow;
There anchoring, Peter chose from man to hide,   185
There hang his head, and view the lazy tide
In its hot slimy channel slowly glide;
Where the small eels that left the deeper way
For the warm shore, within the shallows play;
Where gaping mussels, left upon the mud,   190
Slope their slow passage to the fallen flood;

Here dull and hopeless he'd lie down and trace
How sidelong crabs had scrawled their crooked race;
Or sadly listen to the tuneless cry
Of fishing gull or clanging goldeneye;[7]   195
What time the sea birds to the marsh would come,
And the loud bittern, from the bulrush home,
Gave from the salt-ditch side the bellowing boom.
He nursed the feelings these dull scenes produce,
And loved to stop beside the opening sluice,   200
Where the small stream, confined in narrow bound,
Ran with a dull, unvaried, saddening sound;
Where all presented to the eye or ear
Oppressed the soul with misery, grief, and fear.

    Besides these objects, there were places three,   205
Which Peter seemed with certain dread to see;
When he drew near them he would turn from each,
And loudly whistle till he passed the reach.[8]

    A change of scene to him brought no relief;
In town, 'twas plain, men took him for a thief;   210
The sailors' wives would stop him in the street,
And say, "Now, Peter, thou'st no boy to beat";
Infants at play, when they perceived him, ran,
Warning each other, "That's the wicked man."
He growled an oath, and in an angry tone   215
Cursed the whole place and wished to be alone.

    Alone he was, the same dull scenes in view,
And still more gloomy in his sight they grew.
Though man he hated, yet employed alone
At bootless labor, he would swear and groan,   220
Cursing the shoals[9] that glided by the spot,
And gulls that caught them when his arts could not.

    Cold nervous tremblings shook his sturdy frame,
And strange disease—he couldn't say the name;
Wild were his dreams, and oft he rose in fright,   225
Waked by his view of horrors in the night—

[7] a duck noted for its swift, whistling flight.
[8] The reaches in a river are those parts which extend from point to point (Crabbe).
[9] schools of fish.

Horrors that would the sternest minds amaze,
Horrors that demons might be proud to raise;
And though he felt forsaken, grieved at heart,
To think he lived from all mankind apart;   230
Yet, if a man approached, in terrors he would start.
　　A winter passed since Peter saw the town,
And summer lodgers were again come down;
These, idly curious, with their glasses spied
The ships in bay as anchored for the tide,   235
The river's craft, the bustle of the quay,
And seaport views, which landmen love to see.
　　One, up the river, had a man and boat
Seen day by day, now anchored, now afloat;
Fisher he seemed, yet used no net nor hook;   240
Of seafowl swimming by, no heed he took,
But on the gliding waves still fixed his lazy look:
At certain stations he would view the stream,
As if he stood bewildered in a dream,
Or that some power had chained him for a time,   245
To feel a curse or meditate on crime.
　　This known, some curious, some in pity went,
And others questioned, "Wretch, dost thou repent?"
He heard, he trembled, and in fear resigned
His boat; new terror filled his restless mind,   250
Furious he grew, and up the country ran,
And there they seized him—a distempered man.
Him we received, and to a parish-bed,
Followed and cursed, the groaning man was led.
　　Here when they saw him, whom they used to shun,   255
A lost, lone man, so harassed and undone,
Our gentle females, ever prompt to feel,
Perceived compassion on their anger steal;
His crimes they could not from their memories blot,
But they were grieved, and trembled at his lot.   260
　　A priest too came, to whom his words are told,
And all the signs they shuddered to behold.
　　"Look! look!" they cried, "his limbs with horror shake,
And as he grinds his teeth, what noise they make!
How glare his angry eyes, and yet he's not awake.   265

See! what cold drops upon his forehead stand,
And how he clenches that broad bony hand."
  The priest attending, found he spoke at times
As one alluding to his fears and crimes:
"It was the fall," he muttered, "I can show   270
The manner how—I never struck a blow."
And then aloud—"Unhand me, free my chain;
On oath, he fell—it struck him to the brain—
Why ask my father?—that old man will swear
Against my life; besides, he wasn't there—   275
What, all agreed?—Am I to die today?—
My Lord, in mercy, give me time to pray."
  Then as they watched him, calmer he became,
And grew so weak he couldn't move his frame,
But murmuring spake, while they could see and hear   280
The start of terror and the groan of fear;
See the large dew-beads on his forehead rise,
And the cold death-drop glaze his sunken eyes;
Nor yet he died, but with unwonted force
Seemed with some fancied being to discourse;   285
He knew not us, or with accustomed art
He hid the knowledge, yet exposed his heart;
'Twas part confession and the rest defense,
A madman's tale, with gleams of waking sense.
  "I'll tell you all," he said, "the very day   290
When the old man first placed them in my way:
My father's spirit—he who always tried
To give me trouble, when he lived and died—
When he was gone, he could not be content
To see my days in painful labor spent,   295
But would appoint his meetings, and he made
Me watch at these, and so neglect my trade.
  " 'Twas one hot noon, all silent, still, serene,
No living being had I lately seen;
I paddled up and down and dipped my net,   300
But (such his pleasure) I could nothing get—
A father's pleasure, when his toil was done,
To plague and torture thus an only son!
And so I sat and looked upon the stream,

How it ran on, and felt as in a dream;   305
But dream it was not; no! I fixed my eyes
On the mid-stream and saw the spirits rise;
I saw my father on the water stand,
And hold a thin pale boy in either hand;
And there they glided ghastly on the top   310
Of the salt flood, and never touched a drop;
I would have struck them, but they knew th' intent,
And smiled upon the oar, and down they went.
   "Now, from that day, whenever I began
To dip my net, there stood the hard old man—   315
He and those boys: I humbled me and prayed
They would be gone—they heeded not, but stayed.
Nor could I turn, nor would the boat go by,
But gazing on the spirits, there was I.
They bade me leap to death, but I was loath to die;   320
And every day, as sure as day arose,
Would these three spirits meet me ere the close;
To hear and mark them daily was my doom;
And 'Come,' they said, with weak, sad voices, 'come.'
To row away with all my strength I tried,   325
But there were they, hard by me in the tide,
The three unbodied forms—and 'Come,' still 'come,' they cried.
   "Fathers should pity—but this old man shook
His hoary locks, and froze me by a look.
Thrice, when I struck them, through the water came   330
A hollow groan, that weakened all my frame.
'Father!' said I, 'have mercy.' He replied,
I know not what—the angry spirit lied—
'Didst thou not draw thy knife?' said he. 'Twas true,
But I had pity and my arm withdrew;   335
He cried for mercy which I kindly gave,
But he has no compassion in his grave.
   "There were three places, where they ever rose—
The whole long river has not such as those—
Places accursed, where, if a man remain,   340
He'll see the things which strike him to the brain;
And there they made me on my paddle lean,
And look at them for hours—accursèd scene!

When they would glide to that smooth eddy-space,
Then bid me leap and join them in the place;   345
And at my groans each little villain sprite
Enjoyed my pains and vanished in delight.
    "In one fierce summer day, when my poor brain
Was burning hot and cruel was my pain,
Then came this father-foe, and there he stood   350
With his two boys again upon the flood;
There was more mischief in their eyes, more glee
In their pale faces when they glared at me;
Still did they force me on the oar to rest,
And when they saw me fainting and oppressed,   355
He, with his hand, the old man, scooped the flood,
And there came flame about him mixed with blood;
He bade me stoop and look upon the place,
Then flung the hot-red liquor in my face;
Burning it blazed, and then I roared for pain,   360
I thought the demons would have turned my brain.
    "Still there they stood, and forced me to behold
A place of horrors—they cannot be told—
Where the flood opened, there I heard the shriek
Of tortured guilt—no earthly tongue can speak: 365
'All days alike! for ever!' did they say,
'And unremitted torments every day'—
Yes, so they said."—But here he ceased and gazed
On all around, affrightened and amazed;
And still he tried to speak, and looked in dread   370
Of frightened females gathering round his bed;
Then dropped exhausted and appeared at rest,
Till the strong foe the vital powers possessed;
Then with an inward, broken voice he cried,
"Again they come," and muttered as he died.   375

Selected Bibliography

This is a group of books of general interest on this period. The works given in the first group contain extensive lists of readings on particular topics.

1. George Sherburn, "The Restoration and Eighteenth Century (1660-1789)," in *A Literary History of England*, ed. A. C. Baugh (1948).
2. Bonamy Dobrée, *English Literature in the Early Eighteenth Century, 1700-1740* (1959).
3. A. D. McKillop, *English Literature from Dryden to Burns* (1948).
4. Boris Ford, ed., *From Dryden to Johnson* (1957).
5. Louis I. Bredvold, "The Literature of the Restoration and Eighteenth Century," in *A History of English Literature*, ed. Hardin Craig (1950).
6. H. V. Dyson and John Butt, *Augustans and Romantics, 1689-1830* (1950).

7. J. L. Clifford, *Eighteenth-Century English Literature: Modern Essays in Criticism* (1959).
8. J. L. Clifford and L. A. Landa, eds., *Pope and His Contemporaries: Essays Presented to George Sherburn* (1949).
9. J. R. Sutherland and F. P. Wilson, eds., *Essays on the Eighteenth Century Presented to David Nichol Smith* (1945).
10. R. F. Jones, *et al.*, *The Seventeenth Century: Studies in the History of English Thought and Literature from Bacon to Pope* (1951).
11. R. C. Boys, ed., *Studies in the Literature of the Augustan Age: Essays in Honor of A. E. Case* (1952).
12. *The Age of Johnson: Essays Presented to Chauncey Brewster Tinker* (1949).

13. J. W. H. Atkins, *English Literary Criticism: Seventeenth and Eighteenth Centuries* (1951).
14. Ronald S. Crane, "Neo-Classical Criticism," in *Critics and Criticism, Ancient and Modern*, ed. R. S. Crane (1952).

15. M. H. Abrams, *The Mirror and the Lamp: Romantic Theory and the Critical Tradition* (1953).
16. W. J. Bate, *From Classic to Romantic: Premises of Taste in Eighteenth-Century England* (1946).
17. René Wellek, *A History of Modern Criticism, 1750-1950;* Volume I: "The Later Eighteenth Century" (1955).

18. A. R. Humphreys, *The Augustan World* (1954).
19. Ian Jack, *Augustan Satire* (1952).
20. J. R. Sutherland, *A Preface to Eighteenth-Century Poetry* (1948).

21. An annual bibliography, "English Literature, 1660-1800" has appeared in *Philological Quarterly* since 1926. The lists for 1926-50 are collected in two volumes, ed. L. A. Landa (1950, 1952).

Rinehart Editions